HANDBOOK OF ENTREPRENEURSHIP AND SUSTAINABLE DEVELOPMENT RESEARCH

Handbook of Entrepreneurship and Sustainable Development Research

Edited by

Paula Kyrö

Former Professor, School of Business, Aalto University, Finland

Edward Elgar
PUBLISHING

Cheltenham, UK • Northampton, MA, USA

Published by
Edward Elgar Publishing Limited
The Lypiatts
15 Lansdown Road
Cheltenham
Glos GL50 2JA
UK

Edward Elgar Publishing, Inc.
William Pratt House
9 Dewey Court
Northampton
Massachusetts 01060
USA

Paperback edition 2017

A catalogue record for this book
is available from the British Library

Library of Congress Control Number: 2014947033

This book is available electronically in the **Elgar**online
Business subject collection
DOI 10.4337/9781849808248

ISBN 978 1 84980 823 1 (cased)
ISBN 978 1 84980 824 8 (eBook)
ISBN 978 1 78347 994 8 (paperback)

Typeset by Servis Filmsetting Ltd, Stockport, Cheshire

Contents

Contributors

Sofia Avdeitchikova, The Ratio Institute, Sweden.

Frank-Martin Belz, Chair of Corporate Sustainability, TUM School of Management, Technische Universität München, Germany.

Karin Berglund, Stockholm Business School, Stockholm University, Sweden.

Julia Katharina Binder, Chair of Corporate Sustainability, TUM School of Management, Technische Universität München, Germany.

Toke Bjerregaard, Department of Business Administration, Business and Social Sciences, Aarhus University, Denmark.

Oana Branzei, University of Western Ontario, Richard Ivey School of Business, Canada.

Benedetto Cannatelli, ALTIS-Postgraduate School Business and Society, Università Cattolica del Sacro Cuore, Italy.

Tara Ceranic, University of San Diego, School of Business Administration, USA.

Lars Coenen, Centre for Innovation, Research and Competence in the Learning Economy (CIRCLE), Lund University, Sweden; Nordic Institute for Studies in Innovation, Research and Education (NIFU), Norway.

Marcus Dejardin, Université catholique de Louvain; Department of Economics, University of Namur, Belgium.

Santiago Delgado Calderon, Independent Consultant, Washington, DC, USA.

Javier Delgado-Ceballos, Business and Management Department, Economics and Business School, University of Granada, Spain.

Steffen Farny, School of Business, Aalto University, Finland.

Rosangela Feola, Department of Management and Information Technology, University of Salerno, Italy.

Laura Maria Ferri, ALTIS-Postgraduate School Business and Society, Università Cattolica del Sacro Cuore, Italy.

Vera Ferrón-Vílchez, Business and Management Department, Economics and Business School, University of Granada, Spain.

Samuel Gómez-Haro, Business and Management Department, Economics and Business School, University of Granada, Spain.

Fafani Gribaa, ERFI et CML – Montpellier I and Sousse Universities, Higher Institute of Management of Sousse, Tunisia.

Bengt Johannisson, School of Business and Economics, Linnaeus University, Sweden.

Anders W. Johansson, School of Business and Economics, Faculty of Business, Economics and Design, Linnaeus University, Sweden.

Ganesh Keremane, Centre for Comparative Water Policies and Laws, School of Law, UniSA Business School, University of South Australia, Australia.

Rita Klapper, Manchester Enterprise Centre, Manchester Business School, University of Manchester; Honorary Research Fellow, Sustainability Research Institute, University of Leeds, UK.

Paula Kyrö, School of Business, Aalto University, Finland.

Jakob Lauring, Department of Business Administration, Business and Social Sciences, Aarhus University, Denmark.

Jennifer McKay, Centre for Comparative Water Policies and Laws, School of Law, UniSA Business School, University of South Australia, Australia.

Karim Messeghem, Montpellier I University, France.

Mario Molteni, ALTIS (Postgraduate School Business and Society), Università Cattolica del Sacro Cuore, Italy.

Ivan Montiel, College of Business and Economics, Loyola Marymount University, USA.

Jean Nizet, Department of Political, Social and Communication Sciences, University of Namur, Belgium.

Roberto Parente, Department of Management and Information Technology, University of Salerno, Italy.

Matteo Pedrini, ALTIS (Postgraduate School Business and Society), Università Cattolica del Sacro Cuore, Italy.

Kim Poldner, Institute for Organizational Psychology, University of St Gallen, Switzerland.

Tõnu Roolaht, Faculty of Economics and Business Administration, University of Tartu, Estonia.

Erik Rosell, School of Business and Economics, Linnaeus University, Sweden.

Birgitta Schwartz, Stockholm Business School, Stockholm University, Sweden.

Mauro Sciarelli, Department of Economics, Management and Institution, University of Naples Federico II, Italy.

Elisabeth Sundin, Helix Vinn Excellence Centre, Linköping University, Sweden.

Rebecca Stenberg, Department of Management and Engineering, Linköping University, Sweden.

Mario Tani, Department of Economics, Management and Institution, University of Naples Federico II, Italy.

Malin Tillmar, Division of Business Administration, Department of Management and Engineering; Helix Vinn Excellence Centre, Linköping University, Sweden.

José Manuel de la Torre-Ruiz, Business and Management Department, Economics and Business School, University of Granada, Spain.

Azzedine Tounés, INSEEC Business School, France.

Paul Upham, Centre for Integrated Energy Research and Sustainability Research Institute, University of Leeds, UK.

Denise Van Dam, Department of Political, Social and Communication Sciences, University of Namur, Belgium.

Zhifang Wu, Centre for Comparative Water Policies and Laws, School of Law, UniSA Business School, University of South Australia, Australia.

Foreword

Societal transition toward sustainable development is one of mankind's key challenges in the twenty-first century. Entrepreneurship and sustainable development research, which tries to understand how individuals, organizations and economies can contribute to making this transition successful, has thus become a timely and highly important field of academic study. The current book provides an important contribution to this stream of research and provides insights for academics, practitioners and policy makers.

For academics in the fields of entrepreneurship and sustainable development the book provides an overview of the current state of research and an inspiration to join the sustainable entrepreneurship research community and further develop the field. The studies represented in the book capture multiple levels of analysis (for example, individual, organization, community, economy) and multiple theoretical approaches (for example, cognitive, sociological, economic) and empirical approaches (for example, ethnographic, case study, survey) to sustainable entrepreneurship. Thus, academics from psychology, organization science, sociology and economics gain insights on how their academic discipline can contribute to entrepreneurship and sustainable development research. Both the studies' settings and author teams represent multiple countries from four continents (Europe, North America, Africa and Australia), which illustrates the multifaceted nature of how entrepreneurship can contribute to sustainable development by addressing problems that are often specific for a particular country or region.

Practising entrepreneurs, and investors into sustainable development ventures, can gain valuable insights from the book's studies. For example, the studies outline the conversion of business models toward sustainability, and how new business opportunities that pursue both economic and societal and environmental goals can be recognized. Further, entrepreneurs and investors will find information on how micro-businesses might impact upon sustainable development in local communities, and how new ventures developing sustainable technologies can shape the development of entire industries.

Since a substantial portion of the book is dedicated to the impact of entrepreneurship on societies and economies, there are important implications for policy makers. These include, for example, how in economically less developed countries the environmental intentions of entrepreneurs can be facilitated, and the role of international aid, government intervention and entrepreneurship for fostering societal democratization. Further insights are provided on how public servants can act as entrepreneurs to establish a sustainability policy.

In sum, the diverse collection of chapters presented in this book makes it interesting reading for a large audience, and an inspiring and motivating input for academic research going forward.

Holger Patzelt
Professor of Entrepreneurship, Chair of Entrepreneurship
Technische Universität München
TUM School of Management
Munich

Acknowledgements

When in 2010 I launched the call for the *Handbook of Entrepreneurship and Sustainable Development Research*, I could not have imagined what an exciting but long journey was ahead of me. The interest the call inspired demonstrated the shared understanding of the importance of advancing research on the alliance between entrepreneurship and sustainable development, as well as a need to share views on this among the global research community. Of the suggestions received, it was possible to present here the work of 45 researchers. Their research communities are in 16 countries in Europe, Africa, Australia and North America. It was delightful to perceive that many of the research groups were both cross-national and multidisciplinary. As all chapters were double-blind reviewed, and most of them by two reviewers, the community involved with compiling this book altogether consisted of about 100 scholars. Some of these authors and their research communities have been working on entrepreneurship and sustainability issues for over a decade, but there are also more recently founded research groups and promising younger researchers whose full potential we can only expect to benefit from in the future.

I would like to warmly thank all these contributors, not only the authors of the published chapters but also the whole community, for their important work and patience in the lengthy editing process, and I hope some of these research communities will take responsibility in future to compile a new handbook to follow and share the findings of this expanding field of research.

Finally I would like to thank the School of Business, Aalto University entrepreneurship research community for supporting my ambitious initiative during these years, and to express special thanks to the publication designer, Sari Nyrhinen, who has tirelessly coordinated the writing and editing process.

Paula Kyrö
Tuusula, Finland,
29 March 2014

Introduction: expanding the field of research on entrepreneurship and sustainable development

Paula Kyrö

INCREASING INTEREST IN RESEARCH ON ENTREPRENEURSHIP AND SUSTAINABLE DEVELOPMENT

The combination of entrepreneurship and sustainable development has re-emerged only recently in science and slightly earlier in political debate guided by the Brundtland Commission's report (WCED, 1987), the United Nations Conference on Environment and Development in 1992, and later by the United Nations climate conference in Copenhagen. Since Pastakia's pioneering article in 1998 this discussion has intensified in just a few years in international, peer-reviewed journals as Binder and Belz's analysis in this book (Chapter 2) indicates.

However, the roots of sustainable development in science are as old as those of entrepreneurship itself (Kyrö and Suojanen, 1999; Kyrö, 2001). The very first school of thought in entrepreneurship, the French physiocrats, assumed that economic prosperity was produced by free human beings who by their own efforts, under the conditions of the self-sustaining system of nature, created something new which on its own behalf created economic progress (e.g. Barreto, 1989; Casson, 1982; Wilken, 1979). This fact, even though rarely noticed, seems also to pave the way for the current debate on sustainability and entrepreneurship, bringing along a similar movement from 'sustainable entrepreneurship' to 'making entrepreneurship sustainable', as Hjorth and Steyaert (2009) argue is achieved in social entrepreneurship.

As is typical of a nascent field of research, its understanding, approaches and forms are diverse, and seem to be open to different interpretations in different contexts, as, for example, Johannisson et al. argue in Chapter 5. This contextual bond is also apparent in other chapters of this book. Often entrepreneurship seems to be taken as a transitional tool to tackle the crucial problems calling for change in society and economy. For example, North American and European discourses can be identified. A characteristic of the North American discussion is to take social entrepreneurship as a starting point and then to move forward to, or combine it with, ecological sustainability. In Europe and especially in the Nordic countries social entrepreneurship has its own specific place and ecological discussion is often combined with environmental or institutional economics. Thus the landscape of entrepreneurship and sustainability is coloured by diverse approaches and perspectives.

This diversity was the stimulus to compile this *Handbook* in order to explore and gather these diverse perspectives and thus paint a picture of the past and present understanding of entrepreneurship and sustainable development, to inspire researchers, teachers and policy makers to intentionally develop their own understanding and help them to add their contribution to this landscape.

DIVERSITY OF APPROACHES AND CONCEPTS

Even though the approaches for the alliance between entrepreneurship and sustainable development are diverse, when it comes to sustainable development they seem to be explicitly or implicitly inspired by the United Nations report on *Our Common Future*. It defines sustainable development as 'meeting the needs of the present without compromising the ability of future generations to meet their needs' (WCED, 1987). How to do that and what is the role of entrepreneurship in this process seems to be an underlying question for most of the chapters in this book. Many of them draw their arguments from the transformative capacity or power of entrepreneurship towards more sustainable development in our society, its institutions and practices. Only time will tell if this debate is about to bring 'entrepreneurship for sustainable development' as an umbrella concept for the alliance between entrepreneurship and sustainable development, as some authors suggest (Montiel and Ceranic, Chapter 8; Poldner and Branzei, Chapter 14). Currently we can still identify the relationships between entrepreneurship and sustainable development that are characterized by all 'and', 'within' and 'for' definitions.

Whatever the answer may be, the 'how' and 'role' questions have already broadened our conceptualizing debate today and introduced new concepts alongside the better-known terms 'ecopreneurship', 'environmental entrepreneurship' and 'sustainable entrepreneurship'. For example, 'societal entrepreneurship' is ably introduced in Chapter 5 by Johannisson et al., and 'policy entrepreneurship' is conceptually presented in Chapter 6 by Ganesh Keremane, Jennifer McKay and Zhifang Wu.

Within these questions and diverse concepts the most vivid definitional discussion of this book concerns the 'chicken and egg' question: is the pursuit of economic, social and environmental goals simultaneous or does one or more of them supercede the others. The dynamics between these three is also a fundamental choice in formulating research questions and designs in this book, as is well elaborated in Chapter 15 'Market-driven capabilities and sustainability of alliances by agricultural small and medium-sized enterprises' (Sciarelli and Tani). Struggling between often competing objectives of economic, social and ecological value creation, as for example Binder and Belz (Chapter 2) as well as Cannatelli et al. (Chapter 7) argue, leads us to an increased conceptual complexity that is well demonstrated in this book.

Methodological choices of the chapters as typical of the nascent field of research focus on qualitative methods endeavouring to provide a more profound understanding of and new insights on the topic and the dynamics between its diverse dimensions. However, they also offer some previously lacking empirical evidence on different aspects of entrepreneurship and sustainable development. Thus they also methodologically advance research on the field by elevating it from prescriptive to descriptive research (Hall et al., 2010).

STRUCTURE AND CHAPTERS OF THE BOOK

The book is divided into four parts. Part I contains the chapters that shed light on the historical roots and current conceptual approaches to the alliance between entrepreneurship and sustainable development. Thus it outlines the landscape of past and present research on the topic.

Part II underlines the transformative capacity and power of entrepreneurship for a sustainable society. Like Binder's and Belz's (Chapter 2) aspect of transition, it offers examples of different levels of the impact of entrepreneurship for a sustainable society. Reaching over the previous criticism of the prescriptive nature of current research (Hall et al., 2010), it also offers descriptive empirical evidence of the dynamics between entrepreneurship and sustainable development in and for society. The four chapters in this part draw their ideas from Malawian, Haitian, East-Timorian, Australian and Swedish contexts.

Part III gathers together those chapters that investigate entrepreneurs' drivers, motivators and intentions vis-à-vis sustainable development. Following Patzelt and Shepherd's (2011) pioneering work, the chapters in this part add to our knowledge of the individual-level factors of the opportunity process in the context of sustainable entrepreneurship. As in Part II, based on empirical evidence the chapters also present the current phase of the research on this topic.

Finally, the six chapters in Part IV broaden our view of how sustainability is integrated and embedded in industry- and economy-level research.

PART I HISTORICAL ROOTS AND CURRENT CONCEPTUAL APPROACHES TO THE ALLIANCE BETWEEN ENTREPRENEURSHIP AND SUSTAINABLE DEVELOPMENT

This part starts with a socio-historical study 'To grow or not to grow? Entrepreneurship and sustainable development'. Drawing on environmental economics, Chapter 1 elaborates the less discussed recommendation of the Brundtland Commission's report (WCED, 1987) and the United Nations Conference on Environment and Development (UNCED), namely their recommendation to replace the ideology of continuous economic growth with the principles of sustainable development. Following scientific discussions over time it reveals some misunderstandings in the research on the history of entrepreneurship and builds up an alternative discussion of growth. It also isolates entrepreneurship and ecological economics from other paradigms in environmental economics. As an outcome of this journey the chapter offers us a chronological and theoretical description of how, through entrepreneurship, economy and sustainable development can join hands and produce a new approach to the discussion between economy and welfare. The study also reveals how the social sciences not only say how things are, but also produce the reality around us. Thus the chapter both gives us a historical understanding of the current discussion between entrepreneurship and sustainable development and also demonstrates the transitional nature and transformative power of entrepreneurship in economics.

Chapter 2 written by Julia Katharina Binder and Frank-Martin Belz from the German entrepreneurship research community of TUM School of Management is a conceptual study that delineates what sustainable entrepreneurship is. Its systematic literature review ends up with a definition that reflects five aspects of sustainable entrepreneurship: the sources of opportunities; a process-focused perspective; the individual sustainable entrepreneur; economic, ecological and social value creation; and the transition to a sustainable society. Consequently this chapter offers all researchers an excellent opportunity to reflect their own conceptual understanding of sustainable entrepreneurship.

Together these two chapters provide an overall landscape for understanding the past and present conceptual discussions of entrepreneurship for and also within sustainable development. Thus the reader is well equipped to explore the other chapters of the book and benefit from these fundamental discussions in their own work.

PART II   THE TRANSFORMATIVE APPROACH TO ENTREPRENEURSHIP FOR A SUSTAINABLE SOCIETY

The four chapters in this part underline the transformative capacity and power of entrepreneurship for sustainable development in society. The part is organized according to two different contexts: on the one hand that of developing societies, and on the other hand that of mature democracies with well-established public sectors, assuming that these differences are reflected in how entrepreneurship for sustainable development emerges in these societies.

In Chapter 3, 'Socially sustainable entrepreneurship: a case of entrepreneurial practice in social change and stability', the Danish scholars Toke Bjerregaard and Jakob Lauring argue that social sustainability is an inherent aspect of the entrepreneurial process. Their ethnographic study on the implementation of liberal democracy in Malawi examines the strategies through which entrepreneurs navigate the multiple institutional logics of the spheres in which they operate and, in turn, contributes to both sustaining and changing societal structures. Thus the chapter, drawing on institutional theory, gives us insights into the complexity of a transitional change in society.

The next chapter continues this discussion on democratization processes in fragile nations. Steffen Farny, a German researcher from the Finnish Aalto University, and his colleague Santiago Delgado Calderon from Cornell University, USA, follow socio-historical findings (Kyrö, Chapter 1) on the power of the dominating scientific debates to promote sustainable development. The authors suggest that entrepreneurship could be the missing link for democratization and development in fragile nations. Drawing on the negative experiences of foreign aid, they focus on the change-making side of entrepreneurship and sustainable development, arguing that we lack an understanding of how organizational strategies affect the quality of democratic institutions. Relying on Huang's (2008) findings from China, they suggest that neither international aid nor government intervention, but rather local entrepreneurs, can be the main agents driving societal renewal and accelerating economic liberalization. The findings of their ethnographic content analysis of the institution-building process in Haiti and East Timor, however, indicate that entrepreneurial activity is now supporting a parallel system rather than aiding the development process of a sovereign nation. Thus their study on the one hand verifies the findings of Bjerregaard and Lauring, and on the other reveals the basic assumptions that prevent transformations.

Chapter 5, 'Organizing societal entrepreneurship: a cross-sector challenge', written by a large Swedish research consortium – Bengt Johannisson, Anders W. Johansson, Elisabeth Sundin, Karin Berglund, Erik Rosell, Birgitta Schwartz, Rebecca Stenberg and Malin Tillmar – takes us into the welfare state context. The authors argue that in a welfare economy social enterprising typically appears as a mobilizing and innovative effort that crosses the boundaries between the market, the public sector and the non-profit and voluntary sector. The chapter introduces the notion of 'societal' entrepreneurship and presents an analysis of its features through seven narrations. These narrations are drawn from the consortium's extensive work on the topic in Sweden. The authors propose that societal entrepreneurship has five dualistic features that can be positioned using an institutional framework: (1) the interplay between economic and social values over time; (2) the tension between agency and structure; (3) entrepreneurship as individual initiative or collective mobilization; (4) balancing economies of scale and the beauty of smallness; (5) social venturing as exploiting opportunity or organizing opposition. Thus the chapter offers us a more profound understanding of the notion of societal entrepreneurship in the context of the welfare state.

The last chapter of this part transports us to another continent with the Australian scholars Ganesh Keremane, Jennifer McKay and Zhifang Wu. Chapter 6, 'Public servants as sustainability policy entrepreneurs in Australia: the issues and outcomes', introduces the concept of the sustainability policy entrepreneur rarely dealt with in journals specializing in entrepreneurship. In this case the focus is on water planners who are appointed officials and have adopted the sustainable development philosophy contained in all Australian water and other natural resource legislation since 1992 (NWC, 2004; McKay, 2005). These authors deal with entrepreneurship and sustainable development by selecting a topic that is important in their Australian context and investigating the policy entrepreneur's role in the adoption of changes to water allocations. The findings from their survey of water planners and interviews with other key actors indicate how policy transition is an evolving process, where sustainability policy entrepreneurs have an important role in shaping policy outcomes. Thus the chapter expands our conceptual understanding of the diverse forms of sustainable entrepreneurs and their role in policy processes.

Together these four chapters on the transformative approach introduce the diverse contexts and forms of sustainable entrepreneurs and entrepreneurship. They verify the argument of the Swedish consortium (Johannisson et al., Chapter 5) about the importance of context in understanding the transformative nature of entrepreneurship and sustainable development.

PART III   MOTIVATIONAL AND INTENTIONAL APPROACH TO ENTREPRENEURSHIP AND SUSTAINABLE DEVELOPMENT

This part focuses on an individual entrepreneur in pursuit of sustainable development. All the chapters centre on what makes an individual entrepreneur engage in an entreprenial venture for sustainable development.

In Chapter 7 the Italian researchers Benedetto Cannatelli, Laura Maria Ferri, Matteo Pedrini and Mario Molteni investigate the psychological dimensions leading individuals to the identification of first-person entrepreneurial opportunities for sustainable development. Based on the literature on opportunity recognition they build a set of propositions, and then using grounded theory in the Kenyan context suggest that entrepreneurial knowledge and knowledge of the natural and communal environment play a major role in feasibility assessment, but altruism and the perception of goodwill towards the natural and communal environment constitute the main drivers of the desirability assessment of the opportunity. Their findings indicate that both knowledge and motivation are moderated by the emotional and social involvement of the entrepreneur with the beneficiaries of the initiative. Thus, as called for by Binder and Belz (Chapter 2), this chapter replicates some of the previous findings of Patzelt and Shepherd (2011), increasing their validity, yet it also makes its own specific contribution to the opportunity process research for sustainable development.

Chapter 8, 'Cooking up solutions for climate change: the role of sustainable entrepreneurs', written by Ivan Montiel and Tara Ceranic from the USA, continues the opportunity discussion. The authors suggest that sustainable entrepreneurship is an umbrella under which social and environmental concerns are both addressed equally in the enterprise. The study adopts Zahra et al.'s (2009) typology of three different social entrepreneurs, and adapts it to the sustainability context by investigating how three types of search processes exist among entrepreneurs interested in climate change mitigation. The findings from their multiple case study indicate similarities between entrepreneurs aiming to create social wealth (social entrepreneurs) and those who aim to minimize their footprint (sustainable entrepreneurs). In addition, the findings reveal how enterprises tend to tackle both social and environmental projects at the same time, rather than choosing between the two. Thus the results confirm their claim and bring Zahra et al.'s model into a new context.

The Algerian–Tunisian–French research team of Azzedine Tounés, Fafani Gribaa and Karim Messeghem build 'An exploratory model of the environmental intention of SME directors in Tunisia' in Chapter 9. By combining the theory of planned behaviour of Ajzen (1991) and the entrepreneurial theory of Kuhndt et al. (2004) they explore what kind of relations exist between company directors' environmental intentions and their antecedents in the textile industry in Tunisia. The results of their qualitative survey of 20 company directors give ideas for further research by suggesting the type of connections between intention and the factors likely to explain it. As the authors argue, being able to understand the determining factors of the managers' environmental intentions advances both theoretical and policy development in the field.

In Chapter 10 the Spanish research group of Samuel Gómez-Haro, Vera Ferrón-Vílchez, José Manuel de la Torre-Ruiz and Javier Delgado-Ceballos from the University of Granada investigate what motivates hotel managers to become ecopreneurs. For them, ecopreneurs are entrepreneurs who look for profitable businesses with strong underlying green values. On the basis of Post and Altman's (1994) three categories of motivations, the authors suggest that the motivational factors of ecopreneurs, in addition to compliance-, market- and value-driven motivations, also include the personal environmental values of entrepreneurs (that is, intrinsic motivation). Their case study on the Spanish hostel industry supported this suggestion, but also revealed that the willingness to meet the ecological demands of customers was the main motivator for adopting an advanced environmental management strategy.

In Chapter 11, Rita Klapper and Paul Upham from the UK investigate 'The impact of micro-firm everyday practices on sustainable development in local communities'. This chapter is part of a bigger research project on how entrepreneurial micro business owners contribute to sustainable development by pursuing their own values. The authors argue that comparatively little is known about the role of micro businesses in sustainable development, particularly the ways in which they combine entrepreneurship with environmental protection and social benefit. The authors provide a model that connects micro-firm entrepreneurship and value creation to the economic, social and environmental aspects of sustainable development. The case study findings indicate that these firms are driven by the owner-manager's values, which find their expression in monetary and non-monetary value creation.

PART IV INDUSTRY- AND ECONOMY-ORIENTED APPROACHES TO ENTREPRENEURSHIP AND SUSTAINABLE DEVELOPMENT

Part IV presents six industry- and economy-oriented chapters. The first of these, Chapter 12 by the Italian scholars Roberto Parente and Rosangela Feola, 'The renewable energy industry: competitive landscapes and entrepreneurial roles', argues that in sustainable industry a positive role exists for both 'Emerging Davids' (new entrants) and well-established 'Greening Goliaths' (incumbent firms). They investigate the entry strategies of key players in the emerging renewable energy industry in Italy and how their strategic choices are influenced by the competitive landscapes in which they take place. The chapter contributes to our understanding of the entrepreneurial roles in new industry development by proposing a model for analysing, from a static and a dynamic perspective, the competitive structure of the renewable energy sector.

From the renewable energy industry in Italy we move to Swedish clean technology innovations. In Chapter 13 the researchers Sofia Avdeitchikova from The Ratio Institute and Lars Coenen from the Lund University Centre for Innovation, Research and Competence in the Learning Economy (CIRCLE) research centre in Sweden focus on the interplay of agency and structure in 'Commercializing clean technology innovations: the emergence of new business in an agency–structure perspective'. They argue that research in the entrepreneurship literature has often failed to explain why some new technologies reach markets while others do not, and also why some technological solutions ultimately become industry standards while others quickly disappear from the market. The authors provide an alternative approach to analyse the entrepreneurial process of commercializing 'cleantech' that underlines the duality of structure and agency. The contribution of the chapter lies in making explicit the agency–structure discussion in order to add to our understanding of cleantech as an emergent technological field and the role of entrepreneurs and/or entrepreneurship in shaping this field.

Next, still following the David and Goliath theme, we move from technology to the world of design in Chapter 14 by the Swiss researcher Kim Poldner and the Canadian Oana Branzei entitled 'David versus Goliath: how eco-entrepreneurs transform global ecosystems'. Their study elaborates the micro-practices by which individual human beings can transform global ecosystems. Reporting on a five-year multi-method study of the global ethical fashion industry, the authors expand Tillman Lyle's (1999) framework as they express it 'by marrying it' to the literature on entrepreneuring (Rindova et al., 2009; Steyaert, 2007). As an outcome they propose a theoretical framework that explains how eco-entrepreneurs use material, discursive and connective practices – that is, the artefacts, language and community – to progressively improve the ecosystem they work in.

From design we move in the two following chapters closer to the earth, that is, to the agricultural industry. The Italian scholars Mauro Sciarelli and Mario Tani's Chapter 15 concerns 'Market-driven capabilities and sustainability of alliances by agricultural small and medium-sized enterprises'. The authors argue for the importance of their topic as agricultural entrepreneurs are under pressure to use a more intense, and often less sustainable, way of growing crops. Drawing on Passet's (1996) hierarchical bioeconomy model of sustainability, they compile a framework that builds upon market-driven capabilities and analyse the opportunities and risks related to different agricultural farms' alliances. By adopting the multiple case study method they then investigate what kinds of capabilities are used in successful farmers' alliances. Their results indicate that agricultural alliances do not always succeed in driving agribusinesses toward more sustainable strategies, and they are able to help local development only if the alliance does not involve some other bigger players further down their value chain. According to the authors these results indicate that the bioeconomy model can provide researchers with the needed guidance for assessing if a given model of alliance can really help in sustainable development processes.

In Chapter 16 the Belgian multidisciplinary group of Marcus Dejardin, Jean Nizet and Denise Van Dam investigate organic farmers' entrepreneurial functions. Drawing on the classical work of Schumpeter, Knight and Kirzner they focus on three entrepreneurial functions: innovation, risk-taking and contribution to efficiency. Through the narrated experiences of three organic farmers the authors show how these entrepreneurial functions may be transposed in the practice of organic farming. Thus they bring the industry of organic agriculture into the entrepreneurship discussion by claiming that this evolving industry represents a renewal of agricultural activities, and organic farming can be seen as a way to achieve sustainability in agriculture and, more broadly, in the agro-food industry.

In the last chapter of the book, Chapter 17, Tõnu Roolaht from Estonia introduces us to 'The entrepreneurial contribution of foreign-owned companies to the sustainable development of a small developing host economy'. He investigates how foreign-owned companies support the sustainable development of a small host economy through their entrepreneurial initiatives. The results indicate that foreign-owned companies do indeed foster sustainable entrepreneurship in the small open economy, but the environmental, economic and social dimensions of sustainability are not always perfectly aligned, at least in the short term. The implications of this research for theory are that the sustainable entrepreneurship concept should be viewed as more heterogeneous and multidimensional than several studies assume.

EXPECTATIONS FOR THE FUTURE

As the chapters of this book demonstrate, the alliance between entrepreneurship and sustainable development is an evolving field with diverse meanings depending on the lenses through which we view it. Even though the authors of this book seek to clarify the differences between diverse definitions, and so provide suggestions for drawing boundaries between different concepts and approaches, the complexity and ambiguity remain as a challenge for future research. On the one hand the chapters are good examples of the conceptual diversity, and on the other their voice is similar when it comes to calling for a better understanding of this diversity.

It has become clear that the interest in and concern about entrepreneurship and sustainability issues are globally shared by scientific communities. However it is equally obvious that to flourish and grow this research needs global collaboration, since concepts and forms of entrepreneurship are context-bound and can be developed and adopted only by sharing them among different contexts. There also seems to be a consensus independent of the level of analysis that a transformative aspect is implicitly or explicitly embedded in all concepts and approaches in the field of entrepreneurship and sustainable development. This indicates that perhaps Hjorth's ideas of the movement from 'sustainable entrepreneurship' to 'making entrepreneurship sustainable' is characteristic of the current phase of research (Hjorth and Steyaert, 2009). Perhaps this book also indicates that Hall's (2012) claim that research is rather prescriptive than descriptive has been advanced somewhat by the findings in this handbook. In this nascent, evolving field of research this *Handbook* represents an initial effort to elaborate the view of the global research community, and most certainly new handbooks are needed in future to follow and share the findings of this expanding field of research.

REFERENCES

Ajzen, I. (1991), 'The theory of planned behaviour', *Organizational Behaviour and Human Decision Process*, 50, 179–211.

Barreto, H. (1989), *The Entrepreneur in Microeconomic Theory: Disappearence and Explanation*, London, UK and New York, USA: Routledge.

Casson, M. (1982), *The Entrepreneur: An Economic Theory*, Oxford: Martin Robinson.

Hall, J., G. Daneke and M. Lenox (2010), 'Sustainable development and entrepreneurship: past contributions and future directions', *Journal of Business Venturing*, 25(5), 439–48.

Hjorth, D. and C. Steyaert (eds) (2009), *The Politics and Aesthetics of Entrepreneurship*, Cheltenham, UK and Northampton, MA, USA: Edward Elgar.

Huang, Y. (2008), *Capitalism with Chinese Characteristics: Entrepreneurship and the State*, Cambridge: Cambridge University Press.

Kuhndt, M., V. Türk and M. Herrndorf (2004), 'Stakeholder engagement: an opportunity for SMEs? ', *UNEP industry and environment*, pp. 40–43, October–December.

Kyrö, P. (2001), 'To grow or not to grow? Entrepreneurship and sustainable development', *International Journal of Sustainable Development and World Ecology*, 8, 15–28.

Kyrö, P. and U. Suojanen (1999), 'The relationship between sustainable development and entrepreneurship in the postmodern transition', *International Journal of Entrepreneurship*, 3, 30–52.

McKay, J. (2005), 'Water institutional reforms in Australia', *Water Policy*, 7(1), 35–52.

National Water Commission (NWC) (2004), 'National Water Initiative', www.nwc.gov.au (accessed 28 July 2011).

Passet, R. (1996), *L'Economique et le vivant*, 2nd edn, Paris: Payot.

Pastakia, A. (1998), 'Grassroot ecopreneurs: change agents for a sustainable society', *Journal of Organizational Management*, 11(2), 157–73.

Patzelt, H. and D.A. Shepherd (2011), 'Recognizing opportunities for sustainable development', *Entrepreneurship Theory and Practice*, 35(4), 631–52.

Post, J. and B. Altman (1994), 'Managing the environmental change process: barriers and opportunities', *Journal of Organizational Change Management*, 7(4), 64–81.

Rindova, V., D. Barry and D. Ketchen (2009), 'Entrepreneuring as emancipation', *Academy of Management Review*, 34(3), 477–91.

Steyaert, C. (2007), 'Of course that is not the whole (toy) story: entrepreneurship and the cat's cradle', *Journal of Business Venturing*, 22(5), 733–51.

Tillman Lyle, J. (1999), *Design for Human Eco-Systems: Landscape, Land Use and Natural Resources*, New York: Island Press.

Wilken, P.H. (1979), *Entrepreneurship: A Comparative and Historical Study*, Norwood, NJ: Ablex.

World Commission on Environment and Development (WCED) (1987), *Brundtland Report: Our Common Future*, Oxford: Oxford University Press.

Zahra, S.A., E. Gedajlovic, D. Neubaum and J.M. Shulman (2009), 'A typology of social entrepreneurs: motives, search processes and ethical challenges', *Journal of Business Venturing*, 24, 518–32.

PART I

HISTORICAL ROOTS AND CURRENT CONCEPTUAL APPROACHES TO THE ALLIANCE BETWEEN ENTREPRENEURSHIP AND SUSTAINABLE DEVELOPMENT

1. To grow or not to grow? Entrepreneurship and sustainable development*
Paula Kyrö

GROWTH OR SUSTAINABLE DEVELOPMENT

Growth and its connection with the success of the economy and welfare have been taken for granted throughout the history of industrialization. The main question has been how to grow (e.g. Thurik and Wenekers, 1999). In the modern era this dialogue has taken place between large firms and society. In science this story can be identified in the dialogue between economics and sociology. The role of economics has been to ensure continuous growth in the private sector. Sociology on its own behalf has represented society and has focused on looking after either the side-effects produced by continuous growth or the infrastructure needed for growth (Kyrö, 1999). Its main concerns included employment and equal income distribution. In this dialogue the impact of entrepreneurship and small firms has not been valued. When we arrived at the postmodern transition and noticed that large firms were not creating work for citizens, the dialogue between growth and welfare also turned to include small firms. The ideal of growth were applied and are about to be applied to small firms. In this process the question is not raised, either in the mainstream of economics or even in the paradigms of entrepreneurship, as to whether that growth is desirable or not, even though we have empirical evidence all around us of its destructive consequences.

The question, to grow or not to grow, has thus arisen from a different direction. Since the 1980s we have been involved in another dialogue, that is, the debate between sustainable development and economic growth. The Brundtland Commission's report (WCED, 1987) and the United Nations Conference on Environment and Development (UNCED, 1993) in 1992 both strongly suggested that the ideology of continuous economic growth should be replaced by the principles of sustainable development. This dialogue has strengthened in the field of environmental economics, that is, in institutional school and in ecological economics. Both of them, however, have problems about how to combine the two phenomena of economics and sustainable development.

3

I suggest that through entrepreneurship, economy and sustainable development can join hands with each other and produce a new approach to the discussion between economy and welfare. To delineate this connection, it is necessary to reveal some misinterpretations of the development entrepreneurship and environmental economics theories. The very first misinterpretation concerns the origins of both fields of science. By revealing this misinterpretation we can reach the roots of combining economics and sustainable development. At the same time, however, we create the basis for an alternative discussion of growth. The prerequisite for this is, however, that we follow the development of these paradigms from past to present. This journey isolates the paradigms of entrepreneurship and ecological economics from other paradigms in environmental economics. That is how a renewed connection between Nature and economics can be found.

The final question is, of course: why is this important – why should we look for alternative ideas to growth? The reason for this can also be found in history and its effect on the present day. By evaluating the consequences of growth we can also reflect upon whether these consequences can be regarded as desirable. In this chapter, following the historical development of the paradigms in environmental economics from the eighteenth century until the present day carries out this task. The history reveals how science not only says how things are, but rather also produces the reality. That is why it should also be aware of what kind of reality it regards as valuable. The methodology of social history offers tools for such a journey. I will apply it to the story of growth and its opponent, entrepreneurship and sustainable development.

THE METHODOLOGY OF SOCIAL HISTORY: PAST FOR THE FUTURE

The orientation of social history is multi-scientific and society theoretical. Its research target is society. Social history produces explicit answers to contemporary questions in society (Haapala, 1989). The question of whether to grow or not to grow can be regarded as one of the most critical questions of our day, one which cannot be answered without a multi-scientific approach. Social history therefore offers us an excellent tool to tackle that problem. The most popular research area in social history has been industrialization. This research is now facing a new phase. Culture in its broadest sense has replaced government. Instead of government and power, the emphasis has focused on action, interaction and comparisons. This is exactly what takes place in this chapter.

The problem of growth and connecting sustainable development and economics has been approached as a cultural process. This process has its roots in France during the Enlightenment. From France it expanded and developed along with industrialization. From a historical perspective it can be seen as having undergone two transitions and two eras preceding them (e.g. Dillard, 1967; Beck et al., 1995; Harvey, 1990; Kyrö, 1996; Turner, 1990). The first transition, which is termed here the modern transition, took place at the beginning of industrialization, from the eighteenth to the nineteenth century, when the traditional era closed. Out of this transition developed the modern era, which, for its part, started to come to its end in the 1970s, when the postmodern transition occurred. The development of economics and its consequences can be positioned and analysed through and within these culturally constituted phases (Kyrö, 1999; Kyrö and Suojanen, 1999).

In this process science is not independent of the environment and its incidents, but rather it takes part in constructing the reality around us in interaction with the environment. Culture means a collectively created reality, conscious or unconscious; it is not something that just happened – it is made (Hofstede, 1991; Kyrö, 1996). Through culture, successful patterns of behaviour and values guiding that behaviour will be transferred from the past to the present and on to the future. It is here suggested that growth and its connection with welfare and democracy is one of the most illusionary culturally constituted values ever invented. It is also suggested that this connection is implicit rather than explicit; that is, it is irrational rather than rational.

From this perspective the development of scientific discussions will be followed through time as an interactive, discursive process between scientific descriptions and events in the environment. Such an approach is chronological and theoretical at the same time (Haapala, 1989). The data consists on the one hand of scientific theories, on the other hand the incidents in reality.

The social historical process answers the following questions: (1) What happened? (2) How did it happen? (3) Why did it happen? (4) What was it all about? All of these questions will be asked and also evaluated after reporting the results. Next I report the results of the study. This is a rather unusual choice in historical research, since normally the whole story will be reported. In this chapter, lack of space limits me from doing that. That is why I will present only the summaries of my findings and some of the most critical argument chains.

THE MODERN TRANSITION

Looking for and Losing Nature and the Free Human Being

The roots of environmental economics and entrepreneurship can be traced back to eighteenth-century France to the time known as the Enlightenment. It was a time when society reformed its ideas about itself, Nature and the human being. In France, at the end of the Middle Ages, two systems, feudalism and the crafts system, were coming to an end. People were tired of the court's profligacy and heavy taxation, and the control of mercantilism. Citizens, trade and industry in general started to demand freedom: freedom to decide how to earn a living. Science started to model and describe this new environment. In this diversity, with its new ideas of the human being, are to be found the seeds for entrepreneurship in its broad sense.

Finding difficulties in supporting both its luxurious life and the country's defence, the French court hired a Scottish adventurer, John Law, as secretary of the treasury. He founded a bank with paper money and a trading company. The company soon encountered difficulties and those who had invested in it lost their money. John Law was sacked and a little later the state obtained more responsible treasurers. Richard Cantillon, the Irish-born banker, was one of those who gained from these incidents. He owned shares in the trading company and managed to sell them at a large profit before the bankruptcy in 1720. His ideas of entrepreneurship encompassed these experiences. For him, the entrepreneur is one who identifies the possibility of gaining from the market. He buys at a certain price and sells at an uncertain price. The difference between these two is the profit (Barreto, 1989; Casson, 1982; Kyrö, 1997; Wilken, 1979). The story of Cantillon forms a watershed between the ideas of entrepreneurship and the idols of our modern times.

The first school of entrepreneurship and ecological economics, the French physiocrats, was born to oppose mercantilism and the power of money. In short they opposed the ideas of Cantillon. This is a distinction that has not been generally noted (e.g. Christensen, 1996: 109; http://www.mtsu.edu~^tvs2l; Lindeqvist, 1905; Massa, 1995: 25). For them, wealth came from the land. The land provided the products, which industry only further refined (e.g. http://www.mtsu.edu~^tvs2/quesnay.html; Hobbes, 1660). The entrepreneur was for them a farmer who hired land from landowners and produced raw materials for the artisan. The farmer was the only one who could add to the value of the product in this process. Entrepreneurship referred to a farmer and farming in free circumstances. Later the term 'entrepreneurship' started to be applied to emerging industry. It started to refer to unusual human beings who by their own efforts and thinking, under conditions produced by Nature, created something new which on its own behalf created economic progress (e.g. Barreto, 1989; Casson, 1982; Wilken, 1979). This was the opposite of the traditional idea of the human being as a product of his born place in society, and it was also the opposite of the idea of wealth produced by money and expanding trade.

At the same time as the physiocrats were fighting for their beliefs and ideas in France, Adam Smith was visiting the country. He disagreed with the ideas of the physiocrats, and started to write his famous work *The Wealth of Nations* (1776). Above all, Smith based his ideas on free trade. For him not land but work had the greatest value, and it was of the utmost importance for the wealth of nations to expand the demand for it. Smith thought that by expanding trade it was also possible to satisfy citizens' self-interest and to produce welfare. These thoughts laid the base for the modern era. The circumstances in Britain at that time gave rise to those thoughts: trade and the developing manufacturing sector were important; Britain had all the resources needed to expand its trade. Its welfare was based on its 30 colonies and it thus had access to raw materials. It could control prices and production, it had a cheap or free workforce, technical inventions, and domination of the sea. In these circumstances began the story of economic growth that has most deeply affected our understanding of Nature (Dillard, 1967: 238–40).

In the writings of Adam Smith both entrepreneurship and Nature were lost and the illusion of an 'invisible hand' was created. Smith regarded Nature as an unlimited and free source of resources. Rational equilibrium replaced the human being. These ideas generated three different paradigms in economics in general and in environmental economics in particular. Beside the classical school was born the German historical school, the grandfather of sociology, which started to challenge both the methodology and the consequences of equilibrium theories (e.g. Von Böhm-Bawerk, 1890–91; Schmoller, 1881, 1897 [1884]). The third paradigm followed the physiocrats. Its ideas branched off into ecological economics and entrepreneurship (e.g. Ricardo, 1821). In the modern transition these were still living side by side. But toward the end of the transition the classical school and its followers gained dominance. Their domination was possible because demand was growing. I have summarized the development of these three schools in Table 1.1.

The time limits for this transition are not very exact, as can be seen from Table 1.1, since industrialization took place as a process travelling from country to country, from Britain to the USA and then back to Europe.

Table 1.1   *The development of the 'dicussions' between three paradigms in environmental economics and entrepreneurship*

Modern breaks from traditional – 18th century

	Physiocrats Entrepreneurship and ecological economics 1700– Quesnay Turgot (1727–1781) ↙ ↓ ↘	

The modern transition develops, 18th and 19th centuries

↗	↓	↘
German historical school *Wilhelm Roscher (1817–1894) Bruno Hildebrandt, Karl Knies, Gustav Schmoller (1838–1917) Max Weber (1864–1929)*	Classical school The end of the 18th century *Adam Smith (1723–1790) David Ricardo (1772–1823) Thomas Robert Malthus (1766–1834)*	Entrepreneurship and ecological economics *Sadi Carnot (1796–1832) Patrick Geddes (1854–1932)*
↓ →	← ↓	↓
Early American institutional school *Thorsten Veblen (1857–1929), John R. Commons (1862–1945) Wesley Mitchell*	Neo-classical school *Leon Walras (1834–1910) William Stanley Jevons (1835–1882) Karl Menger (1840–1921)*	The early phase of the Austrian school *Karl Menger (1840–1921) Friedrich von Wieser (1851–1926) Eugen von Böhm-Bawerk (1851–1914) Joseph Schumpeter (1883–1950) (early contribution in Austria in 1910s)*
↓	↓	↓

The modern era 1900–

The contemporary institutional school (1900–) *Institutional economics Harold A. Innesin *Structure-dynamics school Francois Perroux Ordoliberal school Walter Eucken* ↓ → ⇔	← ↓ The contemporary neo-classical school (1945–) *The theory of externalities *Arthur Cecil Pigou (1877–1959)* *Keynesian economics *John Maynard Keynes (1883–1946)*. ⇔ ⇔ ⇔ ⇔ ⇔	The American-Austrian school *Joseph Schumpeter* (later contribution) The American school *Frederick, Barnard Hawley* ↓ ⇔

The postmodern transition

Institutional environmental economics (1950–) *William Kapp *Bruno S. Frey *Peter Söderbaum *Sociology joins environmental economics ↓ ⇔	Neo-classical environmental economics (1960–) *Coase *Baumol ⇔ ⇔ ↓ ⇔ ⇔	Contemporary ecological economics (1950–) *Nicolas Georgescu-Roegen *Kenneth Boulding The entrepreneurship paradigm becomes more versatile, starts to question the paradigm of modern era in economics, search for connection to macro level ⇔ ↓
Global knowledge and the consequences of externalities	The costs of large-scale production	To produce ecologically sustainable development

Perhaps this is the reason why it has been so hard to identify, even in longitudinal analysis, how these different paradigms have developed (Massa, 1995; Raumolin, 1995; Söderbaum, 1993). Perhaps this misunderstanding also prevents one from identifying the existence of an alternative economic idea that could combine both ecological principles and the economy: that is, entrepreneurship. The classical school, however, applied something from physiocrats. It applied Nature's self-sustaining production cycle to the economy. The economy was isolated as a self-sustaining system, which received Nature's raw materials as an unlimited source of wealth (Christensen, 1996; Ricardo, 1821).

The Three Schools in the Modern Transition

Neo-classical school: the story of rationality and growth

The interest of the followers of Adam Smith, the classical and later neo-classical schools lay in macroeconomics and later in the behaviour of the organization in the environment of large-scale enterprises. The main concern lay in the problems of increasing supply as efficiently as possible. The premises for the theories of macroeconomics and, later, of microeconomics relied on the idea of growth, rational actors with full information and their ability to produce work and welfare (Baumol and Blinder, 1985; Bell, 1981; Ricardo, 1821). It was possible to develop this illusion because demand was growing. Smith's ideas of economic success remained predominant throughout the modern era. Nature and the extraordinary, holistic human being disappeared from the economy in the development of the classical school (Daly and Cobb, 1989: 109–10; Ricardo, 1821). These ideas are manifested also in the thoughts of Leon Walras and William Stanley Jevons, and in the later writings of Karl Menger. Nature and the human being persisted during the transition in two directions: Nature in ecological economics and the human being in the paradigm of entrepreneurship. The latter, however, was also mingled in the thoughts of the German historical school.

Ecological economics: follow the physiocrats

Sadi Nicolas Leonard Carnot (1796–1832), discoverer of the first law of thermodynamics, and the Scottish scientist Patrick Geddes (1854–1932), represent ecological economics. Geddes proposed that economics should be rebuilt according to a knowledge of biology, thermodynamics and the doctrine of the physiocrats (http://www.cce.ed.ac.uk/geddes/research.html/; Macdonald, 1999). He claimed that our environment (water, air and land) is public. He understood the fallacy of the growth concept and was concerned about material consumption without reference to the quality of life. For him technology was not anti-ecological, but rather socially embedded. Geddes' holistic ideas and antagonistic views were not appreciated at the time, nor by recent commentators and biographers (Small, 1999). Something in his ideas of a 'public environment', however, continued to live in the thoughts of the German historical school.

The German historical school: challenges to the neo-classical school
The roots of the German historical school and its followers, the institutionalists, can be traced back to the 1850s. Its founder was Wilhelm Roscher (1817–1894) and among its early contributors can be mentioned Bruno Hildebrandt, Karl Knieves and Gustav Schmoller (1838–1917) (Von Böhm-Bawerk, 1890–91; Massa, 1995: 26; Söderbaum, 1993).

The German historical school regarded the development of economics as a collective phenomenon. Its focus was on historical and cultural development, and on institutions. Roscher was in disagreement with the physiocrats and also with the classical school (Von Böhm-Bawerk, 1890–91). For Schmoller (1897 [1884]), mercantilism represented the collective power of society, which formed the basis for all economic progress. These ideas are a manifestation of the difference between the classical school and the historical school in their development right through the modern era until today. Whereas the classical school concentrated on the equilibrium between supply and demand and on international trade, the core for the historical school was the power of the state. The classical school thought that welfare could be produced through a growing demand created through a self-sustaining market system, while the historical school thought that the activities of the public sector were foremost. The debate between these two schools forms the grand story of modern times. It is amazing that both of them are categorized as schools of environmental economics, since neither of them was interested in the environment. If the postmodern transition had not revitalized ecological ideas, it could even be questioned whether either of these schools belongs to environmental economics, even though they most certainly can be regarded as schools of economics. This interpretation would allow us to search for the connection between ecological sustainability and economics from its roots in the physiocrats, and leave the fostered interpretation of modern times behind us. Rather similar ideas can be found in the writings of Ilpo Massa (1995).

The school of the American institutionalists brought the ideas of the German historical school into modern times. Their thoughts were submerged, however, beneath those of Keynesian economics, the most popular in modern era's political decision-making in many Western countries. When ecological economics tried to develop and apply ecological principles to society, the representatives of entrepreneurship on their behalf tried to question the rational equilibrium and defend the role of the human being in economics. Their contributors can be found in the transition in all three different schools. Towards the end of the transition, however, each of the schools chose its main areas of interest. In this process both the classical and the institutional schools finally lost the human being in their descriptions.

Entrepreneurship in the Modern Transition: Trying to Find its Own Path

When Britain lost its position as a leader of industrialization, the story of entrepreneurship revived. It travelled from France to Austria, the USA and Germany. At the turn of the nineteenth and twentieth centuries the ideas of the classical school were questioned. It was noticed that the reality and actors in reality were far more complicated than simply equilibrium, open competition and actors as a rational homogenous group (Von Böhm-Bawerk, 1890–91; Daly and Cobb, 1989; Schmoller, 1881, 1897 [1884]).

Carl Menger is regarded as a founder of the Austrian school. On the other hand, he is also seen as a contributor to the neo-classical school. In the Austrian school he represented subjectivism. An entrepreneur is an individual who can control and coordinate the chain of inputs in the production process. The uniqueness of the entrepreneur lies in his ability to make decisions, acquire knowledge and predict. Action is an insecure process. He also tried to bring subjectivism and insecurity to the neo-classical school with the concept of marginal utility. Menger's follower Friedrich von Wieser (1851–1926) expanded the idea of entrepreneurship into that of the micro unit, the firm. Before him, it had meant a macro-level economic process created by a unique and free human being. Now it started also to refer to a firm. Böhm-Bawark himself also described entrepreneurship. His follower was Joseph Schumpeter (1883–1950), perhaps most quoted contributor to entrepreneurship.

For Schumpeter the core of entrepreneurship is innovation. The entrepreneur combines resources in an innovative manner, thus creating something new. Innovation breaks with old behaviour in a radical manner. The entrepreneur is one who does things in a novel fashion guided by intuition. Schumpeter's contribution can be divided into two phases: the early contribution took place in Austria and the later one in the USA (e.g. Lovio, 1993). For Schumpeter, economic development was endogenous change. For Menger, economic progress led to the development of entrepreneurship; for Schumpeter, entrepreneurship led to economic progress by breaking old, static behaviour and by inventing new ways and methods. It is understandable that Schumpeter emphasized innovativeness, since industrialization in Austria was very leisurely or 'rocky' from the eighteenth century to the Second World War, as some scientists describe it (Cameron, 1995: 298).

From the USA, entrepreneurship travelled back to Europe with Max Weber (1864–1929), the representative of the German historical school. The school did not approve of the idea of a human being as being a 'hedonistic atom' (Hebert and Link, 1988: 102). Their ideas mainly followed those of other contributors of entrepreneurship. Economic development was for them a dynamic process, which broke with old ways of behaviour and created new ones.

Max Weber represents the third generation of this school. For Weber, the entrepreneur represented the opposite of the craftsman's privileged formality. In his descriptions can be found the human being, the firm he runs and the economic process. Previously, entrepreneurship had mainly denoted an individual who produces economic welfare. This is understandable, since in Europe the crafts tried to prevent the founding of firms (for example the Bubble Act in Britain).

Different approaches to entrepreneurship theory building in economics, sociology and psychology developed from these roots. Amazingly few differences can be found between the theories of early contributors. They describe entrepreneurship as a special kind of management and ownership. The entrepreneur is a holistic, extraordinary human being who, by combining resources in a novel way, by applying new knowledge, taking risks and making decisions, creates something new. Some of the theories focus more on ownership, some on management (Barreto, 1989; Dahmen et al., 1994; Kovalainen, 1993; Weber, 1969 [1947]). Towards the end of the transition, the concept of the firm started to enter into the explanations of entrepreneurship. This was followed by the disappearance of entrepreneurship from macro-level explanations.

We can now see how different ideas criss-cross in the transition and, on the other hand, how societies, in this case Western industrializing societies, chose the ideas they regarded as successful. The relationship between these three schools is shown in Table 1.1. The neo-classical school achieved dominance. Its ideas of growth and its influence on welfare seemed to fascinate the most. The institutionalists started to question and debate the classical school. For the classical school, the premise for welfare was growth created by open competition, mass production and rational, homogeneous actors with economic motivation. For the institutionalists, state and collective power was the premise for welfare and economic progress. The role of institutionalists was to control the so-called market, and to create the infrastructure for economic progress, that is, growth. Ecological economics and entrepreneurship, for their part, had their own but at the same time a diminishing identity. Both of them had their bases in the human being as an extraordinary and free actor. Both of them also had a holistic, integrated approach to human beings and society. The difference between them was related to Nature as an explicit phenomenon. Nature seems to have been left on the shoulders of ecological economics alone. It disappeared from all other lines of thought. In the institutionalists it was replaced by collective power; in the neo-classical school the idea of Nature as a self-sustaining system was cloned into economics, and other dimensions of society disappeared. What could not be explained in monetary terms did not have any place in economical explanations. Why this is so amazing is that all these three schools, except entrepreneurship as a separate school, are categorized as schools of environmental economics.

So far I have argued how three different paradigms can be identified, and have also shown their roots and chronological order. I have also tried to show how the choices among and within these paradigms have been made, since these decisions, and the development that followed them, have most deeply influenced the situation we are living in at the moment. Next I will concentrate on the development of the modern era in order to discuss what kind of consequences these decisions produced. Finally, I will proceed to the postmodern transition to show how irrational and ineffective these choices have been. It will be seen how these paradoxes and contradictions start to direct our focus again toward entrepreneurship and ecological principles.

THE DOMINANCE OF GROWTH AND ORDER SUPPRESS ECOLOGICAL THINKING AND ENTREPRENEURSHIP IN THE MODERN ERA

Economic Growth of the Modern Era

The modern era gives us quite a clear picture of society's relationship to ecologically sustainable development and to growth. In the modern era the population has grown exponentially (Miller, 1979: 4–5). This meant growing demand and polarized welfare. Since the 1950s most of the population growth has taken place in the developing countries. Gross domestic product (GDP) has grown too. The time series in most growth research starts in 1820–1860. From the sixteenth to the seventeenth centuries growth is estimated to have fluctuated between 0.1 and 0.3

per cent. After that, with the exception of two world wars, GDP grew all over Europe till the 1970s (1860, 1.6 per cent; 1974, 5.5 per cent). The same trend can be identified in other industrialized countries (e.g. Hjerppe, 1989).

The productivity grew also. More products could be produced with less labour. All kind of transportation grew, by sea, land and air. Growth was expected to reduce the human suffering involved in poverty (Common, 1999). The problem is that instead of helping to alleviate poverty, it increased it (e.g. Giddens, 1997; UNDP, 1999). Open competition also seemed to be an illusion: until 1913 it was reasonably free, but immediately the growth in a country was threatened, it started to use restrictions (Kenwood and Lougheed, 1971). Restrictions mostly affected the welfare of developing countries dominated by agriculture and that of women, thus increasing the inequality between countries.

While industrialization was expanding, another kind of ethos started to spread in Western industrialized countries from the late nineteenth century onwards. This was the dominance of organization. We have implicitly followed the very first interpretation of culture in our lives, that is, 'order'. We have organized our lives and Nature, believing that organizing is a way to secure our existence and our success. In this stream of ideas the relationship between Nature and the human being changed. This was followed by the notion that Nature can be controlled and changed through technology. This line of thought became dominant in the modern era. It had no place for entrepreneurship or ecological ideas, focusing instead on increasing efficiency by organizing production and society (e.g. Etzioni, 1968; Morgan, 1986; Zuboff, 1988).

Three Different Schools Maintain their Places in the Modern Era

The neo-classical school strengthens its domination
In the reality of the modern era, the position of the neo-classical school strengthened as a school of economics as well as a school of environmental economics. Within the school of environmental economics, the focus was turned to looking after economic growth so as to be able to secure employment. This can be noticed when we follow the ideas of two contributors in environmental economics, Arthur Cecil Pigou (1877–1959) and John Maynard Keynes (1883–1946).

Pigou used the term 'externalities' when he referred to the effects produced by the market but left outside its concern. He thought that when prices fall, wealth grows, individuals can consume more and thus production can grow (Arnold, 1999). For him economics could only describe those factors that can be measured in monetary terms, that is, by GDP

(Serafy, 1991). The problem is that in practice these other dimensions were left out of the mainstream discussion of wealth. Daly and Cobb (1989: 52–53) describe this as a spillover effect, not noticed until the 1930s. Pigou was Keynes's mentor and teacher. Keynes introduced the idea of modified capitalism and semi-autonomous actors. He also believed that unemployment was a consequence of a lack of purchasing power. The state can help in this, by increasing demand through controlling investments, savings and interest rates. Keynes strongly influenced the politics of Europe and the USA (Daly and Cobb, 1989: 209).

Entrepreneurship fights for its existence

I have now discussed how two main interests started to dominate reality in Western industrialized countries in the modern era, that is, growth and employment. Society was neither interested in entrepreneurship nor in the environment (for similar conclusions, see for example Barreto, 1989; Massa, 1995). The rationalist story of the power and meaning of growth and order in economics is in fact a different story from that of entrepreneurship and environmental concern. The ideas of Adam Smith have followed us through modern times, even though it has been observed in many contexts that their premises produce paradoxical and controversial consequences when verified empirically.

When this illusion of the possibility for continuous growth, producing employment and wealth, gained dominance, entrepreneurship was not valued. It lost its role as a creator of economic progress. Its focus turned to the new, emerging micro-level phenomenon, the firm, and started to mean small business ownership and management. Within the discussion about entrepreneurship, the American approach gained dominance. Enterprise and profit were extremely clear in this approach (e.g. Barreto, 1989: 37). The macro-level meaning of entrepreneurship was lost and the environmental discussion was silenced.

Institutionalists challenge the neo-classical school but remain marginal

Later, the American institutional school, the structural-dynamics school and the ordoliberal school followed the ideas of the institutionalists. The common feature of the institutionalists was their holistic and multidisciplinary approach and dynamics applied from the physiocrats and later from the representatives of entrepreneurship (http://www.mtsu.edu/tvs2/instit.html).

The American institutionalists emphasized social responsibility and society's role in the economy. Their culmination can be identified in the 1920s and 1930s. They were, however, left on the sidelines when the doctrine of Keynes spread throughout Western countries, but they re-emerged in the 1960s (Söderbaum, 1993). In the 1930s, Harold A. Innes presented how the world economy affected national welfare when its natural resources were overcultivated or overused. According to him, this kind of robbery was followed by a one-sided structure of the economy, and further by the economy's instability. The state's role in controlling and guiding the economy was important, therefore. This has happened, in fact, in developing countries.

As its name suggests, the structural-dynamics school was interested in the structures of national and international economy. Its main contribution was made between the world wars. After the Second World War it was marginalized because of the Keynesian influence. The undeniable merit of this school lies in its endeavour to expand the discussion to cover global development. The home of the ordoliberals is Germany; it also has support in Switzerland. According to this school, the market lacks the ability of self-control; therefore state control is needed.

The institutionalists have given much to environmental economics. They have created the ideas of common responsibility and made explicit the global aspect of this field. Thanks to them the connection between entrepreneurship and environmental economics did not disappear. Even though this connection was modest, it remains open for us to rediscover it in the postmodern transition. Why this is so important will be seen when we start to consider the consequences produced by economic growth. What can be noticed in the scientific discussion of economics in the modern era is that the human actor and Nature as premises still do not interest scientists. These aspects have disappeared from mainstream discussions.

THE POSTMODERN TRANSITION

The Consequences of Growth Show Up

When we look at the empirical evidence resulting from growth, the dilemma between the premises of economics and its consequences can be identified. The mass production techniques used in industry and agriculture have not been employed without consequences. They have affected air, water, land and the welfare of people; in the opposite way, however, to that expected. It is estimated that half of the world's cultivated land will be ruined by the year 2025. Already, 840 million people are malnourished (UNDP, 1999). For the first time food production is also meeting its limits due to the robbery taking place in the sea (Halinen, 1998). We have also experienced changes in the climate, which have global scope. Instead of wealth we have produced poverty and inequality. Instead of employment we have produced unemployment. Western countries woke up when the growth rate of GDP decreased to the level of the 1900s. At the same time unemployment in Organisation for Economic Co-operation and Development (OECD) countries doubled during the 1980s and also in the 1990s (Naschold, 1995: 18).

At the same time it was noticed that large firms and organizations did not produce work. New work was created in small firms or by self-employed citizens. Large firms grew globally, extended and diversified their production chains all over the world, using the criterion of short-term profit. Even though these facts were noticed, societies did not change their behaviour: they started to put even more pressure on growth. It is still thought that by increasing supply we can produce wealth, and the key to that is growth as measured by GDP.

These consequences can be summarized as growing polarizations not only between countries, areas and regions, but also within them. They concern the whole globe, not only poor countries. As a whole, it is a question of the dialogue between growth and wealth, rather than wealth produced by growth. It poses us the question of whether to grow or not to grow. It also concerns questions of global and local. Some essential polarizations are listed below:

1. Polarizations between rich and poor. This gap has been widening since the early nineteenth century (Table 1.2).
2. We may also note that technology has not been a solution for poor countries. In 1993, ten countries accounted for 84 per cent of global research and development expenditures (UNDP, 1999). Industrialized countries use 93.8 per cent of research expenditures, developing countries 6.2 per cent and Africa only 0.3 per cent (Calder and Newell, 1992).
3. Growth and diversified production techniques have caused damage to Nature. The damage has mostly affected poor nations, while rich industrialized countries have received the advantages. There are global changes in the atmosphere. The temperature of the earth has risen. Industrialized countries use most of the energy and thus also cause most of the damage. It is expected however that poor countries will increase their use of energy in the future (Kuusisto et al., 1996: 33). Also the ozone layer is getting thinner. Every year 3 million people die from air pollution and 5 million as a result of water contamination (UNDP, 1999: 22). It should be noted that human beings have produced all these changes. Simulations predict that the consequences of growth will have their major effect in the near future (Miller, 1979).

Table 1.2   Stark disparities between rich and poor in global opportunities

In 1997	Richest 20% of population (%)	Middle 60% of population (%)	Poorest 20% of population (%)
Shares of world GDP	86	13	1
Shares of exports	82	17	1
Shares of foreign direct investments	68	31	1
Shares of internet users	93.3	6.5	0.2

Source: Summarized from UNDP (1999: 2).

How we have reacted to these threats is that the world has been divided into three regional blocs: Asia, North America and Europe (Spybey, 1996). Each of these has started to link up to those nations having a lower GDP; in this way they can access cheap labour and increasing demand.

Leaning on this empirical evidence, it is hard to draw any other conclusion than that modern economics has failed. Its premises have not produced the expected consequences. It is also obvious that these consequences, for the first time, have an inevitably global impact. Geddes' discovery that we have a common environment seems to be verified. This has had some impact on economical explanations as can be seen when we follow their development in the postmodern transition. It should be noticed however that even though there are some voices questioning growth as an idol, we still rely on it as a solution.

The Dialogue between the Paradigms of Environmental Economics Expands in the Postmodern Transition

The neo-classical school starts to notice the environment

The focus in environmental economics turned more to externalities and their effects, but not actually to Nature (Arnold, 1999; Baumol and Blinder, 1985; Coase, 1991; Zylicz, 1991: 385). The premises of the neo-classical school rested on the fundamental presumptions of the classical school. My assumption is that the school has tried to answer the question of how much it costs to use the common environment, or how much it costs to fix the consequences produced by the market. The difference compared to previous ideas is that there is now a readiness to pay some attention to the environment.

Institutionalists are worried about global welfare

There has been a bit of confusion in separating institutionalists from eco-logical economists, since their differences over economic thought about entrepreneurship have not been clear (e.g. Massa, 1995). By following this presentation however, the route of the three different schools can be iden-tified. It helps us to identify, as the influential contributors in the school of institutional environmental economics, William Kapp, Bruno S. Frey and Peter Söderbaum. Such scientists as Daniel Bell, Anthony Giddens and Ulrich Beck also belong to the school of institutional environmental economics. They have produced such concepts as reflective sociology, the risk society and reflective modernization (e.g. Beck et al., 1995; Bell, 1981; Giddens, 1997). Their incontestable contribution concerns global effects: they have brought us the idea that local activities produce global conse-quences, and that what is taking place in and for Western countries affects global welfare, both directly and indirectly.

The difference between the nature of the institutionalists and that of the neo-classical school can be characterized by polarizations. It could be stated that the neo-classical school created economic success for the few – the wealth side of polarizations – while institutionalists for their part were concerned with the ugly side of the polarizations produced by the neo-classical thinking. In the postmodern transition this discussion has ever more closely approached Nature and its limitations.

Direct concern about the environment as Nature can be identified since the 1950s in the ideas of Karl Polanyi and Karl W. Kapp. They show that environmental and social costs have a direct relationship with industrialization and the market economy (Van der Bergh, 1996). Kapp opposed the idea that welfare can be measured in monetary terms (Söderbaum, 1993). According to him, giving a money value to welfare does not solve the problem of choice, nor change the fact that we risk human health and survival (Munda, 1997: 222). Kapp's ideas follow the dialogue which has taken place all throughout the modern era. Frey also continued this dialogue in the 1970s. The value of their contribu-tion can be seen in their questioning the possibility of growth at the explicit level. When the neo-classical school asked how much should be paid for degrading the environment, the institutionalists verified that the consequences of mass production and growth were catastrophic and that society has a responsibility to look after them. Even though both are important and valuable, there still remains the problem of how to combine the economy and ecologically sustainable develop-ment; how to produce ecological sustainability. Both schools neglected the fact that the destruction of nature is carried out by human beings. This means that ecologically sustainable development can also be produced by human behaviour, not by rational equilibrium or by collective structures and institutions. This concerns the fact that Geddes already noticed in claiming that technology is socially constructed. Another fact is that ecological sustainability cannot be produced without ecological premises. This problem cannot be solved by pondering the consequences of destructive behaviour, but rather by describing the conditions and premises for sustainable development. This kind of endeavour can be found in the ideas of the third school, ecological economics. To combine them with economics, however, needs a suitable paradigm in economics. This is entrepreneurship. This final step in my discussion will be taken next.

Ecological economics finds its roots
Georgescu-Roegen, the Anglo-Saxon Kenneth E. Boulding and the French Michel Cepede, the representatives of ecological economics, started to claim that economics should be 'ecologized' (Raumolin, 1995: 45). They tried to find a solution as to how to combine economics and Nature. Georgescu-Roegen claimed that economic theories had totally forgotten the connection between Nature and economics (Christensen, 1996). He applied thermodynamics to economics (Georgescu-Roegen, 1971), and suggested, following the second law of thermodynamics, that the aim of economic activities should be low entropy. Daly suggested that the entropy law is a formalized expression of the general and absolute scarcity that mankind and its economy are subjected to (Van der Bergh, 1996: 21). In conclusion, Georgescu-Roegen suggested that perfect recycling is not possible and that this should be a new law of thermodynamics. Perhaps the most valuable outcome of these thoughts is the realization of the existence of absolute scarcity, not taken seriously by economics before.

Boulding, together with Herman E. Daly, demanded that the economy should rest on evolutionary theories, ecology and thermodynamics (Raumolin, 1995: 47). Boulding claimed that the economy and the biosphere can only survive if short-term-oriented, exploitative, expansive human behaviour is replaced by long-term-oriented, conservative and prudent actions (Van der Bergh, 1996: 17).

With the ideas of these scientists we return to the holistic ideas of the physiocrats, how wealth is produced by human beings within Nature's recycling capacity. Its dependence on the biosphere raises some other issues. During the modern transition the role of Nature was understood mostly through experience and intuitive conclusions. In this transition we actually have concepts to describe these relationships. From the perspective of ecological sustainability they concern ecology, while from the perspective of human behaviour it is suggested that the keys could be found in entrepreneurship. These constitute the raw materials for combining Nature and economics. It should be emphasized however that this is only an option, since it has not been done before; as Bahtin says, it concerns existential knowledge, the possibility of knowledge but not actually existing knowledge.

The Premises for Ecological Sustainability

We can describe the premises for ecological sustainability through the relatively new concept or phenomenon known as the ecosystem. This was introduced by the British ecologist Sir Arthur Tansley in 1935. It describes an ecological community consisting of living organisms – that is, a biological community – together with a physical and chemical environment – that is, a non-living environment – and their relationship to each other in a certain area. In an ecosystem these interact with each other. This interaction produces unpredictable consequences. Even though there are different ideas about the development of an ecosystem, a consensus has been reached concerning certain principles. These are: (1) the sensitivity of the balance of the ecosystem; (2) its local nature; (3) the long-term development required to form a competitive ecosystem able to survive; (4) the unpredictability of the results of outside interventions.

When we combine these ideas with those of the ecological economists, especially with the laws of thermodynamics, we can produce three premises of ecological economics. The first law of thermodynamics states that in a closed system energy does not disappear but only changes its form of existence. The second law of thermodynamics states that a certain amount of this energy cannot be used effectively, some of it always being used in the changing process or for less useful purposes. All living existence on the earth is dependent on energy. Most of it comes from the sun. Energy use is never 100 per cent efficient; a certain amount of energy is always wasted. This is why 100 per cent recycling is not possible. Less changes in the forms of existence therefore means more efficiency. It also means more ecological sustainability. This means short production chains. Short production chains are even more important when we understand the sensitivity and local nature of the ecosystem. Outside interventions are always threats to an eco-balance.

The second premise concerns the absolute scarcity of natural resources. This requires that we use them as efficiently as possible. This means that each product uses as few natural resources as possible and that we use these products for as long as possible.

By combining the empirical evidence – that is, the fact that the destruction of nature is produced by one species only, human beings – we are able to conclude that the achievement of ecological sustainability is thus dependent on the ability of this species to understand the consequences of its choices. It can be assumed that we have the ability and possibility to produce ecological sustainability and control the consequences of our consumption in the ecosystem we are part of. Now we have quite rational reasons and premises for ecological sustainability. They form three principles: (1) as efficient recycling as possible; (2) as efficient use of natural resources as possible; (3) as prolonged use of each form of existence as possible. These principles mean short production chains as far as possible, and prolonged use of each part of the chain as far as possible.

When we compare the results of the modern era to these principles, we can see that from the perspective of ecological sustainability the modern era has produced contrary results. This conclusion can be drawn both by analysing the dialogue between the dominating schools of economics, and by looking at the consequences this dialogue has produced.

In the Postmodern Transition, Entrepreneurship is Looking for its Connection to Society

Now that we have found that the world around us is changing and that the illusion of continuous, implied growth, ever-growing prosperity, full employment and the domination of the Western world with its large companies and institutions is not producing the expected welfare for us, a new stream of discussion is about to flow. There is much similarity between this conversation and that in France during the transition from the traditional to the modern era. In this postmodern transition, entrepreneurship has invaded organization theories, other fields of economics, learning theories and so on, but in its original form (Argyris et al., 1985; Minzberg and Quinn, 1991; Morgan, 1986; Näsi, 1991). In the transition from modern to postmodern, it has found a new object which is a product of the modern era, namely the organization. Time has produced three different kinds of present-day entrepreneurship: (1) the small enterprise, meaning the individual entrepreneur and the entrepreneur's firm; (2) intrapreneurship, meaning an organization's collective behaviour; and (3) individual, self-oriented entrepreneurship, meaning an individual's self-oriented behaviour. Probably entrepreneurship has the same role in this transition as in the previous one. It has been used as an instrument for changing the culture and envisioning a new future. Society is using it as a tool to change its culture (Kyrö, 1997).

Now the discussions about entrepreneurship are looking for mutual

Table 1.3   Changes in entrepreneurship paradigms

Time	Whose society?	Entrepreneurship
Traditional era before 18th century	The nobility's, administered through feudalism, the crafts system and mercantilism * Class society, man's place in society was based on his class at birth	Entrepreneurship started its journey in semantics as an individual – adventurer, risk-taker – project-based assignments from the Crown
Theory building in entrepreneurship starts		
The modern transition at the beginning of 18th century till the shift between 19th and 20th centuries	Citizens' society * feudalism and crafts system broke * liberalism and democracy as idols	Entrepreneur as an individual and entrepreneurship as a creater of economic success (macro-level process) * breaks old models of behaviour and old systems, creates new ways of work and ownership * innovator, coordinator, special kind of observer, takes risks and responsibility for his own life, applies new knowledge
1st change in the paradigm of entrepreneurship		
The modern era 19th and 20th centuries	Society of public sector and large firms * homogenizing democracy * order and unified culture * continuous growth and expanding market as idols * unhistorical era * rationality, efficiency, hierarchy, bureaucracy, control, diversification	Entrepreneurship as small business management and ownership, connection to economics (macro level) was lost
2nd change in the paradigm of entrepreneurship		
Postmodern transition 1970–	Polarized society * rich/poor * health/sick * employed/unemployed * civil servant/entrepreneur	Entrepreneurship three forms and again latent meaning in breaking old models and creating new culture 1. individual entrepreneurship

Table 1.3   (continued)

Time	Whose society?	Entrepreneurship
2nd change in the paradigm of entrepreneurship		
	* individuals v. systems' and organizations' society * local/global * knowledge nobility/ segregated	2. small business management and ownership 3. intrapreneurship = organization's collective behaviour
3rd change in the paradigm of entrepreneurship as an option for the future		
Postmodern era?	Struggle with local and global? Struggle with welfare and growth?	Will entrepreneurship reach a meaning at the macro level? Will entrepreneurship again find ecological principles? Will ecological economics and entrepreneurship meet each other?

bases all around the world. These can be identified as an endeavour to make a contribution not only at the micro level but also at the macro level in society. Still, however, entrepreneurship is not a partner at the same table with economists but rather as a partner in an employment project. There is however the option to notice the different bases which entrepreneurship represents in welfare discussion. In the following section an attempt will be made to show how this dialogue can be constructed. By following the discussion of economics it could be claimed that the dialogue in which entrepreneurship has been participating all through its history concerns economic and rational growth versus extraordinary human beings. By separating these two stories from one another the paradigmatic changes in the theories of entrepreneurship can also be revealed, and an expectation for the future as an option can be formulated.

There have been two shifts in entrepreneurship paradigm building. The first occurred when entrepreneurship lost its connection to the macro level and Nature and started to refer to the small firm. The next was when it expanded to intrapreneurship. We are now waiting for the next shift, that is, the connection back to the macro level again, and finally to ecological economics. This path has been built in Table 1.3.

EVALUATION OF THE JOURNEY INTO HISTORY AND SOME CONCLUSIONS

The aim of this journey has been to see if it is possible to combine economics and ecologically sustainable development. This was approached by asking, as a social-historical process, the question: To grow or not to grow? Social historical methodology attempts to answer the questions: What happened? How did it happen? Why did it happen? What was it all about?

The answer to the question 'What happened?' seems to indicate that the idea that economical growth measured in monetary terms will produce welfare, has been an illusion. The results have been almost the opposite. Paradoxically enough this relationship has been argued through rationality and objectivity, but it seems to be quite irrational compared to the empirical facts available to us.

The question 'How did it happen?' could be answered on these bases. The answer to the first question leads us to conclude that reality is made by scientific descriptions and explanations rather than vice versa. The suggestion that science should also make value statements, instead of just telling how things are, seems to be a reasonable request from this perspective.

Why did it happen? The answer to that seems to be simple. Since economic growth has produced welfare for a few – that is, Western industrialized countries – during the modern era, it has not been questioned, even though empirical evidence had already warned us long ago about its consequences.

What was it all about? To be positive in this final question, I would like to believe that the possibilities and values offered by entrepreneurship in its very first forms, and the tremendous work done by many brilliant scientists over a period of 200 years, will finally be recognized and also valued by the mainstream of economics. This means that economics has the courage to question its very basic premises, such as what efficiency is and how it is measured. Ecologically sustainable development suggests that economic behaviour, also measured by rational and objective yardsticks, means to produce as much wealth as possible with as few resources as possible. If this cannot be measured in contemporary monetary terms, these terms should be re-evaluated. The positive side of this story is that there actually are models and criteria for such an evaluation, if we are willing to learn from history. I hope this story has revealed some ideas for that: the option offered by entrepreneurship and ecological economics.

Finally, as mentioned at the beginning of the discussion, the reader will be the evaluator of the validity of historical research. You will decide how coherently the story has been told, how 'truthful' it seems to be. In the idea of the human being nurtured by entrepreneurship, this means action. Is the picture painted here holistic and reasonable enough to be able to give raw material for acting upon? As Georgescu-Roegen said, being is becoming. If I have succeeded in giving some raw material for new ideas about growth and its consequences, some ideas in rethinking what is valuable and what is not, I think something has been accomplished.

NOTE

*   Originally published 2001 as a shorter version in the *International Journal of Sustainable Development and World Ecology*, 8, 15–28.

REFERENCES

Argyris, C., R. Putnam and D. Mclain Smith (1985), *Action Science*, San Francisco, CA: Jossey-Bass Publishers.

Arnold, J. (1999), 'How is it possible for Pigou to have influenced and contributed to the construction of New Keynesian Economics?', http://tommy.iinet.net.au/essays/ja2.html, accessed 3 July 1999.

Barreto, H. (1989), *The Entrepreneur in Microeconomic Theory. Disappearence and Explanation*, London, UK and New York, USA: Routledge.

Baumol, W.J. and A.S. Blinder (1985), *Economics. Principles and Policy*, 3rd edn, San Diego, CA: Harcourt Brace Jovanovich.

Beck, U., A. Giddens and S. Lash (1995), *Nykyajan jäljillä* (Reflexive Modernization), Tampere: Vastapaino.

Bell, D. (1981), 'Models and reality in economic discourse', in D. Bell and I. Kristol (eds), *The Crisis in Economic Theory*, New York: Basic Books, pp. 46–80.

Van der Bergh, J.C.J.M. (1996), *Ecological Economics and Sustainable Development: Theory, Methods and Applications*, Aldershot, UK and Brookfield, VT, USA: Edward Elgar.

Böhm-Bawerk, E. von (1890–91), 'The historical vs. the deductive method in political economy', transl. H. Leonard, *Annals of the American Academy*, 1 (1890–91), http://socserv2.mcmaster.ca/ econ/ugcm/3113/bawerk/bohm001.html.

Calder, N. and J. Newell (ed.) (1992), *Maapallon tulevaisuus. Tieteen maailma*, edited in Finnish by K. Taipale and R. Taipale, Kopenhagen: Bonneirs Boge A/S.

Cameron, R. (1995), *Maailman taloushistoria paleoliittiselta kaudelta nykypäivään. Teollistumista koskevin osin*, Juva: WSOY Suomen Historiallinen Seura.

Casson, M. (1982), *The Entrepreneur. An Economic Theory*, Oxford: Martin Robertson.

Christensen, P. (1996), 'Classical foundations for a physiological and ecological model of sustainability', in S. Faucheux, D. Pearce and J. Proops (eds), *Models of Sustainable Development*, New Horizons in Environmental Economics, Aldershot, UK and Brookfield, VT, USA: Edward Elgar Publishing, pp. 105–22.

Coase, H.R. (1991), 'Autobiography of Ronald Coase', http://nobel.sdsc.edu/laureates/economy-1991-1-autobio.html/ accessed 10 August 1999.

Common, M.S. (1999), 'Roles for ecology in ecological economics and sustainable development', Chapter 26. http://life.csu.edu.au/esa.esa97/papers/common/common.htm, accessed 19 July 1999.

Dahmen, E., L. Hannah and I.M. Kirzner (1994), *The Dynamics of Entrepreneurship, Crafoord Lectures 5*, Institute of Economic Research, Malmö: Lund University Press.

Daly, H.E. and J.B. Cobb (1989), *For the Common Good: Redirecting the Economy toward Community, the Environment, and a Sustainable Future*, Boston, MA: Beacon Press.

Dillard, D. (1967), *Economic Development of the North Atlantic Community: Historical Introduction to Modern Economics*, Englewood Cliffs, NJ: Prentice-Hall.

Etzioni, A. (1968), *Nykyajan organisaatiot*, Foorum Kirjasto, Helsinki: Kustannusosakeyhtiö Tammi.

Georgescu-Roegen, N. (1971), *The Entropy Law and the Economic Process*, Cambridge, MA: Harvard University Press.

Giddens, A. (1997), *Sociology*, 3rd edn, Cambridge: Polity Press.

Haapala, P. (1989), *Sosiaalihistoria, Johdatus tutkimukseen*, Helsinki: Suomen historiallinen seura.

Halinen, A. (1998), *Riittääkö ruoka? – maailman ravintotilanne*, Fakta Osa 23, Porvoo: WSOY.

Harvey, D. (1990), *The Condition of Postmodernity*, Oxford: Basil Blackwell.

Hebert, R.F. and A.N. Link (1988), *The Entrepreneur. Mainstream Views and Radical Critiques*, 2nd edn, New York: Praeger.

Hjerppe, R. (1989), *The Finnish Economy 1860–1985, Growth and Structural Change*, Helsinki: Bank of Finland, Government Printing Centre.

Hobbes, T. (1660), *The Leviathan*, http://osu.orst.edu/instruct/phl302/texts/hobbes/leviathan-contents.html, accessed 30 March 1999.

Hofstede, G. (1991), *Cultures and Organizations. Software of the Mind. Intercultural Cooperation and its Importance for Survival*, London: McGraw-Hill.

http://www.cce.ed.ac.uk/geddes/research.html/, accessed 2 April 1999.

http://www.mtsu.edu.~tvs2/instit.html.

http://www.mtsu.edu~^tvs2l, accessed 24 March 1999.

http://www.mtsu.edu~^tvs2/quesnay.html, accessed 24 March 1999.

Kenwood, A.G. and A.L. Lougheed (1971), *The Growth of the International Economy 1820–1960*, London: George Allen & Unwin.

Kovalainen, A. (1993), *At The Margins of The Economy, Women's Self Employment in Finland 1960–1990*, Series A 9:1993, Turku School of Economics and Business Administration.

Kuusisto, E., L. Kauppi and P. Heikinheimo (1996), *Ilmastonmuutos ja Suomi*, Helsinki: Yliopistopaino.

Kyrö, P. (1996), 'The points of transition in reforming the understanding and meaning of entrepreneurship', *Academy of Entrepreneurship Journal*, 2(1), 71–94.

Kyrö, P. (1997), *Yrittäjyyden muodot ja tehtävä ajan murroksissa*, Jyväskylä studies in computer science and economics and statistics 38, Lievestuore: University of Jyväskylä.

Kyrö, P. (1999), *Yrittäjyys, talous ja kestävä kehitys*, Taloustieteiden tiedekunta, No. 119/1999, Julkaisuja: Jyväskylä University.

Kyrö, P. (2001), 'To grow or not to grow? Entrepreneurship and sustainable development', *International Journal of Sustainable Development and World Ecology*, 8, 15–28.

Kyrö, P. and U. Suojanen (1999), 'The relationship between sustainable development and entrepreneurship in the postmodern transition', *International Journal of Entrepreneurship*, 3, 30–52.

Lindeqvist, K.O. (1905), *Yleinen historia. Uusi Aika*, Porvoo: WSOY.
Lovio, R. (1993), *Evolution of Firm Communities in New Industries The Case of the Finnish Electronics Industry*, Acta Academiae Oeconomicae Helsingiensis Series A:92, Helsinki: Helsinki School of Economics.
Macdonald, M. (1999), http://www.cce.ed.ac.uk/geddes/Euro.htm, accessed 24 March 1999.
Massa, I. (1995), 'Epävarman yhteiskunnan ympäristöpolitiikka', in I. Massa and O. Rahkonen (eds), *Riskiyhteiskunnan talous: Suomen talouden ekologinen modernisaatio*, Gaudeamus kirja, Helsinki: Hakapaino Oy, pp. 7–38.
Miller, G.T., Jr (1979), *Living in the Environment*, 2nd edn, Belmont, CA: Wadsworth Publishing Company.
Minzberg, H. and J. Quinn (1991), *The Strategy Process: Concepts, Contexts, Cases*, London: Prentice-Hall, International.
Morgan, G. (1986), *Images of Organization*, Beverly Hills, CA: Sage Publications.
Munda, G. (1997), 'Environmental economics, ecological economics, and the concept of sustainable development', *Environmental Values*, 6(2), 213–33.
Naschold, F. (1995), *The Modernization of the Public Sector in Europe: A Comparative Perspective on the Scandinavian Experience*, Helsinki: Ministry of Labour.
Näsi, J. (1991), 'Strategic thinking as doctrine: development of focus areas and new insights', in J. Näsi (ed.), *Arenas of Strategic Thinking*, Helsinki: Foundation for Economic Education, pp. 26–66.
Raumolin, J. (1995), 'Ympäristaloustieteen koulukuntia ja suuntauksia', in I. Massa and O. Rahkonen (eds), *Riskiyhteiskunnan talous: Suomen talouden ekologinen modernisaatio*, Helsinki: Gaudeamus kirja, Hakapaino Oy, pp. 41–96.
Ricardo, D. (1821), *On the Principles of Political Economy and Taxation*, London: John Murray.
Schmoller, G. (1881), 'The idea for justice in political economy', transl. E. Halle and C. Schutz, *Annals of the American Academy of Political and Social Science*, 1, n.s.; German edition, 'Jahrbuch fur Gesetzgebung Verwaltung, und Volkswirtschaft', http://socserv2.socsci.mcmaster.ca/ econ/ugcm/3113/schmoller/justice.
Schmoller, G. (1897 [1884]), *The Mercantile System and its Historical Significance*, English edn, first published 1884 in *Studien uber die withschaftliche Politik Friedrichs des Grossen* (in German), http://socserv2.socsci.mcmaster.ca/ econ/ugcm/3113/schmoller/merkant.
Serafy, S.E. (1991), 'The environment as capital', in R. Constanza (ed.), *Ecological Economics, The Science and Management of Sustainability*, New York: Columbia University Press, pp. 168–75.
Small, M. (1999), 'Vitalistic philosopher – practical visionary – professor of things', http://www.cce.ed.ac.uk/geddes/pg1.htm/, accessed 2 April 1999.
Smith, A. (1776), *The Wealth of Nations*, London: W. Strahan & T. Cadell.
Söderbaum, P. (1993), *Ekologisk ekonomi, Miljö och utveckling i ny belysning*, Lund: Studentlitteratur.
Spybey, T. (1996), *Globalisation and World Society*, Cambridge: Polity Press.
Thurik, R. and S. Wenekers (1999), 'Linking entreprenership and economic growth', European Council for Small Business, 12th Workshop, Lyon, France.
Turner, B.S. (ed.) (1990), *Theories of Modernity and Postmodernity: Theory, Culture and Society*, London: SAGE Publications.
UNCED (1993), *United Nations Conference on Environment and Development, Rio de Janeiro, 3 –14 June 1992*
UNDP (1999), *Human Development Report*, New York: Oxford Unversity Press.
WCED (1987), *Our Common Future (The Brundtland Report)*, World Commission on Environment and Development, Oxford: Oxford University Press.
Weber, M. (1969 [1947]), *The Theory of Social and Economic Organization*, 1st paperback edn 1947, New York: Free Press / Collier-Macmillan.
Wilken, P.H. (1979), *Entrepreneurship, A Comparative and Historical Study*, Norwood, NJ: Ablex Publishing Corporation.

Zuboff, S. (1988), *In the Age of the Smart Machine: The Future of Work and Power*, New York: Basic Books.

Zylicz, T. (1991), 'The role for economic incentives in international allocation of abatement effort', in R. Constanza (ed.), *Ecological Economics, The Science and Management of Sustainability*, New York: Columbia Univeristy Press, 384–99.

2. Sustainable entrepreneurship: what it is
Julia Katharina Binder and Frank-Martin Belz

INTRODUCTION

In 1987 the World Commission on Development and the Environment of the United Nations published the report *Our Common Future*. It defines sustainable development as 'meeting the needs of the present without compromising the ability of future generations to meet their needs' (WCED, 1987: 8). Hereby, the World Commission recognizes interdependencies between the natural environment, human social welfare and economic activity, and the need to establish and maintain a dynamic balance between the three elements. During the 1990s the definition of sustainable development gained wide recognition and support. However, production and consumption patterns remain unsustainable (United Nations, 2002). The scale and nature of human and economic activities exceeds what the planet can physically sustain (World Resources Institute, 2005). Traditionally, entrepreneurship was associated with economic development and wealth generation (e.g. Schumpeter, 1942; Kirzner, 1973), while environmental and social problems were widely neglected. At the nexus of sustainable development and entrepreneurship, Hart and Milstein (1999) were among the first to emphasize the potential of entrepreneurship. They applied the concept of creative destruction (Schumpeter, 1942) as a precondition and the central force for the transition to a sustainable society. They claimed that 'innovators and entrepreneurs will view sustainable development as one of the biggest business opportunities in the history of commerce' (Hart and Milstein, 1999: 25). Whereas sustainable development was often seen as a cost factor impeding competition, the authors provided a new perspective on sustainable development as a source for entrepreneurial opportunities. Following this understanding an increasing number of researchers started devoting their attention to the nexus of sustainable development and entrepreneurship (e.g. Cohen and Winn, 2007; Gibbs, 2009; O'Neill et al., 2009).

The aim of this chapter is to give an overview of the emerging field of sustainable entrepreneurship research. We want to give an answer to the following (deceptively simple) question: What is sustainable entrepreneurship? To this end we conduct a systematic literature review, adopting a transparent and replicable process as suggested by Tranfield et al. (2003). Accordingly, our systematic literature review on sustainable entrepreneurship is organized into three main steps: defining protocols, mapping the field and reporting the findings. The first articles that can be assigned to the topic appeared in the end of the 1990s. However, prior to 2008 just a limited number of 15 articles were published in international, peer-reviewed journals. Since then the number of articles has increased significantly: in the short period between 2009 and 2012 a total of 28 articles were published on sustainable entrepreneurship. The special issue 'Sustainable Development and Entrepreneurship' of the *Journal of Business Venturing* in 2010, co-edited by Daneke et al. (2010) increased the number of articles. More importantly, this special issue in one of the leading and most impactful entrepreneurship journals added legitimacy to the nascent research field. Not surprisingly for a new field of research, there are a variety of different terms for and understandings of sustainable entrepreneurship. Some researchers see it as part of or equal to 'social entrepreneurship' (e.g. Sullivan Mort and Hume, 2009; Berglund and Wigren, 2012; Kury, 2012). Others use sustainable entrepreneurship as synonymous with 'environmental entrepreneurship' and 'ecopreneurship' (e.g. Pastakia, 1998; Isaak, 2002; Schick et al., 2002). Still others embrace sustainable entrepreneurship as the nexus of economic, ecological and social value creation (e.g. Cohen et al., 2008; Kuckertz and Wagner, 2010; Patzelt and Shepherd, 2011). On the one hand, the plurality of terms and approaches add to the creativity of the field. The diversity and openness attracts researchers from different disciplines embracing the topic. On the other hand, the lack of clarity hampers rigorous research. As long as a common understanding of the key term 'sustainable entrepreneurship' is missing, further progress in this stream of research is unlikely, despite ample opportunities. Thus, we want to add clarity to the terminology of sustainable entrepreneurship in this chapter. As a synthesis and result of our review we suggest a definition of sustainable entrepreneurship, which may serve as a common basis for further research in this area. We define sustainable entrepreneurship research as the scholarly examination of how opportunities to bring into existence future goods and services are recognized, developed and exploited, by whom, and with what economic, social and ecological gains.

We proceed as follows. First we look at the origins and related concepts of sustainable entrepreneurship, including conventional entrepreneurship, environmental entrepreneurship and social entrepreneurship. In the main section of the chapter we conduct a systematic literature review on sustainable entrepreneurship. Key concepts of sustainable entrepreneurship include: socio-ecological problems as sources of entrepreneurial opportunities; the process perspective; the individual entrepreneur; the triple bottom line of economic, social and ecological value creation; and transition to a sustainable society. In the final section we give a brief summary and an outlook on further research in the nascent field of sustainable entrepreneurship.

ORIGINS AND RELATED CONCEPTS OF SUSTAINABLE ENTREPRENEURSHIP

Sustainable entrepreneurship is based on and related to conventional entrepreneurship, environmental entrepreneurship and social entrepreneurship. While sustainable entrepreneurship pursues the triple bottom line of economic, social and ecological goals, the other related concepts focus on one or two dimensions. Conventional entrepreneurship is one-dimensional insofar as it mainly puts emphasis on economic goals such as income and profit (Gibb, 1996; Shane, 1996). In contrast, environmental and social forms of entrepreneurship are two-dimensional: environmental entrepreneurship pursues the double bottom line of economic and ecological goals, while social entrepreneurship mainly follows social goals, financed by economic income (Figure 2.1). In this section we briefly introduce the three concepts. In line with the historic development we start with conventional entrepreneurship, and then continue with environmental entrepreneurship and social entrepreneurship. The overview of the three related concepts gives a better understanding for the emergence of sustainable entrepreneurship at the turn of the century and sets the ground for the discussion in the summary section of the chapter.

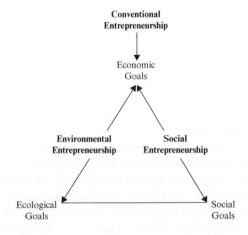

Figure 2.1   Related concepts of sustainable entrepreneurship

Conventional Entrepreneurship

Conventional entrepreneurship research builds on the early works by Schumpeter (1942) and Kirzner (1973). According to Schumpeter, innovation is at the heart of the concept and can be seen as the creative act of combining existing resources in new, valuable ways. Through creative destruction the entrepreneur changes the status quo in a market, thereby creating economic growth (Schumpeter, 1942). Accordingly, Schumpeter refers to the 'creation of opportunities', which he perceives as the 'active' act of creating market disequilibrium (Chiles et al., 2007). For Kirzner, on the other hand, innovation is not a prerequisite for entrepreneurship. Instead, alertness to identify new opportunities is the essential attribute for entrepreneurship in his view (Kirzner, 1973). Thus, Kirzner refers to the 'discovery of opportunities', describing the more 'passive' act of being alert to opportunities that have been overlooked in the past (Kirzner, 1979). Several entrepreneurship researchers have taken a neutral stance towards the two approaches and call for a combination of the two sources, thereby allowing for opportunities either to be created or discovered (McMullen and Shepherd, 2006; Short et al., 2010).

For a long time, the focus of entrepreneurship research has been on the individual entrepreneur. The field was mainly defined in terms of who the entrepreneur is, and what kind of traits and characteristics they have (Gartner, 1988). A notable change in current literature is the emphasis on the nexus of individuals and opportunities, and the process of entrepreneurship (Moroz and Hindle, 2012). One of the most accepted definitions of entrepreneurship comes from Shane and Venkataraman (2000). They define the field of entrepreneurship research as 'the scholarly examination of how, by whom, and with what effects opportunities to create future goods and services are discovered, evaluated, and exploited' (Shane and Venkataraman, 2000: 218).

Key elements of this definition include:

- Opportunities lie at the heart of entrepreneurship. Generally, there are three categories of entrepreneurial opportunities: the creation of new information; the exploitation of market inefficiencies that result from market information asymmetries; and the reaction to shifts in the relative costs and benefits of alternative uses for resources (Drucker, 1985).
- '[B]y whom' refers to the nexus of the individual and opportunities. The recognition of entrepreneurial opportunities is a subjective process (Shane and Venkataraman, 2000), influenced by alertness (Kirzner, 1973) and prior knowledge (Shane, 2003).

- '[D]iscovered, evaluated and exploited' relates to the activity-based process of entrepreneurship (Shane and Venkataraman, 2000; Ucbasaran et al., 2001; Zahra, 2007).
- '[T]o create future goods and services' refers to material and imma- terial services, which are combined in novel ways, and which are not yet offered on the market (Venkataraman, 1997).
- Effects can be any effects, but in most studies on conventional entre- preneurship the output is measured in terms of profits, putting an emphasis on economic goals (Davidsson and Wiklund, 2001).

Environmental Entrepreneurship

The term and the concept of 'environmental entrepreneurship' gained some popularity in the early 1990s (e.g. Blue, 1990; Bennett, 1991; Berle, 1991). However, the initial academic interest in environmental entre- preneurship soon shifted away (Schaltegger, 2002). In 2002, a special issue on environmental entrepreneurship was published in the *Greener Management International Journal*, which contributed to a reignition of interest in the research stream. A substantial problem with environmental entrepreneurship research is its terminology, leading to greater difficul- ties in establishing the phenomenon as a research field. Typical of this is the *Greener Management International Journal* special issue in 2002, in which the same phenomenon was subject to three different terminologies that were used synonymously: Linnanen (2002) termed the phenomenon 'environmental entrepreneurship', Schaltegger (2002) defined it as 'eco- preneurship', while Walley and Taylor (2002) used 'green entrepreneur- ship'. In essence, literature on environmental or green entrepreneurship and ecopreneurship agrees that a double bottom line of environmentally responsible and yet profitable opportunities is at the core of the concept (Larson, 2000; Anderson and Leal, 2001; Meek et al., 2010). This is also reflected in the definition by Dean and McMullen (2007: 58), who coined a definition of environmental entrepreneurship as 'the process of discovering, evaluating, and exploiting economic opportunities that are present in environmentally relevant market failures'. Three elements of this definition are:

- Environmental entrepreneurship as a process, which focuses on discovering, evaluating and exploiting opportunities (Dean and McMullen, 2007).
- The reference to economic opportunities, emphasizing the for-profit nature of environmental entrepreneurship (Larson, 2000; Anderson and Huggins, 2008).

- Environmentally relevant market failures are the source of opportunities, implying that current market offerings are not efficient, and linking to the Kirznerian school of thought (Cohen and Winn, 2007; Dean and McMullen, 2007).

The definition incorporates some characteristics that have been found to be important in environmental entrepreneurship literature (e.g. economic opportunities, environmental market failure), yet the process focus on environmental entrepreneurship is a rather unusual approach of studying the phenomenon.

Similarly to social entrepreneurship, environmental entrepreneurship can be categorized as mission-driven entrepreneurship (Dixon and Clifford, 2007). However, the difference is that in environmental entrepreneurship economic value creation is seen as equally important. This might be surprising, as environmental entrepreneurship often emphasizes the mission of creating environmental value; yet according to the literature environmental entrepreneurs are driven by both the desire to save the environment and the desire to make a profit with their venture (Linnanen, 2002). Accordingly, environmental entrepreneurship can be found in for-profit contexts.

Social Entrepreneurship

The concept of social entrepreneurship first sparked the interest of academic researchers in the late 1990s (Boschee, 1995; Leadbeater, 1997; Dees, 1998; Wallace, 1999). In recent years, social entrepreneurship has enjoyed great popularity among researchers, resulting in a number of published articles in academic journals. Despite its relevance and the significant scientific contribution over the last 15 years, the research field lacks a unified definition and conceptual understanding (Short et al., 2009). This is reflected in a review conducted by Dacin et al. (2010). They identified 37 definitions of social entrepreneurship, revealing discrepancies between the different understandings. As a common ground has yet to emerge, we will adopt the definition of one of the most frequently cited works in social entrepreneurship research, by Dees (1998: 4), who posits that:

> Social entrepreneurs play the role of change agents in the social sector, by: Adopting a mission to create and sustain social value (not just private value); recognizing and relentlessly pursuing new opportunities to serve that mission; engaging in a process of continuous innovation, adaptation, and learning; acting boldly without being limited by resources currently in hand; and exhibiting heightened accountability to the constituencies served and for the outcomes created.

This definition is characterized by the following elements:

- Social entrepreneurs as change agents, referring to the individual's power to reform and revolutionize the social sector (Dees, 1998; Thompson et al., 2000; Chell, 2007).
- The mission to create and sustain social value, implying that the social mission or social value creation is at the heart of social entrepreneurship (Waddock and Post, 1991; Dees, 1998; Austin et al., 2006).
- The social sector, also referred to as the not-for-profit or non-governmental sector, signifying that profit is entirely used to finance the social mission (Cornwall, 1998; Thompson, 2002; Lasprogata and Cotton, 2003).
- Recognizing and pursuing opportunities, where opportunities are considered as possibilities to realize an individual's vision of social value creation (Dees, 1998; Thompson et al., 2000; Sullivan Mort et al., 2003).
- Continuous innovation, creating a link to Schumpeter's concept of innovation as a basis for entrepreneurship (Dees, 1998; Sullivan Mort et al., 2003).

Furthermore, the definition focuses on the individual entrepreneur, rather than taking a process perspective on social entrepreneurship. This reflects the great majority of research in social entrepreneurship, yet several authors have criticized this individual-centered approach (Dorado, 2006; Mair and Marti, 2006). In line with conventional entrepreneurship, these researchers suggest a process perspective on social entrepreneurship.

Despite some major discrepancies in the research of social entrepreneurship, broad agreement exists about its mission. Several authors claim that the social mission is fundamental and central to social entrepreneurship (Dees, 1998; Sullivan Mort et al., 2003; Austin et al., 2006). Consequently, the primary aim of social entrepreneurs lies in creating social value, in the form of products and services that benefit society and have a social impact (Shaw et al., 2002; Mair and Noboa, 2006; Austin et al., 2006).

While many social entrepreneurs realize economic gains with their enterprise, these are by no means the focus of social entrepreneurs. Rather, social entrepreneurs utilize profit returns as a reinvestment of their social mission (Bacq and Janssen, 2011). Although more recent literature has stated that social entrepreneurship can occur in not-for-profit, for-profit and hybrid venture forms (Johnson, 2003; Roper and Cheney, 2005; Murphy and Coombes, 2008), the main focus of researchers in social entrepreneurship is on the not-for-profit sector (Thompson, 2002; Weerawardena and Mort, 2006).

SUSTAINABLE ENTREPRENEURSHIP

Against the background of conventional, social and environmental forms of entrepreneurship, sustainable entrepreneurship emerged in the literature at the end of the 1990s. To give an overview of the emerging field of sustainable entrepreneurship research we conducted a systematic literature review, which differs from traditional narrative reviews. Systematic literature reviews adopt a transparent and replicable process with the aim of providing a thorough knowledge base of research published in a given field, while minimizing the bias of reviewers (Tranfield et al., 2003). 'Transparent' means that the method employed in the literature review process is made explicit. Every step taken in the process is described in sufficient detail. The transparency allows other researchers to replicate the literature review, to repeat it with modifications or to update it. In line with the procedure suggested by Tranfield et al. (2003) and adopted by other management researchers (e.g. Pittaway et al., 2004; Macpherson and Holt, 2007), our systematic literature review on sustainable entrepreneurship is organized into three main stages: defining protocols, mapping the field and reporting the findings.

Defining Protocols

First, we selected two established databases, Science Direct and EBSCO – Business Source Premier. As our review included peer-reviewed journal articles only, these databases were deemed well suited in providing a substantial number of relevant journals in the field of entrepreneurship, for example the *Journal of Business Venturing*; environmental management studies, for example *Business Strategy and the Environment*; as well as social management studies, for example the *Journal of Business Ethics*. The potentially relevant studies were reviewed in a three-step process: (1) database analysis; (2) title and abstract analysis; and (3) relevance analysis. By using the keywords 'sustainable entrepreneurship', 'sustainability entrepreneurship' as well as '(sustainable OR sustainability) AND entrepreneur*', both databases were examined with regard to their title, keywords and abstracts.

In the first step, the inclusion and exclusion criteria were determined. Inclusion criteria were defined as follows: (1) peer-reviewed journal articles; (2) all industry sectors; (3) all articles published until 2012;

(4) conceptual articles; and (5) empirical studies. We decided to exclude articles that: (1) were not peer-reviewed journal articles; (2) were not written in English or German; (3) did not relate to entrepreneurship; and (4) did not relate to sustainability. The database analysis yielded a total number of 576 potentially relevant articles, which were exported to the referencing software programme Citavi for further analysis (see Appendix 2A.1).

In the second step, the title and abstract of each article were reviewed against the predetermined inclusion and exclusion criteria and classified into two categories: 'relevant' for sustainable entrepreneurship (108), and 'not relevant' for sustainable entrepreneurship (468). Articles which were categorized as 'sustainable entrepreneurship' shared the common understanding of 'sustainable' as economic, social and/or environmental sustainability. Articles which were excluded used 'sustainable' in the sense of durable, financial, or in the context of a competitive advantage. Where the abstract alone was not sufficient to classify the article, the entire article was reviewed in order to categorize it into one of the two categories (see Appendix 2A.2).

In the third and last step, each of the articles categorized as 'sustainable entrepreneurship' was analysed in greater depth. First, the duplicates were removed in order to avoid double counting; due to similar search strings a few articles were detected several times by the search engines. Altogether 41 duplicates were removed, which resulted in a total number of 67 articles on sustainable entrepreneurship. In the following, each of the 67 articles was reviewed thoroughly regarding its relevance for sustainable entrepreneurship research. The relevance judgement was made on whether the studies: (1) focused on sustainable entrepreneurship in their paper, that is, articles that only mentioned or just briefly touched on the topic were excluded; and (2) made a theoretical or empirical contribution to sustainable entrepreneurship. Based on the relevance judgement, 43 articles were considered relevant for the field of sustainable entrepreneurship (see Appendix 2A.3).

Mapping the Field

The studies obtained from the systematic review were used as a basis for mapping the field of sustainable entrepreneurship. As said in the beginning, sustainable entrepreneurship is considered to be an emerging research stream. The systematic review supports this statement: according to our finding the first article in the field of sustainable entrepreneurship was published by Pastakia in 1998. In the following ten years, up to 2008, only 14 more articles were detected and deemed relevant for the field of

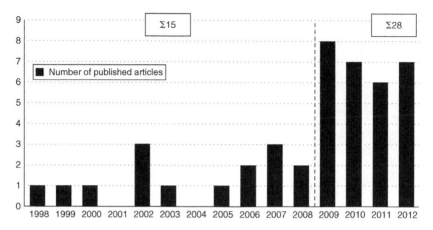

Figure 2.2   Number of journal articles on sustainable entrepreneurship, 1998–2012

sustainable entrepreneurship. This is an average of 1.4 articles per annum. From 2009 onwards, the number increased significantly, with 28 articles that published on sustainable entrepreneurship in international journals between 2009 and 2012 (see Figure 2.2). This is an average of seven articles per annum.

Of the 43 articles, 18 (42 per cent) were published in sustainable business journals such as *Business Strategy and the Environment, Greener Management International* and the *Journal of Cleaner Production*. This is in line with Hall et al. (2010), who maintain that articles on sustainable entrepreneurship are predominantly published by scholars who have a background in sustainable business research, rather than by those specializing in entrepreneurship research. Fifteen articles (35 per cent) were published in entrepreneurship journals, including *Entrepreneurship Theory and Practice*, the *Journal of Business Venturing* and the *Journal of Small Business and Entrepreneurship*. This relatively high number indicates that sustainable entrepreneurship has gained a foothold in mainstream entrepreneurship in recent years. This can also be attributed to the special issue on 'Sustainable Development and Entrepreneurship', which was guest edited by Daneke et al. (2010) and published in the *Journal of Business Venturing*, one of the leading entrepreneurship journals with an impact factor of 3.95. The rest of the identified articles (23 per cent) were published in a variety of other journals from different fields and disciplines (for example, *Environmental Economics and Policy Studies*, the *Journal of Organizational Change Management* and *Procedia Economics and Finance*).

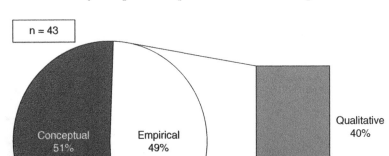

*Figure 2.3   Conceptual and empirical articles on sustainable
entrepreneurship, 1998–2012*

The research methods employed, as reported in the journal articles, were evenly distributed between conceptual and empirical
research (Figure 2.3). A total of 22 articles based their research on
theoretical considerations and were of a purely conceptual nature. The
remaining 21 articles conducted empirical studies, whereof 17 were
qualitative and four were quantitative. The large proportion of conceptual papers and qualitative studies is typical for a nascent, emerging
research field where the focus is on theory development rather than
theory testing (see e.g. Edmondson and McManus, 2007). As the field
grows and matures, we might expect more empirical studies, especially
quantitative research, based on variance models, hypotheses and large
surveys.

Reporting the Findings

The systematic literature review intends to contribute to clarity in sustainable entrepreneurship research and to answer the question 'What
is sustainable entrepreneurship?' Below, the findings of the systematic
review will be discussed, including the terminology and definition of sustainable entrepreneurship; the key concepts of sustainable entrepreneurship research; and the differentiation from related concepts of sustainable
entrepreneurship.

Terminology and definition of sustainable entrepreneurship

In their overview of sustainable entrepreneurship, Hall et al. (2010) pointed to the ambiguous use of the term 'sustainable entrepreneurship'. Their finding can be supported by our systematic review. 'Sustainable' was not only used in the context of the triple bottom line, but also with regard to the financial development, longevity or stability of a business (e.g. Morris, 2001; Kelley, 2011). It is notable from the systematic review that sustainable entrepreneurship receives a great deal of interest from different research disciplines, including entrepreneurship, social business and environmental management research. This leads to a wide array of various definitions of the phenomenon under study. Appendix 2A.4 gives an overview of all definitions identified in the literature review. On the one hand, different disciplines and definitions add to the scientific creativity and diversity of the nascent research stream, which in turn contributes to the development of the field (Shepherd and Patzelt, 2011). On the other hand, the disparity in the terminology and diversity of definitions hampers rigorous research into the phenomenon. This in turn leads to difficulties in identifying the distinctiveness of sustainable entrepreneurship as an independent research stream in the domain of entrepreneurship. Despite the diversity among the definitions of sustainable entrepreneurship (Appendix 4), some patterns emerged from our analysis. For instance, a number of scholars from social and environmental management journals have taken a more narrow stance toward the phenomenon by defining it as 'those entrepreneurial activities in which the central guiding purpose is to make a substantial contribution to sustainable development' (Parrish and Foxon, 2009: 48); as 'the incorporation of all elements of sustainable development, not just some' (Young and Tilley, 2006: 411); or simply as the 'distinct approach to balance the requirements of the triple bottom line' (Schlange, 2009: 18). It is notable that these definitions strongly emphasize the concepts of sustainable development and the triple bottom line, while the entrepreneurial activities remain subordinate to these. However, we found that consensus has been reached among scholars of leading entrepreneurship journals who align the notion of the triple bottom line with more established elements of conventional entrepreneurship. The definitions provided by authors of these journals put equal weight on sustainable development and entrepreneurial activities. Thus, they tend to better capture all the facets of the phenomenon (Table 2.1).

As Table 2.1 shows, Cohen and Winn largely orientated themselves on Shane and Venkataraman (2000) and expanded their definition of conventional entrepreneurship by integrating a sustainable perspective. Accordingly, they defined sustainable entrepreneurship research 'as the

Table 2.1   Definitions of sustainable entrepreneurship in leading entrepreneurship journals

Authors	Journal	Definition
Cohen and Winn (2007: 35)	*Journal of Business Venturing*	'We define sustainable entrepreneurship [research] as the examination of how opportunities to bring into existence "future" goods and services are discovered, created, and exploited, by whom, and with what economic, psychological, social, and environmental consequences.'
Dean and McMullen (2007: 58)	*Journal of Business Venturing*	'The process of discovering, evaluating, and exploiting economic opportunities that are present in market failures which detract from sustainability, including those that are environmentally relevant.'
Hockerts and Wüstenhagen (2010: 482)	*Journal of Business Venturing*	'We thus define sustainable entrepreneurship as the discovery and exploitation of economic opportunities through the generation of market disequilibria that initiate the transformation of a sector towards an environmentally and socially more sustainable state.'
Pacheco et al. (2010: 471)	*Journal of Business Venturing*	'We view sustainable entrepreneurship as the discovery, creation, evaluation, and exploitation of opportunities to create future goods and services that is consistent with sustainable development goals.'
Patzelt and Shepherd (2011: 632)	*Entrepreneurship Theory and Practice*	'Sustainable entrepreneurship is the discovery, creation, and exploitation of opportunities to create future goods and services that sustain the natural and/ or communal environment and provide development gain for others.'

examination of how opportunities to bring into existence "future" goods and services are discovered, created, and exploited, by whom, and with what economic, psychological, social and environmental consequences' (Cohen and Winn, 2007: 35). The close alignment with the terminology of conventional entrepreneurship helps in establishing a common conceptual basis for entrepreneurship as a research domain (Landström and Benner, 2010). The other definitions bear some similarity.

It is notable that consensus has been reached in the articles published in leading journals to term the phenomenon under study 'sustainable entrepreneurship', with the common understanding of 'sustainable' in terms of the triple bottom line (economic, social and ecological). Although this might appear as a matter of course, the importance of a unified terminology for defining and positioning an emergent research stream cannot be underestimated and is far from being self-evident, as the systematic review has shown.

Another similarity is that all definitions emphasize opportunities as the central construct in their description of sustainable entrepreneurship. This is in line with the seminal works by Venkataraman (1997) and Shane and Venkataraman (2000) who emphasize the opportunity-centred approach in their research on entrepreneurship.

Furthermore, all definitions take a process view on sustainable entrepreneurship instead of focusing on the individual entrepreneur. This is in accordance with recent entrepreneurship research, which emphasizes the action-oriented process of entrepreneurship rather than the personality and characteristics of the individual entrepreneur (Bygrave, 2004; Zahra, 2007; Moroz and Hindle, 2012).

A notable finding is that consistency can be found among the definitions with respect to the term 'discovery and exploitation' of opportunities (Table 2.2). It is apparent that all authors employed the term 'discovery' as the first phase of the process, which implies that a Kirznerian view on entrepreneurship has been taken. Accordingly, the opportunities 'just' have to be detected by individuals with a high level of alertness. This relates to the finding that market imperfections are a major source for sustainable entrepreneurial opportunities, which consequently need to be discovered. However, in many cases the challenges of sustainable development require innovation from a Schumpeterian

Table 2.2   Differences between the terminology of the sustainable entrepreneurial process

Authors \ Process activity	Discovery	Creation	Evaluation	Exploitation
Cohen and Winn (2007)	x	x		x
Dean and McMullen (2007)	x		x	x
Hockerts and Wüstenhagen (2010)	x			x
Pacheco et al. (2010)	x	x	x	x
Patzelt and Shepherd (2011)	x	x		x

perspective, suggesting that opportunities need to be created rather than discovered. This has been considered by the authors of three of the definitions, who refer to the Schumpeterian creation of opportunities as the second stage of the process (Cohen and Winn, 2007; Pacheco et al., 2010; Shepherd and Patzelt, 2011). These definitions combine the two views of entrepreneurial opportunities, which is a common approach in modern entrepreneurship research as both types have been found to account for the phenomenon in practice (Chiles et al., 2007; Pacheco et al., 2010).

Having analysed the definitions of sustainable entrepreneurship in greater detail, we suggest the following definition: sustainable entrepreneurship research as the scholarly examination of how opportunities to bring into existence future goods and services are recognized, developed and exploited, by whom, and with what economic, social and ecological gains.

The suggested definition is in close alignment with the ones presented before, yet we suggest employing the neutral term 'recognition' for the description of the sources of opportunities, which allows for opportunities to be either discovered or created. This is in line with entrepreneurship research arguing that both types of opportunities can be present at the same time, thus combining Kirznerian and Schumpeterian opportunities (Holcombe, 1998; Shane and Venkataraman, 2000; Shane, 2003; Pacheco et al., 2010). As our definition emphasizes a process view on the phenomenon, applying both terms one after the other might suggest that the sources appear in a sequential order, rather than in terms of 'either/ or'. Thus, in order to avoid ambiguity, we apply the term 'recognition' for the first phase of the process. Furthermore, we suggest adding the term 'development' for the second phase of the process, where the development of the opportunity has been found to be a core activity for sustainable entrepreneurship (Belz and Binder, 2013). Lastly, our definition refers to gains rather than consequences, as the outcome of the entrepreneurial activity is a proactively managed achievement, rather than a logical effect of a previous occurrence.

Key elements of our definition include:

- The source of opportunities, referring to the sources of opportunities both in the form of alertness to sustainable entrepreneurial opportunities with regard to discovering market failures (e.g. Cohen and Winn, 2007; Dean and McMullen, 2007; Patzelt and Shepherd, 2011), as well as the creation of sustainable entrepreneurial opportunities (Pacheco et al., 2007; Schaltegger and Wagner, 2011).

- A process perspective on sustainable entrepreneurship by examining how opportunities are recognized, developed and exploited (e.g. Dean and McMullen, 2007; Choi and Gray, 2008; Hockerts and Wüstenhagen, 2010).
- Examining by whom opportunities are recognized, developed and exploited, integrating the individual sustainable entrepreneur as a unit of analysis (e.g. Schlange, 2009; Kuckertz and Wagner, 2010; Spence et al., 2011).
- Balancing the economic, social and ecological gains of the sustainable venture (e.g. Cohen et al., 2008; Parrish, 2010).
- Future goods and services, referring to the transformative power of sustainable entrepreneurship (Gibbs, 2009; Parrish and Foxon, 2009; Hockerts and Wüstenhagen, 2010).

The key concepts of sustainable entrepreneurship, derived from the definitions and the analysis of the systematic review, will be discussed in greater detail in the following section.

Key concepts of sustainable entrepreneurship research

Source of opportunities   In line with the high importance attached to entrepreneurial opportunities in conventional entrepreneurship research (e.g. Gaglio and Katz, 2001; Ardichvili et al., 2003; Shane, 2003), literature on sustainable entrepreneurship has started to turn its attention to sustainable entrepreneurial opportunities (Cohen and Winn, 2007; Dean and McMullen, 2007; Patzelt and Shepherd, 2011). In this literature, Patzelt and Shepherd (2011) distinguish between system-level and individual-level factors for explaining sustainable entrepreneurial opportunities.

System-level factors explain the source of sustainable entrepreneurial opportunities to be found in market imperfections (Cohen and Winn, 2007) or market failure (Dean and McMullen, 2007; Shepherd and Patzelt, 2011). According to Cohen and Winn (2007), market imperfections occur when: (1) firms are inefficient, implying that natural resources are not used productively; (2) externalities exist, referring to the negative results of production and consumption on the cost of the natural environment; (3) pricing mechanisms are imperfect, representing the inaccurate pricing for exhaustible and non-renewable resources; or (4) the distribution of information is imperfect, indicating an information asymmetry of individuals (producers and consumers) with regard to resources, markets and opportunities. The authors posit that all four types of market imperfections provide ample opportunities to be discovered by sustainable entrepreneurs.

Similar to this typology, Dean and McMullen (2007) identified five types of environmentally relevant market failures. Among these are, in accordance with Cohen and Winn (2007): (1) externalities; and (2) imperfect distribution of information. Furthermore, the authors suggest that entrepreneurial opportunities for sustainable development can be found in: (3) public goods, as the non-excludability of the public good results in the motivation for individuals to quickly exploit the resource; (4) monopoly power, as firms that do not face competitive pressure are less likely to adopt more sustainable technologies and production methods; and (5) inappropriate government intervention, accusing politicians and regulators of following their own interests with their interventions, without taking the environmental impact of such actions into consideration. The authors suggest that all these market failures are a source for entrepreneurial opportunities which, when exploited, contribute to sustainable development.

A point of criticism of the two papers is that both neglect social development in their analysis of sustainable entrepreneurial opportunities. The focus on environmentally related market imperfection and market failure provide important insights into sources for environmental entrepreneurial opportunities, yet their work should be extended by means of socially relevant market imperfections and failures. The multiple perspectives on entrepreneurial opportunities have been taken account of by Patzelt and Shepherd (2011) who focus on the individual-level factors in their research.

Individual-level factors, as the term implies, focus on the sustainable entrepreneurial opportunities with regard to the individual's prior knowledge and motivation (Patzelt and Shepherd, 2011). Patzelt and Shepherd propose a model for the recognition of third-person sustainable development opportunities, which consists of the two variables 'knowledge of the natural/communal environment' and 'motivation'. These variables are moderated by the 'entrepreneurial knowledge' variable. According to the authors prior knowledge of the natural and communal environment is an important factor for recognizing sustainable development opportunities. Furthermore, the authors posit that prior knowledge of the natural and communal environment is not sufficient: it is complemented by prior knowledge of markets, ways to serve markets and customer problems, that is, entrepreneurial knowledge. Another important factor the authors identified is motivation. Patzelt and Shepherd (2011) propose that in sustainable entrepreneurship, motivation occurs when individuals feel that their or another person's physical or psychological welfare is threatened. Again, this might be moderated by an individual's entrepreneurial knowledge, as individuals with entrepreneurial knowledge might be able to detect the source of the threat, that is, a sustainable development opportunity. Patzelt and Shepherd are the first to look at the individual-level factors of opportunity recognition in sustainable entrepreneurship and their focus on third-person opportunities provides a valuable starting point for further research.

In sum, research in sustainable entrepreneurial opportunities is still in its infancy. The three conceptual papers presented above provide interesting insights, yet more research is needed to account for the important topic of entrepreneurial opportunities for sustainable development. Particularly, the papers presented above focus on the discovery of sustainable entrepreneurial opportunities, while the creation of sustainable entrepreneurial opportunities is largely neglected in their considerations. Furthermore, there is a lack of empirical research that sheds light on the recognition of sustainable entrepreneurial opportunities, including the process, types and antecedents.

A process perspective on sustainable entrepreneurship   Since the turn of the century, research on conventional entrepreneurship has started to emphasize the process view on the phenomenon (Shane and Venkataraman, 2000; Bygrave, 2004; Zahra, 2007). The study of processes is a common approach for understanding the development and change of a given phenomenon (Van de Ven, 1992). The definitions of sustainable entrepreneurship presented in Table 2.1 imply that the process-centred view holds true for the sustainable entrepreneurship literature as well. Yet, out of the 43 relevant papers identified in the systematic review, only three explicitly focus their research on the entrepreneurial process of the sustainable venture (Larson, 2000; Schick et al., 2002; Choi and Gray, 2008).

According to our systematic review, Larson (2000) was the first to examine the process of a sustainable start-up. By focusing on the single case of Walden Paddlers, a kayaking company, the author provides a thorough description of the company's venture process through the lens of the entrepreneur.

In their case study research, Schick et al. (2002) analysed the start-up process of ten businesses with different industrial backgrounds. A particular focus was put on the ecological orientation in the practice of the start-ups. On the basis of their results, the authors offer a differentiation between eco-dedicated, eco-open and eco-reluctant start-ups, which are assumed to vary in the degree of ecological consistency throughout the entrepreneurial process.

Choi and Gray (2008) analysed the venture process of sustainable entrepreneurs by employing Morris et al.'s (2001) framework of the entrepreneurial process. Accordingly, the start-up process in sustainable entrepreneurship involves the same six steps as conventional entrepreneurial processes: (1) identify an opportunity; (2) develop the concept;

(3) determine the required resources; (4) acquire the necessary resources; (5) implement and manage; and (6) harvest the venture. By means of 21 case studies, the authors provide a descriptive overview of events as experienced by the entrepreneurs.

As the review has shown, research focusing on the entrepreneurial process of sustainable start-ups remains considerably small. This is particularly surprising, as all definitions provided in Table 2.1 emphasize the process view on sustainable entrepreneurship. The three articles dealing with sustainable entrepreneurship processes were of an empirical nature, namely case studies. Yet, the findings of this research lack generalization and a theoretical understanding of the sustainability entrepreneurial process. This opens up ample research opportunities in the important key concept of sustainable entrepreneurship from a process perspective.

The individual entrepreneur   Until the turn of the century, the individual-level perspective on entrepreneurship was the dominant research approach in entrepreneurship literature (Ucbasaran et al., 2001). The field was mainly defined in terms of who the entrepreneur is, and what he or she does (Shane and Venkataraman, 2000). As mentioned before, a notable change is that current literature emphasizes the action-oriented process of entrepreneurship (Moroz and Hindle, 2012). Nevertheless, Steyaert (2007) argues for a reintroduction of the individual entrepreneur as one part of the unit of analysis in entrepreneurship research. The literature on sustainable entrepreneurship takes account of this call. A number of papers identified in the systematic review focus on the motivation of entrepreneurs by studying their sustainability orientation (Kuckertz and Wagner, 2010; Wagner, 2012), their vision (Dixon and Clifford, 2007), their commitment (Spence et al., 2011) and their 'perpetual reasoning' (Parrish, 2010). Typical for the nascent stage of sustainable entrepreneurship research, the papers on the motivation of sustainable entrepreneurs differ greatly in their focus.

In their quantitative research, Kuckertz and Wagner (2010) aimed at testing whether there exists a link between sustainability orientation and entrepreneurial orientation. The results of their large-scale survey revealed that sustainability-oriented individuals are not only more likely to recognize a higher number of sustainability entrepreneurial opportunities, but have also been found to be more ambitious in acting upon the identified opportunities. Yet, their results also showed that business education and business experience significantly weakened the positive effects of sustainability orientation for entrepreneurial opportunity recognition and the intention to act upon these opportunities. The authors assumed that with more business experience, the profitability and practicability of sustainable entrepreneurship were perceived as increasingly uneconomical (Kuckertz and Wagner, 2010). Similarly, Wagner (2012) shows that sustainability orientation is not a driver for entrepreneurial intentions. Although sustainability-oriented individuals are more likely to identify sustainability-related opportunities, they do not engage in entrepreneurial activities in order to act upon them.

In a comprehensive North–South comparison by means of case studies, Spence et al. (2011) identified three types of sustainable entrepreneurs, which they referred to as the committed, the aware and the indifferent. As the name implies, committed entrepreneurs are most strongly associated with sustainable development goals and are driven by their sustainable vision and values. Entrepreneurs who belong to the second group of the typology are aware of social and environmental issues, yet these are not the primary mean of their motivation to engage in sustainable entrepreneurial behaviour. They are mainly driven by making profits, with sustainable considerations playing only a subordinate role to the economic ones. Lastly, the indifferent entrepreneurs understand sustainability purely in financial terms and do not take any socio-environmental factors into account. Nevertheless, even the indifferent might unintentionally contribute to sustainable development, when it results in an immediate gain for their business operations.

In his study of entrepreneurial motivations in the context of sustainability, Parrish (2010) derived five rules for successful sustainable organizations from his case studies: resource perpetuation, benefit stacking, strategic satisficing, qualitative management and worthy contribution. Taken together, the author proposes that these rules result in 'perpetual reasoning', a unique interpretative scheme that distinguishes successful from unsuccessful sustainable entrepreneurs. The interpretative scheme can be seen as a reflection of the values, motives and purposes of the sustainable entrepreneurs, which are embedded in the organizational design of the sustainable venture.

To conclude, research focusing on the role of the individual for sustainable entrepreneurship has looked into many different factors that might be suitable to explain the motivation of some individuals to engage in sustainable entrepreneurship. Although this research is exemplary in its use of empirical methods (as compared to the rest of the sustainable entrepreneurship literature), further research should try to replicate some of the findings in order to increase their validity. Furthermore, important future contributions should link individual-level research to research on entrepreneurial processes in order to better account for cause and effect of the phenomenon.

Economic, social and ecological value creation   Historically, entrepreneurship has been operationalized with regard to one dimension, which is the economic performance of the enterprise. The vast majority of conventional entrepreneurship research emphasizes profit creation as the central construct for entrepreneurship (Amit et al., 2000; Davidsson and Wiklund, 2001). As a consequence, value creation is measured in financial terms such as sales, profit or return on investment (ROI) and is seen as maximizing individual utility (Schlange, 2009). In response to the increased demand for sustainability, and the criticism that business accounts for a high proportion of environmental degradation and social injustice (Pigou, 1932; Dorfman, 1993), the traditional understanding of value creation simply in terms of economic gains has been broadened to include non-economic gains as well (Shepherd and Patzelt, 2011).

As sustainability incorporates the notions of economy, environment and society, it comes as no surprise that value creation from a sustainable entrepreneurship perspective shows overlaps with the concepts of conventional, social and environmental entrepreneurship. While each of the concepts emphasizes one or two aspects of sustainable development, sustainable entrepreneurship calls for a holistic perspective on entrepreneurial value creation (Cohen et al., 2008). Consequently, sustainable entrepreneurs need to balance the competing objectives of economic, social and ecological value creation (Schlange, 2007; Parrish, 2010). This leads to an increased complexity for sustainable entrepreneurship in comparison to other forms of entrepreneurship, which might be one-dimensional or two-dimensional in nature. Furthermore, sustainable opportunities for value creation have been classified as 'wicked problems', as they are characterized by high complexity, strong uncertainty associated with the cause and effect of the problem, and difficulties in providing a definitive solution (Lans et al., 2014).

The common measure for sustainability is the triple bottom line, based on Elkington's (1994) finding that the combination of economic, social and ecological benefits results in a win–win–win situation for business, society and the environment. Almost all literature sources identified in the systematic review refer to the triple bottom line as the underlying principle of sustainable entrepreneurship. Proponents of the triple bottom line value the multi-perspectivity as the promise of sustaining the earth and society for future generations (Cohen et al., 2008). Opponents of the triple bottom line criticize that conventional accounting practices cannot capture the notions of society and environment (Brown et al., 2008; Dillard et al., 2005), thereby making it difficult to measure the entrepreneurial performance of sustainable ventures (Tilley and Young, 2009).

In sum, value creation in sustainable entrepreneurship encompasses economic, social and ecological wealth. Balancing the competing goals is a major challenge for sustainable entrepreneurs and results in increased complexity throughout the venture creation (and beyond). Further research should identify adequate metrics that capture the social and ecological dimension, as these are hard to quantify with traditional accounting metrics.

Transition to a sustainable society   An important question in sustainable entrepreneurship research concerns whether sustainable entrepreneurship can have a positive impact on the larger society and environment. Besides the direct benefits of the entrepreneurial activities, which are often on a local or communal level, sustainable entrepreneurship has been found to function as an impetus for the transition to a sustainable society (e.g. Gibbs, 2009; Parrish and Foxon, 2009; Schaltegger and Wagner, 2011).

In their research Hockerts and Wüstenhagen (2010) distinguish between 'Emerging Davids' and 'Greening Goliaths'. While the latter is the attempt of established firms to implement sustainability in their innovation process, the former can be seen as idealistic and radically innovating sustainable start-ups. Although Davids seem more desirable from a sustainability perspective, as they often show a superior performance with regard to one specific social or environmental problem, they tend to remain a niche phenomenon. Usually, Davids initiate sustainability innovations, which are then followed by the established market players. These kinds of Goliaths are less innovative, but have the possibility to serve mass markets and can have a much stronger impact on the transformation beyond the sustainable niche. The findings of the authors imply that neither one nor the other is sufficient to bring about the transition to a sustainable society, but that it is a co-evolution of the two market players, in which the change is triggered by sustainability start-ups and taken up by market incumbents to influence the wider society.

The importance of transformation beyond the sustainable niche has also been emphasized by Gibbs (2009). Building upon Geels's (2005) work on transition management, the author takes a multi-level perspective on sustainable entrepreneurship. Accordingly, sustainable start-ups may occupy sustainable niches, which in turn have the transformative power of changing technological regimes – that is, long-established systems – which largely neglect sustainable issues. This is also expressed by Schaltegger and Wagner (2011), who posit that the role of sustainable entrepreneurship lies in influencing the entire market, which in turn influences society as a whole.

Parrish and Foxon (2009) also assign sustainable entrepreneurship the important role of a catalyst for far-reaching socio-economic transformations. However, the authors refer to the corresponding challenge of immediately satisfying customer needs while at the same time creating and promoting the technologies needed to achieve sustainability. Their research builds on findings of a case from the renewable energy market, which they identify as a catalyst for wider socio-economic transition. Besides the catalytic function, the authors suggest that sustainable enterprises are also taking over the role of gap-fillers. Accordingly, these enterprises are important in filling the socio-ecological gaps that have been left by industry and government.

In conclusion, there is support from research that sustainable entrepreneurship plays a decisive role in the transition towards a sustainable society. Limited empirical evidence in the form of two case studies has been found to support this assumption (Parrish and Foxon, 2009; Plieth et al., 2012). However, most of the research to date remains conceptual (e.g. Gibbs, 2009; Hockerts and Wüstenhagen, 2010; Schaltegger and Wagner, 2011). Hall et al. (2010) criticize that this type of literature is more prescriptive than descriptive and might well be too confident regarding the transformative power of sustainable entrepreneurs.

Sustainable entrepreneurship and related concepts
At the beginning of this chapter we introduced the related concepts of sustainable entrepreneurship. In this section we have provided the results of the systematic review of sustainable entrepreneurship, aiming to contribute to our understanding of 'what it is'. To conclude this section, we will provide a comparison of the three related concepts and sustainable entrepreneurship. At first glance, conventional, environmental and social entrepreneurship share some commonalities with sustainable entrepreneurship, yet when looking at the core of the concepts, the heterogeneity becomes apparent, particularly with regards to the goals and the desired value creation (Figure 2.4).

A crucial point of differentiation between conventional and sustainable entrepreneurship is in the normative goals. While conventional entrepreneurship is mainly driven by the normative goal of profit, sustainable entrepreneurship supports the normative goal of sustainable development, meeting the triple bottom line of economic, social and ecological goals. The different goals also translate into differences in the evaluation of the success of the enterprise. Accordingly, the expected value of conventional entrepreneurship is measured primarily in monetary terms such as profit and return on investment. Sustainable entrepreneurship, on the other hand, is driven by its mission to create socio-ecological value, while at the same time ensuring the profitability of the venture. Consequently, the value is not purely measured in financial terms, but also in the contribu-

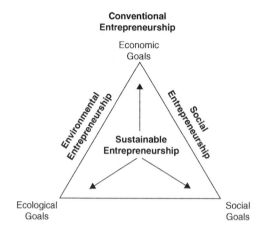

Figure 2.4   Sustainable entrepreneurship and related concepts

tions to society and the environment, which are difficult to quantify and aggregate.

Environmental entrepreneurship and sustainable entrepreneurship are two concepts that are closely interrelated. Both focus on making a profit while aiming at improving environmental conditions with their business. Yet, sustainable entrepreneurship goes one step further by emphasizing the creation of social value in addition to the economic and environmental benefits of the enterprise. This is also the major point of difference, as environmental entrepreneurship can be categorized as two-dimensional ('double bottom line'), while sustainable entrepreneurship employs the well-known focus on and balance of the triple bottom line goals.

For social entrepreneurship the social mission is fundamental and driven by the motivation to benefit society. Sustainable entrepreneurship, on the other hand, is driven by the mission to solve socio-ecological problems while at the same time it is motivated to realize economic gains. The discrepancy in the mission results in differences in the value creation of the two concepts as well. Putting the social mission at the heart of the business, social entrepreneurs will consequently strive for creating social value by, for example, creating social capital, promoting social change or addressing social needs (ends). The main value creation of social entrepreneurship is only one of three aspects in the value creation of sustainable entrepreneurs, as value created in sustainable entrepreneurship needs to incorporate environmental and economic values as well (ends and means). This results in a greater complexity and higher requirements for sustainable entrepreneurs, who will have to balance the triple bottom line in their value creation. The vast majority of the literature on social entrepreneurship focuses on the not-for-profit sector. Although some researchers have posited that social entrepreneurship can occur in both the not-for-profit and the for-profit sectors, the majority of literature remains in the context of not-for-profit. In contrast to that, sustainable entrepreneurship focuses solely on for-profit organizations, which aim to meet the triple bottom line of economic, ecological and social goals.

SUMMARY

The findings of the systematic literature review show that sustainable entrepreneurship is an emerging stream of entrepreneurship literature. The first articles on the topic appeared at the end of the 1990s. However, between 1998 and 2008 only 15 articles were published in international journals. Since 2009, the number of articles published on sustainable entrepreneurship has increased significantly. Although the number of published articles has increased in recent years, sustainable entrepreneurship is still a nascent stream of research. Not surprisingly, an array of different definitions are used for sustainable entrepreneurship, adding to the creativity in the field, but also leading to confusion. However, a notable result of our literature review is that the articles published in mainstream entrepreneurship journals found some common ground for defining sustainable entrepreneurship. As a result of the systematic review, our suggested definition emphasizes the following five aspects:

- The source of opportunities, referring to both the discovery and creation of sustainable entrepreneurial opportunities.
- A process-focused perspective on sustainable entrepreneurship by examining how opportunities are recognized, developed, and exploited.
- Examining by whom opportunities are recognized, developed, and exploited, integrating the individual sustainable entrepreneur as a unit of analysis.
- Balancing the economic, social and ecological gains of the sustainable venture.
- Future goods and services, referring to the transformative power of sustainable entrepreneurship.

The common definition and understanding of the phenomenon under study is an important step towards the establishment of sustainable entrepreneurship as a new stream of research. We hope that our contribution has helped to clarify what sustainable entrepreneurship is in order to enhance research with relevance and rigour in this field. Against the background of our literature review we see ample research opportunities. First of all, we see the need for theory development. Although there are a large number of conceptual papers on sustainable entrepreneurship (Figure 2.3), there are very few authors developing theoretical models. A notable exception is by Patzelt and Shepherd (2011), who develop a theoretical model for recognizing opportunities for sustainable development in a deductive way. Based on existing theories and previous empirical studies they suggest a causal model with the recognition of sustainable development opportunities as a dependent variable, knowledge of natural and communal environment as well as motivation as independent variables, and entrepreneurial knowledge as a moderating variable.

Another example is Belz and Binder (2013), who develop a theoretical model in an inductive way. Based on a multiple case study design (Yin, 2008) they suggest a process model of sustainable entrepreneurship, including five main activities: recognizing socio-ecological problems; recognizing entrepreneurial opportunities; developing an integral sustainable opportunity; funding and forming a sustainable enterprise; creating and entering sustainable markets (Belz and Binder, 2013). This is a start to describing the process of sustainable entrepreneurship and giving an answer to 'How?' and 'What?' questions. Here we see the need to look into each phase of the sustainable entrepreneurial process and give answers to 'Why?' questions to develop variance and causal models as well. As sound theoretical models are developed there is a need to test them with large-scale surveys. Here it might not be easy to draw the sample, since the population of sustainable enterprises is still evolving and not officially registered. Another challenge is measurement of the triple bottom line, pursued in sustainable entrepreneurship. Social and ecological goals are difficult to quantify and aggregate. However, we are certain that these hurdles will be overcome. We hope that our systematic literature review and the suggested definition of sustainable entrepreneurship is a step forward to enhance relevant and yet rigorous research in this nascent field.

ACKNOWLEDGEMENT

Two previous versions of the chapter were reviewed thoroughly by two anonymous reviewers. They provided us with critical and constructive feedback. We would like to thank them for sharing their invaluable comments. It gave us the opportunity to enhance the quality of the chapter. In addition, thanks go to Christoph Baumeister, Markus Hagenmaier, Marianne

Kreissig, Stefanie Preissner, Christina Raasch and Tim Schweisfurth for reading and discussing the second version of the chapter with us in one of the research seminars at the TUM School of Management.

REFERENCES

Amit, R., K.R. MacCrimmon and C. Zietsma (2000), 'Does money matter? Wealth attainment as the motive for initiating growth oriented technology ventures', *Journal of Business Venturing*, 16(2), 119–43.

Anderson, T. and D. Leal (2001), *Free Market Environmentalism*, London: Palgrave Macmillan.

Anderson, T. and L. Huggins (2008), *Greener than Thou: Are You Really an Environmentalist*, Stanford, CA: Hoover Institution Press.

Ardichvili, A., R. Cardozo and S. Ray (2003), 'A theory of entrepreneurial opportunity identification and development', *Journal of Business Venturing*, 18(1), 105–23.

Austin, J., H. Stevenson and J. Wei-Skillern (2006), 'Social and commercial entrepreneurship: same, different, or both?', *Entrepreneurship Theory & Practice*, 30(1), 1–22.

Bacq, S. and F. Janssen (2011), 'The multiple faces of social entrepreneurship: a review of definitional issues based on geographical and thematic criteria', *Entrepreneurship and Regional Development*, 23(5–6), 373–403.

Belz, F.-M. and J.K. Binder (2013), 'A process view on sustainability entrepreneurship: towards a model', SSRN: http://ssrn.com/abstract=2304602, accessed 15 November 2013.

Bennett, S. (1991), *Ecopreneuring: The Complete Guide to Small Business Opportunities from the Environmental Revolution*, New York: Wiley.

Berglund, K. and C. Wigren (2012), 'Soci(et)al entrepreneurship: the shaping of a different story of entrepreneurship', *Tamara – Journal for Critical Organization Inquiry*, 10(1), 9–22.

Berle, G. (1991), *The Green Entrepreneur: Business Opportunities that can Save the Earth and Make You Money*, Blue Ridge Summit, PA: Liberty Hall Press.

Blue, J. (1990), *Ecopreneuring: Managing for Results*, London: Scott Foresman.

Boschee, J. (1995), 'Social entrepreneurship', *Across the Board*, 32(3), 20–3.

Brown, D., J. Dillard and R.S. Marshall (2008), 'Triple bottom line: a business metaphor for a social construct', in J. Dillard, V. Dujon and M.C. King (eds), *Understanding the Social Dimension of Sustainability*, New York: Routledge Press, pp. 211–32.

Bygrave, W.D. (2004), 'The entrepreneurial process', in W. Bygrave and A. Zacharakis (eds), *The Portable MBA in Entrepreneurship*, Hoboken: John Wiley & Sons, pp. 1–27.

Chell, E. (2007), 'Social enterprise and entrepreneurship: towards a convergent theory of the entrepreneurial process', *International Small Business Journal*, 25(1), 5–26.

Chiles, T.H., A.C. Bluedorn and V.K. Gupta (2007), 'Beyond creative destruction and entrepreneurial discovery: a radical Austrian approach to entrepreneurship', *Organization Studies*, 28(4), 467–93.

Choi, D. and E. Gray (2008), 'The venture development processes of "sustainable" entrepreneurs', *Management Research News*, 8(31), 558–69.

Cohen, B. (2006), 'Sustainable valley entrepreneurial ecosystems', *Business Strategy and the Environment*, 15(1), 1–14.

Cohen, B., B. Smith and R. Mitchell (2008), 'Toward a sustainable conceptualization of dependent variables in entrepreneurship research', *Business Strategy and the Environment*, 17(2), 107–19.

Cohen, B. and M. Winn (2007), 'Market imperfections, opportunity and sustainable entrepreneurship', *Journal of Business Venturing*, 22(1), 29–49.

Cornwall, J. (1998), 'The entrepreneur as building block for community', *Journal of Developmental Entrepreneurship*, 3(2), 141–48.

Dacin, P.A., M.T. Dacin and M. Matear (2010), 'Social entrepreneurship: why we don't need a new theory and how we move forward from here', *Academy of Management Perspectives*, 24(2), 36–56.

Daneke, G., J. Hall and M. Lenox (eds) (2010), Special Issue, 'Sustainable Development and Entrepreneurship', *Journal of Business Venturing*, 25(5), 439–540.

Davidsson, P. and J. Wiklund (2001), 'Levels of analysis in entrepreneurship research: current research practice and suggestions for the future', *Entrepreneurship Theory and Practice*, 25(4), 81–100.

Dean, T. and J. McMullen (2007), 'Toward a theory of sustainable entrepreneurship: reducing environmental degradation through entrepreneurial action', *Journal of Business Venturing*, 22(1), 50–76.

De Clercq, D. and M. Voronov (2011), 'Sustainability in entrepreneurship: a tale of two logics', *International Small Business Journal*, 29(4), 322–44.

Dees, J.G. (1998), 'The meaning of social entrepreneurship', contributed from the Social Entrepreneurship Funders Working Group.

Dillard, J., D. Brown and R.S. Marshall (2005), 'An environmentally enlightened accounting', *Accounting Forum*, 29(1), 77–101.

Dixon, S. and A. Clifford (2007), 'Ecopreneurship – a new approach to managing the triple bottom line', *Journal of Organizational Change Management*, 20(3), 326–45.

Dorado, S. (2006), 'Social entrepreneurial ventures: different values so different process of creations, no?', *Journal of Developmental Entrepreneurship*, 11(4), 319–43.

Dorfman, R. (1993), 'Some concepts from welfare economics', in R. Dorfman and N.S. Dorfman (eds), *Economics of the Environment: Selected Readings*, New York: W.W. Norton, pp. 79–96.

Drucker, P. (1985), *Innovation and Entrepreneurship: Practice and Principles*, New York: Harper & Row.

Edmondson, A.C. and S.E. McManus (2007), 'Methodological fit in management field research', *Academy of Management Review*, 32(4), 1155–79.

Elkington, J. (1994), 'Towards the sustainable corporation: win–win–win business strategies for sustainable development', *California Management Review*, 36(2), 90–100.

Gaglio, C.M. and J. Katz (2001), 'The psychological basis of opportunity identification: entrepreneurial alertness', *Small Business Economics*, 16(2), 95–111.

Gartner, W.B. (1988), '"Who is an entrepreneur?" is the wrong question', *American Journal of Small Business*, 12(4), 11–32.

Geels, F. (2005), *Technological Transitions and System Innovations: A Co-evolutionary and Socio-technical Analysis*, Cheltenham, UK and Northampton, MA, USA: Edward Elgar.

Gibb, A.A. (1996), 'Entrepreneurship and small business management: can we afford to neglect them in the twenty-first century business schools?', *British Journal of Management*, 7(4), 309–22.

Gibbs, D. (2009), 'Sustainability entrepreneurs, ecopreneurs and the development of a sustainable economy', *Greener Management International*, 55(Winter), 63–78.

Hall, J., G. Daneke and M. Lenox (2010), 'Sustainable development and entrepreneurship: past contributions and future directions', *Journal of Business Venturing*, 25(5), 439–48.

Hall, J. and M. Wagner (2012), 'Editorial: the challenges and opportunities of sustainable development for entrepreneurship and small business', *Journal of Small Business and Entrepreneurship*, 25(4), 409–16.

Hart, S. and M. Milstein (1999), 'Global sustainability and the creative destruction of industries', *Sloan Management Review*, 41(1), 23–33.

Hockerts, K. and R. Wüstenhagen (2010), 'Greening Goliaths versus emerging Davids: theorizing about the role of incumbents and new entrants in sustainable entrepreneurship', *Journal of Business Venturing*, 25(5), 481–92.

Holcombe, R.G. (1998), 'Entrepreneurship and economic growth', *Quarterly Journal of Austrian Economics*, 1(2), 45–62.

Isaak, R. (2002), 'The making of the ecopreneur', *Greener Management International*, 38(Summer), 81–91.

Johnson, S. (2003), 'Social entrepreneurship literature review', *New Academy Review*, 2(2), 42–56.

Kardos, M. (2012), 'The relationship between entrepreneurship, innovation and sustainable development: research on European Union countries', *Procedia Economics and Finance*, 3, 1030–1035.

Keijzers, G. (2002), 'The transition to the sustainable enterprise', *Journal of Cleaner Production*, 10(4), 349–60.

Kelley, D. (2011), 'Sustainable corporate entrepreneurship: evolving and connecting with the Organization', *Business Horizon*, 54(1), 73–83.

Kirzner, I.M. (1973), *Competition and Entrepreneurship*, Chicago, IL: University of Chicago Press.

Kirzner, I.M. (1979), *Perception, Opportunity, and Profit*, Chicago, IL: University of Chicago Press.

Kuckertz, A. and M. Wagner (2010), 'The influence of sustainability orientation on entrepreneurial intentions: investigating the role of business experience', *Journal of Business Venturing*, 25(2), 524–39.

Kury, K.W. (2012), 'Sustainability meets social entrepreneurship: a path to social change through institutional entrepreneurship', *Journal of Business Insights and Transformation*, 4(3), 64–71.

Landström, H. and M. Benner (2010), 'Entrepreneurship research: a history of scholarly migration', in H. Landström and F. Lohrke (eds), *Historical Foundations of Entrepreneurship Research*, Cheltenham, UK and Northampton, MA, USA: Edward Elgar Publishing, pp. 15–45.

Lans, T., V. Blok and R. Wesselink (2014), 'Learning apart and together: towards an integrated competence framework for sustainable entrepreneurship in higher education', *Journal of Cleaner Production*, 62(1), 37–47.

Larson, A. (2000), 'Sustainable innovation through an entrepreneurship lens', *Business Strategy and the Environment*, 9(5), 304–17.

Lasprogata, G. and M. Cotton (2003), 'Contemplating "enterprise": the business and legal challenges of social entrepreneurship', *American Business Law Journal*, 41(1), 67–114.

Leadbeater, C. (1997), *The Rise of the Social Entrepreneur*, London: Demos.

Linnanen, L. (2002), 'An insider's experiences with environmental entrepreneurship', *Greener Management International*, 38(Summer), 71–81.

Lordkipanidze, M., H. Brezet and M. Backman (2005), 'The entrepreneurial factor in sustainable tourism development', *Journal of Cleaner Production*, 13(8), 787–98.

Lorne, F. (2009), 'Macro-entrepreneurship and sustainable development: the need for innovative solutions for promoting win–win interactions', *Environmental Economics and Policy Studies*, 10(2), 69–85.

Macpherson, A. and R. Holt (2007), 'Knowledge, learning and small-firm growth: a systematic review of the evidence', *Research Policy*, 36(2), 172–92.

Mair, J. and I. Marti (2006), 'Social entrepreneurship research: a source of explanation, prediction, and delight', *Journal of World Business*, 41(1), 36–44.

Mair, J. and E. Noboa (2006), 'Social entrepreneurship: how intentions to create a social venture are formed', in J. Mair, J. Robinson and K. Hockerts (eds), *Social Entrepreneurship*, Basingstoke, UK and New York, USA: Palgrave Macmillan, pp. 121–35.

Mathew, V. (2009), 'Sustainable entrepreneurship in small-scale business: application, concepts and cases', *ICFAI Journal of Entrepreneurship Development*, 6(1), 41–61.

McMullen, J.S. and D.A. Shepherd (2006), 'Entrepreneurial action and the role of uncertainty in the theory of the entrepreneur', *Academy of Management Review*, 31(1), 132–52.

Meek, W.R., D.F. Pacheco and J.G. York (2010), 'The impact of social norms on entrepreneurial action: evidence from the environmental entrepreneurship context', *Journal of Business Venturing*, 25(5), 493–509.

Moroz, P.W. and K. Hindle (2012), 'Entrepreneurship as a process: toward harmonizing multiple perspectives', *Entrepreneurship Theory and Practice*, 36(4), 781–818.

Morris, M.H. (2001), 'The critical role of resources', *Journal of Developmental Entrepreneurship*, 6(2), 5–9.

Morris, M.H., D.F. Kuratko and M. Schindehutte (2001), 'Towards integration: understanding entrepreneurship through frameworks', *International Journal of Entrepreneurship and Innovation*, 2(1), 35–49.

Morrish, S.C., M.P. Miles and M.J. Polonsky (2011), 'An exploratory study of sustainability as a stimulus for corporate entrepreneurship', *Corporate Social Responsibility and Environmental Management*, 18(3), 162–71.

Murphy, P.J. and S.M. Coombes (2008), 'A model of social entrepreneurial discovery', *Journal of Business Ethics*, 87(3), 325–36.

Nagler, J. (2012), 'Entrepreneurs: the world needs you', *Thunderbird International Business Review*, 54(1), 3–5.

O'Neill Jr., G., J. Hershauer and J. Golden (2009), 'The cultural context of sustainability entrepreneurship', *Greener Management International*, 55, 33–46.

Pacheco, D.F., T.J. Dean and D.S. Payne (2010), 'Escaping the green prison: entrepreneurship and the creation of opportunities for sustainable development', *Journal of Business Venturing*, 25(5), 464–80.

Parrish, B. (2010), 'Sustainability-driven entrepreneurship: principles of organization design', *Journal of Business Venturing*, 25(5), 510–23.

Parrish, B. and T. Foxon (2009), 'Sustainability entrepreneurship and equitable transitions to a low-carbon economy', *Greener Management International*, 55, 47–62.

Pastakia, A. (1998), 'Grassroot ecopreneurs: change agents for a sustainable society', *Journal of Organizational Management*, 11(2), 157–73.

Patzelt, H. and D.A. Shepherd (2011), 'Recognizing opportunities for sustainable development', *Entrepreneurship Theory and Practice*, 35(4), 631–52.

Pigou, A.C. (1932), *The Economics of Welfare*, 4th edn, London: Macmillan & Co.

Pittaway, L., M. Robertson, K. Munir, D. Denyer and A. Neely (2004), 'Networking and innovation: a systematic review of the evidence', *International Journal of Management Reviews*, 5–6(3–4), 137–68.

Plieth, H., A.C. Bullinger and E.G. Hansen (2012), 'Sustainable entrepreneurship in the apparel industry: the case of Manomama', *Journal of Corporate Citizenship*, 45, 121–34.

Potocan, V. and M. Mulej (2003), 'Entrepreneurship: between sustainable development and reality', *Public Finance and Management*, 3(2), 241–62.

Rodgers, C. (2010), 'Sustainable entrepreneurship in SMEs: a case study analysis', *Corporate Social Responsibility and Environmental Management*, 17(3), 125–32.

Roper, J. and G. Cheney (2005), 'Leadership, learning, and human resource management: the meaning of social entrepreneurship today', *Corporate Governance: The International Journal for Effective Board Performance*, 5(3), 95–104.

Schaltegger, S. (2002), 'A framework for ecopreneurship', *Greener Management International*, 38, 45–59.

Schaltegger, S. and M. Wagner (2011), 'Sustainable entrepreneurship and sustainability innovation: categories and interactions', *Business Strategy and the Environment*, 20(4), 222–37.

Schick, H., S. Marxen and J. Freimann (2002), 'Sustainability issues for start-up entrepreneurs', *Greener Management International*, 38, 59–70.

Schlange, L.E. (2007), 'What drives sustainable entrepreneurs?', *Indian Journal of Economics and Business*, 6, 35–45.

Schlange, L.E. (2009), 'Stakeholder identification in sustainability entrepreneurship', *Greener Management International*, 55, 13–32.

Schumpeter, J.A. (1942), *Capitalism, Socialism, and Democracy*, New York, USA and London, UK: Harper & Brothers.

Shane, S. (1996), 'Explaining variation in rates of entrepreneurship in the United States 1899–1988', *Journal of Management*, 22(5), 747–81.

Shane, S. (2003), *A General Theory of Entrepreneurship: The Individual–Opportunity Nexus*, Cheltenham, UK and Northampton, MA, USA: Edward Elgar Publishing.

Shane, S. and S. Venkataraman (2000), 'The promise of entrepreneurship as a field of research', *Academy of Management Review*, 25(1), 217–26.

Shaw, E., J. Shaw and M. Wilson (2002), *Unsung Entrepreneurs: Entrepreneurship for Social Gain*, Durham: University of Durham Business School – The Barclays Centre for Entrepreneurship.

Shepherd, D.A. and H. Patzelt (2011), 'Sustainable entrepreneurship: entrepreneurial action linking "what is to be sustained" with "what is to be developed"', *Entrepreneurship: Theory and Practice*, 35(1), 137–63.

Short, J., D.J. Ketchen, C.L. Shook and R.D. Ireland (2010), 'The concept of "opportunity" in entrepreneurship research: past accomplishments and future challenges', *Journal of Management*, 36(1), 40–65.

Short, J.C., T.W. Moss and G.T. Lumpkin (2009), 'Research in social entrepreneurship: past contributions and future opportunities', *Strategic Entrepreneurship Journal*, 3(2), 161–94.

Spence, M., J.B.B. Gherib and V.O. Biwolé (2011), 'Sustainable entrepreneurship: is entrepreneurial will enough? A North–South comparison', *Journal of Business Ethics*, 99(3), 1–33.

Steyaert, C. (2007), 'Of course that is not the whole (toy) story: entrepreneurship and the cat's cradle', *Journal of Business Venturing*, 22(5), 733–51.

Sullivan Mort, G. and M. Hume (2009), 'Editorial to special issue: Sustainability, social entrepreneurship and social change', *Australasian Marketing Journal*, 17(4), 189–93.

Sullivan Mort, G., J. Weerawardena and K. Carnegie (2003), 'Social entrepreneurship: towards conceptualization', *International Journal of Nonprofit and Voluntary Sector Marketing*, 8(1), 76–88.

Thompson, J.L. (2002), 'The world of the social entrepreneur', *International Journal of Public Sector Management*, 15(4/5), 412–31.

Thompson, J.L., G. Alvy and A. Lees (2000), 'Social entrepreneurship: a new look at the people and the potential', *Management Decision*, 38(5), 328–38.

Tilley, F. and F. Young (2009), 'Sustainability entrepreneurs', *Greener Management International*, 55, 79–92.

Tranfield, D., D. Denyer and P. Smart (2003), 'Towards a methodology for developing evidence-informed management knowledge by means of systematic review', *British Journal of Management*, 14(3), 207–22.

Ucbasaran, D., P. Westhead and M. Wright (2001), 'The focus of entrepreneurial research: contextual and process issues', *Entrepreneurship: Theory and Practice*, 25(4), 57–80.

United Nations (2002), 'Report of the world summit on sustainable development', Johannesburg, South Africa, 26 August – 4 September, New York: United Nations.

Van de Ven, A.H. (1992), 'Suggestions for studying strategy process: a research note', *Strategic Management Journal*, 13(Summer Special Issue), 169–88.

Venkataraman, S. (1997), 'The distinctive domain of entrepreneurship research: an editor's perspective', in J. Katz and R. Brockhaus (eds), *Advances in Entrepreneurship, Firm Emergence, and Growth: An Editor's Perspective*, 3rd edn, Greenwich, CT: JAI Press, pp. 119–38.

Waddock, S.A. and J.E. Post (1991), 'Social entrepreneurs and catalytic change', *Public Administration Review*, 51(5), 393–401.

Wagner, M. (2012), 'Ventures for the public good and entrepreneurial intentions: an empirical analysis of sustainability orientation as a determining factor', *Journal of Small Business Venturing*, 25(4), 519–32.

Wagner, M. and S. Schaltegger (2010), 'Classifying entrepreneurship for the public good: empirical analysis of a conceptual framework', *Journal of Small Business and Entrepreneurship*, 23(3), 431–43.

Wallace, S.L. (1999), 'Social entrepreneurship: the role of social purpose enterprises in facilitating community economic development', *Journal of Developmental Entrepreneurship*, 4(2), 153–74.

Walley, E.E. and D.W. Taylor (2002), 'Opportunists, champions, mavericks . . .? A typology of green entrepreneurs', *Greener Management International*, 38, 31–43.

Weerawardena, S. and G. Mort (2006), 'Investigating social entrepreneurship: a multidimensional model', *Journal of World Business*, 41(1), 21–35.

World Commission on Environment and Development (WCED) (1987), *Brundtland Report: Our Common Future*, Oxford: Oxford University Press.

World Resources Institute (2005), *Ecosystems and Human Well-Being: Synthesis Report (Millennium Ecosystem Assessment)*, Washington, DC: Island Press.

Yin, R.K. (2008), *Case Study Research: Design and Methods*, Thousand Oaks, CA: Sage Publications.

Young, W. and F. Tilley (2006), 'Can businesses move beyond efficiency? The shift toward effectiveness and equity in the corporate sustainability debate', *Business Strategy and the Environment*, 15(6), 402–15.

Zahra, S.A. (2007), 'Contextualizing theory building in entrepreneurship research', *Journal of Business Venturing*, 22(3), 443–52.

APPENDIX

Table 2A.1   Science Direct

Search string	Scope	Date of search	Number of entries
'sustainable entrepreneurship' OR 'sustainability entrepreneurship'	Title, Abstract, Keywords	04.09.2013	93
(sustainable OR sustainability) AND entrepreneur*	Title, Abstract, Keywords	04.09.2013	191
Total Science Direct			284

EBSCO Business Source Premier

Search string	Scope	Date of search	Number of entries
'sustainable entrepreneurship' OR 'sustainability entrepreneurship'	Title, Abstract, Keywords	04.09.2013	42
(sustainable OR sustainability) AND entrepreneur*	Title, Abstract, Keywords	04.09.2013	250
Total EBSCO			292

Table 2A.2   Science Direct

Search string	Sustainable	Irrelevant
'sustainable entrepreneurship' OR 'sustainability entrepreneurship'	13	80
(sustainable OR sustainability) AND entrepreneur*	15	176

EBSCO Business Source Premier

Search string	Sustainable	Irrelevant
'sustainable entrepreneurship' OR 'sustainability entrepreneurship'	21	21
(sustainable OR sustainability) AND entrepreneur*	59	191

Table 2A.3   Summary of the systematic review of journal articles retrieval and analysis

	Number of documents
Stage one: database analysis	
Science Direct	284
EBSCO – Business Source Premier	292
Total database analysis	576
Stage two: title and abstract analysis	
Categorized as irrelevant	468
Categorized as sustainable entrepreneurship	108
Duplicates in the category 'sustainable entrepreneurship'	41
Total title and abstract analysis	67
Stage three: relevance analysis	
Sustainable entrepreneurship	67
Not relevant	24
Total relevance analysis	43

Table 2A.4   As retrieved from the systematic literature review

Author	Title	Journal	Year	Definition of SE
Berglund, Karin; Wigren, Caroline	Soci(et)al entrepreneurship: the shaping of a different story of entrepreneurship	*Journal of Critical Postmodern Organization Science*	2012	No definition of SE provided
Choi, David Y.; Gray, Edmund R.	The venture development processes of 'sustainable' entrepreneurs	*Management Research News*	2008	No definition of SE provided; focus on the individual sustainable entrepreneur
Cohen, Boyd	Sustainable valley entrepreneurial ecosystems	*Business Strategy and the Environment*	2006	No definition of SE provided; focus on sustainable entrepreneurial ecosystems
Cohen, Boyd; Winn, Monika I.	Market imperfections, opportunity and sustainable entrepreneurship	*Journal of Business Venturing*	2007	'We define sustainable entrepreneurship [research] as the examination of how opportunities to bring into existence future goods and services are discovered, created, and exploited, by whom, and with what economic, psychological, social, and environmental consequences.'
Cohen, Boyd; Smith, Brock; Mitchell, Ron	Toward a sustainable conceptualization of dependent variables in entrepreneurship research	*Business Strategy and the Environment*	2008	'Under this concept, entrepreneurship research is concerned with discovering (1) why, when, and how opportunities for the creation of goods and services in the future arise in an economy; (2) why, when, and how some are able to discover and exploit these opportunities while others cannot or do not; and finally (3) what are the economic, psychological, social *and environmental* (added) impacts of this pursuit of a future market not only for the pursuer but also for

Authors	Title	Journal	Year	Definition
Dean, Thomas J.; McMullen, Jeffery S.	Toward a theory of sustainable entrepreneurship: Reducing environmental degradation through entrepreneurial action	*Journal of Business Venturing*	2007	the other stakeholders and for society as a whole. Based on Cohen and Winn (2007).' 'Sustainable entrepreneurship is defined to be: the process of discovering, evaluating, and exploiting economic opportunities that are present in market failures which detract from sustainability, including those that are environmentally relevant.'
De Clercq, Dirk; Voronov, Maxim	Sustainability in entrepreneurship: A tale of two logics	*International Small Business Journal*	2011	No definition of SE provided
Dixon, Sarah E. A.; Clifford, Anne	Ecopreneurship – a new approach to managing the triple bottom line	*Journal of Organizational Change Management*	2007	No definition of SE provided
Gibbs, David	Sustainability entrepreneurs, ecopreneurs and the development of a sustainable economy	*Greener Management International*	2009	No definition of SE provided; focus on the individual sustainable entrepreneur
Hall, Jeremy K.; Daneke, Gregory A.; Lenox, Michael J.	Sustainable development and entrepreneurship: Past contributions and future directions	*Journal of Business Venturing*	2010	No definition of SE provided
Hall, Jeremy; Wagner, Marcus	Editorial: The challenges and opportunities of sustainable development for entrepreneurship and small business	*Journal of Small Business & Entrepreneurship*	2012	No definition of SE provided
Hart, Stuart L.; Milstein, Mark B.	Global sustainability and the creative destruction of industries	*Sloan Management Review*	1999	No definition of SE provided

Table 2A.4 (continued)

Author	Title	Journal	Year	Definition of SE
Hockerts, Kai; Wüstenhagen, Rolf	Greening Goliaths versus emerging Davids: theorizing about the role of incumbents and new entrants in sustainable entrepreneurship	*Journal of Business Venturing*	2010	'We thus define sustainable entrepreneurship as the discovery and exploitation of economic opportunities through the generation of market disequilibria that initiate the transformation of a sector towards an environmentally and socially more sustainable state.'
Isaak, Robert	The making of the ecopreneur	*Greener Management International*	2002	No definition of SE provided
Kardos, Mihaela	The relationship between entrepreneurship, innovation and sustainable development: research on European Union countries	*Procedia Economics and Finance*	2012	'The notion of sustainable entrepreneurship . . . has been raised to address the contribution of entrepreneurial activities to solving societal and environmental problems, to sustainable development in a more comprehensive way.'.
Keijzers, Gerard	The transition to the sustainable enterprise	*Journal of Cleaner Production*	2002	No definition of SE provided
Kuckertz, Andreas; Wagner, Marcus	The influence of sustainability orientation on entrepreneurial intentions – Investigating the role of business experience	*Journal of Business Venturing*	2010	Refer to the definitions of Cohen and Winn (2007) and Dean and McMullen (2007)
Kury, Kenneth Wm	Sustainability meets social entrepreneurship: a path to social change through institutional entrepreneurship	*International Journal of Business Insights and Transformation*	2012	'Sustainable and environmental entrepreneurship are more macro in focus and seek to describe interactions in the institutional realm that create opportunities from market failures and work to develop a more sustainable future.'

Author	Title	Journal	Year	Definition
Larson, Andrea L.	Sustainable innovation through an entrepreneurship lens	*Business Strategy and the Environment*	2000	No definition of SE provided
Lordkipanidze, Maia; Brezet, Han; Backman, Mikael	The entrepreneurship factor in sustainable tourism development	*Journal of Cleaner Production*	2005	No definition of SE provided
Lorne, Frank T.	Macro-entrepreneurship and sustainable development: the need for innovative solutions for promoting win-win interactions	*Environmental Economics and Policy Studies*	2009	No definition of SE provided
Mathew, Viju	Sustainable entrepreneurship in small-scale business: application, concepts and cases	*ICFAI Journal of Entrepreneurship Development*	2009	'Sustainable entrepreneurship can be defined as the continuing commitment by businesses to behave ethically and contribute to economic development while improving the quality of life of the workforce, their families, the local and global community as well as future generations.'
Morrish, Sussie C.; Miles, Morgan P.; Polonsky, Michael Jay	An exploratory study of sustainability as a stimulus for corporate entrepreneurship	*Corporate Social Responsibility and Environmental Management*	2011	'Firms that have adopted SCE must exhibit: . . . evidence of all three sustainability components – responsible environmental management, social accountability, and long-term economic performance – as well as the presence of significant innovation with respect to the firm's products, processes, strategies, domain or business model. (Based on Miles et al., 2008)'
Nagler, Jürgen	Entrepreneurs: the world needs you	*Thunderbird International Business Review*	2012	No definition of SE provided

Table 2A.4 (continued)

Author	Title	Journal	Year	Definition of SE
O'Neill Jr, Gerald D.; Hershauer, James C.; Golden, Jay S.	The cultural context of sustainability entrepreneurship	*Greener Management International*	2009	'Sustainability entrepreneurship is a process of venture creation that links the activities of entrepreneurs to the emergence of value-creating enterprises that contribute to the sustainable development of the social–ecological system. An enterprise resulting from this process can be referred to as a sustainability venture.'
Pacheco, Desirée F.; Dean, Thomas J.; Payne, David S.	Escaping the green prison: entrepreneurship and the creation of opportunities for sustainable development	*Journal of Business Venturing*	2010	'We view sustainable entrepreneurship as the discovery, creation, evaluation, and exploitation of opportunities to create future goods and services that is consistent with sustainable development goals.'
Parrish, Bradley D.; Foxon, Timothy J.	Sustainability entrepreneurship and equitable transitions to a low-carbon economy	*Greener Management International*	2009	'Sustainability-driven entrepreneurship describes those entrepreneurial activities in which the central guiding purpose is to make a substantial contribution to sustainable development. More specifically, sustainability entrepreneurs design ventures with the primary intention of contributing to improved environmental quality and social well-being in ways that are mutually supportive.'
Parrish, Bradley D.	Sustainability-driven entrepreneurship: principles of organization design	*Journal of Business Venturing*	2010	No definition of SE provided
Pastakia, Astad	Grassroots ecopreneurs: change agents for a sustainable society	*Journal of Organizational Change Management*	1998	No definition of SE provided; focus on the individual sustainable entrepreneur

Author	Title	Journal	Year	Definition
Patzelt, Holger; Shepherd, Dean A.	Recognizing opportunities for sustainable development	*Entrepreneurship: Theory and Practice*	2011	'Sustainable entrepreneurship is the discovery, creation, and exploitation of opportunities to create future goods and services that sustain the natural and/or communal environment and provide development gain for others.'
Plieth, Hanna; Bullinger, Angelika C.; Hansen, Erik G.	Sustainable entrepreneurship in the apparel industry: the case of Manomama	*Journal of Corporate Citizenship*	2012	No definition of SE provided
Potocan, Vojko; Mulej, Matjaz	Entrepreneurship: between sustainable development and reality	*Public Finance & Management*	2003	No definition of SE provided
Rodgers, Cheryl	Sustainable entrepreneurship in SMEs: a case study analysis	*Corporate Social Responsibility and Environmental Management*	2010	No definition of SE provided
Schaltegger, Stefan; Wagner, Marcus	Sustainable entrepreneurship and sustainability innovation: categories and interactions	*Business Strategy and the Environment*	2011	'Defined more widely, sustainable entrepreneurship can thus be described as an innovative, market-oriented and personality driven form of creating economic and societal value by means of break-through environmentally or socially beneficial market or institutional innovations.'
Schick, Hildegard; Marxen, Sandra; Freimann, Jürgen	Sustainability issues for start-up entrepreneurs	*Greener Management International*	2002	No definition of SE provided
Schlange, Lutz E.	Stakeholder identification in sustainability entrepreneurship	*Greener Management International*	2009	'In other words, entrepreneurial ventures driven by sustainability may be defined by their distinct approach to balance the requirements of the triple bottom line.'

Table 2A.4 (continued)

Author	Title	Journal	Year	Definition of SE
Shepherd, Dean A.; Patzelt, Holger	The new field of sustainable entrepreneurship: studying entrepreneurial action linking 'what is to be sustained' with 'what is to be developed'	*Entrepreneurship: Theory and Practice*	2011	'Sustainable entrepreneurship is focused on the preservation of nature, life support, and community in the pursuit of perceived opportunities to bring into existence future products, processes, and services for gain, where gain is broadly construed to include economic and non-economic gains to individuals, the economy, and society.'
Spence, Martine; Ben Boubaker Gherib, Jouhaina; Ondoua Biwolé, Viviane	Sustainable entrepreneurship: is entrepreneurial will enough? A North–South comparison	*Journal of Business Ethics*	2011	'An innovative, market oriented and personality driven form of value creation by environmentally or socially beneficial innovations and products exceeding the start-up phase of a company (based on Schaltegger and Wagner, 2007).'
Sullivan Mort, Gillian; Hume, Margee	Special Issue: Sustainability, social entrepreneurship and social change	*Australasian Marketing Journal*	2009	No definition of SE provided; focus on social entrepreneurship
Tilley, Fiona; Young, William	Sustainability entrepreneurs	*Greener Management International*	2009	No definition of SE provided; focus on the individual SE entrepreneur

Author	Title	Journal	Year	
Wagner, Marcus	Ventures for the public good and entrepreneurial intentions: an empirical analysis of sustainability orientation as a determining factor	*Journal of Small Business and Entrepreneurship*	2012	'The teleological process aiming at the achievement of sustainable development, by discovering, evaluating and exploiting opportunities and creating value that produces economic prosperity, social cohesion and environmental protection (based on Katsikis and Kyrgidou, 2008).'
Wagner, Marcus; Schaltegger, Stefan	Classifying entrepreneurship for the public good: empirical analysis of a conceptual framework	*Journal of Small Business and Entrepreneurship*	2010	'The term "entrepreneurship for sustainable development" . . . is characterized by some fundamental aspects of entrepreneurial activities which are less oriented towards management systems or technical procedures and focus more on the personal initiative and skills of the entrepreneurial person or team to realize market success with environmental or societal innovations.'
Young, William; Tilley, Fiona	Can businesses move beyond efficiency? The shift toward effectiveness and equity in the corporate sustainability debate	*Business Strategy and the Environment*	2006	'This paper argues that sustainable entrepreneurship is the incorporation of all elements of sustainable development, not just some.'

71

PART II

THE TRANSFORMATIVE APPROACH TO ENTREPRENEURSHIP FOR A SUSTAINABLE SOCIETY

3. Socially sustainable entrepreneurship: a case of entrepreneurial practice in social change and stability

Toke Bjerregaard and Jakob Lauring

INTRODUCTION

Sustainable entrepreneurship is attracting increasing attention in the entrepreneurship literature. In the present chapter we illuminate how small business entrepreneurs engage in activities of importance for social sustainability and development as they undertake entrepreneurial ventures. This chapter thus examines how small-scale entrepreneurial venturing in a developing country contributes to both sustaining and changing societal structures.

Poor people's participation in markets are in many developing countries restricted by 'institutional voids' (Mair and Martí, 2009). In contexts characterized by institutional voids, institutions that support markets are absent or malfunction (Khanna and Palepu, 1997). Extant research primarily differentiates between three types of institutional voids, namely voids that restrict market creation, obstruct market functioning and impede market participation (Mair and Martí, 2009). Voids that impede market creation may comprise weak or absent governance structures, property rights and the rule of law (Mair et al., 2007). Developing countries characterized by institutional voids often lack formal institutions that support market functioning. However, weak formal rules and institutions do not imply an absence of informal, social or cultural-cognitive institutions and norms (Bohannan and Dalton, 1965; Moore, 1978). Developing countries may be characterized by formal institutional voids but may be rich in informal institutions, traditions, customary practices and beliefs which are believed to often impede social and economic development by restricting people from access to the market (Mair and Martí, 2009).

Extant research has focused on how social entrepreneurs such as non-governmental organizations (NGOs) change the informal institutions, traditions, customary norms and practices that are believed to prevent poor people from market participation in developing countries (Mair and Martí, 2009; Martí and Mair, 2009). Hence, social entrepreneurs such as

NGOs recombine available resources and institutions to fill institutional gaps that impede market participation and activity (Mair et al., 2007). Social entrepreneurship can in this perspective be understood as 'a process involving the innovative use and combination of resources to pursue opportunities to catalyse social change and/or address social needs' (Mair and Martí, 2006). Social entrepreneurship, like other entrepreneurial activities, is shaped by the broader institutional contexts and logics in which it is embedded (Marquis and Lounsbury, 2007; Polanyi, 1944). Development actors, as one type of social entrepreneurs, work on building the institutions that support poor people's market participation (Mair and Martí, 2009). While much research has examined the activities of social entrepreneurs such as NGOs, relatively little has been done to elucidate the work of poor people in developing countries as they, through entrepreneurial ventures, cope and work with the institutional environments that supposedly restrict them from market participation.

In the present research we aim to bridge some of this gap. Hence, while this chapter addresses the role of small-scale business entrepreneurs in social stability and change, such a perspective focusing on actors' work with sustaining or changing societal structures has largely been present in the social entrepreneurship literature. Our argument is illustrated by an ethnographic field study that examines the strategies used by small entrepreneurs in an area of extreme resource scarcity to navigate co-existing and potentially contradictory social and market logics. The entrepreneurs cope with and exploit institutional contradictions through their sphere-straddling ventures during institutional change from an economy based on traditional exchange relationships to a situation with an emerging market economy. We examine the strategies through which the entrepreneurs navigate and work with the multiple institutional logics of the different spheres in which they operate in order to facilitate entrepreneurial venturing and, in turn, contribute to both sustaining and changing societal structures. Informal institutional structures and logics were believed by local NGOs to impede economic and social development by demotivating poor people from market participation. However, by examining the actual perceptions and strategies of the local, poor people and their entrepreneurial ventures, we illuminate how customary norms, beliefs and institutions did not merely impose institutional constraints on economic practice, but were used by entrepreneurs to create opportunities for individual value generation.

This chapter proposes an alternative conceptualization of institutional entrepreneurship than the predominant one. Traditionally, institutional entrepreneurship has been conceived as actors' activities with changing social structures to realize opportunities (DiMaggio, 1988), that is, changes that deviate from the established institutions in a field of activity (Battilana et al., 2009). The present study illustrates that institutional entrepreneurship in pluralistic contexts is as much about the activities of actors in maintaining or sustaining societal structures, as it is about changing them. Hence, entrepreneurs bridging pluralistic institutions devise strategies to strike a balance between the logics on which their ventures are based, and thereby work simultaneously with sustaining and changing social structures. Social sustainability concerns are in this perspective a central aspect of the entrepreneurial process (Barth, 1963).

CONCEPTUAL BACKGROUND: A PRACTICE APPROACH TO SOCIAL SUSTAINABILITY IN ENTREPRENEURSHIP

In the present chapter we suggest a conceptualization of institutional entrepreneurship by drawing inspiration from practice theory represented in theories such as Barth's analytic approach to the study of entrepreneurship (Barth, 1963, 1967, 1981). While often associated with the seminal works of central social theorists such as Bourdieu (1977) and Giddens (1979), different strands of practice theory have been gaining ground across the social sciences (Rasche and Chia, 2009; Schatzki et al., 2001), including organization and management studies (Ahrens and Chapman, 2002), strategy research (Jarzabkowski and Spee, 2009) and to some extent the entrepreneurship literature (Steyaert, 2007). The different variants that underlie these developments vary on different dimensions such as the particular conception of and significance granted to structure and action; for example, to what degree theories are more structuralist or interactionalist (Rasche and Chia, 2009). Barth's approach to the study of entrepreneurship may be seen as a precursor to practice theory, which conceives of everyday practice as a form of skilled improvisation where people more or less strategically work with rules, norms and institutions using their knowledge and resources at hand in pursuing more immediate interests and concerns (Wilk and Cliggett, 2007). As noted by Barth (2007), this requires an account of both the sought and unsought consequences of practice for systems.

Barth's (2007) work in anthropology covers more than six decades, which has generated a varied theoretical and empirical production. Whilst initially being an exponent for transactionalism in his earliest works, which portray values, norms and rules as momentary effects of an ongoing flow of transactions and negotiations between people, Barth came to identify his work with practice theory (Barth, 1994, 2007), and reviewers of social theory of economy describe him as a precursor of practice theory (Wilk and Cliggett, 2007). However, practice theorists such as Bourdieu (1977) argued that early transactional approaches did not adequately account for the relationship between formal, institutional structure and action, but tilted towards examining informal social organization (see also Ortner, 1984). Yet, in order to appreciate how his analytic approach is positioned within the broader spectrum of theories of practice, it is useful to account for how it developed among foundational debates on economy, and in particular in response to the tradition of research that conceives of institutional structures as the foundation for economic systems rather than the rational maximizing individual (Polanyi et al., 1957). Hence, to avoid rational economic explanations in this institutional tradition of research on economies and their social embeddedness, change has been explained on the basis of change in structural, institutional forms as opposed to being founded in individual choice. Economies are embedded in institutional spheres and logics which impose constraints and opportunities on entrepreneurial ventures and market activity (Malinowski, 1922; Parry and Bloch, 1989; Polanyi, 1944). In economic anthropology and related fields this view was met with criticism for leaving aside an understanding of how changes in social or institutional forms occur, and the role of individual agency in their reproduction and change. Entrepreneurship was one empirical area of investigation in which these more general analytical and methodological arguments about the study of the social were unfolded by Barth.

According to Barth, the social patterns that emerge in empirical material are rather to be read as tracks in the sand left by a process that has taken place, thereby studying the emergence of institutional formations (Barth, 1981). Hence, what is needed is a generative model that accounts for the generative processes that lead to cultural or institutional forms. The intent was to achieve a greater naturalism in the study of social or institutional forms (Barth, 1992). Thus, conceiving of society as a continuous accomplishment conveys a view of institutions, societal and cultural norms as being more products of practice than its cause (Barth, 1981). Hence, Barth set forth an analytic model based on an understanding of society as something that to a greater extent happens, rather than is; constituting a continuous social organization process rather than a static, monolithic structure (Barth, 1994: 88). This requires the questioning of social or institutional coherence found in given material as something which needs to be accounted for, rather than assumed or something that accounts for (Latour, 2005; Zilber, 2011). Cultural or institutional integration is thus portrayed as always being a work in progress. Even though deviating from them in many respects, his formulations in this vein seem to resonate with some of the arguments set forth by Latour (2005) for a different understanding of the social, whom he also appreciates (Barth, 2002).

This perspective deviates from some institutional theory in the organization literature which has often been based on a notion of institutions as durable, taken-for-granted social structures (Hughes, 1942; Jepperson, 1991). Hence, according to institutional theory it requires an effort to change an institution or social structure (Battilana et al., 2009). Institutional entrepreneurship is then about how actors change institutions to realize valued opportunities (Battilana et al., 2009; DiMaggio, 1988; Eisenstadt, 1980). Research on social entrepreneurship has thus elucidated how microcredit organizations recombine available institutions and resources to create new institutions, or change existing societal norms to facilitate social and economic development (Martí and Mair, 2009).

However, in Barth's perspective societal and cultural structures or institutions are in a process of emergence. In such a perspective it is likely to require an effort to maintain or sustain societal structures as well as changing them. Conceptualizing entrepreneurship in such a perspective conceives of entrepreneurial practice in pluralistic contexts as an ongoing activity, balancing the maintenance and revision of existing institutions and the integration of new institutional structures. Efforts aimed at ensuring social sustainability are thus an inherent aspect of entrepreneurial processes which are bound up with multiple spheres and logics. Actors operating amid institutional contradictions must simultaneously undertake activities to maintain existing institutions and integrate new ones. Hence, rather than being restricted to a few actors, institutional agency is potentially present in all social or economic activities that are bound up with multiple spheres and logics. Institutional entrepreneurs act in alternative ways in relation to established patterns and norms, and thereby generate social and cultural change by manipulating and mobilizing actors and resources in the entrepreneurial process (Barth, 1967: 80).

Extant research has examined how institutional entrepreneurs make use of institutional logics to promote change within a field by transposing institutional elements or logics between fields. Comparatively less research has illuminated those actors that operate in different spheres simultaneously where, according to Martí and Mair (2009), they at the same time have to juggle and navigate multiple and often contradictory logics. However, there is a need for more research on the challenges faced and the skills needed by actors operating across societal spheres and logics (Martí and Mair, 2009: 112). This is often a characteristic of entrepreneurship, which in the words of Barth:

> frequently involves the relationship of persons and institutions in one society with those of an other . . . and the entrepreneur becomes an essential 'broker' in this situation of culture contact. But in the most general sense, one might argue that in the activities of the entrepreneur we may recognize processes which are fundamental to questions of social stability and change, and that their analysis is therefore crucial to anyone who wishes to pursue a dynamic study of society. (Barth, 1963: 3)

According to practice theory, social continuity and change is the product of an articulation process occurring at the macro level of structuring structures as well as the level of actors' transformative praxis (Comaroff, 1985). Novel orders and logics come into being through a process of reorganization (Comaroff, 1985). Social continuity and reorganization takes place through a dialectical articulation process of institutional structure and action which may create a syncretistic institutional *bricolage* (Comaroff, 1985; Lévi-Strauss, 1966). Such a *bricolage* includes both a reproduction of existing institutions and a change with the introduction of new elements; that is, a joining together of distinct systems, themselves dynamic orders of practice and meaning. By using and recombining the institutional logics and resources at hand, brokers in this articulation process partake in the construction of new orders of legitimate social and economic action. Hence, in a practice perspective, the focus is not merely on whether economic action breaks or conforms with a social norm (see Holy and Stuchlik, 1983). Rather, the focus is on which institutional logics and norms are invoked in taking particular actions, whether actors under- or over-perform given norms in their actual interactions and, in turn, reproduce or transform those norms and logics of legitimate action (see Holy and Stuchlik, 1983). This dialectic of institutional system and practice continuously reproduces or transforms institutional spheres of value circulation and channels of conversion and thereby shapes the strategic agency of the entrepreneur (Barth, 1967). Accounting for the dialectical relationship between structural conditions and entrepreneurial practice responds to calls for more research on how action beyond discourse interacts with institutions (Barley, 2008).

Moreover, this concern resonates with current efforts to understand how institutional multiplicity is worked out in micro-practice (Lawrence et al., 2010; Zilber, 2011). Hence, Barth's efforts to combine social and material value, structure and action, continuity and change in an account of the entrepreneurial process resonate with recent efforts to balance the reciprocal relationship between institution and agency in organization studies (Barley and Tolbert, 1997; Jarzabkowski et al., 2009; Lawrence et al., 2010). The project conveys a synthesis of structure and actor perspectives on economic activity (Wilk and Cliggett, 2007).

Whilst the practice perspective implies that multiple actors may partake in the entrepreneurial process, we also recognize that certain actors may be more central to the process than others. Hence, while much institutional research has concentrated on the agency of powerful macro-actors, the empirical choice of this study to focus on individual, small-scale entrepreneurs and their capable actions and interactions aligns well with the practice perspective taken.

In summary, the practice perspective is central to the argument of this chapter as it illuminates how social structures such as institutions are sustained and changed through entrepreneurs' everyday practice, thereby depicting social sustainability issues as integral to entrepreneurship. The approach outlined is grounded on a concern to decipher social patterns in the making, and to connect different levels of analysis (Barth, 1981; Comaroff and Comaroff, 1999; Gluckman, 1955; Powell and Colyvas, 2008). It inserts entrepreneurship into a social ontology of becoming (Nayak and Chia, 2011; Steyaert, 2007). In the following sections we illustrate the value of this perspective by use of an ethnographic field study of how small business entrepreneurs cope with and exploit the institutional contradictions forming the basis for social and economic changes in the wider societal context. This is done by illuminating the entrepreneurs' strategies of balancing the co-existing social and market logics on which their ventures are dependent during a societal transition phase.

METHODOLOGY

Taking the methodological consequence of a practice perspective seriously calls for grounding the research on particular methodologies such as ethnography that captures the constitutive nature of action for structure (Evens and Handelman, 2006; Jarzabkowski et al., 2007; Rasche and Chia, 2009). Ethnographic studies use data collected from various sources, such as participant observation and semi-structured interviews, to provide a detailed and comprehensive account of a particular social context. One strength of the ethnographic approach is that it is exploratory, allowing findings that might not be anticipated from a study of the literature alone. Moreover, ethnographic methodologies are under-represented in entrepreneurship research (Kyrö and Kansikas, 2005). A colleague generously provided us with access to data from five months of fieldwork, used for analyses for this chapter.*

---

* The original dataset was made available at Inge Pasgaard (2004) 'Field report: Ndalalama ndi moyo'. Aarhus University, Denmark.

Participant Observation

In ethnographic participant observation, the researcher aims to gain an understanding of a particular social context from the perspective of the local community. In this study villagers were told that the researcher was interested in the entrepreneurial activities conducted in the village. To facilitate the study, the researcher kept a low profile and avoided asking questions or performing actions that would create atypical social behaviour among the villagers. Through observation and participation, research questions were developed and adapted as a result of information exchanges with the informants and through dialogue with other members of the research team. For the purpose of this study, participant observation also included informal conversations and questions arising spontaneously during daily interactions. Through the use of participant observation, the field researcher gained the trust of the villagers and was able to receive responses to questions relating to sensitive topics such as the practice of witchcraft in the village. Hence, using the research methodology of participant observation enabled the mapping of implicit and sensitive aspects of village life.

Interviews

In addition to participant observation, semi-structured interviews were conducted with most of the families in the village and with individual key informants (Bernard, 1995). More than 100 individuals contributed to the data material. The interviewer tried to guide the interviews based on a standard set of questions; however, the informants were encouraged to raise and discuss additional, related topics. Typically, the interviews took place in open spaces or in villagers' houses and lasted between one and two hours. To minimize the effects of the setting, elitist bias was reduced by interviewing individuals from different levels of the small society.

Early results were regularly discussed and cross-checked with different key informants. Two interpreters assisted during the interviews. Due to their social contacts and local knowledge, the interpreters had a substantial influence on the final results. To minimize these effects their statements and explanations were continuously cross-checked. Hence, interviews were used to discuss activities observed in the village as well as to register the differing opinions of various members in the local setting. Finally, text material and national statistics were used in order to gain a comprehensive understanding of the context.

Data Analysis

Theme analysis as set out in Spradley (1980) was conducted on the collected data. This analysis entailed a thorough and in-depth reading and coding of field notes, interview transcripts and documents, which led to the development of detailed descriptions of the village. The qualitative analysis program Nvivo was used to sort the data according to the central themes linking to the research question. This helped to identify key aspects of the entrepreneurial practices used by the villagers. The coded data provided examples of how entrepreneurs interpret and practice activities that add to the sustainability of the community. In the analysis, the research team relied on triangulation of different data sources for validation.

Research Site and Socio-Economic Context

This ethnographic study was conducted in 2002 in Malawi during a time of continued efforts to implement liberal democracy in the country. Since 1995, the country had been going through a fragile institutional transition process which included attempts to build stronger pillars for democratic governance, such as the development of a market economy. From 1891, Malawi was the British protectorate of Nyasaland. In 1961 the Malawi Congress Party, led by Hastings Kamuzu Banda, gained an overwhelming majority in elections held for a new legislative assembly, and in 1963 Banda was appointed Prime Minister of the self-governing territory of Nyasaland. In 1964, Nyasaland declared independence from Britain and became the independent nation of Malawi. In 1966, Banda became President of the Republic of Malawi and a one-party state was established. During the famine in 1992, the Catholic Church and many Malawians publicly condemned Banda's system of government, and in the same year many donor countries suspended their relief aid due to the country's human rights record. In 1994, Bakili Muluzi, the leader of the United Democratic Front (UDF), was elected president in Malawi's first multi-party elections. In 1995, a new constitution, which ensured multi-party democracy, was instituted in Malawi (Larney, 2001: 69). The current President of Malawi is Bingu wa Mutharika, who was elected in 2004 and leads the Democratic Progressive Party (DPP). Ninety per cent of the population of Malawi lives in rural areas (Larney, 2001: 115). As is the case with many other developing countries, Malawi has many informal institutions, and few of the formal institutions that are necessary to support a modern market economy (Mair and Martí, 2009). Malawi's democratization project is characterized by institutional fragility. The country has been subject to the administration of international actors who have influenced the formulation of national policies and programmes. The international development industry maintains a strong presence in Malawi.

The social and political situation in the village of Muzigo in central Malawi had a few years earlier been the subject of research conducted by an NGO. Due to the availability of this earlier research and its relevance to our study, we chose the village of Muzigo as the focus of our ethnographic research. Previously, work for a nearby poverty alleviation organization operating microcredit programmes showed that the NGO believed that local, customary practices and myths impeded economic and social development. An example of such a practice was the restriction placed on women, preventing them from participating in value-generating activities outside the house. From the perspective of the NGO, economic practice was impeded by institutional voids which were recognized by the local community as occult forces; these forces could function as a leveraging sanction. For the purpose of our ethnographic study we gained access to the local community independently of the NGO. We did this to avoid being perceived by the local community as having preconceived ideas about local beliefs and traditions and the economic practices in the village. If we were seen as independent of the NGO, villagers might be more willing to speak about their perceptions and strategies concerning economic practices, particularly among the less well-off members of the community. Moreover, being associated with an NGO might limit our access to certain kinds of information among the poor. According to several informants, access to start-up capital and hence market participation is hampered by a long history of Western intervention in Malawi, including 50 years of British colonial administration, Western support to Banda under the Cold War, and the international development industry which is still widely present in Malawi. According to the informants, this intervention has led to a lack of belief among the Malawian population in their own resourcefulness and abilities. The field researcher lived part of the time with a family in Muzigo; however, due to a situation of extreme resource scarcity and an average of one death per week due to poverty and starvation-related diseases in Muzigo, it was decided that the field worker should also live part of the time with a comparatively wealthier family on the outskirts of the village.

At the time of this study, the population of the village of Muzigo was approximately 500, the majority of whom belonged to the Thawu tribe. Migrations from other parts of the country and from Zimbabwe and Mozambique had led to increasing numbers of outsiders settling in the area. Traditionally, the distribution of land in Muzigo has been guided by societal structures of inherited status and has followed social obligations as levelling mechanisms. An example of such a tradition is the expectation that wealthy family members are obliged to financially assist their relatives, as well as providing assistance to their less well-off friends and neighbours. Through his power to distribute land, the chief has traditionally been the administrator of the exchange of value. In recent years, this administrative role of the chief has increasingly been replaced by market forces. More land is now available on the financial market, and government institutions are gradually taking over the role of authority previously held by the chief. Our study revealed that villagers increasingly feel less obliged to follow the tradition of economically supporting their relatives and less fortunate households in their immediate surroundings.

Maize production was the primary income source for most of the villagers at the time of the research; however, due to a scarcity of land, most villagers sought to supplement this income. The three most common means of income supplementation were: seasonal farming labour, for which payment was often made in provisions such as maize; the practice of a trade, which included prostitution in the city; and the production of goods, such as bricks and beer. Certain trades and production businesses were nurturing entrepreneurial ventures at the time in Muzigo. These businesses included the trade of meat, wood, hardware and foreign medicine; the credit business; and the production of mango, furniture and textiles. These businesses generated a relatively larger surplus compared to the conventional small-scale business, but also required more substantial start-up capital and involved a higher risk to the entrepreneur.

FINDINGS

In Muzigo, market logic is steadily gaining a more central position in the system of value circulation. This has led to a gradual replacement of the established social logic of rights and obligations. This is conditioned by, and results in, changes in the local power and distribution structure, as the market is being differentiated from local power institutions. As explained by a local person: 'Nowadays, I tell you, there is no one who doesn't like money. Everybody is working to have money. Everyone is looking for money. I tell you . . . And people kill each other for money, I tell you. Not only by magic. Even killing, reality killing.'

In order to create an arena for market exchange in the system of value circulation it is necessary for the entrepreneur to find a balance between the opposing market and social logics which does not slow or obstruct profit generation and which is also in agreement with the traditional practices of the local community. This raises questions concerning the entrepreneur's role as institutional broker in this process and how this role is affected by the traditional beliefs in occult forces. Societal institutions impose constraints and social sanctions on entrepreneurial activity in Malawi by, for instance, restricting women from undertaking value-generating activities outside the home. Women are subject to a variety of social sanctions, for example witchcraft accusations. An accusation of witchcraft might be made if a practice of exchange that challenges the social and cultural norms of the conventional distribution structure is observed. For example, an accusation of witchcraft might be made as a result of jealousy when an individual accumulates power and material resources that are in excess of or in opposition to the established logic of social rights and obligations. However, entrepreneurs' activities are not only affected by institutional changes, but also sustain and transform societal structures. Entrepreneurship in Muzigo is thus constrained, as entrepreneurs attempt to engage in new business ventures in a way that is perceived as non-threatening to the existing institutional structure. The entrepreneurs develop strategies to bridge the institutional contradictions that form the basis for changes in the societal context. Through the ongoing interaction between macro-institutional structures and entrepreneurial practice, different spheres of value circulation are sustained and altered. Questions of importance to social sustainability and development are thus brought to light in the entrepreneurial process.

The Socially Responsible Entrepreneur

Mr Tamula (as of 2002) is the only farmer from the village of Muzigo whose primary income source is mango growing. For this reason, he is known by the villagers as the 'Mango Man'. He is Thawu, born in Muzigo, and in accordance with tradition he inherited his land from his mother's brother. The Mango Man is retired from a job on a large commercial mango plantation. His job at the large plantation provided him with the knowledge to grow mango on his own land, which is uncommon in Muzigo.

Being a local farmer, the Mango Man attracts capital to the village and distributes it through social obligation and a demand for labour power. In addition, Mr Tamula is very active in the local community. He is a member of the Catholic Church, the government party UDF (in power in 2002), connected to the chiefdom as a substitute for his brother and he is the founder of and an important financial contributor to the Muzigo school. The Mango Man is the only person in Muzigo who is a member of all authoritative institutions, and he has achieved these positions mainly as a result of strategic financial investments in important social relations.

By growing mango Mr Tamula is bridging the divide between commercial large-scale plantation farming and common local subsistence farming. Consequently, he is able to save money in the bank, which is unusual for local people. In Muzigo, private land is typically used for growing maize and other food crops, but after changes resulting from the democratization and privatization process after 1994, Mr Tamula has been able to use the openings between the authority of the chiefdoms and the new, emerging market economy to specialize in mango growing. Hence, the Mango Man is one of the few villagers to have embraced the expanding role of the money economy and the centrality taken by the institutional logic of the market in the system of value circulation. According to the Mango Man: 'If you see possibilities for business you should also use them because you have the chance to do something that is good that may otherwise not be done.'

Although his specialized production is based on his education and experience from previous employment as well as the changing economic conditions on a national level, the Mango Man is bridging different institutional domains, according to Barth (1967). This is because Mr Tamula utilized the new opportunity of exchanging money for positions in powerful institutions. The Mango Man is integrating market forces into the traditional hierarchy, thereby building a bridge between the traditional, social logic of rights and obligations and the new logic of market exchange. Based on the new rules governing privatization, Mr Tamula is now able to grow mango, generating profit that he invests to acquire power in the traditional hierarchy, the Church and the government party.

According to Mr Tamula, he is not being an entrepreneur to generate wealth solely for himself. On the contrary, he shares his economic surplus with his family and various social institutions. Mr Tamula meets his financial obligations to his relatives, all of whom live in Muzigo. During interviews, none of his relatives expressed any negative emotions towards him; this was uncommon in the general community when speaking of wealthy family members. To add legitimacy to economic action, Mr Tamula still honours the traditional normative patterns of rights and obligations.

His entrepreneurship practice is based on different social institutions with different conceptions of value. His brokering practice between institutions reflects an intention of capturing influence and power within them. He exploits the tensions between the spheres as a broker in 'cultural contact' in the structural overlap between them (Thornton et al., 2005). He has introduced a new position of Christian advisor to the chief in the traditional hierarchy, he has established a position as a member of the traditional hierarchy within the Catholic Church, and he has introduced a patrilineal line of inheritance within his family and introduced commercial mango production in Muzigo. He has changed institutionalized forms of exchange and conceptions of value by using his position and his social, cultural and material capital within the different fields. The change capability of his entrepreneurial practice is conditioned by its positioning in the structural overlap (Comaroff, 1985; Thornton et al., 2005).

The Economic Entrepreneur

As a member of the Mnuti tribe in Zimbabwe, Hussu was an outsider to Muzigo. In the 1980s he left his home country and most of his relatives in search of opportunities in Malawi. In Muzigo, he asked the chief for a piece of land that he secretly paid for. This transaction was possible only because Hussu was a newcomer and because he disguised the transaction with the chief. As described by a local informant: 'You know he got all his land from paying money. A large area. This land was supposed to be passed on to someone else but the chief gave it to him. You can ask everyone and they will tell you about this.'

Using concealment together with money to acquire a resource traditionally only available through the local hierarchy of inheritance and social obligations, Hussu was bridging different normative spheres. Hussu is the sole provider for his children, his mother-in-law and his wife's brother; he does not engage in social obligations outside this close family. Accordingly, as an outsider, he is able to give priority to new investments without the expectation of financial obligations to his kinsmen. Hussu is able to take a different approach to entrepreneurship than that taken by the Mango Man. His entrepreneurial activities have made him the wealthiest person in Muzigo. Among his possessions are land, a car, a motorcycle, a large house with a fence and an iron gate, and several apartment houses in the village and the nearby town.

Hussu generates the main part of his surplus from credit business and from rental housing. This type of business is unique to the area, since traditionally it is not expected that one would generate profit from people who have less resources than oneself. The traditional system of social obligation directs the flow of money from the fortunate to the less well-off. Hussu, however, is not subject to the local interpretation of the norm of social obligation as practised in Muzigo. When he is asked for money he offers a loan, thereby actively utilizing the tradition of social obligation to expand his business arena. According to Hussu, he is practising the social obligation in such a way that will not discourage hardworking individuals, but rather promote entrepreneurial activity throughout the village. In this way, Hussu is integrating the existing logic of rights and obligations into the new market economy, thereby brokering between two oppositional institutional structures of value distribution.

Having migrated from Zimbabwe to Muzigo has facilitated Hussu's entrepreneurial strategy. As an 'outsider' he is not subject to the traditional social relationships of the village and is able to actively distance himself from fellow villagers. He does not concede to 'begging' and he only opens the large iron gate of his property to a few select fellow villagers. Each day, on his motorbike, he goes to the town where he has friends.

Both of the entrepreneurs, Mr Tamula and Hussu, are bridging social and economic spheres by operating across the embedded contradiction of the social and economic change processes. They base their ventures on the *bricolage* of the meeting between an existing social structure and the new structures in progress (Lévi-Strauss, 1963). Life experiences and unique circumstances of the two entrepreneurs – that is, having employment in the mango industry in the case of Mr Tamula, and migrating from Zimbabwe in the case of Hussu – are the basis of a knowledge differentiation and an understanding of new logics of value and exchange. Each of the entrepreneurs has used their knowledge advantage to progress their business ventures in the existing value-circulation system in Muzigo. Associated with opportunities and financial surplus, however, is the risk of envy and social sanctions.

The Role of Witchcraft in Sustaining Social Structure

Witchcraft is an example of how established institutional structures may hamper the entrepreneurial process, making it a dialectical rather than a linear process including broader societal structures. Confronted with the notion of witchcraft, all of the informants initially denied its existence. However, after being assured that the researcher was not ridiculing the practice or did not consider acknowledging of the powers of the supernatural to be un-Christian, all informants were able to describe situations where their friends or relatives had used or been affected by witchcraft. One informant describes witchcraft or occult forces thus:

> Magic is science. Because if we talk of magic, we talk of something that is there. But for one to understand it, he has to use all his wisdom and all his intelligence to understand it or to discover it . . . Africans have their own science, the *azungus* [white people] have their own science, the azungus have their own magic.

Behaviour associated with the accumulation of wealth and power is deemed anti-social according to the established social logic of rights and obligations, and increases the risk of being exposed to witchcraft as a result of jealousy. Witchcraft is thus a sanction that is activated by the observation of a practice of exchange that breaks with the institutional logic of the conventional distribution structure. Witchcraft has a levelling effect on power and resource distribution. The risk of jealousy is particularly high when individuals accumulate power and material resources that are in excess of the established normative sphere of rights and obligations. If someone owns a car in an area where people are starving, it is considered proof by the villagers that the person is not facing up to his social obligations. Such behaviour opposes the traditional norm that a person should share his property with his less fortunate relatives and others in need. Such a person might become the subject of a witchcraft accusation.

Antidotes to Witchcraft

Mankwala can be described as a witchcraft prophylaxis that offers protection against all dangers from magic. To gain access to the protection offered by *mankwala*, one must be able to afford the protection and also know or have access to a trustworthy *singanga* or witch doctor. Aside from protection through counter-witchcraft, altruistic behaviour is also believed to provide protection from evil magic.

Clearly, successful entrepreneurs become the targets of witchcraft as a result of jealousy. As such, they require strong protection from the potential dangers of evil magic. Hussu's norm-breaking venture is conditioned by and maintains a need for social relations outside the local area. He consciously excludes himself from interaction with the other villagers by building iron walls around his house. He explains that because many villagers cannot pay back what they owe him, they might try to harm him through witchcraft. Hussu considers *mankwala* to be his most effective protection from witchcraft, regardless of the cost, because he has much property to protect. The protective devices that Hussu is using against witchcraft (*mankwala*, secrecy and social distance) are all expensive. His wealth permits him to buy *mankwala* and frees him of social relations in Muzigo. He is able to pursue friendships with more wealthy friends and business contacts in town. Hussu is frequently suspected of using witchcraft, as a result of his prospering business ventures.

In contrast to Hussu, the Mango Man attends to his social obligations in accordance with the established institutional logic of legitimate value circulation. He is socially active in the local community, shares his wealth with relatives, supports the school and has no walls around his house. His reason for producing mango is that he needs money to meet his social obligations. His altruistic approach, however, does not free him entirely from jealousy and the threat of witchcraft. He is making a substantial surplus on his mango production, and the villagers have started to question why he cannot afford a car. A number of informants suggested that Mr Tamula is spending his money on witchcraft. One informant told us: 'He [Mr Tamula] had a job and he could easily have bought a vehicle, but instead he bought *ndondoches* [zombies, to work for him].'

Both the Mango Man and Hussu legitimize individual profit by a concern for social relations and by basing their ventures on the established logic of social rights and obligations. Hussu justifies his creditor business and perceived reluctance to assist the villagers by arguing that they need to learn how to take care of themselves. The Mango Man, in contrast, legitimizes his motive for generating profit as an urge to support his relatives, the school and fellow villagers in Muzigo. Both entrepreneurs, however, do not receive full social acceptance for their business ventures, and due to legitimacy cracks they face suspicion or envy in their social surroundings. Consequently, they are each accused of being concerned with individual material needs at the expense of their social responsibilities, as determined by the established social logic of the system of rights and obligations. Furthermore, they are accused of using witchcraft to attain their success.

Both of the entrepreneurs, Mr Tamula and Hussu, suggest jealousy as an explanation for the resistance they face in the local community. For these entrepreneurs, jealousy indicates a certain adherence to traditionalism, ignorance and inactivity. The entrepreneurs interpret the role of witchcraft very differently to the non-entrepreneurs. The entrepreneurs' understanding of jealousy is that it is a foundation for social exclusion and a reason to direct evil magic against those who know how to integrate institutional changes in their economic and social practice. The villagers, on the contrary, make claims that the entrepreneurs create profit through the use of witchcraft.

In the village of Muzigo in Malawi, the relationship between entrepreneurship, established logic of social obligations, upcoming logic of market exchange and witchcraft is dialectical and dynamic. This ethnographic study illustrates how two entrepreneurs, each using different profit-oriented approaches and business strategies, have been instrumental in integrating new institutional structures of market exchange with social obligations into the existing system of value circulation. By doing so, they have affected changes to the traditional informal system of social levelling and sanctions. Entrepreneurship in Muzigo is conditioned by the entrepreneurs being able to base their ventures on existing institutionalized structures and logics while at the same time establishing links with progressive economic institutions (as illustrated in Figure 3.1). Both of the successful entrepreneurs studied here have had to find a balance between the paradoxes that form the basis for institutional change in Muzigo. In particular,

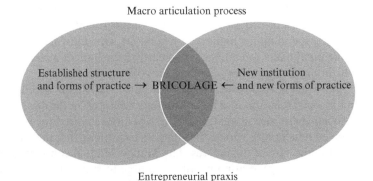

Figure 3.1   Entrepreneurship as a social praxis of maintaining and changing social structures

the role of witchcraft cannot be overlooked and must be integrated in such a process.

Constraints and opportunities in the entrepreneurial process are bound up with the shifting relations between broader societal logics and the changing policies of national and international actors attempting to establish new venues for economic and social development under Malawi's fragile democratization project. In summary, the findings illustrate how institutional changes are not only driven by macro forces and institutional actors at the national or community level, but are also built up from ongoing micro-social interactions with the entrepreneurial process as the nexus. The individual entrepreneurs' ventures sustain established societal structures and integrate new upcoming institutions. As the entrepreneurial ventures are based on contradictory institutions, the entrepreneurs must strike a balance between the social and market logics. Hence, the entrepreneurs working amid institutional contradictions must maintain a balance between the opposing logics on which they are dependent. Imbalances between logics result in witchcraft accusations.

DISCUSSION

The practice perspective is central to the argument of the chapter as it sheds light on how social structures such as institutions are sustained and changed through entrepreneurs' everyday practice, thus portraying social sustainability issues as integral to entrepreneurship. Thereby, the chapter has addressed calls for more research on how entrepreneurship influences and draws upon broader institutional environments and logics (Devereaux Jennings et al., 2009; Garud et al., 2007; Hwang and Powell, 2005; Marquis and Lounsbury, 2007; Phillips and Tracey, 2007; Sarasvathy, 2007; Tillmar, 2006). It sheds light on processes that are not merely restricted to business, but pertain to societal dynamics (Fayolle et al., 2005; Steyaert and Hjorth, 2006; Steyaert and Katz, 2004). The study illuminates the relatively underexplored role of individuals in institutional change and continuity (Battilana, 2006; Battilana et al., 2009). Whilst a practice perspective implies that multiple actors may partake in the entrepreneurial process, we also recognize in this chapter that certain actors may be more central to the process than others. Thus, while some institutional research on change agency has focused on macro-actors such as NGOs as social and institutional entrepreneurs, the empirical choice of this research has been to examine the strategies of individual, small-scale entrepreneurs in balancing different logics through their actions and interactions.

Hence, the present chapter has examined the strategies through which the entrepreneurs navigate and work with the multiple institutional logics of the different spheres in which they operate, in order to facilitate entrepreneurial venturing and contribute to both sustaining and changing institutional structures. The perspective taken by this chapter requires an account of the dialectical relationship between structural conditions and entrepreneurial practice, and responds to calls for more research on micro-action beyond discourse in institutional change and stability (Barley, 2008). Barth (1967) suggested that an analytical and methodological framework for research on entrepreneurship should account for the ways in which relations of exchange and value circulation are produced and reproduced by addressing the entrepreneurial process as it unfolds. Hence, an analytical and methodological approach to entrepreneurship research should be founded on the assumption that the unfolding of interactions and transactions between individuals cannot be deduced from established structures and logics. This implies that entrepreneurial activity is a continuous social process and must be examined iteratively (Barth, 1963: 11–13). It calls for grounding the research in particular methodologies such as ethnography. According to Barth (1963, 1967), a conventional structural analysis based on assumptions of linear causality and predictability will most likely fail to provide insight into the social dynamics and dialectics of the entrepreneurial process. Social patterns are not static social facts, but products of ongoing social processes.

The entrepreneurs presented in this study are brokers in the articulation of the contradictions forming the basis for the changes in the environment. Rather than merely impeding economic action, the entrepreneurs used established institutional structures for individual value generation. As shown, the relation between entrepreneurship, social obligations and cultural institutions – in this case witchcraft – is recursive. The entrepreneurs, through their alternative profit-oriented practices, contribute to the integration of new structures of exchange with regard to social rights and obligations into the existing system of value circulation. The institutional formations or systems stand in a contradictory relationship, and in their intersection an emerging social structure is generated; a *bricolage*. Entrepreneurship in Muzigo is thus characterized by the entrepreneurs being able to base their ventures on existing social structures and simultaneously establishing relations to new structures. The entrepreneur, in other words, has to bridge the institutional oppositions that form the basis for changes. The entrepreneurial ventures are conditioned by operating in the current spheres of exchange (social relations and networks) as well as in upcoming spheres (independent market forces). Institutional change is thus driven by macro forces as well as built up from ongoing micro-social interactions with the entrepreneurial process as the nexus.

The entrepreneurs are actively using contradictory logics, separating different social and economic spheres to create new channels of exchange. They convert barriers of exchange to channels of exchange through their bridging of institutional contradictions. Hence, the two entrepreneurs make their wealthy livelihood by overcoming or using constraints institutionalized in their local society. In order to sustain their business, both of them have been entrepreneurial in overcoming levelling mechanisms in society and escaping traditional exchange modes. Their endurance and success has depended on their achievements as institutional entrepreneurs.

Hence, the stories of the two entrepreneurs illustrate the need to include the broader institutional environments in the study of entrepreneurial processes. Micro and macro processes of institutional change and economic practice interact in highly recursive ways. The study illustrates entrepreneurship as a process of bridging between existing institutional structures and upcoming structures. The focus on the dialectical process of interaction between structural conditions and entrepreneurial agency provides an account that integrates both individual actors and collective social structures.

The local microcredit organization held beliefs that customary practices and myths impede economic development, and practices involving occult forces, such as witchcraft, through social control maintain an egalitarian social structure. However, the study illustrates how customary practices and beliefs did not merely function as constraints, but also held a capacity for individual value generation. Hence, the study illustrates that norms and beliefs associated with witchcraft are not merely traditionalistic and retrospective resistance to change, but multiple, dynamic and part of modern developments (Geschiere, 1997). While the emergence of occult forces in economic practice, highlighting social sustainability concerns, may partly express key transitional moments and social ruptures (Comaroff and Comaroff, 1999; Geschiere, 1997), this however does not necessitate their discontinuity with 'past' or 'traditional' practices (Kapferer, 2003). Social sustainability in entrepreneurship could thus refer to upholding certain societal structures by an equally supporting resource distribution among community members.

Theoretical implications point to possibilities for further research to bridge the turn in institution research to studying how actors' mundane micro activities sustain and alter institutions (Zilber, 2011), and the movement in entrepreneurship research towards conceiving entrepreneurship as an everyday practice of recombining elements. Moreover, by elucidating the importance of satisfying the established social logic of redistribution for the entrepreneurial ventures and thus sustaining the established local social order, the research further contributes to the understanding of sustainability in social development efforts, for example institutional entrepreneurship that introduces social or economic change.

The practical implications of the research highlight the relevance of entrepreneurs' social skills in navigating and embracing multiple, potentially contradictory institutional logics and conceptions of value to acquire legitimacy and resources. It also illustrates the relevance of sustainability concerns for the established local social order in situations where potentially contradictory formal and informal institutions co-exist over time and shape the circulation of value in society and economy.

ACKNOWLEDGEMENT

We wish to thank Inge Pasgaard without whom this chapter would not have been possible.

REFERENCES

Ahrens, T. and C.S. Chapman (2002), 'The structuration of legitimate performance measures and management: day-to-day contests of accountability in a UK restaurant chain', *Management Accounting Research*, 13(2), 151–71.

Barley, S. (2008), 'Coalface institutionalism', in R. Greenwood, C. Oliver, R. Suddaby and K. Sahlin (eds), *The Sage Handbook of Organizational Institutionalism*, Los Angeles, CA, USA; London, UK; New Delhi, India: Sage, pp. 419–518.

Barley, S. and P. Tolbert (1997), 'Institutionalisation and structuration: studying the links between action and institution', *Organization Studies*, 18(1), 93–117.

Barth, F. (1963), *The Role of the Entrepreneur in Social Change in Northern Norway*, 2nd edn, Bergen and Oslo: Universitetsforlaget.

Barth, F. (1967), 'Economic spheres in Darfur', in R. Firth (ed.), *Themes in Economic Anthropology*, London, UK; New York, USA; Sydney, Australia: Tavistock Publications, pp. 149–74.

Barth, F. (1981), *Process and Form in Social Life*, London, UK and Boston, MA, USA: Routledge & Kegan Paul.

Barth, F. (1992), 'Towards greater naturalism in conceptualizing societies', in A. Kuper (ed.), *Conceptualizing Society*, London: Routledge, pp. 17–33.

Barth, F. (1994), *Manifestasjon og prosess*, Oslo: Universitetsforlaget.

Barth, F. (2002), 'An anthropology of knowledge', *Current Anthropology*, 43(1), 1–18.

Barth, F. (2007), 'Overview: sixty years in anthropology', *Annual Review of Anthropology*, 36, 1–16.

Battilana, J. (2006), 'Agency and institutions: the enabling role of individuals' social position', *Organization*, 13(5), 653–76.

Battilana, J., B. Leca and E. Boxenbaum (2009), 'How actors change institutions: towards a theory of institutional entrepreneurship', *Academy of Management Annals*, 3(1), 65–107.

Bernard, R.H. (1995), *Research Methods in Anthropology: Qualitative and Quantitative Approaches*, Thousand Oaks, CA: Sage.

Bohannan, P. and G. Dalton (1965), 'Introduction', in P. Bohannan and G. Dalton (eds), *Markets in Africa*, Garden City, NY: American Museum of Natural History.

Bourdieu, P. (1977), *Outline of a Theory of Practice*, Cambridge, UK and New York, USA: Cambridge University Press.

Comaroff, J. (1985), *Body of Power, Spirit of Resistance: The Culture and History of a South African People*, Chicago, IL: University of Chicago Press.

Comaroff, J. and J.L. Comaroff (1999), 'Occult economies and the violence of abstraction: notes from the South African postcolony', *American Ethnologist*, 26(2), 279–303.

Devereaux Jennings, P., R. Greenwood, M. Lounsbury and R. Suddaby (2009), Call for papers: 'Institutions, entrepreneurs, and communities', *Journal of Business Venturing*.

DiMaggio, P.J. (1988), 'Interest and agency in institutional theory', in L.G. Zucker (ed.), *Institutional Patterns and Organizations: Culture and Environment*, Cambridge, MA: Ballinger, pp. 3–22.

Eisenstadt, S.N. (1980), 'Cultural orientations, institutional entrepreneurs, and social change: comparative analyses of traditional civilisations', *American Journal of Sociology*, 85, 840–69.

Evans, T.M.S. and D. Handelman (2006), *The Manchester School: Practice and Ethnographic Praxis in Anthropology*, New York: Berghahn Books.

Fayolle, A., P. Kyrö and J. Ulijn (2005), 'The entrepreneurship debate in Europe: a matter of history or culture?', in A. Fayolle, P. Kyrö and J. Ulijn (eds), *Entrepreneurship Research in Europe: Perspectives and Outcomes*, Cheltenham, UK and Northampton, MA, USA: Edward Elgar, pp. 1–34.

Garud, R., C. Hardy and S. Maguire (2007), 'Institutional entrepreneurship as embedded agency: an introduction to the special issue', *Organization Studies*, 28, 957–69.

Geschiere, P. (1997), *The Modernity of Witchcraft*, Charlottesville, VA: University Press of Virginia.

Giddens, A. (1979), *Central Problems in Social Theory: Action, Structure, and Contradiction in Social Analysis*, Berkeley, CA: University of California Press.

Gluckman, M. (1955), *Custom and Conflict in Africa*, Oxford: Blackwell.

Holy, L. and M. Stuchlik (1983), *Actions, Norms and Representations: Foundations of Anthropological Inquiry*, Cambridge and London, UK; New York, USA: Cambridge University Press.

Hughes, E.C. (1942), 'The study of institutions', *Social Forces*, 20(3), 307–10.

Hwang, H. and W.W. Powell (2005), 'Institutions and entrepreneurship', in S.A. Alvarez,

R. Agarwal and O. Sorenson (eds), *Handbook of Entrepreneurship Research: Disciplinary Perspectives*, New York: Kluver Publishers, pp. 179–210.

Jarzabkowski, P., J. Balogun and D. Seidl (2007), 'Strategizing: the challenges of a practice perspective', *Human Relations*, 60(1), 5–27.

Jarzabkowski, P., J. Matthiesen and A. Van de Ven (2009), 'Doing which work? A practice approach to institutional pluralism', in T.B. Lawrence, R. Suddaby and B. Leca (eds), *Institutional Work: Actors and Agency in Institutional Studies of Organization*, Cambridge: Cambridge University Press, pp. 284–316.

Jarzabkowski, P. and S.P. Spee (2009), 'Strategy as practice: a review and future research directions', *International Journal of Management Reviews*, 11(1), 69–95.

Jepperson, R.L. (1991), 'Institutions, institutional effects, and institutionalization', in W.W. Powell and P.J. DiMaggio (eds), *The New Institutionalism in Organizational Analysis*, Chicago, IL: University of Chicago Press, pp. 143–63.

Kapferer, B. (2003), 'Sorcery and the shapes of globalization disjunctions and discontinuities: the case of Sri Lanka', in J. Friedman (ed.), *Globalization, the State, and Violence*, Walnut Creek, CA: AltaMira Press, pp. 1–34.

Khanna, T. and K. Palepu (1997), 'Why focused strategies may be wrong for emerging markets', *Harvard Business Review*, 75(4), 41–51.

Kyrö, P. and J. Kansikas (2005), 'Current state of methodology in entrepreneurship research and some expectations for the future', in A. Fayolle, J. Uljin and P. Kyrö (eds), *Entrepreneurship Research in Europe: Perspectives and Outcomes*, Cheltenham, UK and Northampton, MA, USA: Edward Elgar, pp. 121–49.

Larney, K.T. (2001), *Malawi. En politisk og økonomisk oversigt*, Copenhagen: Udenrigsministeriet.

Latour, B. (2005), *Reassembling the Social: An Introduction to Actor-Network-Theory*, Oxford, UK and New York, USA: Oxford University Press.

Lawrence, T.B., R. Suddaby and B. Leca (2010), 'Institutional work: refocusing institutional studies of organization', *Journal of Management Inquiry*, 20(1), 52–8.

Lévi-Strauss (1963), *Structural Anthropology*, New York: Basic Books.

Lévi-Strauss, C. (1966), *The Savage Mind*, Chicago, IL: University of Chicago Press.

Mair, J. and I. Martí (2006), 'Social entrepreneurship research: a source of explanation, prediction, and delight', *Journal of World Business*, 41, 36–44.

Mair, J. and I. Martí (2009), 'Entrepreneurship in and around institutional voids', *Journal of Business Venturing*, 24, 419–35.

Mair, J., I. Martí and K. Ganly (2007), 'Social entrepreneurship: seeing institutional voids as spaces of opportunity', *European Business Forum*, 31, 34–9.

Malinowski, B. (1922), *Argonauts of the Western Pacific*, London: Routledge.

Marquis, C. and M. Lounsbury (2007), 'Vive la résistance: competing logics and the consolidation of U.S. community banking', *Academy of Management Journal*, 50(4), 799–820.

Martí, I. and J. Mair (2009), 'Bringing change into the lives of the poor: entrepreneurship outside traditional boundaries', in T.B. Lawrence, R. Suddaby and B. Leca (eds), *Institutional Work*, Cambridge: Cambridge University Press, pp. 92–119.

Moore, S.F. (1978), *Law as Process: An Anthropological Approach*, London and Henley, UK; Boston, MA, USA: Routledge & Kegan Paul.

Nayak, A. and R.C.H. Chia (2011), 'Thinking becoming and emergence: process philosophy and organization studies', *Research in the Sociology of Organizations*, 32, 281–309.

Ortner, S.B. (1984), 'Theory in anthropology since the Sixties', *Comparative Studies in Society and History*, 26(1), 126–66.

Parry, J. and M. Bloch (1989), *Money and the Morality of Exchange*, Cambridge: Cambridge University Press.

Phillips, N. and P. Tracey (2007), 'Opportunity recognition, entrepreneurial capabilities and bricolage: connecting institutional theory and entrepreneurship in strategic organization', *Strategic Organization*, 5(3), 313–20.

Polanyi, K. (1944), *Great Transformation: The Political and Economic Origins of Our Time*, Boston, MA: Beacon Press.

Polanyi, K., K. Conrad, K. Arensburg and H.W. Pearson (1957), *Trade and Market in the Early Empires; Economies in History and Theory*, Glencoe, IL: Free Press.
Powell, W.W. and J.A. Colyvas (2008), 'Microfoundations of institutional theory', in R. Greenwood, C. Oliver, K. Sahlin and R. Suddaby (eds), *Handbook of Organizational Institutionalism*, London: Sage Publishers, pp. 276–98.
Rasche, A. and R. Chia (2009), 'Researching strategy practices: a genealogical social theory perspective', *Organization Studies*, 30(7), 713–34.
Sarasvathy, S.D. (2007), *Effectuation: Elements of Entrepreneurial Expertise*, Cheltenham, UK and Northampton, MA, USA: Edward Elgar.
Schatzki, T.R., K. Knorr-Cetina and E. von Savigny (2001), *The Practice Turn in Contemporary Theory*, New York: Routledge.
Spradley, J.P. (1980), *Participant Observation*, New York: Holt Rinehart & Winston.
Steyaert, C. (2007), '"Entrepreneuring" as a conceptual attractor? A review of process theories in 20 years of entrepreneurship studies', *Entrepreneurship and Regional Development*, 19(6), 453–77.
Steyaert, C. and D. Hjorth (2006), *Entrepreneurship as Social Change*, Cheltenham, UK and Northampton, MA, USA: Edward Elgar.
Steyaert, C. and J. Katz (2004), 'Reclaiming the space of entrepreneurship in society: geographical, discursive and social dimensions', *Entrepreneurship and Regional Development*, 16, 179–96.
Thornton, P., C. Jones and K. Kury (2005), 'Institutional logics and institutional change in organizations: transformation in accounting, architecture, and publishing', *Research in the Sociology of Organizations*, 23, 125–70.
Tillmar, M. (2006), 'Swedish tribalism and Tanzanian entrepreneurship: preconditions for trust formation', *Entrepreneurship and Regional Development: An International Journal*, 18(2), 91–107.
Wilk, R.R. and L. Cliggett (2007), *Economies and Cultures: Foundations of Economic Anthropology*, 2nd edn, Boulder, CO: Westview Press.
Zilber, T.B. (2011), 'Institutional multiplicity in practice: a tale of two high-tech conferences in Israel', *Organization Science*, 22(6), 1539–59.

4. Entrepreneurship: the missing link for democratization and development in fragile nations?
Steffen Farny and Santiago Delgado Calderon

INTRODUCTION

Voices from development economics and public administration have raised their concern that the sustainable development discussion is addressed from a wrong angle (compare Andrews et al., 2012; Potts et al., 2010). Development economics, traditionally debating factors that promote and constrain economic activity in low-income countries (Gillis et al., 1992), has started to recognize that economic growth has been the exception rather than the rule in developing and least-developed nations (Potts et al., 2010). Despite large influxes of foreign aid, there are only a few cases where countries have been able to move forward, and in some situations the very presence of international aid has aggravated the situation at hand (Riddell, 2007). Huang (2008) points out that rural China is a noteworthy example, demonstrating an alternative path. In this particular case, rural entrepreneurs became the real catalysts for the emergence of the Chinese economy, instead of public enterprises (township and village enterprises) directed and managed by local governments, as is commonly believed (ibid.). Such examples provide some evidence that neither international aid nor government intervention, but rather local entrepreneurs, are (sometimes) the main factors or agents driving societal renewal and accelerating economic liberalization, and are also important in signalling the emergence of democratization processes, rights and freedom (Nicholls, 2008: 94; Huang, 2008).

Alongside the economic development efforts, we have witnessed a move towards democratic progress via the replacement of authoritarian regimes with democracies (Huntington, 1993), a shift that has been labelled the new 'megatrend' in developing countries (Boeninger, 1992). Following Dahl's (1971) characterization of democracy as the government's continuous responsiveness to the preferences of its citizens as political equals, democratization processes refer to the action that 'moves the political system of any given society towards a system of government that ensures peaceful competitive political participation in an environment that guarantees political and civil liberties' (Samarasinghe, 1994: 14). This definition captures the dynamic quality of democratic evolution in any society, but especially in developing countries (ibid.). Yet still mostly neglected has been the relationship between organizations and democracy, which is particularly pertinent because of organizations increasingly interfering in and redefining the notion of the public good (Martí et al., 2008). These organizations' entrepreneurial activities might have positive and counteracting forces to the development of nascent democratic regimes (ibid.).

Currently in the literature we miss an understanding of the dynamism entrepreneurs instill into the process of democratic transitions. So far, entrepreneurship is hardly ever related to poverty, welfare and inequality, or structural transformation (Naudé, 2011). Currently governments support entrepreneurship primarily as a vehicle to drive economic development, but with a top-down emphasis. Gries and Naudé (2011) claim that, in this light, entrepreneurship is a production factor executing two main functions. First, entrepreneurs are a knowledge filter for the commercialization of technology and new knowledge in general (Audretsch et al., 2006); and second, they improve the efficiency of production factor allocation (Acs and Storey, 2004). However, in particular in developing nations, entrepreneurship makes a greater contribution to development (Naudé, 2011). The social change-maker role of entrepreneurs who support democratization processes is not yet widely recognized by governments and policy makers. We lack an understanding of how organizational strategies affect the quality of democratic institutions and, vice versa, how those actors respond (Martí et al., 2008). As Naudé (2011) claims, by neglecting entrepreneurship in the development process, economists fail to appreciate how institutions shape development outcomes.

In order to address this problem, the question arises: What is the role of entrepreneurship for democratization processes in fragile nations? Since institutions are a representation of societal norms, rights and freedom, we study the institution-building process as a mirror of democratization processes. A particularly suitable scenario for analysing entrepreneurship and its role in structural transformation, and development in general, is the post-shock context. A post-shock context – post-conflict[1] and/or post-disaster[2] – portrays an array of fundamental and comprehensive institutional changes (Ahlstrom and Bruton, 2006). We narrow the idea of a shock to either a natural disaster or a serious political conflict violently overthrowing existing structures. After a shock that pushes a state into a condition of fragility, two main tasks need to be implemented: security and economic development; our focus is on the latter aspect. Currently, these shocks are studied either on a macroeconomic level or a household or individual level (Brück et al., 2013), not at the intersection of institution building and entrepreneurship. We are thus concerned with the role that entrepreneurship plays for democratization processes, as an alternative to the interventionist approach common in fragile nations.

Since a consensus seems to exist that institution building is a prerequisite, we intend to contribute to the discussion by analysing the role that entrepreneurship plays in the institution-building process. For that purpose, we chose Haiti and East Timor as two recent, extreme, but different cases where the transformational processes are exceptionally visible. Through ethnographic content analysis we investigate whether the role of entrepreneurship in efforts to build sovereign nations has progressed as the entrepreneurship paradigm evolved in the economic debate.

THE HISTORICAL EVOLUTION OF ENTREPRENEURSHIP AND THE SUSTAINABLE DEVELOPMENT DEBATE

Through the evolution of economic thought, three major streams emerged that are of relevance to sustainable development and entrepreneurship today (Kyrö, 2001). Neo-classical, neo-institutional and evolutionary economics each provide a different rationale for how sustainable development can be achieved. Yet, as socio-historical analysis shows, entrepreneurship continued mainly with the evolutionary economists (ibid.), and only recently has a reintegration into the mainstream development discussion started. Therefore, since the dominant economic debate has excluded entrepreneurship, we are curious as to whether it can be claimed to have an essential role for our future development. We first briefly present the historical development in order to demonstrate the reasons that entrepreneurship has progressed in a separate paradigm.

One could claim that the French physiocrats represent the beginning of entrepreneurship (Kyrö, 2001). They saw nature as the limiting factor for entrepreneurship; hence, a clear connection between the environment and macroeconomic development existed, which was exploited through the act of entrepreneurship. Centuries later during the modern transition – the start of the industrial revolution – Adam Smith claimed that labour, its division and specialization, added the greatest value. He perceived nature as an unlimited and free resource, which from then onwards has been largely disregarded in the economic debate on growth and welfare creation (ibid.). The idea of the rational equilibrium further replaced the predominant role of the human being – the entrepreneur (Daly and Cobb, 1989). Demand and supply forces directed by the 'invisible hand' became the

Table 4.1   Different rationales for sustainable development

	Evolutionary economics	Neo-institutional economics	Neo-classical economics
Rationale for growth/ development	Extraordinary free actors driving progress, no equilibrium forces	Legitimating role of the state	Equilibrating forces of the market
Rationale for sustainability	Human action reason for environmental destruction, though human action also brings solutions for it	Market externalities bring environmental costs, thus externalities have to be reduced	

main explanation for market developments. The three emerging schools – the German historical school (for example, Max Weber), the classical school (Adam Smith, David Ricardo), and ecological economics, the early Austrian school (for example, Karl Menger) – each claimed a different rationality for growth. Fuelled by the start of the industrial revolution, population explosion and a growing demand for manufactured products, the classical school became the dominant paradigm in economics (Kyrö, 2001). Barreto (1989) recognizes the dominance of the classical school as the cause for losing the connection between entrepreneurship and micro-economics. As Table 4.1 depicts, the rational limits of nature continued only in the debate of institutional ecological economists, while the human being continued in the debate on entrepreneurship; no longer were they connected in economic thought (Kyrö, 2001).

As a result, the human agent started to be excluded from the two emerging and dominating schools, institutional theory and classical theory. However, from the time evolutionary economics emerged, it has been strongly drawn towards embracing institutional analysis (Nelson and Nelson, 2002). This development was greatly motivated by the perception that neo-classical growth theory inadequately explains the technological advance and economic development (Nelson and Winter, 1982); the dominant arguments for social welfare and economic progress were the equilibrium forces of the market versus the legitimizing role of the state. Building on the work of Schumpeter, sophisticated scholars in the field have always understood the important role of institutional structures for supporting technological progress, yet have been unable to incorporate institutions on a formal level (Nelson and Nelson, 2002). As a surprising outcome, evolutionary economics has been as limited in the incorporation of institutions as the neo-classical school, even though it was originally designed to replace it for that particular reason (ibid.).

While particularly institutional theorists have thought about society taking care of failures and enabling circumstances for development, in contrast, entrepreneurship has always argued against the equilibrium idea. The idea of the entrepreneur as an extraordinary free actor driving economic progress mainly continued with Schumpeter's followers, referred to as the Austrian school – the least represented school of thought during the modern era. Schumpeter (1934) understood the entrepreneur as an innovator bringing radical change to the market. Disregarding the limiting external natural constraints, the possibility of continued growth increased its dominance in the dominant economic discussions, and entrepreneurship was integrated merely at the organizational level, not as the Schumpeterian entrepreneur (Kyrö, 2001). Kyrö further notes that it is amazing that the classical school and the German historical school are considered schools of environmental economics, since neither of them was interested in the environment per se. Even though nature was acknowledged again in the postmodern transition (since 1970), it is not perceived as a limiting factor; externalities entered the debate through the lens of environmental costs. Both dominant economic schools of thought continue to ignore the human actor as the force of environmental destruction. Consequently it can be claimed that entrepreneurship has been disconnected from the economic debate and the environment throughout the entire modern era including the postmodern transition (ibid.).

Therefore, since the dominant economic debate has excluded entrepreneurship, we are curious as to whether it can be claimed to have an essential role for our future development. The following section will provide arguments to show that recently a reintegration of entrepreneurship into the welfare and development discussion has begun.

THE CURRENT DEBATE ON ENTREPRENEURSHIP AND SUSTAINABLE DEVELOPMENT

In recent years economists and entrepreneurship researchers alike have started to address their original connection. Instead of consideration for the environment acting as a constraint on entrepreneurship, the environment can be ameliorated through an entrepreneurial act (Rammel, 2003). Potts et al. (2010: 376) exemplify the value that entrepreneurship can bring to the environment, for instance 'by shifting resources, by making resource substitutions, by bringing new technologies, or business models to bear on the problem, or by new forms of contracts, organizations or institutions'. Newly emerging environmental challenges require novel ideas and a different set of responses, which are produced by entrepreneurs who create and use new markets (Potts et al., 2010). This is because of the dual impact of entrepreneurs. Economic activity and growth cause environmental stress, though entrepreneurs are the ones creating value out of the resulted friction (Anderson, 1998); and this stress is particularly evident in fragile nations.

How and to what extent entrepreneurship contributes to development is a debated topic. Addressing the gap from a development economist's perspective, the scepticism arises from the diversity of organizational forms that lead to economic productivity (Sun, 2003). These scholars are sceptical about equating growth and productivity to the activities executed by entrepreneurs – mainly resource coordination, new business creation and innovation – and perceive entrepreneurship merely as a means to an end (Naudé, 2011). Moreover, their concern relates to the significant levels of venture activity that are often necessity-based, occur in the informal sector and are difficult to differentiate from the voluntary sector (Bennett, 2010; Maloney, 2004); or the contribution to economic development is simply regarded as minor (Beck et al., 2003). The lack of emphasis on the entrepreneur's role for economic development reflects the perception that other constraints are dominating (Naudé, 2011). The discussion of development economists shows that risks and obstacles in exploiting opportunities are dominating in their studies.

Some entrepreneurship scholars support this view and emphasize the obstacle of institutional uncertainty and its impact on entrepreneurship. The low appreciation of entrepreneurship in the growth debate is also linked to the fact that for a long time entrepreneurship scholars have not perceived the developing-country context as an opportunity. In an uncertain institutional context in developing countries, entrepreneurship has been primarily studied with regard to factors inhibiting opportunities for entrepreneurs (Aidis, 2005; Fogel et al., 2006; Luthans and Ibrayeva, 2006; Manolova et al., 2008). These scholars claim that opportunities are repressed because of the increased risk and complexity levels in unstable institutional environments, leading to more frequent market failures and distortions than in developed countries. Another stream of scholars avoids linking entrepreneurial activity to structural efforts for economic development. As Naudé (2011: 34) notes, 'entrepreneurship scholars almost never relate entrepreneurship to poverty/welfare and inequality, or multidimensional well-being indicators, and only very rarely consider its role in structural transformation'. One of their arguments against linking entrepreneurship and economic development in fragile nations is that entrepreneurship is primarily associated with product and process innovations more likely to be found in mature economies (ibid.). Another reason is that entrepreneurship, in the Schumpeterian sense, leads to radical innovation, while in developing nations replicative entrepreneurship dominates (Baumol et al., 2007). And a third argument is that despite the entrepreneurs' contribution to economic development, they are not the ones kick-starting growth (Pahn et al., 2008). However, in a recent attempt, Tracey and Phillips (2011) identify strategies that entrepreneurs execute to harvest opportunities precisely because of the contextual factors and market disequilibria.

In a nutshell, both domains convey the lack of institutions to be the answer to economic development. Naudé (2011: 37) claims:

> [a] convergence in thinking of development economists and entrepreneurship scholars on the importance of institutions, the heterogeneity of institutions, and the myriad ways in which it may interact and impact on entrepreneurship – and be influenced by entrepreneurship – suggests through the need for 'many recipes' to growth and development that there may indeed be cases where the institutions–entrepreneurship nexus is a constraint.

Since a consensus seems to exist that institution building is a prerequisite, we intend to contribute to the discussion by analysing the role that entrepreneurship plays in the institution-building process. As mentioned before, this process is most evident in the case of failed states, where the primary task is to build institutions and foster economic development. Through interventions, the international community claims to create opportunities for economic development in failed nations. Governments, international institutions such as the United Nations (UN)-related institutions and the World Bank group, as well as international organizations, justify their activity in order to mitigate the local government's limited capacities and capabilities.

Another need for our study is that despite the convergence of thinking between development economists and entrepreneurship scholars, one empirical study questions the viability of this approach. Supporting Naudé's concern that the institution–entrepreneurship nexus can be a constraint, Baliamoune (2009) finds that institutional reform does not seem to matter for the growth effects of entrepreneurship. Studying the interplay of institutional reform and entrepreneurship, the study advocates that financial sector reform enhances the growth of entrepreneurship, but only in the initial stages, having a diminishing effect at a later stage. This evidence finds earlier support by Meyer (2001) who claims that rapidly changing institutions may cause inconsistency between the requirements of the different institutions and further aggravate uncertainty over future institutional changes. Institution-building attempts do not necessarily reduce uncertainty in the institutional context, hence even prohibit an improved investment climate for established businesses.

This result suggests that new or increased economic activity has to come from new actors – entrepreneurs – who create innovative solutions for sustainable and equitable development. Yet, neglecting institution building is no solution either as a fragile nation would slip back into anarchic conditions. We are thus concerned with the role that entrepreneurship plays for advancing growth, providing services and pushing for democratization processes, as an alternative to the interventionist approach common in fragile nations. The sum of these inconsistencies provides sufficient motivation for our study to question the sufficiency of institutional reform in order to achieve equitable growth.

ETHNOGRAPHIC CONTENT ANALYSIS AND THE SELECTION OF THE TEXT

In order to explore the phenomenon of this study – the role of entrepreneurship for democratization processes – we select a comparative case analysis (Yin, 2009) and apply ethnographic content analysis (ECA) (Altheide, 1987; Grbich, 2012). Through ECA we are able to examine each of the documents (given in Table 4.2) in a corpus of its own, and discern thematic patterns that extend across the text (Huckin, 2002). If the two economic schools of thought are dominating the development debate, as the theoretical analysis suggests, we should be able to find evidence in both cases. Therefore, a comparative study of two extreme cases allows us to derive information on the general patterns and dominant debates (see Table 4.2). For this purpose we apply purposive, critical-incident sampling (Neergaard, 2007), typical for ECA (Altheide, 1987).

In ECA texts exemplify the ideal-typical construction of a phenomenon, instead of being representative in any statistical way (Altheide, 1987). We follow the five steps proposed by Grbich (2013: 195). First we located all strategic development documents of the UN and UN-related institutions relevant for the two cases. The official post-shock UN documents are a unique representation of a country's path to democracy and economic development, which do not exist to the same comprehensive degree in other contexts. In each case two documents were published regarding the development path of the country, and additionally in Haiti the post-disaster needs assessment (PDNA) instrument was available, in total 652 pages (see Table 4.2). Compiled under the leadership of the

Table 4.2 Case documents and descriptions

	East Timor (post-conflict)	Haiti (post-disaster)
UN peacekeeping mission	UNTAET, United Nations Transitional Administration in East Timor	MINUSTAH, United Nations Stabilization Mission in Haiti
	25 October 1999 – 20 May 2002 (day of independence)	1 June 2004 – ongoing
Post-shock UN mandate	UNMISET, United Nations Mission of Support to East Timor	IHRC, Interim Haiti Recovery Commission
Shock and date	1999–2002, Self-annexation conflict from Indonesia	January 2010, earthquake near the capital city
UNDP development strategy documents	UNDP (2002a), *East Timor Human Development Report: The Way Ahead* UNDP (2006), *Timor-Leste Human Development Report: The Path out of Poverty*	UNDP (2002b), *La Bonne Gouvernance: Un Defi Majeur Pour Le Developpement Humain Durable En Haïti* [Governance for human development: a major challenge for sustainable human development in Haiti] UNDP (2008), *La vulnérabilité en Haïti: Chemin inévitable vers la pauvreté?* [Vulnerability in Haiti: the inevitable path towards poverty?]
Authors	UNDP East Timor	UNDP Haiti
Post-shock document of the UN mission	–	Post-disaster needs assessment (PDNA) (Government of Haiti, 2010b)

local government, a multi-disciplinary, multi-agency team comprising the World Bank, the Global Facility for Disaster Reduction and Recovery (GFDRR), UN agencies and the European Commission, the PDNA provides a framework for legitimized actions and institution-building efforts (World Bank, 2013). The PDNA first emerged for the Bangladeshi 2007 cyclone and has been applied for all major catastrophes in developing nations ever since. For post-conflict cases such a comprehensive instrument is not available and the UN Development Programme strategy is the best representation existing. These reports are a unique possibility to study the role of entrepreneurship and democratization processes, as the attempt is made to reconstruct a nation *de novo*, and hence provide an ideal-typical construction of the process.

Next, we identified sustainability and economic development as our analytical focus. Our interest was on distinctive patterns that represent the interest of governments – especially the international community's interests – and set the norms for working in this environment (for an enumerative overview see Figure 4A.1 in the Appendix). The overview shows that government and public sector activities are mostly addressed, reaffirming our initial claim that institution building is emphasized in the development efforts and seemingly a prerequisite.

As an outcome, we designed a test protocol to distinguish ideas related to the neo-institutional, neo-classical and environmental economic schools. Typical for ECA is that as the analytical process advances, coding categories emerge (Altheide, 1987, 2004; Witt and Redding, 2009). As we proceeded with the categorization we further refined the protocol to distinguish plans, actions, outcomes and the role of entrepreneurship. As a last step, we conducted a cross-case analysis, interpreting the meaning in its cultural and contextual setting. Our application of ECA in this research is summarized in Table 4.3. Compared to quantitative content analysis, ECA allowed us to focus on ideal-typical construction and to follow up on concepts emerging during the analytical process. It further enabled us to integrate our previous contextual knowledge and analyse across the cases, which enriched the depth of the analysis.

A FRAGILE NATION POST-SHOCK CONTEXT

In order to better understand the role of entrepreneurship for democratization processes, we selected as our context two post-shock fragile nations: a natural disaster and a conflict. Our case examples are Haiti and East Timor because the cases differ in the nature of the shock. While Haiti suffered from a devastating earthquake in January 2010, East Timor suffered from a civil war between Timorese and Indonesians to gain independence during the late 1990s. Our focus on post-shock scenarios in fragile states is due to the fact that development efforts are most visible in this context.

Furthermore, as failed states they exemplify a lack of democratic structures, and have a non-democratic history experiencing unprecedented shocks in the last 20 years. Despite the world's unprecedented increases in wealth and development, around 40 countries have been the victims of either natural or man-made shocks that have caused them to slide into anarchic conditions (Ghani and Lockhart, 2008). This phenomenon

Table 4.3 Quantitative and ethnographic content analysis

	Quantitative content analysis	Ethnographic content analysis (ECA)	ECA as applied in this research
Research goal	Verification	Discovery, verification	Discovery of the role of entrepreneurship; verification of the dominant debate
Reflexive research design	Seldom	Always	Reflexive
Emphasis	Reliability	Validity	Ideal-type construction
Progression from data collection, analysis, interpretation	Serial	Reflexive, circular	Very circular, adding new data and coding categories along the way
Primary researcher involvement	Data analysis and interpretation	All phases	All phases, each author in one country first, then cross-comparison
Sample	Random or stratified	Purposive or theoretical	Purposive, critical incident
Pre-structured categories	All	Some	Three mainstream schools of thought
Training required to collect data	Little	Substantial	All researchers have been engaged with UN activities in the two countries for more than two years, and partly collected (ethnographic) data on site for other purposes
Type of data	Numbers	Numbers, narrative	Published documents
Narrative description and comments	Seldom	Always	Case descriptions of Haiti and East Timor
Concepts emerge during research	Seldom	Always	Mainly in 3rd and 4th step of the Grbich model
Data analysis	Statistical	Textual, statistical	First: textual analysis of each case separately; second: comparative analysis
Data presentation	Tables	Tables and text	Case descriptions, tables and text of the analysis, case comparison

Source: Based on Altheide (1987: 67).

is called state fragility, stemming from the complete or partial absence of political authority (King and Zeng, 2001). State fragility entails that governments are unable to fulfil the basic functions expected from a modern state in the twenty-first century. Lawlessness and violence permeate society in these countries because the state lacks the capacity to hold both the monopoly of violence and administrative control across its territory (Ghani and Lockhart, 2008). Furthermore, in these countries there is complete absence of adequate infrastructure, investments in human capital, service provision and sound management of public finances (ibid.). From this perspective, state fragility can also be conceptualized as the complete breakdown of relationships between the state, citizens and the marketplace (ibid.).

After a shock that pushes a state into a condition of fragility, two main tasks need to be implemented: security and economic development. On the one hand, the state needs to re-establish security by imposing control across its territory. Security should be the most important objective for foreign development actors after a situation like war (Jones et al., 2005). On the other hand, and almost simultaneously, economic (sustainable) development needs to be fostered in order to avoid a slide back to chaos (ibid.). In this chapter, we focus on the latter aspect. Examining the variety of previous studies, we realize that governments of failed states have not been able to cope with the conditions at hand, and in some cases even contributed to deterioration of the situation in instances where states prey on their own populations. Extreme poverty and hunger are widespread; citizens are effectively left to their own devices. As a whole, the situation has been made worse by the fact that failed states experience high population growth, far higher than average world rates (Brown, 2008). In the absence of healthcare, extremely high rates of maternal and child mortality have become widespread (World Bank, 2007).

In this context entrepreneurship occurs in a radically different institutional setting than in a prospering developed nation. The challenge is then to operate in a complete institutional vacuum, characterized by widespread market disruptions and instability while at the same time thriving to jumpstart economic activity. As Table 4.4 summarizes, the contexts in which the UN operated in East Timor and Haiti are similar in many ways, mainly related to these being failed states. Both countries had experienced extremely low levels of development and did not have well-functioning local institutions before the shock. In East Timor, government institutions were run by the Indonesian occupation; and in Haiti the USA, as the largest donor, held much sway over local politics and economic policy. Both countries experienced an interventionist strategy to solve an unprecedented humanitarian emergency. Large flows of internally

Table 4.4   Country-specific facts for Haiti and East Timor

	East Timor / Timor-Leste	Haiti
Country area (position in the world)	14 874 sq km (160th)	27 750 sq km (148th)
Population	1.2 million (159th)	9.9 million (88th)
Median age	18.4 years	21.9 years
Human development index position	134	161
Annual GDP	US$4.2 billion	US$7.9 billion
Annual GDP per capita	US$10 000 (119th)	US$1300 (208th)
Inequality of income distribution – GINI index	31.9 (106th)	59.2 (7th)
Failed States Index (alert: 33 countries)	92.7 (28th)	104.9 (7th)
Post-shock ODA to Reconstruction Fund	42 million	265 million
Total capital inflow (estimates)	n.a.	5–10 billion (spent so far)
Displacement / refugee flows	~ 250 000 refugees, ~75% of population temp. displaced	~ 1 million (mainly internal)
Level of destruction	n.a.	31 out of 32 ministries collapsed

Sources: CIA (2013); UNDP (2013); Fund for Peace (2012); HRF (2010); Beauvais (2001).

displaced people, pockets of violence, widespread looting, food insecurity and destruction permeated societies in these countries. Consequently, the UN missions operating in Haiti and East Timor were endowed with strong mandates. They had the responsibility to stabilize the situation and ensure the distribution of humanitarian relief.

CASE: EAST TIMOR – A FIGHT FOR INDEPENDENCE

At the end of Portuguese colonial rule, Indonesia occupied East Timor in 1975 and prevented the East Timorese from exercising their right to self-determination. This was a case of forceful annexation that was not recognized by the UN (Beauvais, 2001). The international community provided tacit support to Indonesia and avoided bringing up this topic at the Security Council. Support for Indonesia was based on the fact that the Suharto regime was a key partner during the Cold War against the Soviet threat and no single country was willing to sacrifice its commercial relationship with Indonesia at the expense of recognizing East Timorese sovereignty. These factors, coupled with a lack of media coverage, help to explain why it took so long for the international community to act in East Timor.

However, support for Indonesia began to shift in the aftermath of the Santa Cruz massacre on 12 November 1991, when a peaceful East Timorese demonstration was violently put down in front of foreign journalists, sparking international solidarity for the East Timorese cause.

In 1999, following Suharto's fall as a result of the rippling effects of the financial crisis in Indonesia, a UN-supported referendum called for Indonesia to allow the East Timorese to vote for self-determination or for annexation to Indonesia. The election proceeded peacefully, but when the results emerged they revealed that around 80 per cent of the population had voted for independence. These results were met with violence. The UN officials in the country failed to protect the East Timorese people because they underestimated the reaction of pro-Indonesian militias and the support that these groups received from the Indonesian army. Thousands of pro-independence supporters were murdered. Pro-Indonesia militias initiated a systematic campaign to punish and exterminate the Timorese population. The days following the election witnessed chaos, wanton violence against civilians and egregious human rights abuses.

As a result of post-electoral violence, East Timor suffered an unprecedented humanitarian emergency, making stabilization the primary goal of the intervention as is usually the case after a major conflict (Jones et al., 2005). The entire population had been affected by the violence. People fled the country or took refuge in the mountainous regions of the island. Almost 250 000 individuals fled to West Timor and many of them remained under the control of pro-Indonesia militias. East Timor was one of the poorest regions in South East Asia before the crisis; violence and the destruction of medical services aggravated this situation. In the wake of post-electoral violence, cases of severe malnutrition became widespread (FAO, 2008). Food insecurity increased due to the destruction of infrastructure and the disruption of markets. This made it difficult, if not impossible, for the local population to access the little food that was available. The looting of farms and burning of seed was rampant, leading to a serious state of food insecurity. As a result the entire population, around 1 million people, found itself in a desperate humanitarian emergency.

After violence escalated, it was determined that the situation in East

Timor constituted a threat to peace and security, and the process of capacity and institution building started. The Security Council quickly deployed INTERFET (the International Force for East Timor). As a result of abundant resources and a strong peace-enforcement mandate, this mission became an effective instrument for conflict resolution. It established security and stabilized the country shortly after deployment. Once the situation had been considerably stabilized following post-electoral violence, UNTAET (the United Nations Transitional Administration in East Timor) took control over INTERFET's security apparatus. The new mission swiftly moved to continue the implementation of measures attempting to establish law and order (Stevens, 2007). The objective was to facilitate the emergence of legitimate structures through which the population could enforce law and ensure that East Timor transitions away from conflict. As part of this strategy, the rule of law was promoted as one of the most important pillars ensuring the emergence of responsive, accountable and responsible institutions. To accomplish this, several 'transitional judicial packages' were designed and executed (UN, 1999).

CASE: HAITI – A CIRCLE OF FOREIGN INTERVENTIONS AND DEPENDENCY

In the afternoon of 12 January 2010 an earthquake of the magnitude 7.3 on the Richter scale struck Haiti. The epicentre in the vicinity of Port-au-Prince, the most densely populous area of the country, was directly struck by the tectonic movements (Government of Haiti, 2010b). According to Haitian evaluations more than 230000 people lost their lives (ibid.), though estimations are between 46000 and 315000, with a tendency to inflate them (BBC, 2011). The financial effect alone has been evaluated to be 100 per cent of the national gross domestic product (GDP), or US$7.804 billion (Government of Haiti, 2010b), though the socio-psychological and institutional effects are a much greater burden for the development of the country (GoH, 2010a).

Haiti shows a history of political turmoil and mismanagement. In the media the country is often stigmatized to a cynical image – the poorest country of the Western world. Even though numerical measures justify the title, they fail to acknowledge the real misery and tragedy that ultimately resulted in this status. Reviewing the last century, one can only come to the conclusion that national and international policy mistakes triggered a downward spiral, causing its self-sustaining capacity to vanish into thin air. As a failing state close to the US border, Haiti poses deeply rooted challenges to US and UN foreign policy (Erikson, 2004). Two answers are commonly provided as to why Haiti has gone so awry: depending which side has been solicited, the other is to be blamed. On the one hand, the international community with the leadership of the US is perceived as misunderstanding the Haitian context (Girard, 2010). On the other hand, 'many place the blame for Haiti's failure on the country's rulers, especially on the leadership of Aristide and his political party following his restoration in 1994' (Erikson, 2004: 285–6). All the latest enduring presidents, Papa Doc (Francois Duvalier), Bébé Doc (Jean-Claude Duvalier) and Jean-Bertrand Aristide, established paramilitary groups, collected bribes, tortured political opponents, plundered the state, spent vast amounts of money abroad, and destroyed the morality and hope of the Haitian population for a better life (Girard, 2010).

In the last century, the Western world has tried to seize Haiti's vast variety of natural resources. It can be argued that the most severe interference into national Haitian politics has been the US-directed free trade agreement in 1986 (Schuller, 2012). Due to the economic recession in the 1970s, the international aid community subsequently increased their donations and interventions. The spiral of dependency on foreign aid accelerated, and simultaneously anti-American sentiment was spurred. As a politically dependent country, Haiti committed itself to the American initiative of a free trade agreement (Girard, 2010). In retrospect, this event eventually destroyed its last ambitions to spur economic growth and become a self-sustaining country (ibid.). From that year onwards, volatility of the international commodity markets led to periods of cheap imports destroying the local farming sector. Even though those periods were short-term, local production was not resilient enough to survive. Consequently, the international community had to step up to diminish the numbers of hungry stomachs. The aftershocks of the liberalization exist nowadays in the form of cheap imports from the Dominican Republic for almost all agricultural products, and an absence of local industries. All in all, the Haitian population has got used to constant dependence on foreign donations, even for food production.

THE QUEST FOR DEMOCRATIZATION AND DEVELOPMENT: A DEBATE BETWEEN INSTITUTION BUILDING AND MARKET CREATION

The quest for democratization and development centres on a discussion between creating institutional capacity versus market-driven economic liberalization. The majority of planned and executed actions address these concerns through the rationale of sustainable development. 'The task for

East Timor is to ensure investment in human development and stimulate enterprise, while not using oil and gas revenues on current consumption' (UNDP, 2002a: 9). Both missions faced a daunting task on a scale never seen before, mainly to build a state and ensure that democratization processes and economic growth takes hold:

> East Timor's future will depend ultimately on establishing a thriving private sector that can generate output, savings, private investment and trade. Public policy must therefore foster an environment in which the private sector can expand and flourish. (UNDP, 2002a: 63)

> Given the low rate of savings in East Timor and the limited amount of entrepreneurial ability or experience, much of the stimulus for future economic and human development through the formal sector will have to come from foreign direct investment (FDI). Private capital can not only boost productivity but also widen human development choices by allowing the East Timorese to develop their capacities through the training and experience they gain from working in foreign enterprises. (UNDP, 2002a: 66)

In East Timor the result was that UNTAET ended up perceiving its short and long-term goals of humanitarian relief and development respectively as incongruent, rather than complementary to each other. Enterprises were present though this did not preclude the emergence of entrepreneurship. Instead, the strategy relied on foreign direct investment (FDI), and on official development assistance (ODA). The process necessary to arrive at sustainable development can be sequentially divided between a short-term and a long-term strategy. Most interesting, though, the cases show that either an institutional or a market economic perspective is applied in the argumentation for the national development strategy.

EAST TIMOR'S INSTITUTION BUILDING AND MARKET CREATION EFFORTS

In the post-conflict case of East Timor, the long-term goal was to develop local capacity, and hence to prepare East Timor for self-government. It was envisioned that after UNTAET's presence in East Timor, a democracy would be in place along with a set of institutions to perform the basic functions expected from a state in the twenty-first century (UN, 2001). These functions mainly entail the development of state capacity to supply basic public services to citizens, protect them from avoidable harm, enable them to democratically elect their leaders, and provide them with the opportunity to participate in the political process and marketplace. This goal was meant to be achieved by enhancing the participation of the local population in the process of reconstruction, but this did not happen: instead, the UN centralized authority. By involving the East Timorese in decision-making, the mission would have been able to instil representativeness, foster pluralism, promote sustainability and contribute to capacity development – a factor in short supply.

Concerning the market creation activities, the strategy was to rely on a cash influx that would exploit opportunities in the market disequilibrium: 'Given the low rate of savings and the limited amount of entrepreneurial experience, much of the stimulus for economic and human development through the formal sector will have to be based on foreign direct investment' (UNDP, 2002a: 8).

Yet, the strategy was built on unstable ground, as pumping in money had not accelerated economic development in the past: 'While the government invested, the private sector, foreign or domestic, was largely absent. Scarcely any foreign investors entered the province. And even local entrepreneurs were hard to find: by mid-1999 the Board of Investment had registered only 10 projects from domestic investors' (UNDP, 2002a: 56).

The short-term goal to accelerate the process of reconstruction basically entailed the rebuilding of infrastructure, restarting the economy and providing basic services, for which UNTAET hired foreign experts. This was done in response to pressure to deliver visible results. By acting in such a way, UNTAET signalled donors its ability to 'manage for results', which in turn enhanced the UN's reputation in the realm of international security and provided the mission with increased leverage to raise more funds. The idea was that the quick provision of public services and infrastructure would improve UNTAET's legitimacy and would ultimately boost the local economy, and private money would follow public investments. Yet, this goal has proven elusive so far.

The emphasis on institution building and erosion of market failure led to a complete exclusion of the Timorese society in the process. UNTAET faced intense international pressure to minimize political risk and avoid failure at all costs. There was a need to limit the likelihood of anyone hijacking the emerging political system, which would have proved detrimental to the prospects of democracy and to the success of the mission. To thwart such an undemocratic outcome, UNTAET believed that full executive and legislative power should remain within the mission (Beauvais, 2001). Concomitantly, UNTAET circumvented participation of the local population in the process of 'creating' the East Timorese state. However, the negative effect was that this approach forestalled the building of local capacity that would have otherwise been possible if the local population had been allowed to participate: 'The weaknesses in government are mirrored in the private sector and civil society. So far there have been a few initiatives to build private-sector capacity' (UNDP, 2006: 47).

To disregard entrepreneurship in the development process has been justified by the general lack of entrepreneurial capacity in the country, and partly due to governmental failure. Foreign implanted institutions as well as international best practices cannot drive governance, much less foster the conditions necessary for entrepreneurship.

The mistakes of the earlier strategic direction were the exclusion of the actors supposed to implement the change, which has been recognized and addressed, although within the same policy framework. Thus, supporting entrepreneurs becomes merely an economic instrument, instead of acknowledging them as agents of change: 'The Government could encourage entrepreneurs who are interested in delivering services, through tax breaks and access to credit' (UNDP, 2006: 3).

Officially acknowledged in the new 2006 development plan quoted from above, a lesson has been learned and the role of entrepreneurship has been upgraded, as it is increasingly perceived as supportive for the process of building sovereign nations and sustainable development. The new strategy focuses on participation of rural areas and small-scale entrepreneurship: 'Replacing these sources of income will be difficult but some opportunities exist – for example, offering training to local entrepreneurs drawing on the experience of the small enterprise project. What is needed is a dynamic agricultural sector that would itself create more opportunities for off-farm employment' (UNDP, 2006: 30).

As a recent shift, the government is eager to build a more supportive framework for entrepreneurs:

> The Trust Fund for East Timor is funding the Second Small Enterprise Project with $7.5 million. The aim is to generate employment, accelerate economic growth and improve the competitiveness of small and medium enterprises. The project supports five business development centres in Dili, Baucau, Maliana, Oecussi and Maubisse, offering several types of basic management and entrepreneurship courses, lasting from one day to three weeks. To date, over 1000 East Timorese entrepreneurs have attended the training courses, about 70% of them men and 30% women. (UNDP, 2006: 30)

Yet, the failures made in capacity building and institution building are reflected in the fact that the private sector is still in its infancy, and therefore the new strategy is not without risks:

> Whether this new strategy will be effective is open to question since the private sector in Timor-Leste is still at an embryonic stage. It could take up to ten more years for sufficient entrepreneurs to emerge; meanwhile rural communities are

being deprived of many essential services – and of opportunities to increase their incomes and escape from poverty. (UNDP, 2006: 30)

This perception shows that the instrumental value of enterprises is respected, but entrepreneurship is not regarded to contribute to the greater capacity building in order to build a sovereign nation.

HAITI'S INSTITUTION BUILDING AND MARKET CREATION EFFORTS

In the post-disaster case of Haiti, forming a new institution has been the primary strategy. Established by the United Nations to supervise the reconstruction efforts for 18 months, the IHRC (Interim Haitian Reconstruction Commission) has the task to evaluate the damage, losses and needs for the development of Haiti, and to coordinate the transition from recovery to rebuilding of the country; though multiple international agencies and aid conditionality gave little support to building local structures. An overall assessment in 2011, a year after the earthquake, concludes that only 1 per cent of the money disbursed has been given to the Haitian government while the other 99 per cent has financed the UN peacekeeping mission, the international non-governmental organizations (NGOs), private contractors and debt relief (Office of the Special Envoy for Haiti, 2011). On the one hand, required local capacity is lacking; external perception attributes limited capabilities to the local and national government, and further criticizes a lack of transparency on public expenditure. On the other hand, the international community desires strong national institutions to allow for justice in the society, and thus has to invest in building the capacity. However, local Haitian organizations have been fully excluded from the first post-earthquake appeal.

This is shocking, though not surprising, because of the international community's lack of trust in the local entrepreneurs and the private sector. Entrepreneurs are currently rather a threat to the institution-building efforts, due to the idea that a functional market that drives development is non-existent.

> On the individual and sectoral plans (specific population categories) the multiplication of precarious conditions touches all aspects of existence. Job flexibility tends to become the norm with the easiness of relocating companies and large migration flows, rending vulnerable the stability of residence. The growing importance of the vulnerability makes it gradually acquire a systematic character; this concept is positioned in a way as a poverty vector as well as deprivation. (UNDP, 2006: 16)

It is true that a portion of paid employees exists in renowned and formal enterprises and is taken by the most qualified individuals from the labour market. But is also important to count the low end paid jobs: 53% of the whole of salaried individuals – main breadwinner or not – are poor. (UNDP, 2006: 12)

Despite the official analysis that the earthquake damage primarily hampered the private sector, and that 52 per cent of the money invested should be directed towards the social sector (Government of Haiti, 2010b), the strong interventionist policies have not supported the creation of a functional market. In fact, out of the post-earthquake structure arose a parallel quasi-governmental system of international NGOs and transnational organizations administering the reconstruction. Consequently, Haitians perceive the development architecture as a threat to their governmental efforts, lacking resources in contrast to the international response system. Overall, a lack of joint efforts weakens the national sovereignty, erodes legitimacy and creates dependencies.

As in East Timor, the policies in place perceive the entrepreneur merely as a target for development efforts, not as the actor of change:

Put in place an active employment policy based on micro-businesses, strengthening vocational training, particularly for young people, incorporating and implementing the principles of the 'highly labour intensive' (HLI / HIMO) approach, and bringing together Haitian entrepreneurs, the local workforce, and the communities. (Government of Haiti, 2010b: 9)

Launch a short- and long-term national vocational training campaign; a campaign to raise young people's awareness of topics of employment, entrepreneurship, and apprenticeship; and revise training curricula so they correspond to the needs of the job market. (Government of Haiti, 2010b: 16)

While the economic function of entrepreneurship is appreciated, it is disregarded in concrete action steps and even neglected with regard to building the institutional set-up. Hence, it is merely a target of the institutions, not an agent shaping the development process.

In sum, our ethnographic content analysis suggests that the entrepreneur, the human actor interpreting the opportunities, exploiting them and shaping the way policies are realized, has been completely neglected in the efforts. The closest indication of the necessity to include entrepreneurs is the idea of 'accompaniment'. This approach entails that sharing decision-making with the intended beneficiaries could improve the livelihood situation. 'Accompaniment' complements aid effectiveness and human rights principles in a number of ways. It stresses the importance of the Haitian government and its citizens being 'in the driver's seat'. While this concept at least acknowledges the need for entitlement and possessing ownership, it does not clarify any required action.

DIFFERENCES AND SIMILARITIES BETWEEN POST-CONFLICT AND POST-DISASTER DEVELOPMENT EFFORTS

Despite the official acknowledgement that entrepreneurship is required (Naudé, 2011), in fragile nations it is not yet perceived to contribute to active citizenship and the democratization processes that are aimed for in this process of building a sovereign nation. Even though the historical, social and cultural environment, as well as the nature of the shock differed greatly, the role of entrepreneurship is perceived similarly. The analysis indicates that this is due to private enterprises being perceived as a threat to the political development, and therefore entrepreneurship is only addressed as a means for employment creation (see Table 4.5). Several times it was mentioned that the enterprises are predominantly small and with low capacity. The analysis shows that in both cases the collection and distribution of official development aid has been centralized. The management and distribution occurred through the standard procedure of a multi-donor trust fund. Due to the strong control criteria for fund disbursement, the multi-donor trust fund disbursed only 13 per cent in Haiti and 11 per cent in East Timor in the first year to the approved projects (Haiti Reconstruction Fund, 2010).

Entrepreneurship remains to be perceived as a means towards an end, as a suitable tool to increase economic output. While in each case the development strategy is slowly being adjusted, the institutional and market economic perspectives continue to dominate. As a result the mantra remains: maintaining process control leads to the best outcome. It is without doubt that UNTAET's decision to follow an authoritarian approach in order to swiftly provide visible results, minimize risk and, ultimately, prepare the local population for self-government was self-defeating. The centralization of power and exclusion of East Timorese from decision-making isolated UNTAET. Without feedback and policy input from the local population, policies and legislation enacted by UNTAET became devoid of local content and, thus, failed to address the realities on the ground and spur enterprise development. As a result, in some instances, UNTAET policies inadvertently aggravated the impoverished conditions in East Timor and contributed to the emergence of parallel governance structures. Therefore, entrepreneurial activity is now supporting the parallel system rather than aiding the development process of a sovereign nation.

Table 4.5   Role of entrepreneurship in post-shock strategies

	Plans	Activities (selective not exhaustive)	Role of entrepreneurship	Reported outcomes
East Timor (post-conflict)	*Institution building* – halving poverty – empowerment of poor *Market creation* – inclusion of civil society	– decentralization and local governance – capacity development – partnerships and alliances (FDI)	Entrepreneurs as a risk factor (Foreign) entrepreneurs as partners	1. Entrepreneurs a means for job creation 2. Build supportive framework for small enterprises
Haiti (post-disaster)	*Institution building* – active employment policy – environmental resilience – risk and disaster management – access to basic services *Market creation* – reconstruct the economy	– built democratic processes in institutions – empower the Ministry of Environment (subsidies / cross-taxation) – contingency plans and evacuation camps – decentralization of public governance – strengthen private sector capacity – recapitalize – enhance number of jobs	Entrepreneurs not considered Entrepreneurs as job creators	1. Dependency on foreign money flows 2. Need for 'accompaniment', inclusion of locals

Another similarity we encountered in both cases is that the enterprise activity was mentioned, in conjunction with informal sector activities or even directly, with negative environmental consequences. The link to informal activity is not far-fetched as most economic activity in fragile states occurs without official documentation, yet it neglects the beneficial impetus that informal activity gives to start regional economic development. In both cases we found the perception of entrepreneurs as exploiters of resources was mentioned several times in a single sentence. In East Timor entrepreneurs were accused of depleting the oil reserves without contributing to development. In Haiti, their activities were a reason for deforestation. Therefore we claim that the role of entrepreneurship has not seen the same evolution in the post-shock fragile nation context as in developed economies. It is not yet perceived as a contributor to democratization processes and development. The analysis shows that this is mainly due to the presence of the dominant economic schools, neglecting entrepreneurship in the development discussion.

DISCUSSION

In this chapter we argue that currently in post-shock fragile states democratization and development questions are addressed from an economics or institutional perspective, mainly disregarding the entrepreneurship element. This chapter adds to the evolving sustainable entrepreneurship literature by analysing the role that entrepreneurship plays for democratization and development processes. Although entrepreneurship is regarded as contributing to the creation of economic liberalization, social wealth and personal freedom (Nicholls, 2008; Huang, 2008), and entrepreneurship makes an even greater contribution to development (Naudé, 2011), studying the post-shock scenario in fragile nations shows little sign of entrepreneurship driving the democratization process. This is not to say that new economic activity is not to come from new actors – the entrepreneurs – but that current development processes in fragile states follows rather an interventionist agenda with a multiplicity of interests.

From an institutional perspective, what is to be sustained is socially constructed and adopted in the institutions; and those institutions having power, influence and legitimacy is what is to be developed (Shepherd and Patzelt, 2011). In both Haiti and East Timor parallel systems emerged, one money-laden in the hands of foreign institutions, and one without resources in the hands of the local government; for instance, resulting in merely 1 per cent of donor money being channelled through the Haitian government (Farmer, 2012). Our study finds that the closest concept starting to be recognized in this debate is the idea of 'accompaniment'. This approach entails that sharing decision-making with intended beneficiaries could improve the livelihood situation (Schuller, 2012). Additionally, encouraging entrepreneurial behaviour through a problem-driven iterative approach together with – and not over the heads of – beneficiaries, would even more strongly support institution building (Andrews et al., 2012). In such a model, democratization and sustainable development would be entrepreneur-led and not expert-driven (Potts et al., 2010); the latter we have encountered in this chapter. Likewise a co-evolutionary model would build up the absorptive capacity of local institutions, thereby counteracting the vicious circle of pledged money being bypassed due to a lack of capacity and further aggravating the problem (Farmer, 2012). In this study we come to agree with Naudé (2011) that by neglecting entrepreneurship in the development process, economists and policy makers currently fail to appreciate how institutions shape development outcomes.

From a market or neo-classical economics perspective, what is to be sustained is the market impact of entrepreneurship on the environmental dimension; and bringing profit to the individual, organization and economy is what is to be developed (Shepherd and Patzelt, 2011). Both cases demonstrated that enterprises, rather than entrepreneurship, are a means towards increasing economic output and reducing unemployment. Rather than sustaining low environmental impact, micro and small enterprises were perceived as a cause for deforestation in Haiti, and oil depletion in East Timor. In order to sustain a low environmental impact and to develop profits, one possibility is to increase the 'regional entrepreneurial capital', measured by the rate of entrepreneurship (Naudé et al., 2008), which impacts upon economic activity at the micro and meso level (Wennekers et al., 2002). In this respect, our findings indicate:

> what really matters is the existence of entrepreneurial actions to shift meso rules in fundamental ways. . . . So when economists talk of correcting 'market failure', 'negative externalities' and 'public good problems' the general public cannot relate to it. So it is also naive to imagine that environmental problems can be fixed by removing supposed market failures and relying only on price incentives. (Potts et al., 2010: 379)

Whilst a neo-classical perspective perceives enterprises as instruments to remove externalities, an entrepreneurial response would acknowledge the need for experimentation and best practices spread through imitation, collaboration and selection, hence shifting the meso rules. This idea indicates adopting a co-creational model as suitable because it is sceptical on the notion of exogenous constraints and emphasizes what can be achieved through entrepreneurial behaviour (Potts et al., 2010).

The comparative analysis further suggests that the nature of the shock seems to play a rather marginal role, but the socio-historical and pre-shock context significantly influences the development process. Both cases exemplify the current external interventionist strategy dominating in the fragile nations context, only minor raise contextual factors. That a shift would be beneficial is starting to be realized by scholars from public administration and institution building (Andrews et al., 2012), and ecological economics (Potts et al., 2010). Humans are ecologically destructive, although they perceive and exploit the resulting opportunities through entrepreneurial activities (Penn, 2003). Our contribution is to point out that entrepreneurship theory has valuable contributions to support the future of the democratization and development discussion in fragile nations.

CONCLUSION

This study reports on the role of entrepreneurship for democratization processes in two fragile nations, Haiti and East Timor. Our aim was to contribute to the discussion by analysing its role in the institution-building process. In the theoretical analysis we argued for two dominating positions shaping the development debate, being the institutional and neoclassical economics perspectives. Our ethnographic content analysis found additional evidence for this dominance. As a result the study showed that control is valued, instead of empowerment of locally independent institutions, actors and processes. The role of entrepreneurship in this debate is that of a purely economic perspective of entrepreneurship as a target for job creation. Hence the study indicates that in post-shock fragile nations the main strategy to achieve development remains heavily focused on the reconstitution of government institutions, while ignoring indigenous entrepreneurial activities that spring up to cope with the conditions at hand and boost the fragile local economy.

While previous research suggests that entrepreneurs are agents driving societal renewal and economic liberalization, and are a sign of democratization processes, rights and freedom (Nicholls, 2008: 94; Huang, 2008), our findings would indicate that this role of entrepreneurship has to be acknowledged in the first place. Therefore, we point to a deficiency in the current approach to democratization processes, which is the neglect of entrepreneurship's transformative power. Thus, rethinking current development practices seems necessary. We agree with the ideas of previous authors that entrepreneurship could contribute to democratization and development processes, if it was acknowledged much more broadly in the first place. The co-evolution of economic and environmental relations, enabled through the entrepreneur, is more important than stressing 'hard' environmental constraints (Potts et al., 2010).

A major weakness in this study arises from the limited availability of strategic documents that are supported by the decision-makers, and also available to the actors operating in the fragile nations. For the future this indicates that valuable data could also be obtained through more longitudinal and ethnographic methods. More research attention should also be given to impactful small-scale initiatives that occur despite the current development agenda, thus providing an indication that an alternative model could be more suitable. Furthermore, at the moment we lack an understanding of the entrepreneurial activities in the informal sector that initiate positive development. Probably the critical question for future research is: How can co-evolution occur? First indications can be found in the entrepreneurship research domain that looks at entrepreneurial enactment or the contextualization of entrepreneurship research.

ACKNOWLEDGEMENTS

The authors are grateful to Vera Haataja and an anonymous reviewer for their valuable comments and suggestions. We would like to express our sincerest appreciation to the editor Paula Kyrö for her recommendations and guidance throughout the process.

NOTES

1. Conflict is 'the systematic use of armed violence for criminal and/or political objectives; it is well known to have devastating impacts on well-being and development' (Brück et al., 2013: 2).
2. A natural disaster is commonly defined as the 'impact of an extreme natural event on an exposed, vulnerable society. If impacts exceed an affected region's coping capacity thereby necessitating interregional or international help, a large disaster is said to have occurred' (Mechler, 2003: 10).

REFERENCES

Acs, Z.J. and D. Storey (2004), 'Introduction: entrepreneurship and economic development', *Regional Studies*, 38(8), 871–77.
Ahlstrom, D. and G.D. Bruton (2006), 'Venture capital in emerging economies: networks and institutional change', *Entrepreneurship: Theory and Practice*, 30(2), 299–320.
Aidis, R. (2005), 'Institutional barriers to small- and medium-sized enterprise operations in transition countries', *Small Business Economics*, 25(4), 305–17.

Altheide, D.L. (1987), 'Reflections: ethnographic content analysis', *Qualitative Sociology*, 10(1), 65–77.

Altheide, D.L. (2004), 'Consuming terrorism', *Symbolic Interaction*, 27(3), 289–308.

Anderson, A.R. (1998), 'Cultivating the Garden of Eden: environmental entrepreneuring', *Journal of Organizational Change Management*, 11(2), 135–44.

Andrews, M., L. Pritchett and M. Woolcock (2012), 'Escaping capability traps through problem-driven iterative adaptation (PDIA)', Center for International Development at Harvard University, Working Paper, 240.

Audretsch, D.B., M.C. Keilbach and E.E. Lehmann (2006), *Entrepreneurship and Economic Growth*, Oxford: Oxford University Press.

Baliamoune, M.N. (2009), 'Entrepreneurship and reforms in developing countries', UNU-WIDER Research Paper RP2009/04, World Institute for Development Economic Research (UNU-WIDER).

Barreto, H. (1989), *The Entrepreneur in Microeconomic Theory: Disappearance and Explanation*, London, UK and New York, USA: Routledge.

Baumol, W.J., R.E. Litan and C.J. Schramm (2007), *Good Capitalism, Bad Capitalism and the Economics of Growth and Prosperity*, New Haven, CT: Yale University Press.

BBC (2011), 'Report challenges Haiti earthquake death toll', http://www.bbc.co.uk/news/world-us-canada-13606720, accessed 16 January 2013.

Beauvais, J.C. (2001), 'Benevolent despotism: a critique of UN state-building in East Timor', *New York University Journal of International Law and Politics*, 33, 1101–178.

Beck, T., A. Demirguc-Kunt and R. Levine (2003), 'Small and medium enterprises, growth, and poverty: cross-country evidence', World Bank Policy Research Working Paper 3178, December.

Bennett, J. (2010), 'Informal firms in developing countries: entrepreneurial stepping stone or consolation prize?', *Small Business Economics*, 34(1), 53–63.

Boeninger, E. (1992), 'Governance and development: issues and constraints', *World Bank Proceedings of the World Bank Annual Conference on Development Economics 1991*, Washington, DC.

Brown, L.R. (2008), *Plan B 3.0: Mobilizing to Save Civilization*, New York: W.W. Norton.

Brück, T., W. Naudé and P. Verwimp (2013), 'Business under fire: entrepreneurship and violent conflict in developing countries', *Journal of Conflict Resolution*, 57(1), 3–19.

CIA (2013), 'The World Factbook', https://www.cia.gov/library/publications/the-world-factbook/geos/xx.html, accessed 10 June 2013.

Dahl, R.A. (1971), *Polyarchy, Participation and Opposition*, New Haven, CT: Yale University Press.

Daly, H.E. and J.B. Cobb (1989), *For the Common Good: Redirecting the Economy toward Community, the Environment, and a Sustainable Future*, Boston, MA: Beacon Press.

Erikson, D. (2004), 'The Haiti dilemma', *Brown Journal of World Affairs*, 10(2), 285–97.

Farmer, P. (2012), 'Foreword', in M. Schuller (ed.), *Killing with Kindness: Haiti, International Aid, and NGOs*, New Brunswick, NJ: Rutgers University Press, pp. xi–xii.

Fogel, K., A. Hawk, R. Morck and B. Yeung (2006), 'Institutional obstacles to entrepreneurship', in M. Casson, B. Yeung, A. Basu and N. Wadeson (eds), *The Oxford Handbook of Entrepreneurship*, Oxford: Oxford University Press, pp. 540–79.

Food and Agriculture Organization (FAO) (2008), *FAO/WFP Crop and Food Supply Assessment Mission to Timor-Leste Special Report*, Rome: World Food Programme.

Fund for Peace (2012), 'The Failed States Index', http://ffp.statesindex.org/rankings-2012-sortable, accessed 10 June 2013.

Ghani, A. and C. Lockhart (2008), *Fixing Failed States: A Framework for Rebuilding a Fractured World*, Oxford, UK and New York, USA: Oxford University Press.

Gillis, M., D.H. Perkins, M. Roemer and D.R. Snodgrass (1992), *Economics of Development*, 3rd edn, New York: WW Norton & Company.

Girard, P. (2010), *Haiti: The Tumultuous History – From Pearl of the Caribbean to Broken Nation*, New York: Palgrave Macmillan.

Government of Haiti (GoH) (2010a), *Action Plan for National Recovery and Development of Haiti*, Port-au-Prince: Government of Haiti.
Government of Haiti (2010b), *Haiti Earthquake PDNA: Assessment of Damage, Losses, General and Sectoral Needs*, Haiti: Government of Haiti.
Grbich, C. (2012), *Qualitative Data Analysis: An Introduction*, Thousand Oaks, CA: SAGE Publications.
Gries, T. and W. Naudé (2011), 'Entrepreneurship and human development: a capability approach', *Journal of Public Economics*, 95, 216–24.
Haiti Reconstruction Fund (HRF) (2010), 'Rebuilding together: six months progress report June 17 – December 16 2010', Port-au-Prince: Haiti Reconstruction Fund Secretariat, http://www.haitireconstructionfund.org/documents/annual_quarterly/en, accessed 10 June 2012.
Huang, Y. (2008), *Capitalism with Chinese Characteristics: Entrepreneurship and the State*, Cambridge: Cambridge University Press.
Huckin, T. (2002), 'Textual silence and the discourse of homelessness', *Discourse and Society*, 13(3), 347–72.
Huntington, S.P. (1993), *The Third Wave: Democratization in the Late Twentieth Century*, Vol. 4, Norman, OK: University of Oklahoma Press.
Jones, S.G., J.M. Wilson, A. Rathmell and K.J. Riley (2005), *What Have We Learned About Establishing Internal Security in Nation-Building?*, Santa Monica, CA: Rand Corporation.
King, G. and L. Zeng (2001), 'Improving forecasts of state failure', *World Politics*, 53(4), 623–58.
Kyrö, P. (2001), 'To grow or not to grow', *International Journal of Sustainable Development and World Ecology*, 8, 15–28.
Luthans, F. and E.S. Ibrayeva (2006), 'Entrepreneurial self-efficacy in central Asian transition economies: quantitative and qualitative analysis', *Journal of International Business Studies*, 37(1), 92–110.
Maloney, W. (2004), 'Informality revisited', *World Development*, 32, 1159–178.
Manolova, T.S., R.V. Eunni and B.S. Gyoshev (2008), 'Institutional environments for entrepreneurship: evidence from emerging economies in Eastern Europe', *Entrepreneurship: Theory and Practice*, 32(1), 203–18.
Martí, I., Etzion, D. and Leca, B. (2008), 'Theoretical approaches for studying corporations, democracy, and the public good', *Journal of Management Inquiry*, 17(3), 148–51.
Mechler, D. (2003), 'Natural disaster risk management and financing disaster losses in developing countries', Doctoral dissertation, Universität Fridericiana zu Karlsruhe.
Meyer, K. (2001), 'Institutions, transaction costs, and entry mode choice in Eastern Europe', *Journal of International Business Studies*, 32(2), 357–67.
Naudé, W. (2011), 'Entrepreneurship is not a binding constraint on growth and development in the poorest countries', *World Development*, 39(1), 33–44.
Naudé, W., T. Gries, E. Wood and A. Meintjies (2008), 'Regional determinants of entrepreneurial start-ups in a developing country', *Entrepreneurship and Regional Development*, 20(2), 111–24.
Neergaard, H. (2007), 'Sampling in entrepreneurial settings', in H. Neergaard and J.P. Ulhoi (eds), *Handbook of Qualitative Research Methods in Entrepreneurship*, Cheltenham, UK and Northampton, MA, USA: Edward Elgar Publishing, pp. 253–78.
Nelson, R.R. and K. Nelson (2002), 'Technology, institutions, and innovation systems', *Research Policy*, 31(2), 265–72.
Nelson, R.R. and S.G. Winter (1982), *An Evolutionary Theory of Economic Change*, Cambridge, MA: Harvard University Press.
Nicholls, A. (ed.) (2008), *Social Entrepreneurship: New Models of Sustainable Social Change*, Oxford: Oxford University Press.
Office of the Special Envoy for Haiti (2011), *Has Aid Changed? Channeling Assistance to Haiti before and after the Earthquake*, New York: United Nations Office of the Special Envoy for Haiti.
Pahn, P.P., S. Venkataraman and S.R. Velamuri (2008), *Entrepreneurship in Emerging*

Regions around the World: Theory, Evidence and Implications, Cheltenham, UK and Northampton, MA, USA: Edward Elgar Publishing.

Penn, D. (2003), 'The evolutionary roots of our environmental problems: towards a Darwinian ecology', *Quarterly Review of Biology*, 78(3), 275–301.

Potts, J., J. Foster and A. Straton (2010), 'An entrepreneurial model of economic and environmental co-evolution', *Ecological Economics*, 70, 375–83.

Rammel, C. (2003), 'Sustainable development and innovation: lessons from the Red Queen', *International Journal of Sustainable Development*, 6(4), 395–416.

Riddell, R. (2007), *Does Foreign Aid Really Work?*, New York: Oxford University Press.

Samarasinghe, S.W.R. de A. (1994), 'Democracy and democratization in developing countries', Data for Decision Making Project, Department of Population and International Health, Harvard School of Public Health, Boston, MA, http://www.hsph.harvard.edu/ihsg/publications/pdf/No-7-1.PDF, accessed 8 October 2013.

Schuller, M. (2012), *Killing with Kindness: Haiti, International Aid, and NGOs*, New Brunswick, NJ: Rutgers University Press.

Schumpeter, J.A. (1934), *The Theory of Economic Development*, Cambridge, MA: Harvard University.

Shepherd, D.A. and H. Patzelt (2011), 'The new field of sustainable entrepreneurship: studying entrepreneurial action linking "What is to be sustained" with "What is to be developed"', *Entrepreneurship Theory and Practice*, 35(1), 137–63.

Stevens, D. (2007), 'Strength through diversity: the combined naval role in Operation Stabilize', Working Paper 20, Canberra: Sea Power Center.

Sun, L. (ed.) (2003), *Ownership and Governance of Enterprises: Recent Innovative Developments*, Basingstoke: Palgrave Macmillan.

Tracey, P. and N. Phillips (2011), 'Entrepreneurship in emerging markets: strategies for new venture creation in uncertain institutional contexts', *Management International Review*, 51, 23–39.

UN (1999), *Security Council resolution 1264 on the deployment of INTERFET in East Timor S/RES/1264*, New York.

UN (2001), 'East Timor-UNTAET: facts and figures', http://www.un.org/en/peacekeeping/missions/past/etimor/UntaetF.htm, accessed 23 December 2001.

UNDP (2002a), *East Timor Human Development Report: The Way Ahead*, Dili, East Timor: United Nations Development Programme.

UNDP (2002b), *La Bonne Gouvernance: Un Defi Majeur Pour Le Developpement Humain Durable En Haiti* [Governance for human development: a major challenge for sustainable human development in Haiti].

UNDP (2006), *Timor-Leste Human Development Report: Path out of Poverty*, Dili, Timor-Leste: United Nations Development Programme.

UNDP (2008), *La vulnérabilité en Haïti: Chemin inévitable vers la pauvreté?* [Vulnerability in Haiti: the inevitable path towards poverty?]

UNDP (2013), *Human Development Report: The Rise of the South: Human Progress in a Diverse World*, New York: United Nations Development Programme.

Wennekers, A.R.M., L.M. Uhlaner and A.R. Thurik (2002), 'Entrepreneurship and its conditions: a macro perspective', *International Journal of Entrepreneurship Education*, 1(1), 25–64.

Witt, M.A. and G. Redding (2009), 'Culture, meaning, and institutions: executive rationale in Germany and Japan', *Journal of International Business Studies*, 40(5), 859–885.

World Bank (2007), *Global Monitoring Report 2007 Millennium Development Goals: Confronting the Challenges of Gender Equality and Fragile States*, Washington, DC: World Bank Group.

World Bank (2013), 'Damage and loss assessments', http://web.worldbank.org/WBSITE/EXTERNAL/TOPICS/EXTURBANDEVELOPMENT/EXTDISMGMT/0,contentMDK:20196047~menuPK:1415429~pagePK:210058~piPK:210062~theSitePK:341015,00.html, accessed 18 June 2013.

Yin, R. (2009), *Case Study Research: Design and Methods*, 4th edn, Thousand Oaks, CA: SAGE.

APPENDIX

Sources: top: Government of Haiti (2010b); bottom: UNDP (2006).

Figure 4A.1 Enumerative content overview in selected official post-shock documents

5. Organizing societal entrepreneurship: a cross-sector challenge[1]

Bengt Johannisson, Anders W. Johansson, Elisabeth Sundin, Karin Berglund, Erik Rosell, Birgitta Schwartz, Rebecca Stenberg and Malin Tillmar

SOCIETAL ENTREPRENEURSHIP

As clearly demonstrated by for example Nicholls (2010), the majority of approaches to entrepreneurship as a social phenomenon, more specifically to 'social entrepreneurship', position the phenomenon against business venturing. Others, notably Dey and Steyaert (2010), argue that entrepreneurship in general and social entrepreneurship in particular should be kept open to different understandings. A nuanced vocabulary may guide such an ambition. Here we thus put forward 'societal entrepreneurship' as such an open concept. This to our mind focuses on entrepreneurship as a mode of organizing rather than on the ends and means of non-commercial innovative activity that are usually targeted in social entrepreneurship research. Specifically, we argue that societal entrepreneurship as creative organizing occurs at the intersections between the private, public, and non-profit and voluntary (NPVO) sectors. Social and societal entrepreneurship of course have similarities, such as a social intention and concern for shortcomings in society and its formal institutions. But there are also differences between the two phenomena which invite different conceptual frameworks as well as methodologies.

First, societal entrepreneurship embraces change on both the macro level, for example institutions, and on the micro level – that is, in people's everyday life. Dependent on sector, people are identified as customers, clients or citizens; that is, demanding, docile or concerned individuals with varying rights and obligations. Social entrepreneurship, in contrast, often focuses on the (formal) organization level. Second, societal entrepreneurship's concern for organizing implies that it is oriented towards the mobilization of people, (social) innovations and opportunity enactment. Social entrepreneurship in the literature is often considered as a way to correct failures made by the market and/or the public sector without changing their basic structure. Third, societal entrepreneurship has other neighbours than social entrepreneurship, which are mainly related to market-driven entrepreneurship. These neighbours include 'institutional entrepreneurship' that builds institutions (Garud et al., 2007; Hardy and Maguire, 2008; Czarniawska, 2009) as well as 'extreme entrepreneurship' that explicitly challenges institutions (Johannisson and Wigren, 2006). Fourth, having these neighbours signals that how societal entrepreneurship is studied and practised is very much dependent on context. This context sensitivity calls for the more fine-tuned modes of inquiry that are usually adopted in social entrepreneurship research.

In Sweden, a mature welfare economy with well-established private, public and NPVO sectors, there has been a growing interest in societal entrepreneurship. This means that we have learnt lessons which we think are important to share. Our aim is thus to articulate the concept of societal entrepreneurship by, first, providing a more elaborate, yet tentative, conceptual framework; and second, offering a number of empirical illustrations of how (local) entrepreneurial initiatives are enacted in the same (Swedish) cultural and institutional setting. The movements within and between the sectors of society which we associate with societal entrepreneurship are reflected by different vocabularies and practices that are only to some extent mutually recognized by the agents in the three sectors. More often, management principles and practices originating in the private sector colonize the public sector as new public management (NPM) (see e.g. Brunsson and Jacobsson, 2000; Christensen and Laegreid, 2002). However, environmental and social concerns which earlier typically resided in the NPVO and public sectors are now appropriated by private companies as corporate social responsibility (CSR) (see e.g. Sahlin-Andersson, 2006; Schwartz and Tilling, 2009; Dobers and Halme, 2009). Still, to be properly labelled, it concerns how the effects of outsourcing from the public sector affect the private as well as the NPVO sector.

Our chapter is organized as follows. In the next section we elaborate upon our conceptualization of 'societal entrepreneurship' by paying due respect to its dependence on context. Tentatively, we frame societal entrepreneurship by a number of dualities that we associate with it, and also summarize our understanding of the different rationales which guide each sector. Considering our concern for context, we begin our next empirical section by presenting some distinct features of the Swedish setting that accommodate our empirical cases. Before turning to our concrete cases we also provide an overview of our diverse modes of inquiry. Then we invite the reader to seven narrations on different aspects of societal entrepreneurship. Thereafter we bring out insights gained in our empirical research by reviewing the dualities that carry our conceptual points of departure.

The lessons are then used to further refine our arguments for recognizing societal entrepreneurship as an important perspective on the renewal of society in the interest of its citizens.

INQUIRING INTO SOCIETAL ENTREPRENEURSHIP: THE NEED FOR A CONTEXTUALIZED AND DIVERSE APPROACH

In their creative organizing, social initiatives often challenge established institutions and sometimes even establish their own domains. In their disrespect for established structures they reflect a more general development. While the industrial era was characterized by dominant producers thriving on economies of scale and scope in expanding welfare states, the prevailing post-industrial digitalized era indicates 'street-smartness', including for example user-driven product innovation, improvisation as regards organizing production and local solutions to challenges. Entrepreneurial practice then means that rather than being locked into iron cages created by institutions (DiMaggio and Powell, 1983), the actors concerned poach on their ground.

The size dimension may be as relevant as the sector dimension, and time may be most important when making sense out of the manifold contemporary appearances of societal entrepreneurship. The ways in which entrepreneurship presents originate in the entrepreneurship of yesterday. Accordingly, many welfare institutions were once enacted as societal entrepreneurship. The criticism of these established, once entrepreneurial, solutions proves a need for continuous societal entrepreneurship.

The need for a language that can produce a proper vocabulary for capturing societal entrepreneurship is thus urgent. But, as stated above, we do not want to close the conceptual window too early and therefore we, like Eisenhardt (1989), use own cases to offer a conclusive theory. Staying faithful to our contextual view, we rather want to reflect upon our tales from the field and encourage both researchers and practitioners to use them as analogies and not as illustrations of a definite analytical framework. Conversations on a number of dualities then appear as a proper point of departure (Achtenhagen and Melin, 2003). Thus we present below five dualities that frame individual, organizational or societal features.

1. The interplay between economic and social values over time. The pre-industrial era was based on the rural context of recognizing social values while the industrial era emphasized urbanization, eco-

nomic value and contract. Applying Tönnies' (1965) vocabulary, a *Gemeinschaft* order was replaced by a *Gesellschaft* order. Societal entrepreneurship may recreate a balance between these two modes of organizing society.

2. The creative tension between agency and structure (Giddens, 1984), where the expansion of the domain of entrepreneurship invites further agents as well as infusing them with self-confidence, provides more variety as regards the way of crafting new practices. Actors are thus empowered by institutional entrepreneurship and societal entrepreneurship jointly.

3. The ongoing debate over whether entrepreneurship is a phenomenon mainly associated with individual initiative or collective mobilization inspires a reframing of both the driving forces and the modes of organizing for innovation and renewal. Where individuals as participants in social movements cross the boundaries between societal sectors, individual initiatives unite into collective efforts.

4. The industrial era and its established institutions were dominated by big organizations, and large scale was celebrated because of its efficiency as well as its impact. Size was seen as a solution but over time created problems and alienation. Could societal entrepreneurship be a new, challenging way to deal with a situation where smallness is not just beautiful (Schumacher, 1975) but also needed to create the diversity that sustainability calls for?

5. Although entrepreneurship in a welfare state is usually associated with the creation and exploitation of opportunity it could also be seen as a reaction to and a protest against dominating structures and attitudes – something expressed as a necessity.

Besides these five dualities, our tentative conceptual framework rests on the rationales that guide the operations of the three sectors that societal venturing encompasses. Elsewhere we elaborate what we address as 'sector logic' (Berglund et al., 2012) and, since this is greatly dominated by its institutions, we relate to the literature on institutional logic (see e.g. Thornton and Ocasio, 1999).

As Table 5.1 indicates, the sectors vary radically with respect to the 'aspect' or dimensions of the logic that monitors it. Obviously, the real challenge of the venturing that societal entrepreneurship encompasses is to organize the operations so that they become effective without violating any of the rules of the sectors involved so that the necessary triple legitimacy is lost. Our argument is that the field research needed to substantiate how this organizing is achieved calls for a methodology lying very close to the people and practices that enact societal ventures.

Table 5.1   Aspects of sector logics

	Private sector	Public sector	NPVO sector
Institutional pillars	Normative	Regulative	Cognitive/cultural
Time perspective	Short-term	Long term	Short and long term
Focal form of capital	Financial	Human	Social
Interaction rationale	Calculative	Ideational/ calculative	Ideational/genuine
Commitment	Voice/exit	Loyalty	Involvement
Control	Output	Process	Culture
Innovation	Advancing technologies	Ongoing reforming	Mobilizing human capacities
Outlook	Global	Local	Glocal

Source: Berglund and Johannisson (2012, Table 1.1, p. 11).

PROVIDING DIVERSITY WITHIN A NATIONAL CONTEXT: SWEDISH EMPIRICAL CASES

The Swedish Context

Societal entrepreneurship as venturing is influenced by and influences its broader context. In order to make sense out of the cases presented below we have to briefly comment upon the Swedish labour market, the Swedish welfare system and its civil society. A high share of the Swedish population is on the labour market. In 2009, 81 per cent of women and 88 per cent of men aged 20–64 were employed or self-employed (Statistics Sweden, 2010). Sweden also scores high in international comparisons of living standards and quality of life, and as regards equality between men and women. In contrast, as indicated, Sweden does not come out well in international entrepreneurship rankings (GEM, 2010). The reasons for this are much debated and often related to the welfare state, which in the Scandinavian setting means that care obligations are more often handled by the state than by relatives and the NPVO sector (Berggren and Trägårdh, 2009). The consequences of a highly institutionalized setting from an entrepreneurship perspective are dual, in both creating a labour market and taking away business opportunities. The degree of social engagement, however, seems in an international perspective to be as high in Sweden as in other countries (Wijkström, 2011).

The origins of the Swedish welfare state are often found in societal entrepreneurship through politicians, trade unions and popular movements. Some were transformed into public sector organizations (such as libraries), while others stayed outside (such as the trade unions and sports associations). The public sector itself is under constant reorganization. In Sweden societal entrepreneurship has for a long time been associated with people's attachment to place (Johannisson and Nilsson, 1989). While this cultural profile obviously reflects a *Gemeinschaft* community, the formal way of organizing social services from above rather reflects values and practices guided by *Gesellschaft* norms. This paradoxical constitution of Swedish society makes it, in our opinion, especially interesting for research into societal entrepreneurship.

Proposing Spatial, Organizational and Methodological Variation

Here we tell the stories of seven Swedish enactments of societal entrepreneurship; see Table 5.2 for an overview. Paying attention to spatial and organizational variation calls for a narrative approach. Stories are by necessity located in time and place and therefore emphasize the importance of context (Ricoeur, 1984; Polkinghorne, 1988). Using stories from different contexts also allows us to demonstrate the scope of societal entrepreneurship. The plot of our text, focusing on five different dualities characterizing societal entrepreneurship, contributes to defining and to some extent closing it as a new concept. As stories are, however, always open to new interpretations, those narrated by us act as a power of example (cf. Flyvbjerg, 1991) beyond our conceptualization. In addition, they call for more stories about societal entrepreneurship to be told.

To illustrate that we see the move between different sectors in society as the most typical marker of societal entrepreneurship, Table 5.2 reports such cross-overs. The seven narrations also describe alternative organizational forms. Yet our empirical report is in no way a complete odyssey through the archipelago of societal entrepreneurship. Nevertheless, we argue that these seven cases together provide enough variation to present societal entrepreneurship as an opening concept and give input to its further refinement.

Researchers benefit from collaboration beyond the academic community when making excursions to contexts where societal entrepreneurship is studied empirically. Then joint knowledge is created. This epistemological and moral standpoint represents what is addressed as 'interactive' research, which is well established in the Scandinavian setting (see for example Nielsen and Svensson, 2006; Johannisson, 2014). Interactive research has its own identity in the family of approaches where there is interplay between researchers and subjects. While the more institutionalized 'action research' (Reason and Bradbury, 2001) is mainly concerned

Table 5.2   *Geographical, organizational and methodological variation in*
societal entrepreneurship (SE)

Case	Geographical scope	Organizational cross-overs	Methodological approach
Fair Trade	International	Fair trade market as SE by non-profit organization enacted by small private firm	In-depth interviewing, shadowing; mentoring, ongoing dialogue, observing participant
The Moon House	National and international	Spectacular idea as SE emerging into a quadruple helix organization net	Participating observer, in-depth interviewing, shadowing, enactive research
Public Markets	National and local	Small private firm as SE replacing public sector organization and being replaced by big private firm	In-depth interviewing
The Ice Web skridsko.net	National and local	Non-profit organization enacting SE embracing several sectors' activities	Auto-ethnography, enactive research
ALW	Local and national	Enacting SE by key actors with changing organizational forms (private-public sector)	Retrospective studies or archival (secondary) data, supplementary in-depth interviewing
Macken	Local, potentially national	Local co-operative as SE solving public sector problems	In-depth interviewing, observant participation, shadowing, diary dialogue, dwelling
SIP	Local and national	Project-based SE enacted by network and hybrid organization	Participating observation and enactive research

with the rights of those concerned to influence the research process, 'collaborative' research (Adler et al., 2004) may be primarily considered as a dialogue between experts.

Taking the interactive ambition seriously, the Organizing Societal Entrepreneurship in Sweden (OSIS) research community has in several cases established formal agreements (and associated funding) with a number of organizations and social businesses covered by the different cases. The specific research questions brought up in each case and the conceptualization accordingly called for have of course decided what kind of interactive approach has been adopted. This is in line with the strong belief that knowledge creation in the field of societal entrepreneurship as a complex social phenomenon calls for close-up studies where the contextual setting can be further considered through those concerned.

As Table 5.2 shows, the different kinds of interactive methods used vary from the more traditional in-depth interviewing to more seldom used auto-ethnography. In the Ice Web case the author reports on her own experiences of being an active member of an ice skating organization in her private life. This is close to 'enactive research', which appears in several cases, meaning that the process studied is initiated and 'managed' by the researcher (Johannisson, 2011). In some cases the researcher has entered the studied organization and taken part in the activities, becoming a 'temporal' member of the organization in order to catch the unspoken features of societal entrepreneurship. In one case the researcher has 'shadowed' the social entrepreneur to see him operate in practice; and in another case the entrepreneur and the researcher organized a web-based daily dialogue. These conversations were combined with the researcher dwelling – that is, 'hanging around' – in the context of the social venture.

THE SEVEN NARRATIVES

Fair Trade on Trial

Our first story, told by Birgitta Schwartz, is based on a study of a small Swedish retailer of Fair Trade cotton products produced in India and narrates how different actors in both India and Sweden (inter)act and negotiate. The case shows how the Fair Trade label is interpreted by actors in the private sector belonging to different contexts, like Sweden and India, as well as by actors in the NPVO sector.

The Fair Trade market as societal entrepreneurship reveals that the private sector and the NPVO sector meet when actors from both sectors interplay. The story tells us that the Fair Trade label and certification processes (www.fairtrade.net) developed by actors in the non-profit sector in Europe are diffused to Fair Trade farmers and suppliers in India in order to control the improvement of working conditions and environmental issues. The Fair Trade norms include increasing the influence of the workers, and the awareness of environmental issues. The Fair Trade label could be seen as the tool for changing the institutions in Indian society.

According to an Indian Fair Trade supplier, the label makes the supplier reliable and trustworthy in relations with customers such as European companies. A large Swedish retailer, which also sells a range of Fair Trade labelled products, sees this label and other sustainability management standards as necessary in its relations with suppliers and customers. However, the retailer also carries out its own audits of Indian suppliers, because it does not rely on certification processes made by Indian auditors. 'We do both, because it is possible to copy a paper [certificate] or to buy it' (Interview, purchaser). So, even if the Indian supplier carries out all the necessary audits with a third party, some customers still carry out their own audits on site. He says, 'so we have independent audits like some customers, we tell them that we got certified, but they still send their auditors to audit . . . and because of that . . . our factory is open 24 hours for customers to come check and see' (Interview, chief executive officer, Indian Fair Trade supplier). This shows that the Swedish retailer sees legitimacy and control as important when it appropriates the Fair Trade idea. The retailer acts in relation to values and norms in the Swedish context where management standards and control systems are popular and legitimated practices in companies.

Yet, is it really possible to create a good company in low-income countries through institutionalized management standards which are developed in a Western society? Standards are spread very rapidly, compared with norms, which develop by socialization processes over a long time and require particular social conditions to emerge at all (Brunsson and Jacobsson, 2000). Schwartz's study also shows that the diffusion process is not easy to handle for small companies. Their suppliers in India are tough businesspeople guided by a profit-maximizing logic, who often take advantage of the (Swedish) societal entrepreneurs' lack of business experience. The foreign societal entrepreneurs are in the Indian context forced to make business according to the profit-maximizing logic, while at the same time as promoters of Fair Trade they try to change this logic because of its exploitation of workers. This 'Fair Trade paradox' shows that societal entrepreneurship is framed by a global economic discourse. The Indian Fair Trade producers embedded in the Indian private sector and context are, as Holm (1995) states, conditioned by the very institutions that provide the framework for their actions. Neither is this consequence of the Fair Trade business taken up by the NGOs.

Flying to the Moon while Keeping the House: Dreams Coming True

The Moon House case, studied and reported by Karin Berglund, has no straightforward social or societal connections. The first question that usually comes into people's minds when they are introduced to the idea of a house on the moon is, Karin Berglund tells us, 'Why?' The answer given by Mikael Genberg, the entrepreneur, is: 'because there is a vision'. And the vision is to create a moment of reflection, considering how to make life on earth better.

'When the house is standing there on the moon people can see the inhospitable environment. Perhaps they then realize that it is high time for us to be a little more concerned about our own environment. Starting to take a bit more care of mother earth' (cited from a seminar, in Berglund et al., 2007: 271).

The idea with the Moon House is quite simple. The task is to put a miniature of a typical red Swedish cottage on the moon. But, even if the idea is clear-cut, the carrying out of the idea has proved to be challenging. The house cannot be built, by craftspeople, on the moon, but needs to be transported in an unpiloted lunar module that is sent to the moon. As there is limited 'space' in the module, the house will be put in a box not larger than the size of six milk cartons and with a maximum weight of 5 kilos. The logic of technical and aeronautic restraint is, if not always easy to understand in detail, very easy to understand in terms of limitations for what it is possible to do. Nevertheless, the Moon House was seen by the Swedish Space Corporation not only as a possible idea to carry through, but also as an opportunity for making the Swedish space industry known for its competence in delivering new and sustainable solutions for the future. The idea has been formalized by the non-profit association 'Friends of the Moon House' and the private company 'Luna Resort', but can above all be seen as an extensive informal network consisting of numerous activities which have attracted four strong interests: industry, non-governmental organizations (NGOs), governmental agencies and academia. This also makes up the second point, relating to societal entrepreneurship, namely, that it takes 'togetherness' to make such an entrepreneurial project work. This collective work has come to be a trademark of the project, gathering people from the private, public, non-profit and voluntary sectors. The project has so far created a number of landmarks, as for instance the erection of a red house on the Globe, the national sports arena in Stockholm, has gained great publicity and has contributed to developing contacts with international actors such as the National Aeronautics and Space Administration (NASA).

The idea and the activities initiated in the project have, in a positive sense, provoked public and potential co-entrepreneurs. The project has also demonstrated that entrepreneurship can be seen as a balancing act between creativity and imitation, between creating an identity and using the entrepreneur epithet to gain legitimacy, and also between discovering an idea and creating opportunities based on it (Berglund et al., 2007).

Moreover, the Moon House has formed an empirical example of the role of resistance in entrepreneurial processes, demonstrating that resistance may be a requirement for entrepreneurship to continue and flourish (Berglund and Gaddefors, 2010).

Public Markets in the Health Services

The next story originates in a study carried out by Malin Tillmar and concerns the reorganization of the public sector, that is, changes in the way the welfare system is enacted. In the Scandinavian welfare states, many societal entrepreneurs have been active in the public sector, aiming for example at improving healthcare services (Sundin and Tillmar, 2008). Currently, an increasing portion of health and care services are outsourced to private organizations, competing on the public market. This implies that small-scale societal entrepreneurs also act on these markets.

As a case in point, a home for the elderly run by four nurses in a middle-sized Swedish municipality was studied. When the home for the elderly where they worked as managers was about to be closed down, the four nurses decided to start their own firm in the sector. This was in 1994, and they describe, in retrospect, that 'We had great visions about how to give the elderly a home-like environment and live on their own. We were the only large home to do something like this at the time' (One of the entrepreneurs).

The four nurses had well-functioning cooperation with the municipality. The municipality was also very happy with this home for the elderly, and spoke about it during interviews as well as on other public occasions as a success story and a good example. One of the reasons for the high quality delivered was the amount of time the nurses put into the company: 'Yes, I guess that is always the case with business owners. You work around the clock' (One of the entrepreneurs).

However, in 2003 the situation became insecure. The contract with the municipality expired and a public procurement procedure started. A large international corporation made a lower bid on the unit run by the nurses. Thus, the nurses lost their contract:

> At first we were sad more than anything. It really was awful having to give up something that you know is really good, because it was, especially for those living there. But you can't continue thinking about it, you would just get angry . . . You would become a so-called zealot. (One of the entrepreneurs)

Since the nursing home was opened in 1994, the municipality has replicated the concept in all its homes. The entrepreneurs are positive about the fact that the municipality has learnt from them, but also think that they should have been given the opportunity to develop their ideas further. They think that small-scale providers are needed. Despite that, they did not have any plans to start a new care business.

It seems as if a great deal of commitment and energy mobilized in the name of societal entrepreneurship is lost in the transition involving not just the public sector but also, through the construction of public markets, private sector organizations. Size also seems to be of importance here, something that we will return to below.

Icy Initiatives in the Ice Web – and No Warm Reception

Our fourth story is founded – literally – on thin ice. This study made by Rebecca Stenberg concerning societal entrepreneurship stands out because it has societal and social dimensions, although the actors involved seem to be guided by their self-interest.

Scandinavia offers extremely favourable conditions for tour skating on natural ice. Tour skating can be done as a nature experience, as social recreation, as a sport or as a thrilling adventure, both in clubs and as a commercial tourism experience. Regardless of motive it is important to take measures to stay safe on the ice by gathering information on ice quality, weather and other tour conditions. For ice guides and tour leaders this information gathering and analysis used to take a considerable amount of time to carry out until some tour skating enthusiasts, who also happened to work professionally with computer systems and programming, created the federation and website Skridskonätet (www.skridsko.net), designed for information exchange about ice conditions, tour possibilities, tour experiences and safety. The website was launched in 2006 and grew to become the world's largest tour skating website, with 35 000 members of 80 tour skating clubs all over Northern Europe as users. In order to support reporting and clear communication, much of the vocabulary used is standardized. But there are also 'free zones' for reporting in one's own words, the use of poetry, pictures and films from tours.

However, Skridskonätet's databases are not only useful for creating opportunities for having fun on the ice, or reading about other people's adventures. They can also be seen as tools for facilitating physical and social activities and thereby promoting public health. A considerable amount of knowledge about ice and ice safety is gathered, analysed and presented to the members, to the media and interested rescue organizations, by a board appointed by Skridskonätet. It is therefore a source of up-to-date information for the Swedish Sea Rescue Society, which uses it for ice rescue planning and estimates of where ice rescues might be needed.

Thereby Skridskonätet can be seen as a societal entrepreneurial activity in a new and unusual field of social entrepreneurship, adding safety as a new objective to the social values of soci(et)al entrepreneurship (Mair and Martí, 2006; Dey and Steyaert, 2010). It is an initiative that not only embraces the activities of different sectors as non-profit, public and commercial activities, but also facilitates mutual urban and rural interests, for example in good skating conditions combined with possibilities for sleeping accommodation in youth hostels normally closed during the winter. The use of the databases by voluntary or commercial actors is uncontroversial as long as they contribute as much information as they take. Controversies, however, remain between institutional processes and entrepreneurial interests, which actors at Skridskonätet try to settle.

One example of the conflict between legitimacy and marginalization is that the relevant and up-to-date information for everybody who utilizes the ice covered by Skridsko.net cannot be used officially by the rescue services, since it comes from hobby activities. A second example is the conflict between robustness and capacity (Stenumgaard and Larsson, 2010). Standardization also calls attention to the third conflict, between mimetic institutional isomorphism pressures (DiMaggio and Powell, 1983). On the one hand, measurability and comparisons are facilitated by technical development and devices made for outdoor usage; and on the other hand the tour skaters in their capacity as free spirits of adventure want to control their own identity construction. Standards for the information exchange are agreed on by all participating clubs. The question is how the central values and the concurrent identities as tour skaters will survive and transform due to the standardization. Would cooperation with authorities make demands for even more standardization? Will there still be a free spirit of adventure out there – the spirit which calls us out on our beloved ice?

ALW: Entrepreneurship in the Name of the Children

The Astrid Lindgren World (ALW) is yet another way of materializing societal entrepreneurship. Its story is told by Bengt Johannisson and Elisabeth Sundin.[2] In the beginning of the 1980s three families in the small Swedish town of Vimmerby constructed small houses based on one of the stories (*Emil in Katthult*) told by Astrid Lindgren, the world-famous author of children's literature, for their own children to play in, in the vicinity of their own houses. ALW has a history of steady expansion up to today (2012), and the park now covers a huge area outside the town. Every summer it has around half a million visitors coming from all over the world. Its successful trajectory is an outcome of 'creative tensions':

that is, collaboration but also conflict between different stakeholders representing, besides the three sectors, the author and her family. The fights, or maybe rather the discussions and arguments, mainly concern who are the legitimate interpreters of the legacy of Astrid Lindgren. She herself always put the interests of children first and underlined the importance of play and creativity (cf. Johannisson, 2010).

The development of ALW can be defined in phases according to the changing dominant ownership. During its first ten years, 1979–1988, the three pioneering families acted as grass-roots entrepreneurs. The municipality was supportive, but without enthusiasm, although Astrid Lindgren herself blessed the initiative. The unprecedented success of acquiring 100 000 visitors in 1988 made it an attractive business opportunity for several more resourceful actors. Thus, during the second phase, 1989–1994, a private regional company became the majority shareholder in ALW. The personal consent of Astrid Lindgren, who herself had no formal ownership, was the key to the takeover. After only three years, in 1992, the private company ran into financial problems. The municipality then mobilized financial resources to supplement two more new owners: an insurance company, which had interests to protect due to the private company failure; and an organization belonging to the temperance moment that could associate with the message of some of the stories materialized in ALW.

A new phase began when the private and NPVO owners left in 1994 and made the municipality the sole proprietor. That last and present (2012) phase began in 2010 when the Lindgren family (Astrid Lindgren herself died in 2002) insisted on taking over the ownership of ALW. Since the family already possessed all the copyrights associated with the author's work, this change meant that the ownership of ALW became an integrated part of the heritage of Astrid Lindgren.

We want to highlight two aspects of the making of the event park as a societal venture. To begin with, the construction and importance of a social capital originating in one person, Astrid Lindgren. The relations to her both enabled and restricted the venturing as an economic project. The second aspect has to do with the basic personal ideas of the author. Her key concern – to care for and protect children, all children, through her stories and through ALW – mainly relates to a rural context. Jointly, these two aspects pinpoint the importance of place as an emotional attractor and highlight the question of whether, and how, social and cultural capital become place-specific (cf. Borch et al., 2008; Sundin, 2011). The ALW case hints at another intriguing question: is it possible and desirable to create sustainable entrepreneurship that is not subject to tension and turbulence? A trajectory combining periods of stable change and disruptive movements appears to be the most reliable (re)construction of the long-term and successful development of ALW.

Macken: Environmental and Social Concern as a Business Challenge

In the social enterprise Macken, Bengt Johannisson tracks how societal entrepreneurship as a practice is enacted. The co-operative was established in 2005 by a journalist and teacher at the local folk high school with a passion for co-operative ideas and environmental protection. Starting with refurbishing feasible items from the municipal dump, additional social value is created by having Swedish craftsmen, who have been excluded for social or physical reasons from the labour market, team up with immigrant craftsmen with similar work experience. This arrangement empowers the marginalized members of both groups by re-establishing their self-respect on the job. In addition, the new Swedes learn their new culture and language in a supportive setting. Macken's operations also include a 'social' incubator for nascent entrepreneurs who can test their emerging venture as 'intrapreneurs' in Macken's business centre.

From its very start Macken had to put on an organizational dress characterized by improvisation and social *bricolage* (Barrett, 1998; Baker and Nelson, 2005; Johannisson and Olaison, 2007; Di Dominico et al., 2010). This mode of organizing made it possible to bridge between an overly bureaucratized public sector and a demanding private sector on one hand, and the constantly changing and specific needs and dreams of discriminated-against ethnic and new Swedes on the other. Macken's ambition to fill gaps in the elaborate Swedish societal texture invites continuous social and organizational innovativeness. The personal commitment of the 20-person staff and a generous voluntary sector, as well as further public European Union (EU) and Swedish funding, provide the human, social and financial capital needed for enacting Macken's mode of societal entrepreneurship.

After its formative years, Macken's organization has developed into a dual structure by combining the original organic and volatile informal practice with a structure including a professional financial administration and regular meetings with all personnel. The latter structure is to a great extent the outcome of the voluntary involvement of two business angels. The creative tension between their commercial experience and Macken's original social mission has made the business angels much more aware of values besides economic ones, and the volunteers at Macken have become more effective in the interest of their own social ambitions. Macken also has an active board with an external chairperson, and further supportive structures include coaches for the nascent entrepreneurs at the business centre and a broader network, 'Macken's Friends', that includes people from different constituencies in the regional context. The business centre itself is run as a joint venture with the municipality as a provider of needed financial capital. In return Macken offers new ways of operating public activities. It also inspires the market to find ways for turning social activities into commercial ones, for good or bad (cf. Miller and Wesley, 2010). In its own context, that of social enterprises, Macken in 2013 has become one of the franchisors in a national project that aims at enacting social franchising in Sweden.

SIP: Embodying the Practice of Societal Entrepreneurship

The network organization SIP (Societal change In Practice) studied by Erik Rosell has, in a way similar to that of Macken, over the years become a recognized platform for a diverse range of development projects. The organization has its base in Växjö, but the projects undertaken mobilize and reach people in the wider municipality, and sometimes even have national or international coverage.

It all started back in 2001–2002. A group of young people got together to organize what they all agreed were 'funny projects'. Among other things, art exhibitions and so called LAN (Local Area Network) parties,[3] were arranged. The informal group of youngsters soon drew the attention of the politicians in the region. 'If you start an association, we can support you', was the message from the local politicians when they visited a LAN party on New Year's Eve 2001. Soon after, the association Tech Group was established. The name signalled a focus on digital media, as this subject area was the basis for most of the projects that were initiated early on. For example, the project Computer Support at Home was launched, where young people helped senior citizens to solve computer problems at their homes. Another project was Girl Tech, where the initial aim was to support the use of digital media by teenage girls. Later the activities within the project broadened to include such areas as supporting entrepreneurship and leadership among young women, with the overall aim of promoting equality in society. The name Tech Group was changed to Societal change In Practice (SIP) in order to better reflect the broader scope of the association. The projects were now directed towards all kinds of social issues, such as equality, sustainability and the integration of social groups which in some way had been left outside mainstream society. For example, the Funkibator project, an incubator for people with physical handicaps, has been granted funding from the state.

Over time SIP developed into an organizer of social projects. Members of the SIP network constantly engage in new projects and involve new people and new associations in the network organization. They create arenas for their target groups and promote the sharing of experience, network building and development of joint visions of how to best promote a specific interest in society. By producing information material to target groups in society, SIP creates and communicates knowledge on subjects like entrepreneurship, equality between the sexes and other topics. When SIP presents itself, the fusion of entrepreneurial energy with a commitment to take responsibility for and actively engage in the development of our society becomes clear:

> Right now there are a great number of social changes going on, involving new thoughts blending with established ideas . . . To many people these changes seem intimidating. For us in SIP they mean endless opportunities to build a smarter and more fun society. SIP is always democratic and includes a great deal of cockiness and love. We DO and ARE what our name says. (www. natverketsip.se/omsip.php, 11 August 2009, Erik Rosell's translation)

SIP's message is obviously that everybody can make a change if they are given the opportunity to experiment, create and develop their personal interests.

REVISITING PROPOSED DUALITIES: LESSONS FROM THE FIELD

The seven narratives reveal several faces of societal entrepreneurship, a diversity which invites further reflection on the issues brought up in the introductory sections. The soci(et)al ventures approached, on the one hand, originate in the cracks and gaps in and between established structures and sectors; and on the other hand, bring promises of institutional change. The special concern in the narrations is how processes that cross the boundaries between the three sectors emerge and relate. In several cases, like Fair Trade, Public Markets and Macken, the shortcomings of the established sectors have been the main trigger for the initiative. This does not mean that the initiatives originate in intentional strategizing. The entrepreneurs on public markets are inspired by a combination of general concern about their professional field and personal curiosity. In other cases personal interest and 'play' have been mentioned by the agents themselves as the main motivations for getting involved. This is illustrated by the Ice Web, ALW and SIP cases. In the Moon House project the artist/ entrepreneur practised imagination and associated experimenting. Several stories demonstrate that the need for 'street smartness' is even greater in societal initiatives than in any commercial venture. This should not, however, come as a surprise, considering that many societal ventures are concerned with basic everyday-life challenges that, as much as speculative projecting, should be associated with entrepreneurship (see e.g. Steyaert and Katz, 2004).

Returning to the dualities introduced above, the co-existence of *Gemeinschaft* and *Gesellschaft* is especially salient in the Fair Trade case where the efforts to integrate social values and commercial activities combine with the ambition to limit the misuse of people and nature. The actors behind the Moon House try to redefine market-driven resources, not only financial and material, but also immaterial ones such as influence, and use them for artistic and existential purposes. Public Markets appears as an initiative to replace public sector activities with small-scale entrepreneurial ones that are able to bring professionals closer to those being cared for. The narratives testify that this does not have to be interpreted as another mode for the market to colonize society but can rather be seen as an attempt to reintroduce *Gemeinschaft*-oriented values and practices that contemporary urbanized modernization has eroded. Icy initiatives are constructed bottom-up as a movement guided by *Gemeinschaft* ideals and social cohesion, primarily caring for the safety of people enjoying what nature offers. *Gesellschaft* norms are adopted mainly to gain legitimacy. ALW can on the one hand be seen as an endeavour to transform symbolic resources into economic value, and on the other as using commercial venturing as a means for preserving a cultural *Gemeinschaft* heritage. Macken and SIP are both driven by the vision of a society where people who are marginalized by the rules of a *Gesellschaft*-oriented economy are brought back to the centre by way of practices that are guided by *Gemeinschaft* norms.

Entrepreneurial initiatives, whether soci(et)al or not, originate in a strong belief in human agency. Our narratives also suggest different ways of coping with existing and resisting structures. Measures include ignoring or exploiting them (SIP), forging a partnership with them (Macken), infiltrating and trying to change the structures from the inside (Public Markets) or building new structures (for example, the Ice Web). These cases accordingly demonstrate the affiliation between soci(et)al and institutional entrepreneurship. Still, while institutional entrepreneurship according to DiMaggio (1988) is resource driven and oriented towards the market, soci(et)al entrepreneurship is carried by the vision of creating a better world and of people being able to and responsible for doing that. The market is a tough competitor, as the Public Markets case demonstrates; or a great seducer, as we have learnt from the ALW story, whose success is based on its ability to create markets – albeit not intentionally to begin with.

The duality between individual and collective efforts appears in all cases. The Fair Trade story presents a small-scale female entrepreneur working on her own, yet collaborating with the collective Fair Trade certification organization in order to gain the necessary legitimacy. The Moon House project was enacted by a single entrepreneur but carried on very much as a collective effort, spontaneously crystallizing into an emerging structure out of intensive and expansive personal networking. Public Markets in the health sector was an entrepreneurial effort encouraged by a public sector initiative but actualized by a group of entrepreneurial nurses carried by personal commitment. The Ice Web appears more than the other cases as an original collective effort, very much depending, however, on the commitment of individual members with specific skills and contributions. ALW was envisioned and materialized by three families, that is, a second-order collective. Its ownership shifted several times over its existence but was until recently characterized by partnerships. In spite of this collective mobilization, ALW still remains closely tied to a single person – the author Astrid Lindgren – which motivates a dialogue between collectivism and individualism. Macken and SIP are driven by the idea of a democratic society and thus give much space for everyday entrepreneurship, which makes their operations appear as collectivistic endeavours. Nevertheless, on as well as behind the stage there are individuals who are filled with commitment and dedication to a social cause, using the organizations as arenas for their own identity-making. Even if soci(et)al entrepreneurship is considered to epitomize human collective effort and responsibility, its dependence on individual actors thus remains. Anything else would, as the saying goes, be like performing *Hamlet* the play without Hamlet the character.

Keeping it small and 'beautiful' guided the initiative behind Public Markets in the health sector as a reaction to pressure towards large-scale public markets. However, the small-scale operations that the story describes could not be protected against the offensive of big companies in the field. As much as for commercial ventures, quantitative growth is for societal entrepreneurial initiatives an indicator of success, at least a way to create visibility and legitimacy. Still, our stories also report resistance toward this pressure for growth. The Fair Trade case reports such experiences, although the small company has so far managed to ward off the attacks. The Ice Web operates on an (inter)national scale, but as a federation of independent clubs it has managed to balance local identity and smallness on the one hand, and the need for standardization and concerted large-scale operations on the other. Macken has established local subsidiaries and considers introducing a franchising concept that will make it into a national operation. At the same time its local social organization is being diversified and decentralized in order to keep each operation manageable. SIP combines local and national initiatives and presents itself as small or large according to what challenge is taken on. As a young organization inhabited by young people, SIP can adopt this experiential practice. The joint lesson from our stories is that by keeping the boundary between the soci(et)al projecting and the context fuzzy, smallness and largeness may coexist.

Finally, do these cases illustrate opportunity-driven or necessity-driven entrepreneurship? Initiatives like the Moon House, ALW and SIP appear as quite spontaneous initiatives driven by pleasure, by a wish to do something fun that also challenges existing institutions. In Sweden, as a welfare state, opportunity entrepreneurship dominates necessity entrepreneurship as defined by the market. Several of the initiatives we have studied also redefined the creation of societal values as opportunities, not just referring to such ambitions in order to gain legitimacy. The Moon House project made evident the need to widen our horizons in order to be able to create a new world (see Spinosa et al., 1997), and SIP established itself as a regular contributor to the local welfare system – which in line with Wijkström's and Einarsson's findings (2006) can be interpreted as a consequence of NPM strategies in many municipalities. In contrast, the Fair Trade venture originated in serious societal global concerns, while the Ice Web took off from national and public markets and Macken from local needs. Yet, all these specific initiatives were presented as both opportunities and opposition against the dominant order, reflecting responsibilities.

Not surprisingly, the insights gained in each case study vary considerably, something that the overview of the findings in Table 5.3 reminds us of. There the lessons from the stories told in the cases are summarized with respect to their proposed contributions to our understanding of societal entrepreneurship as creative and contextualized organizing. Our original dualities have, in our view, remained as relevant analytical tools to reflect upon these empirical experiences.

BEYOND DUALITIES AND CONTEXTUALITY AS NARRATED INQUIRIES INTO SOCIETAL ENTREPRENEURSHIP

Obviously the attachment to place remains across different forms of societal entrepreneurship in Sweden, but varies considerably with respect to how this attachment evolves, due to varying cultural embeddedness from the instigation of the societal venture to its present status. Our findings

Table 5.3   Comprehensive lessons from the empirical cases

	Fair Trade	The Moon House	Public Markets	The Ice Web
Outcomes of societal entrepreneurship	Fair trading and standardization as a contradictory practice across cultural and institutional orders	Ongoing balancing of tensions between creativity and imitation, provocation and resistance	Imported managerial standards closes the public sector to local initiatives	Strong sectors reduce the absorptive capacity for initiatives from below
	ALW	Macken	SIP	
Outcomes of societal entrepreneurship	The imprints of societal entrepreneurship pattern differently in long and short time perspectives	Organizational innovativeness creates a pressure for institutional change	Incessant societal venturing feeds inspiration, creativity and learning	

suggest that there is a need for further inquiry into how societal venturing establishes its own practices while emerging.

The making of societal entrepreneurship dressed as everyday operations demonstrates a special kind of dynamics. In order to identify its features our image of entrepreneurship has to be reconsidered. Steyaert (2007) argues that the social phenomenon that we study as genuinely processual should rightfully be addressed as 'entrepreneuring'. Accordingly, we elsewhere propose a practice framework as a proper conceptual base for further conceptual elaboration (Johannisson, 2011). The field research needed to reveal societal entrepreneuring as a practice must, as several cases attempt, apply a methodology that comes very close to those concerned. Only an adequate mode of inquiry makes it possible to reveal the micro-dynamics of how the structure and logic of the different sectors in society restrict, enforce and even enact societal entrepreneurship.

We thus argue that the dualities that the cases reveal, in the same way as paradoxes (cf. Van de Ven and Poole, 1988), offer an appropriate way of making a complex reality comprehensible. Keeping context in mind reminds us of the need to practise reflexivity in scientific work. If we argue with Czarniawska (2004: 6–10) that narratives in their own right represent (a kind of) knowledge, we become even more convinced that stories as told here provide an appropriate way of gaining insight into societal entrepreneurship. Through 'translation' our experiences can be applied to new settings (see Czarniawska and Sevón, 1996). While bluecopying is always impossible, especially in the context of entrepreneurial projecting (Johansson, 2010), analogy is generally feasible (Johannisson, 2011).

Studies of social and societal entrepreneurship obviously have the potential to give voice to actors and groups that are excluded from the established arenas as well as from the heroic stories of (market) entrepreneurs. What is more, our interactive approach, recognizing those enacting societal projects not just as interlocutors but as active contributors to a deeper understanding of societal entrepreneurship, brings those once marginalized into the centre of knowledge creation. The broad repertoire of field reports presented above also demonstrates that initiatives from below may create movements that not only bridge social and physical space, as the Fair Trade case demonstrates, but also mental space, as clearly illustrated by the Moon House project. Our contribution to the general field of entrepreneurship is thus to narrate how arenas for many other forms of entrepreneurship emerge out of and remain embedded in the societal texture.

Dominating discourses concerning society constrain the freedom and possibilities of actions for certain groups or kinds of people. Discourses tell us how things are expected to be done, what is possible and what is not, who is supposed to be responsible for what, and consequently who is included and who is excluded from the public debate. By being sensitive to groups of people who in some way feel marginalized, but also to their own ideas, arenas are created where alternative definitions are made and alternative voices heard. The change that new dialogues initiate inevitably means that contemporary societal structures are questioned and eventually rebuilt. Obviously, we need to reflect on the seminal article by William Baumol (1990) where he states that the way productive and unproductive as well as destructive entrepreneurship are distributed reflects the (national) institutional setting. If we recognize that entrepreneurial capabilities are evenly distributed over all nations and places, the limited commercial entrepreneurial activity instigated by Swedes is most probably due to their involvement in other kinds of entrepreneurship, not least societal ones, as we have tried to demonstrate here. Such a proposition definitely invites further research.

NOTES

1. The research reported here was carried out within OSIS (Organizing Societal Entrepreneurship in Sweden), a research programme financed by the Swedish Knowledge Foundation. A more elaborate report appears in Berglund et al. (2012).

2. Astrid Lindgren's works have been frequently analysed in both research (see e.g. Kümmerling-Meibauer and Surmatz, 2011) and the (Swedish) mass media. A research project taking a special interest in the cultural heritage of Astrid Lindgren was reported in 2010. In a volume edited by Leif Jonsson an original interpretation of ALW as a social enterprise was made by Bengt Johannisson and Elisabeth Sundin (2010).
3. A Local Area Network is a computer network that connects computers and people in a limited geographical area. A LAN party is an event where this technology is used, to play computer games.

REFERENCES

Achtenhagen, L. and L. Melin (2003), 'Managing the homogeneity–heterogeneity duality', in A. Pettigrew et al. (eds), *Innovative Forms of Organizing: An International Perspective*, London: Sage.

Adler, N., A.B. Shani and A. Styhre (eds) (2004), *Collaborative Research in Organizations: Foundations for Learning: Change and Theoretical Development*, Thousand Oaks, CA: Sage.

Baker, T. and R. Nelson (2005), 'Creating something from nothing: resource construction through entrepreneurial bricolage', *Administrative Science Quarterly*, 50(3), 329–66.

Barrett, F.J. (1998), 'Creativity and improvisation in jazz and organizations: implications for organizational learning', *Organization Science*, 9(5), 605–22.

Baumol, W.J. (1990), 'Entrepreneurship: productive, unproductive, and destructive', *Journal of Political Economy*, 98(5), 893–921.

Berggren, H. and L. Trägårdh (2009), *Är svensken människa: gemenskap och oberoende i det moderna Sverige*, Stockholm: Norstedt.

Berglund, K., M. Dahlin and A.W. Johansson (2007), 'Walking a tightrope between artistry and entrepreneurship – the stories of Hotel Woodpecker, Otter Inn and Luna Resort', *Journal of Enterprising Communities: People and Places in the Global Economy*, 1(3), 268–84.

Berglund, K. and J. Gaddefors (2010), 'Entrepreneurship requires resistance to be mobilized', in F. Bill, B. Bjerke and A.W. Johansson (eds), *(De)Mobilizing Entrepreneurship – Exploring Entrepreneurial Thinking and Action*, Cheltenham, UK and Northampton, MA, USA: Edward Elgar, pp. 140–57.

Berglund, K. and B. Johannisson (2012), 'Introduction: in the beginning was societal entrepreneurship', in K. Berglund, B. Johannisson and B. Schwartz (eds), *Societal Entrepreneurship – Positioning, Penetrating, Promoting*, Cheltenham, UK and Northampton, MA, USA: Edward Elgar, pp. 1–27.

Berglund, K., B. Johannisson and B. Schwartz (eds) (2012), *Societal Entrepreneurship – Positioning, Penetrating, Promoting*, Cheltenham, UK and Northampton, MA, USA: Edward Elgar.

Borch, O.J., A. Førde, L. Rønning, I.K. Vestrum and G.A. Alsos (2008), 'Resource configuration and creative practices of community entrepreneurship', *Journal of Enterprising Communities: People and Places in the Global Economy*, 2(2), 100–23.

Brunsson, N. and B. Jacobsson (eds) (2000), *A World of Standards*, Oxford: Oxford University Press.

Christensen, T. and P. Laegreid (2002), *New Public Management: The Transformation of Ideas and Practice*, Aldershot: Ashgate.

Czarniawska, B. (2004), *Narratives in Social Science Research*, London: Sage.

Czarniawska, B. (2009), 'Emerging institutions: pyramids or anthills?', *Organization Studies*, 30(4), 423–41.

Czarniawska, B. and G. Sevón (1996), *Translating Organizational Change*, Berlin: de Gruyter.

Dey, P. and C. Steyaert (2010), 'The politics of narrating social entrepreneurship', *Journal of Enterprising Communities: People and Places in the Global Economy*, 4(1), 85–108.

Di Dominico, M., H. Haugh and P. Tracey (2010), 'Social bricolage: theorizing social value creation in social enterprises', *Entrepreneurship Theory and Practice*, 34(4), 681–704.

DiMaggio, P. (1988), 'Interest and agency in institutional theory', in L. Zucker (ed.), *Institutional Patterns and Culture*, Cambridge, MA: Ballinger, pp. 3–22.

DiMaggio, P.J. and W.W. Powell (1983), 'The iron cage revisited: institutional isomorphism and collective rationality in organizational fields', *American Sociological Review*, 48(2), 147–60.

Dobers, P. and M. Halme (2009), 'Corporate social responsibility and developing countries', *Corporate Social Responsibility and Environmental Management*, Special Issue: CSR and Developing Countries Perspectives, 16(5), 237–49.

Eisenhardt, C. (1989), 'Building theories from case study research', *Academy of Management Review*, 14(4), 532–50.

Fairtrade, http://www.fairtrade.net/aims_of_fairtrade_standards.html (accessed 30 December 2010).

Flyvbjerg, B. (1991), *Rationalitet og magt*, Bind 1, Det konkretes videnskap, Copenhagen: Akademisk Forlag.

Garud, R., C. Hardy and S. Maguire (2007), 'Institutional entrepreneurship as embedded agency: an introduction to the special issue', *Organization Studies*, 28(7), 957–69.

GEM (2010), *Global Entrepreneurship Monitor*.

Giddens, A. (1984), *The Constitution of Society*, Cambridge: Polity Press.

Hardy, C. and S. Maguire (2008), 'Institutional entrepreneurship', in R. Greeenwood, C. Oliver, R. Suddaby and K. Sahlin (eds), *The Sage Handbook of Organizational Institutionalism*, Los Angeles, CA: Sage, pp. 218–42.

Holm, P. (1995), 'The dynamics of institutionalization: transformation processes in Norwegian fisheries', *Administrative Science Quarterly*, 40(3), 398–422.

Johannisson, B. (2014), 'The practice approach and interactive research in entrepreneurship and small-scale-venturing', in M. Brännback and A. Carsrud (eds), *Research Methods in Small Business*, Cheltenham, UK and Northampton, MA, USA: Edward Elgar.

Johannisson, B. (2011), 'Towards a practice theory of entrepreneuring', *Small Business Economics*, 36(2), 135–50.

Johannisson, B. and A. Nilsson (1989), 'Community entrepreneurship – leadership for local economic development', *Entrepreneurship and Regional Development*, 1, 1–19.

Johannisson, B. and L. Olaison (2007), 'The moment of truth – reconstructing entrepreneurship and social capital in the eye of the storm', *Review of Social Economy*, 65(1), 55–78.

Johannisson, B. and E. Sundin (2010), 'Astrid Lindgrens Värld', in L. Jonsson (ed.), *Astrid Lindgrens världar i Vimmerby, En studie om kulturarv och samhällsutveckling*, Lund: Nordic Academic Press, pp. 150–68.

Johannisson, B. and C. Wigren (2006), 'The dynamics of community identity making in an industrial district: the Spirit of Gnosjö revisited', in C. Steyaert and D. Hjorth (eds), *Entrepreneurship as Social Change: a Third Movements in Entrepreneurship Book*, Cheltenham, UK and Northampton, MA, USA: Edward Elgar, pp. 188–209.

Johansson, A.W. (2010), 'Innovation, creativity and imitation', in F. Bill, B. Bjerke and A.W. Johansson (eds), *(De)mobilizing the Entrepreneurship Discourse, Exploring Entrepreneurial Thinking and Action*, Cheltenham, UK and Northampton, MA, USA: Edward Elgar, pp. 123–39.

Kümmerling-Meibauer, B. and A. Surmatz (eds) (2011), *Beyond Pippi Longstocking. Intermedial and International Aspects of Astrid Lindgren's Works*, London, UK and New York, USA: Routledge.

Mair, J. and I. Martí (2006), 'Social entrepreneurship research: a source of explanation, prediction, and delight', *Journal of World Business*, 41(1), 36–44.

Miller, T.L. and C.L. Wesley II (2010), 'Assessing mission and resources of social change: an organizational identity perspective on social venture capitalists' decision criteria', *Entrepreneurship Theory and Practice*, 34(4),705–33.

Nicholls, A. (2010), 'The legitimacy of social entrepreneurship: reflexive isomorphism in a pre-paradigmatic field', *Entrepreneurship Theory and Practice*, 34(4), 611–33.

Nielsen, K.A. and L. Svensson (2006), *Action Research and Interactive Research: Beyond Practice and Theory*, Maastricht: Shaker.

Polkinghorne, D.E. (1988), *Narrative Knowing and the Human Sciences*, New York: State University.

Reason, P. and H. Bradbury (2001), 'Introduction', in P. Reason and H. Bradbury (eds), *Handbook of Action Research: Participative Inquiry and Practice*, Thousand Oaks, CA: Sage, pp. 1–14.

Ricoeur, P. (1984), *Time and Narrative*, Vol. 1, Chicago, IL: University of Chicago Press.

Sahlin-Andersson, K. (2006), 'Corporate social responsibility: a trend and a movement, but of what and for what?', *Corporate Governance Journal*, 6(5), 595–608.

Schumacher, E.F. (1975), *Small is Beautiful: A Study of Economics as if People Mattered*, New York: Harper & Row.

Schwartz, B. and K. Tilling (2009), '"ISO-lating" corporate social responsibility in the organizational context: a dissenting interpretation of ISO 26000', *Corporate Social Responsibility and Environmental Management*, Special Issue: CSR and Developing Countries Perspectives, 16(5), 289–99.

Spinosa, C., F. Flores and H. Dreyfus (1997), *Disclosing New Worlds: Entrepreneurship, Democratic Action and the Cultivation of Solidarity*, Cambridge, MA: MIT Press.

Statistics Sweden (2010), 'Women and men: figures and facts'.

Stenumgaard, P. and E.G. Larsson (2010), 'Robustness and capacity – two contradictory properties for wireless communications in security and crisis management', National Symposium on Technology and Methodology for Security and Crisis Management (TAMSEC), 27–28 October.

Steyaert, C. (2007), 'Entrepreneuring as a conceptual attractor? A review of process theories in 20 years of entrepreneurship studies', *Entrepreneurship and Regional Development*, 19(6), 453–77.

Steyaert, C. and J. Katz (2004), 'Reclaiming the space of entrepreneurship in society: geographical, discursive and social dimensions', *Entrepreneurship and Regional Development*, 116(3), 179–96.

Sundin, E. (2011), 'Entrepreneurship and social and community care', *Journal of Enterprising Communities: People and Places in the Global Economy*.

Sundin, E. and M. Tillmar (2008), 'A nurse and a civil servant changing institutions: entrepreneurial processes in different public sector organizations', *Scandinavian Journal Management*, 24, 113–24.

Thornton, P.A. and W. Ocasio (1999), 'Institutional logics and the historical contingency of power in organizations', *American Journal of Sociology*, 105(3), 801–43.

Tönnies, F. (1965), *Community and Association*, London: Routledge & Kegan Paul.

Van de Ven, A.H. and M.S. Poole (1988), 'Paradoxical requirements for a theory of change', in R.E. Quinn and K.S. Cameron (eds), *Paradox and Transformation, Toward a Theory of Change in Organization and Management*, Cambridge, MA: Ballinger, pp. 19–63.

Wijkström, F. (2011), '"Charity speak and business talk", the on-going hybridization of civil society', in F. Wijkström and A. Zimmer (eds), *Nordic Civil Society at a Cross-Roads, Transforming the Popular Movement Tradition*, Baden-Baden: Nomos, pp. 27–54.

Wijkström, F. and T. Einarsson (2006), *Från nationalstat till näringsliv? Det civila samhällets organisationsliv i förändring*, Stockholm: EFI.

6. Public servants as sustainability policy entrepreneurs in Australia: the issues and outcomes

Ganesh Keremane, Jennifer McKay and Zhifang Wu

INTRODUCTION

Freshwater and its allocation between competing users and uses has always been conflict ridden, but the intensity of these conflicts has escalated in recent history because of increased urbanization, changes in diet, increased population and several local factors (Dirksen, 2002). The escalation of conflict in Australia has been the result of relatively recent policies since 1994 that require ecologically sustainable development (ESD) to be pursued. This in practice means that the environment is now a player and must be considered in water allocation processes (McKay, 2010). Australia has several well-developed state and national processes to incorporate this policy, and the technique selected is the regional water allocation plan. These are set up under several state laws and in practice require communication with existing water users as to setting limits on extraction to be within the ESD rule. For example in South Australia, which has the most comprehensible approach to water management in Australia, the water allocation plans are developed by the Natural Resources Management Board (NRMB) with significant contributions from the community in the region to address ESD principles of the *Natural Resources Management Act*, 2004 (Hughes and McKay, 2009). After several iterations based on community feedback the Minister for Environment and Conservation (currently Minister for Sustainability, Environment and Conservation) approves the final plan for implementation by the NRMB.

However there will be conflicts over reduced or changed water allocations as agreed on in the plan. This is where the role of sustainability policy entrepreneurs becomes important. As observed by Hughes and McKay (2009) the regions that achieve less conflict in water plan adoption are those with some key policy entrepreneurs in situ. Hence the goal of this chapter is to elucidate the role of sustainability policy entrepreneurs in the context of the adoption of changes to water allocations in a region. The data used in our study is based on an internet survey of the water planners in Australia and a case study based on intensive interviews with key actors. The internet survey was conducted in order to understand what role water planners as sustainability policy entrepreneurs play in achieving ESD and its implementation across Australia. The survey findings are then supplemented by a case study focusing on individual(s) within governmental bureaucracies who help or influence a policy change process; in this case, adoption of a water allocation plan in the south-east of South Australia. A brief review on policy entrepreneurs and their role in the policy process is presented before the actual empirical results.

POLICY ENTREPRENEURS AND THEIR ROLE IN THE POLICY PROCESS

The terms 'entrepreneur' and 'entrepreneurship' have been appearing in the public policy and management literatures since the 1960s (Roberts and King, 1989) and since then entrepreneurs have been described in many different ways: as policy entrepreneurs, political entrepreneurs, programme entrepreneurs, bureaucratic entrepreneurs, administrative and executive entrepreneurs, and issue entrepreneurs (Roberts and King, 1989); and as change agents, policy advocates, boundary spanners and visionary leaders (Huitema and Meijerink, 2009; Huitema et al., 2011). Roberts and King (1989) separated public entrepreneurs into four different types in terms of their behavioural patterns: (1) political entrepreneurs, who hold elected leadership positions in government; (2) executive entrepreneurs, who hold appointed leadership positions in government; (3) bureaucratic entrepreneurs, who hold formal positions in government, although not leadership positions; and (4) policy entrepreneurs, who work from outside the formal governmental system to introduce, translate and implement innovative ideas into public sector practice.

In the present case the focus is on water planners, who as Teodoro (2009) describes, are public agency administrators and/or high-profile appointed officials promoting a particular public policy (Howard, 2001). The most common term used to describe these individuals in the public policy and management literatures is bureaucratic entrepreneurs. Teske and Schneider (1994: 3) describe bureaucratic entrepreneurs as 'actors who help propel dynamic policy change in their community'. Huitema et al. (2011: 718) note that bureaucratic policy entrepreneurs instigate, implement and sometimes block transitions; they describe them as individuals from within government seeking change, who may be politicians or bureaucrats. Crow (2010) describes them as individuals who promote policy change, and the people who influence the policy process effectively. These individuals can affect shifts in water resource management through a set of strategies, such as advocating new ideas, defining and reframing problems, coalition building, mobilizing public opinion, network management and specifying policy alternatives (Roberts and King, 1991; Huitema and Meijerink, 2009). They invest their time, knowledge and skills into instigating and implementing a policy change (Huitema et al., 2011) and have energies and talents that could influence alternative spheres of political activity (Schneider and Teske, 1992: 737).

According to Howard (2001), in Australian public policy literature the focus has largely been on the entrepreneurial activity in areas of government, and policy entrepreneurs are often identified as elected representatives or high-profile appointed officials. The author describes them as 'administrative entrepreneurs' who are non-elected officials, who work inside of government to move policy solutions, and at times attempt to compensate for a lack of interest in a policy issue on the part of elected representatives. In this case the focus is on water planners who are appointed officials, who have adopted the sustainable development philosophy placed in all Australian water and other natural resource laws since 1992 (NWC, 2004; McKay, 2005). Therefore in our study we call them 'sustainability policy entrepreneurs'.

In Australia sustainability policy entrepreneurs can be clustered into two groups (McKay, 2010): (1) informal entrepreneurs (including public servants at local and regional level, state-based public servants, Commonwealth-based public servants, members of industry or commodity groups or water user groups, and members of environmental groups); and (2) formal court-based officers. Therefore, 'sustainability policy entrepreneurs' for the purpose of this research refers to local-level and state-based public servants who go beyond their job to unite the region and its communities of water users and in so doing influence water policy transitions. Furthermore, the status quo is that the relevant department administering the water legislation in each state is responsible for preparing the water plans; and the water planners using best available science, social and economic analysis and community input prepare the water allocation plans to accommodate and fulfil the legal requirements to achieve ESD. The next section has more discussion about ESD and the classification of sustainability policy entrepreneurs in Australia.

However not all bureaucrats meet these requirements. According to Teodoro (2009), career mobility affects the probability of administrators and bureaucrats emerging as policy entrepreneurs. He further argues that the likelihood of them initiating innovations in their agencies is directly related to their professional involvement. Furthermore, these individuals cannot influence the policy change process on their own (Roberts and King, 1991): they need to build policy networks with the other members of the policy-making community to 'build their credibility and determine what arguments will persuade others to support their policy ideas' (Mintrom, 1997: 739).

Roberts and King (1991: 151) point out that policy entrepreneurs participate in the first three stages: develop a new idea, translate it into a more formal statement (such as a proposal, bill or law), and then help to implement it into public practice as a new programme. Teske and Schneider (1994) are cautious about the role of bureaucratic policy entrepreneurs in the policy process and suggest that 'even though entrepreneurs play a critical role in importing and formulating new policies, ultimately their success is tied to how well policies are carried out' (p. 332). Therefore it is important to research the factors influencing the adoption of any policy change, the present case being the adoption of changes to water allocations in the south-east of South Australia.

ECOLOGICALLY SUSTAINABLE DEVELOPMENT AND CLASSIFICATION OF SUSTAINABILITY POLICY ENTREPRENEURS IN AUSTRALIA

There is now a history of 17 years in the use of the term 'ecologically sustainable development' (ESD) in Australian policy. This was heavily influenced by the 1987 publication of *Our Common Future* and its definition of sustainable development (Brundtland, 1987). In addition, the international environmental movement in the late 1980s and early 1990s also prompted the Australian government to commission working groups to determine how ESD could be implemented locally. As a result the National Strategy for Ecologically Sustainable Development (NSESD) was released in 1992, which is the most prominent first use of the term in an official Australian context. The Strategy defined ESD as 'using, conserving and enhancing the community's resources so that ecological processes, on which life depends, are maintained, and the total quality of life, now and in the future, can be increased' (NSESD, 1992).

About water resources management in Australia, the Strategy articulates the challenge as 'to develop and manage in an integrated way, the quality and quantity of surface and groundwater resources, and to develop mechanisms for water resource management which aim to maintain ecological systems while meeting economic, social and community needs'. To address this challenge the National Water Initiative (NWI) which is Australia's blueprint for water reform, includes objectives and commitments to specific actions across eight interrelated elements of water management; and the first objective is to 'prepare water plans with provision for the environment' (NWC, 2004). Consequently, the mechanism used to achieve ESD within the water sector has been legally mandated regional water allocation plans. Hence, each state has set in train different processes to achieve ESD; the principal legislation applicable to each state and territory are also different, and so are the type of plans (see Table 6.1).

The responsibility for preparing the water plans in most states is with the relevant department administering the water legislation, except in South Australia where the Natural Resources Management Boards are charged with the responsibility (Hamstead et al., 2008). Ultimately, it is the water planners who prepare the water allocation plans to accommodate and fulfil the legal requirements to achieve ESD; hence they have been made sustainability policy entrepreneurs by statute (McKay, 2010). The classification of sustainability policy entrepreneurs in Australia includes two groups: the first are the informal entrepreneurs who recognize demand for innovations and then expend resources and take risks to make policy (Teodoro, 2009). The second group are the formal court-based officers (McKay, 2010) who are bound by rules of judicial practice and will not be discussed here. Suffice it to say that some judges become very activist in promoting the ideal of the law and adopt wide, expansive views of the concept of sustainable development; and others less so (Preston, 2010). Hence this classification looks at the criteria as going above and beyond their job to promote the water plan in a region which will generally reduce water allocations to all users. The focus of this study is informal entrepreneurs and McKay (2011) suggests there are six groups of informal sustainability policy entrepreneurs in Australia. However this chapter focuses on one group: public servants who mostly function at the local, regional and/or state level.

POLICY ENTREPRENEURS' ROLE IN ADOPTION OF CHANGES TO WATER ALLOCATIONS: EMPIRICAL INSIGHTS

To better understand the role of sustainability policy entrepreneurs in the context of the adoption of changes to water allocations, the empirical study involved two components: (1) an internet survey of water planners in all Australian states and territories; and (2) a case study conducted in the south-east region of South Australia, commonly referred to as the Limestone Coast. The focus is on implementing the Lower Limestone Coast Water Allocation Plan (LLCWAP).

Table 6.1   Principal water management agencies and laws applicable to each state and territory

State/ territory	Lead jurisdictional body for water management	Principal legislation	Type of plan
Australian Capital Territory	Environment ACT	Water Resources Act 1998	Water resources management plan
New South Wales	Department of Natural Resources	Water Management Act 2000; Water Act 1912	Water sharing plan
Northern Territory	Department of Natural Resources, Environment and the Arts	Water Act 1992	Water allocation plan
Queensland	Department of Natural Resources, Mines and Water	Water Act 2000; Wild Rivers Act 2005; Integrated Planning Act 1997	Water resource plan
South Australia	Department of Water (now part of DEWNR)	Natural Resources Management Act 2004; Groundwater (Border Agreement) Act 1985	Water allocation plan
Tasmania	Department of Primary Industries and Water	Water Management Act 1999	Water management plan
Victoria	Department of Sustainability and Environ- ment	Water Act 1989; Groundwater (Border Agreement) Act 1985	Regional sustainable water strategies
Western Australia	Department of Water	Rights in Water and Irrigation Act 1914	Water management plan/water allocation plan

Source: National Water Commission (2011).

While the survey findings provide the water planners' perspective about the complex water planning process and the challenges faced while negotiating the changes in water allocation with the introduction of new users such as the environment, the case study demonstrates how individuals within governmental bureaucracies can influence adoption of a water allocation plan in a region; the Lower Limestone Coast in this case.

An Internet Survey of Informal Sustainability Policy Entrepreneurs in Australia

Water management in Australia is a complex process that falls within the power of the states, and hence there are many laws. The governance arrangements are complex with at least 14 different types of legal forms of water supply businesses (McKay, 2007: 151). Furthermore, the water governance structures have undergone notable transformation since the 1994 Council of Australian Government (COAG) reforms, and since then the Australian states have been directed to achieve ESD; the means used to achieve ESD has been legally mandated regional water allocation plans. Therefore an internet survey of water in various water management regions of Australia was conducted.

The respondents were selected as expert professionals involved in the planning process in various water management authorities around the country. They all held senior positions in their organization or department – Director, Policy and Planning; Senior Policy Officer; Senior Water Planning Officer; Manager, Water Planning – and had university or postgraduate degrees in subjects including environmental science, hydrology, law and geography, water science and business administration. All of them were involved in developing and implementing the water plans in their regions and had close links with the local communities, guaranteeing a sufficient involvement of local communities in relevant water planning processes in their region.

Initial contact with the respondents was established by a snowballing exercise and thorough desk research of the information available in print or published on the website of the respective state departments dealing with water planning. As a result, a list of 40 potential respondents was generated who were then contacted via telephone and/or email to check their availability and interest in participating in the study. This exercise was time-consuming because states like Queensland and Victoria were battling with floods when the study was initiated. Additionally, the Australian public sector (APS) reforms, particularly the project related to strengthening the workforce by encouraging employees to expand

Table 6.2   State-wise break-up of the respondents

State or territory	No. of potential participants	No. of final respondents
Australian Capital Territory	1	1
New South Wales	11	6
Northern Territory	3	0
Queensland	4	2
South Australia	8	6
Tasmania	6	2
Victoria	4	3
Western Australia	3	3
Total	40	23

their career experience, has led to changes in work location (for example, interdepartmental moves) and changes in work type (for example, from policy to service delivery) (Moran, 2010). Consequently, the people who were initially involved in water planning in these states and territories had either changed their work location or work type and were not available. Therefore getting the list of water planners was challenging, resulting in a relatively low number of respondents (Table 6.2).

The survey asked planners cast in the role of drafting the water allocation plans questions related to different aspects of Australian water management, such as federalism equity and sustainability in Australian water management (Keremane et al., 2012). But keeping in mind the goal of this chapter, only the findings related to water planners' perceptions about the issues and/or challenges in achieving sustainable water management and allocation in Australia are discussed below.

Even though water institutions in Australia are far more advanced than in many other countries, in the context of achieving ESD there are still some aspects that are yet to be fully achieved. The federal and the state governments recognize that there is no identifiable point where they can say that they have achieved ESD. For that reason, the survey asked the water planners:

- What are the major obstacles to achieve sustainable water management in your region?
- Which sector and/or factors shape and direct sustainable water management and allocation in your region?
- How much effort is put into and what is the level of difficulty in achieving the ESD principles?

Table 6.3   Obstacles to achieving sustainable water management and allocation

Obstacles to achieving sustainable water management and allocation	Ranking order	Factors directing sustainable water resource management	Ranking order
Conflict between different user groups	1	Environmental concerns	1
		Community perception	2
Limited supply of water	2	Financial pressure	3
Poor coordination between government agencies and departments	3	Powerful and influential individuals	4
Complexity of regulations and compliance regimens	3		
Poor economic return on irrigated products	4		

Note: The ranking order is based on ordinal ranking technique used to create a score by reversing the number order.

The water planners were presented with rank order type questions, and the results are discussed below.

Conflict between different user groups was considered to be the major obstacle, followed by limited supply of water (Table 6.3). This can be attributed to the worst drought to hit Australia, in 2006, which had an adverse impact on water availability and a profound influence on policy decisions in Australia, thereby causing hardship for rural and urban communities (Beeton et al., 2006). Conflicts over water allocation in Australia can be for different reasons. Bowmer (2007) lists a few, such as costing and pricing; paying for infrastructure when no water is delivered; exit fees imposed by irrigation corporations; effects of water trading on health of regional communities; conditions under which environmental water might be purchased from irrigators; rural to urban transfers; and the use of water for electricity generation across state borders. Irrespective of the reasons for conflict, sustainability policy entrepreneurs play a very important role in resolving the conflicts. They invest their time, knowledge and skills into resolving these conflicts through stakeholder negotiations before a water plan can be adopted (MacDonald and Young, 2000). They are able to do this because of their close links with the communities developed over time, and also their networks with the other members of the policy-making community (Roberts and King, 1991; Mintrom, 1997). Poor coordination between government agencies and departments, and the complexity of regulations and compliance regimes, were pointed out as other important factors impeding achieving ESD and sustainable water management.

The water planners were asked similar questions about the factors directing sustainable water resource management in their region (Table 6.3). The respondents identified 'environment' as being the major factor. Respondents reckoned community perceptions about sustainability in general and water management in particular were the next important factor directing sustainable water management in Australia. This is mainly because when drafting a water plan or policy, the planners place more emphasis on the environmental dimensions of sustainability, because they are bound by the legal requirements to achieve ESD introduced into Australian law in the form of the Intergovernmental Agreement on the Environment, 1992 and the related National Strategy on Ecologically Sustainable Development (McKay, 2010). On the other hand, from a community perspective water in regional communities is commonly linked with the social dimensions of sustainability: that is, ensuring communities have enough water to remain healthy and sustain their lifestyle (Wright, 2002). But all the dimensions of sustainability – social, economic and environmental – are intrinsically related, and therefore any water planning or policy development process should take into account all three dimensions of sustainability.

Case Study: Implementation of the Lower Limestone Coast Water Allocation Plan

This section presents a case study of a policy transition to regulate forestry water use in the south-east of the South Australia region with particular reference to implementing the Lower Limestone Coast Water Allocation Plan (LLCWAP). The case study demonstrates how a window of opportunity (for example, review of the water allocation plan, stakeholder conflicts, intensity of water use) was utilized by sustainability policy entrepreneurs to initiate a change process to encourage progress towards sustainable water management in the region.

The data was collected by interviewing key actors from within governmental bureaucracies who have played important roles in achieving this policy change. These individuals, as sustainability policy entrepreneurs, led a discussion amongst the key stakeholders to try to reach a policy position relating to the inclusion of forestry in the water allocation plans that was acceptable to all parties. They were able to exercise influence over the policy process because they were able to gather political and managerial support resulting from their strategic social and policy networks (Taylor et al., 2011). In addition, South Australia is considered a leader in reform within Australia, taking the lead on many policy issues including water management, and so provides valuable opportunities for analysis. The state also has the most coherent approach of the Australian states to water management (Hughes and McKay, 2009).

The context

The south-east of South Australia (also known as the Limestone Coast region) covers an area of approximately 28 000 sq. km bounded by the Victorian border to the east, the Southern Ocean to the south and the Coorong to the west. The region relies heavily on its unique groundwater resources which include two extensive regional aquifer systems separated by a clay aquitard: (1) the unconfined aquifer which is the principal resource for municipal, industrial and irrigation water use; and (2) the confined aquifer utilized mainly for municipal needs, and to a lesser extent for agricultural needs. The key economic activities supported by these resources include plantation forestry, viticulture, agriculture, dairy and aquaculture (SENRMB, 2012). But forestry plantations in the region expanded rapidly due to the federal government's Managed Investment Scheme (MIS) that allowed tax deductions for contributions to forestry Managed Investment Schemes. This induced rapid land use change and created pressure on the local water resources, resulting in water table decline. Therefore since the 1970s groundwater regulation via prescription of the water resources has been introduced in the state of South Australia. According to the *Natural Resources Management Act* 2004 [Sec 76(1)], where a water resource has been prescribed the respective regional Natural Resources Management Board (NRMB) – in this case the South East NRMB – should prepare a water allocation plan (WAP) for each of the prescribed water resources in its region. The Act also requires that the NRMB reviews the plan at least once during each period of five years following its adoption (*NRM Act* 2004, Sec 81). See Box 6.1 for more details about water planning in South Australia.

Meanwhile, the Intergovernmental Agreement on a National Water Initiative (NWI) also required significant water intercepting activities including forestry plantations to be accounted for and managed (NWC, 2004). Therefore, the review of the LLCWAP provided a window of opportunity to initiate a policy change that recognizes forestry as a water-affecting activity which therefore should be accounted for and be licensed like other water users in the region. This plan is the result of merging the operational plans for Comaum-Caroline, Lacepede Kongorong and Naracoorte Ranges into a single new plan for the Lower Limestone Coast Prescribed Wells Area (PWA). The entire development process is complex and has run since 2004 (see Table 6.4).

BOX 6.1   WATER PLANNING IN SOUTH AUSTRALIA

Water planning at regional level in South Australia was mentioned in the Water Resources Act 1990 and Catchment Water Management Act 1995. However it was clearly defined in the Water Resources Act 1997 (sections 101 and 107) and the Act also introduced the term 'Water Allocation Plan (WAP)' and established that a permit was required for any water-affecting activities including commercial forestry (with the amendment of the Act in 2004). Currently, water resources management in South Australia is governed by the Natural Resources Management Act 2004 (implemented from July 2005) which replaced the Water Resources Act 1997 and also introduced further changes required by the National Water Initiative (NWI) signed by the COAG in 2004.

Currently there are 27 prescribed water resources in South Australia; 20 of the prescribed water resources have existing water allocation plans, four are managed under the Water Resources (Penrice Exemption) Regulation 1997, and water allocation plans are being prepared for the remaining areas.

Water allocation plans set the principles or rules under which consumptive pools, entitlements and allocations are created. They also set out the water-affecting activities that require a permit or approval, such as drilling a bore or constructing a dam. The Department for Water (DFW) assists NRM boards in the preparation of water allocation plans by providing data (hydrogeological and hydrological) and advice about licensing, permits, legislation, policy and intergovernmental agreements. The NRM Act 2004 requires, for any WAP, a public consultation once the plan has been drafted consisting of a public meeting and written submissions (section 79). Accordingly, once the NRM board prepare a draft WAP, the community is consulted on the draft plan and the Minister is required to consider all submissions prior to adoption of the draft plan. Once community consultation has been completed, WAPs are adopted by the relevant Minister and they then become government policy.

Source: http://www.waterforgood.sa.gov.au/water-planning/ (accessed 27 November 2013).

Nevertheless, the focus in this context is more on the period from 2008, because until then the development process at the local level was deadlocked (see Table 6.4). This happened because of two things: (1) the absence of legislation to enable the government to license forestry, which meant there was a need to make legislative changes to the existing *NRM Act* 2004; and (2) strong opposition from the forestry lobby groups in the region to the science explaining the impact of commercial forestry on the region's groundwater resources. They dismissed the findings of Benyon and Doody (2004) who reported that there was compelling evidence to prove that commercial forestry causes reductions in run-off through interception of the canopy and also through draw-down on shallow aquifers. As a result the then Minister for Water sought a whole-of-government approach and decided to form

Table 6.4   History of the development of LLC WAP to account for forestry water use

2004	June: LLC WAP review process began, development of the Concept Statement to amend the 2001 LLC WAP to provide for regulating forestry water use
	October: Community information and consultation based on the Concept Statement
2005	September: A1 Community consultation for the draft LLC WAP
2006	May–December: Forestry facilitated stakeholder process held as part of the LLC WAP review
	July: Volumetric conversion reports released
2007	December: A2 consultation on the draft LLC WAP 2008
	November: Meeting between farming groups and Minister for Forests regarding LLC WAP
	December: Meeting between farming groups and Environment Minister and establishment of an Inter-Departmental Committee (IDC) to review state policy on forestry water use
2008	**Transition of Policy Development Process**
	Establishment of an IDC to review state policy on forestry water use
2009	June: IDC releases state-wide policy framework for managing the water resource impacts of plantation forests and Introduction in Parliament of the NRM (Commercial Forestry) Bill 2009
2010	February: Establishment of the LLC WAP Taskforce
	March: South Australian state elections
	September: Establishment of a Reference Group consisting of 8 local industry representatives
	November: NRM (Commercial Forests) Amendment Bill 2010 reintroduced in Parliament
2011	July–September: Debate in Parliament on the NRM (Commercial Forests) Amendment Bill 2010
	September: NRM (Commercial Forests) Amendment Bill 2010 introduced in the Legislative Council
	November: Second reading of the NRM (Commercial Forests) Amendment Bill 2010 and the Legislative Council agreed to the bill and NRM (Commercial Forests) Amendment Act 2011 is passed
2012	February: Lower Limestone Coast Water Allocation Plan Policy Principles released
	May–July: LLCWAP Reference Group formed, Reference Group met for a series of workshops and provided recommendations to the SE NRM Board for their consideration when deciding policy for inclusion into the draft amended LLC WAP
2013	Public consultation on the draft amended LLC WAP

Sources: SENRMB and personal interviews with key actors.

an interdepartmental committee (IDC) to look into this matter. This marked the beginning of the transition of the policy development process from the local to the state level, and also the time when policy entrepreneurs employed strategies such as recognizing and exploiting windows of opportunity and orchestrating and managing networks (Huitema and Meijerink, 2010) in influencing the change process. Here it is important to note that even though water planners are made sustainability policy entrepreneurs by statute, not all meet the requirements of 'policy entrepreneurs' discussed in the previous section. Only a few go above and beyond their job description to promote the water plan in a region, and the people interviewed during this study fit in that category. They were able to have influence because of intrinsic motivation and commitment rather than their formal job description (Howell and Higgins, 1990). Figure 6.1 presents the stages of the transition process and indicates the strategies employed by policy entrepreneurs to achieve the desired outcome of a policy change.

The approach
As discussed earlier in the chapter, policy entrepreneurs are individuals (or groups) who play a critical role in driving a process to effect change, and in the context of Australian water management this is called the 'champion phenomenon' (Commonwealth of Australia, 2002). Irrespective of the change or transition they are involved in, the approach or the process of influence is mostly similar, and involves establishing direction, aligning resources, generating motivation and providing inspiration (Taylor et al., 2011). This is similar to the 'model of influence' (see Cohen and Bradford, 2005) which was developed by the authors as a guide to create win–win situations when dealing with individuals, groups or organizations with different viewpoints, as in the present case of regulating forestry in the south-east. The water and forestry debate in the south-east involves multiple stakeholders – farmers, the forestry industry, the NRMB, the state government, urban water users, politicians – and finding common ground was always going to be difficult. Nevertheless, this was achieved due to the efforts of policy entrepreneurs who went above and beyond their formal job description to build bridges between the stakeholder groups. The result is a most impressive and world-leading legislation that recognizes forestry as a water-affecting activity and is now accounted for in the water plans of the south-east.

To quote the words of one policy entrepreneur representing the Department for Water (now part of the Department of Environment, Water and Natural Resources (DEWNR)), who played a key role in the entire process:

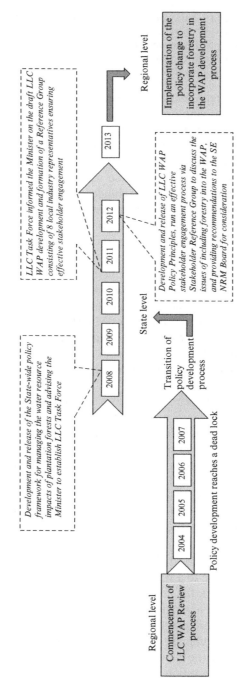

Note: The call-outs indicate the contributions by sustainability policy entrepreneurs at different stages of policy development.

Figure 6.1 Forestry policy change process in the south-east of South Australia and influence of policy entrepreneurs

Policies cannot be done in a dark room. We have to connect with the people, listen to their concerns, and work with them to reaching [*sic*] an acceptable solution. Accordingly, in this case we listened to [forestry] industry concerns, worked with all stakeholders, took time to resolve matters of principle, and kept early conversations at the outcome level.

As another key actor representing the department pointed out during the interviews: 'The underlying objective is to balance the triple bottom line issues, i.e. manage the water resources sustainably. To achieve this, the mentality of winners and losers needed to be replaced by identifying acceptable outcome [*sic*] for all parties.'

Thus, one thing that is clear from these statements is that the key strategy is effective community and stakeholder engagement (Xu et al., 2013). The National Water Commission agrees, and in its 2011 assessment report (NWC, 2011: 7) the Commission recommends 'recognizing the value of local knowledge and the importance of regional implementation, and review [*sic*] institutional arrangements and capacity to enable effective engagement at the local level'. This is an approach which the South Australian government has already adopted in the case of the South-East. The federal government now acknowledges the importance of tapping into local knowledge and the Water Minister Tony Burke (2013) recently announced the plan to recruit six Commonwealth Environmental Water local engagement officers in the basin states who will be based in local communities and work with the locals on how best to use the environmental water.

Although the approach appears simple, it is not so easy. According to Cohen and Bradford (2005: 17), 'a more deliberate and conscious approach is needed, including careful diagnosis of the other's interests, assessment of what resources you possess, and paying attention to the relationship with all parties involved'. In the present case, this was achieved through various initiatives at the state level (see Table 6.4) including forming the Water Resources and Forests Inter-Departmental Committee (IDC), the Lower Limestone Coast (LLC) Taskforce, and a Reference Group with members representing different peak industry bodies in the region to advise the LLC task force. Forming an IDC was a very important milestone in the entire process because it revived the whole LLCWAP policy development process that had come to a standstill. It was the IDC that released a state-wide policy framework for managing the water resource impacts of plantation forests in 2009. This framework supported the licensing of commercial forests in areas where plantation forests have a significant impact on water resources at a catchment and sub-catchment scale. Forming an LLC Taskforce to manage the water impacts of plantation forestry in the region was also an IDC suggestion.

Even though the IDC recommended 'licensing of commercial forests' there was no enabling legislation to implement this policy. This required making legislative changes to the existing *Natural Resources Management Act (NRM Act* 2004); accordingly the *Natural Resources Management (Commercial Forests) Amendment Bill* 2010 was first introduced to parliament in June 2009 and the *Natural Resources Management (Commercial Forests) Amendment Act*, 2011 was passed in November 2011. The forest water licensing and permit systems were designed to integrate with existing water licences and permits under the *NRM Act*. This supports the earlier argument that policy entrepreneurs alone cannot bring about a policy change. As evidenced in this case, other factors such as organizational capacity, legislative professionalism and policy networks also play important roles in influencing the adoption of changes to water allocations in a region. Even though key actors played an important role this would not have been possible without the legislative changes made to the *NRM Act* 2004. Equally important is having suitable policy networks. In this case the IDC and the Taskforce had representatives from the Department of the Premier and Cabinet, the DEWNR (then known as Department of Water, Land and Biodiversity Conservation), and the Department of Primary Industries and Resources SA (PIRSA), South East Natural Resources Management Board (SENRMB) and the Department of Treasury and Finance, ensuring a whole-of-government approach was in place. In addition, the Reference Group to the Taskforce included representatives from peak industry bodies from the forestry, wine, dairy, potato and dryland farming industries to ensure all stakeholders were involved in the process.

The other important milestone has been the release of Lower Limestone Coast Water Allocation Plan Policy principles providing the guidance for the SENRMB on drafting the LLCWAP. The LLC Taskforce in consultation with the Reference Group was responsible for preparing the Lower Limestone Coast Water Allocation Plan Policy Issues Discussion Paper. Following public consultation on the Discussion Paper, the policies put forward were amended after further discussion with the LLC Taskforce and Reference Group. In February 2012, the final Lower Limestone Coast Water Allocation Plan Policy Principles were released by the Minister for Sustainability, Environment and Conservation (hereafter: the Minister). These included the high-level Policy Principles and more specific guidelines related to water resources and plantation management, providing the guidance for the SENRMB on drafting the LLCWAP. During this period the Taskforce organized another independent science review (even though the science had been independently reviewed by the IDC in 2009), mainly to address the constant opposition by the forestry lobby groups.

The implementation
Following the release of the Policy Principles, the development of the LLCWAP was transferred back to the SENRMB which then formed the LLCWAP Reference Group, a formal subcommittee to assist in developing water policy options. The Reference Group has met several times to review water allocation plans, and the draft LLCWAP has been submitted to the Minister for approval. The LLCWAP was adopted by the Minister on 26 November 2013.

CONCLUSIONS

In the present era of climate change, sustainable management and development of water resources is important to preparing societies' ability to adapt and increase resilience to climate change uncertainty. This requires policy and governance shifts, and changes in the way water concerns are addressed, including the adoption of changes to water allocations. In this context, the role of policy entrepreneurs – individuals representing the decision-makers, the bureaucrats – will be crucial. Accordingly our study examined the role of policy entrepreneurs in designing a public policy while focusing on strategies and innovations to encourage sustainable water management in Australia.

The findings of the internet survey show water planners' perspectives about the complex water planning process and the challenges faced while negotiating changes in water allocation to achieve ESD. The results reveal that while water planners agree that water plans are the right way to approach sustainable water policy in Australia, they raise some concerns about the development of the water plan, such as unfairness in the processes for public consultation, lack of use of local knowledge and uncertainties in the science. These findings echo some of the NWC assessment report findings, such as 'objectives specified in plans need to be clear and measurable' (NWC, 2011).

The case study focuses on showing how context (for example, water conflicts) influences the contribution of policy entrepreneurs in South Australia, and the strategies used to achieve sustainable water management in their jurisdiction. It touches upon the concerns raised during the internet survey in that it shows how a transparent and enhanced consultation process can tackle the challenges highlighted by the water planners. The case study also elucidates how policy transition is an evolving process, and that sustainability policy entrepreneurs have a key role in shaping policy outcomes, and they have to do more than what their job or position demands. At the same time, it is also evident that policy entrepreneurs single-handedly cannot influence a policy change.

Our study found that it was the combination of the personal attributes (for example, leadership qualities) and strategies adopted by the key policy actors, and the contextual factors (for example, window of opportunity, legislative environment, policy and social networks) that were instrumental in influencing the change process. Therefore, the most influential strategy in this case (policy change to regulate forestry water use) was developing trust, long-term relationships with key stakeholders, mutual understanding of the issues, having continuous interactions with the stakeholders (consultations) and, most importantly, maintaining transparency throughout the process.

Finally, even though the findings are limited by the fact that this research is conducted in a particular region and is unique to the south-east of South Australia, there are opportunities for other regions to learn from the process that has run since 2004.

ACKNOWLEDGEMENT

The authors acknowledge the funding from the National Centre for Groundwater Research and Training (NCGRT) for this study. We also thank the water planners for their time and for participating in the survey.

REFERENCES

Beeton, R.J.S., K.I. Buckley, G.J. Jones, D. Morgan, R.E. Reichelt and D. Trewin (2006), *Australia State of the Environment 2006*, Australian State of the Environment Committee 2006, Independent report to the Australian Government Minister for the Environment and Heritage, Department of the Environment and Heritage, Canberra.

Benyon, R. and T.M. Doody (2004), 'Water use by tree plantations in South East SA', Technical Report 148, CSIRO Forestry and Forest Products, Mt Gambier, Australia.

Bowmer, K.H. (2007), 'Water and conflict resolution: from smoke filled rooms to public participation', in A.L. Wilson, R.L. Dehaan, R.J. Watts, K.J. Page, K.H. Bowmer and A. Curtis (eds), *Proceedings of the 5th Australian Stream Management Conference. Australian rivers: making a difference*, Charles Sturt University, Thurgoona, New South Wales, pp. 25–30.

Brundtland, G.H. (1987), *Our Common Future*, Report of the World Commission on Environment and Development, Oxford: Oxford University Press.

Burke, Tony (2013), 'Local engagement officers for environmental watering', press release, 6 February, Australian Government, Canberra.

Cohen, A.R. and D.L. Bradford (2005), *Influence without Authority*, Hoboken, NJ: John Wiley & Sons.

Commonwealth of Australia (2002), 'The value of water: inquiry into Australia's management of urban water', Report of the Senate Environment, Communications, Information Technology and the Arts References Committee, Commonwealth of Australia, Canberra.

Crow, D.A. (2010), 'Policy entrepreneurs, issue experts, and water rights policy change in Colorado', *Review of Policy Research*, 27(3), 299–315.

Dirksen, W. (2002), 'Water management structures in Europe', *Irrigation and Drainage*, 51(3), 199–211.

Hamstead, M., C. Baldwin and V. O'Keefe (2008), 'Water allocation planning in Australia: current practices and lessons learned', Waterlines Occasional paper No. 6, National Water Commission, Canberra.

Howard, C. (2001), 'Bureaucrats in the social policy process: administrative policy entrepreneurs and the case of Working Nation', *Australian Journal of Public Administration*, 60(3), 56–65.

Howell, J. and C. Higgins (1990), 'Champions of technological innovation', *Administrative Science Quarterly*, 35(2), 317–41.

Hughes, S. and J. McKay (2009), 'The contribution of actors to achieving sustainability in Australia through water policy transitions', in D. Huitema and S. Meijerink (eds), *Water Policy Entrepreneurs: A Research Companion to Water Transitions around the Globe*, Cheltenham, UK and Northampton, MA, USA: Edward Elgar Publishing, pp. 175–92.

Huitema, D., L. Lebel and S. Meijerink (2011), 'The strategies of policy entrepreneurs in water transitions around the world', *Water Policy*, 13(5), 717–33.

Huitema, D. and S. Meijerink (eds) (2009), *Water Policy Entrepreneurs: A Research Companion to Water Transitions around the Globe*, Cheltenham, UK and Northampton, MA, USA: Edward Elgar Publishing.

Huitema, D. and S. Meijerink (2010), 'Realizing water transitions: the role of policy entrepreneurs in water policy change', *Ecology and Society*, 15(2), available at www.ecologyandsociety.org, accessed 10 August 2011.

Keremane, G.B, J. McKay and Z. Wu (2012), 'Sustainable water planning in Australia: a survey of attitudes of our sustainability water policy entrepreneurs', *Water: Journal of the Australian Water Association*, 39(5), 62–5.

MacDonald, D.H. and M. Young (2000), 'A case study of the Murray–Darling Basin', Final Report for the International Water Management Institute, Policy and Economic Review Unit, CSIRO Land and Water, Australia.

McKay, J. (2005), 'Water institutional reforms in Australia', *Water Policy*, 7(1), 35–52.

McKay, J. (2007), 'Groundwater as the Cinderella of water laws, policies and institutions in Australia', in S. Ragone (ed.), *The Global Importance of Groundwater in the 21st Century: Proceedings of the International Symposium on Groundwater Sustainability*, Westerville, National Groundwater Association, pp. 321–27.

McKay, J. (2010), 'Some Australian examples of the integration of environmental, economic and social considerations into decision making – the jurisprudence of facts and context', in D. French (ed.), *Global Justice and Sustainable Development*, Leiden: BRILL, pp. 327–39.

McKay, J. (2011), 'Australian water allocation plans and the sustainability objective-conflicts and conflict-resolution measures', *Hydrological Sciences Journal*, 56(4), 615–629.

Mintrom, M. (1997), 'Policy entrepreneurs and the diffusion of innovation', *American Journal of Political Science*, 41(3), 738–70.

Moran, T. (2010), 'Ahead of the game: blueprint for the reform of Australian Government administration', Department of the Prime Minister and Cabinet, Canberra.

National Strategy for Ecologically Sustainable Development (NSESD) (1992), available at http://www.environment.gov.au, accessed 28 July 2011.

National Water Commission (NWC) (2004), *National Water Initiative*, available at www.nwc.gov.au, accessed 28 July 2011.

National Water Commission (NWC) (2011), 'The National Water Initiative – securing Australia's water future: 2011 assessment', Canberra: NWC.

Preston, B.J. (2010), 'Reflection on water use and justice', in J. McKay, G. Keremane and A. Gray (eds), *Picturing Freshwater Justice in Rural Australia*, Queensland: CRC Irrigation Futures, pp. 84–99.

Roberts, N.C. and P.J. King (1989), 'Public entrepreneurship: a typology', paper presented to the Academy of Management Meetings, Public Sector Division, Washington, DC, available at http://calhoun.nps.edu/public/bitstream/handle/10945/29055/publicentrepren e00robe.pdf?sequence=1, accessed 28 July 2011.

Roberts, N.C. and P.J. King (1991), 'Policy entrepreneurs: their activity structure and function in the policy process', *Journal of Public Administration Research and Theory*, 1(2), 147–75.

Schneider, M. and P. Teske (1992), 'Toward a theory of the political entrepreneur: evidence from local government', *American Political Science Review*, 86(3), 737–47.

South East Natural Resources Management Board (SENRMB) (2012), 'Water planning in the South East', Fact Sheet, available at http://www.senrm.sa.gov.au/, accessed 20 September 2012.

Taylor, A., C. Cocklin, R. Brown and E. Wilson-Evered (2011), 'An investigation of champion-driven leaderships processes', *Leadership Quarterly*, 22(2), 412–33.

Teodoro, M.P. (2009), 'Bureaucratic job mobility and the diffusion of innovations', *American Journal of Political Science*, 53(1), 175–89.

Teske, P. and M. Schneider (1994), 'The bureaucratic entrepreneur: the case of city managers', *Public Administration Review*, 54(4), 331–40.

Wright, A. (2002), 'Sustainable water supplies for remote communities of indigenous people: the first step-water conservation', CRC for Water Quality and Treatment, Salisbury, South Australia.

Xu, C., J. McKay and G.B. Keremane (2013), 'The political difficulties in incorporating plantation forestry as a water affecting activity – a case study in South Australia', paper presented at the National Groundwater Association 2013 Summit, 28 April – 1 May, San Antonio, TX, USA.

PART III

MOTIVATIONAL AND INTENTIONAL APPROACH TO ENTREPRENEURSHIP AND SUSTAINABLE DEVELOPMENT

7. Recognizing first-person opportunities for sustainable development

Benedetto Cannatelli, Laura Maria Ferri, Matteo Pedrini and Mario Molteni

INTRODUCTION

Opportunity recognition has been acknowledged as one of the most relevant topics in the entrepreneurial process. Specifically, entrepreneurial opportunities are defined as 'situations in which new goods, services, raw materials, and organizing methods can be introduced and sold at greater than their costs of production' (Shane and Venkataraman, 2000: 220). Opportunity recognition acts as a trigger for the entire entrepreneurial process by uncovering a prospective pattern for the entrepreneurial initiative (Shane and Venkataraman, 2000; McMullen and Shepherd, 2006; Baron, 2006). Although this topic has been widely explored within the traditional entrepreneurship domain, the adaptability of opportunity recognition to new forms of entrepreneurial initiatives – such as entrepreneurship for sustainable development – has been overlooked.

Sustainable development (which includes preservation of the ecosystem, reduction of degradation and deforestation) has been acknowledged as a priority at all latitudes by the global community (WCED, 1987; Hall et al., 2010). Within this urgency, entrepreneurship has been advocated by a number of scholars as a key element for counteracting negative social and environmental trends (Brown, 2006; Homer-Dixon, 2006; Lovins et al., 2004; Vaitheeswaran, 2003).

The emergence of entrepreneurial initiatives aimed at addressing long-standing social and environmental issues has been attracting the attention of scholars in the entrepreneurship field (Hall et al., 2010; Parrish, 2010; York and Venkataraman, 2010). The simultaneous pursuit of economic, social and environmental goals enhances the complexity of the opportunity recognition process by including new variables in the original model. Although traditional entrepreneurial opportunities are mostly assessed based on their profitability, opportunity recognition for sustainable development implies the additional pursuit of social and environmental benefits. In this perspective, understanding how and why some individuals foresee how to 'connect the dots' (Baron, 2006) to generate economic, social and environmental value simultaneously is of critical importance to support entrepreneurship as a means of social and environmental development. A better understanding of opportunity recognition for sustainable development may lead to increased entrepreneurial actions in geographic areas in which economic, social and environmental development is of primary concern. Following McMullen and Shepherd (2006) and Patzelt and Shepherd (2011), this chapter adopts a psychological perspective on opportunity recognition (Cohen and Winn, 2007; Child et al., 2007; Mitchell et al., 2002).

In a milestone contribution, McMullen and Shepherd (2006) suggested a two-stage model to explain entrepreneurial opportunity recognition, based on the identification of third-person opportunity and first-person opportunity. They assumed individual knowledge and motivation as antecedents of the development of entrepreneurial intention. The third-person opportunity refers to the first stage, when individuals recognize potential patterns for traditional entrepreneurial initiatives. The first-person opportunity refers to the second stage of entrepreneurial intention. It is developed as a result of a personal assessment based on feasibility and desirability. This model is rooted in Aristotle's 'practical syllogism', which equals action and intention. Thus it conceives first-person opportunity recognition, entrepreneurial intention and entrepreneurial action as stages that stand beyond opportunity recognition. Although we are aware of the conceptual distinction between these three concepts since, for example, entrepreneurial action requires other contingencies than intention alone to occur, for the purpose of this chapter we group them as stages that stand beyond opportunity recognition, thus falling beyond the focus of the research.

More recently, Patzelt and Shepherd (2011) revised the first stage of the model proposed by McMullen and Shepherd (2006) – the identification of a third-person opportunity – and adapted it to entrepreneurship for sustainable development. Specifically, they suggested entrepreneurial knowledge as a moderator of the main relationships. In this chapter we focus instead on the second stage of the model (the first-person opportunity recognition), to detect psychological triggers which are uniquely linked to the simultaneous pursuit of social, environmental and economic gains.

Relying on early-stage entrepreneurs is consistent with our purpose of elaborating existing theory by getting direct, empirical evidence of the factors leading individuals to engage in entrepreneurial action. In this perspective, grounded theory is employed to suggest new relationships among constructs. Such a methodological approach is consistent with the purpose of analysing 'the actual production of meanings and concepts used by social actors in real settings' (Gephart, 2004: 457). Although grounded theory is mostly used to generate new theory from scratch, it can be adopted to further extend existing models by 'shoot[ing] for the elaboration of existing theory rather than untethered new theory' (Suddaby, 2006: 635). Grounded theory allows us to deal with the high conceptual density of the relationships and the constructs implied by our research question, which focuses on the drivers to the identification of first-person entrepreneurial opportunities for sustainable development. The chapter proceeds as follows. First, we provide a literature review on entrepreneurship for sustainable development and opportunity recognition. Next, we present the research setting and methodology used for our purpose. We present the theoretical model and its key factors and then investigate how they are treated in actual opportunity recognition processes. We then discuss theoretical and managerial implications. Finally, we present limitations and indications for further research.

ENTREPRENEURSHIP FOR SUSTAINABLE DEVELOPMENT AND OPPORTUNITY RECOGNITION

Our review covers literature on entrepreneurship for sustainable development and entrepreneurial opportunity recognition. Combining extant knowledge at the interaction between these two areas was a key step to identify the research gap that our study addresses. A better understanding of the factors leading individuals to pursue entrepreneurial opportunities for sustainable development may provide useful insights for academics and policy makers. Indeed, it may suggest directions for educational, training and supportive initiatives to foster entrepreneurship to promote simultaneous economic, social and environmental development.

In the following section, we discuss entrepreneurship for sustainable development in order to clear up potential definitional ambiguities and clarify the research domain. Then we recall extant literature on opportunity recognition and state the research question that drives the study.

ENTREPRENEURSHIP FOR SUSTAINABLE DEVELOPMENT

Over the last decade, the nexus between economic activity and social and environmental improvement has gained increasing attention within the academic community. This debate resulted in a significant amount of research exploring causal links between these topics (Austin et al., 2006;

Drayton, 2002; Peredo and Chrisman, 2006). Worldwide events and long-standing issues are rapidly changing the global socio-economic landscape, such as the financial crisis and increasing poverty. These dynamics induced practitioners and academics to question how entrepreneurial activity can enhance social and environmental welfare on a large scale, especially in underdeveloped geographic areas (Yunus, 2010; Nicholls, 2006). Contributions may be ideally positioned along a continuum whose variance is predicted by the equilibrium between profit and social aims, ranging from corporate social responsibility (CSR), which is usually associated with existing for-profit-oriented businesses, to social entrepreneurship, which refers to entrepreneurial ventures whose primary goal is value creation for society. However, a wide range of approaches may be found in-between the two extremes.

This chapter focuses on the notion of entrepreneurship for sustainable development defined by Shepherd and Patzelt (2011: 137) as 'entrepreneurship [which] is focused on the preservation of nature, life support, and community in the pursuit of perceived opportunities to bring into existence future products, processes, and services for gain, where gain is broadly construed to include economic and non-economic gains to individuals, the economy, and society'. Therefore, it provides a follow-up to a growing stream within the entrepreneurship literature (Hall et al., 2010; Parrish, 2010; York and Venkataraman, 2010).

Compared to the constructs of CSR and social entrepreneurship, entrepreneurship for sustainable development presents some peculiarities worth recalling in order to clear up potential ambiguity and set the boundaries of this study. First, the strong focus on entrepreneurial action distinguishes entrepreneurship for sustainable development from CSR, which does not necessarily refer to socially and environmentally friendly activities pursued by entrepreneurs. Conversely, the CSR domain is usually targeted to the social engagement of large organizations (Shepherd and Patzelt, 2011; Baron, 2007). Second, compared to the notion of social entrepreneurship, entrepreneurship for sustainable development assumes a wider range of objectives to be pursued simultaneously.

Although social entrepreneurs are mainly concerned with social issues such as poverty, health or education, entrepreneurship for sustainable development assumes the simultaneous pursuit of a triple bottom line, namely, economic, social and environmental goals (Shepherd and Patzelt, 2011; Pacheco et al., 2010; Hall et al., 2010; Cohen and Winn, 2007). This multi-fold approach has relevant implications in distinguishing it from social entrepreneurship, in particular regarding the profit motives beyond the two constructs. Specifically, although a wide-accepted definition of social entrepreneurship has yet to appear, most authors – especially early contributors from the American tradition, the social enterprise school (Bacq and Janssen, 2011) – agree on the full primacy of social over economic motives, including activities that are not self-sustainable (relying therefore to a different extent on grants, volunteer labour and donations). Indeed, such a definition prevents initiatives with financially sustainable business models from distributing their profits to investors (Yunus, 2010; Dees, 1998; Peredo and McLean, 2006; Austin et al., 2006). However, profit motives are normally included within the domain of entrepreneurship for sustainable development as a means of promoting economic, social and environmental conditions (Dean and McMullen, 2007).

However, this approach to entrepreneurship – known as the panacea hypothesis – has been largely debated on a prescriptive rather than a descriptive base. The consequence of this has been the occurrence of anecdotal rather than empirical support for how and why entrepreneurial activity can actually address social and environmental issues (Hall et al., 2010; Shepherd and Patzelt, 2011). In this scenario, Shepherd and Patzelt (2011) identified three perspectives that scholars may pursue to improve the understanding of entrepreneurial action within the sustainable development domain, namely: the economics perspective, which focuses on the natural environment-related market imperfections that allow the emergence of opportunities; the institutional perspective, which examines how entrepreneurs may foster institutional changes toward the adoption of sustainable practices; and the psychological perspective, which focuses mainly on entrepreneurial cognition (Cohen and Winn, 2007; Child et al., 2007; Mitchell et al., 2002).

This study assumes the third perspective – the psychological perspective – by responding to Patzelt and Shepherd's call (2011) for a deeper understanding of first-person opportunity recognition leading to entrepreneurial action for sustainable development. Consistently with the methodological approach predicted by grounded theory, we converged toward Patzelt and Shepherd's perspective as a result of an ongoing, dynamic interaction between data collected and extant theory. In the next section, we integrate previous theoretical work on entrepreneurial opportunity recognition which emerged as theoretically relevant as the analysis proceeded.

OPPORTUNITY RECOGNITION

Exploring psychological mechanisms leading to entrepreneurial action requires approaching entrepreneurship at the individual level rather than the system level. On the one hand, the system-level approach focuses on the consequences of exploiting entrepreneurial opportunities in terms of the health of the economic system (Kirzner, 1973; Schumpeter, 1934), thus disregarding those who actually carry on the entrepreneurial activity. On the other hand, the individual-level approach attempts an understanding of why some individuals are more likely to pursue entrepreneurial opportunities than others.

In the field of study approaching the individual level, scholars from the psychological approach attempt to address this question by leveraging the concept of uncertainty – rather than personality or position held within the organization – to be faced by the prospective entrepreneur in the decision-making process (McMullen and Shepherd, 2006). This theoretical framework, known as the theory of the entrepreneur, conceptualizes uncertainty in two complementary ways.

The first approach – typically referred as the Austrian economists' scholarship – suggests that entrepreneurial action is the result of psychological factors which drive a lower perception of uncertainty (Kirzner, 1989; Mises, 1949; Pasour, 1989). According to this approach, entrepreneurs are distinguished from non-entrepreneurs based on the knowledge held about a specific market or environment, which reduces their perception of uncertainty and increases their judgement about the feasibility of action. The second approach – that of non-Austrian economists – assumes entrepreneurial action in a slightly different way, precisely as a result of a personal higher willingness to overcome uncertainty (Knight, 1921; Schumpeter, 1934). According to this approach, given a certain level of uncertainty affecting a group of individuals, entrepreneurs are those who are more willing to engage in entrepreneurial actions because they have higher motivation. Because of that, personal desire for entrepreneurial opportunities is higher in entrepreneurs than in non-entrepreneurs.

McMullen and Shepherd (2006) provided a synthesis of the two approaches, proposing a model suggesting entrepreneurial action as a function of knowledge and motivation. Specifically, their model suggests entrepreneurial opportunity recognition – then leading to entrepreneurial action – as a result of two steps. The first step is the recognition of third-person opportunities, where uncertainty, defined as ignorance, is overcome through prior knowledge and awareness of the domain in which such opportunity arises. The second step is the recognition of a first-person opportunity, where uncertainty, intended as doubt, is overcome by feasibility and desirability assessments leading the individual to entrepreneurial action (McMullen and Shepherd, 2006).

This model provides a useful explanation of how opportunity recognition (thus entrepreneurial action) occurs in the traditional entrepreneurship domain, whereas its adequacy in predicting how opportunities are identified when social and environmental motives assume primary importance still needs confirmation. In this vein, Shepherd and Patzelt (2011) emphasized avenues for further research, suggesting a deep exploration of the desirability and feasibility assessment dynamics for first-person opportunity recognition in entrepreneurship for sustainable development. In this perspective, the two authors provided an initial contribution by advancing a theoretical model suggesting how recognition of third-person opportunities may occur in the sustainable opportunity domain. Specifically, the model predicts knowledge of the natural/communal environment on the one hand, and altruism and perception of threat to the natural and communal environment on the other, as independent variables affecting recognition of third-person opportunities for sustainable development. Moreover, this model is enriched by the presence of entrepreneurial knowledge moderating the relationships. The choice to rely on McMullen and Shepherd's model as the main basis to integrate our research has been suggested by initial evidence which emerged in the early stages of the research process. Several interviews with the prospective entrepreneurs who took part in the research assumed knowledge and motivation arguments to be main drivers in the opportunity recognition process. For example, in retracing her personal story a participant recalled that the problem she was going to tackle with her new venture 'has always been something myself and my family have struggled with for many years. Such a situation kept us in an helpless condition . . . just when the frustration became unsustainable I realized that doing something myself would have been the only way to improve the condition of my community'. Indeed, another participant recalled how 'being an expert in mastering the agriculture techniques required by the specific climate of [his] region allowed him to conceive a solution which would have remained otherwise hidden'. These – plus other similar input we received in the early process of information gathering – moved us to design our research around the model proposed by McMullen and Shepherd (2006).

This study aims at contributing to this path by advancing a model predicting knowledge and motivation leading to recognition of first-person opportunities – and thus, to entrepreneurial intention – in the sustainable development domain. Therefore, our research question is the following: What factors lead individuals to recognize first-person entrepreneurial opportunities for sustainable development? In the next section, we describe the methods and criteria that guided us in collecting and analysing the data.

METHODS

To address our research question we assume an abductive approach – consistent with grounded theory – by providing evidence from 36 prospective entrepreneurs for sustainable development through an in-depth approach (Suddaby, 2006). Since studies on opportunity recognition for sustainable development are in the nascent stage, the methodology was chosen after various models and methods were investigated. Grounded theory was deemed adequate for this study (Glaser and Strauss, 1967; Miles and Huberman, 1984). The purpose of grounded theory is 'the discovery of theory from data that is systematically obtained from research' (Glaser and Strauss, 1967: 5). Though the methodology was initially recommended to investigate uncharted topics, later approaches discussed the reliability of the methodology to elaborate and to modify existing theory, also through systematic interaction between empirical evidence and existing constructs (Strauss and Corbin, 1998). Moreover, this approach is particularly suited for addressing research questions requiring detailed analysis of the phenomenon to be studied (Kreiner et al., 2009). In this study, we use grounded theory to address the need for a coherent theoretical framework for first-person opportunity recognition in entrepreneurship for sustainable development.

Theoretical Sampling

To develop a theory of first-person opportunity recognition for sustainable entrepreneurship, we relied on 36 entrepreneurs (2011 candidates) enrolled in an MBA programme on entrepreneurship held in Nairobi, Kenya. This educational programme, run by a local university in partnership with two other academic institutions (in Italy and India), was awarded the 2012 Ashoka U – Cordes Innovation Award.[1] Relying on prospective and early-stage entrepreneurs is consistent with the aim of exploring the first-person opportunity recognition process. Applying to the MBA programme required students to submit an executive summary of a sustainable, entrepreneurial idea that they were expected to get off the ground right after the end of the programme, which thus classified them as early-stage entrepreneurs. Ideas that demonstrated more attention to the triple bottom line – that is, simultaneously pursuing economic, social and environmental objectives – were preferred in the selection process.

Priority was given to projects demonstrating a strong balance among the three dimensions rather than to ideas in which social or environmental motives prevailed over the economic one or vice versa. In this sense, business models that could be demonstrated to be financially sustainable were preferred, since the declared purpose of the supporting institutions was 'to foster the creation of a new class of African entrepreneurs able to cope with social and environmental sustainability with financial and economic soundness' (from the university's website). Therefore, students had not only already recognized the existence of a third-person opportunity for entrepreneurial action, but had also already moved through the feasibility and desirability assessments by developing their own business plan and applying to the MBA programme.

According to McMullen and Shepherd (2006) and Shepherd et al. (2007), these students can be ideally positioned in the second stage of the opportunity recognition model, since they had overcome the doubt and 'form(ed) the belief that this represents an opportunity for them personally (first-person opportunity belief)' (Shepherd and Patzelt, 2011: 152). This selection allowed a focus on cases with 'rare' qualities, allowing processes that can exist in other contexts to emerge sharply (Eisenhardt, 1989; Pettigrew, 1990; Pratt et al., 2006; Tracey and Jarvis, 2007; Kreiner et al., 2009).

As shown in Table 7.1, 36 entrepreneurs were included in the study, thus accounting for an equal number of business proposals. Entrepreneurial initiatives ranged across different sectors, from education to wood manufacturing and waste management. In Table 7.1, the profiles of the MBA students are outlined, and a summary of each entrepreneurial project is provided.

Data Collection

To guarantee the validity and reliability of the results, data were collected from multiple sources (Eisenhardt, 1989). Specifically, preliminary analysis was based on the three-page executive summaries students had submitted to apply to the MBA programme. Since at that time students were not aware of the research project, the executive summaries constituted an unbiased source of data. In addition, the business plan developed as the final assignment of the programme constituted a further documental source of data. The business plans, which total 1110 pages of documentary information, were a relevant source of information for full comprehension of the business models, financial sustainability and impact generated by each idea.

To complement the data collected, semi-structured interviews were conducted with each entrepreneur enrolled in the MBA programme. The 36 interviews, which lasted 40 minutes on average, were divided among the authors and digitally recorded. The interviewers took notes about their impressions to account for perception-related data. Consistently with the

Table 7.1   A list of entrepreneurs and sustainable business ideas

	Citizenship	Gender	Birth	Entrepreneurial purpose
1	Kenya	Female	1971	Microfinance in rural Kenya
2	Uganda	Female	1987	Micro health insurance in Uganda
3	Ethiopia	Male	1981	Bamboo manufacture in Ethiopia
4	Kenya	Male	n.a.	Services for small-scale farmers in rural Kenya
5	Sudan	Male	1981	Rural clinic in Southern Sudan
6	Mali	Male	1972	Vocational training centre in Mali
7	Rwanda	Female	1972	Centre for woman training in Rwanda
8	Ghana	Male	1974	Cassava cultivation in Ghana
9	Sierra Leone	Male	1967	Cassava flour factory in Sierra Leone
10	Sudan	Male	1976	Oil production from groundnuts in Sudan
11	Italy	Female	1983	Fair Trade wine production
12	Ethiopia	Male	1979	Training centre for women in Ethiopia
13	Rwanda	Male	n.a.	Maize production and poultry farming in Rwanda
14	Togo	Male	1973	Vocational training and small business creation for young people in Togo
15	Sierra Leone	Male	1973	Training centre in Sierra Leone
16	Uganda	Male	1973	Coffee co-operative enhancement in Uganda
17	Kenya	Female	1972	Fresh milk and poultry meat production in Kenya
18	Congo	Male	1983	Small scale cooperatives to produce Aloe Vera in Congo
19	Uganda	Female	1984	Poultry eggs production in Uganda
20	Kenya	Male	1973	Craftsmanship, breeding and farming for young jobless in Kenya
21	Kenya	Male	1970	Garbage collection and recycling in Mombasa
22	Rwanda	Female	1975	Homecare of elderly in Rwanda
23	Ethiopia	Male	1981	Kindergarten in Ethiopia
24	Mauritius	Male	1975	Production of high-quality paper in Mauritius
25	Kenya	Female	1976	Auto repair services in Kenya
26	Cameroon	Female	1965	Secondary school in Cameroon
27	Nigeria	Female	1978	Training centre in Nigeria
28	Italy	Male	1987	Training in catering competencies in Kenya
29	Rwanda	Male	1974	Technical skills education centre in Rwanda
30	Ghana	Male	1974	Sustainable tourism in Volta region in Ghana
31	Sudan	Male	1978	Poultry producing farm in South Sudan
32	Ghana	Male	1976	Vocational training centre for young jobless in Ghana
33	Rwanda	Female	1982	Agribusiness in Rwanda
34	Italy	Female	1986	Production of clothes in Kenya
35	Mauritius	Male	1985	CSR trust fund in current employer in Mauritius
36	Rwanda	Female	1971	Biogas production in Rwanda

grounded theory methodology, data were analysed for as long as data collection proceeded, and the interview protocol evolved over time to include systematically new constructs emerging in previous interviews (Yin, 1989; Eisenhardt, 1989; Kreiner et al., 2006).

Furthermore, two of the authors taught courses during the MBA programme and engaged in informal discussions with the entrepreneurs. At that time, this was not with any specific study purpose, since the courses were taught when the study was still at the design stage and the dialogues occurred as part of regular communication between professors and students. This facilitated a deeper understanding of the contextual aspects, and gave insights into students' motivation, sensitivity and other personal aspects.

Data Analysis

Data analysis was conducted through open, axial and selective coding.

Open coding

Open coding process was adopted for as long as data collection proceeded. The authors were involved in selecting and naming categories. Each author examined the data collected to identify key aspects and newly codified concepts, which were deemed relevant to understand the process of first-person opportunity recognition for sustainable development.

The coding process required a constant dialogue among the authors and a regular comparison with previous literature, in order to solve problems of interpretation and to reach agreement on the identified categories and their contributions to theoretical development. In analysing the data, transcripts and documentary and observational evidences from each potential entrepreneur were then organized into categories. Each concept was labelled with a term often based on the language of the interviewee. Concepts formed the basis of the coding frame.

Next, the concepts were used to develop categories and then, progressively, a smaller number of overall themes. Therefore, the analysis allowed a shift from a case-by-case approach to a construct-by-construct standpoint. In this sense, the newly identified concepts in each case were added and combined to overcome the authors' and the single-case biases. The process was not linear, as the synthesis into one theoretical model needed an iterative comparison not only among cases and contexts but also with previous theoretical models. No concepts were deemed significant for the construction of a new theoretical proposal until the authors had reached agreement on their reliability, materiality and relevance. Once agreement was achieved, the concepts were grouped into categories, to organize similar individual issues.

This phase required moving iteratively between data and existing theory to come to meaningful conceptual categories (Eisenhardt, 1989; Tracey and Jarvis, 2007). As observed by Eisenhardt (1989), tying emergent theory to extant literature enhances the internal validity, generalizability and theoretical level. The new conceptualization was then discussed and interpreted with implications derived for theory and practice. As a result, the process led to the identification of seven categories. Table 7.2 relates concepts that emerged through the open coding process with the categories thereby identified.

Axial coding
In the second step of our analysis, the authors axially codified the data. Although in practice open and axial coding processes do not occur separately – rather, they are mostly intertwined – for the sake of clarity we present them here as discrete steps.

At this stage, causal relationships and interconnections between categories and concepts are identified. Indeed, the aim of the second stage was to build explicit connections between categories and subcategories at a dimensional level. In analysing relationships, several techniques were adopted to remain focused on the research problem (Creswell, 2003; Glaser and Strauss, 1967; Yin, 1994). Conceptual mapping was employed as an analytical tool to organize and analyse data. This technique promotes pattern matching and the effective categorization of data (see Figure 7.1).

The relationships among concepts and categories emerged along the analysis are drawn in the conceptual map reported in Figure 7.1. Sketching out a map uncovering links among categories allowed a better understanding of the interdependence between the 'structure' and the 'process' of the phenomena studied (Strauss and Corbin, 1998). For example, we realized that being part of the community to be served (structure) allows an individual to mitigate market risk (process) by virtue of their deep understanding of the psychological and cultural dynamics underlying beneficiaries' behaviour. This process resulted in the understanding of how, when, why and with what consequences a specific phenomenon may occur, therefore providing the basis for the last stage of the analysis.

Selective coding
In the third step of the analysis, theory was integrated and refined. Data collected through interviews with the entrepreneurs allowed psychological drivers to entrepreneurial action to emerge sharply, providing important insights into how and why individuals may recognize and develop the

Table 7.2   Concepts and categories resulting from the open coding process

Concept code	Concept label	Category label	Quotations
11	Moral imperative to support others	Altruism	'therefore it's sort of natural to me to wonder how can I be of help for other people'
18	Self-realization from helping others		
15	Identification with the community	Social involvement	'it was an issue concerning my whole community . . . we couldn't have waited longer than that, since our health condition was at stake'
10	Interaction with the community		
04.	Dependence from the community		
02.	Family links	Emotional involvement	'when I realized that my brothers were experiencing that, I felt kind of "pushed" to think something to alleviate their pain . . . I think everybody would feel the same'
14.	Friendship links		
17.	Moving experiences		
07.	Technical expertise	Entrepreneurial knowledge	'I've been a salesmen for the past 10 years, therefore I knew what to expect and I believe – at the end of the day – that our expectations are definitely reasonable'
13.	Selling expertise		
08.	Negotiation		
05.	Need for social reward	Perception of goodwill of the natural and communal environment	'and, to be fair, feeling the gratitude of my people is often what motivates me the most in keeping on my activity'
09.	Being a positive example to the others		
01.	Business opportunity	First-person opportunity recognition	'therefore I decided to quit my day-job to fully commit myself in bringing this idea off the ground. The opportunity is there, and I'm confident I have good chances to make it working well'
03.	Undertaking action		
16.	Mitigating risk		
19.	Challenging the status quo		
06.	Belonging to a community	Knowledge of the natural and communal environment	'I think the main advantage I have compared to foreign organizations coming here to alleviate a bad situation is that I've been living here for 34 years, which implies a deep, intense empathy between myself and my people'
12.	Belonging to a geographical area		

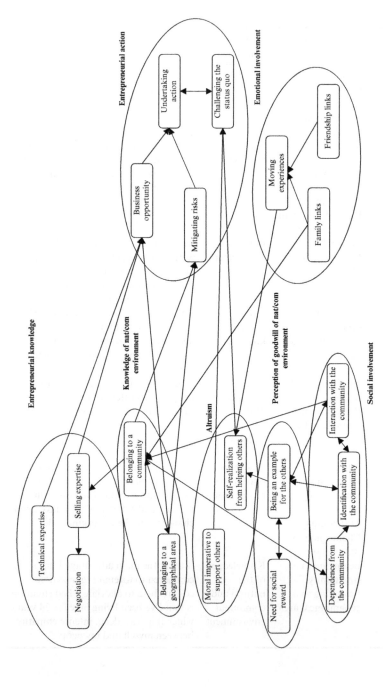

Figure 7.1   Conceptual map resulting from axial coding

intention to pursue first-person opportunities for sustainable development, which counted as a core category of the study. This is consistent with the original purpose of the study, which was to follow up the study by Patzelt and Shepherd (2011), who explained how context-specific knowledge and motivation – moderated by entrepreneurial knowledge – may lead to individuals identifying opportunities for sustainable development.

FINDINGS

Model and Summary of Results

Findings from our research are now presented along the three steps envisaged by the grounded theory methodology, namely open, axial and selective coding. Our model focuses on the next step to the Patzelt and Shepherd's model and explains what drives individuals to overcome doubt through feasibility and desirability assessments, thus conceiving the opportunity for sustainable development previously identified as a 'generic' option as a feasible and desirable option for themselves. Our model resulting from selective coding is reported in Figure 7.2.

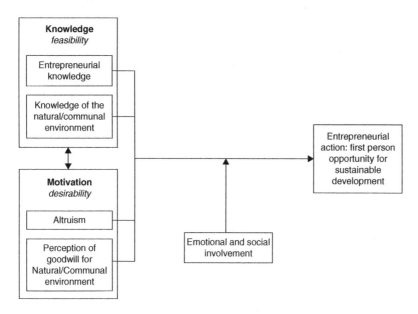

Figure 7.2 A conceptual model for first-person opportunity recognition in entrepreneurship for sustainable development

Consistent with McMullen and Shepherd (2006), our model suggests that knowledge and motivation are the main drivers of entrepreneurial action. More specifically, findings suggest that entrepreneurial knowledge and knowledge of the natural and communal environment play the main roles in the feasibility assessment; while altruism and perception of goodwill for the natural and communal environment constitute the main factors around which the desirability assessment takes place. Moreover, our findings emphasize the role of an individual's emotional and social involvement as additional constructs moderating these relationships. Our model is further discussed below, together with extracts from the interviews with the entrepreneurs so as to provide evidence for the logic behind each relationship.

Knowledge: Feasibility Assessment

Entrepreneurial knowledge

Entrepreneurial knowledge includes knowledge of markets, ways to serve markets and customer problems (Shane, 2000; Patzelt and Shepherd, 2011). This dimension is included in Patzelt and Shepherd's (2011) model for third-person opportunity recognition. However, while in the model entrepreneurial knowledge is predicted to moderate the main relationship among knowledge, motivation and likelihood to recognize generic (third-person) opportunities for sustainable development, our data suggest that entrepreneurial knowledge exerts a direct effect when an opportunity is assessed as feasible for the individual themself (first-person opportunity). In this regard, several entrepreneurs emphasized how the decision to start their own activity was led by a deep understanding of how to serve a specific market, which resulted from previous experiences of the entrepreneurs in the industry.

Being familiar with the needs underlying a specific value proposition and the mechanisms beyond extant solutions is of critical importance for increasing individuals' commitment to and confidence in the goals of the entrepreneurial initiative (McCarthy et al., 1993; Dimov, 2010). This idea is well expressed in the entrepreneurs' own words:

> I did my studies, my degree in Business Administration, and in 2009 I had worked for one year before developing my idea and join[ing] this programme [MBA]. So during my work in this microfinance organization we helped a lot of women to start up their own business, and I understood the dynamics. (Entrepreneur #12)

> I know how to run a school because I've been a teacher for most of my life . . . I studied Sociology, then I had a Master's in Business Administration, then I specialized in Human Resources. Then I taught in schools in Ghana before coming to this MBA [programme]. (Entrepreneur #32)

This experience counts as the main discriminating factor between the two subsequent stages of the opportunity recognition process: although in the third-person opportunity domain entrepreneurial knowledge may assume low intensity and may be based mostly on theoretical notions about a specific process, the development of entrepreneurial intention (recognition of a first-person opportunity) requires knowledge to reach a higher level for the individual to invest their time and engage with the risks underlying entrepreneurship (Palich and Bagby, 1995; Shane, 2000).

This requirement is even more critical for entrepreneurial opportunities for sustainable development, which imply higher complexity and call for highly innovative solutions due to the long-standing issues at stake. Some entrepreneurs in the education and health sectors remarked on this point regarding the social needs entrepreneurs aim at addressing:

> In 2010 I was working in a high school and then in hospital where I was in charge of social work. And by doing this job, I had to visit the community where people lived, and I experienced and got to know how women are suffering in these communities . . . I wanted to provide some support under the form of courses because normally they are women who did not have the chance to continue their studies. The way to help them was to give them some education. They needed the knowledge. They needed courses. (Entrepreneur #7)

> I knew about this business opportunity when I went on holiday to . . . and I felt sick and I was trying to find out where I could go for medical check-up, and it wasn't easy, then I went to one clinic, and I did some blood testing. I didn't get my results on that very same day because there were problems with medical equipment, and I was told to come the following day. So I wondered, 'Wow what is happening?' so I thought there were need for medical service. And I also thought about the poor who cannot afford to travel to go to a good place for . . . good health care service. (Entrepreneur #5)

> I worked in a hospital before. Actually, I held a degree in a management organization, and I worked for this organization which has insurance, hospital, and health care facilities together. I saw people coming without insurance, and I realized that there are people going into poverty because they cannot afford insurance for health care . . . I saw people in need in the hospital I was working in. (Entrepreneur #2)

These findings reinforce the relevance of entrepreneurial knowledge for the framework of opportunity recognition for sustainable development: if its occurrence enhances the likelihood that knowledge of the natural and communal environment and motivation lead to the identification of third-person opportunity by moderating their relationships, when it comes to the first person, entrepreneurial knowledge assumes a primary role by providing the individual with a set of information and technical skills that reduce their perception of uncertainty, thus pushing them toward entrepreneurial action.

Knowledge of the natural and communal environment
The third-person opportunity in the field of entrepreneurship for sustainable development has also been explained through the knowledge of the natural and communal environment (Patzelt and Shepherd, 2011). In this sense, the more the individual is aware of and sustains the resources, services and potential threats in the natural environment (Cooper and Daily, 1997; Goodland, 1995) as well as the characteristics of the culture, groups and places that distinguish the community (Etzioni, 1996; Spicer, 2001), the more they are able to recognize entrepreneurial opportunities.

This relationship holds true even in the second stage of the opportunity recognition process, as part of the feasibility assessment. If prior knowledge of problems in the natural and communal environment were found to play an important role in the recognition of opportunities that sustain that environment (Patzelt and Shepherd, 2011), first-person opportunities are identified through a deeper understanding of such problems and of the reasons why previous attempts – by either private (market) or public (government) organizations – failed at solving or even at reducing them. As in the words of one interviewee: 'There is no institution, particularly where I live. I decided to start the business just to help them [women] . . . There are problems; there are no organizations. There is no coordination' (Entrepreneur #12).

Deep comprehension of the factors that prevented former attempts from coping with the social or environmental issues further strengthen the knowledge of the natural and communal environment, thus constituting the critical background for the personal intent to solve a specific issue. Being conscious of how and why previous attempts failed in accomplishing their mission induces prospective entrepreneurs to design their own business models around alternative mechanisms to provide effective solutions to the social problem:

> No schools in Ghana have this idea to generate an entrepreneurial mind into the young people. So, my school is going to be different because I want to give students entrepreneurial skills . . . We are also going to use a percentage of the profit to give scholarship to poor who are already working and cannot afford to. So we are trying to influence the Ghanian educational policy. (Entrepreneur #32)

Further understanding of the natural and communal environment is also related to the venture's consciousness of the need to challenge the status quo in order to reach its goal. Thus, not only the understanding of failures but also the knowledge of what should be changed in the environment represents a key dimension to push the prospective entrepreneur to take action. This element is well described by another entrepreneur: 'I'm Kenyan, and most of the business in my country does have a social orientation. With my business, I want to provide a model to my government that can introduce a national policy that could increase the social impact of firms' (Entrepreneur #25).

In light of the evidence from the interviews, we propose that entrepreneurial knowledge and knowledge of the natural and communal environment, as described above, play a primary role in the running of feasibility assessments for engaging in entrepreneurial action for sustainable development.

Motivation: Desirability Assessment

Altruism

Previous literature suggests that the intention to improve another person's welfare helps in recognizing sustainable development opportunities (Penner et al., 2005; Patzelt and Shepherd, 2011). Evidence from the present study extends the validity of this relation to the first-person opportunity domain, emphasizing that entrepreneurial action in sustainable development settings may leverage higher motivation as a consequence of a stronger willingness to personally contribute to improving others' social conditions.

In the words of several entrepreneurs: 'Why don't [I] make my idea of business more social and make it more for the people rather than just for those who are funding the project?' (Entrepreneur #3). And, 'My business idea is very simple. It is about how to help rural farmers who cultivate cassava to add value to their product, so that their family will become very sustainable and profitable to the people in the village' (Entrepreneur #8).

In the case of the first-person opportunity, prior personal sensitiveness to indigent people strengthens one's attention to others and acts as a powerful spur for enhancing the desirability assessment and therefore drives the prospective entrepreneur to undertake action:

> Personally, I have always had a natural inclination to come to the aid of my brothers and sisters in humanity in difficult situations. Therefore, I consider myself more as a social entrepreneur. Then, I think that the social nature of my business idea is an eloquent testimony. (Entrepreneur #6)

> I'm not so concerned about profit, but I have more interest in creating value for my community. I'm going to create employability for my brothers and sisters, and I want to use the profit to finance educational programmes because, in the long term, I want to create stability in the local economy. I want to produce and sell cooking oil in the local context to provide products at a lower price than

> now, this being economic sustainable and, at the same time, giving access to oil also to my people. (Entrepreneur #10)

According to Tan et al. (2005), altruism does not clash with the opportunity to pursue personal gain. On the contrary, altruism can coexist with profit motives that, in this perspective, may 'include not only cash but also intangible profits such as improved health or less denuded rainforests' (p. 358). In this vein, the relevance of altruism in opportunity recognition is not limited to feeding awareness of social and environmental issues. Rather, altruism plays an active role in inducing individuals to pass through desirability assessments to engage in entrepreneurial action by putting social, non-self-interest concerns alongside regular economic expectations. This attitude was further confirmed by the business proposal submitted by the prospective entrepreneurs, revealing opportunities that, in some cases, may appear suboptimal from a mere rational-economic perspective.

Perception of goodwill for natural and communal environment
Motivations to entrepreneurial action for sustainable development were also related to awareness of generating a positive impact on the natural and communal environment. This result is different from what has been suggested in previous literature, where opportunity recognition for sustainable development was related to threats from the natural and communal environment (Patzelt and Shepherd, 2011). Indeed, people involved in the study were more concerned about the benefits they were able to provide through their business, rather than being pushed by a sense of urgency or personal responsibility for the threats to societal and environmental well-being:

> There is also a government appreciation because of our environmental awareness and benefits compared to that of other different furniture business which use other kind of wood and often cut trees which are in extinction. There is also a second benefit, because the bamboo is easier to work also for, for instance, women. (Entrepreneur #3)

> My idea is social because the involvement in society that allows my community to benefit from my entrepreneurial activity. This fulfils me more than anything else. (Entrepreneur #30)

In this perspective, the individual's concerns about the natural and communal environment rely on opposite drivers depending on the stage of the opportunity recognition process. As discussed earlier, Patzelt and Shepherd (2011) suggested that awareness of social or environmental issues is pushed by concerns about possible future, dramatic scenarios that will be faced by the next generations as a consequence of the current negligence of civil society. In their article, the concept of threat is described in three possible forms: threats to the need for competence, threats to the need for relatedness and threats to the need for autonomy. Although the threats may have a minor role in the desirability assessment, the evidence from the study indicates the superiority of a positive or proactive attitude toward the decision to engage in entrepreneurial activity – such as an intangible reward like personal gratitude – compared to a 'responsive' approach. The latter approach, which normally constitutes the main source of social activism initiatives, is a much weaker driver in fostering entrepreneurial action.

Interaction between Knowledge and Motivation

The model depicted in Figure 7.1 shows a reciprocal, direct relationship between knowledge and motivation. Evidence collected among prospective entrepreneurs supports such interaction.

The first direction of the relationship – knowledge affecting motivation – stems from a greater consciousness of the potential positive externalities that may be generated by the entrepreneurial venture. An entrepreneur emphasized this point explicitly, suggesting that the process of gaining entrepreneurial knowledge gave him opportunities to gain better awareness of broad social issues, thus enhancing his motivation:

> Initially, I did my BSc in Agricultural Engineering and Mechanization, so my background is on agricultural issues (conservation, irrigation, focused on this area). But after I had worked for a Catholic organization I came to see this issue about management, and it opened my eyes to see these social issues. It would have never occurred without that experience. (Entrepreneur #3)

However, in some cases, a high level of personal motivation constituted the driver to fill a knowledge gap, inducing the prospective entrepreneur to undertake initiatives to improve the entrepreneurial knowledge needed to run the feasibility assessment:

> I was thinking how to come up with something new to reduce the poverty in my community and, once I have had my business idea, I spent a couple of months thinking on how to bring my idea into reality. I was afraid about how to implement my business idea because I knew I need more skills, technical skills, and this is the reason why I decided to attend a management master [programme]. (Entrepreneur #10)

Moderating Variables

The theoretical model we propose includes other constructs – social and emotional involvement – that, in turn, moderate the relationship of first-person opportunity recognition with knowledge and motivation. Evidence collected from interviews, documents and by direct observation suggest that the degree of involvement experienced by prospective entrepreneurs – in terms of social acceptance by the local civil society and emotional closeness with target beneficiaries – enhances the likelihood that feasibility and desirability assessments will lead the individual to engage in entrepreneurial action.

Social involvement

By 'social involvement', we indicate here the degree of acceptance acknowledged for an individual by the community in which they are establishing their venture. This definition refers to the notions of network and cultural embeddedness put forward by Zukin and DiMaggio (1990) and later recalled by Kistruck and Beamish (2010), which in turn refers to 'strong or weak ties that form interdependencies between actors' (network embeddedness) and 'more macro-level shared meanings and beliefs about appropriate roles and actions' (cultural embeddedness). Evidence provided by data collected from our sample suggests that socially involved entrepreneurs are more likely to positively assess feasibility than those with lower levels of social involvement.

Sharing commonalities (that is, cultural, racial, religious, and so on) and holding social ties with the target community in many cases facilitates access to relevant information or to effective supply and distribution channels, thus enhancing the positive relation of entrepreneurial and context-specific knowledge in the development of entrepreneurial intention:

> Developing my business idea in the community where I live helps me because I know the people and it is easier to make them open up during my interviews. (Entrepreneur #2)

> For myself, who was grown in that village, won't be a problem getting access to the resources I need from them [locals] since they are confident that I won't betray them, since we share mostly the same condition. (Entrepreneur #31)

Wide acceptance by people in the community in which the venture will operate, the understanding of values and cultures dominant in the local area, and the support guaranteed by a network of long-standing relationships represent features that affect the feasibility assessment by enhancing or decreasing the direct effect of knowledge on the development of entrepreneurial intention and subsequent engagement in action.

Some interviewees showed how confidence in the target community's collaboration and acceptance enhanced their confidence to reach their expectations by lowering their perception of risk, thus making the opportunity more attractive: 'I believe in my people. I believe in my community; they will provide me the support I need. Because of that the profit of my business has to return to my community and my business must increase the global conditions of my community' (Entrepreneur #25).

Emotional involvement
However, our model predicts emotional involvement moderating the relationship between motivation and first-person opportunities in sustainable development contexts. Emotional involvement, which indicates the degree of positive feelings that an individual has for others, emerged in most cases as a construct improving an individual's motivation effect on the likelihood of recognizing a first-person opportunity for sustainable development.

High levels of emotional involvement enhance the desirability assessment by increasing individual expectations of benefits for the target beneficiaries. In the individual perspective, such expectations assume higher intensity as a consequence of the value that the beneficiaries assume for the entrepreneur himself or herself. Indeed, higher levels of emotional involvement have been detected among entrepreneurs targeting the primary people with whom the entrepreneurs were emotionally close (families, clans, and so on). In these cases, motivation assumed primary relevance in the development of entrepreneurial intention, which was often confirmed by the choice to adopt business models that were overtly socially or environmentally oriented:

> Personally, I have always had the desire to come to the aid of my brothers and sisters in humanity in difficult situations. Therefore, I consider myself more as a social entrepreneur. Then, I think that the social nature of my business idea is an eloquent testimony. (Entrepreneur #6)
>
> I'm not so concerned about profit, but I have more interest in creating value for my community. I'm going to create employability for my brothers and sisters, and I want to use profit to finance educational programmes because, in the long term, I want to create stability in the local economy. I want to produce and sell cooking oil in local context to provide products at a lower price than now, this being economic sustainable and, at the same time, giving access to oil also to my people. (Entrepreneur #10)

However, a review of the business proposals submitted by the prospective entrepreneurs before they enrolled in the programme suggested that they intended to pursue opportunities that were suboptimal from a rational-economic perspective. In these cases, part of the interview session turned on the feasibility of the entrepreneurial opportunity to isolate the motivational factors pushing the prospective entrepreneur toward entrepreneurial action by favouring overconfidence on the feasibility assessment. In this vein, emotional involvement emerged as related to an overly optimistic assessment of the business opportunity regardless of objective constraints that would lead to discarding the venture.

DISCUSSION

Findings presented in the previous section provide evidence about the drivers of first-person entrepreneurial action in the sustainable development domain. Extant literature connecting the opportunity recognition process with entrepreneurial action acknowledged a primary role for knowledge and motivation in driving individuals to take initial steps in creating a business (McMullen and Shepherd, 2006; Shane et al., 2003; Krueger, 2000). Adopting a cognitive approach to opportunity recognition, McMullen and Shepherd (2006) suggested that knowledge and motivation were necessary to overcome uncertainty along two steps of the process, in which the prospective entrepreneur recognizes a general opportunity to be exploited by a third person (the first step), to eventually realize that it may constitute a business opportunity for himself or herself (the second step).

The present chapter contributes to the literature on opportunity recognition by focusing on the emerging stream of entrepreneurship for sustainable development (Baron and Ensley, 2006; Kirzner, 1979). Previous studies explored cognitive drivers to entrepreneurial action mostly within the traditional domain of commercial (or business) entrepreneurship. Our study aims at following up the work by Patzelt and Shepherd (2011) that proposed a set of propositions explaining the drivers for recognizing third-person entrepreneurial opportunities in the sustainable development domain. Specifically, we shifted to the first-person opportunity stage through a qualitative, in-depth study targeting 36 prospective entrepreneurs enrolled in an MBA programme in Nairobi, Kenya.

Our model extends previous studies by combining constructs that had an active role in the opportunity recognition process with new subdimensions of knowledge and motivation that lead individuals to directly undertake entrepreneurial action. Specifically, our findings suggest that entrepreneurial knowledge and knowledge of the natural and communal environment directly influence entrepreneurial action. Regarding the former (entrepreneurial knowledge), evidence suggests that it exerts a direct impact on entrepreneurial action without having any moderating effect on other relationships; this does not conflict with the model proposed by Patzelt and Shepherd (2011) that suggested a moderating effect in the third-person stage. The shift of entrepreneurial knowledge from a moderating to a direct role in recognizing opportunities for sustainable development can be ascribed to the different forms of uncertainty that individuals have to deal with in the third- and first-person stages. Indeed, while recognizing third-person opportunity requires individuals overcoming radical uncertainty or ignorance based on their prior knowledge (McMullen and Shepherd, 2006), in this context, a high degree of entrepreneurial knowledge enhances the identification of an opportunity by allowing them to 'connect the dots' of their prior knowledge in more effective ways, uncovering relations that may remain hidden (Patzelt and Shepherd, 2011). In the first-person stage (instead), uncertainty assumes the form of doubt requiring individuals to perform a feasibility assessment to evaluate their suitability for the opportunity itself. This assessment assumes entrepreneurial knowledge is a necessary element in the decision-making process since such knowledge provides the set of criteria according to which the opportunity will be judged. However, the knowledge of the natural and communal environment construct emerged as strongly related to the knowledge of the reasons why previous attempts failed to respond to natural and communal needs and of possible alternative mechanisms that could fill this gap.

Regarding motivation, our model suggests that altruism and perception of goodwill of natural and communal environment are the main drivers of the desirability assessment of the entrepreneurial opportunity. Not surprisingly, altruism was previously discussed by Patzelt and Shepherd (2011) as a key dimension of motivation for identifying third-person opportunities for sustainable development. Our data suggest that altruism is a key driver even in the desirability assessment stage, when the prospective entrepreneur decides whether their desire for helping others may overcome the action-specific uncertainty.

A slight difference with the work of Patzelt and Shepherd (2011) can be found in the construct of perception of goodwill towards the natural and communal environment. Although in the third-person stage entrepreneurs are motivated to identify opportunities in response to a threat they perceive in their environment, our findings suggest that when assessing the desirability of their action individuals are motivated by the perception that they will be rewarded with the approval of the beneficiaries who will appreciate the individuals' initiative. This specificity may constitute a difference from traditional, commercial entrepreneurs who may pursue legitimacy of their action.

Last, our model includes two moderating variables, social and emotional involvement, that affect, in turn, the effects of knowledge and motivation on entrepreneurial action. Although social involvement favours the identification of first-person entrepreneurial opportunities for sustainable development by facilitating access and confidence in resources and relationships locally available (thus enhancing the feasibility and desirability assessments), emotional involvement may allow the emergence of trade-offs between a higher level of motivation and an overestimation of the economic feasibility of the opportunity to be pursued. This construct, distinct from mere altruism – since it implies a commitment to a specific group of people who are emotionally linked, compared to a more generic attitude to sustain people in need – may assume different degrees of relevance in different entrepreneurial profiles. This potential trade-off calls for attention from public and private institutions supporting entrepreneurship for sustainable development, which may develop policies to counterbalance this risk of overconfidence.

LIMITATIONS AND FUTURE RESEARCH

The present study was designed as a qualitative study, aimed at generating new theory rather than testing and validating extant relationships (Eisenhardt, 1989). The outcome consists of a set of theoretical propositions linking individuals' knowledge and motivation to their ability to identify first-person opportunities and engage in entrepreneurial action. However, research on opportunity recognition assuming social and environmental criteria with higher or the same relevance of economic goals is in its initial stages and deserves further attention. Future research opportunities may stem from this initial study: starting from Patzelt and Shepherd's (2011) and our work, researchers may 'operationalize' constructs and test the models empirically to obtain statistical confirmation.

In terms of practical implications (though needing statistical confirmation), our findings provide an initial indication of the entrepreneurial profiles more likely to engage in action. The taxonomy proposed by Zahra et al. (2009) – who proposed three profiles of social entrepreneurs: social bricoleur, social constructionist and social engineer – is recalled here and transposed to the setting of entrepreneurship for sustainable development. According to Zahra et al. (2009), the three profiles differ in the scope of their action, which mainly depends on their orientation, with the social bricoleur more local and community-driven, and the social engineer more global and issue-driven.

Most individuals in our sample reflected the characteristics of the bricoleur profile, as they were mostly part of the community they aim to serve and their business models are often sized for their target community. Alternative entrepreneurial profiles – such as social constructionist and social engineer – are excluded by our study. Being aware of this limitation, a possible implication is that bricoleurs may find a higher level of emotional involvement than constructionist and engineers, since those in the former category are usually driven by the community they aim to serve rather than the social or environmental issue they aim at challenging.

This consideration opens up two research questions worth addressing in future studies: first, how can the downsides of high levels of emotional involvement for the social bricoleur be properly managed? Second, how can social bricoleurs be encouraged to give up a strictly local focus in favour of a scaling-up approach that could benefit society at large?

Regarding limitations, against the benefits recalled in the methodology section, theoretical sampling has a specific downside that may prevent potential divergences from emerging clearly. Further research may take such differences into account and explore whether different social entrepreneur typologies require different levels of knowledge and motivation to engage in entrepreneurial action (Zahra et al., 2009; Smith and Stevens, 2010).

A further element that fell outside the domain of this study regards the effect that the equilibrium among the goals of a triple bottom line may exert on the process of opportunity recognition. Different configurations among economic, social and environmental objectives may lead to different priorities in the feasibility and desirability assessments, resulting in different likelihoods in recognizing opportunities for sustainable development. Future research may consider the effects that individuals' attitudes and opportunity characteristics – such as the potential for profitability and the potential for value creation – exert on first-person opportunity recognition processes.

NOTE

1. The Ashoka U – Cordes Innovation Award acknowledges international teaching and partnership practices that are innovative and replicable and that make a significant impact on society.

REFERENCES

Austin, J., H. Stevenson and J. Wei-Ski-llern (2006), 'Social and commercial entrepreneurship: same, different, or both?', *Entrepreneurship Theory and Practice*, 30(1), 1–22.

Bacq, S. and F. Janssen (2011), 'The multiple faces of social entrepreneurship: a review of definitional issues based on geographical and thematic criteria', *Entrepreneurship and Regional Development*, 23(5–6), 373–403.

Baron, R.A. (2006), 'Opportunity recognition as pattern recognition: how entrepreneurs "connect the dots: to identify new business opportunities"', *Academy of Management Perspectives*, 20(1), 104.

Baron, R. (2007), 'Entrepreneurship: a process perspective', in J. Baum, M. Frese and R. Baron (eds), *The Psychology of Entrepreneurship*, Mahwah, NJ: Erlbaum, pp. 19–39.

Baron, R. and M. Ensley (2006), 'Opportunity recognition as the detection of meaningful patterns: evidence from comparisons of novice and experienced entrepreneurs', *Management Science*, 52, 1331–44.

Brown, R. (2006), 'State entrepreneurship in Singapore: prospects for regional economic power?', in Y. Cassis and I.P. Minoglou (eds), *Country Studies in Entrepreneurship: A Historical Perspective*, New York: Palgrave, pp. 123–46.

Child, J., Y. Lu and T. Tsai (2007), 'Institutional entrepreneurship in building an environmental protection system for the People's Republic of China', *Organization Studies*, 28(7), 1013–34.

Cohen, B. and M. Winn (2007), 'Market imperfections, opportunity, and sustainable entrepreneurship', *Journal of Business Venturing*, 22(1), 29–49.

Cooper, A.C. and C.M. Daily (1997), 'Entrepreneurial teams', in D.L. Sexton and R.W. Smilor (eds), *Entrepreneurship 2000*, Chicago, IL: Upstart Publishing Company, pp. 127–50.

Creswell, J.W. (2003), *Research Design: Qualitative, Quantitative, and Mixed Methods Approaches*, Thousand Oaks, CA: Sage.

Dean, T.J. and J.S. McMullen (2007), 'Toward a theory of sustainable entrepreneurship: reducing environmental degradation through entrepreneurial action', *Journal of Business Venturing*, 22(1), 50–76.

Dees, J.G. (1998), 'Enterprising nonprofits: what do you do when traditional sources of funding fall short?', *Harvard Business Review*, 76(2), 55–67.

Dimov, D. (2010), 'Nascent entrepreneurs and venture emergence: opportunity confidence, human capital, and early planning', *Journal of Management Studies*, 47(6), 1123–53.

Drayton, W. (2002), 'The citizen sector: becoming as entrepreneurial and competitive as business', *California Management Review*, 44(3), 120–32.

Eisenhardt, K.M. (1989), 'Building theories from case study research', *Academy of Management Review*, 14, 532–50.

Etzioni, A. (1996), *The New Golden Rule: Community and Morality in a Democratic Society*, New York: Basic Books.

Gephart, R. (2004), 'Qualitative research and the *Academy of Management Journal*', *Academy of Management Journal*, 47, 454–62.

Glaser, B. and A. Strauss (1967), *The Discovery of Grounded Theory: Strategies for Qualitative Research*, Chicago, IL: Aldine.

Goodland, R. (1995), 'The concept of environmental sustainability', *Annual Review of Ecology and Systematics*, 26, 1–24.

Hall, J.K., G.A. Daneke and M.J. Lenox (2010), 'Sustainable development and entrepreneurship: past contributions and future directions', *Journal of Business Venturing*, 25(5), 439–48.

Homer-Dixon, T. (2006), *The Upside of Down: Catastrophe, Creativity, and the Renewal of Civilization*, New York: Random House.

Kirzner, I. (1973), *Competition and Entrepreneurship*, Chicago, IL: University of Chicago Press.

Kirzner, I.M. (1979), *Perception, Opportunity and Profit*, Chicago, IL: University of Chicago Press.

Kirzner, I. (1989), *Discovery, Capitalism, and Distributive Justice*, Oxford: Blackwell.

Kistruck, G.M. and P.W. Beamish (2010), 'The interplay of form, structure, and embeddedness in social intrapreneurship', *Entrepreneurship: Theory and Practice*, 34(4), 735–61.

Knight, F.H. (1921), *Risk, Uncertainty, and Profit*, Boston, MA: Houghton Mifflin.

Kreiner, G.E., E.C. Hollensbe and M.L. Sheep (2006), 'Where is the "me" among the "we"?

Identity work and the search for optimal balance', *Academy of Management Journal*, 49, 1031–57.

Kreiner, G., E. Hollensbe and M. Sheep (2009), 'Balancing borders and bridges: negotiating the work–home interface via boundary work tactics', *Academy of Management Journal*, 52, 704–30.

Krueger, N.F. (2000), 'The cognitive infrastructure of opportunity emergence', *Entrepreneurship Theory and Practice*, 24, 5–23.

Lovins, A., E.K. Datta, O. Bustnes, J.G. Koomey and N.J. Glasgow (2004), *Winning the Oil Endgame*, Snowmass, CO: Rocky Mountain Institute.

McCarthy, D.J., S.M. Puffer and S.V. Shekshnia (1993), 'The resurgence of an entrepreneurial class in Russia', *Journal of Management Inquiry*, 2(2), 125–37.

McMullen, J.S. and D.A. Shepherd (2006), 'Entrepreneurial action and the role of uncertainty in the theory of the entrepreneur', *Academy of Management Review*, 31(1), 132–52.

Miles, M. and A. Huberman (1984), *Qualitative Data Analysis*, Beverly Hills, CA: Sage.

Mises, L.W. (1949), *Human Action: A Treatise on Economics*, 3rd rev. edn, New York: Regnery.

Mitchell, R.K., J.B. Smith, E.A. Morse, K.W. Seawright, A.M. Peredo and B. McKenzie (2002), 'Are entrepreneurial cognitions universal? Assessing entrepreneurial cognitions across cultures', *Entrepreneurship Theory and Practice*, 26(4), 9–32.

Nicholls, A. (2006), 'Social entrepreneurship', in D. Jones-Evans and S. Carter (eds), *Enterprise and Small Business: Principles, Practice and Policy*, 2nd edn, Harlow: FT Prentice Hall, pp. 220–42.

Pacheco, D.F., T.J. Dean and D.S. Payne (2010), 'Escaping the green prison: entrepreneurship and the creation of opportunities for sustainable development', *Journal of Business Venturing*, 25(5), 464–80.

Palich, L.E. and D.R. Bagby (1995), 'Using cognitive theory to explain entrepreneurial risk-taking: challenging the conventional wisdom', *Journal of Business Venturing*, 10, 435–38.

Parrish, B.D. (2010), 'Sustainability-driven entrepreneurship: Principles of organization design', *Journal of Business Venturing*, 25(5), 510–23.

Pasour, E.C., Jr (1989), 'The efficient-markets hypothesis and entrepreneurship', *Review of Austrian Economics*, 3, 95–108.

Patzelt, H. and D.A. Shepherd (2011), 'Recognizing opportunities for sustainable development', *Entrepreneurship Theory and Practice*, 35(4), 631–52.

Penner, L.A., J.F. Dovidio, J.A. Piliavin and D.A. Schroeder (2005), 'Pro-social behavior: multilevel perspectives', *Annual Review of Psychology*, 56, 365–92.

Peredo, A.M. and J.J. Chrisman (2006), 'Toward a theory of community based enterprise', *Academy of Management Review*, 31, 309–28.

Peredo, A.M. and M. McLean (2006), 'Social entrepreneurship: a critical review of the concept', *Journal of World Business*, 41, 56–65.

Pettigrew, A.M. (1990), 'Longitudinal field research on change: theory and practice', *Organization Science*, 1(3), 267–92.

Pratt, M.G., K.W. Rockmann and J.B. Kaufmann (2006), 'Constructing professional identity: the role of work and identity learning cycles in the customization of identity among medical residents', *Academy of Management Journal*, 49, 235–62.

Schumpeter, J.A. (1934), *The Theory of Economic Development*, Cambridge, MA: Harvard University Press.

Shane, S. (2000), 'Prior knowledge and the discovery of entrepreneurial opportunities', *Organization Science*, 11(4), 448–69.

Shane, S., E.A. Locke and C.J. Collins (2003), 'Entrepreneurial motivation', *Human Resource Management Review*, 13(2), 257–79.

Shane, S. and S. Venkataraman (2000), 'The promise of entrepreneurship as a field of research', *Academy of Management Review*, 25, 217–26.

Shepherd, D.A., J.S. McMullen and P.D. Jennings (2007), 'Formation of opportunity beliefs: a coherence theory perspective', *Strategic Entrepreneurship Journal*, 1(1–2), 75–95.

Shepherd, D.A. and H. Patzelt (2011), 'The new field of sustainable entrepreneurship:

studying entrepreneurial action linking "What is to be sustained" with "What is to be developed"', *Entrepreneurship Theory and Practice*, 35(1), 137–63.

Smith, B. and C. Stevens (2010), 'Different types of social entrepreneurship: the role of geography and structural embeddedness on measurement and scaling of social value', *Entrepreneurship and Regional Development*, 22, 575–98.

Spicer, M. (2001), *Public Administration and the State: A Postmodern Perspective*, Tuscaloosa, AL: University of Alabama Press.

Strauss, A., and J. Corbin (1998), *Basics of qualitative research: Techniques and Procedures for Developing Grounded Theory*, 2nd edn, Thousand Oaks, CA: Sage.

Suddaby, R. (2006), 'What grounded theory is not', *Academy of Management Journal*, 49(4), 633–42.

Tan, W., J. Williams and T. Tan (2005), 'Defining the "social" in "social entrepreneurship": altruism and entrepreneurship', *International Entrepreneurship and Management Journal*, 1, 353–65.

Tracey, P. and O. Jarvis (2007), 'Toward a theory of social venture franchising', *Entrepreneurship Theory and Practice*, 31, 667–85.

Vaitheeswaran, V.V. (2003), *Power to the People: How the Coming Energy Revolution Will Transform Industry, Change Our Lives, and Maybe Even Save the Planet*, New York: Farrar, Straus & Giroux.

WCED (1987), *Our Common Future*, Oxford: Oxford University Press.

Yin, R. (1989), *Case Study Research: Design and Methods*, Newbury Park, CA: Sage Publishing.

Yin, R. (1994), *Case Study Research: Design and Methods*, 2nd edn, Thousand Oaks, CA: Sage Publishing.

York, J.G. and S. Venkataraman (2010), 'The entrepreneur–environment nexus: uncertainty, innovation and allocation', *Journal of Business Venturing*, 25(5), 449–63.

Yunus, M. (2010), *Building Social Business: The New Kind of Capitalism That Serves Humanity's Most Pressing Needs*, New York: Public Affairs.

Zahra, S., E. Gedajlovic, D. Neubaum and J. Shulman (2009), 'A typology of social entrepreneurs: motives, search processes and ethical challenges', *Journal of Business Venturing*, 24, 519–32.

Zukin, S. and P. DiMaggio (1990), *Structures of Capital: The Social Organization of the Economy*, Cambridge: Cambridge University Press.

8. Cooking up solutions for climate change: the role of sustainable entrepreneurs
Ivan Montiel* and Tara Ceranic

INTRODUCTION

The evidence that human activity is accelerating climate change has given birth to a whole new set of environmental concerns that remain at the core of society's anxiety about the future. The issue has become a focal point on governmental agendas around the world. In December 2009 the United Nations, along with global leaders from around the world, convened at the Climate Change Conference in Copenhagen, Denmark with hopes of reaching: (1) a binding international resolution for the reduction of greenhouse gases emissions; and (2) a set of agreed-upon strategies aimed at helping developing countries reduce their emissions (Cop15, 2009). Climate change is directly tied to economic growth and it is predicted to have tangible impacts on the planet within a few years, if not already (Gore, 2006). These predictions are bringing the climate change issue to the top of the list on organizations' sustainability agendas.

Not only have governments been involved in attempting to mitigate issues around climate change, but entrepreneurs and businesses have also addressed the challenge. Private industry has developed strategies to reduce carbon footprints, and it is important to understand the existing motivations for businesses to begin taking action on this issue.

Our research focuses on sustainable actions being driven by a particular type of entrepreneur and we propose a classification of these individuals based on Zahra's typology of social entrepreneurs (Zahra et al., 2009). Specifically, we are interested in what different mechanisms explain the involvement and entrepreneurial activities of enterprises involved in climate change mitigation strategies. In order to undertake this, we classify and describe different sustainable entrepreneurs for climate change mitigation and the enterprises they have created. First, we provide a clarification of the definitions surrounding the different types of social and environmental entrepreneurship and adapt social entrepreneurship definitions to frame sustainable entrepreneurship. Next, we explain Zahra et al.'s (2009) framework on social entrepreneurship which states that there are three types of social entrepreneurs who often destroy dated systems and replace them with those that are newer and more suitable to society's current needs. These three types of entrepreneurs – bricoleurs, constructionists and engineers – vary in the way they discover social opportunities, determine their impact on a broader social system, and assemble the resources needed to pursue these opportunities. Finally, we adopt Zahra et al.'s (2009) framework and by using a case study approach investigate how these three types of search processes exist in the context of sustainable entrepreneurs interested in climate change mitigation.

SOCIAL, ENVIRONMENTAL AND SUSTAINABLE ENTREPRENEURS

Various descriptions and definitions exist regarding entrepreneurship, as well as the enterprises that serve to address and solve social or environmental issues. This section provides clarification of the most commonly used terms in the area: social entrepreneurship, environmental entrepreneurship and sustainable entrepreneurship. It also highlights their overlapping foundations and similar aims.

Social Entrepreneurship

Researchers in the fields of corporate social responsibility and entrepreneurship have introduced the social entrepreneurship concept, describing social entrepreneurs as individuals concerned with reconfiguring resources in order to achieve specific social objectives. The success of social entrepreneurs is measured by the extent to which they achieve 'social transformation' (Alvord et al., 2004). Social entrepreneurs are characterized by very particular traits such as a special type of leadership, being socially driven, a passion to realize their vision and a strong ethical fibre, which allows them to combine resources to address social problems (Mair and Marti, 2006).

The term 'social entrepreneurship' has grown in popularity in recent years, partially due to Muhammad Yunus being awarded the 2006 Nobel Peace Prize for his work in founding the Grameen Bank in 1976. The Grameen Bank started to catalyse social and economic development in Bangladesh by providing microcredit to the urban and rural poor who often are without collateral (Yunus and Jolis, 2003). The bank has expanded globally and his model has been used as a benchmark for microcredit organizations across the globe.

Environmental Entrepreneurship

Environmental entrepreneurship is defined as 'the process of discovering, evaluating and exploiting economic opportunities that are present in environmentally relevant market failures' (Dean and McMullen, 2007: 58). Examples of environmental entrepreneurs are found in a variety of fields, and the waste management sector is no exception. It continues to provide a multitude of examples as new, cutting-edge businesses have emerged with innovative ways to reuse and/or recycle different types of refuse and materials (Meek et al., 2010). In some instances, the market failures and negative environmental impacts that environmental entrepreneurs address are caused by the issues surrounding global poverty and inequality issues. In these cases, both the social and the environmental goals of entrepreneurs are completely integrated and there are common social and environmental justice goals.

Sustainable Entrepreneurship

Similar to environmental entrepreneurship, recent research has also introduced the term 'sustainable entrepreneurship' to describe business initiatives with an environmental and social drive. For instance, Dean and McMullen (2007) describe sustainable entrepreneurship as a broader term that embraces environmental entrepreneurship but also includes social dimensions. Sustainable entrepreneurship is the process of discovering, evaluating and exploiting economic opportunities that are present in market failures which detract from sustainability. Unlike environmental entrepreneurship, the opportunities sought are not necessarily environmental in nature or even environmentally relevant (although many are). These market failures refer to inefficient firms, externalities, flawed pricing systems and information asymmetries (Cohen and Winn, 2007).

Uniting the Concepts

Corporate sustainability scholars identify a multidimensional construct formed by three interconnected pillars: the economic, the social and the environmental (Montiel, 2008). The social and environmental pillars are more commonly emphasized than the economic pillars in sustainability research and practitioner discussions (Montiel and Delgado-Ceballos, 2014). However, it is critical that the economic dimension is also integrated in the discussions. Bansal (2005) defines the corporate sustainability economic dimension as achieving economic prosperity through value creation: 'Firms create value through goods and services they produce.

Therefore, firms increase the value created by improving the effectiveness of those goods and services efficiently' (p. 200).

If we consider sustainability as a composite of economic, social and environmental dimensions, we may also identify social and environmental entrepreneurs as a subset of sustainable entrepreneurs. In fact, the social and environmental dimensions tend to evolve together and can be almost impossible to disentangle. For instance, in the case of the Grameen Bank and Yunus, the social development created by the bank will not only help individuals with personal economic plights, but will also help Bangladesh socially and environmentally by having a positive impact on decreasing environmental degradation, since the social wealth created by the loans will also alleviate environmental pressures derived from poverty. In addition, without economic prosperity through value creation a social enterprise like the Grameen Bank would not be sustainable. Hence, sustainable entrepreneurs come under a broad umbrella under which social and environmental entrepreneurs also fall. Different terms are used in different cases depending on the pillar that is most emphasized, even though all cases may fall under the umbrella of sustainable entrepreneurship.

A CLASSIFICATION OF SOCIAL ENTREPRENEURS

The previous definitions and descriptions highlight the conflated and, at times, confusing terminology utilized in the realm of entrepreneurship as well as social and environmental initiatives. We propose that frameworks and theories previously developed in the field of social entrepreneurship can be adapted specifically to the case of sustainable entrepreneurship. Therefore, in our proposed classification of sustainable entrepreneurs we use the Zahra et al. (2009) categorization of social entrepreneurs' search processes as the context for understanding entrepreneurs focusing on climate change mitigation. Zahra et al. (2009) highlight three types of social entrepreneurs – social bricoleurs, social constructionists and social engineers – each of which differ by scale, scope and focus. Below we provide further details of Zahra's categories.

Zahra's Social Entrepreneurial Classifications

Zahra et al. (2009) use Hayek (1945) as their theoretical inspiration for the discussion of social bricoleurs. They point to Hayek's (1945) proposition that 'entrepreneurial activities can only be discovered and acted upon at very local levels' (Zahra et al., 2009: 524) and, as such, social bricoleurs are those entrepreneurs that perceive and act upon opportunities to address a local social need which they are motivated to address while having the expertise and resources to do so. Although the solutions proposed by social bricoleurs are sometimes small in both scale and scope, it is important to note that these entrepreneurs are often motivated by bringing social wealth to their communities as well as by addressing what Zahra et al. (2009) call 'serious social problems' (p. 524). One interesting note about social bricoleurs, according to Zahra et al. (2009), is that they can be difficult to locate or observe due to a tendency to become embedded in the location in which they operate. They are often singularly focused on their enterprise and have no desire to upscale it or to further commercialize it.

Kirzner (1973) is the theoretical inspiration for the description of social constructionists by Zahra et al. (2009). Kirzner (1973) stressed the importance of an entrepreneur's ability to find opportunities that they are able to leverage, in contrast to the local focus advocated by Hayek (1945) and the social bricoleurs. Social constructionists create enterprises that deal with social issues otherwise ignored by non-governmental organizations (NGOs), government and business (Zahra et al., 2009). The typical social constructionist designs an enterprise that is scalable (Grant, 1996), as opposed to the intensely local focus of the social bricoleur. They are also motivated by the aspiration to create social wealth while creating equilibrium within large social systems (Zahra et al., 2009).

Finally, Schumpeter (1942) is the theoretical inspiration for social engineers, because they utilize creative destruction in order to fix the social issues they see. Social engineers recognize social problems and aim to solve them via 'revolutionary change'; these entrepreneurs are seen as the most driven of the three by Zahra et al. (2009: 526). The issues that social engineers tackle are large relative to those dealt with by bricoleurs and constructionists. Social engineers also face a particularly difficult challenge, because 'the nature of the reforms they introduce are usually a threat to the interests of established institutions and are sometimes seen as subversive and illegitimate' (Zahra et al., 2009: 526).

Integrating the Sustainability Dimension

The social classifications by Zahra et al. (2009) serve as the foundation for the proposed categorization of sustainable bricoleurs, sustainable constructionists and sustainable engineers. The move from 'social' to 'sustainable' specifically highlights the importance of climate change mitigation practices by entrepreneurs. Table 8.1 summarizes the suggested typology and the main characteristics of sustainable bricoleurs, sustainable constructionists and sustainable engineers, following the same structure that Zahra et al. (2009) used for social entrepreneurs. The next sections

Table 8.1   A typology of sustainable entrepreneurship

Type	Sustainable bricoleur	Sustainable constructionist	Sustainable engineer
Theoretical inspiration	Hayek	Kirzner	Schumpeter
Scale	Small scale	Small to large scale	Large scale
Scope	Local	Local to national	National to international
Significance	Their actions help maintain harmony in the face of sustainability problems	They mend the sustainability fabric where it is torn, address acute sustainability needs within broader sustainability structures	They seek to rip apart existing structures and replace then with new ones. They represent an important force for social change
Source of discretion	Being on the spot with the skills to address local problems not on other 'radars'	They address needs left unaddressed. They may be seen as a 'release valve' preventing negative publicity or sustainability problems that adversely affect existing business organizations	Popular support to the extent that existing structures are incapable of addressing important sustainability needs

Source: Adapted from Zahra et al. (2009).

are devoted to describing our method, and how our *ex ante* case study analyses were mapped into Zahra's social entrepreneurship model.

METHODS

We utilized the case study approach for this research in order to better understand the dynamics present in specific entrepreneurial settings (Eisenhardt, 1989; Yin, 2002). This approach allowed for detailed within-case analyses via write-ups that led the authors to be what Eisenhardt (1989) described as 'intimately familiar with each case as a stand-alone entity' (p. 540). This understanding led to the emergence of descriptions of each of the types of entrepreneurs that, in turn, yielded the links to Zahra's model (Zahra et al., 2009). Case studies directly represent the real-world and practical context of models (Baumgärtner et al., 2008) thus making them an appropriate methodological choice for this research.

Selection of Cases

The case studies we utilized were selected not only due to the unique characteristics of the enterprise, but also for the particularities of the founding entrepreneurs. Both authors have been collaborating on case writing for some time and we realized that there were convergences and differences in how the three companies analysed dealt with the issues of climate change. We identified all three cases as companies with a sustainable entrepreneurship component, but with differences in their approaches. At the same time, we were learning and reading about theories, definitions and conceptual models of social entrepreneurship, and identified similarities between the categorization used by Zahra et al. and our three cases studies. We therefore adapt Zahra's model to our three case study analysis. While analysing these cases, we were able to better understand the characteristics of the founders of the enterprises and the differences among the mechanisms used to establish sustainability policies, their scope and scale, and the mobilized resources. These differences were then mapped on to Zahra's social entrepreneurship model.

RESULTS

Table 8.2 maps the different traits defined by Zahra's model and how those relate to the types of sustainable bricoleurs, constructionists and engineers in our three cases.

Type I: The Sustainable Bricoleur

We view sustainable bricoleurs as those entrepreneurs who have identified a local need to improve the sustainability of business systems and are using their expertise and resources to address the problem. Sustainable bricoleurs may start with a general goal of good corporate citizenship that is then drilled down to a level of greater specificity. For example, the sustainable bricoleur may opt to include social responsibility focused on stakeholders such as employees and customers, or they may consider the natural environment with a focus on climate change-related issues.

Table 8.2   Cases of sustainable entrepreneurs for climate change mitigation

Type	Sustainable bricoleur	Sustainable constructionist	Sustainable engineer
Case	Grenada Chocolate Company	Sierra Nevada Brewing Co.	WVO technology (e.g. Veg Rev)
Scale	Small	Small to large	Large
Scope	Grenada community (local)	California and the United States (local to national)	WVO initiatives worldwide (international)
Significance	Its actions help maintain harmony in Grenada regarding sustainability issues (renewable energy, organic farming)	It mends the sustainability fabric where it is torn by becoming the first 100% solar power brewery, applying novel water saving techniques	It seeks to rip apart existing structures (petrol as the only alternative to run vehicles) and replace with new ones (waste veggie oil technology). It represents an important source of social change
Source of discretion	Address local problems not on 'other' radars: help the locals in Grenada	Address needs left unaddressed: become energy self-sufficient with renewable sources	Popular support comes from users wanting to use other fuels to address important sustainable needs
Interaction between government and business	No interaction	Took advantage of federal and state incentives	Alternative model to what was promoted by government
Taking advantage of locality	Uniquely suited for organic farming and community engagement	Local availability of original brewery components	Progressive mindset, availability of space and capital to engage in WVO vehicle conversion

The following is a description of Mott Green and his factory. The Grenada Chocolate Company is a small, solar-powered, employee co-operative located in the Caribbean, and serves as a clear example of the sustainable bricoleur.

Mott Green and Grenada Chocolate Company

Grenada Chocolate Company (GCC) was founded in 1999 by Mott Green and two friends (Edmond Brown and Doug Browne) on the Caribbean island of Grenada and has seen the demand for its chocolates skyrocket in recent years. GCC is one of the few companies in the world to produce bean-to-bar chocolates, that is, cocoa grown in its own fields and converted to chocolate all in one place: the company's solar-powered factory. Mott's main goals by bringing GCC into existence were twofold: to help the local economy and, for perhaps the first time in history, to make it possible for those who grow cocoa beans to also make the chocolate – and consume it. Before GCC, the people of Grenada had only eaten milk chocolate from the USA and Europe. They did not know much about fine dark chocolate, even though their country produces some of the most superb cocoa beans available in the world. With such quality regional beans, GCC has sold its chocolate to the people of Grenada and the tourists who visit, allowing the income generated from the sale of the cocoa products to remain in Grenada. The founders never intended the sustainably produced organic chocolate to be sold in large quantities to the international market. Their intention from the beginning was to introduce the delectable chocolate to the people who call the island home, while showcasing the gourmet chocolate to visitors. With tourism as the country's largest industry, Mott and his crew wanted to give visitors yet another reason to return to the gorgeous island in order to further stimulate the local economy. The rich bittersweet flavour and fruity cocoa notes of the chocolate attracted visitors, who fell in love with GCC's product, which in turn fuelled additional tourism to the island.

GCC's beans are grown at Belmont Estate on its 100 acre farm, located 1 mile from the GCC factory. All of its beans are completely organic, as is the sugar and vanilla used as additional ingredients. The high cost of pesticides led local farmers to rely on preventative maintenance rather than chemicals, allowing GCC to immediately be certified organic by the United States Department of Agriculture (USDA) National Organic Program (NOP), as well as by BCS Oko-Garantie GmbH, an independent and private controlling agency which certifies organic products worldwide in accordance with various regulations and private standards. According to the USDA, 'organic food is produced by farmers who emphasize the use of renewable resources and the conservation of soil and water to enhance environmental quality for future generations'. Organic food is produced without using most conventional pesticides, fertilizers made with synthetic ingredients or sewage sludge, bioengineering, or ionizing radiation. Before a product can be labelled 'organic', a government-approved certifier inspects the farm where the food is grown to make sure the farmer is following all the rules necessary to meet USDA organic standards.

All of GCC's other ingredients are certified organic as well. The tiny amount of soy lecithin necessary in the production process is made from non-GMO (genetically modified organism) soybeans. The sugar comes from an organic raw sugar growers' co-operative in Paraguay, and the vanilla beans are grown biodynamically in Costa Rica. Biodynamic farming is a holistic traditional farming technique used to cultivate the highest quality of products. In addition, practices such as crop rotation, composting and biodynamic farming integrate agricultural, biological and ecological scientific knowledge into crop rotation, compost production, and soil and animal practices. A product that is certified biodynamic exceeds the standards and regulations for organic certified farming.

GCC and climate change
The overloaded power grid of Grenada is not completely reliable. Outages occur once or twice a month, typically for an entire day at a time, which combined with the founders' dedication to sustainable technology, led the company to install several photovoltaic (PV) solar panels to supply the electricity used by its chocolate-making machines. The power system at GCC was entirely fashioned by Mott Green. Sixteen 120 watt PV modules were installed on the roof of the factory and on the ground next to the building. As a result, GCC has 6920 watts of photovoltaic power from the PV panels. These are connected to large, deep-cycle batteries and various controls, and provide the majority of the factory's electricity needs. GCC does use grid power and a propane-fuelled generator to supplement and back up its system at times when there is cloudy weather. The system powers the air conditioning required in two special rooms: the moulding room and the wrapping room. These two rooms are a key factor to operations as they are the heart of the process producing 300 pounds of chocolate and cocoa powder every week. Chocolate making is a 24-hour a day activity, and the machines require constant power, so the combination of the grid, the solar panels and the generator allows GCC to run at full capacity without concern that its machines will stop running in the middle of production.

GCC is not only reducing its carbon footprint by generating its own electricity with its solar grid system, but its bean-to-bar business model is also part of its plan. Since GCC manufactures chocolate where cocoa beans grow, it immediately lowers the carbon footprint associated with the production of a conventional chocolate bar. Before GCC, cocoa beans grown in Grenada were transported thousands of miles to Europe or North America. Now, cocoa beans do not travel around the world for consumption, but rather remain on the island to become high-end chocolate bars.

GCC is a clear example of a sustainable bricoleur. As summarized in Table 8.1, from a local and small-scale approach, GCC has developed a social enterprise that also involves sustainability practices to reduce its carbon footprint and its impact on climate change. Its actions help to maintain harmony in the face of the sustainability issues faced by developing nations, since they have been on the spot with the appropriate skills to address local programmes not taken into account on other 'radars' (Zahra et al., 2009). From a motivation perspective, GCC began from a social entrepreneurial approach, helping people in Grenada first, but its commitment to corporate social responsibility has been transferred to helping the natural environment, which led to the use of solar panels to reduce its carbon footprint, as well as to the use of organic ingredients. GCC was easily able to implement all of its sustainable technologies without any regulatory obstacles from the Grenadian government, and the unique location of the island allowed it to easily implement organic farming that directly benefited the local community.

Type II: The Sustainable Constructionist

Social constructionists build and operate alternative structures to provide goods and services addressing needs that governments, agencies and businesses cannot (Zahra et al., 2009). Adapting this definition to sustainable constructionists for climate change yields entrepreneurs building and operating alternative structures to provide goods and services addressing environmental concerns that governments and other agencies cannot. A clear example of this is Ken Grossman, founder of Chico, California-based Sierra Nevada Brewing Co. (SNBC). Grossman has made significant efforts to change the way beer is produced and aims specifically to reduce his organization's impact on the environment. The amount of waste that a brewery produces would be too difficult for the local government of Chico, California to reclaim. Therefore, SNBC took responsibility for the waste it generates and using the available resources, including government subsidies, it is moving closer and closer to a zero carbon and wastewater footprint.

Ken Grossman and Sierra Nevada Brewing Co.
Starting with the dedication of the founder, owner and chief executive officer (CEO), Ken Grossman, SNBC had a very strong commitment to reducing its impact on the environment. In 1976, Ken opened The Home Brew Shop in Chico, California where he sold home-brewing equipment

and materials and shared his advice, while planning to open his own brewery at some point in the future. The future arrived in 1979, and Sierra Nevada Brewing Company (SNBC) was born. Named for the mountains that are Ken's favourite hiking grounds, Ken and co-founder Paul Camusi built the original Sierra Nevada brewery using dairy tanks, a soft-drink bottler and salvaged equipment from other breweries that had ceased their operations.

On 15 November 1980, SNBC brewed the first batch of its still popular beer, Sierra Nevada Pale Ale. Within a decade, demand outgrew the original brewery, and SNBC moved to their current site. The heart of the new brewery was a German 100-barrel copper brew house that Ken had shipped to Chico following a trip to Germany. In 1997, the German brew house could no longer meet the capacity demand, and coppersmiths were brought in to match new kettles to the originals.

SNBC and climate change
SNBC has developed different programmes to reduce its carbon footprint. In 2005 it completed a carbon dioxide recovery system that captures carbon dioxide and circulates it back to the plant. One year later, the company set up a comprehensive programme to account for all the greenhouse gas emissions associated with plant operations (including its onsite restaurant and concert venue). This inventory was reported to the California Climate Action Registry.

In 2007, Sierra Nevada Brewing Company started the process of becoming the first 100 per cent solar-powered brewery in the United States. The California Solar Initiative partially funded Sierra Nevada Brewing Company's 503 kW solar arrays. This original installation was housed on top of the SNBC parking garage and contained a tracking feature that maximized the time spent facing the sun. The addition of the newer installation resulted in of one of the largest private solar arrays in the United States. The project started on 16 September 2007, and was completed in 2008. The company gained 1.4 MW of AC power for the brewery.

For solar energy system installations, 100 per cent of the value of the system could be claimed as a property tax exclusion for certain types of systems installed between 1 January 1999 and 31 December 2009. The California Solar Initiative, Go Solar, California!, was overseen by the California Public Utilities Commission and offered financial incentives for solar installations based on the expected performance of a given solar installation. The government of California also implemented two incentive alternatives for solar customers: the Expected Performance Based Buydown (EPBB) and the Performance Based Initiative. Each of these incentives offered payments to organizations based upon the amount of energy produced.

SNBC also implemented a programme to reuse spent vegetable oil from its restaurant in the form of biodiesel for its local and long-haul delivery trucks. Measures such as these have garnered the company the Waste Reduction Awards Program (WRAP) award from the State of California every year since 2001. In 2002, SNBC received recognition as one of the top ten recipients of the WRAP of the Year Award for its waste reduction programmes. In 2005, SNBC received California Governor Arnold Schwarzenegger's Governor's Environmental and Economic Leadership Award, which recognizes Californians and California-based organizations and businesses that are working voluntarily to conserve resources or improve the environment. In 2006, SNBC was the first brewing company to join the California Climate Action Registry, a group of organizations distinguished by demonstrating leadership in voluntarily taking action to abate climate change. Members of the programme are required to track, report and certify greenhouse gas emissions on an annual basis.

SNBC's recycling even extended to byproducts of the brewing process. The spent hops, grain and yeast were collected and used as feed for local dairy and beef cows at California State University, Chico's farm. The reusing and recycling continued, as the compost from the cow manure was used as fertilizer for the experimental hop field at SNBC.

The solar panel initiatives and biodiesel helped SNBC's goal of reducing its carbon footprint. SNBC utilized existing governmental regulations and incentives to develop its sustainable technology, and some of its success comes from its ingenuity in repurposing local machinery and resources. In addition, its overall sustainability mindset has driven it to behave as a sustainable constructionist for climate change.

Type III: The Sustainable Engineer

The third group of social entrepreneurs described by Zahra et al. (2009) are the social engineers. Social engineers create newer, more effective social systems designed to replace existing ones when they are ill-suited to address significant social needs. These entrepreneurs are more aligned with radical innovators. For instance, in the context of initiatives to improve climate change, the sustainable engineer is the kind of entrepreneur that will innovate and try to replace existing technology that contributes to the emission of greenhouse gases for cleaner technology.

The example we offer here is that of the promoters and users of waste vegetable oil (WVO) as an alternative to petrol-run vehicles. The vehicle combustion process is one of the principal contributors to climate change, and increased awareness, combined with rising gas prices, has spurred an interest in alternative fuels such as electric-powered vehicles and the use of biodiesel. An alternative to the use of biodiesel is the use of WVO or rendered animal fats as fuel. This 'underground' activity has proliferated in the United States and advocates believe that more than 250 000 Americans are running their vehicles on cooking oil (Halper, 2008).

WVO as a fuel

WVO as a fuel consists of used vegetable oils generally taken from restaurants that are then processed into fuel for WVO converted vehicles. Food bits are filtered out of the restaurants' WVO and it is converted into straight vegetable oil, SVO, which will not clog a car's engine. WVO only works in diesel engines; therefore, regular petrol-powered vehicles cannot be used. The process of converting a vehicle into a WVO vehicle is the implementation of the WVO system which, according to Calais and Clark, involves installing several new components in the existing engine (Calais and Clark, 2001). Some businesses such as Lovecraft Bio-Fuels in Los Angeles are now specializing in installing the WVO conversion systems, providing oil, fuel and maintenance. Other companies such as Greasercar and Frybird provide conversion kits for individuals who prefer to install the system themselves.

There are several environmental benefits associated with the use of WVO as fuel. Unlike fossil fuels, vegetable-based fuels burn cleaner and are non-toxic (Grabianowski, 2008). WVO fuels do not contain sulphur, and are 'carbon-neutral' as the vegetables grown to produce oil consume more carbon dioxide than is released when the oil burns (Layton, 2009). Not only do WVO users find cost efficiencies in their use of WVO, but restaurants that provide users with WVO do as well. Considering that restaurants incur costs when disposing of WVO, if WVO users take it off their hands, restaurants may experience cost efficiency by no longer having to pay for WVO disposal. As of June 2011 a gallon of diesel fuel was priced at about $3.95. A gallon of waste vegetable oil, the stuff restaurants use in their fryers, costs almost nothing (Layton, 2009). It becomes 'fiscally advantageous' to use WVO, since this means lowering emissions and recycling wasted oil which would otherwise just be thrown away, and at a price to the business. Other entrepreneurs have also emerged from this, becoming middlemen between restaurants and WVO users.

Even though this clean technology seems to be a good alternative to the traditional vehicles, government regulations appear to create barriers rather than incentives for WVO. Government agencies would like fuel sellers to be licensed, instead of people fuelling up by forming a relationship with a local restaurant (Kuhn, 2006). In the state of California, for example, it is required by law for WVO users to have a licence in order to take WVO from local restaurants. Biofuel users who want to collect vegetable oil have to apply for a licence from the meat and poultry inspection branch of the California Department of Food and Agriculture. Similar processes exist in other states:

> In at least two cases, one in Illinois and one in North Carolina, grease-car owners have been told they need to register as 'fuel receivers' a designation usually reserved for companies in the fuel business. To become a 'fuel receiver' you have to buy a $2500 bond up-front as a guarantee that you'll pay your taxes. (Layton, 2009)

What concerns the state governments is not the users finding alternative ways to use fuel, but the tax that is being lost in the process, which is crucial revenue for the state and local government to use in maintaining their highways and roads.

The biggest obstacle is a simple lack of infrastructure to deal adequately with WVO as fuel. In some states, people can sign up to pre-pay fuel taxes when they make the switch to WVO, but that requires an established system to collect and tag that money as WVO-connected, which many states are not yet set up to accomplish. This is why these users get stuck within the framework for other types of fuels and end up being labelled as 'fuel receivers'. WVO advocates state that such regulation would make it hard for most people to keep their 'veggie-cars' fuelled, because few people would be lucky enough to have a licensed seller nearby to top up their tank.

In addition, the Environmental Protection Agency (EPA) announced that using WVO as fuel is a violation of the Clean Air Act, and that modifying a car for WVO subjects the owner to a $2570 fine (Norman, 2006). Also, in California, the government classified WVO B100 fuel (a mix of 80 per cent veggie oil and 20 per cent alcohol) as a 'blend stock'. Blend stock is any substance used for compounding petrol, including natural petroleum, catalytically reformed products and additives, rather than a fuel itself (Washburn, 2008), leaving retailers unsure of the legality of selling it. Moreover, new federal tax credits for biodiesel seem to exclude B100.

With the volatile price of oil in recent years, and many consumers seeking to reduce their carbon footprint:

> Congress has decreed that the country must be using 21 billion gallons of 'advanced' biofuels a year by 2022. Washington is backing that goal with tax breaks, loan guarantees and scores of millions of dollars in grants, with more support expected in upcoming energy bills. These inducements and the vast potential market have stimulated investments of more than $3 billion and spawned a new industry. (Carey, 2009)

There are many benefits that can arise from switching from oil to biofuels. One of the most direct benefits is that the fuel will be generated from crops that are grown directly for fuel purposes, rather than extracting oil, which damages the environment. This will in turn lead to many job opportunities and growth for companies and consumers. Also, since the biofuel will be domestically made, there would be a significant decline in the dependence on foreign oil. However, one of the problems of growing crops for fuel is the competition for these crops as a source of energy and food. The WVO technology does not compete with food resources, because it was waste oil that would have been discharged to a treatment plant otherwise.

Veg Rev and climate change
Veg Rev, founded by William Hibbits and David Shelhart, began its activities in 2004 with the goal to help people reduce their carbon footprint by converting vehicles to WVO. The founders describe WVO as a non-toxic, biodegradable, sustainable, locally sourced and plentiful resource that burns cleaner than traditional biodiesel. Veg Rev first started conversions with individual customers, but businesses are now becoming interested in the technology. The two founders claim to be in the business of 'vehicle fuel reassignment surgery', and can be seen as sustainable engineers for their efforts to help spread the use of WVO as fuel and help interested parties in the conversion process of their vehicles.

Veg Rev specializes in designing systems that enabling any diesel vehicle to run on WVO (Veg Rev, 2008). It also instals WVO kits from any of the major WVO kit providers, sells filtered WVO and does repairs on anything 'veggie' related; for example, changing fuel filters, replacing and upgrading fuel lines to biodiesel grade, troubleshooting faulty systems, and completing conversions that other mechanics were unable to complete. One of their recent customers, Andre Larzul, owner of three restaurants in the Bay Area (Alamo Square Seafood Grill, Blue Jay and Café Revolution), converted his Mercedes truck to WVO. This investment paid back in just a couple of months and the restaurants are now able to use their own waste oil for all their transportation and delivery tasks.

Veg Rev illustrates the emergence of new business opportunities from the perspective of a specific environmental challenge: climate change. The company has identified a niche market of customers who are willing to invest in the conversion of diesel vehicles into WVO technology. Along with the users, they have become sustainable engineers by recognizing systemic problems with existing social structures, and addressing them by introducing revolutionary changes (Zahra et al., 2009). Veg Rev created a new realm in terms of business and government relations in the state of

California because of the novelty of its product. It challenged the status quo and proposed an alternate model to what was in place in terms of the availability of fuel, and was able to take advantage of the locality due to the progressive mindset of the locals and their willingness to invest in WVO vehicle conversion.

DISCUSSION AND CONCLUSIONS

Following the Zahra et al. (2009) framework we have identified three types of sustainable entrepreneurs that specifically engage in climate change mitigation via their enterprises. In order to apply the framework we present three different enterprises, each illustrating one of the three typologies: sustainable bricoleurs, sustainable constructionists and sustainable engineers. Our research broadens the concepts of social bricoleurs, constructionists and engineers described by Zahra et al. (2009), to issues of corporate sustainability.

In the case of sustainable bricoleurs, local, small-scale initiatives are implemented. As the Grenada Chocolate Company illustrates, these entrepreneurs are embedded in an area and are on the spot with the skills needed to address social problems that otherwise would not be addressed. These types of initiatives might be more likely found in developing regions which many view as 'under the radar'. In cases of sustainable constructionists, larger-scale initiatives are utilized to reduce the carbon footprint. As illustrated by the Sierra Nevada Brewing Co., businesses see the need to attempt to solve unaddressed issues (Zahra et al., 2009) such as solar power on a large scale in private enterprise. In the case of sustainable engineers, there is a recognition that existing structures are simply not able to address important sustainability needs such as alternative fuels to run vehicles. The case of WVO and businesses such as Veg Rev, which specialize in the conversion of diesel vehicles to WVO technology, illustrate this type of business. When looking at the descriptions of each of these three types of entrepreneurs it is clear that they all have common traits. Not only do they all share the same motivation of becoming better corporate citizens, but they all also desire to make environmental improvements via various applications of their entrepreneurial skills.

Through the cases of Sierra Nevada Brewing Co. and Veg Rev we are able to analyse the government–business interactions that help or deter the adoption of sustainable strategies for climate change mitigation. On the one hand, we outline how some sustainable entrepreneurs such as Sierra Nevada have been able to facilitate the pursuit of sustainability goals by receiving some governmental incentives and tax breaks from both the state government of California and the federal government. On the other hand, WVO technology has encountered obstacles, specifically in California, but also throughout the United States. Rather than providing incentives to users of WVO technology, some governmental agencies seem to have introduced obstacles for the efficient diffusion of such practices. One might think that when it comes to radical innovations with huge potential for positive environmental impacts, such as the use of WVO, there would be acceptance of the technology. Unfortunately, WVO was been received with resistance since it provides competition for the oil industry. Sustainable engineers such as those with WVO-related enterprises might have obstacles to overcome, especially during the early diffusion of the technology. An extensive education campaign of the benefits of such technologies might increase the acceptance rate by external stakeholders, that is, governmental agencies at different levels, competitors and potential customers in general.

This chapter also highlights the dynamic interactions that exist between governments and businesses that are proactively trying to reduce their own carbon footprint. On the one hand, we illustrate the role that California state government incentives played in the process of our sustainable constructionist case from Sierra Nevada Brewing Co. by helping it achieve its carbon footprint minimization goals. On the other hand, we present some of the common pitfalls and obstacles that many have experienced while interacting with public sector organizations, including the state of California, while attempting to solve climate change issues.

Our study is not without limitations. We have utilized a qualitative approach that classifies three cases into an existing framework of social entrepreneurs. Although this categorization is helpful to understand mechanisms of sustainable entrepreneurship, we realize that the classifications are not always precise. Some entrepreneurs may share characteristics of bricoleurs, but others may be more aligned with sustainable engineers. In addition, we base our chapter on three single enterprises and realize that expanding the study to more cases or including quantitative approaches could be beneficial in future studies.

Contributions

This study points out similarities between entrepreneurs that aim to create social wealth (social entrepreneurs) with those that aim to minimize their footprint (sustainable entrepreneurs). We show that Zahra's typology is clearly applicable to sustainable entrepreneurs and their enterprises via three case studies. In addition, we illustrate how these types of enterprises tend to tackle both social and environmental projects at the same time, rather than choosing between the two. We see sustainable entrepreneurship as an umbrella under which social and environmental concerns are both addressed equally in the enterprise.

Our study is also useful for managers, policy makers and governmental agencies as an illustration of how proactive enterprises have faced the climate change challenge. It can provide a source of inspiration for new innovations to help minimize the carbon footprint of enterprises across the globe. Future studies may focus on quantitative explorations of different types of sustainable entrepreneurs to measure the real impact and the potential to reduce environmental and social impacts that each type of entrepreneur has. In addition, comparative studies of different types of entrepreneurs can bring more light to the question of which type of entrepreneurs works better under different sustainability challenges. Finally, our study raises some questions regarding the involvement of governmental agencies on the facilitation or hampering of new sustainable initiatives towards climate change mitigation.

It is our intention that the framework provided by this study helps to clarify the different entrepreneurial motivations for the incorporation of sustainability into an enterprise. Additionally, we hope that the three cases described shed light on how it is that entrepreneurs can use their resources and influence to implement sustainability practices in their particular enterprises in order to mitigate climate change.

NOTE

* Corresponding author (imontiel@lmu.edu).

REFERENCES

Alvord, S.H., D.L. Brown and C.W. Letts (2004), 'Social entrepreneurship and societal transformation', *Journal of Applied Behavioral Science*, 40(3), 260–82.

Bansal, P. (2005), 'Evolving sustainably: a longitudinal study of corporate sustainable development', *Strategic Management Journal*, 26(3), 197–218.

Baumgärtner, S., C. Becker, F. Karin, B. Müller and M. Quaas (2008),'Relating the philosophy and practices of ecological economics: the role of concepts, models, and case studies in inter- and transdiciplinary sustainability research', *Ecological Economics*, 67(3), 384–93.

Calais, P. and A. Clark (2001), 'Waste vegetable oil as a diesel replacement fuel', http://www.shortcircuit.com.au/warfa/paper/paper.htm.

Carey, J. (2009), 'The biofuel bubble', *Business Week*, April, http://www.businessweek.com/magazine/content/09_17/b4128038014860.htm.

Cohen, B. and M. Winn (2007), 'Market imperfections, opportunities and sustainable entrepreneurship', *Journal of Business Venturing*, 22, 29–49.

Cop15 (2009), United Nations Climate Change Conference, 7–18 December, http://en.cop15.dk/.

Dean, T.D. and J.F. McMullen (2007), 'Toward a theory of sustainable entrepreneurship: reducing environmental degradation through entrepreneurial action', *Journal of Business Venturing*, 22, 50–76.

Eisenhardt, K.M. (1989), 'Building theories from case research', *Academy of Management Review*, 14, 532–50.

Gore, A. (2006), *An Inconvenient Truth: The Planetary Emergency of Global Warming and What We Can Do About It*, Emmanus, PA: Rodale Press.

Grabianowski, E. (2008), 'Can I really burn vegetable oil in my car?' Howstuffworks.com, http://auto.howstuffworks.com/vegetable-oil-fuel1.htm.

Grant, R.M. (1996), 'Toward a knowledge-based theory of the firm', *Strategic Management Journal*, 17, 109–22.

Halper, E. (2008), 'Vegetable oil fuel cars – and tax bills', *Los Angeles Times*, 6 May, http://www.latimes.com/news/local/la-me-vegoil6 2008may06,0,5223509,print.story.

Hayek, F.A. (1945), 'The use of knowledge in society', *American Economic Review*, 35, 519–30.

Kirzner, I. (1973), *Competition and Entrepreneurship*, Chicago, IL: University of Chicago Press.

Kuhn, P. (2006), 'Can vegetable-oil cars save the world?', *CNN Money*, 24 July, http://money.cnn.com/2006/07/21/news/economy/vegetable_cars/index.htm.

Layton, J. (2009), 'Are grease cars legal?' Howstuffworks.com, http://auto.howstuffworks.com/grease-car1.htm.

Mair, J. and I. Marti (2006), 'Social entrepreneurship research: a source of explanation, prediction, and delight', *Journal of World Business*, 41(1), 36–44.

Meek, W., D. Pacheco and J. York (2010), 'The impact of social norms on entrepreneurial action: evidence from the environmental entrepreneurship context', *Journal of Business Venturing*, 25, 493–509.

Montiel, I. (2008), 'Corporate social responsibility and corporate sustainability: separate pasts, common futures', *Organization & Environment*, 21(3), 245–69.

Montiel, I. and J. Delgado-Ceballos (2014), 'Defining and measuring Corporate Sustainability: Are we there yet?', *Organization & Environment*, 27(2), 113–39.

Norman, J. (2006), 'Grease is the word', *New York Times*, 23 July, http://www.nytimes.com/2006/07/23/automobiles/23AUTO.html?_r=2&pagewanted=2&ei=5070&en=d13689 1e9159166c&ex=1153800000.

Schumpeter, J.A. (1942), *The Theory of Economic Development*, London: Oxford University Press.

Veg Rev (2008), 'Vegetable oil fuel systems', www.vegrev.com.

Washburn, J. (2008), 'Fill your tank with vegetable oil', Money Central, MSN, 28 June, http://moneycentral.msn.com/content/Savinganddebt/Saveonacar/P115218.asp.

Yin, R. (2002), *Case Study Research*, 3rd edn, Thousand Oaks, CA: Sage Publications.

Yunus, M. and A. Jolis (2003), *The Banker to the Poor: Micro-Lending and the Battle against World Poverty*, New York: PublicAffairs.

Zahra, S.A., E. Gedajlovic, D. Neubaum and J.M. Shulman (2009), 'A typology of social entrepreneurs: Motives, search processes and ethical challenges', *Journal of Business Venturing*, 24, 518–32.

9. An exploratory model of the environmental intention of SME directors in Tunisia
Azzedine Tounés, Fafani Gribaa and Karim Messeghem

INTRODUCTION

Research into entrepreneurship and environment has constantly attracted the attention of the scientific community (Bansal and Roth, 2000; Kuckertz and Wagner, 2010). The emergence of the field of sustainable entrepreneurship has increased the theoretical and empirical themes of entrepreneurship. Whilst, at the same time, being associated with the concepts and the theories found in this, sustainable entrepreneurship also includes innovation and the issues relating to sustainability. According to Meek et al. (2010), the aim of this emerging field is to study the processes of sustainable entrepreneurial actions. Consequently, it is searching for solutions to societal and ecological preoccupations (Kuckertz and Wagner, 2010).

For Cordano and Frieze (2000), the growing importance of environmental questions has led managers to question the mechanisms for integrating them into entrepreneurial strategies. According to Ivanaj and McIntyre (2006), the study of the behavioural processes of elaborating sustainable strategies offers a privileged field of investigation. Because it implicates changes in visions, values and attitudes, environmental behaviour remains difficult to comprehend (Flannery and May, 2000). This is why researchers specialized in organization and environment have to pay more attention to how the main decision-makers act, their intentions being on purpose, expressed or noticed by others (Starik and Marcus, 2000).

Even if, as Cordano and Frieze (2000) and Martin-Pena et al. (2010) confirm, a consensus of opinion seems to exist relating to the necessity of evaluating the environmental consequences of company activities, we know little about the behavioural intention of managers with regard to the environment. According to Flannery and May (2000), it is essential to comprehend the intention to understand the changes necessary in the perspective of an ecologically sustainable organization. The intention applied in the field of the environment still remains little explored despite its major role in predicting the different types of behaviour within the disciplines of psycho-sociology, marketing, human resources management and entrepreneurship. Understanding the explanatory factors in environmental intention provides information on a major phase in the sustainable behaviour process. For Ajzen (1991, 2002), it is the best predictor of future behaviour.

The aim of this chapter is to explore the relations between the environmental intention of small and medium-sized enterprise (SME) directors and its determinants in the textile clothing sector of the Sahel region in Tunisia. It was not our objective to measure the intensity or the validity of these connections, but rather to understand the nature of the factors predicting the environmental intention. From a qualitative deductive viewpoint, our target was therefore to recognize the theoretic dimensions of this.

This chapter consists of four main sections. The first presents the theoretical framework of the research. It describes the intention as a trigger for the cognitive process that predicts the environmental behaviour. The conceptual framework highlights two complementary theories: the theory of planned behaviour (Ajzen, 1991) and the entrepreneurial theory (Kuhndt et al., 2004). In the next section, we propose the hypotheses that are likely to contain the determinants of environmental intention. Then we show the research methodology and discuss the choice of the study sample. We highlight the operational strategy, the investigation tool and the analysis techniques used. We also review the main results in the inquiry. In the fourth part, we have discussed these depending on their relevance to the literature used. We summarize the analysis by presenting an exploratory model of the environmental intention of directors of Tunisian SME in the textile clothing sector. We conclude the chapter with the contributions, the limitations and the perspectives in this research.

A THEORETICAL FRAMEWORK BASED ON THE PSYCHOLOGY OF SUSTAINABLE ENTREPRENEURSHIP

The psychology of sustainable development can effectively be used to explain responsible behaviour (Schmuck and Schultz, 2002). Combined with other social sciences, it plays a crucial role as the world moves towards sustainable ways of acting (Oskamp and Schultz, 2006). Psycho-sociology is particularly relevant for predicting behaviour. It explains the process whereby individual and contextual factors influence intention. A psychological approach based on the study of this in the field of sustainable entrepreneurship produces results that are relevant for the practices of the entrepreneurs and the theories of environmental management (Martin-Pena et al., 2010). For this, Ajzen's theory of planned behaviour was successfully used to support environmental intention (Kurland, 1995; Cordano and Frieze, 2000; Flannery and May, 2000).

We have combined another theory with that of planned behaviour, taken from the field of entrepreneurship. The entrepreneurial theory (Kuhndt et al., 2004) analyses the variables of environmental behaviour from the individual characteristics. Before justifying the retained theoretical framework, we present our definition of environmental intention.

A Definition of Environmental Intention

According to Searle (1980), actions are made up of a mental component and a physical one. The mental component contains the intention. Ganascia (1996) confirms that most cognitive activities are conceived intentionally in the sense that they respond to an intention, that is to say an aim. For Cossette (2004), people act consciously in an intentional way with the aim of reaching their targets. The *Dictionnaire de la langue française* (Le Robert Plus, 2012) defines intention 'as the fact of proposing a certain objective'. It originates from the Latin word *intendere* which signifies 'to aim at'. It designates the will to aim at a certain objective.

Intention is used for behavioural studies in entrepreneurship, marketing, human resources, philosophy and law. In law, a crime is legally recognized when it is under the control and the will of its perpetrator (Stefani et al., 1997). Committing an act is not in itself the fact that generates criminal responsibility (Desportes and Le Gunehec, 1997). The doctrine informs us that intention is a monolithic and varied notion where the will to accomplish an act is particularly present (Pradel, 1995).

Philosophical sciences take a particular interest in this concept. According to Boyer (1997: 269), 'moral philosophy requires an elaborated theory of intention, if only to not deprive the "ethics of intention" of their sense (not purely consequentialist) and to create the legal and oral concept of personal responsibility'. In the view of Fisette (1997), conceptual multiplicity accentuates the divergences. However, for this author, three irreducible usages have been distinguished. 'Adverbial use' signifies that we do everything intentionally. 'Substantive use' implies that the intention is formed well before the targeted action is carried out. Finally, the use 'acting with an intention' designates the individual's attitude with regard to the relationship between the action and the expected result. The individual assesses the advantages and the inconveniences of a desirable action according to his or her beliefs and limitations.

In the field of entrepreneurship, intention is the probability that an individual will act according to given behaviour (Ajzen and Fishbein, 1980). From the viewpoint of Ajzen (1991), intentions are supposed to denote the motivational factors which influence behaviour. The stronger they are, the more probable it will be that they can be achieved. According to Davidsson (1995), entrepreneurial intention is determined by the conviction that an entrepreneurial career is a preferable alternative for oneself. It orientates the action towards an objective of venture creation (Bird, 1992). Entrepreneurial intention is a type of personal will (Tounés, 2003; Vesalainen and Pihkala, 1999) which includes the ends and the means (Krueger and Carsrud, 1993). It represents a cognitive process which is developed from motivations, needs, values and beliefs. This process is strongly influenced by situational variables (Learned, 1992; Vesalainen and Pihkala, 1999).

In sustainable entrepreneurship, few studies define environmental intention. In a special issue of the *Academy of Management Journal*, it is surprising that two articles concerned with this subject – those of Cordano and Frieze (2000) and Flannery and May (2000) – do not provide a definition for the intention. According to Kuckertz and Wagner (2010), it is important to distinguish 'sustainable entrepreneurial intention' from 'conventional entrepreneurial intention'. According to Hines et al. (1986), the concept of environmental intention indicates the will to act or to behave in a certain way. It represents an interaction between the cognitive variables (capacity for action, knowledge of strategies and their achievement) and the personal variables (attitudes, self-control and personal responsibility). This concept facilitates the realization of environmental behaviour and appears at the moment when a person publically declares that they wish to accomplish an action. For Martin-Pena et al. (2010), environmental intention determines the way in which managers respond to environmental issues.

In our opinion, environmental intention is an important phase in the cognitive process of environmental behaviour. It is an individual will resulting from personal characteristics and socio-cultural, political and economic contexts. Our views coincide with the 'substantive' and 'acting with intention' usages. This is concerned with the intention of acting in the future with an assessment of the expected results of the desired behaviour.

The Theory of Planned Behaviour (Ajzen, 1991)

This theory is based on the model of reasoned action of Ajzen and Fishbein (1980). It specifies that the individual's intention has a central role in the development of behaviour. Ajzen (1991) states that the intention of adopt-

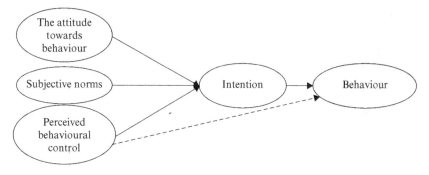

Source: Ajzen (1991).

Figure 9.1   The theory of planned behaviour

ing a behaviour determines the action. Although it is little used to study ethical decision-making (Flannery and May, 2000), the theory of planned behaviour has been successfully used to study environmental intention (Kuckertz and Wagner, 2010). In the view of Martin-Pena et al. (2010: 298), this theory is the starting point for analysing the relations between the relationship between the company manager's environmental intention and their behaviour. Ajzen (1991) confirms that his theory predicts behaviour through three groups of individual or contextual factors (Figure 9.1): the attitude towards the desired behaviour, the subjective norms and the perceived behavioural control.

The attitude towards the expected behaviour implies the degree of evaluation (favourable or unfavourable) that the individual makes; it depends on the estimated results of this behaviour. According to Crozier and Friedberg (1977: 463), the attitude is an attribute which enables an understanding of the chosen behaviour. It represents 'the bridge between the observable conduct of individuals and the structure of unobservable values which orientate them'. For Gergen et al. (1992), the knowledge of the attitudes of an individual towards another person or an object makes it possible to predict their behaviour. The more favourable the attitude is, the stronger the possibility will be that the intention becomes a reality.

According to Meek et al. (2010), social norms are the unwritten rules of conduct in groups. They must be shared by the other members and receive their approbation. Sociology researchers suggest that the majority of individuals belonging to a group believe in the norms that are part of it. The subjective norms concern the influence of the reference groups (family, friends, colleagues, and so on) on individuals' behaviour. They result from the way the pressure from the reference groups is perceived, and the desire (or the constraint) involved in conforming to it. Meek et al. (2010) emphasized that the conformity here refers to individuals' motivation to act according to the rules in society.

Following the theory of planned behaviour, intention can only be expressed if it is under the control of the individual's will. This is why Ajzen (1991) has included in the theory of Ajzen and Fishbein (1980) a third predictive variable: perceived behavioural control. Associated with intention, this makes it possible to directly predict behaviour. It has been empirically shown that if the behaviour is not connected with the factors that the individual cannot master, intention can predict it more precisely. Cordano and Frieze (2000) point out that within the field of sustainable entrepreneurship, managers who have limited power have a weak perception of future behavioural control, and because of this do not take measures to reduce the pollution caused by their activities.

The importance of attitudes associated with behaviour, subjective norms and perceived behavioural control for predicting intention varies depending on the context. For some contexts, only attitudes count; for others, attitudes act at the same time as the behavioural control; and in other cases, the three predictors contribute in an independent way. Apart from this theory of intention, the process of adopting environmental practices has been studied, taking into account the company directors' characteristics that improve our understanding of environmental intention.

Entrepreneurial Theory (Kuhndt et al., 2004)

This theory postulates that the personality and the characteristics of an entrepreneur define their degree of adoption of sustainable behaviour. Contrary to authors arguing that the sustainable commitment of firms is only determined by organizational specificities, a study by the European Observatory for SMEs (European Commission, 2002) highlights the influence of the entrepreneur's personal choices. Within the field of corporate social responsibility, an entrepreneur's cognitive characteristics have a preponderant influence on the integration of social and ecological objectives into decisional strategies (Quairel and Auberger, 2005).

The functions, the beliefs and the characteristics of managers are essential for explaining the sustainable commitment of SMEs (Ben Boubaker-Gherib, 2009; Paradas, 2006). Spence et al. (2007: 28) showed that this is influenced by their values, their entrepreneurial orientation and their perceptions of the environment: 'Firms strongly committed to sustainable development are managed by entrepreneurs who have a long term vision . . . they have an increased entrepreneurial orientation'. Flannery and May (2000) maintain that research on organizational ethics and environmental psychology associates individual and situational factors in order to model environmental intention. To predict that of students and former students of management and engineering schools, Kuckertz and Wagner (2010) paid particular attention to their sustainability orientation.

Entrepreneurial theory represents a relevant conceptual framework for studying company directors' environmental intention. The two theoretical frameworks supporting environmental intention are complementary. The planned behaviour theory is particularly adapted to operationalizing its antecedents. The entrepreneurial theory is well adapted to include individual variables. The theoretical connections have been made, and we will now develop our research hypotheses.

RESEARCH HYPOTHESES

According to Ajzen (1991) the impact of attitudes and perceptions of behavioural intention can be effectively explained through a system of hypotheses. The hypothetico-deductive models elaborated on the basis of the theory of planned behaviour successfully describe intention (Krueger et al., 2000). We have adopted a deductive approach to design a model of environmental intention. This can be described thanks to four homogeneous groups of hypotheses. Three categories of factors explain environmental intention through the theory of planned behaviour. They are: attitudes associated with the required behaviour, subjective norms and perceived behavioural control. A fourth group relating to the entrepreneurial theory analyses this intention through entrepreneurial orientation.

The attitudes associated with behaviour are part of the expected consequences of this behaviour. The subjective norms are considered through the pressure of the company's internal and external stakeholders and the cultural values of the entrepreneurs. The behavioural control emanates from the manager's perceptions of his or her own environmental abilities and the availability (or unavailability) of required resources. The manager's entrepreneurial orientation is shown through proactivity and risk-taking propensity.

Attitudes Towards Environmental Behaviour

The intentions are better understood through specific attitudes. In the view of Cordano and Frieze (2000), researchers from different disciplines confirm that managers' attitudes significantly influence them to prevent pollution. In the same way, according to Flannery and May (2000), company directors' attitudes have a positive effect on their intentions of treating wastewater that has been made dangerous by their industries.

There are three types of attitudes: cognitive, conative and affective (Gergen et al., 1992). The affective component is of particular interest. It relates to the favourable or unfavourable feeling that an individual expresses with regard to certain behaviour. Within the framework of our study, this shows the predictable consequences (positive or negative) of adopting envisaged environmental policies. The desired benefits are 'A consequence nevertheless sufficiently important to explain that the vast majority of SMEs already implicated in the environment have the intention either of continuing their commitment or increasing it' (Habhab-Rave, 2008: 12). The search for profits, a better image (Bansal and Roth, 2000) and a strategy of differentiation (Hamdoun, 2008) are the advantages sought in environmental management. Thus, referring to the theory of Ajzen, we have formulated the first hypothesis of the exploratory model:

Hypothesis H1: The positive consequences expected from desired behaviour positively influence the environmental intentions of company directors.

Subjective Norms Converging with the Determinist Approach

According to Vallerand (1994), these norms represent the expectations concerning the behaviour to be adopted during a socialization process. They designate the effect of other people's behaviour on our own behaviour (Gergen et al., 1992). From the viewpoint of Ajzen (1991), they reflect the perceptions of the pressures from important people concerning the targeted behaviour. These norms represent the importance that the individual gives to the approbation of these people and the individuals' desire (difficulty) to conform to this.

In the field of social responsibility, the determinist approach considers that company directors' behavioural changes result from the pressure and the constraints taking place in companies. In the field of sustainable entrepreneurship, environmental behaviour is a theme appropriated when implementing the theory of planned behaviour. The complex nature of the issues of sustainability, the effects associated with the different social, legal and organizational influences, constrain managers' environmental behaviour (Martin-Pena et al., 2010). Managers have to provide adequate solutions to satisfy the interests of the stakeholders (Banerjee, 2001) and maintain better relations with them (Bansal and Roth, 2000). Moreover, the regulatory mechanisms in force determine the intentions and the perceptions of the company directors. Inappropriate legislation could make it necessary for them to adopt reactive strategies rather than preventive ones (Bansal and Roth, 2000). This is particularly true for SMEs that limit themselves to a strict respect for the legislation (Noci and Verganti, 1999).

Finally, to gain a better understanding of entrepreneurial activities in the field of the environment, it is necessary to analyse not only the stakeholders who are implicated, but also their cultural foothold and their relations with the influential social system. According to Meek et al. (2010), we know little of the role that social norms play in the emergence of sustainable entrepreneurship. However, they point out that these social norms are connected with the individual's value system. If this value system is in favour of protecting an ecological environment, these norms have an influence on the probability of undertaking actions in the environmental field. The culture or the country in which an entrepreneur lives has a considerable influence on whether they will exploit an opportunity. For Bansal and Roth (2000), an employer is more inclined towards strategic changes that are compatible with their own values and perceptions of ecology. In the view of Flannery and May (2000), the moral obligations of company directors in the American metal industry influence their ethical intentions.

We propose that the perceptions of social pressures brought to bear by the different stakeholders explain the environmental intentions of heads of companies. We have also examined the importance of the cultural values of company heads in conforming to these pressures. The related hypotheses can be set out as follows:

Hypothesis H2a: The pressures of the external stakeholders positively influence the environmental intentions of company directors.

Hypothesis H2b: The pressures of the internal stakeholders positively influence the environmental intentions of company directors.

Hypothesis H2c: The cultural values of the company directors positively influence the environmental intentions of company directors.

Perceived Behavioural Control Corresponding to a Voluntarist Approach

The hypothetico-deductive models based on this control are a valuable tool for understanding intention (Krueger and Brazeal, 1994). In the view of Ajzen (1991), this corresponds to the perceived ease in achieving a given behaviour. The author has made a distinction between the internal and external factors of perceived behavioural control.

The internal factors concern entrepreneurial skills. According to Bird

(1992), intention necessitates the ability to verify the feasibility of an entrepreneurial project. From the viewpoint of Hungerford and Volk (1990), environmental knowledge has a direct impact on the adoption of responsible behaviour. An individual is more inclined to begin an action if they can handle the problem they are faced with. For Flannery and May (2000), the knowledge, skills and abilities of managers are essential when deciding to set up a system for treating and evacuating wastewater. Environmental intention therefore requires a perception of the aptitudes that facilitate the desired behaviour. These are acquired through specialized training (Tkachev and Kolvereid, 1999).

Moreover, Martin-Pena et al. (2010) confirm that similar past experiences in the field of the environment can be a determining factor in the perceptions of the director's organizational strategies. According to Flannery and May (2000), past experience increases the manager's confidence and the level of intention to treat toxic water. In the view of Cordano and Frieze (2000), several studies of the theory of planned behaviour have included past behaviour as an explicative variable in intentional models. Although this could not be the direct reason for setting up future behaviour, the absence of similar past behaviour can strengthen the resistance to it being accomplished.

For Cordano and Frieze (2000), the implementation of environmental behaviour represents a critical dimension implying cooperation with several stakeholders. Because of the simultaneous influence of individual and contextual factors; it is difficult to study the ethical decision-making process in the industrial sector (Flannery and May, 2000). More particularly, the Tunisian textile clothing sector lacks human skills, generates pollution requiring confirmed skills to reduce it, and is subject to strong demands from foreign contractors. These specificities give greater importance to past behaviour as an explanation of intention (Ajzen, 2002). We have therefore formulated two hypotheses:

Hypothesis H3a: The perceptions of environmental aptitudes acquired as a result of specific training programmes positively influence the environmental intention of company directors.

Hypothesis H3b: The perceptions of environmental aptitudes acquired during similar past experiences positively influence the environmental intention of company directors.

The external factors of perceived behavioural control are contextual. The company directors actively participate in building their future through a judicious control of the environment (Sharma, 2000; Aragón-

Corréa and Sharma, 2003). Environmental intention may have no effect if directors see obstacles preventing them from attaining the resources in the sector. The weakness of human and financial resources represents an obstacle to the commitment to sustainable entrepreneurship. According to Meek et al. (2010), public financial incentives directly influence environmental commitment in the industrial sectors. In the view of Del Brio and Junquera (2003), the industrial sectors require that employees and managers be well trained, with the appropriate competencies. Moreover, the perceptions of the entrepreneur regarding the ease (or the difficulty) of access to information, advice and support can act on their intention (Tounés, 2003). This helps them in their environmental approaches. We have set out the following hypothesis:

Hypothesis H4: Perceptions of the availability of resources (information, advice, support, finance and human resources) positively influence the environmental intention of company directors.

Entrepreneurial Orientation

For Miller (1983), the entrepreneurial orientation of the SMEs functioning in the competitive sectors mainly depends on the personalities of their company heads. It is strategic quality that is important for their success. According to Bouchard and Basso (2011), entrepreneurial orientation is the will of the director to identify, assess and exploit growth opportunities. For Spence et al. (2007), it is a necessary condition for the heads of SMEs to become committed to sustainable development. Those that are strongly committed show a greater degree of innovation and creativity than those who are less committed.

For Knight and Cavusgil (2005), entrepreneurial orientation is a managerial vision, a tendency to innovate and a proactive competitive attitude. According to a study by the European Commission (2002: 44), 'it is the more innovative and proactive firms that integrate their sustainable activities into their growth strategies'. From the viewpoint of Filion (1991), proactive behaviour is a characteristic of an entrepreneur who has an orientated professional life. Rather than reacting to events, proactivity is a tendency for a company to initiate changes in its different strategies (Aragón-Correa, 1998). It involves anticipation and a vision of the desired future. For Becherer and Maurer (1999), a proactive personality is orientated towards the market and adopts an audacious and aggressive marketing approach.

In the view of Bouchard and Basso (2011), entrepreneurial orientation is significantly correlated with the personality of the director. Kuckertz and Wagner (2010) confirm that the introduction of an individual sustainable orientation into the models of entrepreneurial intention can increase their explicative power. In the process of adopting environmental behaviour, heads of companies showed a propensity for risk-taking (Sharma, 2000). Therefore, and referring to the framework of Lumpkin and Dess (1996), we propose that the entrepreneurial orientation of a director of a Tunisian SME can be appreciated through risk-taking and proactivity:

Hypothesis H5a: Proactivity positively influences the environmental intention of company directors.

Hypothesis H5b: The risk-taking propensity positively influences the environmental intention of company directors.

Thanks to the literature taken from the field of entrepreneurship, psycho-psychology, sustainable development and corporate social responsibility, we have identified four groups of hypotheses likely to determine environmental intention. We will now present the research protocol that confirms or refutes the relevance of the constructed relations.

THE RESEARCH DESIGN

In the environmental field, as Starik and Marcus (2000) confirm, the extraction, manufacturing and processing industries seem to have particularly caught the attention of researchers. Environmental issues are closely linked to industrial activities (Martin-Pena et al., 2010). We were interested in a processing industry that manufactures textile clothing for the general public. We targeted industrial companies in the textile clothing sector in the Tunisian Sahel region.

On the one hand, the sector is confronted with a large array of ecological issues which increase the possibility of expressing environmental intention. On the other hand, the environmental challenges in this sector are particularly numerous because of the materials and the production procedures used. The media regularly reports ecological and sanitary catastrophes caused by these companies. What is more, they are particularly targeted because of the demands for normalization on the part of their foreign contractors.

Study Sample

We deliberately chose a single sector so as to obtain a certain amount of homogeneity in the environmental preoccupations confronting the company managers (Flannery and May, 2000). The environmental impacts occasioned by their activities are quite alike (Bansal and Roth, 2000). The companies in this sector offer products that are approximately similar. In Tunisia, there are 2086 firms in the textile clothing sector, which is 36 per cent of all the national manufacturers (APII, 2011). Companies with ten or more employees represent more than 40 per cent of the total workforce of the Tunisian manufacturing industry, that is, 198 280 jobs. We chose the Sahel geographical zone, which has the largest number of firms in this sector, that is, 889 companies (44 per cent of all the national textile clothing firms).

We used the database of the National Agency for Environmental Protection (ANPE). We requested information on the companies that had been aided by this organization to carry out environmental practices. We excluded those that belong to foreign groups; their head offices are often instigators of sustainable development strategies. Finally, the survey was made up of 148 firms geographically divided between Sousse (87), Monastir (52) and Mahdia (9). We contacted 82 and succeeded in interviewing 20 of them, that is, a quarter. Despite many reminders by telephone and email, it was not possible to increase the level of response. The fields of activity concerned are manufacturing, dyeing, serigraphy (screen-printing) and bleaching. The dividing-up of the companies according to their principal characteristics is shown in the Appendix, Table 9A.1.

A Qualitative-Deductive Framework with an Exploratory Aim

The rarity of works on environmental intention led us to choose an exploratory approach. The operating strategy was based on a qualitative-deductive approach. According to Huberman and Miles (2003), the qualitative approach is particularly adapted to constructing hypotheses on rarely studied issues. Moreover, research on environmental behaviour has been mainly based on European or American populations (Starik and Marcus, 2000), excluding those from Tunisia. 'The qualitative approach examines the phenomena in depth and accepts the contextual specificities and differences in a contextual situation' (Wacheux, 1996: 15). The final argument which justifies this experimental framework was the will to develop constructs for environmental intention and its explanatory variables.

The survey took place in the second quarter of 2010. We carried out semi-directive interviews face to face with the company directors. According to Blanchet and Gottman (1992: 43), a semi-directive interview 'is the preferred tool in the exploratory phase of a survey . . . it is itself an exploratory process . . . The exploratory interviews have the function of highlighting the aspects of the phenomenon that the researcher cannot spontaneously consider and to complete the work directions suggested by its readings'. The interviews lasted between 45 minutes and 1 hour and 15 minutes. They were recorded, then transcribed as the interviews continued. A summary sheet representing the main data was filled in for each interview.

Investigation Tool and Analysis Techniques

The interview guide was based on five themes (Appendix, Box 9A.1). The first, contained in question 2, aimed to enrich our conceptual approach to environmental intention previously explained in this chapter. The second theme enquired into the nature of the attitudes of the company directors with regard to the envisaged behaviour. Question 12 was created to study the relevance of the hypothesis H1. The third theme was concerned with the different pressures from the stakeholders as well as the will (the difficulty) of company directors to conform to them; it was also concerned with the dominant cultural traits which can determine the environmental intention. Questions 3, 4, 5, 6 and 8 made it possible to collect the data necessary to give an opinion on the conformity of the hypotheses H2a, H2b and H2c compared with the theoretical developments used.

The fourth theme concerns the perceptions of the difficulty or the ease in adopting environmental intention. Questions 9 and 10 analysed the nature of the hypotheses H3a, H3b and H4 as well as how they concurred with the literary review. Finally, the last theme deals with the company directors' personal characteristics seen through their entrepreneurial orientation. Questions 7 and 11 were formulated to verify the relevance of the hypotheses H5a and H5b.

We undertook an analysis of the lexical content to gain an in-depth understanding of the social and psychological phenomena (Chenitz and Swanson, 1986). This was based on the postulate that the repetition of elements in the discourse (words, expressions or similar significations) revealed the 'centre of interest' of the actors (Thietart, 2003). The data collected was processed with the software Sphinx. The discourse element was our unit of analysis. The technique used an analysis of the frequency of the appearance of words in an isolated way or in association with other words. We therefore showed the repetitions of words and key expressions so as to interpret the discourses of the company directors. This technique looks at the type and the richness of the vocabulary used. By using frameworks for counting and analysing the frequency of appearances, we intersected the vertical analysis (interview by interview) and the horizontal analysis (theme by theme). Before discussing our analyses, we will succinctly present our results.

RESULTS

Situated within the context of the textile clothing industry of the Tunisian Sahel region, the results of our study indicate that the hypotheses H1, H2a, H3a, H3b, H4, H5a and H5b are relevant and concur with the review of the literature. The favourable desired consequences of the required behaviour, the pressure on the part of public authorities and the foreign contractors, the perceptions of environmental aptitudes and the availability of different resources, and finally the entrepreneurial orientation, positively influence the environmental intention of company directors.

On the other hand, our investigations informed us that two hypotheses were not relevant for predicting their environmental intention. The pressure of employees (H2b) and the cultural values of the company directors (H2c) did not conform to the literature used to support the proposed hypotheses.

The interviews with the heads of companies brought to light two influencing factors which were not sufficiently or not at all identified in our literature review. The entrepreneur models and the desire to imitate them, as well as the nature of the activity, have a positive effect on environmental intention. Therefore, we can propose two new hypotheses:

Hypothesis H6: The nature of the activity positively influences the environmental intention of company directors.

Hypothesis H7: Knowledge of the entrepreneur models and the desire to imitate them positively influences the environmental intention of company directors.

ANALYSES AND DISCUSSION

In the theoretical section, we pointed to the rarity of the definition of the concept of environmental intention in sustainable entrepreneurship. According to Kuckertz and Wagner (2010), it is important to operationalize this concept to overcome this deficit. We formulated our own definition to provide a theoretical framework that was appropriate for our issue. We wished to enhance the concept of environmental intention by examining the significances expressed by the managers.

The lexical processing of 20 interviews revealed that this concept pointed to a will to take action, confirming one of the main attributes that we retained in our own definition (Appendix, Table 9A.2). For the directors of firms A, F, L, M and S, this concerned the will to adopt environmental approaches. For those in the companies G, N and P, intention was the sincerity to act correctly. According to the heads of companies K, P and T, it signified the personal desire to protect the environment. For the directors of C, J and R, environmental intention denotes having an idea for protecting the environment. Finally, there was a vision of the perpetuity of the environment, by the directors of F and I. We will now proceed to examine the discourses to analyse the antecedents of environmental intention. These were distributed according to factors that were relevant, rejected or generated.

The Relevant Factors

The attitude towards the desired environmental behaviour was analysed by studying the expected results. The company director's expectations are absolutely fundamental in the process of implementing practices for environmental protection (Cordano and Frieze, 2000). According to the director of company E, 'It is obvious that the potential advantages are invisible. On the contrary, the absence of environmental policies is shown in the weak reliability of our activities'. On the whole, the improvement in legitimacy and image vis-à-vis the external stakeholders, a more efficient organization for production, a reduction in pollution in the workplace and a differentiation strategy take precedence over financial gain and growth in market share (increase in sales, growth in market share and productivity).

According to Kuckertz and Wagner (2010), individuals showing a strong environmental orientation generally seek non-monetary advantages. However, not being mutually exclusive, economic profitability is associated with environmental requirements (Martin-Pena et al., 2010). Two managers also wished to reduce their energy consumption through their intention to set up an environmental system. The expected results influence the environmental intention. This result concurs with those of the studies of Bansal and Roth (2000), the ACFCI (2006) and Flannery and May (2000).

According to Meek et al. (2010), the results of research on the impact of subjective norms on the setting up of business are contradictory. The analyses of the survey inform us that environmental organizations, public authorities and foreign contractors exercised considerable pressure on the companies studied. The intention of adopting a measure or an environmental policy often boils down to a respect for regulations (Bansal and Roth, 2000; Cordano and Frieze, 2000; Sharma, 2000). 'Regulatory motivation is, for SMEs and large firms alike, the prime motivation for including social and environmental preoccupations in their management' (Quairel and Auberger, 2005: 8). Thus, among the nine managers declaring compliance with the recommendations of public agencies, the director of company C said that 'The national agency for environmental protection (ANPE) required us to purchase this water treatment plant to improve the quality of the water discharged into the environment'. The director of company I, specialized in dyeing and fading jeans, stated that 'the ANPE recommended from the start of our activity installing a water treatment plant because of the dangerous nature of the chemical substances we use'.

The pressure from foreign contractors is considerable for companies. They play a major role in the implementation of certification standards. According to the director of company G, 'Foreign clients require us to undertake the process of obtaining ISO 14001 certification . . . Renowned clients require environmental certification'. The director of company K made a similar remark; in fact: 'the most well-known foreign clients in the jeans industry choose certified subcontractors . . . For this reason we are going to try to obtain the ISO 14001'. The fear of losing the foreign contractors drives the intentions.

Perceptions of environmental abilities can facilitate the realization of the intention. For the managers of K, M, O and P, experience in the field of textiles is a trigger for environmental intention (Appendix, Table 9A.3). The director of company M stated that 'my experience as an employee in a clothing company has been beneficial . . . I already have an idea of environmental practices to reduce production costs'. The head of firm P confirmed that 'my experience as director of a textile company has a direct impact . . . I know the stages in the preparation of the subsidy dossier and the suppliers of the water treatment plants'. The positive impact of previous professional experience on environmental intention is in accordance with the research by Cordano and Frieze (2000). Finally, specialized training and having qualified personnel had an impact on the environmental certification process.

The availability of the financial means is the main resource which contributes to the development of environmental intention for half of the managers. In the context of the Tunisian textile clothing sector, access to public subsidies to acquire water treatment plants had accelerated the cognitive process of environmental intention of six of them. The head of company J stated that 'the existence of state subsidies has strengthened my intention'. Moreover, benefiting from information, advice and support from the specialized services largely conditions this intention. 'The main problem', the director of company E told us, 'is the absence of information on the possibilities of implementing environmental policies and the generated profits'. Time is a necessary 'input' for managers having the intention of obtaining ISO 14001 certification. For the head of company D, 'Sometimes training coincides with working hours and in that case, we have to postpone the sessions'.

The analysis of the discourses showed that the entrepreneurial orientation of company directors largely explains intention (Appendix, Table 9A.4). This result confirms the findings of Kuckertz and Wagner (2010). Fourteen company heads anticipated the requirements of the public authorities and environmental organizations. The head of company P announced, 'I set up a waste water treatment plant mainly to anticipate the regulations, because if I hadn't undertaken this action, I would have had the environmental organizations on my back'. Anticipating the legislation can produce a competitive advantage (Bansal and Roth, 2000; Martin-Pena et al., 2010).

Three employers had adopted the ISO 14001 standard with the aim of getting ahead of the competition and winning market share. The director of firm D noted that 'the ISO 14001 certification will enable me to get ahead of the competition in my sector. Few textile companies are certified 14001 . . . It is an opportunity to have something more than them'. The director of company G added, 'I want to remain in first place in the market . . . I would really like to start measures before the others . . . Foreign clients require certification and labels'. The head of company L clearly expressed his viewpoint: 'we are working very hard to remain the leaders in our sector. Our solid foundations will enable us to grow rapidly and we are really orientated towards the markets and the clients . . . ISO 14001 will increase our share of the foreign market'. Obtaining certification and normalization is an important measure in environmental management (Martin-Pena et al., 2010; Meek et al., 2010). It offers entrepreneurs the opportunity to improve their competitiveness (Bansal and Roth, 2000).

Nine employers said that they had taken a financial risk (bank loan) for their industrial investments. Among these, three confirmed that this risk was worsened by breakdowns due to a lack of personnel training. The director of firm G stated: 'The risk run was caused by the employees' lack of knowledge on how to use the products for neutralizing the water . . . This could lead to wastages'. Three of the company directors noted the risk of not being able to repay their loans. Bouchard and Basso (2011) confirm that when SMEs are in competition in hostile environments, they have a tendency to adopt strategies orientated towards innovation, proactivity and risk-taking.

The Rejected and Generated Factors

Entrepreneurs do not perceive the pressures from internal stakeholders. Employees do not represent a social influence on environmental intention. The views of employees are barely considered in the organizational management of the Tunisian textile clothing sector; their role is limited to making proposals. The analysis of the interview with the director of firm C reflects the position of the managers with regard to them: 'It was my engineer who gave me advice on how to use solar energy . . . Ear muffs were purchased when this was proposed by the personnel'.

The same thing applies from a cultural or religious point of view. Apart from their impacts on two directors, these factors did not play a fundamental role in the will to undertake environmental procedures. The results of the influence of social norms on pro-environmental behaviour are contradictory depending on the context and the type of people studied (Flannery and May, 2000).

The type of activity proves to be a determining factor in the development of environmental intention. This confirmation is in accordance with the study by Sharma (2000). In industry, the fields of activity seem to discriminate against environmental behaviours. According to the author, the fields of activity influence the choice of entrepreneurial strategies of the firms in the industry of hydrocarbons in Canada, depending on whether they are specialized upstream or downstream of the production chain. According to Sharma, these fields of activity differentiate between the choice of entrepreneurial strategies of firms in the hydrocarbon industry in Canada depending on whether they are specialized in working at the beginning or at the end of the production chain.

Twelve of the companies wash out textiles; they are more concerned with the recycling of wastewater. For the director of firm G, 'The style of our activity generates a huge amount of pollution due to the fading operations . . . This influenced our will to install a treatment plant for waste water'. The director of firm B stated that: 'Nobody obliged me to recycle the waste or buy ear muffs for my employees . . . Our activity generates too much noise and waste so we have to recycle and buy ear muffs'.

The successful experiences of other employers are an encouragement for directors to take responsible actions (Granovetter, 1985). It is generally admitted that entrepreneurs' models have considerable influence on the decisions of future entrepreneurs (Van Auken et al., 2006; Meek et al., 2010). They affect entrepreneurial intentions by changing the attitudes, the beliefs and the perceived abilities to succeed in a new company. The empirical study shows the desire of the managers of firms H, J, N, O and S to imitate entrepreneurs who have adopted environmental practices.

The peers influence individuals' systems of values and, in the same way, their perceptions of desirability (Shapero and Sokol, 1982). Observing the behaviour of other entrepreneurs can cause an individual to act differently: 'Social perception is also influenced by the context in which we observe the actions of others . . . Those who are already committed despite the ambiguity of the situation' (Gergen et al., 1992: 44, 239).

A Relevant Model of the Environmental Intention of Company Directors of SMEs in the Tunisian Textile Clothing Industry

The exploratory model of environmental intention combines the components of the theory of planned behaviour and that of entrepreneurial theory. Although it is little used in the field of sustainable entrepreneurship, the theory of planned behaviour has been used with success to study environmental intention (Cordano and Frieze, 2000; Flannery and May, 2000). Our research demonstrates the strength of the entrepreneurial theory and the theory of planned behaviour. Unifying these two frameworks produces hypotheses which concurred with the literature analysed.

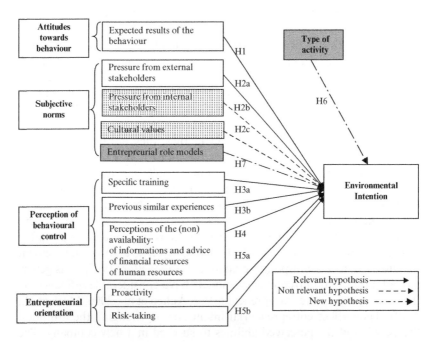

Figure 9.2   An exploratory model of the environmental intention of company directors of Tunisian SMEs

By distinguishing four groups of explicative factors, the relations proposed have been illustrated in Figure 9.2. The new hypotheses are in dark grey and the non-relevant hypotheses are in dotted grey.

CONCLUSION

It is particularly important to clarify the intentional process leading to environmental behaviour (Flannery and May, 2000; Martin-Pena et al., 2010). A particularly interesting theoretic contribution of this research has been to provide a definition of environmental intention. Understanding the type (and not the intensity and the statistical significance) of the connections between environmental intention on the one hand, and attitudes, subjective norms and perceived behavioural control on the other hand, makes it possible to comprehend the theoretic dimensions of this intention. This is expressed by personal characteristics where the individual will is preponderant. It must be situated in organizational, cultural, political and economic contexts.

The model that was created highlighted the importance of considering three levels of analysis for predicting the environmental intention of a company director: the individual, organizational and interorganizational levels. A company is managed by the employer (individual), functions with and for its workforce (organizational), in relation with other companies and public institutions, and is of course rooted in its natural environment (interorganizational). Identifying and managing the role of each actor at each level is essential in order to attain sustainability (Bansal and Roth, 2000). The association of these three interpretive keys enables different theoretic perspectives to be envisaged on the basis of a multidisciplinary approach (Bansal and Roth, 2000). It is necessary to make connections between the organizational theories and those relating to the process of environmental intention (Starik and Marcus, 2000). Sustainable entrepreneurship is an emerging field involving economic, institutional and sociological perspectives (Meek et al., 2010).

Although research into sustainable entrepreneurship is becoming more and more frequent as Kuckertz and Wagner (2010) confirm, it has not as yet been totally included in the vast theoretical, conceptual and empirical corpus studying entrepreneurial behaviour, intentions, attitudes and social norms. According to these authors, using the principal theories of entrepreneurship to explain the issues of sustainable development further enriches the conceptual models in the field of sustainable entrepreneurship. By combining the theory of planned behaviour of Ajzen (1991), borrowed from psycho-sociology, with the entrepreneurial theory of Kuhndt et al. (2004), taken from the field of entrepreneurship, we have created a new theoretical framework for predicting environmental behaviour.

The model's relevance from a managerial viewpoint enables public policies to be improved. Understanding the determinant factors in environmental intention contributes to elaborating adequate systems that aim to reduce the harmful effects of industrial activities on the environment and on the employees. As for the public authorities, the study of the process of managerial commitment to the implementation of environmental measures offers an adequate tool with which to improve their interventions. Identifying the entrepreneurs showing an environmental intention contributes to the creation of a support system responding to their problem issues relating to water treatment, to waste from dyeing, and from printing and bleaching fabrics.

It has been indicated that public actions must facilitate access to financial, informational and human resources. Creating training programmes specialized in the implementation of environmental measures and practices are recommended by entrepreneurs. The relevance of the created model shows that heads of companies are proactive (versus reactive) with regards to the environment. In order to encourage this proactivity it would first be necessary to carry out operations for developing awareness on the part of company directors of the textile clothing industry. It is important to provide information about the challenges involved in this, not only to conform to the legislation, but also to improve company competitiveness (Bansal and Roth, 2000; Martin-Pena et al., 2010).

Although offering an appropriate initial framework for understanding environmental intention, the model created presents two types of limits, relating to the real essence of the subject studied and also the research protocol. The time lag between intention and behaviour is a limit inherent to the subject. The intentional perspective is not a necessary and sufficient condition for the process of environmental behaviour to be undertaken. It is a snapshot at a precise moment and in a given context. Even if it is 'subjected to the requirement of stability' (Bratman, 1997: 255), its chronological time lag separating it from behaviour could prevent it from being achieved. Every intention, even a sufficiently strong one, as Gauthier (1997) confirms, cannot be a guarantee that the corresponding act will be accomplished. In the view of Kuckertz and Wagner (2010), this can happen months or even years later.

This research is a first stage in a large project to explain the types of connections between intention and the factors likely to explain it. The data collected and the investigation protocol adopted cannot conclude on the reliability and the validity of the model, but made it possible only to reach a conclusion on the relevance of the hypotheses formulated. The potential involved in the field of sustainable entrepreneurship means that more rigorous research designs will need to be adopted. Large-scale empirical studies will contribute to development in this field (Kuckertz and Wagner, 2010). The perspective would be to test the explicative power of the model. From a hypothetico-deductive context, we will examine its predictive validity from a representative sample of companies in the Tunisian textile clothing sector. The variables in the model will be mainly expressed by multi-item scales, with a view to confirming or refuting the hypotheses proposed.

For the obvious reason that the people interviewed were similar, the model was used for the Tunisian textile clothing sector. Its relevance is not representative of all the industrial sectors concerned by the environmental challenges. An interesting subject for future research is to explore the specificities of the particular sectors in order to contextualize the model and strengthen our knowledge of the environmental intention. An examination of environmental intention certainly makes it possible to understand why individuals decide to become entrepreneurs, but above all, why they choose activities with societal benefits (Meek et al., 2010).

Moreover, we know little about the impact of environmental ethics on the intensity of this intention. Do individuals preoccupied by environmental issues reveal a greater intention than those who are not (Kuckertz and Wagner, 2010)? A project that particularly interests us is to study environmental intention in an educative context. To our knowledge, there have been no studies in Tunisia or France on the environmental intention of students following university courses specialized in the fields of sustainable entrepreneurship, corporate social responsibility and sustainable development. Is the training given designed to develop the process of sustainable behaviour?

REFERENCES

Agency for the Promotion of Industry and Innovation (APII) (2011), 'Directory of industrial companies', http://www.tunisieindustrie.nat.tn/fr, accessed 25 July 2011.

Ajzen, I. (1991), 'The theory of planned behaviour', *Organizational Behaviour and Human Decision Process*, 50, 179–211.

Ajzen, I., (2002), 'Residual effects of past on later behavior: habituation and reasoned action perspectives', *Personality and Social Psychology Review*, 6(2), 107–22.

Ajzen, I. and M. Fishbein (1980), *Understanding Attitudes and Predicting Social Behavior*, Englewood Cliffs, NJ: Prentice-Hall.

Aragón-Correa, J.A. (1998), 'Strategic proactivity and firm approach to the natural environment', *Academy of Management Journal*, 4(5), 556–67.

Aragón-Correa, J.A. and S. Sharma (2003), 'A contingent resource-based view of proactive corporate environmental strategy', *Academy of Management Review*, 28(1), 71–88.

Assemblée des Chambres Françaises de Commerce et d'Industrie (ACFCI) (2006), 'La prise en compte du développement durable et de la responsabilité sociétale de l'entreprise (DD/RSE) par les PME-PMI', Paris.

Banerjee, S.B. (2001), 'Managerial perceptions of corporate environmentalism: interpretations from industry and strategic implications for organizations', *Journal of Management Studies*, 38(4), 489–513.

Bansal, P. and K. Roth (2000), 'Why companies do green: a model of ecological responsiveness', *Academy of Management Journal*, 43(4), 717–36.

Becherer, R.C. and J.G. Maurer (1999), 'The proactive personality disposition and entrepreneurial behavior among small company presidents', *Journal of Small Business Management*, 37(1), 28–36.

Ben Boubaker-Gherib, J. (2009), 'De l'efficacité des systèmes incitatifs pour l'engagement des entreprises dans le Développement Durable: cas des entreprises tunisiennes', Conference 'énergie, changement climatique et développement durable', Tunis, June.

Bird, B.J. (1992), 'The operation of intentions in time: the emergence of the new venture', *Entrepreneurship Theory and Practice*, 17(1), 11–20.

Blanchet, A. and A. Gottman (1992), *L'Enquête et ses méthodes: l'entretien*, Paris: Nathan.

Bouchard, V. and O. Basso (2011), 'Exploring the links between entrepreneurial orientation and intrapreneurship in SMEs', *Journal of Small Business and Enterprise Development*, 18(2), 219–31.

Boyer, A. (1997), 'Le partage de l'intention', in J.-P. Dupuy and P. Livet (eds), *Les limites de la rationalité: rationalité, éthique et cognition*, Paris: La Découverte, pp. 267–75.

Bratman, M.-E. (1997), 'Intention partagée et obligation mutuelle', in J.-P. Dupuy and P. Livet (eds), *Les limites de la rationalité: rationalité, éthique et cognition*, Paris: La Découverte, pp. 246–66.

Chenitz, W.C. and J. Swanson (1986), *From Practice to Grounded Theory: Qualitative Research in Nursing*, Menlo Park, CA: Addison-Wesley.

Cordano, M. and I.H. Frieze (2000), 'Pollution reduction preferences of US environmental managers: applying Ajzen's theory of planned behavior', *Academy of Management Journal*, 43(4), 627–41.

Cossette, P. (2004), *L'organisation, une perspective cognitiviste*, Quebec: Éditions les Presses de l'Université Laval, Collection Sciences de l'Administration.

Crozier, M. and E. Friedberg (1977), *L'acteur et le système*, Paris: Editions du Seuil.

Davidsson, P. (1995), 'Determinants of entrepreneurial intentions', RENT IX.

Del Brio, J.A. and B. Junquera (2003), 'A review of the literature on environmental innovation management in SMEs: implication for public policies', *Technovation*, 32(12), 939–48.

Desportes, F. and F. Le Gunehec (1997), *Le nouveau droit pénal: droit pénal général*, Paris: Economica.

European Commission (2002), 'European SMEs and social and environmental responsibility', Observatory of European SMEs, No. 4.

Filion, L.-J. (1991), *Visions et relations: clefs du succès de l'entrepreneur*, Montréal: Editions de l'entrepreneur.

Fisette, D. (1997), 'Intentionnalité collective, rationalité et action', in J.-P. Dupuy and P. Livet (eds), *Les limites de la rationalité: rationalité, éthique et cognition*, Paris: La Découverte, pp. 348–64.

Flannery, B.L. and D.R. May (2000), 'Environmental ethical decision making in the US metal-finishing industry', *Academy of Management Journal*, 43(4), 642–62.

Ganascia, J.G. (1996), *Les sciences cognitives*, Paris: Flammarion.

Gauthier, D. (1997), 'Intention et délibération', in J.-P. Dupuy and P. Livet (eds), *Les limites de la rationalité: rationalité, éthique et cognition*, Paris: La Découverte, pp. 59–75.

Gergen, K.J., M.M. Gergen and S. Jurtas (1992), *Psychologie sociale*, Quebec: Editions Etude Vivantes.

Granovetter, M. (1985), 'Economic action and social structure: the problem of embeddedness', *American Journal of Sociology*, 91(3), 481–510.

Habhab-Rave, S. (2008), 'Les dirigeants face à l'environnement: comment réconcilier environnement naturel et opportunités stratégiques?', 5th Conference of ADERSE, Grenoble.

Hamdoun, M. (2008), 'Le comportement écologique des entreprises chimiques tunisiennes: Un passage obligé ou un choix délibéré', 17th Conference of AIMS, Nice.

Hines, J.M., H.R. Hungerford and A.N. Tomera (1986), 'Analysis and synthesis of research on responsible pro-environmental behaviour: a meta-analysis', *Journal of Environmental Education*, 18(2), 1–8.

Huberman, A.M. and M.B. Miles (2003), *Analyse des données qualitatives*, Brussels: Editions De Boeck.

Hungerford, H.R. and T.L. Volk (1990), 'Changing learner behavior through environmental education', *Journal of Environmental Education*, 21(3), 8–21.

Ivanaj, V. and J. McIntyre (2006), 'Multinational enterprises and sustainable development: a review of strategy process research', Multinational Enterprise and Sustainable Development: Strategic Tool for Competitiveness, Tech Center for International Business Education and Research (CIBER), Atlanta, Georgia, October.

Knight, G.A. and S.T. Cavusgil (2005), 'A taxonomy of born-global firms', *Management International Review*, 45, 83–110.

Krueger, N.F. and D.V. Brazeal (1994), 'Entrepreneurial potential and potential entrepreneurs', *Entrepreneurship Theory and Practice*, spring, 91–104.

Krueger, N.F. and A.L. Carsrud (1993), 'Entrepreneurial intentions: applying the theory of planned behaviour', *Entrepreneurship and Regional Development*, 5, 315–30.

Krueger, N.F., M.D. Reilly and A.L. Carsrud (2000), 'Competing models of entrepreneurship intentions', *Journal of Business Venturing*, 15, 411–32.

Kuckertz, A. and M. Wagner (2010), 'The influence of sustainability orientation on entrepreneurial intentions – investigating the role of business experience', *Journal of Business Venturing*, 25(5), 524–39.

Kuhndt, M., V. Türk and M. Herrndorf (2004), 'Stakeholder engagement: an opportunity for SMEs?', *UNEP Industry and Environment*, October–December, 40–43.

Kurland, N.B. (1995), 'Ethical intentions and the theories of reasoned action and planned behavior', *Journal of Applied Social Psychology*, 25, 297–313.

Learned, K.E. (1992), 'What happened before the organization? A model of organization formation', *Entrepreneurship Theory and Practice*, 17(1), 39–48.

Le Robert Plus (2012), *Dictionnaire de la langue française*, Paris: Le Robert.

Lumpkin, G.T. and G.G. Dess (1996), 'Clarifying the entrepreneurial orientation construct and linking it to performance', *Academy of Management Review*, 21(1), 135–72.

Martin-Pena, M.L., E. Diaz-Garrido and J.M. Sanchez-Lopez (2010), 'Relation between management's behavioural intentions toward the environment and environmental actions', *Journal of Environmental Planning and Management*, 53(3), 297–315.

Meek, R.W., D.F. Pacheco and J.G. York (2010), 'The impact of social norms on entrepreneurial action: Evidence from the environmental entrepreneurship context', *Journal of Business Venturing*, 25(5), 493–509.

Miller, D. (1983), 'The correlates of entrepreneurship in three types of firms', *Management Science*, 29(7), 770–92.

Noci, G. and R. Verganti (1999), 'Managing "green" product innovation in small firms', *R&D Management*, 29(2), 3–15.

Oskamp, S. and P.W. Schultz (2006), 'Using psychological science to achieve ecological sustainability', in S.I. Donaldson, D.E. Berger and K. Pezdek (eds), *Applied Psychology: New Frontiers and Rewarding Careers*, Mahwah, NJ: Laurence Erlbaum Associates, pp. 81–106.

Paradas, A. (2006), 'Perception du développement durable par des dirigeants de petites entreprises: résultats d'enquêtes', 8th CIFEPME, Fribourg, Switzerland.

Pradel, J. (1995), *Droit pénal général*, 10th edn, Paris: Editions Cujas.

Quairel, F. and M.N. Auberger (2005), 'Management responsable et PME: Une relecture du concept de responsabilité sociétale de l'entreprise', *Revue des sciences de gestion*, 211–212, 111–26.

Schmuck, P. and P.W. Schultz (2002), *Psychology of Sustainable Development*, Boston, MA: Kluwer Academic Publishers Group.

Searle, J.R. (1980), 'Minds, brains, and programs', *Behavioral and Brain Sciences*, 3, 417–24.

Shapero, A. and L. Sokol (1982), 'The social dimensions of entrepreneurship', *Encyclopedia of Entrepreneurship*, Englewood Cliffs, NJ: Prentice Hall, pp. 72–90.

Sharma, S. (2000), 'Managerial interpretations and organizational context as predictors of corporate choice of environmental strategy', *Academy of Management Journal*, 43(4), 681–97.

Spence, M., J. Ben Boubaker Gherib and B. Ondoua (2007), 'Développement durable et PME. Une étude exploratoire des déterminants de leur engagement', *Revue internationale PME*, 20(3–4), 17–42.

Starik, M. and A. Marcus (2000), 'Introduction to the special research forum on the management of organizations in the natural environment: a field emerging from multiple paths, with many challenges ahead', *Academy of Management Journal*, 43(4), 539–46.

Stefani, G., G. Levasseur and B. Bouloc (1997), *Droit pénal général*, 16th edn, Paris: Editions Dalloz.

Thietart, R.A. (2003), *Méthodes de recherche en management*, Paris: Editions Dunod, Collection Gestion Sup.

Tkachev, A. and L. Kolvereid (1999), 'Self-employment intentions among Russian students', *Entrepreneurship and Regional Development*, 11(3), 269–80.

Tounés, A. (2003), 'L'intention entrepreneuriale des étudiants – une recherche comparative entre des étudiants suivants des formations en entrepreneuriat (bac+5) et des étudiants en DESS CAAE', PhD thesis, Rouen University.

Vallerand, J. (1994), *Les fondements de la psychologie sociale*, Paris: Gaëtan Morin.

Van Auken, H., F.L. Fry and P. Stephens (2006), 'The influence of role models on entrepreneurial intentions', *Journal of Developmental Entrepreneurship*, 11(2), 157–67.

Vesalainen, J. and T. Pihkala (1999), 'Motivation structure and entrepreneurial intentions', Frontiers of Entrepreneurship Research Conference, Darla Moore School of Business, University of South Carolina, USA.

Wacheux, F. (1996), *Méthodes qualitatives et recherche en gestion*, Paris: Économica.

APPENDIX

Table 9A.1   Descriptive characteristics of the sample

SME	Year of creation/ takeover	Activity	Employees number	International transactions
A	1949	Dyeing on knit fabric	180	Total exporter
B	1970	Seat covers, mats, carpets and other products and accessories	65	Partial exporter
C	1980	Baby items, swimming costumes, children's clothes	220	Partial exporter
D	1985	Manufacture of chemical products for the textile industry	145	Non-exporter
E	1986	Packaging and dyeing	100	Total exporter
F	1990	Dyeing, bleaching, serigraphy and embroidery	30	Total exporter
G	1990	Bleaching	100	Total exporter
H	1993	Corset manufacture, swimming costumes and underwear	132	Total exporter
I	1995	Dyeing and jeans bleaching	50	Partial exporter
J	1995	Manufacture of dresses, skirts and children's clothes	70	Total exporter
K	1995	Treatment of manufactured items dyeing, bleaching and serigraphy	86	Partial exporter
L	1999	Treatment of manufactured items dyeing, bleaching and serigraphy	70	Total exporter
M	1999	Manufacture of swimming costumes and underwear	105	Partial exporter
N	1999	Production of textiles	180	Total exporter
O	2000	Clothing manufacture	220	Total exporter
P	2002	Textile finishing, products for treating woven fabrics: bleaching, dyeing, printing	59	Total exporter
Q	2004	Treatment of manufactured items dyeing, bleaching and serigraphy	54	Total exporter
R	2004	Clothing manufacture and bleaching	150	Total exporter
S	2005	Ready to wear clothing manufacture, washing and special treatments	110	Total exporter
T	2006	Treatment of manufactured items (dyeing, bleaching and serigraphy)	100	Partial exporter

---

BOX 9A.1   INTERVIEW GUIDE

1. What are the measures and the environmental policies that you have implemented in your company?
2. Can you define what you understand by 'environmental intention'?
3. Did you have this environmental intention because of a personal will, to imitate your competitors, because of the influence of clients, of certain groups of people or public or political organizations?
4. Which are the groups of people and organizations that have influenced your intention?
5. Have you had the intention of implementing environmental measures or policies for cultural, social, political and/or economic reasons?
6. Have your faith and your religious convictions influenced your intention of adopting environmental measures or policies?
7. Have you had the intention of adopting environmental measures and policies to get ahead of your competitors or anticipate the changes in regulations etc.?
8. Have your international activities influenced your intention of adopting environmental measures and policies?
9. In your opinion, what are the factors that have facilitated (accelerated) your intention of adopting environmental measures and policies?
10. In your opinion, what are the factors that have made it difficult to adopt environmental measures or policies?
11. When planning to adopt environmental measures and policies, what are the risks run by Tunisian company heads?
12. What are the expected results that you could hope to achieve when adopting environmental measures or policies?

Table 9A.2   Key words for the analysis of content of the intention concept

Key word	Frequency
Will	5
Sincerity	3
Personal desire	3
Having an idea	3
Positive thinking	2
Commitment	2
Looking for solutions	2
Vision of permanence	2
Making profits, minimizing energy consumption	2
Phase before commitment	1
Entrepreneurial orientation	1
Personal disposition	1
Degree of awareness	1
Total	28

Note: A company director can evoke more than one key idea.

Table 9A.3   Perceptions of principal environmental abilities and resources for achieving the behaviour

	Frequency
Existence of financial means	11
ANPE subsidies	6
Lack of time	6
Access to information and advice	5
Previous experience in the sector	4
ANPE support	4
Specialized training	3
Personnel skills	2
Total	41

Note: A company director can evoke more than one principal perception.

Table 9A.4   Analysis of the frequency of key ideas relative to entrepreneurial orientation

	Frequency
Proactivity	
Anticipate the regulations	14
Act in advance, before the competitors	3
Initiate the competitors	3
Protect themselves from sanctions, fines and pressure from public authorities	3
Obey the regulations	2
Avoid pollution	2
Anticipate the requirements of foreign clients	2
Increase the market share	2
Protect the employees against pollution	1
Total	32
Risk-taking	
Financial risk	9
Temporal cost	6
Risk of non-reimbursement of loan	3
Risk of non-availability or lack of skills on the part of personnel	3
Cost of training for employees	2
Total	23

Note: A company director can evoke more than one key idea.

10. What motivates hotel managers to become ecopreneurs: a case study on the Spanish tourism sector

Samuel Gómez-Haro, Vera Ferrón-Vílchez, José Manuel de la Torre-Ruiz and Javier Delgado-Ceballos

INTRODUCTION

Environmental problems such as global warming, the depletion of the ozone layer and air pollution in large cities are of increasing public concern. These problems are usually linked to business activity, and in the last few decades a large number of companies worldwide have implemented environmental practices.

Environmental management presents an opportunity for companies to improve their image (Christmann, 2004) and increase the efficiency of their production processes (Christmann, 2000; Hart, 1995). Conversely, not considering environmental issues can have the opposite effect on company strategy, and a lack of concern for the environment can lead to a competitive disadvantage.

Many managers do consider environmental protection as part of their decision-making process. Entrepreneurial activity that contributes to socio-economic development and change (Zahra, 1995) is one option by which companies achieve sustainable growth (Anderson, 1998). The term used by the research literature for environmental, social and economic development by entrepreneurs (e.g., Dixon and Clifford, 2007) is 'ecopreneurship'. The purpose of ecopreneurship is to create solutions that protect the environment and tackle social problems to create sustainable development using the same economic, social and environmental pillars advocated in Elkington's 'triple bottom line' (Elkington, 1998). Ecopreneurship can therefore be considered a way for new ventures to simultaneously focus on sustainability, economic growth and social welfare (WTTC, 2012).

Stringent environmental regulations, corporate social responsibility and the achievement of improvements in efficiency are key reasons to include environmental issues in company decision-making (Balabanis et al., 1998; Bansal and Roth, 2000). Doing so leads to progressively greener organizations rather than a 'big bang' movement towards global sustainability (Hart and Milstein, 1999), and ecopreneurs play an important role in this change process (Anderson, 1998).

The ecopreneurship phenomenon is indicative of the progressive approach of green business toward achieving change (Pastakia, 1998). The interaction between the environmental activities of companies, corporate social responsibility and institutions could potentially be a way of achieving sustainable development (Seelos and Mair, 2005a). Ecopreneurship, through the selling of green products or services, can therefore be defined as entrepreneurial activity with an environmental focus (Schaltegger, 2002).

Sustainability is a key factor in environmental activities (Isaak, 2002; Kirkwood and Walton, 2010; Walley and Taylor, 2002), and ecopreneurs have assumed leadership of this field. Research is attempting to answer key questions regarding the factors that motivate ecopreuneurs (Dixon and Clifford, 2007; Kirkwood and Walton, 2010) by studying varying perspectives. This chapter examines entrepreneurial motivation and how ecopreneurs identify environmental concern and protection as a business opportunity.

This chapter first presents a brief theoretical review of environmental concerns and entrepreneurship. It then analyses the main motivating factors for ecopreneurs outlined in research literature. The next section uses a case study to discuss ecopreneurship in the hotel sector, including the reasons and methodology used. The results of the case analysis are then given. The final section offers conclusions, contributions and future areas for research.

ADDRESSING ENVIRONMENTAL CONCERNS OF ENTREPRENEURIAL ACTIVITIES

Environmental concerns within the public and private sector have increased over recent years. Environmental issues can have negative impacts that directly affect economic activity. For instance, increasing stringent environmental regulations (that is, compliance with Kyoto Protocol requirements) have caused many firms to consider ways to decrease negative environmental impacts and to improve business activity. Environmental issues are also of societal concern, and companies are increasingly incorporating environmental issues into their organizational strategy at all levels (Banerjee, 2001), with varying degrees of proactiveness. This proactivity is described as 'the company's tendency to initiate changes in its various strategic policies rather than to react to events' (Aragón-Correa,

1998: 557). The environmental strategy of a firm can be considered on a continuum ranging from non-compliance with environmental legal requirements to environmentally advanced behaviour (Roome, 1992).

Although adopting proactive environmental strategies and corresponding organizational changes can increase costs (Kolk and Pinkse, 2008), activities that prevent negative impacts are a potential way to gain competitive advantage (Banerjee, 2003) through the creation of new organizational capabilities (Hart, 1995; Christmann, 2000; Darnall and Edwards, 2006). Anticipating and internalizing negative environmental impacts could engender the development of a rare, valuable and inimitable capability (Barney, 1991) that achieves a sustainable competitive advantage. Based on this achievement, the company can both protect the environment and profit from its newly enhanced reputation.

The phenomenon of entrepreneurship encompasses 'acts of organisational creation, renewal, or innovation that occurs within or outside an existing organisation' (Sharma and Chrisman, 1999: 17). Entrepreneurship has been defined as 'those individuals or groups of individuals, acting independently or as part of a corporate system, who create new organisations, or instigate renewal or innovation within an existing organisation' (Sharma and Chrisman, 1999: 17). There are entrepreneurs who have considerable concern for environmental issues and world change (Meadows, 1994); however, there is no common definition for this specific business philosophy. Isaak (1997) stated that entrepreneurial organizations with a high level of environmental concern are 'system-transforming, socially committed break-through ventures' (Isaak, 1997: 25). Ecopreneurs are those entrepreneurs who start for-profit business with strong underlying green values and who sell green products or services based on the principle of sustainability (Isaak, 2002; Walley and Taylor, 2002). The term 'ecopreneur' is therefore used to represent those entrepreneurs whose three main concerns are the protection of the environment, social problems and economic profitability.

Ecopreneurial organizations differ significantly from other organizations. Through ecopreneurship, companies are able to create and develop economically viable businesses that respect environmental and social values (Dixon and Clifford, 2007). Ecopreneurial organizations manage their resources and business opportunities by focusing on environmental commitment (Keogh and Polonsky, 1998). Combining entrepreneurialism with a high level of involvement in the regulatory, political, social and environmental context contributes to their success (Mair and Marti, 2004). There are ecopreneurs who initiate business with existing green values, while others adopt environmental goals after business initiation (McKeiver and Gadenne, 2005; Rao, 2008; Schaper, 2002) by creating new green product lines or through organizational and strategic regeneration (Guth and Ginsberg, 1990; Sharma and Chrisman, 1999). In the next section, we examine the link between entrepreneurship and environmental concern and ecopreneural manager motivation.

ECOPRENEURIAL MOTIVATION

Once the concept of ecopreneurship is defined, it is essential to analyse what motivates ecopreneurs. Ecopreneurs are 'crucial agents of change' (Walley and Taylor, 2002) who exert critical force in facilitating change (Cohen and Winn, 2007). Research has provided possible explanations as to why an entrepreneur might become an ecopreneur. Post and Altman (1994) identified three key motivators for environmental change in business behaviour: compliance-based environmentalism, market-driven environmentalism and value-driven environmentalism.

First, compliance-based environmentalism is based on the idea that ecopreneurship is a result of stringent government rules and regulations. Companies must comply with mandatory environmental regulations, regardless of ecological motivation. Environmental regulatory pressure, however, can provide an incentive to improve internal efficiency, especially through innovative resource productivity (Porter and Van der Linde, 1995). When obligated (not motivated) by law to follow advanced environmental approaches, ecopreneurs mostly agree with stringent environmental regulations because of ecological concerns.

Second, companies receive economic incentives for making environmentally conscious strategic decisions. Companies attempt to find innovative, cost-effective and sustainable solutions to current social and environmental problems. Several studies have argued that implementing advanced environmental approaches in internal processes can improve productivity and efficiency (Aragón-Correa, 1998; Brío et al., 2001; Buchholz et al., 1992; Post and Altman, 1994). Although implementing advanced environmental practices can incur cost increases (Lanoie and Tanguay, 2000), ecopreneurs could be motivated to improve internal processes that decrease a company's negative environmental impacts while improving efficiency and productivity rates.

Finally, value-driven environmentalism describes growing consumer demand for environmentally friendly products and services. Increasing ecological and environmental concern (Laroche et al., 2001) is causing consumers to lose confidence in large companies interested more in economic profitability than in their effect on society or the environment. Consumers expect a high level of social and environmental responsibility

(Webb et al., 2008), and by combining social purposes with for-profit philosophy, ecopreneurs are able to provide business solutions for these environmental and social needs (Seelos and Mair, 2005a, 2005b), perceive these new ecological demands and satisfy this increasing market segment (Cohen and Winn, 2007; Sharma, 2000).

There is a fourth motivator for ecopreneurialism related to the three already discussed. According to Linnanen (2002), ecopreneurs can be classified using two independent variables: their personal values concerning their wish to improve environmental quality, and their ability to identify environmental protection as an opportunity to improve business performance. Improved business performance can be associated with market- and value-driven factors, but personal environmental values offer additional motivational factors to those proposed by Post and Altman (1994). One of the main characteristics of ecopreneurs is strong ethical reasoning (Linnanen, 2002). To become an effective ecopreneur, it is essential to convey environmental values to the entire organization. Convincing decision-makers (Anderson and Bateman, 2000) and employees (Fernández et al., 2003) of the benefits of environmentally focused business strategy is fundamental for effective implementation. Ecopreneurs need commitment from employees whose practical knowledge of daily manufacturing processes often pioneers an organization's proactive environmental activity (Hanna et al., 2000; Ramus and Steger, 2000). Support and leadership from top-level management (that is, ecopreneurs) is essential to ensure environmentally conscious behaviour within organizations (Zutshi and Sohal, 2004). Ecopreneurs who convey an environmentally focused vision and model personal commitment will inspire others to support their mission (Portugal and Yukl, 1994). Ecopreneurs can motivate employees to comply with environmental protection goals through a relationship built on confidence and trust. Figure 10.1 shows the continuum of ecopreneurial motivational factors.

We suggest that the motivational factors increasing the number of ecopreneurs in business today include not only regulatory demands, the achievement of eco-efficiency and the increasing environmental concerns of consumers, but also the personal environmental values of entrepreneurs (that is, intrinsic motivation). To illustrate this, a case study from the tourism industry will be examined, as the environment forms a significant part of this industry's product.

We analyse a small Spanish firm that exemplifies ecopreneurial motivation and how this business philosophy can generate multiple organizational capabilities to the competitive advantage of the company. This environmental philosophy epitomizes the contribution that ecopreneurship can make to sustainable development.

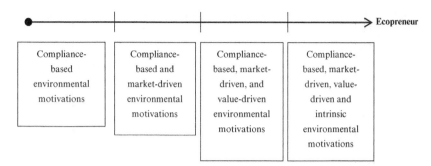

Figure 10.1   The continuum of ecopreneurial motivation

ECOPRENEURSHIP IN THE HOTEL INDUSTRY

Environmental Concerns in the Hotel Industry

Studies addressing company environmental strategy have traditionally focused on the direct impact on the natural environment of sectors such as mining, chemicals or manufacturing. Despite a need for major research on these businesses and the environment (Starik and Marcus, 2000), research over the last few decades has also included the service industries and, specifically, the tourism sector (Alvarez-Gil et al., 2001). Environmental regulation in the tourism sector is minimal (Alvarez-Gil et al., 2001) compared to industries that are more heavily scrutinized, and companies are able to use their environmental practices to appeal to consumer demand and to differentiate themselves from competitors. The service sector, particularly tourism, has not traditionally been of great concern regarding environmental impact and has been termed the 'silent destroyer of the environment' (Alvarez-Gil et al., 2001). However, this opinion has changed dramatically in the last decade (Claver et al., 2007). The accommodation industry (hotels, hostels, and so on) consumes large amounts of energy. The use of fossil fuel rather than renewable energy means that hotels emit polluting gases that directly affect global warming. A typical hotel can emit between 160 and 200 kg/m^2 per room per floor of carbon dioxide (CO_2), and some European hotels emit as much as 13.6 megatonnes of CO_2 (Bohdanowicz, 2005).

   The growth of mass tourism in Spain over the last 50 years has spread to new rural and natural areas, where 50 per cent of the harmful effects are considered irreversible. Customers are demanding a greater respect for the environment, and their satisfaction depends on the sustainability of the environment, natural attractions and landscape. The survival of hotels and quality tourist destinations depends on industry commitment to sustainability. Conflict results when industrial development impacts upon environmental efforts necessary for the continuity of tourism (Chan and Wong, 2006; Mihalic, 2000; Urtasun and Gutierrez, 2006). Although the hotel sector causes less pollution than some industries (Kirk, 1995), environmental issues still have a critical impact. An excessive increase in temperature related to climate change can have a negative impact on a destination's desirability, for example (Berritella et al., 2006).

The hotel sector was chosen as an example for four reasons. First, tourism is a sector of great economic importance in Andalusia (and Spain in general). Spanish tourism ranks third in the world, behind the US and Japan. Further, Andalusia received over 22 million tourists, with an estimated income of €15000 million in 2009 (Andalusia Tourism, 2010). Second, in addition to providing accommodation, the hotel sector supports all tourist attractions by offering entertainment and activities (Deng et al., 1992). Third, the hotel sector is undergoing a process of global integration and concentration that is increasing industry competition. This global integration has seen the emergence and development of several environmental initiatives, certification requirements and programmes (for example, Green Globe; the International Hotel Environmental Initiative – IHEI; Q for Quality of the Institute for Spanish Tourism Quality – ICTE) that aim to update and homogenize environmental efforts. Box 10.1 shows several characteristics of the hotel sector that differ from industrial activities.

Finally, companies from the tourism sector are more willing to adapt to environmental requirements than those in manufacturing because they cannot operate in a contaminated environment (Mihalic, 2000).

BOX 10.1   SPECIFIC CHARACTERISTICS OF THE HOTEL SECTOR

1. The hotel sector lacks flexibility in its product offering (i.e., beds per night) because capacity is limited.
2. The product is perishable – a room reservation cannot be stored for later use.
3. The product or service must be consumed at the production point. Services can be exported to other locations that provide the necessary environmental conditions.
4. The negative externalities are not exportable. Damage to the environment occurs in the same location as consumption and degrades service quality and revenue.

Source: Burkart and Medlik (1981).

Conservation is vital for the tourism sector because the environment is part of the product being sold. This is even more applicable in established tourist destinations such as Andalusia, where there is an ongoing struggle to lessen the negative impact from over half a century of intensive exploitation, increased international competition from new destinations and the potential for loss of revenue (Mihalic, 2000). Environmental degradation has called into question the continuity and development of the accommodation sector. These distinguishing industry factors call for management education and mobilization around environmental protection issues.

Sustainable tourism is dependent upon the implementation of practices beyond legal compliance that are aligned with global expectations and reforms. Hotels must now establish recycling targets and measures that reduce energy and water consumption. Sustainable, routine, evolutionary practices, as opposed to revolutionary practices, will be increasingly pervasive and more effective in dealing with environmental and socio-cultural problems (Weaver, 2012).

Firms offering accommodation consume energy, water and other natural resources on a daily basis. The voluntary adoption of proactive environmental practices and initiatives positively affects hotel activity for two reasons: relief from stakeholder pressure, and management perception of the potential benefits that an enhanced reputation can bring. The World Tourism Organization (1998: 21) states that:

> the development of sustainable tourism responds to the needs of tourists and the host regions, as well as protecting and improving future opportunities; it is focused on the management of all resources and therefore satisfies all economic, social and aesthetic needs, as well as respecting cultural integrity, essential ecological processes, biological diversity and life support systems.

Reducing environmental impact may be viewed positively by green consumers who demand more environmental concern from companies. Over 33 per cent of travellers are prepared to pay more for environmentally friendly tourism services, and this percentage is expected to grow over the next two decades (UNWTO, 2011). Voluntary environmental action may therefore improve brand image and provide competitive advantage (Bohdanowicz, 2005). Adopting voluntary environmental programmes can reduce costs and increase efficiency for companies offering accommodation by minimizing waste and resource consumption.

This chapter focuses on hotel management motivation for the adoption of environmental practices. More than 80 per cent of Spanish hotels are independent, small companies with less than ten employees (Observatory of Telecommunications and Information Society, 2007). The willingness of a manager to adopt environmental practices depends on whether management attitudes and knowledge align with customer preferences and regulations (Bohdanowicz, 2005). Managers of independent hotels have autonomous decision-making power and flexibility in meeting consumer demands. Attitude and vision are key factors in determining ecopreneurial behaviour. Available resources and company size can make the additional effort involved in adopting environmental strategies difficult (Sharma and Vredenburg, 1998). It is especially interesting, therefore, to analyse what motivates hotel managers to become ecopreneurs.

A Case Study of Spanish Ecopreneurship: Costa Azul Hostel

The entrepreneur and environmental management literature focuses on case study analysis (Dixon and Clifford, 2007; Ferrón-Vílchez et al., 2012) or small samples with less than ten cases (e.g., de Bruin and Lewis, 2005; Freimann et al., 2005; Pastakia, 1998; Schaltegger, 2002). Case studies have been used because there is scarce research in this area (Dixon and Clifford, 2007; Ferrón-Vílchez et al., 2012). In this particular case study, direct contact with entrepreneurs provided easy access and valuable insight to the organization over the research period. Costa Azul Hostel offers accommodation in the tourism centre of Granada (Andalusia, southern Spain).

The company is renowned for its environmentally friendly and socially oriented management style. In both the regional Andalusian and national Spanish market, Costa Azul Hostel is the only hostel to comply with the three main Spanish accommodation standards: Q for Quality (the most important certification for Spanish accommodation companies), ISO 9001 (certification of the quality management system) and ISO 14001 (certification of the environmental management system). Recent literature suggests that quality and environmental management depend on excellence and sustainability because there are philosophical and procedural similarities: continuous improvement, zero defects and zero emissions, a high grade of formalization (Brío et al., 2001; Harrington et al., 2008; Ferrón-Vílchez et al., 2010), and synergies between quality and environmental practices that positively impact upon the performance of firms (Brío et al., 2001, 2002; Ferrón-Vílchez et al., 2010). Quality and environmental management are required to achieve sustainability, strategic placement and competitive advantage.

Costa Azul Hostel is a unique example of a micro-business with entrepreneurial and strategic vision in the Spanish accommodation industry. Founded in 1965, this company has more than 50 years of experience in the hotel industry, 100 per cent Andalusian investment and a team composed of two managers (the owners) and seven non-managerial employees.

Business activities involve a balanced and ongoing search for economic development, environmental integrity and social well-being, establishing the company as an environmental leader in Andalusia's accommodation sector. Costa Azul Hostel is an example of how a business, through organizational and strategic renovation (Guth and Ginsberg, 1990; Sharma and Chrisman, 1999), can adopt an ecopreneurial orientation based on sustainability and economic development.

The case study used primary and secondary data collected from informal interviews with the entrepreneurs and follow-up research (special thanks to the Ogea sisters, chief executive officers of Costa Azul hostel). Three main information sources were used. First, the literature was used to contextualize some environmental problems affecting the tourism sector. Second, an in-depth interview was conducted with the manager of Costa Azul Hostel to analyse the motivation for being an ecopreneur. Questions established in recent research by Kirkwood and Walton (2010) were posed to better understand the motivation for ecopreneurs: (1) What motivates people to become ecopreneurs? (2) Which motivators are most important to ecopreneurs? (3) What is the impact of green values on those starting (and running) a business? (4) Do these motivations differ from the general population of entrepreneurs? How? Third, we had the chance of visiting the hotel and conducting some informal conversations with both the employees and the managers to compare previously collected data. We used this information to reflect on motivation for ecopreneurial action and the distinctive attributes of ecopreneurship (in a small and medium-sized enterprise, SME, context).

ANALYSIS OF COSTA AZUL HOSTEL

For the managers of Costa Azul, the location of a green hostel (for marketing, advertising and publicity purposes) in Granada, and having the recognition of being the only hostel in Spain engaged in quality and environmental protection with the three certifications, motivated them to implement environmentally friendly practices. The management of Costa Azul identify three main motivators for the adoption of ecopreneurial strategy:

1. environmental responsibility as a way of life for management;
2. improved management efficiency through the adoption of ecopreneurial strategy;
3. to demonstrate that small companies can develop environmentally and socially valued initiatives.

Costa Azul Hostel complies with the four motivators illustrated in the continuum in Figure 10.1.

The Compliance and Market-Driven Motivation of Costa Azul Hostel

Implementing an environmental management system in compliance with certification requirements has contributed in two ways to compliance and market-driven motivation. Environmental certification supports the compliance-based aspect of motivation, which is satisfied by the implementation of certification. Cost savings from better monitoring of inputs, energy and waste minimization have satisfied the market-driven aspect of motivation. The management of Costa Azul Hostel have become aware, through experience, that collaboration in environmental protection results in improvements in daily business. They are convinced that any company (no matter how small) can implement management practices that protect the natural environment. Operations at the hostel illustrate the environmental protection and quality concerns of management. Ecologically friendly products in use include the following:

- products (that is, shower gel and shampoo) that comply with standard environmental requirements;
- containers for recycling paper, glass and batteries;
- recycled paper and other office stationery;
- food and beverages made from 100 per cent organically farmed products; and
- promoting the use of bicycles or Segways (self-balancing human transporters) instead of automobiles.

The manager stressed that: 'it is important to note that we did not obtain any governmental subsidy to implement our environmental and quality management systems, but the initial environmental investment costs were rapidly recovered'. By complying with environmental standards of certification, the management has learned how to improve daily business processes. For example, Costa Azul experienced savings on hostel maintenance, and other unexpected economic rewards quickly emerged (energy and water savings, and an increase in business).

Value-Driven Motivation of Costa Azul Hostel

Costa Azul's management consider that environmental certification is evidence of a commitment to meet the increasing demand for environmentally responsible behaviour. The current financial crisis is affecting the tourist sector, and Costa Azul believes that client satisfaction, in the form of a pleasant visitor experience, leads to increased client loyalty. Clients convey good experiences and environmental service perceptions to family members and friends, and Costa Azul values the positive feedback it receives from clients in the form of satisfaction and quality surveys or direct congratulations and encouragement of their business philosophy. The management commented: 'incidentally, clients are surprised that a tourist establishment as small as our hostel has obtained the certifications'. Positive advertising and external recognition of the hostel has increased, and it has been recognized for its environmentally friendly behaviour by the Association of Accommodations of Granada.

Intrinsic Motivations of Costa Azul Hostel

For the successful ecopreneurial orientation of the company, it was necessary to involve all employees in the environmental commitment. One of the Ogea sisters said, 'We have to understand, accept and adopt the environmental commitment as part of our lives; in fact, society starts with oneself'. Employees receive environmental training in the use and maintenance of ecological products as a key part of their job. The management is also committed to communicating the environmentally proactive approach to customers, suppliers and other competitors to promote understanding, acceptance and the value of environmental management in their business environment. Table 10.1 illustrates Costa Azul's communication to various stakeholders.

The Ogea sisters express great satisfaction with the results of the ecopreneurial strategy. The management consider this approach to be the company's greatest asset and source of competitive advantage for continued success in the hospitality industry. They believe that this is the way to achieve a balance between environmental sustainability and profitability.

CONCLUSIONS

In this chapter, we have analysed some of the motivators that lead managers to become ecopreneurs and what managers perceive as the social and economic impacts of ecopreneurial behaviour. The case study analysis of the motivation of the management and owners of a small company in the Spanish hostel industry revealed that the willingness to meet the ecological demands of customers was the main motivator for adopting an advanced environmental management strategy.

In addition to compliance-driven, market-driven and value-driven

*Table 10.1   How does Costa Azul Hostel communicate its environmental
concern?*

Agents	How do you communicate your concern to this agent?	The manager said. . .
Clients	Client relationships are direct, and thus, managers have the opportunity to explain their ecological concerns and the environmental certification process, from the initial decision to the certification.	'Sharing the business project with clients by explaining how to use energy (air conditioning, light, water and gas) well; dispose of towels, and recycle paper, glass and batteries'. The managers also stressed the importance of customer demand for green service providers with a certain level of environmental commitment. This has strengthened the company's position regarding competitors.
Suppliers	Costa Azul Hostel only uses inputs that comply with equipment parameters to limit waste generation. Several suppliers co-operated after discovery of this requirement.	'Sharing the business project with our suppliers by clarifying our requirements for inputs'.
Competitors	Management believes that any tourist establishment must be concerned with environmental issues and environmental management practices, regardless of size. As Granada is a global tourist destination, companies have a responsibility to maintain environmental standards.	'Sharing the business project with our competitors by showing how essential it is that the project becomes the norm'.

motivators, we also proposed a fourth driver related to intrinsic motivations, expanding on the work of Post and Altman (1994), and developed a continuum of motivations for becoming an ecopreneur.

Costa Azul Hostel's management maintain that adopting the role of ecopreneur benefits the business. The management have taken advantage of an increase in green clients who demand an environmentally friendly service. By being the only hostel to enforce three main quality standards, the hostel has created a valuable way to differentiate itself from its competitors. The management recognize that environmental practices have reduced operational costs through closer monitoring of inputs and energy. The Costa Azul Hostel illustrates that being small is not an obstacle to enforcing an advanced environmental management strategy.

Recent literature on ecopreneurship addresses a greener approach to business (Pastakia, 1998), which is a potential path towards sustainable development because ecopreneurship is a vehicle for social change (Anderson, 1998). The research contributes to the emerging dialogue on a new business paradigm, verifying that ecopreneurs have wider motivations than merely the exploitation of a niche market. With values, reputations and a way of life related to being environmentally aware, employees, customers and supplier involvement can all contribute to a firm's successful sustainable development strategy.

ACKNOWLEDGEMENTS

This work has been partially funded by the Spanish Ministry of Education (project ECO2010-20483) and the Regional Government of Andalusia (project P11-SEJ-7988). The authors want to thank the members of the research group, 'Innovation, Sustainability and Business Development' (SEJ-481), for their help and comments. In addition, the authors want to sincerely acknowledge the book's editors for contributing beneficial suggestions and providing the opportunity to elaborate this chapter.

REFERENCES

Alvarez-Gil, M.J., J. Burgos-Jiménez and J.J. Céspedes-Lorente (2001), 'An analysis of environmental management, organizational context and performance of Spanish hotels', *Omega*, 29, 457–71.

Andalusia Tourism (2010), *2009 Andalusian Tourism Report*, Ministry of Tourism, Trade and Sports, Junta de Andalucía.

Anderson, A.R. (1998), 'Cultivating the Garden of Eden: environmental entrepreneuring', *Journal of Organizational Change Management*, 11(2), 135–44.

Anderson, L.M. and T.S. Bateman (2000), 'Individual environment initiative: championing natural environment issues in US business organizations', *Academy of Management Journal*, 45(4), 548–70.

Aragón-Correa, J.A. (1998), 'Strategic proactivity and firm approach to the natural environment', *Academy of Management Journal*, 41, 558–67.

Balabanis, G., H.C. Phillips and J. Lyall (1998), 'Corporate social responsibility and economic performance in the top British companies: are they linked?', *European Business Review*, 98(1), 25–44.

Banerjee, S.B. (2001), 'Managerial perceptions of corporate environmentalism: interpretations from industry and strategic implications for organizations', *Journal of Management Studies*, 38, 489–513.

Banerjee, S.B. (2003), 'Who sustains whose development? Sustainable development and the reinvention of nature', *Organization Studies*, 24, 143–80.

Bansal, P. and K. Roth (2000), 'Why companies go green: a model of ecological responsiveness', *Academy of Management Journal*, 43(4), 717–36.

Barney, J.B. (1991), 'Firm resources and sustained competitive advantage', *Journal of Management*, 17, 99–120.

Berritella, M., A. Bigano, R. Roson and R.S.J. Tol (2006), 'A general equilibrium analysis of climate change impacts on tourism', *Tourism Management*, 27(5), 913–24.

Bohdanowicz, P. (2005), 'European hoteliers' environmental attitudes: Greening the business', *Cornell Hotel and Restaurant Administration Quarterly*, 46, 188–204.

Brío, J.A., E. Fernández and B. Junquera (2002), 'Sinergias ISO1400 / ISO9000 prevención de riesgos laborales en las empresas industriales españolas: Un estudio empírico', *Cuadernos de Economía y Dirección de la Empresa*, 11, 59–78.

Brío, J.A., E. Fernández, B. Junquera and C.J. Vázquez (2001), 'Joint adoption of ISO 14000-ISO 9000 occupational risk prevention practices in Spanish industrial companies: a descriptive study', *Total Quality Management*, 12(6), 669–86.

Buchholz, R., A. Marcus and J. Post (1992), *Managing Environmental Issues; A Case Book*, Englewood Cliffs, NJ: Prentice-Hall.

Burkart, A. and S. Medlik (1981), *Tourism: Past, Present and Future*, London: Heinemann.

Chan, E.S.W. and S.C.K. Wong (2006), 'Motivations for ISO 14001 in the hotel industry', *Tourism Management*, 27, 481–92.

Christmann, P. (2000), 'Effects of "best practices" of environmental management on cost advantage: the role of complementary assets', *Academy of Management Journal*, 43, 663–80.

Christmann, P. (2004), 'Multinational companies and the natural environment: determinants of global environmental policy standardization', *Academy of Management Journal*, 47, 747–60.

Claver, E., J.F. Molina, J. Pereira and M.D. López (2007), 'Environmental strategies and their impact on hotel perfomance', *Journal of Sustainable Tourism*, 15, 663–79.

Cohen, B. and M. Winn (2007), 'Market imperfections, opportunity and sustainable entrepreneurship', *Journal of Business Venturing*, 22(1), 29–49.

Darnall, N. and D. Edwards Jr. (2006), 'Predicting the cost of environmental management system adoption: the role of capabilities, resources and ownership structure', *Strategic Management Journal*, 27, 301–20.

de Bruin, A. and K. Lewis (2005), 'Green entrepreneurship in New Zealand: a microenterprise focus', in M. Schaper (ed.), *Green Entrepreneurship in New Zealand: A Micro-Enterprise Focus*, Aldershot: Ashgate Publishing.

Deng, S.L., C. Ryan and L. Moutinho (1992), 'Canadian hoteliers and their attitudes towards environmental issues', *International Journal of Hospitality Management*, 11(3), 225–37.

Dixon, S. and A. Clifford (2007), 'Ecopreneurship – a new approach to managing the triple bottom line', *Journal of Organizational Change Management*, 20(3), 326–45.

Elkington, J. (1998), *Cannibals with Forks: the Triple Bottom Line of 21st Century Business*, San Francisco, CA: Wiley.

Fernández, E., B. Junquera and M. Ordiz (2003), 'Organizational culture and human resources in the environmental issue: a review of the literature', *International Journal of Human Resource Management*, 14(4), 634–56.

Ferrón-Vílchez, V., J.M. de la Torre-Ruiz and J.A. Aragón-Correa (2010), 'Calidad y algo más: el efecto conjunto de la gestión de la calidad y medioambiental en la rentabilidad de la empresa', *Revista Española de Financiación y Contabilidad*, 34(148), 655–75.

Ferrón-Vílchez, V., J.M. de la Torre-Ruiz, N. Ortiz-Martínez de Mandojana and J. Aguilera-Caracuel (2012), 'Spanish hotel industry leadership on climate change mitigation', in D.R. Gallagher (ed.), *Environmental Leadership: A Reference Book*, Thousand Oaks, CA: SAGE Publications, pp. 617–25.

Freimann, J., S. Marxen and H Schick (2005), 'Sustainability in the start-up process', in M. Schaper (ed.), *Sustainability in the Start-Up Process*, Aldershot: Ashgate Publishing, pp. 149–64.

Guth, W.D. and A. Ginsberg (1990), 'Guest editors' introduction: corporate entrepreneurship', *Strategic Management Journal*, 11(Summer), 5–15.

Hanna, M.D., R. Newman and P. Johnson (2000), 'Linking operational and environmental improvement through employee involvement', *International Journal of Operations and Production Management*, 20(2), 148.

Harrington, D., M. Khanna and G. Deltas (2008), 'Striving to be green: the adoption of total quality environmental management', *Applied Economics*, 40(23), 2995–3007.

Hart, S.L. (1995), 'A natural-resource-based view of the firm', *Academy of Management Review*, 20, 986–1014.

Hart, S.L. and M.B. Milstein (1999), 'Global sustainability and the creative destruction of industries', *Sloan Management Review*, 41(1), 23–33.

Isaak, R. (1997), 'Globalisation and green entrepreneurship', *Greener Management International*, 2, 80–90.

Isaak, R. (2002), 'The making of the ecopreneur', *Greener Management International*, 38(Summer), 81–91.

Keogh, P. and M. Polonsky (1998), 'Environmental commitment: a basis for environmental entrepreneurship?', *Journal of Organizational Change Management*, 11(1), 38–49.

Kirk, D. (1995), 'Environmental management in hotels', *Contemporary Hospitality Management*, 7, 3–8.

Kirkwood, J. and S. Walton (2010), 'What motivates ecopreneurs to start businesses?', *International Journal of Entrepreneurial Behaviour and Research*, 16(3), 204–228.

Kolk, A. and J. Pinkse (2008), 'A perspective on multinational enterprises and climate change: learning from "an inconvenient truth"?', *Journal of International Business Studies*, 39, 1359–378.

Lanoie, P. and G. Tanguay (2000), 'Factors leading to green profitability: ten case studies', *Greener Management International*, 31, 39–50.

Laroche, M., J. Bergeron and G. Barbaro-Forleo (2001), 'Targeting consumers who are willing to pay more for environmentally friendly products', *Journal of Consumer Marketing*, 18(6), 503–20.

Linnanen, L. (2002), 'An insider's experiences with environmental entrepreneurship', *Greener Management International*, 38(Summer), 71–80.

Mair, J. and I. Marti (2004), 'Social entrepreneurship: what are we talking about? A framework for future research', IESE Business School, University of Navarra, Barcelona.

McKeiver, C. and D. Gadenne (2005), 'Environmental management systems in small and medium businesses', *International Small Business Journal*, 23(5), 513–37.

Meadows, D.H. (1994), 'Seeing the population issue whole', in L.A. Mazur (ed.), *Beyond the Numbers*, Washington, DC: Island Press, p. 22.

Mihalič, T. (2000), 'Environmental management of a tourist destination: a factor of tourism competitiveness', *Tourism Management*, 21, 65–78.

Observatory of Telecommunications and Information Society (Observatorio de las telecomunicaciones y la Sociedad de la Información-Entidad Pública Empresarial) (2007), 'Diagnóstico tecnológico sector hotelero 2007', www.red.es.

Pastakia, A. (1998), 'Grassroots ecopreneurs: change agents for a sustainable society', *Journal of Organizational Change Management*, 11(2), 157–73.

Porter, M.E. and C. van der Linde (1995), 'Toward a new conception of the environment–competitiveness relationship', *Journal of Economic Perspectives*, 9(4), 97–118.

Portugal, E. and G. Yukl (1994), 'Perspectives on environmental leadership', *Leadership Quarterly*, 5, 271–76.

Post, J. and B. Altman (1994), 'Managing the environmental change process: barriers and opportunities', *Journal of Organizational Change Management*, 7(4), 64–81.

Ramus, C.A. and U. Steger (2000), 'The roles of supervisory support behaviors and environmental policy in employee "ecoinitiatives" at leading-edge European companies', *Academy of Management Journal*, 43(4), 605–26.

Rao, P. (2008), 'Environmental initiatives undertaken by entrepreneurs in the Phillipines', *Journal of Entrepreneurship*, 1(1), 73–81.

Roome, N. (1992), 'Developing environmental management strategies', *Business Strategy and the Environment*, 1, 11–24.

Schaltegger, S. (2002), 'A framework for ecopreneurship: leading bioneers and environmental managers to ecopreneurship', *Greener Management International*, 38(Summer), 45–58.

Schaper, M. (2002), 'Small firms and environmental management: predictors of green purchasing in Western Australian pharmacies', *International Small Business Journal*, 20(3), 235–51.

Seelos, C. and J. Mair (2005a), 'Sustainable development, sustainable profit', *European Business Forum*, 20, 49–53.

Seelos, C. and J. Mair (2005b), 'Entrepreneurs in service of the poor – models for business contributions to sustainable development', *Business Horizons*, 48(3), 241–46.

Sharma, P. and J.J. Chrisman (1999), 'Toward a reconciliation of the definitional issues in the field of corporate entrepreneurship', *Entrepreneurship Theory and Practice*, 23(3), 11–27.

Sharma, S. (2000), 'Managerial interpretations and organizational context as predictors of corporate choice of environmental strategy', *Academy of Management Journal*, 43, 681–97.

Sharma, S. and H. Vredenburg (1998), 'Proactive corporate environmental strategy and the development of competitively valuable organizational capabilities', *Strategic Management Journal*, 19, 729–53.

Starik, M. and A.A. Marcus (2000), 'Introduction to the special research forum on the management of organizations in the natural environment: a field emerging from multiple paths, with many challenges ahead', *Academy of Management Journal*, 43(4), 539–46.

United Nations World Tourism Organization (UNWTO) (2011), 'Tourism: investing in energy and resource efficiency', *Green Economy Report – Tourism Chapter*, http://sdt.unwto.org/sites/all/files/pdf/11.0_tourism.pdf, accessed 5 May 2012.

Urtasun, A. and I. Gutiérrez (2006), 'Tourism agglomeration and its impact on social welfare: an empirical approach to the Spanish case', *Tourism Management*, 27, 901–12.

Walley, E. and D.D. Taylor (2002), 'Opportunists, champions, mavericks . . .? A typology of green entrepreneurs', *Greener Management International*, 38(Summer), 31–43.

Weaver, D.B. (2012), 'Organic, incremental and induced paths to sustainable mass tourism convergence', *Tourism Management*, 33, 1030–1037.

Webb, D.J., L.A. Mohr and K.E. Harris (2008), 'A re-examination of socially responsible consumption and its measurement', *Journal of Business Research*, 61(2), 91–8.

World Tourism Organization (WTO) (1998), *Guide for Local Authorities on Developing Sustainable Tourism*, Madrid: World Tourism Organization.

World Travel and Tourism Council (WTTC) (2012), http://www.wttc.org/site_media/uploads/downloads/Progress_Priorities_2011_2012.pdf.

Zahra, S.A. (1995), 'Corporate entrepreneurship and financial performance: the case of management leveraged buyouts', *Journal of Business Venturing*, 10, 225–47.

Zutshi, A. and A.S. Sohal (2004), 'Adoption and maintenance of environmental management systems: critical success factors', *Management of Environmental Quality*, 15(4), 399–419.

11. The impact of micro-firm everyday practices on sustainable development in local communities
Rita Klapper and Paul Upham

INTRODUCTION

While micro firms are normally discussed in light of their function as providers of employment and substantial research has explored their various roles in the economy, little has been said about their responsibilities and capabilities in sustainable development processes vis-à-vis entrepreneurship. Indeed, more generally, as Hall et al. (2010: 339) state: 'To date, the academic discourse on sustainable development within the entrepreneurship literature has been sparse'. Moreover, although the Brundtland Commission (1987) acknowledged at an early stage in the discourse of sustainable development the role that the micro-firm sector could (and indeed must) play, as Crals and Vereeck (2011) observe, it remains far from clear that small businesses can afford the time required to follow any one of the plethora of sustainability certification processes and guides now available. Indeed the sheer quantity of assistance on offer itself has the potential to confuse. One UK database, for example, lists over 500 environmental accounting software tools (Environment Tools, 2013). Some considerable degree of specialist knowledge and time is required to meaningfully differentiate between these offers, despite their potential to routinize data collection and to guide on action. Similarly it is difficult to imagine many small businesses, particularly of micro scale, using official guidance such as the Department for Environment, Food and Rural Affairs (Defra)'s (2006) environmental key performance indicators, as these again require considerable understanding and time to make sense of and to use.

Yet as we emphasize below, the role of small and medium-sized organizations (SMEs) in the UK (and European) economy is profound. A variety of SME definitions exist across Europe. Increasingly, classifications follow the European definition of an SME as a company that employs up to 250 people and fulfils certain criteria of independence. Smaller businesses, that is, companies that employ up to ten people, are also referred to as micro businesses. In many cases small and medium-sized enterprises are rooted in their local communities, and their owners and employees may for this reason alone be expected to show a particular interest in their local environment. Moreover, Hutchinson and Hutchinson (1997) conclude that sustainability is not possible without the involvement of the SME sector. An SME's shorter lines of managerial communication and its flexibility to work in niche markets should make it an ideal partner in the environmental agenda.

Much corporate sustainability research has focused on the economic and environmental dimension of sustainability, particularly the latter (e.g. Adeoti, 2000; Friedman et al., 2000). Indeed the *Oxford English Dictionary* (Oxford Dictionaries, 2011), classifying sustainability as a derivative of the adjective 'sustainable', defines the latter environmentally, as 'able to be maintained at a certain rate or level', or in a more environmental direction 'conserving an ecological balance by avoiding depletion of natural resources' (Oxford Dictionaries, 2011). For a discussion of the concept of sustainability and its origins see, for instance, Shrivastava and Kennelly (2013). Relatedly, Hall et al. (2010) find that much of the recent sustainable entrepreneurship literature has been published in sustainable development and environmental management journals rather than journals specializing in entrepreneurship theory. However, as Shaw and Kidd (2001) and Seidl (2000) have emphasized, the most widely shared view of sustainable development includes non-environmental components: issues of quality of life, social equity and economic health. Indeed, as Upham (2000a) suggests, the concept of sustainable development was deliberately framed by the World Commission on Environment and Development (1987) so that it would engender wide political purchase at the general level of definition. It was never intended to only appeal to those with environmental priorities. With a broad definition of sustainable development in mind, this chapter explores the economic, socio-cultural and environmental contribution of two micro businesses in the North-West of England.

Here we examine how the practices of micro firms may simultaneously achieve the multiple dimensions of sustainable development, specifically focusing on the impact of micro-firm everyday practices on sustainable development in local communities. The chapter, firstly, aims to provide a reassessment, or different perspective, of the view that SMEs have little time for sustainable development. Secondly, there appears to be little conceptual work in the direction of a holistic model that combines the economic, social and environmental dimensions of sustainable development in specific connection to the role of micro business. We suggest that relative environmental impact reduction at this micro scale of business is more likely to arise from an expression of personal and professional values in the context of resource scarcity than it is from the use of systematized environmental knowledge tools.

The chapter first briefly introduces the literature on the integrated social, economic and environmental dimensions of sustainable development and approaches to facilitating environmental management by SMEs. This is followed by an overview of the study area, that is, Cheshire in the North-West of England, together with an explanation of the research methodology employed and description of the cases. The cases are then considered in the light of Bruyat's theory of entrepreneurial value creation and the relationship of this to the three dimensions of sustainable development. Given the observation that in our cases there is a consistency or congruency between these constituent parts of the picture, we go on to question the value of codified certification and standards-based approaches to sustainable development at this scale of business; not in principle, but simply in recognition of the conditions involved. We highlight the need to shape the wider conditions of the business environment so as to bring micro firms into pro-sustainability orientations.

SMEs AND THE DIMENSIONS OF SUSTAINABILITY

Economic Dimensions

As Adeoti (2000) highlights, there are typically considered to be three broad categories of problems associated with sustainable development: environmental, economic and social. The economic importance of micro firms is well established. Given that employment generation is one of the primary aims of the economic development process, much attention has been given to the economic dimension of micro firms in the national and regional economy. Strategies for the promotion of small-scale industries have focused mainly on policies promoting employment generation, entrepreneurship development, and training and skills acquisition. Local, regional and national governments have increasingly realized that SMEs are a vital part of the economy with regard to their net contribution to employment and job creation (Atkinson and Storey, 1994; Curran, 2000; Parker, 2001; Phelps, 1996; Reynolds et al., 1999; UK Round Table on Sustainable Development, 1999). In terms of the distribution of employees across enterprise size, there were some 4.5 million SMEs in the UK at the beginning of 2011, an extra 1 million relative to 1999. Of these SMEs in 2011, 62.4 per cent were sole proprietorships (3 364 020 enterprises), 99.2 per cent were categorized as small (0–49 people) and 0.7 per cent were medium-sized (50–249 people). Only 0.1 per cent of UK private sector firms are large, employing 250 people and above. Small enterprises accounted for 46.2 per cent of private sector employment and

48.8 per cent of private sector turnover at the start of 2011. In 2011, SMEs in total account for 58.8 per cent of UK private sector employment and 48.8 per cent of private sector turnover (BIS, 2011).

Social Dimension

To date, the social dimension of sustainable development appears to have been explored primarily in terms of indicators (for a discussion see Bell et al., 2000; Levett, 1998; MacGillivary et al., 2000). This is a theme reflected in indicators adopted by the UK government in 1996, revised in 1999 to reflect social issues (DETR, 1999a), with iterations through to Defra's sustainable development indicators of 2010 (Defra, 2010). Subsequently a new set of streamlined sustainability indicators went through a process of consultation, with the intention of supporting the government's approach to 'mainstreaming sustainable development'. These were published in mid-2013 (Defra, 2013).

On a regional level within an entrepreneurial context, the emphasis has been on micro firms taking over a social role as recipients for labour released due to rationalization, down-scaling and decentralization amongst larger businesses, management buy-outs, and the introduction of new technologies (Council of Europe, 1994; Curran and Storey, 1994). This has given micro firms particular prominence in many urban and rural communities, where it is argued that small and micro businesses are essential for the social benefits they can bring to these areas. In fact, they have been credited with bringing economic diversity, resulting in communities being less susceptible to economic downturn. Similarly, it has been argued that small firms tend to 'promote improved employer–employee relationships and greater community involvement' (UK Round Table on Sustainable Development, 1999: 2). Very little of this, however, is explored within the context of sustainable development.

Environmental Dimension

However, it is also likely that the micro-firm sector makes a significant contribution to environmental degradation, although only rough estimates are available. Albeit that small companies may only have a limited individual environmental impact, taken together their impact is likely to be substantial. Considering the UK and Netherlands, Rutherford et al. (2000) refer to an estimate that 70 per cent of industrial pollution is created by small firms, and 60 per cent of carbon emissions from industry can be attributed to SMEs (Hillary, 2000).

Earlier studies emphasized that micro firms need support and encouragement if they are to improve environmental performance (e.g. BCC, 1996; Bianchi and Noci, 1998; Petts, 2000; Rutherford et al., 2000). At the same time, these firms have for at least the last decade been subject to cost pressures that may reduce some forms of environmental impact; notably reducing waste, increasing recycling and taking prompt action to comply with new legislation (Klapper, 2001; Petts, 2000). Yet, Petts' (2000) research has shown that it is difficult to find direct business resonances with sustainable development concepts, even when managers have personal environmental concerns, and even in companies which are particularly concerned with environment management.

Reviewing the 2003–2008 literature on environmental interventions directed at SMEs, Parker et al. (2009) make a number of important points: that SMEs vary greatly in many different respects; that this has a significant bearing on the effectiveness of particular types of intervention; and that this in turn underlies the conflicting nature of the results found by intervention studies in the literature. Parker et al. further argue for both segmentation of SMEs when targeting interventions, and a mutually supportive mix of legislation, regulation and voluntary tools. They observe at least four types of SME orientation for which different intervention mixes are likely to be effective: profit, regulatory compliance, advantage seeking and environment-driven. Our purpose here is (1) to point in the direction of a fifth type, one where personal and entrepreneurial values are oriented towards commercial success through the provision of quality in the broadest sense; (2) to suggest that this orientation can deliver environmental benefits without the need for specific intervention; and (3) to suggest that, if intervention is an objective, then connection to the quality-oriented aspect of entrepreneurial value creation offers an entry point. In order to show this, we need to examine the detail of firm-level value creation, which qualitative in-depth case studies can help to provide. Hence in the next sections we drop down to the micro level of individual firms, where our main focus lies in this chapter.

AN APPROACH TO VALUE CREATION

In this section we conceptually integrate and graphically illustrate entrepreneurial value creation by small businesses in the context of the three dimensions of sustainable development. In terms of the process of value creation, we use a French perspective provided by Bruyat and Julien (2001). The latter extended Bruyat (1993) to define entrepreneurship as concerning the relationship between the individual and value creation ('l'objet scientifique étudié dans le champ de l'entreprenership est la dialogique individu/creation de valeur') (Bruyat, 1993: 57). Bruyat's concept is in turn based on Gartner's (1985) four-variable model of entrepreneurship, comprising the individual, the process, the environment and the enterprise. Bruyat's approach suggests that new value is created in terms of more or less intense change in the environment directly related to the entrepreneurial process (Verstraete and Fayolle, 2005). In other words, Bruyat argued that at the heart of the entrepreneurial process we find the act of value creation, as a result of the interaction between the individual and their environment. As Bruyat and Julien (2001) elaborate, at the beginning of the process we have the individual defining themself in relation to the structure, that is, the organization that is being created. Hence the individual is both constrained and created by the object that they construct, in a dialogic process between the two entities that form a system.

Figures 11.1 to 11.3 portray the above process of value creation graphically, incrementally introducing elements until the later culmination in Figure 11.3, in which the various elements of the cases are present. In Figure 11.1, the individual entrepreneur seeks to create economic value through a process of establishing an organization, the company. This organizational structure both constrains and liberates the entrepreneur: they must act within a variety of institutionalized norms and structures, but this frees them to create. In Figure 11.2, economic value is created through this process, which then has the potential to support the entrepreneur in a cycle of further value creation. In Figure 11.3, we set this process in the context of the three dimensions of sustainable development, in which social benefit derives from economic value and both rely on environmental services. We can expand on this, to note, first, that this is an ideal – it assumes the economic activity is socially benign; and second,

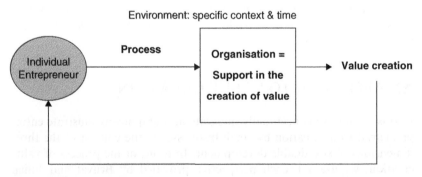

Source: Bruyat and Julien (2001).

Figure 11.1   The conceptualization of value creation

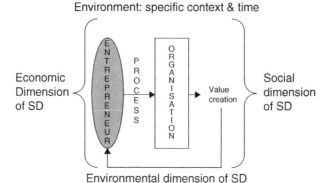

Figure 11.2   The application of Bruyat and Julien's (2001) model in the context of sustainable development

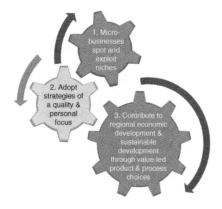

Figure 11.3   The contribution of low-impact micro firms to sustainable development

that the environmental impact of this activity will largely be proportional to the intensity of resource use and waste generation.

What is at issue here, however, is how the practices of micro firms may simultaneously achieve the multiple dimensions of sustainable development. Thus our research aimed to explore the impact of micro-firm everyday practices on sustainable development in local communities. In the following sections we first consider the two case studies and then, based on our findings, develop a holistic model that integrates the economic, social and environmental dimension of sustainable development in relation to value creation by small business. Recognizing the key role of value and values in this model, we discuss the implications of this for the nature of the sustainability related assistance that is offered to micro firms.

CASE STUDY METHODOLOGY

In terms of the chosen method, following the recommendations of Perry (2001), when explanation of causal links are too complex for survey or experimental methods, case research may be employed as an appropriate approach for an investigation of a contemporary, dynamic phenomenon such as sustainable development and its emerging body of knowledge. This approach is also in line with that of Jones (2000), who suggested that case studies on 'value-based' firms would be a good starting point for further research into sustainable development. A further reason for using a case-based research design lies in its capacity to deliver focused and detailed insights.

Case research tends to be of an explanatory, theory-building nature. A multiple case design was chosen, to provide more robust evidence regarding the phenomena, with a focus on the contribution of micro firms to sustainable development. This corresponds to Jensen and Rodgers's (2001) reasoning that comparative case analysis and 'replication across the cases' may produce both unique and consensus findings. Furthermore as Perry (2001) points out, a minimum of between two and four cases is acceptable for case research. Pluralism of research methods and combining them in a given study has long been advocated by authors such as Denzin and Lincoln (1998) and Montealegre (1999). Thus, data collected for each case included organizational information and documents. In addition, semi-structured interviews were conducted with the owner-managers, and one of the co-authors spent several months observing the entrepreneurial activities in both businesses, and participating in some of the social activities launched by the Haslington business owners.

In terms of the region chosen, the two micro businesses examined in this chapter are based in Cheshire (now termed Cheshire East after an administrative boundary change) in the North-West (NW) of England. The NW region contains almost 7 million inhabitants and 252 000 businesses, with a £119 billion economy: the UK's largest regional economy and larger than the individual economies of 15 European Union (EU) member states (NWDA, 2011). Although the partnership 4NW took on some of the coordination functions of the Regional Development Agency (RDA) (4NW, 2010), the abolition of the RDAs by the Conservative–LibDem coalition government and the ending of 4NW has made it more difficult to readily access regional statistical information. Nonetheless, we know that in 2000, Cheshire contributed one-sixth of North-West gross domestic product (GDP) (Cheshire County Council, 1999) and the region had one of the highest GDPs in the country (NWDA, 2000). Yet the region is also known to have substantial variations in economic performance: geographically, sectorally and within various communities. There are significant concentrations of unemployment, and as of 2006, 9 per cent of the working age population lived on 'Incapacity Benefit': at 400 000 people this was the largest number of any UK region (NWDA, 2006). The North-West also has the local authorities with the lowest house prices, and the unitary authority (a city-region administrative unit) with the lowest male life expectancy in England (ONS, 2012). At the same time, regional bodies have nonetheless positioned sustainability within their economic discourse and ambitions, and in general there is considerable commitment to recognizing both the intrinsic and the economic value of environmental protection (4NW, 2010).

The North-West picture is mixed when examining new start-ups and enterprise survival. On the one hand the North-West has enjoyed higher rates of new business start-ups than the UK average, ranking only behind London, the South-East and the South-West. On the other hand the region has the UK's second-lowest survival rate for start-ups, ranking just behind the North-East (NWDA, 2001b; Segal Quince Wicksteed Ltd, 1999). In 1997 the North-West had over 207 000 SMEs (defined as companies employing between 1 and 299 employees), which represents an increase of about 40 per cent since 1993.

The catering sector was chosen due to one of the co-authors' involvement in the start-up of a business in that sector, and several months were spent observing the creation of one of the firms, as well as active involvement in some of the social activities launched by the business owners. A second small catering firm in the neighbouring village served to benchmark the observations and findings.

Both firms discussed in this chapter thus belong to the catering sector, which will differ in impact profile from other sectors, such as those involved in manufacturing. This needs to be borne in mind when considering the wider, particularly theoretical, implications of the results. Moreover our purpose here is not to advocate a non-codified approach to the environmental management of micro businesses per se, but rather to emphasize that owner-managers' values and quality-driven practices may be aligned with the sustainability agenda. In other words these agendas, embodied in the personal values and the identity of the entrepreneurs, not only offer potential entry points for shaping firm behaviour in the direction of sustainability, but may already be doing so. Company selection was thus made on the basis of personal contact. In general, the two chosen cases are typical of many UK micro firms in different sectors in terms of size, their focus on survival, their resource scarcity, and in respect of the fact that they are owner-manager-driven: that is, the values of the entrepreneur dictate the company strategy.

The Case Study Firms

In this section we provide a short, descriptive overview of the two firms. These are micro firms in the catering sector, of likely low environmental impact relative to manufacturing enterprises, and chosen to illustrate our particular points of interest. They are likely in many ways to be typical of similar firms in other sectors, though environmental impact types will vary across sectors.

The first firm is a bakery with adjoining café located in a village in Cheshire. The company was established in November 2000 and is run by two female owner-managers. Prior to establishment, the owner-managers had each already run a small business. One of these delivered general supplies to the people in the local community, particularly 'personalized goods' (orders for sandwiches, drinks, crisps) to an industrial site nearby. After four years the owner-manager sold the business, as by her own account: 'I was working 12–14 hours a day but only working for the VAT man'. The second owner-manager is a fully trained nurse who previously ran a graphics design business with her husband for 16 years. Her main task lay in marketing the organization. She described her main motivation for setting up the business as: 'I had had enough, wanted something different'.

Prior to setting up the bakery, the proprietors conducted a market survey in the local area to assess whether there would be a need for the kind of business they had in mind. They took a systematic approach, as they felt 'we had only one chance to get good data, unbiased data'. They sent out 3500 questionnaires of which 24 per cent were returned to them. The responses were very encouraging and supported the owner-managers' view that the village needed the type of business that they had envisaged. This centres on a range of traditional, but also Continental-style breads, bread rolls, pies, quiches, sliced meats and cakes. One of their specialities is yeast-, wheat- and gluten-free bread. Similarly, they bake sugar-free cakes and sell sugar-free jams for a number of diabetic customers in the surrounding villages. For those who want to bake their own bread they offer a range of organic flours and yeasts. Thus, while offering conventional lines (not all detailed here), they are catering to a number of particular food-related niches.

The second firm is a delicatessen run by a male Armenian who had

owned a number of businesses before, some in catering and some in manufacturing. The owner has an MPhil in quantum chemistry, did very little
market research prior to opening the delicatessen, but followed his 'gut
instinct' that there would be demand for 'a Continental-style delicatessen
in a middle class area'. He argued: 'I had a rough idea that demand would
be greater than supply'. This is very much in line with Brouthers et al.
(1998), Cooper (1981) and Julien (1994), who have emphasized 'intuition'
of the owner-manager as well as the 'first hand feel' for the realities of
customers as key issues in a small business. The owner's main motivation
for becoming self-employed was financial: he had to support his family,
which took preference over pursuing a career in quantum chemistry. He
does not, however, rule out that his future might lie in going back to his
chemistry background. The delicatessen sells a wide range of Continental
produce ranging from cakes (prepared on the premises), different types of
breads, cheese and sliced meat, to a vast range of speciality conserves such
as vintage garlic. It also sells a wide range of alcoholic beverages. Between
four and five different meals are offered per day such as salads, pasta
and rice dishes, all of which stress the different flavours of a cuisine not
traditionally found in Britain.

FINDINGS

In this section we elaborate on our findings from the case analysis in terms
of the conventional, threefold sustainable development dimensions; the
results are displayed in Figure 11.3.

Niche Exploitation

Examining the two cases, the first point to note is that the owner-managers
have been successful in spotting gaps in the local market. They have set
up companies that are flexible enough to capitalize upon existing and new
opportunities. Both companies have established themselves as providers
of specialist products and services in niches which would not be worth
exploration by large companies: 'There are other companies who do it
but who don't do our products' (delicatessen). In both businesses the
owner-managers display a drive to offer 'something different', something
innovative to the customer:

> I believe in the intelligence of my customers and that innovations pay off in
> the longer term. We have to be different in packaging, origin and quality of
> our products. Different in terms of what has been available before and what
> is available now . . . I need to emphasise the difference of the place. I need to

bring added value for the customer to stay longer in the shop, to look around, buy more. (delicatessen)

In practical terms, this involves offering every customer a cup of coffee, cappuccino or espresso, or a cold drink, upon arrival, with the opportunity to try different speciality products.

Similarly the proprietors of the bakery emphasize being different and operating on quality as the two key values on which their business is based. Before setting up the business, they visited a number of outlets selling bakery equipment as well as bakeries and delicatessens. They concluded, however, that it was 'much of a muchness', with the products 'very boring', and decided that they wanted to offer their customers something different: 'We were not prepared to stick with the premixed product range, we want to offer our customers a good variety and choice of products and we want to use only the best ingredients'.

Socio-Economic Co-Benefits

The strategy of opportunity-spotting and niche exploitation provides the micro businesses with – and helps them maintain – a competitive advantage which has paved the way to long-term profit potential and survival. In terms of contribution to the local economy, both businesses successfully support the owner-managers together with a number of staff. The bakery employs four staff and the delicatessen six people (not all full-time). Thus both small businesses make a positive contribution to the regional economy. In fact, to ensure further growth and profit potential, both small businesses are in the process of diversifying their range of customers by targeting supply to local large-scale companies. This diversification relies in part on their local reputations and a willingness to supply innovative and personalized products and services to the surrounding community. With competitiveness and sustainable development both being promoted as key aspects of the regional strategies of the then Northwest Regional Development Agency (NWDA) (2001b, 2001c), the cases illustrate how micro firms support and promote the multiple dimensions of sustainable development.

The businesses are inextricably linked to the local community, through not only monetary flows but also social ties in family, near and extended networks. One of the bakery owner-managers founded the charity Neighbours in Distress, which is aimed at old-age pensioners (OAPs) in wheelchairs. Events such as the Sponsored Dogwalk which take place every year aim to raise money for the charity. Similarly, the other owner-manager founded the Haslington Companion, a group of people who look after abled-bodied OAPs. The bakery offers a special meal deal twice a week for OAPs, the aim of which is to offer a well-balanced meal. These activities are very much in line with the type of community involvement of micro firms as stressed by the UK Round Table on Sustainable Development (1999) and the NWDA (NWDA, 2001a, 2001b, 2001c).

Environmental Co-Benefits

Most of the research that focuses on micro firms and environmental issues has explored environmental management systems and tools such as life cycle analysis and total quality environmental management (see e.g. Banerjee, 2001; Wolters et al., 1997). The wider literature dealing with corporate environmental management and corporate social responsibility is collectively large. However, neither case discussed here follows any codified environmental management approach. What both small businesses have in common, however, is their interest in delivering products of high quality to the local community. In addition, the bakery places a special emphasis on providing products that are free of artificial ingredients. This emphasis on high-quality products expresses a care for the well-being of the customers and an interest in the quality of the local environment, but it is expressed as much through health and quality discourses as through reference to environmental protection or the use of codified systems.

This mixed discourse (including practice) is also very much in line with long-standing UK government strategy that promotes better health for all, arguing that we need to address pollution, unhealthy lifestyles, poverty and 'worklessness' (DETR, 1999a). Given the emphasis on providing first-rate quality products to their customers, these two businesses act very much in accord with policies that aim to generate a link between health and sustainable development. In fact, as UK strategy has long argued, in particular, at the local level sustainable development and health strategies must reinforce each other (DETR, 1999b). In this regard, these small businesses are indeed making their contribution to achieving sustainable development on a local level, as expressed in terms of government discourse.

Nonetheless, in line with other research that has shown that recycling is the most commonly performed activity among micro firms (see e.g. Banerjee, 2001) the two cases show that although neither of the businesses explicitly tries to formally take on board greener ideas, they both make an effort to participate in recycling initiatives. The delicatessen, for instance, uses recycled wrapping paper and tends to buy wrapping paper from sustainable resources. At the bakery business, cardboard boxes are recycled. Bread that cannot be sold is distributed to the Salvation Army or given to a bird sanctuary. Throughout, there is a theme of environmental co-benefits; for example, most patently in the bakery's recycling of off-cuts to provide a double income and avoid waste disposal costs: 'To recycle what would have been waste you create double products, create something else and sell it.'

All these activities show a certain degree of environmental awareness that appears to be as much born of a need for economic behaviour in the widest sense: a desire to minimize wastage and to prosper in conditions of resource scarcity. There is, however, no genuine desire in either business to install anything remotely resembling an environmental management system. The owner-managers appear to be satisfied with the environmental credentials of their businesses. In contrast, the environmental practitioner and academic discussion of the environmental contribution of businesses has given considerable attention to environmental management systems and formal codes. Yet it has long been recognized that it is very difficult to motivate micro firms to become involved in these. In fact, the proprietors felt that such a system would have no relevance for their business as they were too small and were doing already their best to minimize the effect on the local environment. In this regard it is quite possible that many minor initiatives pursued in micro firms are overlooked and are undervalued, as they do not conform to standardized norms. Arguably, this may distort the reality and create a generally gloomy picture of the contribution of micro firms to the pursuit of sustainable development.

DISCUSSION

Working closely with the micro-firm cases, we have shown that the multiple dimensions of sustainable development, at least in terms of the usual conception, are in effect furthered through the normal pursuit of entrepreneurial objectives. While we cannot generalize to firms with inherently higher environmental impacts, this does beg the question of how environmental performance might be improved in such a context. In general, options include: regulations, financial incentives, influencing consumer demand for specific products or behaviours, providing assistance or education, plus commitments to general business objectives, and also the degree of personal environmental commitment held by owner-managers (Parker et al., 2009). Our contribution here lies in the latter space, as our findings emphasize that aligning personal values and beliefs with the three dimensions of sustainable development need not necessarily be the outcome of a planned, strategized enterprise creation and development process, but rather can emerge out of the entrepreneurial everyday practice. On the basis of participative involvement in two micro enterprises by the lead author, we have witnessed how business creation and development, not led by environmental values alone, can still lead to positive environmental, social and economic outcomes in an integrated (one might say 'natural') way, due to the owner-manager leading this process in line with their beliefs, vision and values. Building on this observation, we wonder whether this perspective might offer more scope for effective interventions, particularly at the micro and service end of the business size and type spectrum, than environmentally explicit approaches.

Of course this begs the further question of how best to support such practice, and we do not address this question in detail here. In the absence of extensive micro regulation, options include supporting pro-environmental consumer norms (Parker et al., 2009) and peer messaging, as we know that environmental awareness among the totality of SMEs is influenced by and related to their networks (Schaefer et al., 2011), and that there is potential for inducing positive environmental norms in communities that involve such businesses (Moraes et al., 2010).

In general we concur with Chen et al. (1997) and Shrivastava (1995), who emphasize the vision and/or values of an owner-manager as instrumental in determining an organization's strategic direction. Shrivastava and Kennelly (2013) have also emphasized the importance of 'place' in bringing enterprise and sustainability together. We emphasize that these are somewhat differing approaches to values management. Coulter (2000) suggests that having a core set of values can influence the way an organization does its business, defining values-based management as: 'an approach to managing an entrepreneurial venture that entails establishing, promoting, and practising shared values. An organization's values reflect what it stands for and what it believes in' (Coulter, 2000: 111). Shared organizational values may promote a variety of purposes which guide decisions and actions, shape employee behaviour, influence marketing efforts and assist in building team spirit in organizations. These values may range from an interest in the health of customers to the provision of top-quality products and services, to involvement in the community. However, significantly, here we are witnessing not a strategic process of values management, but a set of interconnected, more or less conscious processes that nonetheless lead to relatively positive outcomes across the three dimensions of sustainability (while acknowledging that most human activity inevitably has some degree of negative environmental impact).

In Figure 11.3, we summarize the way in which business creation and the maintenance of competitive advantage contributes to the objectives of long-term profit potential, survival, well-being of the regional economy, as well as to the implementation of aspects of regional and central government policy in pursuit of sustainable development. The values of the micro-firm owners, their desire to offer products which are different, innovative, personalized and of top quality, as well as their wish to maintain environmental quality and contribute to the well-being of the customers, are shown as informing the choice and identification of the niches in which they operate, contributing to further competitive advantage. This helps to generate long-term profit potential and better opportunities to survive locally, which again contributes to the well-being of the local economy.

In achieving this, the firms make no recourse to environmental management tools, but rather appear to rely on tacit knowledge (Polanyi, 2009), likely derived from a variety of sources and directed by a range of more or less congruent personal and professional values. Indeed the role of tacit knowledge in environmental decision-making per se, and in a micro-firm context, relative to the use of explicit and codified knowledge, is something that merits closer attention by those with an interest in facilitating pro-environmental company behaviour. One potential research direction, for example, is to explore the potential role of heuristics in the popular sense of 'rules of thumb'. This would include readily memorable notions such as the waste hierarchy, 'reduce, reuse, recycle' (Environment Agency, 2012), which condense a large body of empirically derived knowledge into short principles. A similar approach has been followed by The Natural Step (Upham, 2000a, 2000b), which has sought to simplify the wide array of sustainable development and environmental assessment issues into a set of principles that, while best used to orient environmental decision-making tools rather than on their own, are nonetheless educationally helpful (Upham, 2000a, 2000b, 2000c, 2000d). Other directions for research include, as referred to above, supporting pro-environmental consumer norms (Parker et al., 2009) and also community norms (Moraes et al., 2010), as well as making use of peer networks (Schaefer et al., 2011). These are not exclusive options, though, and both the theoretical and practical aspects of integrating entrepreneurial and environmental norms and behaviour need closer attention.

CONCLUSIONS

This research has investigated the impact of micro-firm everyday practices on sustainable development in local communities in the UK, and we discussed how entrepreneurial value creation in two small businesses in Cheshire has contributed to the three dimensions of sustainable development through pursuit of entrepreneurial and personal values, in the absence of environmental management tools. Though we acknowledge that these particular cases are relatively low environmental impact operations, they are typical of UK micro firms in making little use of such tools, and in their commitment to providing quality as well as responding to niche opportunities. At issue is the extent to which a variety of personal commitments might be better mobilized in pursuit of sustainability, given the difficulty in securing the use of formal environmental management approaches.

To this end, here we have thought about sustainability from an entrepreneurial practice perspective, highlighting the contribution of micro firms despite a relatively unplanned, unstrategized approach to sustainable development. Most studies of environmental management in and by SMEs have emphasized a single dimension of sustainable development – the environment – and advocate environmentally informed, conscious, rational planning and management for sustainability. The conceptual model described above adopts a perspective that views the economic, social and environmental dimensions of sustainable development from the standpoint of economic value creation. Most economic activity has negative environmental impacts of some type and duration, and we are very much aware of the need to reduce this. To this end, it is worth exploring alternative ways of promoting and thinking about what is increasingly described as sustainable entrepreneurship. This chapter has made a case for exploring in greater depth in future research the tacit, including cognitive, dimensions of the interface between entrepreneurship and sustainable development as expressed in day-to-day entrepreneurial practice.

Given the importance of the values of a micro-firm owner for the strategies and further development of the organization, further work should assess the importance of a range of values for such firms within the framework of sustainable development concepts, and how they relate to the owner-manager's identity and their personal constructs, which ultimately drive the venture creation and development. Here we mean values of different types: economic, environmental and social as well as personal and professional. This work might explore connections between the personal attributes of owner-managers, their educational habitus and professional experience and their pro-environmental, or pro-sustainability, commitments. This may include gender terms, contrasting male and female owner-managers and the influence of gender on behaviour relevant to sustainable development. As Seidl (2000) argues: 'sustainable development cannot occur if the contribution of women to the economy and their knowledge about environmental problems and solutions remain veiled'. More generally, a number of gender differences may be found when surveying men and women as to their reasons for starting businesses (Shane and Kolvereid, 1991). Environmental and social commitment also tend to be closely connected in the general population (Stern and Dietz, 1994), with significant gender differences among, for example, students' beliefs about consequences of economic and other activity for self, others and the biosphere (Stern et al., 1993).

Finally, the cases discussed here hint at the ways in which successful micro firms may target niches in which they have a realistic chance that their value-based management will create competitive advantage. This has the potential to lead to long-term profit potential, economic survival and, within a wider context, to add to the economic well-being of a region. There is plenty more work to be done to understand how best to facilitate these processes, such that they align with sustainability imperatives, as these continue to build in strength and urgency globally.

REFERENCES

4NW (2010), 'Sustainable economic development: North West case studies', 4NW, http://www.4nw.org.uk/downloads/documents/jul_10/4nw_1277989065_SED_Case_studies-June_2010.pdf. Also see http://www.4nw.org.uk/articles/article.php?page_id=759 and http://www.4nw.org.uk/articles/article.php?page_id=760 [no longer available].

Adeoti, J.O. (2000), 'Small enterprise promotion and sustainable development: an attempt at integration', *Journal of Developmental Entrepreneurship*, 5(1), 57–72.

Atkinson, J. and D. Storey (1994), 'Small firms and employment', in J. Atkinson and D. Storey (eds), *Employment, The Small Firm and The Labour Market*, London: Routledge, pp. 1–28.

Banerjee, S.B. (2001), *Corporate Environmental Strategies and Actions Management Decision*, 39(1), 36–44.

BCC (1996), 'Effective business support, a UK strategy; phase two', London: BCC.

Bell, S., S. Morse and F. Nunan (2000), 'Sustainability indicators: measuring the immeasurable', *Local Government Studies*, 26(2), 138–140.

Bianchi, R. and G. Noci (1998), 'Greening SMEs' competitiveness', *Small Business Economics*, 11, 269–81.

BIS (2011), 'Business population estimates for the UK and regions 2011', Department for Business Innovation and Skills, London, http://www.bis.gov.uk/analysis/statistics/business-population-estimates, accessed 8 May 2012.

Brouthers, K.D., F. Andriessen and I. Nicolaes (1998), 'Driving blind: strategic decision-making in small companies', *Long Range Planning*, 31(1), 13–138.

Brundtland Commission (1987), *Report of the World Commission on Environment and Development: Our Common Future*, New York: United Nations, http://www.un-documents.net/our-common-future.pdf, accessed 6 November 2013.

Bruyat, C. (1993), 'Création d'Entreprise: contributions épistémologiques et modélisation', Thèse pour le Doctorat de Sciences de Gestion, ESA – Université Grenoble II, Grenoble.

Bruyat, C. and P.A. Julien (2001), 'Defining the field of entrepreneurship', *Journal of Business Venturing*, 16(2), 165–80.

Chen, S.Y., B.R. Sawyer and F.P. Williams (1997), 'Reinforcing ethical decision making through corporate culture', *Journal of Business Ethics*, 16(8), 855–65.

Cheshire County Council (1999), 'Cheshire current facts and figures, economic information unemployment', Ec I 2, October.

Cooper, A. (1981), 'Strategic management: new ventures and small business', *Long Range Planning*, 14(5), 39–45.

Coulter, M. (2000), *Entrepreneurship in Action*, Upper Saddle River, NJ: Prentice Hall.

Council of Europe (1994), *The Promotion of Small and Medium-Sized Enterprises in the European Union*, Strasbourg: Council of Europe Press.

Crals, E. and L. Vereeck (2011), 'Sustainable entrepreneurship in SMEs. Theory and practice', http://www.scribd.com/doc/48311365/Sustainable-entrepreneurship-in-SMEs.

Curran, J. (2000), 'What is small business policy in the UK for? Evaluation and assessing small business policies', *International Small Business Journal*, 18(3), 36–56.

Curran, J. and D. Storey (1994), 'The location of small and medium enterprises: are there urban–rural differences?', in J. Curran and D. Storey (eds), *Small Firms in Urban and Rural Locations*, London: Routledge, pp. 1–16.

Denzin, N. and Y. Lincoln (eds) (1998), *The Landscape of Qualitative Research*, Thousand Oaks, CA: Sage.

Defra (2006), 'Environmental key performance indicators: reporting guidelines for UK business', London: Defra, http://archive.defra.gov.uk/environment/business/reporting/pdf/envkpi-guidelines.pdf.

Defra (2010), 'Measuring progress: sustainable development indicators', London: Defra, http://sd.defra.gov.uk/progress/national/annual-review/, accessed 6 November 2013.

Defra (2013), 'Sustainable development indicators', London: Defra, http://sd.defra.gov.uk/2013/07/new-sustainable-development-indicators-published/, accessed 6 November 2013.

DETR (1999a), 'A better quality of life: a strategy for sustainable development for the United Kingdom', London: DETR.

DETR (1999b), 'Supplementary guidance to Regional Development Agencies', 14 April, www.local-regions.detr.gov.uk/rdas/rdasup/index.htm [no longer available].

Environment Agency (2012), 'Waste hierarchy – frequently asked questions', http://www.environment-agency.gov.uk/business/regulation/129223.aspx.

Environment Tools (2013), 'Environmental software tools directory', Abingdon, http://www.environmenttools.co.uk/.

Friedman, A.L., S. Miles and C. Adams (2000), 'Small and medium sized enterprises and the environment: evaluation of a specific initiative aimed at all small and medium sized enterprises', *Journal of Small Business and Enterprise Development*, 7(4), 325–38.

Gartner, W.B. (1985), 'A conceptual framework for describing the phenomenon of new venture creation', *Academy of Management Review*, 10(4), 696–706.

Hall, J.K., G.A. Daneke and M.J. Lenox (2010), 'Sustainable development and entrepreneurship: past contributions and future directions', *Journal of Business Venturing*, 25, 439–48.

Hillary, H. (2000), *Small and Medium-Sized Enterprises and the Environment: Business Imperatives*, Sheffield: Greenleaf Publishing.

Hutchinson, A. and F. Hutchinson (1997), *Environmental Business Management*, London: McGraw-Hill Publishing Company.

Jensen, J.L. and R. Rodgers (2001), 'Cumulating the intellectual gold of case study research', *Public Administration Review*, 61(2), 235–46.

Jones, D.R. (2000), 'A cultural development strategy for sustainability', *GMI*, 31, 71–85.

Julien, P.A. (1994), 'Small businesses as a research subject: reflections on knowledge of small businesses and its effects on economic theory', *Small Business Economics*, 5, 157–66.

Klapper, R. (2001), 'Small and medium sized enterprises and sustainable development: the case of two European regions: Tyne and Wear and Emscher Lippe', unpublished MPhil dissertation.

Levett, R. (1998), 'Sustainability indicators – integrating quality of life and environmental protection', *J.R. Statistical Society A*, 161(3), 291–302.

MacGillivary, A., C. Weston, C. Unsworth and M. Stott (2000), 'Communities count! A step by step guide to community sustainability indicators', *Local Economy*, 14(4), 375–90.

Montealegre, R. (1999), 'A case for more case study research in the implementation of information technology in less-developed countries', *Information Technology for Development*, 8, 199–207.

Moraes, C., M. Carrigan and S. Leek (2010), 'Reducing plastic bag consumption: a community approach to social marketing', 2010 European Conference of the Association for Consumer Research, 30 June – 3 July, Royal Holloway, University of London.

NWDA (2000), *North West Objective 3 Regional Development Plan*, Manchester: Pion Economics, June.
NWDA (2001a), 'England's North West – a strategy towards 2020', www.nwda.co.uk/strategy/strat/documents/adhead.pdf, accessed October 2002 [no longer available].
NWDA (2001b), 'North West England Objective 2 SPD Chapter 10 Cross cutting priorities', www.eurofundingnw.org.uk/, accessed October 2002 [no longer available].
NWDA (2001c), 'Strategic vision', www.englandsnorthwest2020.com, accessed September 2002.
NWDA (2006), 'Northwest Regional Economic Strategy – 2006 baseline report', Manchester: North West Regional Development Agency [no longer available online].
ONS (2012), 'Summary: Regional Profiles – Social Indicators – North West – February 2012', Office of National Statistics, http://www.ons.gov.uk/ons/rel/regional-trends/region-and-country-profiles/social-indicators/social-indicators---north-west.html.
Oxford Dictionaries (2011), http://oxforddictionaries.com/view/entry/m_en_gb0833570#m_en_gb0833570.006, accessed 8 May 2012.
Parker, C., J. Redmond and M. Simpson (2009), 'Review of interventions to encourage SMEs to make environmental improvements', *Environment and Planning C: Government and Policy*, 27(2), 279–301.
Parker, R. (2001), 'The myth of the entrepreneurial economy: employment and innovation in small firms', *Work, Employment and Society*, 15(2), 373–84.
Perry, C. (2001), 'Case research in marketing', *Marketing Review*, 1, 303–23.
Petts, J. (2000), 'Smaller enterprises and the environment organisational learning potential', in S. Fineman (ed.), *The Business of Greening*, Routledge: London, pp. 153–69.
Phelps, N.A. (1996), 'Small firms and local economic development in South London', *Local Economy*, 11(3), 202–21.
Polanyi, K. (2009), *The Tacit Dimension*, Chicago, IL: University of Chicago Press.
Reynolds, P.D., M. Hay and S.M. Camp (1999), *Global Entrepreneurship Monitor*, Kansas City, MO: Kauffman Center for Entrepreneurial Leadership.
Rutherford, R., R.A. Blackburn and L.J. Spence (2000), 'Environmental management and the small firm', *Internal Journal of Entrepreneurial Behaviour & Research*, 6(6), 310–25.
Schaefer, A., S. Williams and R. Blundel (2011), 'SMEs' construction of climate change risks: the role of networks and values', SMEs: Moving Towards Sustainable Development, International Conference, 20–22 October, Montreal, Canada.
Segal Quince Wicksteed Ltd (1999), 'Review of business development needs in the North West', A final report to the North West Development Agency (NWDA), Stockport.
Seidl, I. (2000), 'A step to endorse sustainability', *International Journal of Social Economics*, 27(7–10), 768–87.
Shane, S. and L. Kolvereid (1991), 'An exploratory examination of the reasons leading to new firm formation across country and gender', *Journal of Business Venturing*, 6(6), 431–446.
Shaw, D. and S. Kidd (2001), 'Sustainable development and environmental partnership at the regional scale: the case of Sustainability North West', *European Environment*, 11, 111–123.
Shrivastava, P. (1995), 'Environmental Technologies and competitive advantage', *Strategic Management Journal*, 16, 183–200.
Shrivastava, P. and J.J. Kennelly (2013), 'Sustainability and place-based enterprise', *Organization and Environment*, 26, 83–101.
Stern, P.C. and T. Dietz (1994), 'The value basis of environmental concern', *Journal of Social Issues*, 50(3), 65–84.
Stern, P., T. Dietz and L. Kalof (1993), 'Value orientations, gender, and environmental concern', *Environment and Behavior*, 25(3), 322–48.
UK Round Table on Sustainable Development (1999), *Small and Medium Sized Enterprises*, London: DETR.
Upham, P. (2000a), 'Scientific consensus on sustainability: the case of The Natural Step', *Sustainable Development*, 8, 180–190.

Upham, P. (2000b), 'An assessment of The Natural Step theory of sustainability', *Journal of Cleaner Production*, 8(6), 445–54.

Upham, P. (2000c), 'LCA from a sustainability perspective; reply to the Letter to the Editor by K.-H. Robèrt, J. Holmberg and U. Lundqvist', *International Journal of Life Cycle Assessment*, 5(4), 193.

Upham, P. (2000d), 'LCA and post-hoc application of sustainability criteria: the case of The Natural Step', *International Journal of Life Cycle Assessment*, 5(2), 68–72.

Verstraete, T. and A. Fayolle (2005), 'Paradigmes and Entrepreneuriat', *Review de l'Entrepreneuriat*, 4(1), 33–52, http://asso.nordnet.fr/r-e/RE0401tv_af.pdf, accessed 6 November 2013.

Wolters, T., P. James and M. Bouman (1997), 'Stepping stones for integrated chain management in the firm', *Business Strategy and the Environment*, 6, 121–32.

World Commission on Environment and Development (WCED) (1987), *Our Common Future*, Oxford: Oxford University Press.

PART IV

INDUSTRY- AND ECONOMY-ORIENTED APPROACHES TO ENTREPRENEURSHIP AND SUSTAINABLE DEVELOPMENT

12. The renewable energy industry: competitive landscapes and entrepreneurial roles

Roberto Parente* and Rosangela Feola*

INTRODUCTION

Emerging societal needs are a source of pressure for the development of new technology (Arthur, 2009). Improvements in existing products and services very often are not sufficient to narrow the gap and consequently the search for an entirely new technology paradigm starts, and usually ends with the emergence of a new industry (Day, 2000). The speed and effectiveness of this process of replacement depends on the one hand on technological and scientific progress, and on efficacious business strategies on the other. If it is true to say that new technological paradigms are the outcome of the combination of old and new knowledge (Arthur, 2009), it is also true to say that firms, by means of entry strategy decisions (Ghemawat, 1991), can select and foster the production of such new knowledge (Nelson and Winter, 1982). Unfortunately entrants to the new industry have to bear considerable risks. The time the development of a new technology takes, the amount of investments required and the possibility of being surpassed by competing technology platforms, are just a few of the sources of risk. Investments in such a scenario, where development trajectories are unknown and unknowable (Zeckhauser, 2006), are usually limited and will tend to follow rules that are very different from standard financial models.

If competitors move late and/or with incremental investments only, the new industry will develop very slowly. The complexity of interaction between the scientific and technological knowledge domain and the business rules domain can cripple the process, leading to a sense of frustration among the supporters of the new industry (UNEP, 2010).

The renewable energy industry seems to fit exactly into this scenario. Despite the rising concern about the negative impact of global warming, fossil fuels still represent the dominant paradigm in the energy-producing field (IEA, 2010). The perspective of entry strategies into a new industry followed by competitors, either those already dominating related industries (incumbents), or those wishing to enter the field (newcomers), could shed light on the reasons why new industry develops or fails to develop over time. Academic debate on the issue has a very long track record. According to the Schumpeterian line of thought (Schumpeter, 1934) the dominant paradigm of analysis is that new entrepreneurial ventures will be the vehicles introducing new technology onto the market, and in the long run will replace the old population of existing firms (incumbents) that have grown thanks to mature technologies (Hannan and Freeman, 1977). This approach has been questioned, and very recently, with specific regard to sustainable industry; it has been posited that a positive role for both young 'Davids' and well-established 'Goliaths' can feasibly exist (Hockerts and Wüstenhagen, 2010).

In order to understand entrepreneurial roles (young 'Davids', and old 'Goliaths' capable of readapting to new scenarios) in innovative industries, such as that of renewable energy, the concept of entry strategies (and related issues) needs to be reflected upon and elaborated. By analysing recent changes in how competition is structured, the objective of the chapter is to explore issues relating to entry strategy paths of key players in the renewable energy sector in order to understand the entrepreneurial role in a new industry.

The chapter proceeds as follows. The following section describes the renewable energy sector and clarifies the focus of the chapter. Next, we provide a review of existing literature on entry strategies in new industries and on 'competitive landscapes' structures, in order to define the theoretical frame of reference. After that, we specify our research methodology. Finally, we present the empirical research and the results and end with a discussion of the study's limitations, implications and conclusions.

THE RENEWABLE ENERGY INDUSTRY

Global climate change and the accelerating depletion of natural resources are just two of several phenomena indicating that the world is not well aligned to the concept of sustainable development. The term 'sustainable development' was first coined at the United Nations Conference on the Human Environment in 1972 and later gained prominence by way of a report to the United Nations by the World Commission on Environment and Development (WCED, 1987), chaired by Norwegian Prime Minister Gro Harlem Brundtland. The report defines sustainable development as 'development that meets the needs of the present generation without compromising the ability of future generations to meet their own needs'. The central point of this definition is that all natural systems have limits, and that human well-being requires living within those limits. Sustainable development implies that renewable sources should be used wherever possible and non-renewable resources should be husbanded to extend their viability for generations to come (Hall et al., 2010). The use of renewable sources is considered a key factor in sustainable development as they are able to reconcile environmental issues with economic growth (Lund, 2007; Dincer, 2000).

The term 'renewable energy sources' refers to all sources of energy that can be continually and naturally replenished as they are produced by physical or chemical mechanisms of the planet by the direct or indirect effect of solar energy. Unlike fossil fuels that are finite resources, renewable sources can be regarded as unlimited resources. Furthermore, fossil fuels cause air, water and soil pollution and produce greenhouse gases that contribute to global warming. Renewable energy resources offer clean alternatives to fossil fuels. They produce little or no pollution or greenhouse gases, and they will never run out. The use of renewable energy is not new. More than 150 years ago, wood, which is one form of biomass, supplied up to 90 per cent of our energy needs. But the interest in renewable energy has grown more quickly in recent years as a result of higher prices for oil and natural gas, and a number of other factors and changes occurring in the electricity system, encouraging its use. These factors can be traced to:

- environmental problems and growing social awareness towards these issues;
- the growth of demand for electricity;
- technological development and reduction in the cost of energy from renewable sources;
- government support for renewable energy sources.

Renewable energy plays an important role in the supply of energy and produces many positive effects on the economic system, defined as 'multiple dividend' (De Paoli and Lorenzoni, 1999). Such positive effects of renewable energy can be distinguished in:

- reduction of dependence on external providers of energy, with a consequent increase of security of supply;
- increased diversification of energy sources, with strong benefits for the security of electricity supply but also for reduction of the risks of fluctuations in prices;
- reduction of atmospheric pollutants. When renewable energy sources are used, the demand for fossil fuels is reduced. Unlike fossil

fuels, renewable sources of energy do not directly emit greenhouse gases;
- contribution to the sustainability of economic activity in the long run;
- replacement of imported input and equipment with facilities that enable domestic employment;
- ability to develop new businesses by encouraging local entrepreneurship and promoting employment growth.

Some negative factors exist regarding renewable energy sources, rendering them not an exclusive but a complementary resource in the energy supply. Renewable energy is generally more expensive than fossil fuels. Renewable resources are often located in remote areas, and it is expensive to build power lines to the cities where the electricity they produce is needed. The use of renewable sources is also limited by the fact that they are not always available, as their availability depends on particular climate and natural conditions. Renewable energy sources generally include solar, wind, hydropower, energy flows, wave and tidal energy, energy from biomass, geothermal energy and waste. More accurately, they can be distinguished as non-renewable fuels and renewable fuels. The former include hydropower, wind, solar and geothermal energy whose availability is related to peculiar climatic conditions. Renewable fuels are those continuously produced by nature (biomass) or from human activity (fuels derived from biodegradable urban and industrial waste).

Renewable energy has become a priority for governments of both industrialized and emerging economies. Countries are gradually recognizing the potential role of renewable energy within a portfolio of low-carbon and cost-competitive energy technologies capable of responding to the emerging major challenges of climate change, energy security and access to energy. Nevertheless, despite the rising concern about renewable energy, fossil fuels still represent the dominant paradigm in the energy-producing field, and currently renewable energy sources have a small global market share: only 18.5 per cent of worldwide production for energy in the electricity sector is met using renewable energy sources (IEA, 2010). In this perspective it might be interesting to analyse the reasons for this slow growth of the renewable energy sector. In our opinion, the perspective of entry strategies followed by competitors – either those already dominating related industries (incumbents), or those wishing to enter the field (newcomers) – could shed light on the reasons why new industry develops or fails to develop over time.

THEORETICAL FRAME OF REFERENCE

Entry Strategies in New Industries

Exploiting entrepreneurial opportunity requires an appropriate strategy in order to create maximum wealth and sustainable competitive advantage (Ireland et al., 2001; Hitt et al., 2001). Since the order of entry into a new industry can influence players' performance (Lambkin, 1988), entry strategies are at the foundation of a strategic approach to entrepreneurial opportunity exploitation. The essence of entry strategy is to gain sustainable competitive advantage in a new industry (Porter, 1985), and is defined by two main strategic decision-making drivers (Ghemawat, 1991; Lieberman and Montgomery, 1990; Lilien and Yoon, 1990):

- timing of entry: that is, decisions about when to enter new technology sectors (moving early versus late);
- level of commitment: that is, decisions about entity of investment made to enter new technology, sectors/segments (large investment versus incremental).

Decision-making relative to these elements defines three basic strategic options available for firms (Mitchell and Singh, 1992; Mitchell, 1989) (Figure 12.1):

- learning strategy, which means moving through successive steps in the accumulation of necessary resources. In this way, a firm opens a window to an emerging technology but also maintains the flexibility necessary to change in response to further technological development and to market reaction;
- growth strategy, where attempts are made to pursue entrepreneurial opportunity rapidly, anticipating competitors and acquiring first-mover advantages;
- deferring strategy, which imply the decision not to consider at all (Mode 1), or at least to postpone further investments until the time when technological and market uncertainties of the new industry are less significant (Mode 2).

Entry strategy choice clearly defines different kinds of roles in new industry development. Would-be pioneers in the industry consider growth strategy as their first option; likewise, potential early entrants will follow learning strategy investment in order to actively seek new opportunities;

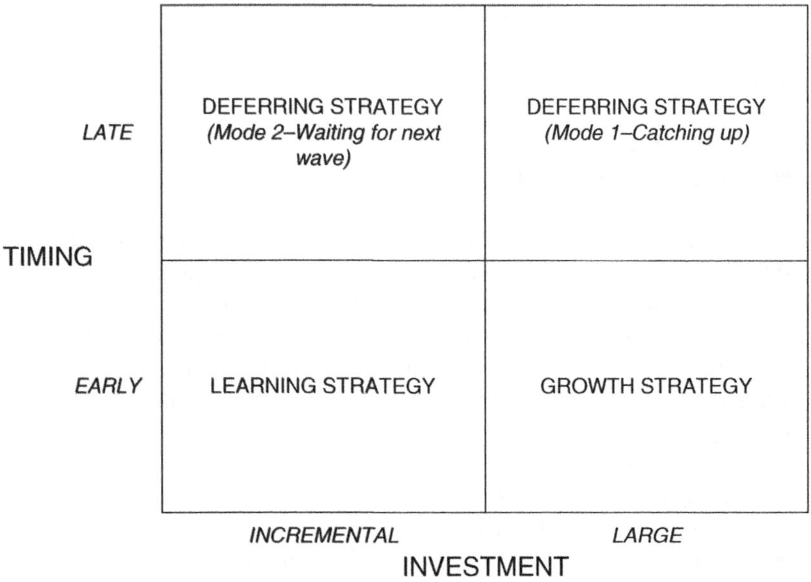

	INCREMENTAL	LARGE
LATE	DEFERRING STRATEGY *(Mode 2–Waiting for next wave)*	DEFERRING STRATEGY *(Mode 1–Catching up)*
EARLY	LEARNING STRATEGY	GROWTH STRATEGY

TIMING

INCREMENTAL   *LARGE*

INVESTMENT

Figure 12.1   Strategic entry options

while late entrants will defer their investment in a new technology for as long as possible.

Nature of Entrepreneurial Opportunity and Entrepreneurial Champions

When and how intensive the economic players' commitment will be in the development of new technology represents just one side of the coin. The issue of who the dominant player of such development will be is equally important. From this point of view, the key question becomes the differences in strategic approaches on the part of incumbents from related industry and new entrants. Will it be, for example, only the former to act as pioneer in the industry, pursuing a straightforward growth strategy?

The most influential theoretical paradigm on this issue is the 'population ecology framework' (Hannan and Freeman, 1977). The findings of this model indicate that new firms could easily be comfortable in dealing with fundamentally new technology. Start-ups of new industries are, as a matter of fact, often associated with high start-up rates of new small firms, which often show greater flexibility and are better able to react to stimuli from the environment (Baumol et al., 2007; Audretsch et al., 2002; Arend, 1999; Swaminathan, 1998; Geroski, 1995; Tushman and Anderson, 1990).

In contrast, well-established firms (incumbents) often show a more limited ability to perceive emerging opportunities because of a series of obstacles to face in the process of change (Hill and Rothaermel, 2003). One of the main obstacles is organizational inertia, which prevents successful, well-established firms from changing their strategies and their organizational routines. Another reason for the failure of existing firms in the pursuit of new entrepreneurial opportunities is connected to the different systems of incentives for incumbents and new entrants. According to this view, in fact, even if the incumbents perceive the potential of change, rationally they may be induced to invest in incremental improvements that leverage the knowledge base they already possess to consolidate the positions acquired in the sectors where they operate (Helfat, 1997).

Although the idea is still widely accepted that entrepreneurial new ventures are the engine of economic change (Carree and Thurik, 2006), there is evidence that in some cases incumbents are able to intercept new entrepreneurial opportunity through adequately diversified strategies. Corporate entrepreneurship philosophy and practice (Ahuja and Lampert, 2001) put in place by incumbents could explain why sometimes they also become pioneers and leaders in new industry. Through investments in complementary assets to their technology base they might be able to understand very quickly the right trajectory with which to address their vast resources (Wu et al., 2014). On the other hand, it has been stated that open innovation strategies, leverage on the acquisition of external knowledge, may enable large companies to lead new industry (Chesbrough, 2006).

It should be clear that novelty per se is not a guarantee of success and that intelligent incumbents can play a key role in developing new industry (Acs and Audretsch, 1988). One of the main paradigms used to explain the interplay between new and old firms is the dynamic perspective. Hockerts and Wüstenhagen (2010), for example, propose that early in the transformation of an industry towards sustainability, new entrants, 'Emerging Davids' as the authors call them, are more likely to pursue opportunities for sustainability. Eventually, incumbent firms respond to new entrants and adopt sustainability practices. These 'Greening Goliaths' are less progressive but have considerable impact due to their existing market presence. Ultimately, new entrants and incumbents co-evolve, creating incentives and competitive positions that allow both to survive. Hockerts and Wüstenhagen therefore argue that progress in creating sustainable industries and economies will soon rely on an interplay of entrepreneurial entry and the transformation of incumbent players.

Competitive Landscapes and Entrepreneurial Process

To reconcile different paradigms relative to pioneers in new industry, the entrepreneurial process perspectives may prove useful. Sarasvathy et al. (2005) argue that entrepreneurial opportunities are not at all similar. Some entrepreneurial opportunities are simply discovered, others have to be created. If entrepreneurial opportunities have to be created, because an enterprise cannot leverage on an existing well-functioning business model, serendipity is the driver of a firm's success much more than strategic planning and execution (Denrell et al., 2003). Entrepreneurially based new ventures might be much more familiar with such a peculiar entrepreneurial process. This is basically a process of exploration of new knowledge (essentially technology knowledge) domains (Alvarez and Barney, 2008). The consequence of this entrepreneurial process is that the possibility for incumbents to successfully explore new technology domains is closely linked to the nature of the competences needed to nurture such new technology. The more the new set of competences is radically different from those they already master, the more difficult it is for them to play a role in the new technological paths.

Another interesting perspective clarifying the varying nature of the entrepreneurial process in different sets, is that of 'competitive landscapes' (Kauffman, 1993). The actions of the firms are embedded in competitive landscapes that can be complex to a greater or lesser extent according to sources of uncertainty and the wealth of intersection points between such sources. The highest level of complexity ('rugged landscapes') is when a lot of technology trajectories unrelated to each other exist and this will present a multi-peak design in strategies. A low level of complexity ('smooth landscapes') is when investments in technology trajectories are additive, and this will present a single-peak strategy (Levinthal and Warglien, 1999) (Figure 12.2).

The concept of competitive landscapes can be useful for predicting the dynamics of new industry development, since competitive landscapes change over time. Usually a multi-peak, rugged landscapes, evolves along time in a single-peak, smooth landscape, through an evolutionary process of variety production/selection of specific technology platforms (Nelson and Winter, 1982).

The basic question now is as follows: in an environment that allows multi-peak design strategy (rugged landscapes), which are the areas best suited for new entrepreneurial ventures, and which are the areas (if any) for entrepreneurial initiatives of incumbents from related industries? Our assumption is that the nature of the technology trajectories clearly defines the entrepreneurial roles in the new technology developments. As much as

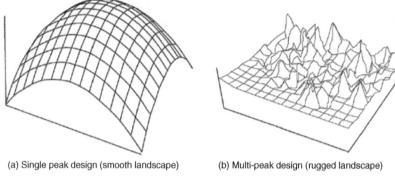

<table>
(a) Single peak design (smooth landscape)   (b) Multi-peak design (rugged landscape)
</table>

(a) Single peak design (smooth landscape)   (b) Multi-peak design (rugged landscape)

Source: Levinthal and Warglien (1999).

Figure 12.2   Landscape fitness according to the degree of interaction

the technology trajectories intersect with the technology base (in a broad sense) of incumbents, as much as they can contribute to new industry development.

Coming back to the basic strategic options about entry strategy and integrating them with the construct of competitive landscapes, we can identify five different kinds of entrepreneurial process:

- standby landscape;
- entrepreneurial learning leading process;
- entrepreneurial growth leading process;
- corporate learning leading process;
- corporate growth leading process.

Standby industries are characterized by low or nil investments. These conditions will apply when landscapes are 'smooth' and where the single-peak investment strategy has already been identified and pursued in the past. Potential competence-destroying technologies are still to be confirmed from the scientific and technological point of view. Entrepreneurial learning leading industries are characterized by moderate investments, mainly from new entrepreneurial firms. This scenario occurs where competitive landscapes are 'rugged' and there is room for diversified investment strategies. Competence-destroying technologies are many and they compete with one another with no clear advantage associated to any of them. Entrepreneurial growth industries are characterized by strong investment policies made especially by new entrants. Competitive landscapes are 'rugged' but competing technology platforms are few. Corporate learning industries are characterized by moderate investments made by incumbents in a 'rugged' environment. Corporate growth industries are characterized by strong investments made especially by incumbents. Competitive landscapes are becoming less 'rugged': a specific winning technology has been selected by competitors and the competence needed to manage such new technology can be borrowed, at least in part, from the portfolio of consolidated competence of the incumbents.

To further develop our proposition, the competitive landscape construct will be applied to the renewable energy sector in order to understand the entrepreneurial roles in a new industry.

RESEARCH METHODOLOGY

The objective of the chapter is to explore issues relating to the entry strategy of key players in the renewable energy sector in order to understand the entrepreneurial role in a new industry. The focus of the chapter is an Italian case. Italy is one of the main actors in the international renewable energy scenario. According to the latest Ren21 Report, in 2012, with an installed capacity of 29 GW, Italy ranked fifth in the world (REN21, 2013). Italy shows excellent performance in all areas of the renewable sector: it occupies second place, after Germany, for photovoltaic installed power and per-capita capacity; fifth place in geothermic production and investments in the sector; seventh place for the growth of wind power capacity; and ninth place for bio-power generation.

The methodology used to investigate entry strategies in the renewable energy sector is mainly qualitative, which is well suited to exploratory investigations where the objective is not to validate a research proposition but to explore and develop a proposition (Eisenhardt, 1989; Miles and Huberman, 1994). To conduct our research, we collected data on the dynamics of development in each segment of the sector, and on the structure of competition in terms of dominant players. Data for the research were gathered from a variety of secondary sources. In particular, data on the development of the renewable energy sector were collected from studies and annual reports provided by institutional organizations of the sector: ENEA (Italian National Agency for New Technologies, Energy and Sustainable Economic Development), AEEG (Italian Regulatory Authority for Electricity Gas and Water) and GSE (Energy Service Authority). Data on the structure of competition were obtained from databases and internal reports provided by Italian industry associations (Italian Wind Energy Association, Renewable Energy

Producers Association). Data from single sources were analysed separately and compared in order to obtain as realistic a picture as possible of the industry. To define competitive landscapes in the renewable energy sector we used the following data:

- the average growth rate of each renewable technology in the period 2005–2009, measured by the power installed during the period;
- the average growth rate of the electricity sector in Italy in the period 2005–2009, measured by the power installed during the period;
- the impact of newcomers in each technology, measured by the contribution of newcomers to the total production of renewable energy in each segment.

The term 'newcomers' was defined on the basis of three elements: year of constitution of firm; core business activity; and independence from incumbents.

In our study newcomers are start-up companies constituted after the deregulation process of the electric sector (after 1990), with core business in one or more renewable technologies, and independent from incumbent firms. Incumbents are electricity operators integrating traditional activity in non-renewable energy technologies with investments in new renewable technologies.

DATA ANALYSIS AND FINDINGS

Having analysed collected data, our findings show that in Italy, production of renewable energy in 2009 reached about 68 TWh, representing 20 per cent of total consumption and with a growth rate of 13 per cent compared to 2008 (ENEA, 2010; AEEG, 2010). See Table 12.1.

From a trend analysis of the sector during the period 2005–2009 in terms of installed power (Table 12.2), the sector confirms the trend shown in Table 12.1.

With the exception of photovoltaic energy, which during the period evidenced a boom, the annual average growth rate of the sector was about 14 per cent. In particular, it emerged that wind, biomass and waste, and photovoltaic are the businesses with the biggest growth rate in the period (respectively 39.77 per cent, 13.64 per cent, 890.2 per cent). Geothermal and hydroelectric are more stable. With regard to the traditional electricity sector, the average annual growth rate, in terms of installed power, was about 3.8 per cent (Terna SPA, 2013).

The renewable energy industry is a complex and heterogeneous system,

Table 12.1   Italian production of electricity (GWh)

	2005	2006	2007	2008	2009
Total thermo-electric production	246918	255420	258811	253806	218247
Renewable production	49863	52239	49411	59720	67458
Biomass and waste	6155	6745	6954	7523	7740
Wind	2343	2971	4034	4861	6087
Photovoltaic	4	2	39	193	750
Geothermal	5325	5527	5569	5520	5347
Hydro	36067	36994	32815	41623	47534
Hydro (pumping)	6860	6431	5666	5604	4209
Total production	303672	314090	313888	319129	289914

Source: AEEG (2010).

Table 12.2   Italian installed power (MW)

	2005	2006	2007	2008	2009
Biomass	1200.00	1256.60	1336.80	1555.30	2018.50
Wind	1639.00	1908.00	2714.00	3538.00	4898.00
Photovoltaic	25.10	45.00	86.80	431.50	1142.30
Geothermal	711.00	711.00	711.00	711.00	737.00
Hydro	17326.00	17412.00	17458.60	17623.48	17721.47
Total	20901.10	21332.60	22307.20	23859.28	26517.27

Source: Data from GSE (Gestore Servizi Energetici).

with the presence of many players involved in the different phases of the value chain (technology development, plant construction, installation, energy production and distribution) distinguished by different dimensions, strategies and business models, portfolios of sources, technological and financial capacity. An analysis of the segment of renewable energy production highlighted the following categories of operators (Marangoni, 2010):

- Traditional global players: some of the biggest players in Europe (such as Enel, Edf, Rwe, E.ON), operating in Italy through business units focused on renewables (Enel Green Power, EDF Energies

Nouvelles, Rwe Innogy, E.ON Climate and Renewables). The players operate using a diversified portfolio of renewable sources and a global strategy. They integrate traditional activity in non-renewable energy technology with investments in new technology, such as wind and solar energy.

- Pure renewables: a group of companies made up of two types of firms – newcomers and international groups focused on renewable energy. Newcomers are usually independent and privately owned Italian-based firms, operating in the energy industry after the deregulating process (Alerion, Moncada, Actelios, IVPC, HFV, Terni, and so on). Renewable energy is their core business. The smallest are involved in just one kind of technology. Some medium-sized companies have gradually expanded their business; for example Moncada which operates in wind and solar energy with a strategy of vertical integration in the production of photovoltaic panels. International groups are focused on renewables with reference to the Italian market (International Power Renewables, Acciona, Iberdrola Renewables, SSE Renewables, Solon Q-Cell, Solarwatt). They are usually large companies with interests in different kinds of new technologies (Table 12.3).

The analysis of the competitive structure of the renewable energy industry shows that the former Italian electricity sector monopoly (Enel), is the main operator in the production of hydroelectric and geothermal energy, with a market share of 56 and 100 per cent of total production,

Table 12.3   Pure renewables and traditional global players

	Business model	Investments	Financial capability	Portfolio sources
Pure renewable	Start-up Small business Financial subject Diversified firms	Local or national Limited inter-national presence	Slow-medium High leverage Collaboration with financial subjects or other subjects of the sector	Focus on one/two technologies R&D limited or focused
Traditional global player	Big electric players Local utilities Oil and gas players	National and inter-national Emergent economies	Financial solidity Self-financing Credit capacity Collaboration with international players	Presence on more technologies Strong R&D

Source: Marangoni (2010).

respectively. In the wind segment, International Power, the largest electricity operator in Great Britain, is the main producer, with a market share of 17.1 per cent; while A2A, a local utility, is the number one operator in biomass and waste energy. Newcomers have a remarkable market share in biomass and waste (81 per cent), and a more limited share in the wind sector (48 per cent). In hydroelectric energy, newcomers have a small market share of about 18.2 per cent. The photovoltaic segment presents a peculiar structure due to public support in production, promoting especially small and domestic photovoltaic installations. The structure of the photovoltaic segment is characterized by the presence of a large number of newcomers having the prevalent share of production. In particular, new electric operators specialized in photovoltaic have about 94 per cent of the market share. Only four traditional incumbents are involved in photovoltaic technology, with a dedicated business unit (Enel with Enel Green Power, Edison with Edison Energie Speciali, EDF with Edf EN Italia, Sorgenia with Sorgenia Solar), having a small market share (about 6 per cent).

A Framework to Identify Competitive Landscapes in the Renewable Energy Industry

As outlined in the previous paragraph, different technologies vary in terms of growth rate and dominant players. Table 12.4 summarizes those differences.

On the basis of the data collected we elaborate a diagram that identifies five different competitive landscapes, with regard to the role of incumbents and newcomers (Figure 12.3). The diagram has been built on three key variables:

Table 12.4   A comparison of renewable energy technologies (%)

	Annual market growth rate (2005/2009)	Newcomers' market share
Biomass	13.64	81.00
Wind	39.77	48.00
Photovoltaic	890.20	94.00
Geothermal	0.73	0.00
Hydro	0.46	18.20
Average of the sector (without photovoltaic)	13.65	48.24

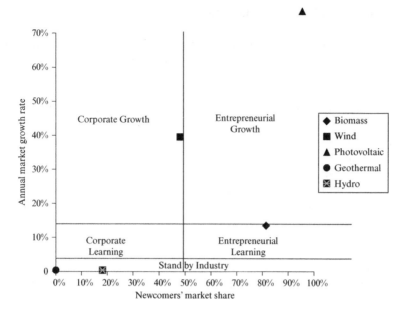

Figure 12.3   Competitive landscapes in the renewable energy industry

- average growth rate of Italian energy sector in the period 2005–2009 (3.8 per cent);
- average growth rate of the renewable sector in the period 2005–2009 (13.65 per cent);
- newcomers' market share in the renewable sector in 2009 (48.24 per cent).

Standby Industry

Geothermal and hydro follow this business structure. Both can be considered as the 'old' green technologies in the renewable energy industry. In other words, according to the technology available today, no further sources of economically viable production can be found without huge investments in infrastructure, with economic and/or environmental costs too high to be accepted. In such conditions, low growth rates and a limited presence of newcomers are the most obvious results. Nevertheless, new technology paths can change the situation, repositioning water kinetics and warm natural land as competitive energy sources able to attract new investments. To date, due to the immaturity of such technologies, projects ongoing in this direction are relegated to laboratory testing of concept development.

Entrepreneurial Learning Leading Industry

Biomass and waste are characterized by a slow growth rate but also by the relevant role of newcomers, generally small firms. This structure of the biomass sector is the result of two main elements: technologies used for the exploitation of biomass, and the procurement process of biomass. As concerns the first element, technologies currently available have reached a high level of development that ensures high efficiency of plant and high profitability of investment. On the other hand, current technologies concern large- and small-scale plants: for this reason, investment is also possible for small players generally having limited financial resources. As concerns the second element, the procurement process of biomass is a lengthy and complex process, involving different subjects operating in different phases (production and collection, storage and treatment, transportation and supply to energy producers). For these reasons the presence in the area and the direct contact with different subjects involved in the procurement process is a key factor for the production of energy from biomass. In this perspective, small firms have many advantages from their strong link with the area and local providers of biomass.

Entrepreneurial Growth Leading Industry

Some technologies, such as the photovoltaic category, have experienced a boom, with newcomers being predominant. The main factors include the system of public support to investment, and the level of technological development. In more general terms, the two aspects are strongly related because public support plays an important role in the diffusion of a specific technology in the event of its not being fully competitive with other available technologies. In the case of photovoltaic, related technologies are actually more expensive and still in the development phase. In recent years, solar and in particular photovoltaic technologies have made important progress, but further developments are also possible and the maturity stage is still far away. These characteristics of photovoltaic technologies, on the one hand, explain the behaviour of big players operating in the sector either through exploration investment – that is, investment to preside over a sector with high potential of development but actually not economically viable – or through investments in research projects. On the other hand, the high cost of photovoltaic energy explains public support for investments. The Italian support system for photovoltaic energy is based on feed-in tariff mechanisms. The mechanism consists of an incentive proportional to the electricity produced by the photovoltaic plant. The cost of the incentive is covered by a component of the present electricity tariff structure. The

tariffs, fixed for 20 years, are added to revenues of energy fed into the grid
if the system operator chooses sale, or saving on bills in the case of a net-
metering system (for plants up to 20 kW). Tariffs are designed to promote
small plants (distributed generation) and architectural integration; major
incentives are awarded to plants of small dimensions, and the amount of
incentives decrease with the increase in plant dimensions. Incentives make
investment convenient in the photovoltaic sector by reducing the differen-
tial of cost between traditional and photovoltaic energy and stimulating
investments mainly by small operators.

Corporate Growth Leading Industry

Wind is another interesting technology, showing a significant growth
rate and with a more limited role of newcomers, which are in many cases
medium-sized firms. The high growth rate shown by the sector is the result
of technological maturity reached during recent years: wind technology is,
among new renewable sources, more mature, and competitive compared
to traditional sources. In more general terms, wind technology is the
most convenient for the production of renewable energy, because it has
the lowest single cost, a lower ratio of land occupied compared to energy
produced, and potential parallel use of land where plants are installed.
At the same time the particular characteristics and complexity of plants,
requiring large amounts of investment, explain the limited presence of
newcomers, which generally have limited financial resources, and the presence in the sector of incumbent firms, that is, large players generally with
the necessary resources to set up wind farms.

Corporate Learning Leading Industry

This competitive landscape is characterized by a limited growth rate and
the dominant presence of big players. None of the renewable energy technologies, in the analysed period, shows a similar situation.

CONCLUSIONS AND IMPLICATIONS

The concept of competitive landscape appears a useful tool to analyse
the structure of competition in a given sector, not only from a static
but also from a dynamic perspective to investigate the evolution of such
landscape. The case of wind energy is emblematic of change in the competitive landscape. A few years ago newcomers commanded the largest
market share in the industry. Up to 2004, the wind industry could in fact

be classified as an entrepreneurial growth kind of industry with newcomers holding a market share of about 64 per cent. In the period 2000–2005 the wind sector was characterized by significant technology development. This was the main cause of the transition from a 'rugged' competitive landscape to a 'smooth' one. In the period involved we can observe two main trends:

- the increase in turbine size, reaching their maximum limit in 2005, as transport and installation constraints impede further increase;
- the convergence of technology in the direction of a dominant, more efficient, highly reliable model, the outcome of extensive testing and certification, and having high investment costs.

During the period there was a shift from a prototype production to mass production. Changes in technological aspects were accompanied by relevant change in the structure of competition: during the period 2000–2004, newcomers had a predominant role; in the following period, incumbent firms became dominant players, and the entry rate of newcomers decreased.

The evidence is consistent with the above-mentioned 'Davids' and 'Goliaths' model developed by Hockerts and Wüstenhagen (2010) concerning the role of incumbents and new entrants in sustainable entrepreneurship. The authors maintain that there are two types of organizations that engage in sustainable entrepreneurship: namely, 'Emerging Davids' and 'Greening Goliaths'. The former refer to small firms that tend to be recently founded and have a relatively small market share. The latter refer to large incumbent firms who tend to be older and have a relatively high market share. The authors suggest that in the early stage of an industry's transformation towards sustainability, small firms and new entrants, 'Emerging Davids', are more likely to pursue sustainability opportunities. Incumbent firms, 'Greening Goliaths', respond to the new entrants and adopt sustainability practices. 'Greening Goliaths' are less progressive but have considerable impact due to their existing market presence. Ultimately, new entrants and incumbents co-evolve, creating incentives and competitive positions that allow both new entrants and incumbents to survive. Hockerts and Wüstenhagen argue that progress in creating sustainable industries and economies will rely on an interplay, a co-evolution, between incumbents and newcomers.

According to such findings, one interesting area of research would be that of monitoring changes in technology fields now classified as standby industries (geothermal and water kinetics). Will these become entrepreneurial opportunities for newcomers or, in consideration of the existing solid technology base, will they become the incumbents to lead the industry?

The concept of competitive landscape could be used to explain the transition from one phase to another. In our opinion, the main factors influencing the time and direction of such transition are:

- the nature of technology on which a sector is based;
- uncertainty relative to technology competitiveness;
- availability of complementary resources and technologies;
- diffusion, distribution and market perspectives.

Policy makers could play an incisive role in this context: public support for innovation could modify the above-mentioned variables, the way in which they interact and the development of a specific competitive landscape. Solar energy, for example, in Italy has benefited from generous public incentives to the amount of €1.5 billion in 2009. Such incentives have overcome the barriers to the diffusion and adoption of really new technologies by the market (Day, 2000), stimulating investments mainly by small operators.

In short, as we have attempted to show, the role of entrepreneurship is clearly fundamental and the implications for sustainable entrepreneurship are manifold. Supported by a policy of incentives, the renewable energy industry, ecologically and economically sustainable, is undoubtedly a great challenge for young innovative entrepreneurs ('Davids' or newcomers) and at the same time an attractive proposition for more traditional large firms ('Goliaths' or incumbents) obliged to keep pace with their smaller counterparts in contributing to sustainable development within the renewable energy competitive landscape.

Our research has important implications for policy makers and for the definition of adequate policies to stimulate the development of the renewable energy sector. Policy makers have to define policies aiming to stimulate entrepreneurship initiatives in the renewable energy sector and, at the same time, cooperation between newcomers and incumbents.

The chapter proposes a model to analyse, from a static and a dynamic perspective, the competitive structure of the renewable energy sector. However, it does not analyse how different factors, such as public incentives, science and technology investments, influence the dynamics of competitive landscapes. A fertile area for further research might consist in exploring the conditions which clarify the ways in which such factors could end in the development of the corporate and/or entrepreneurial growth kind of landscapes.

ACKNOWLEDGEMENT

The chapter is the result of the research activity carried out within the project Smart Grids with Distributed System Polygeneration (POLIGRID), financed by the Regione Campania (POR Campania 2007/2013, Actions IV and V); Scientific Responsible Prof. A. Piccolo – University of Salerno.

NOTE

*   Although the chapter is the result of joint research, the 'Introduction' and the sections 'The renewable energy industry' and 'Theoretical frame of reference' are attributable to Roberto Parente; the sections 'Research methodology', 'Data analysis and findings' and 'Conclusions and implications' are attributable to Rosangela Feola.

REFERENCES

Acs, Z.J. and D.B. Audretsch (1988), 'Innovation in large and small firms: an empirical analysis', *American Economic Review*, 78(4), 678–90.

Agenzia nazionale per le nuove tecnologie, l'energia e lo sviluppo economico sostenibile (ENEA) (2010), 'Rapporto Energia e Ambiente. Analisi e Scenari 2009', http://www.enea.it/it/produzione-scientifica/rapporto-energia-e-ambiente-1.

Ahuja, G. and C.M. Lampert (2001), 'Entrepreneurship in the large corporation: a longitudinal study of how established firms create breakthrough inventions', *Strategic Management Journal*, 22(6–7), 521–43.

Alvarez, S.A. and J. Barney (2008), 'Opportunity, organizations and entrepreneurship', *Strategic Entrepreneurship Journal*, 2(3), 171–73.

Arend, R.J. (1999), 'Emergence of entrepreneurs following exogenous technological change', *Strategic Management Journal*, 20(1), 31–47.

Arthur, W.B. (2009), *The Nature of Technology: What it Is and How it Evolves*, New York: Free Press and Penguin Books.

Audretsch, D., R. Thurik, I. Verheul and S. Wennekers (2002), 'Understanding entrepreneurship across countries and over time', in D. Audretsch, R. Thurik, I. Verheul and S. Wennekers (eds), *Entrepreneurship: Determinants and Policy in a European–US Comparison*, Economics of Science, Technology and Innovation, Vol. 27, Boston, MA: Kluwer Academic Publishers, pp. 1–10.

Autorità per l'Energia Elettrica e il Gas (AEEG) (2010), 'Relazione Annuale sullo stato dei servizi e sull'attività svolta', http://www.autorita.energia.it/it/pubblicazioni/altre_pubblicaz.htm.

Baumol, W.J., E.L. Robert and C.J. Schramm (2007), *Good Capitalism, Bad Capitalism and the Economics of Growth and Prosperity*, New Haven, CT: Yale University Press.

Carree, M. and R. Thurik (2006), 'Understanding the role of entrepreneurship for economic growth', in M.A. Carree and A.R. Thurik (eds), *The Handbook of Entrepreneurship and Economic Growth*, International Library of Entrepreneurship Series, Cheltenham, UK and Northampton, MA, USA: Edward Elgar Publishing, pp. ix–xix.

Chesbrough, H. (2006), *Open Business Models. How to Thrive in the New Innovation Landscape*, Cambridge, MA: Harvard Business School Press.

Day, G.S. (2000), 'Assessing future markets for new technologies', in G.S. Day, P.J.H.

Schoemaker and R.E. Gunther (eds), *Wharton on Managing Emerging Technologies*, New York: Wiley Day, pp. 127–49.

De Paoli, L. and A. Lorenzoni (1999), *Economia e politica delle fonti rinnovabili e della cogenerazione*, Milan: Franco Angeli.

Denrell, J., C. Fang and S. Winter (2003), 'The economics of strategic opportunity', *Strategic Management Journal*, 24(10), 977–90.

Dincer, I. (2000), 'Renewable energy and sustainable development: a crucial review', *Renewable and Sustainable Energy Reviews*, 4(2), 157–75.

Eisenhardt, K.M. (1989), 'Building theories from case study research', *Academy of Management Review*, 11(4), 532–51.

Geroski, P. (1995), 'What do we know about entry?', *International Journal of Industrial Organization*, 13(4), 421–40.

Ghemawat, P. (1991), *Commitment: The Dynamic of Strategy*, New York: Free Press.

Hall, J.K., G.A. Daneke and M.J. Lenox (2010), 'Sustainable development and entrepreneurship: past contributions and future directions', *Journal of Business Venturing*, 25(5), 439–48.

Hannan, M. and J. Freeman (1977), 'The population ecology of organizations', *American Journal of Sociology*, 82(5), 929–64.

Helfat, C.E. (1997), 'Know-how and asset complementarity and dynamic capability accumulation: the case of R&D', *Strategic Management Journal*, 18(5), 339–60.

Hill, C.W.L. and F.T. Rothaermel (2003), 'The performance of incumbent firms in the face of radical technological innovation', *Academy of Management Review*, 28(2), 257–74.

Hitt, M.A., R.D. Ireland, S.M. Camp and D.L. Sexton (2001), 'Guest editors' introduction to the special issue strategic entrepreneurship: entrepreneurial strategies for wealth creation', *Strategic Management Journal*, 22(6–7), 479–91.

Hockerts, K. and R. Wüstenhagen (2010), 'Greening Goliaths versus emerging Davids: theorizing about the role of incumbents and new entrants in sustainable entrepreneurship', *Journal of Business Venturing*, 25(5), 481–92.

International Energy Agency (IEA) (2010), 'Renewable information 2010', http://www.oecd-ilibrary.org/content/book/renew-2010-en.

Ireland, R.D., M.A. Hitt, S.M. Camp and D.L. Sexton (2001), 'Integrating entrepreneurship and strategic management actions to create firm wealth', *Academy of Management Executive*, 15(1), 49–63.

Kauffman, S. (1993), *The Origins of Order*, Oxford: Oxford University Press.

Lambkin, M. (1988), 'Order of entry and performance in new markets', *Strategic Management Journal*, 9(Summer), 127–40.

Levinthal, D.A. and M. Warglien (1999), 'Landscape design: designing for local action in complex worlds', *Organization Science*, 10(3), 342–58.

Lieberman, M.B. and D.B. Montgomery (1990), 'Strategy of market entry: to pioneer or follow?', in H.E. Glass (ed.) *Handbook of Business Strategy*, 2nd edn, New York: Warren, Gorham & Lamont, pp. 21–9.

Lilien, G.L. and E. Yoon (1990), 'The timing of competitive market entry: an exploratory study of new industrial products', *Management Science*, 36(5), 568–85.

Lund, H. (2007), 'Renewable energy strategies for sustainable development', *Energy*, 32(6), 912–19.

Marangoni, A. (2010), *L'industria italiana delle rinnovabili, tra convenienza aziendale e politiche di sistema, Irex Annual Report 2010*, Milan: Althesys.

Miles, M.B. and M.A. Huberman (1994), *Qualitative Data Analysis*, Thousand Oaks, CA: Sage.

Mitchell, W. (1989), 'Whether and when? Probability and timing of incumbents' entry into emerging industrial subfields', *Administrative Science Quarterly*, 34(2), 208–30.

Mitchell, W. and K. Singh (1992), 'Incumbents' use of pre-entry alliances before expansion into new technical subfields of an industry', *Journal of Economic Behavior and Organization*, 18(3), 347–72.

Nelson, R.R. and S.G. Winter (1982), *An Evolutionary Theory of Economic Change*, Cambridge, MA: Belknap Harward Press.

Porter, M.E. (1985), *Competitive Advantage*, New York: Free Press.

Renewable Energy Policy Network for the 21st Century (REN21) (2013), 'Renewables 2013, Global Status Report', http://www.ren21.net/REN21Activities/GlobalStatusReport.aspx.

Sarasvathy, S., N. Dew, S.R. Velamuri and S. Venkataraman (2005), 'Three views of entrepreneurial opportunity', in Z.J. Acs and D.B. Audretsch (eds), *Handbook of Entrepreneurship Research*, New York: Springer, pp. 141–60.

Schumpeter, J.A. (1934), *The Theory of Economic Development*, Cambridge, MA: Harvard University Press.

Swaminathan, A. (1998), 'Entry into new market segments in mature industries: endogenous and exogenous segmentation in the US brewing industry', *Strategic Management Journal*, 19(4), 389–404.

Terna SPA (2013), 'Dati storici', http://www.terna.it/default/Home/SISTEMA_ELETTRICO/statistiche/dati_storici.aspx.

Tushman, M.L. and P. Anderson (1990), 'Technological discontinuities and dominant design: a cyclical model for technological change', *Administrative Science Quarterly*, 35(1), 604–33.

United Nations Environment Programme (UNEP) (2010), 'Global trends in sustainable energy investments 2010', http://www.unep.org/publications/contents/title_search.asp?search=global+trend&image.x=0&image.y=0.

World Commission on Environment and Development (WCED) (1987), *Our Common Future. Report of the World Commission on Environment and Development* (Brundtland Report), Oxford: Oxford University Press.

Wu, B., W. Zhixi and D.A. Levinthal (2014), 'Complementary assets as pipes and prisms: innovation incentives and trajectory choices', *Strategic Management Journal*, 35(9), 1257–78.

Zeckhauser, R. (2006), 'Investing in the unknown and unknowable', *Capitalism and Society*, 1(2), 1–39.

13. Commercializing clean technology innovations: the emergence of new business in an agency–structure perspective
*Sofia Avdeitchikova and Lars Coenen**

INTRODUCTION

Since the 1970s, environment and energy-related problems have moved to centre stage on many political, business and research agendas. The notion of sustainable development has emerged as the dominant global discourse to adapt societies and economies to novel modes of production and consumption in areas such as transport, energy, housing, agriculture and food. For such shifts, new technology and technological change is considered of critical importance. In other words, clean technology (cleantech) is seen as indispensable to solve or at least abate an environmental and energy crisis without abandoning possibilities for progress and economic growth. This, however, does not imply that sustainable development can be readily achieved through a 'technical fix'. The innovation and commercial introduction of new technology are inherently uncertain processes that fail more often than they succeed.

Following information technology and biotechnology, clean technology is often heralded in policy and investment circles as the new general purpose or platform technology to give rise to growing market opportunities for firms, regions and nations. Similar to its predecessors, initial enthusiasm may have outpaced a more fundamental understanding of the nature and characteristics of this emerging field. It is probably fair to say that a common definition of the cleantech concept is yet to be agreed upon. In a comprehensive literature review carried out in 2008 by the Swedish National Board for Industrial and Technical Development (NUTEK) (since 2009 merged into the Swedish Agency for Economic and Regional Growth), it was concluded that cleantech indicates a broader notion than environmental technology. While environmental technologies are primarily defined in relation to environmental regulatory pressures, cleantech is supposed to be more market oriented. Moreover, it is acknowledged that the concept, in principle, stretches across all industries (including services).

What makes the concept peculiar is that it concerns a relative notion. It is defined in relation to other alternatives by offering a better solution from an environmental point of view. By way of summarizing, NUTEK (2008) defines cleantech as embracing a diverse range of products, services, and processes across industries that are inherently designed to: (1) provide superior performance at lower costs; (2) greatly reduce or eliminate negative ecological impact; and (3) improve the productive and responsible use of natural resources. This resonates with a more academic definition, where cleantech is defined as products and services that use technology to compete favourably on price and performance while reducing pollution, waste and the use of natural resources (Burtis et al., 2006; Cooke, 2008).

Studies on the commercialization of new technology in entrepreneurship literature have often failed to explain why some new technologies reach markets while others do not, as well as why some technological solutions ultimately become industry standards while others quickly disappear from the market (Garud and Karnøe, 2003). Technology commercialization models are often linear, based on technology-push logic, and focus rather exclusively on micro-level issues such as characteristics of technology and product, entrepreneurial experience and access to resources. The original idea of the process of commercializing a new technology (Bush, 1945) is that innovation starts with basic research, followed by applied research and development, and ends with production and diffusion. This model has been very influential within the research community and, despite it being criticized for providing a simplistic and linear view of getting new technologies on the market, subsequent studies of technology commercialization have been largely building upon the same model (e.g. Utterback, 1974; Rogers, 1983; Jolly, 1997). This relates also to the observation that the main part of entrepreneurship literature today continues to treat entrepreneurs as operating within a certain (stable) system of actors and institutions (Shane and Venkataraman, 2003; Johannisson and Wigren, 2006), despite the historical foundations of the entrepreneurship research field which emphasized entrepreneurs as a source of structural change and renewal in the economy.

This chapter takes stock with a linear approach to cleantech commercialization processes and, instead, suggests an alternative approach to analyse the entrepreneurial process of commercializing cleantech. In particular, this approach underlines the duality concerning structure and agency that entrepreneurs tend to encounter in the commercialization of cleantech. Counter to the seemingly appealing simplicity of linear commercialization models, this framework seeks to acknowledge the complexity and uncertainty involved in bringing new technology to the market. First, there is the risk of technological spillover that may prevent the entrepreneur from capturing the full value of an innovation (Wüstenhagen et al., 2008). Second, there is often a lack of internalization of environmental cost benefits that accrue from cleantech and eco-innovation (Rennings, 2000). Thirdly, there is a fundamental uncertainty about the complex and multidimensional shifts considered necessary to adapt societies and economies to sustainable modes of production and consumption in areas such as transport, energy, housing, agriculture and food. The latter two are of particular significance for entrepreneurs' possibilities to capitalize on innovations in cleantech, and this makes the commercialization process fundamentally different from that of other types of technological innovations. In particular it reveals the importance of acknowledging the influence of prevailing social and economic systems on entrepreneurial action and strategies, and perhaps more importantly, the ability of entrepreneurs to adapt to and/or influence such social and economic systems and, through that agency, overcome barriers to commercializing cleantech (Dean and McMullen, 2007).

Given its particularities, clean technology provides a potentially insightful context to study the intersection between the agency that is enacted by entrepreneurs to shape their own paths and the structures that influence these actions. This resonates with the more general arguments by Low and MacMillan (1988) and Davidsson and Wiklund (2001) who argue that entrepreneurship research needs to increasingly adopt a multi-level perspective, due to the embeddedness of entrepreneurs in multiple fields and systems. To deal with the seemingly paradoxical notion of embedded agency, the chapter compares two literatures that address the structure–agency duality in the context of innovation and technological change, namely, socio-technical transitions and institutional entrepreneurship.

The objective of this chapter is to identify how agency and structure interplay in the process of commercializing cleantech. To do so, the chapter reviews two literature streams that each depart from different starting points. Whereas the institutional entrepreneurship literature often departs from the micro level of individual or organizational action, the socio-technical transitions literature departs from a systems perspective on technological change. The contribution of the chapter lies in making explicit the agency–structure discussion in the different approaches in order to add to our understanding of cleantech as an emergent technological field, and the role of entrepreneurs and/or entrepreneurship in shaping this field. By reviewing the recent knowledge development in the area, we also identify two possible ways in which these literature streams can enrich each other: namely, by incorporating the transition process in the institutional entrepreneurship literature-based analytical models, and by incorporating entrepreneur (and incumbent) strategies in socio-technical transition literature-based analytical models.

Following this introduction, the next two sections will introduce and review the main literatures, that is, sustainability transitions and institutional entrepreneurship literature respectively. A reflexive discussion on the review carried out in the chapter is then provided, followed by conclusions and suggestions for further research.

SOCIO-TECHNICAL SYSTEMS AND SUSTAINABILITY TRANSITIONS

In the past decade, the literature on sustainability transitions has made a considerable contribution in understanding the complex and multi-dimensional shifts considered necessary to prepare and adapt societies for sustainable development. Transition is here understood as shifts or 'system innovations' between distinctive socio-technical configurations encompassing not only new technologies but also corresponding changes in markets, user practices, policy and cultural discourses and governing institutions (Geels et al., 2008). Geels and Schot (2010) characterize transitions according to the following characteristics: (1) co-evolution and multiple changes in socio-technical systems or configurations; (2) multi-actor interactions between social groups including entrepreneurs, firms, user groups, scientific communities, policy makers, social movements and special interest groups; (3) 'radical' change in terms of scope of change (not speed); and (4) long-term processes over 40–50-year periods. One of the strengths of transition analysis has been its capacity to deal with structure–agency duality via co-evolutionary long-term trajectories of socio-technical change, illustrating how systemic contexts can act as both barriers and enablers for technological change.

Following the tradition of ecological modernization it has been explicit in pointing to technology and innovation as crucial instruments to adapt capitalist, industrial societies to fit within the earth's ecological carrying capacity (Langhelle, 2000). On the one hand, it acknowledges the difficulties that purposeful structural change to ecological sustainability faces because of lock-in and path-dependence (Geels, 2010). For example, Unruh (2000) argues that lock-ins in fossil fuel-based energy systems have created persistent market and policy failures that can inhibit the diffusion of carbon-saving technologies despite their apparent environmental and economic advantages. On the other hand, the sustainability transitions literature acknowledges the importance of radical, path-breaking innovations that lead to cracks, tensions and windows of opportunities vis-à-vis such lock-ins. On an overall level, this literature investigates and emphasizes mechanisms that induce change as well as inertia in technology-driven sustainable development.

Proponents of socio-technical systems have argued for more explicit attention to the adoption and use of innovations and new technologies (see also Rekers, 2010) and the (potentially transformative) impacts on society in a broader sense (Geels, 2004). Instead of limiting the user side merely to a selection environment, the socio-technical systems approach places (new) technology in a context of societal functions (for example, transport, communication, nutrition). Socio-technical systems are thus understood as the elements necessary to fulfil societal functions in relation to the production, distribution and use of technology. A strength of the socio-technical system framework lies with its ability to reconcile the structure–agency duality in transformative technological change. Long periods of relative stability and technology optimization are followed by relatively short periods of structural change and technological upheaval (Anderson and Tushman, 1990). In this process a paradigm shift takes place where existing structures are broken down and new ones emerge. Within the literature on socio-technical systems, the so-called 'multi-level perspective' helps to explain this dynamic process of change in a way that does justice not only to the structural inertia or sluggishness of technological change, but also to the sudden discontinuities when radical novelty emerges. In offering a perspective that allows for 'small' activities to matter a lot in the face of 'large' challenges, such as climate change and resource scarcity, the approach embraces a tone of (technology-based) optimism and pragmatism.

Multi-Level Perspective on Socio-Technical Systems: Regime, Niche and Landscape

The multi-level perspective differentiates between landscapes, regimes and niches as three different levels through which transitions evolve. A central tenet in the framework concerns the stabilizing influence of a socio-technical regime on innovation dynamics and technological change. Here, a regime is defined as 'the coherent complex of scientific knowledge, engineering practices, production process technologies, product characteristics, skills and procedures, established user needs, regulatory requirements, institutions and infrastructures' (Rip and Kemp, 1998: 338). The multi-level perspective conceptualizes sustainability transitions as regime shifts from existing unsustainable regimes (in, for example, energy, transport, housing, and so on) to sustainable ones. Arguably the best-known example of such a regime shift concerns the decarbonization of energy and transport systems in light of climate change (Verbong et al., 2008). By its very nature a regime seeks to retain its configuration, allowing only for incremental, path-following innovation that 'resists' the broad, transformative and structural change implied by a transition. Regime pressure or selection provides an explanatory framework for technological lock-in (Unruh, 2000) or the prevalence of sustaining innovation. Conversely it can be used to identify barriers to disruptive innovation (Christensen, 1997).

In contrast, the second level in the multi-level perspective, 'niches', act as 'incubation spaces' for radical path-breaking innovation yet immersed in uncertainty and experimental disorder. These are 'protected spaces in which actors learn about novel technologies and their uses' (Geels, 2002: 365) and that nurture novelty creation and protect radical innovations against mainstream market selection. Finally, the landscape level represents the exogenous environment that influences both regimes and niches. In the literature, the landscape has been defined as a 'set of heterogeneous factors, such as oil prices, economic growth, wars, emigration, broad political coalitions, cultural and normative values, environmental problems' (Geels, 2002: 1260). The multi-level perspective has been criticized for some ambiguity in empirical studies with regard to the delineations of the three levels (Smith et al., 2005; Markard and Truffer, 2008; Genus and Coles, 2008), and for conflating the respective levels with alternative models of aggregation and geographical scales (Coenen et al., 2012). Nonetheless, its strength is that sustainability transitions can be explained by the interplay of stabilizing mechanisms at the regime level, combined with the emergence of radical innovations at the niche level (Coenen and Diaz Lopez, 2010).

This particular feature fits very well with the challenges and opportunities for commercialization of clean technology in a combined micro (agency) and macro (structure) framework. In the following section we will first review studies focused on the regime level to unpack specific barriers for the commercialization of cleantech. This is followed by an overview of insights following from studies on niche dynamics to identify drivers for breakthrough innovation in cleantech. These insights are subsequently merged into a framework that specifies barriers and drivers to commercialization of cleantech against the backdrop of an evolving sustainability transition over time. The rationale for doing so is, we argue, that commercialization strategies need to take account of the particular stage of a transition pathway and the particular opportunities and challenges that follow from this for an entrepreneur involved in commercializing cleantech.

Regime Based Barriers to Commercializing Clean Technology Innovations

For the purpose of identifying a number of potential regime-based barriers to commercializing cleantech, we identify the following factors (based on Kemp et al., 1998): (1) technology and infrastructure factors; (2) government policy and regulatory framework; (3) demand factors; (4) production factors; and (5) undesirable societal and environmental effects of new technology. One of the hallmarks of the regime notion is that it emphasizes how different factors are interrelated and mutually reinforcing, thus strengthening its stabilization effects. But for explanatory purposes it makes sense to first disentangle the different factors and discuss their respective effects.

Technological and infrastructure barriers concern the relatively suboptimal performance of new technology in terms of user functionality as well as the need for facilitative, complementary technology or supporting infrastructure that perhaps is not available yet or expensive to use (Utterback, 1994). Often new technology does not diffuse into large-scale application until a dominant design is established, allowing for economies of scale. A good example concerns the commercial introduction of electric vehicles (Cowan and Hulten, 1996), where ill-developed battery technology and uncertain and sceptical consumer behaviour constitute critical bottlenecks in the competition with combustion-engine vehicles. A positive example of how this barrier has been overcome is provided by the case of biofuels (bio-ethanol) in Sweden. An important disincentive for consumers to purchase more environmentally friendly flexi-fuel vehicles was the limited availability of biofuels at filling stations. Government regulation obliged filling stations over a certain size to include biofuel in their product portfolio, after which the sales of flexi-fuel vehicles sharply increased (Hillman et al., 2008).

Also, government policy may be a barrier when it provides unclear or contradictory signals concerning the need for specific new technology. When there is no clear future vision that helps to guide technology developers, entrepreneurs and investors, this infringes on their innovation journey towards sustainable development (Negro et al., 2008). While the Dutch have had a rich tradition in windmill construction, the country belongs to one of the laggards in terms of wind power generation and industry development. Breukers and Wolsink (1997) point to highly volatile public support for wind power as an important cause for this missed opportunity. Obviously, government policy can also facilitate the development of new technology when taking a future-oriented and more proactive stance in terms of sustainable development (Porter and Van der Linde, 1995), illustrated by the stringent recycling legislation in Germany, which has induced incumbent firms to develop less packaging-intensive products, which are both lower in cost and sought after in the marketplace.

In terms of demand factors, Kemp et al. (1998) refer to persistent values and attitudes among manufacturers and consumers that reinforce the familiar and eschew unfamiliar alternatives (for example, resistance to car-sharing, born out of the value of individual freedom that supposedly comes with the possession and use of a car). This relates also to economic barriers on the demand side vis-à-vis prospective users' preferences, risk aversion and willingness to pay for new technologies that have not proven their worth (Kemp et al., 1998).

On the production side, potential barriers also exist. Sunk investments and existing competence in existing facilities may constitute an important impediment for firms to invest in setting up a technical and organizational production structure for a new technology, from scratch. Industrial bio-technology is often mentioned as a promising technology to make chemical production processes more cost- and eco-efficient as it allows for the use of green instead of fossil feedstock, and direct production pathways of chemical substances instead of indirect, more polluting routes. However, most chemical firms remain wary of introducing this technology because of the formidable upfront costs involved in redesigning and re-engineering the production process.

Finally, it is possible that new, clean technology very well may solve certain environmental problems but at the same time give rise to new ones. Such backlash problems may frustrate the introduction of a new technology or, in the worst case, annihilate its chances for commercial success. The recent discussion over crops for food or fuel serves as an example of this.

Role of Niches to Induce Regime Shift

Whereas regime-level factors may be used to identify structural barriers to the commercialization of cleantech, the socio-technical transitions literature identifies niches as the key level where transformative change may take place. Raven (2005) makes a distinction between market and technological niches. Market niches can be seen as new application domains, understood as selection environments that employ different selection criteria or have substantially different resources to deploy compared to mainstream markets (Levinthal, 1998). These differences may in turn give rise to the development of a new technology trajectory. Raven (2005) remains critical of the dominant focus on the demand side and, instead, conceptualizes niches as being situated between variation and selection environments, thus stressing the interplay between technology generation(s) and its application(s).

Niches are often created and nurtured in a purposeful manner in order to induce regime shift, referred to as strategic niche management. Kemp et al. (1998: 186) define it as 'the creation, development and controlled

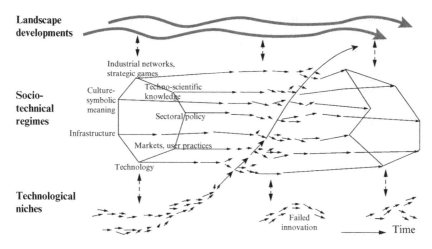

Source: Geels (2002).

Figure 13.1   A multi-level perspective on technological shifts

phase-out of protected spaces for the development and use of promising technologies by means of experimentation', with the aim of learning about the desirability of the new technology and enhancing the further development and the rate of application of the new technology.

Figure 13.1 illustrates how regime-niche interaction shifts over time in the context of a sustainability transition, and how this matters for commercialization strategies for cleantech. According to Geels (2002), a successful regime shift (to sustainability) through niche substitution takes the shape of an S-curve (see Figure 13.1).

Over time, niche stability increases and creates sufficient momentum to compete and challenge the existing regime until ultimately the niche has transformed (made a transition) into a dominant regime. Drawing on Deuten (2003) and Rotmans et al. (2001), this process of emerging stability can be divided into different phases. At the initial, predevelopment phase, niche actors are largely disconnected and acting independently of one another. During take-off, ad hoc network formation takes place, facilitating interaction and exchange of expectations. However, actors still very much act independently of one another, guided by individual expectations. Learning processes are primarily focused on technical issues and user dimensions. At the acceleration phase, social networks have established a critical mass in terms of size and density which enables group-think. Collective action becomes prevalent and group-based rules (institutions) are established. At this point, learning processes are primarily geared to government policy and regulation, industrial development and societal and environmental impact. Finally, during stabilization, the niche has evolved into a regime that consists of established networks, shared expectations and collectively endorsed institutions.

To summarize, the socio-technical transitions literature suggests that the introduction of radically new and green technology involves the build-up of a supporting socio-technical system of production, diffusion and use for clean technologies in the face of resistance and competition from non-sustainable alternatives (that is, a socio-technical system). While this literature highlights the role of entrepreneurs as system builders, it remains silent on the entrepreneurial strategies that could support such a system build-up (Markard and Truffer, 2008). Instead, the analytical focus is directed to processes of niche formation for radical new technology. The following section will review the literature on institutional entrepreneurship to accommodate for a micro-level perspective.

Entrepreneurial Action and Institutional Structures

Recently, we have seen an emerging academic interest in the role of entrepreneurs and entrepreneurship in sustainable development (e.g. Schaper, 2005; Cohen and Winn, 2007; Dean and McMullen, 2007; Wüstenhagen et al., 2008 and the *Journal of Organizational Change Management* Special Issue on environmental entrepreneurship in 2008), focusing on such issues as the nature, motivations and strategies of sustainability oriented entrepreneurs, as well as the context and framework conditions for sustainability oriented entrepreneurship. A variety of concepts have been introduced that aim to describe sustainability driven entrepreneurship and individuals engaging in this activity, such as 'environmental entrepreneurs', 'green entrepreneurs' and 'eco-entrepreneurs'. The exact definition varies between authors, but the common denominator is that these entrepreneurs conduct commercial activities that have an overall positive effect on the natural environment and the move towards a more sustainable future (Schaper, 2005). More specifically, we know from the history of technological change that entrepreneurs, next to researchers and engineers, play a central role in turning inventions into commercially successful innovations (Hughes, 1983). Entrepreneurs, following Schumpeter (1934), are considered to be a driving force for realizing fundamental change in society through 'the process of creative destruction' which involves the discovery and exploitation of new combinations of technologies, products, markets, processes and organizational forms that create (revolutionary) changes in the economy.

Entrepreneurial young firms also have some important advantages compared to larger and more established firms, especially in a changing technological environment. They are considered to be more alert to recognizing business opportunities that arise from market failures, such as environmental degradation (Dean and McMullen, 2007). They are also viewed as more capable to act upon these business opportunities than larger, more established firms that frequently exhibit resistance to change, often as a result of hierarchical organizational structures, inertia and vested financial interests in current ways of doing things (Aldrich and Auster, 1986; Garud et al., 2007). On a more general level, young and small firms can more easily adapt to a changing (technological, market, political, and so on) environment than larger established firms (Aldrich and Ruef, 2006) and thus are more likely to be successful in turbulent environments. At the same time, we know little about how such entrepreneurial actions interplay with institutional structures and how these influence institutional change. These are questions that during the last couple of decades have started receiving academic attention, notably with the emergence of the institutional entrepreneurship literature. In the following section we discuss the theory development relating entrepreneurial action to institutional-level change and its limitations, and present the collective action model as a stepping stone towards understanding the process of new technology commercialization.

RELATING INSTITUTIONAL CHANGE TO ENTREPRENEURIAL ACTION: THE INSTITUTIONAL ENTREPRENEURSHIP LITERATURE

Our knowledge on the interaction between the individual and firm level on the one hand, and the institutional and system level on the other hand, has advanced significantly with the development of the literature on institutional entrepreneurship. Literature on this topic has originated from institutional theory, which has mainly paid attention to the constraints imposed by institutions on the system in which actors operate. From the perspective of institutional theory, fixed institutions create stability and reduce uncertainty for actors in a system, which means that legitimacy is created by adhering to the institutional environment in terms of current practices, norms, standards, values, and so on. By using insights from the stabilizing role of institutions, the literature on institutional entrepreneurship aims to explain how organizations can take actions to shape, change or overthrow the institutions, despite pressure towards stasis. The so-called 'institutional entrepreneurs' are seen as actors who can serve as catalysts for system change by taking the lead and giving direction for structural change in society. Thus, institutional entrepreneurs must both break with the existing rules, practices and institutional logics, and institutionalize the alternative rules, practices and logics they are championing (Garud and Karnoe, 2001). Institutional entrepreneurship framework has, for example, been applied to understanding the transformation of the healthcare sector in the US during the 1990s (Scott et al., 2000), the global computer software industry in the late 1990s (Garud et al., 2002), and the professional business service market (Greenwood and Suddaby, 2006).

The usefulness of the institutional entrepreneurship framework has however been limited by several important factors. First, the applicability of concepts and theories originally used to explain the constraining influence of institutional structures on human behaviour to explaining how individuals generate new institutions has in itself been questioned. At the heart of this criticism is what has been called the 'paradox of embedded agency'. If, as institutional theory asserts, behaviour is substantially shaped by taken-for-granted institutional prescriptions, how can actors envision and enact changes to the contexts in which they are embedded? A central weakness of institutional theory for explaining institutional change driven by entrepreneurial action has therefore been its limited ability to adequately explain how and why actors shaped by (that is, embedded within) institutional structures become motivated and enabled to promote change in those structures (Greenwood and Suddaby, 2006; Garud et al., 2007).

Second, the institutional entrepreneurship framework is based on the assumption of entrepreneurs' ability to resist and neglect the pressure from current institutions in order to achieve institutional change, an action that requires a great extent of organizational power and legitimacy to be able to influence the system context and survive the negative influences. Young and small entrepreneurial firms are in this respect particularly disadvantaged, because of the liabilities of smallness and newness that they are facing. Entrepreneurs often lack financial resources, skills of owners and workers, organizational structure, legitimacy and established relationships with key stakeholders that they can leverage (Aldrich and Auster, 1986; Aldrich and Fiol, 1994). This means that entrepreneurs that challenge the status quo of the sector have to interact with extremely sceptical external resource holders (suppliers, creditors, customers, and so on), while competing with incumbent firms that are committed to, invested in and advantaged by existing ways of doing things in a particular field (Landström, 2005; Garud et al., 2007). In other words, large companies or powerful networks of organizations will have a much better chance of achieving institutional change than smaller and younger companies. Not surprisingly, most of the empirical studies on institutional entrepreneurship to date have focused on large and established firms.

Additionally, studies that use institutional entrepreneurship as analytical framework tend to promote 'heroic' models of actors that have been criticized as being 'ahistorical, decontextualized and universalistic' (Garud et al., 2007: 961). Moreover, by emphasizing the intentionality of action, these studies pay little attention to the unintended consequences of actions that are important components of institutional change. Increasingly, therefore, entrepreneurship scholars have argued that institutional change is not produced by lone entrepreneurs because they do not have the resources, power or legitimacy to produce industrial transformation and institutional change (Aldrich and Fiol, 1994; Van de Ven, 2005). Instead, entrepreneurs operate collectively in order to create the capacity to shape the system environment in a favourable form. Thus, the framework of collective action (e.g. Aldrich and Ruef, 2006; Hargrave and Van de Ven, 2006), or what Van de Ven (2005) has referred to as the 'running in packs' strategy, has become increasingly influential.

Collective Action Model of Institutional Change

The collective action perspective's standpoint is that although entrepreneurial actions induce institutional-level transformations, the latter are not a product of actions of a specific individual or organization. Rather it is a collective action by many people and organizations that jointly – in cooperation and competition – create conditions that transform institutions (Aldrich, 2010). In a similar vein, Van de Ven (2005) argues that entrepreneurs 'run in packs', which means that they simultaneously cooperate and compete with others as they develop and commercialize their innovation. While entrepreneurs compete with their rivals for technological superiority, they at the same time cooperate with them to influence their institutional context and in standard setting activities.

Aldrich and Fiol (1994) describe the process of transforming emerging technologies into new industries as a process of gaining cognitive and socio-political legitimacy. Cognitive legitimacy refers to the taken-for-granted assumption that an institutional change is desirable, proper and appropriate within a widely shared system of norms and values. Socio-political legitimacy consists of endorsements and the support of key constituents, such as financial investors, government officials, consumers and others who play key roles in developing and implementing an innovation (Hargrave and Van de Ven, 2006). This means that entrepreneurs have to strive to gain legitimacy with different groups of stakeholders to get access to resources, markets, and so on, as well as to be perceived as serious and trustworthy. For entrepreneurs within the cleantech sector this appears to be particularly important, because of the diverse set of involved stakeholders.

The primary concern of the collective action model of institutional innovation is how new institutional arrangements emerge from interactions among interdependent partisan agents. The collective action model 'examines the construction of new institutions through the political behaviour of many actors who play diverse and partisan roles in the organizational field or network that emerges around a social movement or technological innovation' (Hargrave and Van de Ven, 2006: 868). Collective action represents a dialectic model of change and focuses on how an established thesis (the established technology and the system around it) is confronted with an anti-thesis (disruptive innovation) to lead to a synthesis, which becomes the thesis for the new dialectic cycle, that is, the new status quo (Van de Ven and Poole, 1995).

As such, the collective action model has been very instrumental for our understanding of the complexity of institutional change, particularly by uncovering the multifaceted micro-level processes and bringing attention to the role of conflict, power and political behaviour in institutional transformation processes. The collective action approach is today one of the dominant models for understanding technological change and new industry formation and has paved the way for further theoretical development within the field of innovation and science and technology studies (e.g. Bergek et al., 2008). At the same time, this perspective has been lacking some of the conceptual precision and concrete analytical tools, especially with regards to explaining the system-level dynamics (Hargrave and Van de Ven, 2006).

Due to the complementary nature of these two research streams, we argue that they can be integrated, or at least cross-fertilized, in order to shed more light on the process and outcomes of the commercialization of clean technology innovations. Looking at the recent developments in the research field, two approaches seem to be particularly fruitful. One is *incorporating the transition process perspective* in the institutional entrepreneurship model to enhance understanding of the system-level shift. More specifically, this implies putting entrepreneurial action in the context of the specific phase of socio-technical transition of the technological field. Another approach is to deepen the understanding of micro-level processes and the outcomes that these subsequently generate by explicitly *incorporating the strategies of entrepreneurs* (and incumbents) into the sustainability transition model (Parrish and Foxon, 2009; Smink et al., 2011). We elaborate on this below and discuss some possible paths for further research.

DISCUSSION AND CONCLUSION

In this chapter we have argued that the commercialization process of cleantech needs to take account of an agency–structure duality. On the one hand, entrepreneurs are embedded in institutional and organizational contexts that enable and constrain their actions, while on the other hand, they need to mindfully diverge from certain rules and structures in order to create and realize the opportunities that cleantech may offer. We have reviewed two streams of literature that both aim to conceptualize this process: the (institutional) entrepreneurship and collective action literature, and the socio-technical sustainability transitions literature. It follows from both literatures that one-dimensional technology-based commercialization processes fail to account for the structural barriers that clean technology faces and run the risk of creating heroic accounts of voluntaristic action. Moreover, such straightforward commercialization strategies often neglect the wider entrepreneurial strategies that are adopted by entrepreneurs to forge change in the area of clean technologies.

Adopting a top-down perspective, the transitions literature points to a structural 'resistance to change' that prevailing regimes in socio-technical systems create. Entrepreneurs involved in the commercialization of clean technology thus encounter an uneven playing field. The incumbents with whom they need to compete benefit from being embedded in a more matured and structurized socio-technical system. Incumbent technologies may thus profit from standardization, economies of scale, conducive regulatory frameworks, habitual consumer behaviour, sunk investment, accumulated skills and competences, and so on. According to the transitions approach, these barriers act in a mutually reinforcing way, allowing for systemic lock-in and path-dependency in existing technological fields. This means that emerging clean technologies often face a number of these difficulties simultaneously, which in turn create considerable barriers to entry for newcomers and entrepreneurs. Similarly, the literature on institutional entrepreneurship emphasizes the resistance to (disruptive) change found in existing institutional structures when radical innovations are introduced. Here, a similar logic can be found in the sense that the individual entrepreneur struggles against systemic 'liability to newness'. While such liabilities may be unpacked into specific barriers such as lacking skills, inappropriate organizational structures or sceptical stakeholders, entrepreneurs often encounter these barriers as an ensemble rather than singularly.

This may explain why only a few of the technological innovations that are taken to the market ultimately are adapted and achieve broad commercial success. Commercialization strategies need to take account of the particular stage of a transition pathway and the particular opportunities and challenges that follow from this for an entrepreneur involved in commercializing technology-based innovations. The appropriate commercialization strategies for the firms will differ depending on the stage of the transition that the system is at in terms of, for instance, the state of public awareness and attitudes, governmental regulations, consumer behaviour, and so on. When it comes to the development of the clean technology sector, this is especially relevant to consider because of the different stages of development of different parts of the sector; while some have already started to consolidate, such as the wind turbine manufacturing industry, many others are still characterized by a high degree of experimentation and new entries (Wüstenhagen et al., 2008).

Instead of a simple technology commercialization strategy, the commercialization of clean technology needs to take account of the institutional work needed to rewrite the rules of the game. In order to succeed in bringing a clean technology to the market, entrepreneurs need to work actively in changing the systemic context in which their technology is embedded. This may seem a paradoxical and daunting task, especially when entrepreneurship is seen as an activity carried out single-handedly by individuals. As such, it points to the need for collective action by and among entrepreneurs and in cooperation with other stakeholders. At this point, the reviewed literatures seem to take different positions with regard to how such collective action is conceptualized. While the transition literature primarily deals with the context conditions in which collective action takes place, the literature on institutional entrepreneurship is more geared to the processes by which entrepreneurs forge change. In doing so, the literatures hold the potential to complement each other.

The transitions literature suggests that transformative change originates from niches that act as protective spaces for emergent technologies to mature up to a point when they are able to compete with incumbent technologies in a competitive market environment. In other words, the niche environment provides an alternative context, counter to that of a regime in a socio-technical system, which allows for stakeholders, including cleantech entrepreneurs, to engage in experimentation and learning processes that should ultimately facilitate the emergent technology to become competitive with incumbent technologies. In concrete terms this suggests that the commercialization of clean technologies can be seen as entrepreneurial experimentation carried out in heterogeneous learning networks of actors which have different knowledge, capabilities, resources and expectations. These networks include entrepreneurs, producers, users, regulators and societal groups. Protection of experiments is, however, crucial in light of the immature or embryonic state of the socio-technical configuration. Such protection could be arranged through policy support (subsidies) or by cooperating with resourceful 'user' stakeholders. The field of clean technology provides many examples of this, for example the use of alternative fuels and/or vehicles in municipal car fleets, the introduction of photovoltaic solar cells in space applications, or living-lab demonstration sites for sustainable urban development and housing.

Dependent on the level of maturity of the technology, the rationale to such experiments may be to discover user preferences; to raise public, industrial and policy awareness and stimulate debate; to promote the adoption of the technology in new markets; and so on. The niche environment is conducive to such processes because the institutional and organizational environment is (still) loosely configured and articulated. Counter to the more hostile regime environment, it allows for immature technologies to exist and to evolve through social learning. Here, user–producer learning should be particularly emphasized. Users have to integrate new technologies in their practices, organizations and routines. This requires alignment and adjustment from both sides. As Geels (2004: 902) puts it, 'new technologies need to be "tamed" to fit in concrete routines and application contexts (including existing artefacts). Such domestication involves symbolic work, practical work, in which users integrate the artefact in their user practices, and cognitive work, which includes learning about the artefact'. In sum, the niche and regime concepts help us to analyse how context matters for the commercialization of cleantech, avoiding heroic and voluntaristic accounts that studies of institutional entrepreneurship have been criticized of. At the same time, the behaviour of individuals and organizations often remains black-boxed in analyses of niche experiments. In other words, there is a lack of attention for the micro foundations of transitions that yield agency to forge change (see also Farla et al., 2012). It is at the level of micro foundations that institutional entrepreneurship may complement transitions literature.

To understand and explain commercialization processes in cleantech, the role of the actions and relationships of single individuals and organizations in a systemic context need to be more closely examined. So far, in transition studies entrepreneurs are seen as components of a system rather than as purposive and mindful agents. How and why entrepreneurs become purposive, motivated and enabled to promote systemic change has remained largely unaddressed. Their presence, emergence, but also disappearance has been assumed rather than explained. Instead of focusing on the individual attributes of entrepreneurs, the institutional entrepreneurship literature allows us to look at these processes as a two-way process between intention and emergence, or agency and structure. This reconceptualizes entrepreneurs in cleantech as reflective change agents who push for change but at the same time adapt to changes in their environment. This opens up room for an appreciation and realization that entrepreneurship is not just about 'taking a technology to the market', but rather about generating and sustaining collective learning processes (Sotarauta and Pulkkinen, 2011). As such, considering institutional entrepreneurship in a context of niche experimentation provides a framework that allows us to analyse how agency and structure interplay in the process of commercializing cleantech.

This opens up a number of questions that could be of interest for future research. The first set of questions is about who the entrepreneurs in cleantech really are. Instead of preselecting the actors according to their formal position, our conceptualization would call for a search on the basis of process. It would allow for identifying entrepreneurs not just in the private domain but also in the public sector or civil society. Moreover it would allow for the possibility to consider cleantech commercialization as a multi-actor phenomenon that unfolds like a relay where no single actor is in charge from 'day one' to the end (Sotarauta and Pulkkinen, 2011). The second set of questions relates to the environments in which commercialization of cleantech takes place and how these environments may help but also hinder entrepreneurs to emerge, operate and learn their skills. Ultimately, to repeat and conclude, it is in the interplay between mindful agents and structuring contexts that commercialization processes take place, operating in between macro and micro issues.

NOTE

* Corresponding author.

REFERENCES

Aldrich, H.E. (2010), 'Beam me up, Scott(ie)! Institutional theorists' struggles with the emergent nature of entrepreneurship', *Research in the Sociology of Work*, 21, 329–64.

Aldrich, H.E. and E.R. Auster (1986), 'Even dwarfs started small: liabilities of age and size and their strategic implications', in B.M. Staw and L.L. Cummings (eds), *Research in Organizational Behavior*, New York: JAI Press, pp. 165–98.

Aldrich, H.E. and M.C. Fiol (1994), 'Fools rush in? The institutional context of industry creation', *Academy of Management Review*, 19(4), 645–70.

Aldrich, H. and M. Ruef (2006), *Organizations Evolving*, London: Sage.

Anderson, P. and M.L. Tushman (1990), 'Technological discontinuities and dominant designs: a cyclical model of technological change', *Administrative Science Quarterly*, 35(4), 604–33.

Bergek, A., S. Jacobsson, B. Carlsson, S. Lindmark and A. Rickne (2008), 'Analyzing the functional dynamics of technological innovation systems: a scheme of analysis', *Research Policy*, 37, 407–29.

Breukers, S. and M. Wolsink (1997), 'Wind power implementation in changing institutional landscapes: an international comparison', *Energy Policy*, 35(5), 2737–750.

Burtis, P., R. Epstein and N. Parker (2006), *Creating Cleantech Clusters*, San Francisco, CA: Natural Resources Defence Association.

Bush, V. (1945), *Science: The Endless Frontier*, Washington, DC: US Government Printing Office.

Christensen, C. (1997), *The Innovator's Dilemma: When New Technologies Cause Great Firms to Fail*, Boston, MA: Harvard Business Press.

Coenen, L., P. Benneworth and B. Truffer (2012), 'Toward a spatial perspective on sustainability transitions', *Research Policy*, 41, 968–79.

Coenen, L. and F. Diaz Lopez (2010), 'Comparing systems approaches to innovation and technological change for sustainable and competitive economies: an explorative study into conceptual commonalities, differences and complementarities', *Journal of Cleaner Production*, 18(2), 1149–160.

Cohen, B. and M.I. Winn (2007), 'Market imperfections, opportunity and sustainable entrepreneurship', *Journal of Business Venturing*, 22(1), 29–49.

Cooke, P. (2008), 'Cleantech and an analysis of the platform nature of life sciences: further reflections upon platform policies', *European Planning Studies*, 16(3), 375–93.

Cowan, R. and S. Hulten (1996), 'Escaping lock-in: the case of the electric vehicle', *Technological Forecasting and Social Change*, 53(1), 61–79.

Davidsson, P. and J. Wiklund (2001), 'Levels of analysis in entrepreneurship research: current research practice and suggestions for the future', *Entrepreneurship Theory and Practice*, 25(4), 81–100.

Dean, T.J. and J.S. McMullen (2007), 'Toward a theory of sustainable entrepreneurship: reducing environmental degradation through entrepreneurial action', *Journal of Business Venturing*, 22(1), 50–76.

Deuten, J.J. (2003), *Cosmopolitanising Technology: A Study of Four Emerging Technological Regimes*, Enschede: Twente University Press.

Farla, J., J. Markard, R. Raven and L. Coenen (2012), 'Sustainability transitions in the making: a closer look at actors, strategies and resources', *Technological Forecasting and Social Change*, 79(6), 991–98.

Garud, R., C. Hardy and S. Maguire (2007), 'Institutional entrepreneurship as embedded agency: an introduction to the special issue', *Organization Studies*, 28(7), 957–69.

Garud, R., S. Jain and A. Kumaraswamy (2002), 'Orchestrating institutional processes for technology sponsorship: the case of Sun Microsystems and Java', *Academy of Management Journal*, 45, 196–214.

Garud, R. and P. Karnøe (2001), 'Path creation as a process of mindful deviation', in R. Garud and P. Karnøe (eds), *Path Dependence and Creation*, Mahwah, NJ: Lawrence Earlbaum Associates, pp. 1–38.

Garud, R. and P. Karnøe (2003), 'Bricolage versus breakthrough: distributed and embedded agency in technology entrepreneurship', *Research Policy*, 32, 277–300.

Geels, F. (2002), 'Technological transitions as evolutionary reconfiguration processes: a multi-level perspective and a case-study', *Research Policy*, 31, 1257–274.

Geels, F. (2004), 'From sectoral systems of innovation to socio-technical systems: insights about dynamics and change from sociology and institutional theory', *Research Policy*, 33, 897–920.

Geels, F.W. (2010), 'Ontologies, socio-technical transitions (to sustainability), and the multi-level perspective', *Research Policy*, 39(4), 495–510.

Geels, F., M. Hekkert and S. Jacobsson (2008), 'The dynamics of sustainable innovation journeys', *Technology Analysis and Strategic Management*, 20(5), 521–36.

Geels, F. and J. Schot (2010), 'The dynamics of socio-technical transitions: a socio-technical perspective', in J. Grin, J. Rotmans and J. Schot (eds), *Transitions to Sustainable Development: New Directions in the Study of Long Term Transformative Change*, London: Routledge, pp. 11–104.

Genus, A. and P. Coles (2008), 'Rethinking the multi-level perspective of technological transitions', *Research Policy*, 37, 1436–445.

Greenwood, R. and R. Suddaby (2006), 'Institutional entrepreneurship in mature fields: the Big Five accounting firms', *Academy of Management Journal*, 49, 27–48.

Hargrave, T.I. and A.H. Van de Ven (2006), 'A collective action model of institutional innovation', *Academy of Management Review*, 31(4), 864–88.

Hillman, K.M., R.A.A. Suurs, M.P. Hekkert and B.A. Sanden (2008), 'Cumulative causation in biofuels development: a critical comparison of the Netherlands and Sweden', *Technology Analysis and Strategic Management*, 20(5), 593–612.

Hughes, J. (1983), *Networks of Power*, Baltimore, MD: Johns Hopkins Press.

Johannisson, B. and C. Wigren (2006), 'Extreme entrepreneurs: challenging the institutional framework', in P.R. Christensen and Poulfelt (eds), *Managing Complexity and Change in SMEs: Frontiers in European Research*, Cheltenham, UK and Northampton, MA, USA: Edward Elgar Publishing, pp. 156–79.

Jolly, V.K. (1997), *Commercializing New Technologies: Getting from Mind to Market*, Boston, MA: Harvard Business School Press.

Kemp, R., J.W. Schot and R. Hoogma (1998), 'Regime shifts to sustainability through processes of niche formation: the approach of strategic niche management', *Technology Analysis and Strategic Management*, 10(2), 175–95.

Landström, H. (2005), *Pioneers in Entrepreneurship and Small Business Research*, New York: Springer.

Langhelle, O. (2000), 'Why ecological modernisation and sustainable development should not be conflated', *Journal of Environmental Policy and Planning*, 2(4), 303–22.

Levinthal, D.A. (1998), 'The slow pace of rapid technological change: gradualism and punctuation in technological change', *Industrial and Corporate Change*, 7(2), 217–47.

Low, M.B. and I.C. MacMillan (1988), 'Entrepreneurship: past research and future challenges', *Journal of Management*, 35, 139–61.

Markard, J. and B. Truffer (2008), 'Technological innovation systems and the multi-level perspective: towards an integrated framework', *Research Policy*, 37, 596–615.

Negro, S.O., M.P. Hekkert and R.E.H.M. Smits (2008), 'Stimulating renewable energy technologies by innovation policy', *Science and Public Policy*, 35(6), 403–16.

Parrish, B.D. and T.J. Foxon (2009), 'Sustainability entrepreneurship and equitable transitions to a low-carbon economy', *Greener Management International*, 55, 47–62.

Porter, M. and C. van der Linde (1995), 'Towards a new conception of the environment–competitiveness relationship', *Journal of Economic Perspectives*, 9(4), 97–118.

Raven, R. (2005), 'Strategic niche management for biomass', PhD thesis, Technical University Eindhoven, the Netherlands.

Rekers, J. (2010), 'Introducing innovations: the role of market intermediaries and institutions in culture and science-based industries', paper presented at the DRUID summer conference 2010, London.

Rennings, K. (2000), 'Redefining innovation: eco-innovation research and the contribution from ecological economics', *Ecological Economics*, 32(2), 319–32.

Rip, A. and R. Kemp (1998), 'Technological Change', in S. Rayner and E.L. Malone (eds), *Human Choice and Climate Change: Resources and Technology*, Columbus, OH: Battelle Press.

Rogers, E.M. (1983), *Diffusion of Innovations*, New York: Free Press.

Rotmans, J., R. Kemp and M. van Asselt (2001), 'More evolution than revolution: transition management in public policy', *Foresight*, 3(1), 15–31.

Schaper, M. (2005), *Making Ecopreneurs: Developing Sustainable Entrepreneurship*, Aldershot: Ashgate Publishing.

Schumpeter, J. (1934), *The Theory of Economic Development*, Cambridge, MA: Harvard University Press.

Scott, W.R., M. Ruef, P.J. Mendel and C.A. Caronna (2000), *Institutional Change and Healthcare Organizations: From Professional Dominance to Managed Care*, Chicago, IL: University of Chicago Press.

Shane, S. and S. Venkataraman (2003), 'Guest editors' introduction to the special issue on technology entrepreneurship', *Research Policy*, 32(2), 181–4.

Smink, M.M., M.P. Hekkert and S.O. Negro (2011), 'Keeping sustainable innovation on a leash: exploring incumbents' strategies with regard to disruptive innovation', ISU Working Paper #11.07.

Smith, A.G., A.C. Stirling and F.G.H. Berkhout (2005), 'The governance of sustainable socio-technical transitions', *Research Policy*, 34(10), 1491–510.

Sotarauta, M. and R. Pulkkinen (2011), 'Institutional entrepreneurship for knowledge regions: in search of a fresh set of questions for regional innovation studies', *Environment and Planning C: Government and Policy*, 29, 96–112.

Unruh, G.C. (2000), 'Understanding carbon lock-in', *Energy Policy*, 28, 817–30.

Utterback, J. (1974), 'Innovation in industry and the diffusion of technology', *Science*, 183, 620–26.

Utterback, J. (1994), *Mastering the Dynamics of Innovation*, Boston, MA: Harvard Business School Press.

Van de Ven, A.H. (2005), 'Running in packs to develop knowledge-intensive technologies', *MIS Quarterly*, 29, 2.

Van de Ven, A.H. and M.S. Poole (1995), 'Explaining development and change in organizations', *Academy of Management Review*, 20(3), 510–40.

Verbong, G., F.W. Geels and R. Raven (2008), 'Multi-niche analysis of dynamics and policies in Dutch renewable energy innovation journeys (1970–2006): hype-cycles, closed networks and technology-focused learning', *Technology Analysis and Strategic Management*, 20(5), 555–73.

Wüstenhagen, R., S. Sharma, M. Starik and R. Wuebker (2008), 'Sustainability, innovation and entrepreneurship: introduction to the volume', in R. Wüstenhagen, S. Sharma, M. Starik and R. Wuebker (eds), *Sustainable Innovation and Entrepreneurship*, Cheltenham, UK and Northampton, MA, USA: Edward Elgar Publishing, pp. 1–26.

14. David versus Goliath: how eco-entrepreneurs transform global ecosystems
Kim Poldner* and Oana Branzei

> There is nothing average about entrepreneurship. Entrepreneurship is not about central tendencies; it is about extremes. Entrepreneurship is not about what is likely; it is about what is possible. It is not about ordinary; it is about extraordinary. The common denominator . . . is their recognition, realization, and reaping of more value than anyone else (the market) could have anticipated.
> (Isenberg, 2013)

DAVID VERSUS GOLIATH

Several recent theories underscore a David versus Goliath effect (Hockerts and Wüstenhagen, 2010), arguing that socially and environmentally minded entrepreneurs could and perhaps should take on the giant problems of our time (Isenberg, 2013). These eco-entrepreneurs, some argue, make the impossible possible (Nicholls, 2008) by introducing alternative models, developing new markets (Isenberg, 2013) and pioneering movements for social change (Waddock, 2008). We too ask, and provide one additional answer, about how such Davids succeed against the odds.

Entrepreneuring involves imagination, translation and, ultimately, the creation of a better future that few others can anticipate or are willing to enact (Rindova et al., 2009). Entrepreneuring also enables 'creative and expressible performance' (Aggestam, 2007: 32). Most studies have so far confined the aesthetic function of entrepreneurship to creative industries (Henry, 2007), but entrepreneurship more generally is a work of art (Hjorth and Steyaert, 2009; Warren and Anderson, 2009). Acting entrepreneurially 'liberates human potential and encourages imagination and initiative to create personal and social wealth' (Fleischmann, 2006). As 'artists', entrepreneurs do not merely appreciate beauty; they can help to make the beauty they see accessible to many others. Recasting entrepreneuring as a series of fundamentally aesthetic acts (Steyaert, 2004, 2007; Steyaert and Hjorth, 2006) draws attention to the intuitive and the imaginative, which are necessary for envisioning and enacting a better future.

We suggest that entrepreneurs striving for the greater good require and rely on aesthetics; those working at the fringes of natural and human ecosystems especially need to first see and make sense of their environment in novel or different ways (Whiteman and Cooper, 2000, 2011) and then translate their understanding into specific practices that enable others to follow suit (Klein, 2013). Such entrepreneurs have to capture and pass on their appreciation of beauty to complex, and often consumption-oriented value chains (Poldner, 2013).

While rare, such entrepreneurs can be very influential. At times they can enable entire sectors to move towards a more sustainable future. For example, Ray Anderson, deemed the 'greenest CEO [chief executive officer] in America', turned his billion-dollar carpet company into a model of sustainability and eventually tipped the entire industry over to more sustainable practices. His *New York Times* eulogy (Vitello, 2011) and his retrospective interviews (TED.com, 2011) boil down his quest to a handful of aesthetic practices: he materially, discursively and connectively took on the proverbial Goliath, and defeated it. Our chapter shows that Ray Anderson's approach is more common than we may think. Most Davids in our study follow the same progression of material, discursive and connective practices to make room for what they whole-heartedly feel is a much more sustainable way to do business.

Our arguments are induced and illustrated in the empirical context of the ethical fashion industry, but our theoretical propositions speak more broadly to a growing stream of literature that celebrates the aesthetic foundations and functions of entrepreneuring. We contribute to this stream by explaining how seemingly small aesthetic acts can transform large ecosystems.

Our chapter complements extant theories of entrepreneuring, especially emancipation-based accounts (Rindova et al., 2009) and effectuation-based accounts (Sarasvathy, 2008), which have already reclaimed the human being as a central actor and main goal of doing business. We add explanatory power to these theories by showing how three specific aesthetic practices continuously renew the human agency and purpose of business, especially when the future we desire requires radical departures from the present we know. The repertoire of aesthetic practices we introduce below also takes a next step towards what Sarasvathy (2012) calls 'worldmaking', that is, the making of new worlds; given the beauty all around us, the framework outlined here urges us to develop research streams that appreciate and translate the inherent beauty of nature and people into a more sustainable way of doing business.

AESTHETIC PRACTICES

Aesthetics (Stecker, 2010) play an important role in nature (Parsons, 2008), society (Lamarque and Olsen, 2003) and organizations (Guillen, 1997). The concept of aesthetics has been adopted by organization scholars in different ways: some see it as a way to immerse and integrate the self within the broader ecosystem (Whiteman and Cooper, 2011), and others regard it as a process of individual becoming (Warren and Anderson, 2009) and identity-building (Shipley, 2009).

While conceptualizations and contributions differ across studies, most of the existing applications have in common an emphasis on what aesthetic practices can add (dimensions, effectiveness, outcomes; see Table 14.1). The underlying premise is that in order to transform appreciation into actionable knowledge (Taylor and Hansen, 2005) or leverage the beautiful to create superior organizational outcomes (Weggeman et al., 2007), all we need is to 'engage our senses' and 'appeal more to the heart than to the head' (Warren and Anderson, 2009: 161).

Any venturing process, some argue, triggers a cycle of aesthetic becoming (Hjorth and Steyaert, 2009; Steyaert, 2007), and aesthetic practices are particularly important for entrepreneurs who need to 'connect the everyday with the artistic' (Steyaert, 2004: 9). But we still know little about how precisely entrepreneurs do so, especially eco-entrepreneurs who seek to 'increase the possibilities of life that are not yet known' (Weiskopf and Steyaert, 2009: 200).

Our working premise is that eco-entrepreneurs successfully tackle intractable social and environmental problems and work effectively at extremes (Isenberg, 2013) because their close proximity to nature and people helps them to appreciate beauty and translate it into organizational outcomes (Ivanova et al., 2013). These eco-entrepreneurs, we further argue and show, not only develop unique aesthetic practices to reconnect with their natural environment (Whiteman and Cooper, 2011) but also deploy these aesthetic practices to transform the global ecosystems they interact with (Poldner et al., 2011).

ECOSYSTEMS

The definition of 'ecosystem' varies broadly (see Slocombe, 1991 for a multidisciplinary review; and Slocombe, 1993: 296 for disciplinary definitions), but most conceptualizations underscore their multidimensionality and the multiplicity of the benefits they engender. In this chapter, we adopt Jorgesen's (2007) definition of an ecosystem as 'a dynamic complex

Table 14.1 Aesthetics practices in organizations

Authors	Studies	Key arguments	Conceptualization	Contribution
Taylor and Hansen (2005)	Theory review	Aesthetics is an alternate method of knowledge creation in organizational studies.	'Aesthetics is concerned with knowledge that is created from our sensory experiences' (2005:1212).	'Aesthetics offers a look at alternative ways of expressing and making meanings that deeply influence organizational actions, behaviours and understandings' (2005: 1227).
Strati (1992, 1999)	Conceptual paper	The feeling of beauty is one of the factors that structure organizations.	'Personal idiosyncracies, specific modes of interpretating events, different views of what to do and when to do it, and the ceaseless negotiation of values, symbols and organizational practices' (1999: 13).	Shifts focus to intuitive and evocative by explaining how human senses structure perception (1999: 13–14).
Guillen (1997)	Conceptual paper	Any act of organizing has aesthetic dimensions.	General features; technical features; ideological features.	'Our understanding of the inner logic of organizational studies, as well as of their effectiveness and impact, will be enhanced with taking the aesthetic dimension into account' (1997: 29).
Weggeman et al. (2007)	Research paper	Organizational performance is enhanced by the beauty of products and services, and indirectly by the aesthetics of organizational work processes (2007: 346).	Process aesthetics; product aesthetics; aesthetic sensibility.	Aesthetics enhance both the beauty and the performance of organizations (2007: 350).

Table 14.1   (continued)

Authors	Studies	Key arguments	Conceptualization	Contribution
Hjorth and Steyaert (2009)	Edited volume introduction	Entrepreneurship studies can keep its own agenda creative and focused on the passionate act of entrepreneuring (2009: 8).	Imagining; envisioning; creating.	'How is the entrepreneurial process created as a work of art in the ensemble of time and place?' (2009: 2).
Warren and Anderson (2009)	Conceptual paper	'The entrepreneurial identity is profoundly aesthetic . . . couched in terms that appeal more to the heart than to the head' (2009: 151).	'Engaging emotions, appealing to senses' (2009: 148).	'We can see a beauty of entrepreneurship mirrored in practices, savour its nature in the production of entrepreneurial identity and reflect on stories. These forms of meanings are aesthetic because they engage our senses' (2009: 161).

of plants, animals and micro-organism communities and the non-living environment, interacting as a functional unit. Humans are an integral part of ecosystems' (p. 20). We take a human ecology point of view and focus on the ways in which human (inter)actions fit within, adapt to and influence the resources in their environment, including 'the range of (other) people's choices . . . including access to income and employment opportunities, education and health, and a clean and safe physical environment' (World Bank, 1991).

All ecosystem approaches have several core characteristics in common: according to Slocombe (1993: 297), ecosystems are holistic, comprehensive and transdisciplinary; they include people and their activities; they undergo complex, dynamic cycles of change, including self-organization, cause-and-effect relationships and feedback loops; and they entail at least implicit ethics of care, quality, well-being and integrity.

Ecosystem research focuses on preserving the whole as it is (Odum, 1969), minimizing or remediating the negative impacts of environmental change (Kothbauer, 1992), and preventing stressors (Rapport et al., 1985).

Ecosystems also 'determine how functional the individual is in his or her environment' (Slocombe, 1993), and what options individuals can pursue (Bronfenbrenner, 1979; Pardeck, 1988). However, ecosystems can also be improved: even the largest and most complex ecosystems are still amenable, and sometimes highly sensitive, to individual action (Paolucci et al., 1977).

Eco-entrepreneurs can and do deliberately redesign ecosystems to better serve the purposes of both people and nature (Poldner et al., 2011). The greater the actors' ecological embeddedness in the land and the ecosystem (Whiteman and Cooper, 2000: 1265), the better their ecological sense-making (Whiteman and Cooper, 2011) and their propensity to effect positive change. Individual actions can set off positive feedback loops and improve the ways in which many others fit within, or interact with, the ecosystem (Lustermann, 1985). The resulting acceleration effect, critical for radical social change more generally (Plowman et al., 2007), explains why seemingly small acts such as aesthetics, grace and ceremony (Reason, 2007) can have system-changing (Gnanadason, 2005) – even world-making (Sarasvathy, 2012) – consequences. Yet we still know little about which of, or how, these small acts matter. We marry Tillman Lyle's ecosystem design intervention with the literature on entrepreneuring (Rindova et al., 2009; Steyaert, 2007), especially the aesthetic approaches to entrepreneuring which we review in Table 14.1 to explain how socially and environmentally minded entrepreneurs rely on aesthetic practices to subtly yet significantly reshape the ecosystems they inhabit (Kaplan and Murray, 2008).

CONTEXT

We focus on the ethical fashion industry, which emerged and evolved since the early 2000s, first as bold responses to specific social and environmental concerns (Branzei and Poldner, 2012), then as a fringe social movement and counterpoint to the known limitations of traditional fashion, and eventually as a desirable strategy for the largest fashion brands (Thopte and Poldner, 2014). Within one decade, eco-entrepreneurs have challenged and changed our collective sense of what is fashionable, the fashion artefacts, the sourcing and distribution of fashion, and ultimately the consumption patterns (Poldner, 2013): 'the old rules of fashion no longer apply – style at the price of people and the planet is not beauty-ful. When shopping for feel-good fashion, keep these fundamentals at top of mind (and heart)' (Zoe, 2012).

Most eco-entrepreneurs in the ethical fashion industry were prototypical Davids: most lacked, and some openly rejected, the strengths that had given traditional fashion its global prominence and profitability. Instead, these eco-entrepreneurs felt a strong drive to develop garments that did not exploit people or nature, for example by prohibiting child labour in their production chains and insisting on paying their workers a fair wage. They experimented with radically new forms of exchange, piecing together alternative supply chains that were humane, transparent and self-sustaining; and radically new forms of discourse, learning how to talk about the difference they were making. They also formed communities of consumption and practice that amplified their positive impact in manifold ways; these communities spanned new forms of relationships between designers, producers and consumers (Ivanova et al., 2013).

If beauty was in the eye of the beholder, these eco-entrepreneurs surely appreciated and confidently translated the beauty they saw (and wanted to preserve and enhance) in nature and people. Using a multi-method approach, we induced how these eco-entrepreneurs skillfully developed and deployed three different types of aesthetic micro-practices. Before defining and illustrating these aesthetic micro-practices we describe our methodology.

RESEARCH DESIGN AND METHODS

The first author was also an industry insider and pioneer; her own experience as an ethical fashion entrepreneur offered a rich real-time understanding of the industry and facilitated personal connections with many of the 58 entrepreneurs we followed over time. The blog that she kept between 2008 and 2010 and her auto-ethnographical account (Poldner, 2013) helped to 'try out' some of our initial insights and adjust subsequent interpretations. The second author was a traditional academic, steeped in the literature on social innovation and social transformation, who helped to develop and execute a complex research design and acted as a devil's advocate throughout the data collection and analysis. Our research design was an iterative process: we describe our qualitative methodology, the sources of data, our longitudinal sampling approach and how we analysed our data.

Method

We combined an industry-level netnography (Kozinets, 2009) that helped us to track the development of the social movement (Davis et al., 2005) with a comparative case study design (Eisenhardt and Graebner, 2007) that systematically sampled eco-entrepreneurs based on start-up time, size, success and status. The findings we present below were replicated across these intended contrasts and across several additional distinctions that emerged during our interviews.

Netnography is a qualitative method introduced to organizational studies in the mid-1990s by cultural anthropologists interested in researching consumer behaviour in internet-based communities. An early review of the method (Kozinets, 1998) summarizes its origins, uses and evaluative standards. The express aim of netnography, according to Kozinets (1998) is to enable 'a contextually-situated study of the consumer behaviour of virtual communities and cyberculture', whereby the researcher becomes 'for a time and in an unpredictable way, an active part of the face-to-face relationships in that community' (Van Maanen, 1998: 9). The 'data' collected during a netnography, as in other types of ethnography, consists of the researchers' field notes, combined with the 'artefacts' of the culture or community they observe. In our case, textual data included stated goals, real-time reflections and interviews given by the entrepreneurs we studied, as well as commentaries by their critics and customers. Visual data included pictures and video presentations of their collections. Our field notes included observations made independently by the two authors about textual and visual data, albeit from different points of view (the first author being an insider and the second author being an outsider to the industry).

Kozinets (1998) explains that online interactions are deliberate self-presentations, whereby protagonists can 'pre-edit' their emotions and reflections. To capture the raw and/or emerging interpretations we complemented the netnographic approach with a traditional comparative case study methodology (Eisenhardt and Graebner, 2007). Unlike the typical Eisenhardt method, which selects and compares cases along predetermined dimensions, we sought to document as many and as diverse cases as possible. During the early stages of the industry when we began our study it was too early for anyone to know which models will prevail, let alone which ecosystem features these models will engage. Furthermore, there was significant change over time, as many models were in flux, experimenting with alternative approaches. We followed all cases longitudinally, but a small subset evolved a particularly rich and theoretically revealing set of ecosystem interactions. This dual qualitative methodology, initially recommended by Leonard-Barton (1990) to mitigate shortcomings of the comparative case study method, helped us to flesh out some of the key dynamics inherent in ecosystem change and to understand how and why they differed across the eco-entrepreneurs we followed.

Sources and Sampling

The eco-entrepreneurs we studied varied in their cultural background and artistic inspiration, from retro to forward; in their products, from shoes to clothes to jewellery and accessories; in their form, from non-profit to for-profit and everything in between; and in their business models, covering a wide array of revenue, sourcing and distribution approaches. Most were boutique sellers, albeit some had grown the number and network of outlets. A handful developed and commercialized prêt-à-porter collections, but these were short-lived endeavours even for the few who gave them a try. Some had built global brands; and a few eventually sold to and/or were absorbed by large, prestigious, traditional fashion brands (Thopte and Poldner, 2014). For each case we tracked the founding eco-entrepreneur over time, using multiple in-person interviews and rich archival information, including third-party reviews and interviews, blogs and posts, photographs and video footage of their collections.

Analysis

We used both traditional text-based analysis and visual methods to collect and analyse the data for each eco-entrepreneur. With a few exceptions of entrepreneurs who explicitly consented to being identified as the protagonists of their own stories (Branzei and Poldner, 2012; Ivanova et al., 2013), we preserved the confidentiality of the informants by disguising their identity (using either the city where each launched the first collection as a pseudonym, or the country where they started when there was no duplication).

We started our analyses with five key informants: protagonists who started early and went through multiple, often significant, changes in their designs, product, brand and business model. Once we induced the three types of aesthetic micro-practices, we used a dual case study methodology (Leonard-Barton, 1990), replicating the induced dimensions across all the remaining 53 cases. The first micro-practice was present in every single one of the longitudinal case studies; the second was present to some degree in 37 of the 58 (64 per cent) and fully fledged only in 22 (38 per cent) of the cases. The third micro-practice was virtually universal: everyone talked about the benefits of being part of a broader, dynamic and socially minded community; however, only about half (55 per cent) of our protagonists had taken any steps themselves to initiate a new community or a new type of connection with any of their stakeholders.

We then went back to our five key informants to further understand how each of these aesthetic micro-practices influenced global ecosystems, asking process questions like: How did each eco-entrepreneur make use of material, discursive or connective micro-practices? How had each eco-entrepreneur's reliance on these different micro-practices evolved over time? How could others tell whether this eco-entrepreneur engaged in this aesthetic micro-practice? How exactly has each one of these aesthetic micro-practices changed the global ecosystem? Then, once again, we went back to the remaining 53 cases to verify whether the same causality held (Leonard-Barton, 1990). We confirmed that the three micro-practices were distinguishable by their effects, and influenced the global ecosystems through distinct mechanisms.

FINDINGS

Among the few studies that have previously explored how individuals deliberately try to improve their ecosystems, Tillman Lyle's framework was particularly fitting for the journeys of the 58 eco-entrepreneurs. This framework suggests that ecosystems can be designed and developed by individuals, and that this process unfolds in three distinct and consecutive stages.

First, individuals let their imagination reign; they anticipate alternative possibilities and let themselves fall in love with some, but not all of the options they see. Tillman Lyle labels this initial stage 'romancing' and describes it as:

> a spirit of boundless anticipation. Fragments of images of what might be, light up all around us and myriad pathways flicker into the haze. It is all confusing, challenging, stimulating, intriguing, daunting, enormously exciting . . . this is a time for letting impressions sink in . . . for questions not answers. (Tillman Lyle, 1999: 136)

Romancing is different from insight because it involves deliberate contemplation, even the cultivation of possibilities that others may not see at all, let alone entertain as desirable or feasible. It is similar to emancipatory theories in that the individual actively engages in a process of dreaming (Rindova et al., 2009); it is also similar to effectuation in that the individual takes active control over the direction of their dreams (Sarasvathy, 2008). But while both emancipation and effectuation privilege the protagonist, romancing is fundamentally about improving the ecosystem.

Once individuals arrive at one insight that stands out among the rest, they proceed to the second stage, which Tillman Lyle refers to as 'making precise'. During this second stage, designers 'deal with landscapes small enough to be perceived and understood in their entireties [and piece together] a gestalt resource inventory' (Tillman Lyle, 1999: 146).

Importantly, the focus is not on a piece or part of the whole, but rather on a subset of parts that fully replicates the functionality of the whole. This subset is rich enough to allow designers to figure out which specific features and qualities are actionable and pilot cause-and-effect relations, yet small enough that any unintended or adverse reactions can be contained and repaired. Making precise is different from structuring: the designer's main goal is neither to impose new types of exchanges nor to impose a different order on pre-existing exchanges. Rather, the goal is to understand deeply and articulate clearly the effects that specific exchanges can have on the ecosystem as a whole.

Only after the designer has developed mastery of the features and qualities that can tip the ecosystem in the direction they desire, do they advance to the third and final stage. In this stage, which Tillman Lyle calls 'generalizing', the designer develops a kit of alternatives that could be combined in various ways to shape the final plan, by looking at each problem and sub-problem from differing points of view (Tillman Lyle, 1999: 162). Generalizing is different from scaling because every step forward requires recalibration; the precision gained in the second step does not become a foregone conclusion in this third stage. Rather, designers cycle back and forth, shifting the features and qualities they choose to enhance the connectivity and functionality of the ecosystem overall.

AESTHETIC MICRO-PRACTICES

We induced three different types of aesthetic micro-practices, each of which could be identified by its observable consequences, and influenced the global ecosystem through a distinct mechanism. To preface our findings, we found evidence of material, discursive and connective aesthetic micro-practices. The vast majority of eco-entrepreneurs developed either material or discursive practices first; only a few started by championing and convening new forms of communities. The largest, most successful or highest-status eco-entrepreneurs had mastered all three, and often practised them in conjunction. However, in our data we have evidence that any one of the three types of practices could be sufficient to help eco-entrepreneurs move in the direction of their dreams.

What was particularly interesting in our data is that these three aesthetic micro-practices did not automatically yield returns: rather, the benefits accruing to the eco-entrepreneur hinged on the extent to which these practices modified the global ecosystem in the first place. Put differently, entrepreneurs felt the results of their actions by the reaction of the global ecosystem: the more significant the change in the global ecosystem, the

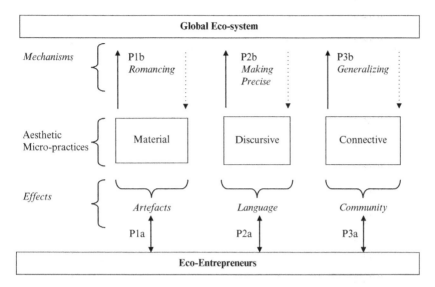

Figure 14.1   Theoretical framework

greater the rewards accruing to the eco-entrepreneur. That is, the benefits of materiality practices were greater for designers who had more successfully romanced the global ecosystem (for example, London; see Poldner et al., 2011), the benefits of discursive practices were greater for designers who had made the global ecosystem more precise (for example, Paris; see Branzei and Poldner, 2012; Rio, see Ivanova et al., 2013), and the benefits of connective micro-practices loomed larger for designers who had excelled at generalizing. Our theoretical framework, shown in Figure 14.1, visualizes this action–reaction loop. Table 14.2 summarizes and illustrates the propositions.

Material Micro-Practices

Each entrepreneur's unique understanding of beauty is materially expressed in the artefacts that they create. Different textures, colours and combinations echo and translate the aspects they perceive as beautiful in their ecosystems (Ivanova et al., 2013). Artefacts embody an entrepreneur's way of seeing the world and come closest to who the entrepreneurs really are: they provide a direct if subjective channel for communicating one's identity (Poldner, 2013). One important characteristic of an ethical fashion product is the 'savoir faire' of the region where it has been produced, especially critical for designers that collaborate with communities to create, source and/or produce the artefacts.

Table 14.2 Propositions

Stages of ecosystem design	Observable effects	Aesthetic micro-practices	Proposition	Illustration
Romancing: 'A spirit of boundless anticipation. Fragments of images of what might be, light up all around us and myriad pathways flicker into the haze. It is all confusing, challenging, stimulating, intriguing, daunting, enormously exciting . . . this is a time for letting impressions sink in . . . for questions not answers' (Tillman Lyle, 1999: 136).	Artefacts		P1a	'In 1989, I fell in love with a Senegalese man. I moved to Senegal and had a son with him, but after a while we each went our own way. By that time I had fallen in love with the city of St Louis and the people there who had become my friends. Inspired by their Muslim culture and innovative ways to recycle waste, I started creating clothing out of praying mats and trash materials' (Senegal).
		Material micro-practices	P1b	'People in Senegal are poor, they hardly have jobs and earn very little money. When I went back home to the UK to visit family, people were enthusiastic about my clothes and I sold some of them. Together with friends in St Louis, I started creating fashion products and I sell these back home in a local shop. I love to experiment with different fabrics and create pieces out of what is considered waste. The process of creating them together with friends to develop these items, is amazing: it has really awakened the artist in me! It also gives me a good feeling to be able to do something for the people who have given me so much over the years. And this project is a great way to finance my travels!' (Senegal).
Making precise: 'We deal with landscapes small enough to be perceived and understood in their entireties . . . In a gestalt resource inventory, then, we identify the	Language		P2a	'We are crazy about our sneakers and really started with the idea to make the best sneakers in the world. Not in the way most companies do, but in a good way, ethical and environmentally sustainable. But when we wanted to source materials to make the sneakers, we found that there was hardly anything available. We had to work with local farmers and rubber tappers in the Amazon to obtain organic cotton and

carrying capacities of the site to support varying human use . . . We also identify specific features and qualities that will influence the design. [This stage relies] heavily on the expertise of the designer because a great many judgments and decisions are made, more or less implicitly, by him alone' (Tillman Lyle, 1999: 146).

Discursive micro-practices

P2b

natural rubber to create a proper value chain. The first time we presented our sample sneakers, five years ago, was at a regular trade fair, not an ethical one. We simply presented the product and only told the story of the process when talking to potential buyers. It worked because in the first place, people loved our product, to them the story was a bonus. Over time, we found that the rubber doesn't sustain as leather does. So even though we always try out the most environmentally and socially friendly options, our sneakers must look good and be of good quality. This means that with some models, we had to start producing them in leather. We know this doesn't appeal to all customers, e.g. people who are vegan, but for us the product comes first. We keep on researching other possibilities, innovations and qualities with one objective: to constantly improve our product' (Paris).

'When we started the company, we found out that farmers in Paraguay were not allowed to grow organic cotton. We needed a lot of time to lobby and convince our government to change the law as to enable farmers to grow it. The main argument we could bring up, was that growing organic cotton would give these farmers an opportunity to survive. It takes a few years to convert to organic cotton, because the soil has to clean up from pesticides. But now, we have hundreds of farmer families growing this crop. The raw fibre goes through a process of ginning and spinning and then we weave garments out of it and sell them. Not to overseas markets, but locally. In the department store in Asuncion and in our own shop which is on our headquarters' premises. Just like the law and growing organic in this country, we had to develop a market and educate consumers. It has not been easy, but the hard work has brought us where we are now' (Paraguay).

Table 14.2 (continued)

Stages of ecosystem design	Observable effects	Aesthetic micro-practices	Proposition	Illustration
Generalizing: 'A task of assembly . . . by looking at each of the problem and sub-problem from differing points of view, the designer developed a kit of alternatives that could be combined in various ways to shape the final plan' (Tillman Lyle, 1999: 162).	Community		P3a	'I was so shocked when I visited this community and found that a large group of women had been suffering from abuse. Even though I am not from this part of India, I decided to move here and help them. I found out that they possess great knowledge of handicraft techniques such as embroidery and realized the potential to make fashion items with them. The farmers in the area provide the organic cotton we use and the young women create the products. It helps them to regain their self-esteem and see future perspectives. Some of them have left to get formal education and came back to be mentors of the younger ones. By now, the community is flourishing and we have even been able to build a hospital. For us, the fashion items we make, provide us with the resources to do what we really want to do: help the women in this community' (Ecuador).
		Connective micro-practices	P3b	'I think we were the first that asked the seamstresses to put their signatures in the T-shirts. We wanted to move away from anonymity and connect them to the end consumer who bought the shirts. On our website, people can find photos of these wonderful ladies and get a glimpse of their work environment. But we wanted to bring the different people in the value chain closer together and decided to fly some of them over to Paris. On a Saturday afternoon, consumers could come into the store and meet the seamstresses. For them it was very special to meet the people behind their much loved piece of clothing. And for the seamstresses it was quite an experience as well. They had never been out of their own community, let alone step in a

356

plane and fly to the other side of the world! A side effect was that other brands also directly got in touch with our value chain. This has led to other companies knocking on our door to make use of it. Not just the small brands, but bigger ones too who have found that our people do quality work. Collaborating with them has given us fresh perspectives on the work we are doing and has helped us to improve our value chain' (Rio).

There are several differences between the UK community and the German community of ethical fashion entrepreneurs (Schiller-Merkens, 2009). Brands in the UK organized themselves in a body that organizes projects and campaigns to promote eco-fashion in the UK, often in collaboration with government agencies, providing the UK network with some legitimacy. Esthetica is the green fashion fair where these brands present themselves, but it is only one event in a range of different projects. In Germany, some people have started a green fashion event and invited brands to present themselves there. These are not just German brands, but brands from other countries too that often meet each other for the first time at this particular event. These brands refer much less to each other on their respective websites and are not as interconnected as the UK community is. This interconnectivity has allowed small brands to source fabrics together because they cannot reach the necessary quantities required by the industry on their own. We see something similar happening in the Netherlands, where a community of small companies has been able to afford Fair Trade certification as a group. Such certification is important to them, but too expensive, and joining forces is a perfect solution to get access to the value chains they need to create their collections.

The partial views that these artefacts retain and reflect the aesthetic vision of the global ecosystem each eco-designer had romanced. The more romancing, the more compelling the artefact. However this is not merely a matter of quantity or degree: eco-entrepreneurs vary widely in what aspects they see and how they bring them forward: how they material-ize their appreciation of beauty into a specific artefact. While some copy a pattern or colour scheme or design directly onto for example a dress, seeking to preserve the authenticity of the work, others look for different degrees of contrast by emphasizing paradoxes.

The materiality of the artefact embodies an alternative way of seeing the global ecosystem, forcing others to pay close attention to what one sees as important; this can vary from threats of oil spills (Toronto) to seasons in one's life (Vancouver) to endangered species (London). Some designers bring out multiple features of complex ecosystems and the need to keep these features in their naturally occurring balance (Paris). But materiality is directly and universally observable in each one of the artefacts eco-entrepreneurs produce. Most artefacts convey powerful messages, and some are deliberately used as signals (Ivanova et al., 2013).

Proposition 1a: Artefacts encapsulate and translate a specific feature that an eco-entrepreneur finds beautiful in nature or people.

By helping others to see (and sometimes also fall in love) with the features eco-entrepreneurs appreciate most, these artefacts influence the ecosystem itself. In a memorable example, one of our key informants, London, con-fesses her straddling of entrepreneuring and activism for endangered species, and how her activist friends envied her ability to draw attention to the plight of bees, bats or bacteria through her modern award-winning designs. As London grows aware of and alert to the power her artefacts have, she inten-sifies romancing, for example by crafting fictional stories about the endan-gered species her collections feature, allowing her customers to identify with them. With each additional collection, London romances the chosen species more and more, by imbuing them with human motives and agency. Her arte-facts take on the colour, shape and texture of these species, literally enabling customers to slip into the skin of, for example, seahorses.

This material loop typically works for each collection (most designers focus on different themes or features of the ecosystem in different collec-tions); some focus on natural features (like wind or rain; Rio), others on social ones (like the financial crisis or the contrast between ethnicities; Rio), and a few even draw attention to the symbiotic relationship between natural features and social ones (like the nomadic life we risk when we condone oil sand exploration; Toronto).

Proposition 1b: Romancing a feature of the ecosystem enhances the effect of the material micro-practices used to embody that feature.

Discursive Micro-Practices

As with entrepreneurs more generally, eco-entrepreneurs in the ethical fashion industries rely on discursive practices (Faulkner and Runde, 2009; Kaplan and Murray, 2008; Steyaert and Katz, 2004). Because entrepreneurial opportunities are embedded in complex webs of understanding, they come with thick, context-specific interpretations (Whiteman and Cooper, 2000, 2011).

Language allows eco-entrepreneurs to identify and understand how specific subsets of the ecosystem function. It also allows them to describe the parties and the exchanges that characterize that ecosystem. Our protagonists often developed a new way to talk about the ecosystem, borrowing analogies and metaphors – for example, London often describes 'how the bees think' – or identifying phenomena for which they did not yet have adequate words.

Proposition 2a: Language encapsulates and translates a subset that an eco-entrepreneur finds beautiful in the nature or people.

Language is not static. As the movement takes shape, language is actively used as a resource (Poldner and Veenswijk, 2011). In some cases the discourse becomes more precise as eco-entrepreneurs go to the grassroots (the natural or social ecosystem); this is all about the facts and explaining the ways in which the facts matter. In other cases the discourse gets more precise as eco-entrepreneurs articulate ways in which the ecosystem resembles the producer, or the consumer; this is all about fiction – helping others to imagine specific instances and impacts. Discursive micro-practices creatively combine fact and fiction to help eco-entrepreneurs, and everyone they interact with, to closely monitor and model specific relationships in the ecosystem.

In our study, the linguistic repertoire expands and shrinks to match the subset of the specific ecosystem eco-entrepreneurs attend to. Similar to the political use of discourse in social movements (Davis et al., 2005; Lounsbury, 2005; Scully and Creed, 2005), our protagonists try out the power of words on different parties, and adjust their repertoire (Hirschman, 1995) to get closer and closer to the natural and/or social inner workings of the ecosystem itself; the better they understand the fact, the more persuasive their fiction gets, and vice versa:

Proposition 2b: Making a subset of the ecosystem precise enhances the effect of the discursive micro-practices used to speak about that subset.

Connective Micro-Practices

The ethical fashion industry brings together a global network of people who try to earn a living by creating fashion while living up to their own values and the broader ecosystem. By coming together, eco-entrepreneurs internalize, and some even habitualize, a way of being that keeps them connected to one another and to the broader ecosystem (Berger and Luckmann, 1967; Schiller-Merkens, 2009).

This coming together is not automatic; it requires deliberate and sometimes unusual forms of convening (Poldner, 2013), for example by gathering in nature or in the community as an alternative to the traditional catwalk (Poldner and Veenswijk, 2011) or by using rich natural and social symbols to contextualize the traditional catwalk (Ivanova et al., 2013). One of the most powerful examples is Paris, who curated local exhibitions in Rio de Janeiro and brought them all the way to Paris. Paris also partnered with numerous artists to create dramatic renditions and deliberate interpretations of the art so that he could further engage specific micro-communities.

Community brings a sense of completeness to the aesthetic micro-practice by identifying what is consistent and important for the ecosystem as a whole. Connective micro-practices focus on the preservation and replication of the whole, such as the *favelas* in Brazil or the deserted fabric mills close to the city of London. Sometimes eco-entrepreneurs deliberately bring multiple communities together or set up novel or different occasions to foster community where none previously existed.

Proposition 3a: Community encapsulates and translates the whole that an eco-entrepreneur finds beautiful in nature or people.

Tillman Lyle (1999: 162) describes the last stage of ecosystem design as 'a task of assembly', where individuals take on different, even diverging points of view in order to find a consistent and generalizable core. Community fosters such plurality, without forgoing a sense of commonality and togetherness. Eco-entrepreneurs showcase a broad variety of ecosystems during, for example, catwalk shows: in our cases we saw milk-fibre sweaters and money enrobed in sustainable plastic jewellery. Some protagonists sought to capture in a single and symbolic necklace the plight of the resource curse in Congo, while others bottled up the essence of wind into a best-selling fragrance.

Only about half of our protagonists took deliberate steps to convene or foster community, but everyone felt part of at least one community, and often multiple ones. The majority of our protagonists credited these communities with a sense of continuity and stability in their personal journey: whenever the going got tough, they had people who understood what they hoped to accomplish, people who clearly cared about and shared a sense of beauty worth fighting for.

Compared to the ecosystem overall, these communities were small (typically under 100 people), but they offered valuable beachheads into much larger portions of ecosystems that the eco-entrepreneurs could not yet understand or access. For example, community gave eco-entrepreneurs access to different sources of materials, created institutes to develop new materials, and opened opportunities to pool scarce resources together to carve out alternative value chains. Eco-entrepreneurs did all this through reaching out to peers who were part of the same community.

This furthered generalizing: broadening the reach and impact of one's artefact or discourse. But it also enhanced the effect of one's connective micro-practices, by plugging eco-entrepreneurs into a rapidly growing movement, which brought together a variety of ecosystems that helped to push everyone's ideas past a tipping point (Thopte and Poldner, 2014).

Proposition 3b: Generalizing the ecosystem as a whole enhances the effect of the connective micro-practices used to foster community.

DISCUSSION

Theoretical Contributions

We join a growing number of studies that grapple with the possibility of social and environmental change against all odds and propose sustainable entrepreneurship as the emerging Davids that successfully take on and accelerate social change. Hockerts and Wüstenhagen (2010: 481) suggest that it is not merely David against Goliath, but often the interplay between the two that generates large-scale transformation. Because Goliaths adapt to these emerging Davids (see also Thopte and Poldner, 2014), small acts get progressively amplified and therefore can quickly reach a point where the system tips over. There is a growing list of industries, from chemicals to forestry to fisheries to food, where emerging Davids experimented with new practices and ushered in new self-regulation, which surely (and not so slowly) tipped the industry over to much more sustainable practices.

We extend these arguments to more prototypical Davids, who are not only under-resourced and ill-prepared to compete traditionally, but are radically different to begin with and therefore willingly reject the strengths and repertoires their rivals possess. The ethical fashion industry provided us with a perfect context where we could observe the flight in real time, and there were dozens and by now hundreds of Davids allowing us multiple comparisons and contrasts as this industry evolved. Yet despite great variety, both by design and by discovery, we found surprising similarity in what made these eco-entrepreneurs so successful.

Our primary contribution is the induction of three types of aesthetic micro-practices that gradually tackle features, subsets and whole ecosystems. The three micro-practices are not unique to our empirical context: entrepreneurs in general rely on material, discursive and connective practices to effectuate (Sarasvathy, 2008) and emancipate (Rindova et al., 2009). These micro-practices have also been shown to be particularly fitting and effective in social entrepreneurship (Nicholls, 2008) and sustainable entrepreneurship (Hockerts and Wüstenhagen, 2010). Our unique contribution is explaining how these aesthetic micro-practices enable individuals to transform global ecosystems. Specifically, we explain how eco-entrepreneurs use the fruits of material, discursive and connective practices – that is, the artefacts, language and community – to progressively improve the ecosystem they work in. Perhaps more importantly, each improvement amplifies the possibilities for social change, by helping these eco-entrepreneurs single out and take on the next feature, subset or whole they would like to see changed for the better.

Our multi-method study is developed in a single and unique context: the ethical fashion industry. Aesthetics come within easy reach in this industry because the fashion products themselves are embodiments of beauty, and eco-entrepreneurs start with and evolve strong aesthetic identities. Aesthetic levels are prevalent in this setting, as different parties attempt to win over consumers' expectations and evaluations of what is beautiful and why it is deemed beautiful (De Klerk and Lubbe, 2008). Aesthetics also play a major role in many other design-driven industries, and some would argue that any product and any design elicits at least some aesthetic action and reaction.

Future Research

Our findings suggest that aesthetic micro-practices are helpful starting places for singling out critical needs for social change and they provide effective ways to keep up with ever-changing needs once radical transformation gets under way. From the vantage point of our answer, the next logical step is to explicitly explore the role of aesthetic micro-practices for socially and environmentally minded entrepreneurs in other settings. We also need to inquire more generally into whether, when and why these aesthetic micro-practices can effectively substitute and even subvert existing (but questionable) ways of doing business. We are just beginning to think how aesthetic repertoires can engender synergies with more traditional cognitive practices in organizations.

From the vantage point of our questioning – what makes Davids successful – aesthetic micro-processes open even more research venues. Aesthetic micro-practices are the proverbial tip of the iceberg, and only one of the ways in which change agents go about large-scale transformation. More interesting than the 'what', however, is the 'how' in our findings. We suggest that one reason why aesthetic micro-practices are so effective is because they can be customized by any individual to fit any stage of the ecosystem they are trying to redesign. Another reason is that aesthetic micro-processes can trigger self-amplifying loops: as the beauty one sees in nature or people gets recognized by many others, change agents can sharpen their tools and broaden their toolkit. We would like to encourage researchers studying cognitive micro-practices to also inquire whether and how they too can interact with global ecosystems.

Finally, we feel that it is high time for us to take one step beyond our individual-centric models of entrepreneurship and to ask how effectuation and emancipation can be broadened to also include interactions between human agents and the natural and social ecosystems they inhabit, and often attempt to change for the better.

CONCLUSION

Approaching radical social change from an ecosystem view moves us beyond an individual-centric view of human agency and helps us understand how the social and environmental context motivates (Gagliardi, 1996; Guillet de Monthoux et al., 2007) and transforms its natural and social ecosystem (Plowman et al., 2007). Our focus on aesthetic micro-practices suggests that seemingly small acts can effectively turn large ecosystems around, even when protagonists lack or reject all of the traditional approaches and capabilities that make their rivals successful within the existing ecosystem. We elaborate on the emerging organizational concept of aesthetic micro-practices, tracing their observable effects in the form of artefacts, language and community; we then explain the mechanisms by which these aesthetic micro-practices help to transform global ecosystems. Our hope is that the growing attention to aesthetics within both ecosystem studies and entrepreneurship studies will create additional opportunities to marry these streams of research and further theorize and observe how human beings go about making their world a better place for everyone.

ACKNOWLEDGEMENTS

Financial support from the Social Sciences and Humanities Research Council, and the Ivey Business School, Western University, Canada is gratefully acknowledged.

NOTE

* Corresponding author. This work is a fully collaborative effort: the authors contributed equally.

REFERENCES

Aggestam, M. (2007), 'Art entrepreneurship in the Scandinavian music industry', in C. Henry (ed.), *Entrepreneurship in the Creative Industries: An International Perspective*, Cheltenham, UK and Northampton, MA, USA: Edward Elgar Publishing, pp. 30–53.

Berger, L. and T. Luckmann (1967), *The Social Construction of Reality: A Treatise in the Sociology of Knowledge*, New York: Anchor Books.

Branzei, O. and K. Poldner (2012), *Veja: Sneakers with a Conscience*, London, Ontaria: Ivey Publishing.

Bronfenbrenner, U. (1979), *The Ecology of Human Development: Experiments by Nature and Design*, Cambridge, MA: Harvard University Press.

Davis, G., D. McAdam, W.R. Scott and M.D. Zald (2005), *Social Movements and Organization Theory*, Cambridge Studies in Contentious Politics, New York: Cambridge University Press.

De Klerk, H. and S. Lubbe (2008), 'Female consumers' evaluation of apparel quality: exploring the importance of aesthetics', *Journal of Fashion Marketing and Management*, 12(1), 36–50.

Eisenhardt, K. and M. Graebner (2007), 'Theory building from cases: opportunities and challenges', *Academy of Management Journal*, 50(1), 25–32.

Faulkner, P. and J. Runde (2009), 'On the identity of technological objects and user innovations in function', *Academy of Management Review*, 34(3), 442–62.

Fleischmann, F. (2006), 'Entrepreneurship as emancipation: the history of an idea', lecture delivered at the Free University of Berlin, 12 July.

Gagliardi, P. (1996), 'Exploring the aesthetic side of organizational life', in S. Clegg, C. Hard, and W. Nord (eds), *Handbook of Organizational Studies*, London: Sage, pp. 565–80.

Gnanadason, A. (2005), 'Listen to the women!', *Listen to the Earth, World Council of Churches*, Volume 111 of Risk Book Series, Indiana University.

Guillen, M. (1997), 'Scientific management's lost aesthetic: architecture, organization and the Taylorized beauty of the mechanical', *Administrative Science Quarterly*, 42(4), 682–715.

Guillet de Monthoux, P., C. Gustafsson and S.-E. Sjöstrand (2007), *Aesthetic Leadership: Managing Fields of Flow in Art and Business*, London: Palgrave Macmillan.

Henry, C. (2007), *Entrepreneurship in the Creative Industries: An International Perspective*, Cheltenham, UK and Northampton, MA, USA: Edward Elgar Publishing.

Hirschman, A. (1995), *A Propensity to Self-subversion*, Cambridge, MA: Harvard University Press.

Hjorth, D. and C. Steyaert (2009), *The Politics and Aesthetics of Entrepreneurship: A Fourth*

Movement in Entrepreneurship Book, Cheltenham, UK and Northampton, MA, USA: Edward Elgar Publishing.

Hockerts, K. and R. Wüstenhagen (2010), 'Greening Goliaths versus emerging Davids: theorizing about the role of incumbents and new entrants in sustainable entrepreneurship', *Journal of Business Venturing*, 25(5), 481–92.

Isenberg, D. (2013), *Worthless, Impossible, and Stupid: How Contrarian Entrepreneurs Create and Capture Extraordinary Value*, Boston, MA: Harvard Business Review Press.

Ivanova, O., K. Poldner and O. Branzei (2013), 'Touch and feel: signals that make a difference', *Journal of Corporate Citizenship*, Special Issue on Sustainable Luxury, 52, 102–130.

Jorgesen, S.E. (2007), 'An integrated ecosystem theory', *Annals of the European Academy of Science*, Liège: EAS Publishing House, pp. 19–33, http://www.eurasc.org/annals/docs/Jorgensen_TeamR_f(15).pdf.

Kaplan, S. and F. Murray (2008), 'Entrepreneurship and the construction of value in biotechnology', in N. Philips, G. Sewell and D. Grifiths (eds), *Technology and Organization: Essays in Honour of Joan Woodward*, Research in the Sociology of Organizations, Vol. 29, Bingley, UK: Emerald Group Publishing, pp. 107–47.

Klein, G. (2013), *Seeing What Others Don't: The Remarkable Ways We Gain Insights*, New York: Public Affairs.

Kothbauer, M. (1992), 'National and provincial park management responses to external threats in Ontario', Wilfrid Laurier University.

Kozinets, R. (1998), 'On netnography: initial reflections on consumer research investigations of cyberculture', in J.W. Alba and J.W. Hutchinson (eds), *NA – Advances in Consumer Research*, Vol. 25, Provo, UT: Association for Consumer Research, pp. 366–71.

Kozinets, R. (2009), *Netnography: Doing Ethnographic Research Online*, London: Sage.

Lamarque, P. and S.H. Olsen (2003), *Aesthetics and the Philosophy of Art: The Analytic Tradition*, Malden, MA: Wiley-Blackwell.

Leonard-Barton, D. (1990), 'A dual methodology for case studies: Synergistic use of a longitudinal single site with replicated multiple sites', *Organization Science*, 1(3), 248–266.

Lounsbury, M. (2005), 'Institutional variation in the evolution of social movements: competing logics and the spread of recycling advocacy groups', in G. Davis, D. McAdam, W.R. Scott and M.D. Zald (eds), *Social Movements and Organization Theory*, New York: Cambridge University Press.

Lustermann, D. (1985), 'An eco-systematic approach to family-school problems', *American Journal of Family Therapy*, 13(1), 22–30.

Nicholls, A. (2008), *Social Entrepreneurship: New Models of Sustainable Social Change*, Oxford: University Press.

Odum, E. (1969), 'The strategy of eco-system development', *Science*, 164, 262–270.

Paolucci, B., O. Hall and N. Axinn (1977), *Family Decision-Making: An Eco-system Approach*, New York: John Wiley & Sons.

Pardeck, J. (1988), 'Social treatment through an ecological approach', *Clinical Social Work Journal*, 16(1), 92–104.

Parsons, G. (2008), *Aesthetics and Nature*, London: Bloomsbury.

Plowman, D.A., L.K. Baker, T.E. Beck, M. Kulkarni, S.T. Solansky and D.V. Travis (2007), 'Radical change accidentally: the emergence and amplification of small change', *Academy of Management Journal*, 50(3), 515–43.

Poldner, K. (2013), 'Un-dress: stories of ethical fashion entrepreneuring', unpublished dissertation, University of St Gallen.

Poldner, K., O. Branzei and C. Steyaert (2011), 'Shecopreneuring: stitching global ecosystems in the ethical fashion industry', in A. Marcus, P. Shrivastava, S. Sharma and S. Pogutz (eds), *Cross-Sector Leadership for the Green Economy: Integrating Research and Practice on Sustainable Enterprise*, New York: Palgrave Macmillan, pp. 157–73.

Poldner, K. and M. Veenswijk (2011), 'ModaFusion on the global catwalk: a narrative approach to studying the ethical fashion industry', *International Journal of Small Business and Entrepreneurship*, 14(2), 230–44.

Rapport, D., H. Regier and T.C. Hutchinson (1985), 'Eco-system behavior under stress', *American Naturalist*, 125, 617–40.

Reason, P. (2007), 'Education for ecology: science, aesthetics, spirit and ceremony', *Management Learning*, 38(1), 27–44.

Rindova, V., D. Barry and D. Ketchen (2009), 'Entrepreneuring as emancipation', *Academy of Management Review*, 34(3), 477–91.

Sarasvathy, S. (2008), *Effectuation: Elements of Entrepreneurial Expertise*, New Horizons in Entrepreneurship, Cheltenham, UK and Northampton, MA, USA: Edward Elgar Publishing.

Sarasvathy, S. (2012), 'Worldmaking', in J.A. Katz and A.C. Corbett (eds), *Entrepreneurial Action, Advances in Entrepreneurship, Firm Emergence and Growth*, Vol. 14, Bingley, UK: Emerald Group Publishing, pp. 1–24.

Schiller-Merkens, M. (2009), *Green is The New Black: The Emergence of an Ethical Field in the UK and Germany*, Mannheim: University of Mannheim.

Scully, M. and D. Creed (2005), 'Subventing our stories of subversion', in G. Davis, D. McAdam, W.R. Scott and M.D. Zald (eds), *Social Movements and Organization Theory*, New York: Cambridge University Press.

Shipley, J.W. (2009), 'Aesthetic of the entrepreneur: Afro-Cosmopolitan rap and moral circulation in Accra, Ghana', *Anthropology Quarterly*, 82(3), 631–68.

Slocombe, D. (1991), *An Annotated, Multidisciplinary Bibliography of Eco-system Approaches*, Waterloo, Ontario and Sacramento, CA, USA: Wilfrid Laurier University Cold Regions Research Centre and IUCN/CESP.

Slocombe, D. (1993), 'Environmental planning, eco-system science and eco-system approaches for integrating environment and development', *Environmental Management*, 17(3), 289–303.

Stecker, R. (2010), *Aesthetics and the Philosophy of Art*, Lanham, MD: Rowman & Littlefield Publishers.

Steyaert, C. (2004), 'The prosaics of entrepreneurship', in D. Hjorth and C. Steyaert (eds), *Narrative and Discursive Approaches in Entrepreneurship*, A Second Movements in Entrepreneurship Book, Cheltenham, UK and Northampton, MA, USA: Edward Elgar.

Steyaert, C. (2007), 'Of course that is not the whole (toy) story: entrepreneurship and the cat's cradle', *Journal of Business Venturing*, 22, 733–51.

Steyaert, C. and D. Hjorth (2006), *Entrepreneurship as Social Change*, A Movements in Entrepreneurship Book; Cheltenham, UK and Northampton, MA, USA: Edward Elgar.

Steyaert, C. and J. Katz (2004), 'Reclaiming the space of entrepreneurship in society: geographical, discursive and social dimensions', *Entrepreneurship and Regional Development*, 16, 179–96.

Strati, A. (1992), 'Aesthetic understanding of organizational life', *Academy of Management Review*, 17(3), 568–81.

Strati, A. (1999), *Organization and Aesthetics*, London: SAGE Publications.

Taylor, S. and H. Hansen (2005), 'Finding form: looking at the field of organizational aesthetics', *Journal of Management Studies*, 42(6), 1211–31.

TED.com (2011), 'Ray Anderson: the business logic of sustainability', http://www.ted.com/talks/ray_anderson_on_the_business_logic_of_sustainability, accessed 5 March 2014.

Thopte, I. and K. Poldner (2014), 'David and Goliath in sustainable fashion: strategic business alliances in the UK fashion industry', *International Journal of Strategic Business Alliances*, 3(2–3), 179–200.

Tillman Lyle, J. (1999), *Design for Human Eco-Systems: Landscape, Land Use and Natural Resources*, Washington, DC: Island Press.

Van Maanen, J. (1988), *Tales of the Field: On Writing Ethnography*, Chicago, IL, USA and London, UK: University of Chicago Press.

Vitello, P. (2011), 'Ray Anderson, businessman turned environmentalist, dies at 77', http://www.nytimes.com/2011/08/11/business/ray-anderson-a-carpet-innovator-dies-at-77.html?_r=4&ref=paulvitello&, accessed 5 March 2014.

Waddock, S. (2008), *The Difference Makers: How Social and Institutional Entrepreneurs Created the Corporate Responsibility Movement*, Sheffield: Greenleaf Publishing.

Warren, L. and A. Anderson (2009), 'Playing the fool? An aesthetic performance of an entrepreneurial identity', in D. Hjorth and C. Steyaert (eds), *The Politics and Aesthetics of Entrepreneurship*, Cheltenham, UK and Northampton, MA, USA: Edward Elgar Publishing, pp. 148–61.

Weggeman, M.C.D.P., I. Lammers and H.A. Akkermans (2007), 'Aesthetics from a design perspective', *Journal of Organizational Change Management*, 20(3), 346–58.

Weiskopf, R. and C. Steyaert (2009), 'Metamorphoses in entrepreneurship studies: towards affirmative politics of entrepreneuring', in D. Hjorth and C. Steyaert (eds), *The Politics and Aesthetics of Entrepreneurship*, A Fourth Movements in Entrepreneurship Book, Cheltenham, UK and Northampton, MA, USA: Edward Elgar.

Whiteman, G. and W. Cooper (2000), 'Ecological embeddedness', *Academy of Management Journal*, 43(6), 1265–82.

Whiteman, G. and W. Cooper (2011), 'Ecological sensemaking', *Academy of Management Journal*, 54(5), 889–911.

World Bank (1991), 'Human Development Report', http://econ.worldbank.org/WBSITE/EXTERNAL/EXTDEC/EXTRESEARCH/EXTWDRS/0,,contentMDK:20227703~pagePK:478093~piPK:477627~theSitePK:477624,00.html, accessed 24 January 2014.

Zoe, H. (2012), 'Eco-fashionista Bianca Alexander on feel-good style in the snowy season', http://www.huffingtonpost.com/zoe-helene/bianca-alexander-eco-fashion_b_2225224.html#s1880422&title=GLORIOUS_MORN_Upcycled, accessed 5 March 2014.

15. Market-driven capabilities and sustainability of alliances by agricultural small and medium-sized enterprises
Mauro Sciarelli and Mario Tani*

INTRODUCTION

The role of small agricultural enterprises and their effects on sustainable rural development have been studied both in developing countries (Ruben et al., 2006; Latouche, 2007) and in developed ones (McCullough et al., 2008; Tasch, 2009). Agricultural enterprises in developed countries face problems driving them towards a more intense, and often less sustainable, way of growing crops.

Maybe the most relevant problem derives from the fact that modern big food retailers demand a stable and large supply of fresh, raw and processed materials, ensuring year-round availability (Reardon et al., 2008). When small farmers cannot warrant a large and continuous stream of products, they have to sell their crops to raw commodities' brokers (Dolan and Humphrey, 2002) that further sell them to industrial processors or to distributors (Maloni and Brown, 2006). In fact, farmers are players in a more complex supply chain with a really small negotiation power (King and Phumpiu, 1996). Farmers use alliances and agreements to increase their negotiation power in order to keep a competitive position in the market, but it is not so obvious what are the effects of these strategies on sustainability of agricultural practices.

To deepen our understanding of the sustainability of different models of alliances this chapter adopts the bioeconomy model of sustainability (Passet, 1996) to evaluate how the different agricultural alliances follow its hierarchical order of economical, environmental and social dimensions, and what kind of capabilities are needed to create and sustain a competitive advantage in these alliances.

First we analyse the main impacts of agricultural practices on sustainable development processes, then we compile a framework that builds upon market-driven capabilities to analyse opportunities and risks related to agricultural farms' alliances. Finally we adopt the multiple case study method to investigate what kinds of capabilities are used in successful farmers' alliances.

THREE DIMENSIONS OF SUSTAINABILITY

The concept of sustainable development traces back to the Brundtland Report (WCED, 1987) that considers a development process to be sustainable only if it 'meet(s) the needs of the present without compromising the ability of future generations to meet their own needs' (WCED, 1987: 43). Thus the concept of sustainability includes future generations as stakeholders in today's enterprises (Freeman, 1984). Since then several authors have modelled the concept of sustainability using multidimensional frameworks, assuming that different dimensions of sustainability could be assessed separately (Hopwood et al., 2005; Pawlowski, 2008). The most widely used approach in this stream of research is Elkington's 'triple bottom line' (1992, 1997) which identifies three pillars of sustainability: economic, environmental and social sustainability.

This model acknowledges that sustainability cannot be limited to the natural resources and the heritage that we pass on to future generations, but has to consider also the effects that development processes have on two other dimensions: the economic and the social. The three pillars are usually presented as the vertex of a triangle and they are usually considered to have a similar value. This model has been criticized because it supports the notion that each perspective can be considered apart from the other two, neglecting to see the strong intertwining between them (Lehtonen, 2006). Moreover, the model provides no guidance on how to arbitrate between the unavoidably conflicting objectives of economical rationalism (profitability), social justice and ecological equilibrium (Upton, 2002).

In order to assess these factors the 'bioeconomy' model (Passet, 1996; Lehtonen, 2006) was developed. It represents sustainable development as three concentric circles: the innermost circle for economic sustainability, the middle one for social and the outermost for the environmental dimension (see Figure 15.1).

The bioeconomy model defines economic activities as the core of sustainable development. They are needed in order to increase the quality of life, but at the same time they must be carried on without endangering the social dimension, and both of them must be acted upon without sacrificing the environment and the natural resources (Lehtonen, 2006). Thus the bioeconomy model has a clear hierarchy where the economic and social dimensions set the limits to economic decision-making processes. This hierarchy helps managers to factor in the sustainability effects of their decision-making processes (Drucker, 1967) and can be used as a criterion of sustainability in assessing different kinds of agricultural alliances.

This model indicates that the various dimensions of the sustainability

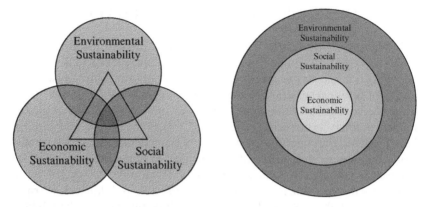

Source: Based on Lehtonen (2006).

Figure 15.1   The triple bottom line and the bioeconomy models

should be taken into account in sequence, rather than at the same time. Using the bioeconomy model we think it is possible to build a framework to comprehend whether the management's actions are capable of being sustainable, and of remaining sustainable over time.

THE PROBLEMS OF SUSTAINABLE DEVELOPMENT AND AGRICULTURAL PRACTICES

Agricultural practices and the development of rural areas have been considered among the core issues in sustainable development since the early 1990s (Lélé, 1991; Schaller, 1993; Yunlong and Smit, 1994). The focus of these studies has been on the links between land and crops, on one side, and the protection of the local environment on the other.

Farmers have to be more competitive in the modern markets led by modern retailers and open to international competition. Some authors have found that most of the new agronomic practices have negative environmental impacts that are not taken into account in farmers' decision-making processes (Tillman et al., 2002; Bennett and Balvanera, 2007). As a consequence there have been several negative effects on soils, groundwater, and on human health as well (Rasul and Thapa, 2004).

McCullough et al. (2008) have identified three main strategies that farmers can use to be more competitive. As a first line of action, farmers may increase the use of chemicals in order to grow more crops, and also higher-quality crops. Farmers use chemicals to reduce impacts from pests and plant diseases, but these also have some negative effects. The utilization of chemicals can have dangerous effects on human health, so they have been regulated in the European Union. These regulations have banned some chemicals and strongly limited the use of others, through setting maximum residue limits (MRLs) in foodstuffs marketed in the union since 1976 (Council Directive, 76/895/EEC).

Moreover chemical treatments can lead to soil overexploitation, making it less and less fertile and, therefore, requiring stronger and stronger treatments to keep up with the new productivity levels (Rasul and Thapa, 2004). Some authors (Latouche, 2007; Tasch, 2009) highlight that in the long run chemicals limit farmers' available strategies and could be considered as a real dependence. Another negative impact of chemicals on soil and water is linked to pesticide drift (Skinner et al., 1997), usually associated with air-based deployment techniques.

A second option farmers have is to enhance productivity by using agricultural machinery and greenhouses. Farmers use machinery to increase productivity in order to counter the increased competition rising out of the lower wages in developing countries; moreover they can use greenhouses to stabilize the production of crops during the year. On the other hand, these practices imply a greater utilization of fossil fuels and more emissions of carbon dioxide (CO_2). These impacts could be reduced through renewable biofuels, mainly cellulosic ethanol, but these lead to displacing crops from food to other uses (Robertson et al., 2008). A third road open for farmers looking to produce more crops is to grow high-yield cultivars or pest-resistant ones, but they can have a nefarious impact on biodiversity (Dale et al., 2002).

A different way to help small and medium-sized agricultural enterprises increase their competitiveness has been developed around a different set of agronomic practices, the so-called integrated farming systems (IFSs). IFSs are being developed so as to avoid, as much as possible, dangers to the environment (El Titi and Ipach, 1989; Behera and Mahapatra, 1999). IFSs aim to solve productivity by focusing actions on two main aspects: they ask farmers to use more environmentally friendly production techniques, and to use natural and biological pest control methods.

The first set of activities asks farmers to substitute intensive production of a single crop with other practices that reduce the needs of fertilizers, such as crop rotation and using intra-row seeding to increase the amount of nutrients in the soils. A similar practice asks farmers to use their fields to raise animals such as goats, or sometimes fish. Deike et al. (2008) have found that while these practices can be successful in reducing environmental impacts, on the other hand they may have several negative economic consequences in asking farmers to reduce automation.

On the pest control side, IFSs ask farmers to use more biologically friendly practices instead of chemical treatments. Some examples are mating disruption, or using selected pheromones to inhibit pest reproduction cycles; and biological control, with the deliberate introduction of predatory insects in the field, such as ladybirds, to reduce pest pressure on crops. Biological control practices can be as effective as chemical treatments but they have a deeper impact on the agricultural enterprise's operations as they require entrepreneurs to pay more attention in selecting the right time frame for each application and the right species for the specific pests they have to counter.

The attention to sustainable rural development has gone beyond the agronomic practices to take into account the managerial side of the agricultural farm. Authors affirm that the agricultural enterprises have to walk a fine line in sustainable development processes. These enterprises should help to improve the local area's quality of life (McCullough et al., 2008), without compromising cultural identity and traditions in the local area (Yunlong and Smit, 1994); for example they can help in creating new jobs linked to the rural traditions.

Carbone et al. (2005) have highlighted how the economic perspective and the more relational one are difficult to separate; similar to what has been observed in family firms (see Mussolino, 2008). According to this stream of research, if development processes involving agricultural firms are to be successful they have to be built upon the synergistic linkages connecting these enterprises with other actors in the local communities, and they should try to increase cooperation in the area (Van der Ploeg et al., 2000).

Other authors go one step further (Senni, 2005; Di Iacovo, 2008), acknowledging that being tightly related to the local community, agricultural enterprises should have a central role in rural development processes. These researchers, building upon the concept of multifunctionality in agriculture, acknowledge that the agricultural enterprise can be a vehicle to regenerative welfare experiences where the farms become a tool for sustaining social development processes in a given area (Di Iacovo, 2007). For example, an agribusiness employing ex-convicts or mentally disabled people can help to integrate them into the society.

These elements show that to successfully manage agricultural enterprises in a sustainable way can be difficult, as these enterprises are driven toward less sustainable models of doing business by their role in the supply chain.

THE DIMENSIONS OF SUSTAINABILITY IN DIFFERENT MODELS OF ALLIANCES IN AGRICULTURE

Agricultural entrepreneurs, especially so for the small and medium-sized ones, have to face several changes in the supply chain structure and in their relationship with the final customer that ask them to be more competitive (King and Phumpiu, 1996). These changes can be classified by three main factors. The first one is the decreased value customers perceive in quality marks (Lenucci, 2009). As a consequence, modern customers value the crop's place of origin less and less. This phases out a source of differentiation that farmers could use in their strategies, and further lessens their negotiating power with distributors and retailers.

The reduced negotiating power is even more threatening when seen in the light of new technologies and the increased potential in sourcing derived from the modern organization of logistics (McCullough et al., 2008). These new technologies enable international competitors from European countries, and from the Mediterranean area too, to sell their products in the various European local markets where they can successfully compete by exploiting a cost-leadership strategy based on their lower wages.

The third factor, seen as a natural evolution of the agricultural market (Reardon et al., 2003), is related to big food retailers becoming the main grocery channel of distribution. Dealing with bigger players down the supply chains lowers the small farmers' negotiating power even more, and endangers their strategic independence as these distributors focus on having a stable and large supply of fresh, raw materials, and processed ones too, ensuring year-round availability (Reardon et al., 2008). Small farmers cannot meet these conditions (Dolan and Humphrey, 2002), so they sell their crops to raw commodities brokers that will later aggregate those from different areas and sell them to industrial processors or to distributors (Maloni and Brown, 2006).

The compound effect of these three factors is that small and medium-sized agricultural entrepreneurs have very little negotiation power as they have to confront those bigger and more efficient distributors that the consumers are used to buying from.

One method that farmers have used to increase their negotiation power has been to create alliances (Sporleder, 1992; Farrell and Tozer, 1996). Moreover, alliances are the small agricultural entrepreneur's main source of market information (Smeltzer et al., 1988) and they are used to share innovation costs and transfer knowledge about new ways to exploit existing technologies (Sivadas and Dwyer, 2000; Audretchs, 2001).

Table 15.1   Alliance models between agricultural enterprises

Horizontal alliances	Vertical alliances	Suppy chain-redefining alliances
Production-oriented horizontal alliances	Price-setting vertical alliances	Ethical purchasing groups
Processing-oriented horizontal alliances		Farmers' markets
		Community-supported agriculture

Obviously, including in agriculture, the survival of an alliance is based upon developing a mutual trust between the partners (Gall and Schroder, 2006). In order to avoid free-ridership, alliances use tight production regulations with two main effects: to lessen the menace of opportunistic behaviours by some members; and to increase and standardize the quality of crops each partner shares with the others.

We divide alliances between horizontal ones, if the partners are agricultural entrepreneurs; and vertical ones, when they are used to tighten links between some agricultural enterprises and other players in their supply chain (Holmlund and Fulton, 1999). A third class of alliance is the so-called alternative food supply chain, or short food supply chain, where producers enter into direct contact with consumers (Marsden et al., 2000; Renting et al., 2003; Ilbery and Maye, 2005). The full breadth of the agricultural alliances is summed up in Table 15.1.

In horizontal alliances, farmers can get together to share resources, machinery and farm equipment. The advantage of these alliances is that production resources are needed only for a limited time each year, so they can be shared if production is scheduled properly.

These alliances let farmers have access to more costly, and more effective, technologies such as new machinery, or Global Positioning System (GPS) to optimize planting procedures. Moreover partners can pool their needs for chemical treatments so to lower the price they pay, further reducing the overall costs of production. These alliances also help farmers to fulfil demand by big food retailers, so they have been supported by the European Union through the structure of producers' organizations in the reform of agricultural common market (Cioffi and Coppola, 2008).

In processing-oriented horizontal alliances, producers get together in order to process their crops into more complex products (such as fresh-cut products, or tomato sauce), using a brand to differentiate them. On the other hand, if the farmer enters one of these alliances he becomes a raw materials supplier. These alliances often ask farmers to focus their production on specific crops with a better yield in transformation processes, thus limiting the farmers' possibility to adopt IFSs. Also, if these cultivars cannot be easily sold in the fresh commodities markets, farmers are actually reducing their strategic independence.

The bigger alliances are able to establish both types of horizontal alliances. Each participant will decide which of his crops will be sold to modern distributors through a group activity, and which will be used in processing.

Vertical alliances consist of creating a stable relationship with a processing firm or with a distributor, and they are often seen as a win–win situation. The farmers can sell their own products even before starting to sow them; they get access to detailed instructions on which crops to sow from their partners; and usually they are supported by one or more expert technicians employed by the partner. If these alliances are signed with processing enterprises, farmers have the further advantage of getting free access to higher-quality, and often still patented, crop varieties. Processing enterprises, and distributors too, will be able to reduce the inherent risks of not being supplied the needed quantities of the cultivars they are looking for, while tightening their control in the supply chain.

In the third class of alliances, agricultural enterprises involve customers to start a process to redefine the supply chain itself, cutting off the distribution players and sharing the crop's value only between the producer and consumers (Payne, 2002).

These alliances can be structured according to three main models – ethical purchasing groups, community supported agriculture and farmers' markets – which all satisfy the modern customer need of a local vision of quality linked to a greater awareness of health risks inherent in intense production systems (Gilg and Battershill, 1998; Marsden et al., 2000). All these alliances can help in shifting customers' perceptions of quality on issues such as authenticity, tradition and healthiness of the crops (Holloway and Kneafsey, 2000), thus creating barriers to imitation (Barney, 1991; Ilbery and Kneafsey, 2000) that get stronger through repeated interactions with the consumers (Venn et al., 2006), helping farmers in implementing a successful differentiation strategy (Norberg-Hodge, 1999).

These practices help agricultural firms in creating a more balanced ecosystem (Norberg-Hodge, 1999) which leads to greater protection of environmental sustainability (Hinrichs et al., 2004), and to reduce their ecological footprint. On the other hand they involve more active participation from the customers, and some authors hold that they will have only a limited impact on the market structure (Tippins et al., 2002).

The various models of alliances described in this section highlight that agricultural entrepreneurs can choose several ways to overcome the natural limitations of their enterprises by entering stable, and mutually advantageous, relationships to increase the value of their crops or to access new markets. At the same time these alliances carry some hindrances with them, so in order to evaluate their potential for creating a competitive advantage we look at how they will be able to help the enterprise relate with the other players in the supply chain.

MARKET-DRIVEN CAPABILITIES IN DEVELOPING SUSTAINABLE ALLIANCES

'Market-driven management' (Shapiro, 1988; Day, 1994) is a strategic management approach focusing attention on the relationships the firm has with the other players in the market in order to satisfy customer needs and to support innovation processes (Drucker, 1954). Relationships are a useful way for an enterprise to get access to new resources, letting the enterprise exploit windows of opportunity that would otherwise be closed to it (Hamel and Prahalad, 1994), and helping it to create a virtuous circle of learning processes (Nonaka and Takeuchi, 1997).

Managers should factor in relationships in order to shape a strategic path for creating, and sustaining (Amit and Schoemaker, 1993), a competitive advantage over competitors (Peteraf and Barney, 2003). Using alliances and networks at the core of strategies has two indirect advantages: first of all they encourage enterprises to intensify their web of relationships so to have a more relevant role in the network, and enable them to have easier access to new alliance opportunities; and second, being embedded in a network of relationships helps the entrepreneur to create relation-specific capabilities (Dyer and Hatch, 2006), thus further reducing the opportunism risks inherent in every strategic alliance.

According to this perspective, the enterprise should create several points of contact with the other players in the market and in the supply chain (Slater and Narver, 1999). Managers should create an interface with customers that involves several different internal functions, according to the specific need of a given interaction. In this way customers will access the right competences for satisfying their needs.

Sciarelli (2008) affirms that a market-driven management approach asks managers to organize and use resources and capabilities to create, and sustain over time, an offer of products and services that customers value more than those of competitors.

These actions can result in new and innovative processes. Sometimes they can even lead the enterprise to redefine the market structure, changing its role in the value chain. This redefinition should be directed to better satisfying customers' needs, taking into account market evolution and identifying consumers' latent needs ahead of competitors.

This approach asks managers to develop several capabilities in order to correctly manage the enterprise's relationships. Management should be able to understand the evolution of the market as a whole (outside-in capabilities); this knowledge about the market should be used in strategy definition processes and in marketing policies (spanning capabilities), and to take advantage of any still not fully exploited resources, skills and knowledge of the enterprise or its partners (inside-out capabilities) (Day, 1994).

Using market-driven management (MDM) as a guide to assess strategies requires entrepreneurs to focus on outside-in capabilities. These capabilities can be further subdivided into three main classes. First there are the channel-bonding capabilities, the skills and knowledge needed to benefit from close relationships with other market players and to exploit them to foster innovation processes (Sivadas and Dwyer, 2000). Second, there are the customer-linking capabilities, skills needed to create and maintain close relationships with customers (Day, 1994). And third, we have the market-sensing capabilities, needed to correctly assess market evolution into strategic path-definition processes and to sustain competitive advantages and anticipate demand bubble creation (Corniani, 2002).

Using the market-driven perspective it is clear that the alliances the enterprise forms will be able to help the enterprise in reaching a competitive advantage by developing managerial outside-in capabilities. Moreover, looking outside the enterprise should help managers to broaden their strategic perspective beyond the economic sphere to also take into account the impacts that the enterprise's activities will have on the local communities.

A FRAMEWORK TO ANALYSE ALLIANCES' SUSTAINABILITY IN AGRICULTURE

In order to more thoroughly understand the effects of alliance models on sustainability, using the bioeconomy perspective on sustainable development, we have designed an interpretative framework shown in Figure 15.2.

This framework builds upon market-driven management to analyse opportunities and risks of agricultural enterprises' alliances and agreements in the current European market. According to market-driven management, alliances can help enterprises in gaining a sustainable competitive advantage when they help them to focus on developing and

Figure 15.2   Market-driven capabilities and sustainability perspectives

exploiting market-driven capabilities. So the baseline of our framework is to have a tool helping managers to be, first of all, successful in their own markets. Alliances will help the managerial action sustainability if they support, or factor in, the various circles of the bioeconomy model in the management decision-making processes.

The inner circle is linked to economical sustainability. Efforts in this perspective have been historically rooted, as shown in the section on 'The problems of sustainable development and agricultural practices', to increase the land's productivity (McCullough et al., 2008). Increased productivity can help agribusiness entrepreneurs if it is matched by the increased profitability (Upton, 2002) related to lower operative costs or increased negotiating power.

Another advantage the agricultural enterprise needs in order to be sustainable is to be strategically independent (Latouche, 2007; Tasch, 2009). When the agricultural enterprise is strategically independent it will be able to gather more value out of the crops and it will have the decision-making power to focus on the effects its own choices have on the other, intertwined, perspectives (Lehtonen, 2006).

The social perspective is the second dimension in the bioeconomy model. Attention to the social dimension is needed to ensure that enterprises are able to preserve their role in the society, while creating economic value without endangering the ecosystem (Yunlong and Smit, 1994; McCullough et al., 2008).

A first indicator of the alliance potential in this dimension is related to preserving the connections between each enterprise and its own local environment as a source of jobs in the rural area, carrying on a function that closes the gap between the economical and the social perspectives.

A second indicator, more in the social perspective, consists of the alliance capability in creating synergies between several social actors in the local community (Van der Ploeg et al., 2000; Carbone et al., 2005), increasing the social capital available in the area (Lin, 2001). Ultimately, according to Di Iacovo (2007), we should consider more valuable those alliance types that usually result in some kind of regenerative welfare process; we have thus decided to use this factor as a separate indicator of sustainability.

In the outermost circle of the bioeconomy model we have the perspective of environmental sustainability. The first element to consider in the environmental sustainability dimension is related to avoiding intensive agricultural practices, as they can have dire effects on the environment (Rasul and Thapa, 2004) which are often unnoticed by the farmers themselves in the short run (Tillman et al., 2002).

A second element to consider is the alliance driving entrepreneurs toward IFSs, as these practices are more environmentally conscious than traditional ones (Behera and Mahapatra, 1999). Last but not least, we have decided to make a separate note of the alliances asking managers to help in protecting local area biodiversity (Dale et al., 2002), as it is needed both for protecting the environment and for preserving local area traditions.

METHODOLOGY

We have developed a multiple case study of alliances involving Italian agricultural small and medium-sized enterprises to evaluate how the different agricultural alliances follow the hierarchical order of economic, environmental and social dimensions, and what kinds of capabilities are needed to create and sustain a competitive advantage in these alliances. Italy is a good nation to investigate the sustainability of agricultural alliances as, according to Eurostat, more professional agricultural enterprises can be classified as small and medium-sized commercial agricultural holdings than in the other European countries. At the same time, the modern food retailers are still not too concentrated (the sum of the three biggest players in food retailing in Italy accounted for only 27 per cent of the market in 2008 using DG Agri data). Combining these two factors we have an interesting macroenvironment where agricultural enterprises can choose between several different alliance models to increase their sustainability.

The selection process followed a theoretical replication procedure as we selected one successful implementation in each of five different classes of alliances (Glaser and Strauss, 1967). These cases have been investigated using two main sources of data. Primary data were collected using direct informal interviews with farmers and other partners, mostly collected during the 2010 MacFrut, the biggest Italian agricultural convention and exhibition; our secondary data sources were the alliance websites, if

Table 15.2   Alliance models and data sources of the related cases

Alliance model	Example	Primary data		Secondary data
		DI	MF'10	Website
PrdHA	APO Lucania	Yes	Yes	
PrcHA	CO.PAD.OR.	Yes	Yes	Yes
Prd&PrcHA	AOP Apofruit	Yes	Yes	Yes
PrSVA	ER High-Quality Durum Wheat Agreement	Yes		
FM	Campagna Amica	Yes	Yes	Yes

Notes: PrdHA = production-oriented horizontal alliances; PrcHA = processing-oriented horizontal alliances; Prd&PrcHA = production-oriented and processing-oriented horizontal alliances; PrSVA = price-setting vertical alliances; FM = farmers' markets; DI = direct interviews with farmers; MF'10 = interviews and leaflets taken at MacFrut 2010.

available. The only notable exceptions to these data-gathering processes were related to the Solarelli initiative by Apofruit, where we had no direct interview with the farmers. Table 15.2 sums up the data sources used in the various cases and how they relate to each type of alliance.

THE RESULTS OF OUR MULTIPLE CASE STUDY

Production-Oriented Horizontal Alliance

This class is made of all those alliances where agricultural entrepreneurs come together to increase their negotiating power and to create a critical mass that makes them able to sell their crops to big food retailers. We call this a 'production-oriented horizontal alliance'.

The case we selected for this class is APO Lucania, a producer organization located in the local area of Potenza, in southern Italy. It is a co-operative and it was founded in 2005. APO Lucania coordinates the activities of 162 small farmers operating in the Basilicata region, and in the Puglia region too, growing fruit and vegetables, mainly tomatoes.

This alliance enforces a strict protocol of maximum residue limits to reduce the risk of free-riding behaviour and to increase product quality. These strict protocols help agricultural entrepreneurs to work together, and increase the level of trust each single entrepreneur has in the producers' organization as a whole, helping them in developing channel-bonding capabilities. Farmers also have to accept frequent controls by agronomists working for the producers' organization that, using the internal laboratories as well, can help them to reduce costs and damage from pests through early treatments while checking for chemical residues.

The co-operative sells crops in Italy through some large retailers, although its most important customers are exporters of fruit and vegetables to food importers in Central Europe, mainly in Germany, and in Russia. These contracts shield management and farmers from being exposed to the other players in the value chain, so they cannot develop customer-linking or market-sensing capabilities.

During 2010 the co-operative decided to counter increasingly intense foreign competition (mainly from Spain, Portugal and Algeria) creating a local centre for direct sales to customers, a weak form of short food supply chain.

This alliance has proven to be successful in increasing farmers' profitability but it has limited their own strategic independence. APO Lucania management is aware of this 'cost' and is trying to use direct sales to increase farmers' links with local customers.

Looking at the social dimension, we found that this alliance is focused on a given local area where they are successful in creating new jobs and in increasing cooperation between local actors. Looking at the effects in the environmental circle, we found that agricultural entrepreneurs are asked to focus on a limited number of crops in order to be viable partners for the big food retailers.

Processing-Oriented Horizontal Alliances

This class of alliances includes all the alliances where agricultural enterprises partner to process their products in order to increase their value for the customers. In this class we selected one of the largest co-operatives in Italy: CO.PAD.OR. from Parma. CO.PAD.OR. was founded in 1987 when a group of farmers in Parma and Piacenza acquired a processing plant for producing tomato paste and sauce. Today its partners cultivate around 4000 hectares of land, resulting in more than 300 000 tonnes of tomatoes in a harvesting campaign concentrated in just 60 days. Agronomists are used to ensure the quality of the crops sold to the alliance, at the same time helping the partners by performing chemical, physical and microbiological tests.

To reduce free-ridership, CO.PAD.OR. sets prices by linking them to a set of quality indicators that producers know beforehand. This helps to generate trust between the producers and to develop channel-bonding capabilities.

CO.PAD.OR. succeeds in creating the other two classes of capabilities prescribed by the market-driven management approach. It has strongly invested in creating brand awareness for its products through the Berni brand, and has developed market-sensing capabilities too as its management has been ready to innovate and follow new requests from the market, creating new products as the Conditoast in the Condiriso line of products, or the new grilled vegetables lines. On the negative side these capabilities are developed at the plant level and only occasionally do they trickle down to agricultural entrepreneurs.

The CO.PAD.OR. experience is a mixed blessing in terms of social sustainability as the processing plant has been able to create new jobs and it has been useful to attract new investments by other industrial enterprises wanting to share infrastructure; but these advantages are in the processing plant area not in the rural areas where the farms operate.

We found mixed results in the environmental sustainability perspective too, as CO.PAD.OR. uses price policies to push producers into selecting, growing and selling a small group of high-yield crops in tomatoes, vegetables and fruit. At the same time we found positive effects related to the short harvesting campaign and the low utilization of greenhouses, two choices that strongly reduce CO_2 emissions.

Production-Oriented and Processing-Oriented Horizontal Alliances

This is the class of those, mainly very big, alliances where producers partner to obtain both the advantages in negotiating power linked to a greater mass of crops and the advantages related to an increased added value that goes with processing the crops. Most of the time these alliances present themselves in the form of an association of producers' organizations (AOP).

In this class we selected the case of the AOP Apofruit Italia. It is based in Cesena and sells more than 300000 tonnes of products, mostly fruits, for total revenues of over €250 million. It has also started a dedicated organic production line using a subsidiary, Canova Srl, which has access to three dedicated processing plants and two logistics platforms in Italy.

In 2009 it created the Canova brand to invest in fresh-cut products, dealing mostly in pre-cooked meals with the brand Almaverde Bio, and in 2010 it complemented this with a Fresh Cut Product business unit for the Fruit on the Beach project. This latter project consists in providing fresh-cut fruit to retailers, including beach resorts, on the Adriatic coast during the summer.

The year 2010 saw the AOP launching a new brand, Solarelli. Solarelli is a line of fresh, unprocessed products that are marketed under a specific brand and sold in big food retailers chains. The turning point, compared with similar previous initiatives, is that the co-operative has provided the business unit with a budget dedicated to promoting the brand in the prime-time TV shows in order to develop a differentiation strategy that can help increase this alliance's negotiating power.

Apofruit management succeeds in developing market-driven capabilities as it has the necessary managerial and financial resources to hold its own in negotiations with the other value-chain players. On the other hand the agricultural entrepreneurs interact only with Apofruit, thus they are not able to develop relationships with other market players.

Being part of the alliances, farmers get a premium price compared to the usual market price for the same crops, so they can successfully exploit the alliance to increase their profitability. Moreover, Apofruit does not bind farmers with multi-year contracts, leaving them more independent. On the other hand this strategic independence seems to be only nominal, because to gain access to the most valued product lines, such as the Canova and Solarelli brands, agricultural entrepreneurs must follow a strict production protocol.

In addition, the higher prices and the sales reliability helps entrepreneurs in creating new, and also more stable, jobs in the various local areas, but we found no Apofruit policy on this, and there are none for the creation of synergistic links in the local area. Apofruit uses some of its brands to deal explicitly with environmental sustainability related issues, but does not factor these issues into most of its other brands.

Price-Setting Vertical Alliance

These are vertical alliances where the agricultural enterprises and some other players in the value chain agree beforehand to fix prices, and which crops to grow, so as to reduce the related risks. The case we chose is the Emilia-Romagna's High-Quality Durum Wheat Agreement, an agreement between Barilla SpA and ten different producer organizations supported by the Emilia-Romagna region. Barilla commits to buy 70 000 tonnes of wheat, leaving producers the option to choose between three alternative price-setting mechanisms at the time of signing the agreement. According to Emilia-Romagna region estimates, producers will get a premium of 30 per cent compared to current market prices. This agreement has been much welcomed by agricultural entrepreneurs, but it exhibits some problems.

While the agreement tightens the link between the processor, Barilla and the farmers, and increases their channel-bonding capabilities, it requires agricultural entrepreneurs to grow only those specific cultivars that Barilla wants to buy, both limiting their independence and preventing them from developing any market-sensing capability. Customer-linking capabilities are never taken into account.

As for the previous class of alliances, the higher prices and the reliability of sales makes the farmers more able to support the local area by creating new jobs, but there are no other effects in the social sustainability circle. This agreement has a negative evaluation in terms of environmental sustainability as the strict protocol of agronomic controls is only designed to increase the quality of the specific cultivars of wheat grown, without taking into account integrated farming systems or the effect on biodiversity.

Farmers' Markets

Farmers' markets are part of the short food supply chain (SFSC) alliances, those alliances where agricultural entrepreneurs become partners in order to sell directly to the consumer, cutting out other players from the value chain. We chose a farmers' market as they are the most widespread model of these alliances, and they require farmers to be involved with both customers and other producers. We chose to analyse Fondazione di Campagna Amica, a non-profit organization promoted by Coldiretti; this SFSC experience, labelled 'Mercati di Campagna Amica', touches various locations in Naples and its local area.

Farmers can sell in these markets only if they let organizers control the quality and safety of their products, raw or processed, and if they let the organization investigate the quantities they can actually grow in their fields. Another rule farmers must follow is that they cannot lower prices below 70 per cent of the average sale price of the same varieties, as observed by daily national public monitoring. Organizers use these safeguards to reduce free-ridership and to stop any attempt at price-based competition.

Obviously farmers' markets help agricultural entrepreneurs in developing channel-bonding capabilities, but they are useful in developing customer-linking capabilities too, thanks to repeated interactions with customers. Moreover, the continuous relationship with customers helps small agricultural enterprises in diversifying their own production in order to capture a greater share of the food budget from each single client, deterring intensive production practices and indirectly benefiting biodiversity. This last effect is stronger as the entrepreneurs tend to focus on local crop varieties in order to differentiate themselves against the big food retailers and their loss-leader or so-called 'Hi-Low' strategies (Lal and Rao, 1997). Furthermore, thanks to continuous interactions with customers the agricultural entrepreneur learns the needs and the tastes of his clients, helping to increase his relational capital and the related market-sensing capabilities.

This alliance helps the entrepreneurs to increase crop profitability, helping them to make their small and medium-sized enterprises viable businesses. On the other hand they usually do not successfully create new jobs; even if they do succeed in helping farmers to create synergies with other local actors that can use these markets as a meeting point, and in some cases as a place where they can play live music or organize small educational lessons on various topics. As a last source of differentiation, Fondazione di Campagna Amica requires farmers to use only IFSs to gain access to the market.

Summary of the Results of the Multiple Case Study

Table 15.3 represents how the various examples of alliances are evaluated, using our interpretative framework. It shows how the traditional models of alliances, represented by the first three cases, are usually able to help farmers reach a better economical sustainability.

On the other hand the model shows that they are not so useful in developing the market-driven capabilities beyond the channel-bonding ones. This harsh evaluation can be moderated in those horizontal alliances with a process orientation, as it asks farmers to appoint professional management to take care of the plant and the relationships with the new distribution channels. The problem is that these competences do not usually trickle down to the farmers themselves, so they become more and more tightly bound to the processing plant itself, further limiting their long-run strategic independence.

A more negative evaluation has been given to vertical alliances, in our case an agreement proposed by a pasta producer. These alliances appear to address only the economical perspective of sustainability, while they do not make any progress at all towards the other types of sustainability.

An interesting result has been found in the case related to the short food supply chain. This farmers' market can help the small and medium-sized agribusinesses to be environmentally and economically sustainable, but they still do not succeed in being fully successful in the social dimension of sustainability. Moreover this alliance model can help in creating a deeper consumer involvement in an agricultural enterprise's management, so farmers can interact with consumers and develop both customer-linking capabilities and market-sensing ones.

CONCLUSIONS

In this chapter we have developed a framework for assessing how the various alliances between agricultural business help entrepreneurs to

Table 15.3 Case results using the interpretative framework

Alliance model	Market-driven capabilities			Economical sustainability		Social sustainability			Environmental sustainability		
	ChBnd	CstLnk	MktSns	Prof.	Ind.	Jobs	Snrg	RgWlf	NIP	IFS	Biodiv
APO – Lucania	Yes	Yes[1]		Yes		Yes	Yes			Yes	
CO.PAD.OR.	Yes	Yes[1]	Yes[1]	Yes	Yes	Yes	Yes[1]		Yes		
AOP Apofruit	Yes	Yes[1]	Yes[1]	Yes	Yes[2]	Yes			Yes[2]	Yes[2]	
ER High-Quality Durum Wheat Agreement	Yes			Yes		Yes					
Campagna Amica	Yes	Yes		Yes	Yes	**	Yes		Yes	Yes	Yes

Notes: ChBnd = channel-bonding capabilities; CstLnk = customer-linking capabilities; MktSns = market-sensing capabilities. Prof. = increase in enterprises' profitability; Ind. = increase in strategic independence; Jobs = new jobs created in local communities; Snrg = synergies between local actors; RgWlf = regenerative welfare; NIP = avoiding intensive productions techniques; IFS = integrated farming system; Biodiv = ecosystems' biodiversity defence.

Yes = the assessment is mostly positive; Yes[1] = the assessment is considered positive for the alliance itself but not for each single farmer; Yes[2] = the assessment is mostly negative but the alliance can have some business units that get a positive assessment.

** = this lack of effects can be explained by the nature of these firms as microenterprises.

develop the capabilities needed to manage successfully their enterprises, and how they drive entrepreneurs onto a sustainable development path according to the model developed by Passet (1996).

Using the framework we have shown how various alliances models have different effects on the sustainability of agricultural enterprises. Most of the alliances can successfully help the agricultural enterprise to partially overcome its structural difficulties (mostly low added value and low negotiating power) but only some of them succeed in helping the entrepreneurs become more strategically independent, and this usually happens when the enterprises succeed in becoming more visible in the final market (thanks to branding strategies or to a direct relationship with customers). In these latter cases entrepreneurs can develop the needed capabilities to interact with the market and to sense market evolution, increasing their chances of sustaining competitive advantage over time.

Moreover the cases show how agricultural alliances do not always succeed in driving agribusinesses toward more sustainable strategies; and even when they succeed in preserving the social structure of the rural areas they can create synergies with other local actors only if the alliance does not involve some other bigger players down the value chain.

Our case confirms the literature on farmers' markets as a more involving experience, helping entrepreneurs to create and leverage market-driven capabilities around a more balanced process involving all three sustainability dimensions.

Ultimately, the case studies show the importance for agricultural enterprises of having relationships with all the other value-chain players, and that the more they build up relationships with customers, the more they become able to align their strategies to capture the increased value that customers ascribe to sustainability. On the other hand we have to remember that our analysis does not employ a literal replication procedure, so our results are not confirmed by multiple observations of the same phenomena.

THEORETICAL AND PRACTICAL IMPLICATIONS

The framework and the cases presented here have several interesting theoretical and practical implications. The research shows that traditional alliances, represented by the first three cases, deprive the local area of distinct value and help enterprises to reach only economical sustainability.

This chapter's main theoretical implication is to highlight that the bioeconomy model can provide researchers with the necessary guidance in assessing whether a given model of alliance can help in sustainable development processes. Furthermore the cases seem to show how the more entrepreneurs succeed in developing market-driven capabilities, the more they are able to align their strategies to sustainable development processes.

This research can have several practical implications too. It basically holds that agricultural entrepreneurs entering alliance models should not only look at the short-term profitability, but to be successful in the long run the agricultural entrepreneurs should look for alliance models helping them to develop a broader set of capabilities. It shows that the modern agricultural entrepreneur can be successful in redefining the supply chain and in cutting out the various intermediaries (see the case on Mercati di Campagna Amica) but to accomplish this the entrepreneur must go beyond the concept of 'farmer' to become more involved in creating a network of relationships with other farmers and with customers as well, or (see the CO.PAD.OR. case) must be able to hire people with those skills.

NOTE

* This work should be considered as the result of a joint effort by Mauro Sciarelli and Mario Tani. The sections on 'The dimensions of sustainability in different models of alliances in agriculture' and 'Market-driven capabilities in developing sustainable alliances' are mainly the work of Mauro Sciarelli. The sections on 'Three dimensions of sustainability' and 'The problems of sustainable development and agricultural practices' are mainly the work of Mario Tani.

REFERENCES

Amit, R. and P.J.H. Schoemaker (1993), 'Strategic assets and organizational rent', *Strategic Management Journal*, 14, 33–46.
Audretchs, D.B. (2001), 'Research issues relating to structure, competition, and performance of small technology-based firms', *Small Business Economics*, 16(1), 37–51.
Barney, J.B. (1991), 'Firm resources and sustained competitive advantage', *Journal of Management*, 17, 99–120.
Behera, U.K. and I.C. Mahapatra (1999), 'Income and employment generation for small and marginal farmers through integrated farming systems', *Indian Journal of Agronomy*, 44(3), 431–9.
Bennett, E.M. and P. Balvanera (2007), 'The future of production systems in a globalized world', *Frontiers in Ecology and the Environment*, 5(4), 191–8.
Carbone, A., M. Gaito and S. Senni (2005), *Quale mercato per i prodotti dell'agricoltura sociale?*, Rome: AIAB.
Cioffi, A. and A. Coppola (2008), 'Il ruolo delle Organizzazioni di Produttori nel settore ortofrutticolo: un'analisi delle possibilità di sviluppo nello scenario di riforma della PAC', proceedings of the XLV Convegno di Studi della SIDEA, Politiche per i sistemi agricoli di fronte ai cambiamenti: obiettivi, strumenti, istituzioni, Portici, 25–27 September.
Corniani, M. (2002), 'Demand-bubble management, corporate culture and market complexity', *Symphonya: Emerging Issues in Management*, 1, 87–98.

Dale, P.J., B. Clarke and M.G. Fontes (2002), 'Potential for the environmental impact of transgenic crops', *Nature Biotechnology*, 20(June), 567–74.

Day, G.S. (1994), 'The capabilities of market-driven organizations', *Journal of Marketing*, 58(4), 37–52.

Deike, S., B. Pallutt and O. Christen (2008), 'Investigations on the energy efficiency of organic and integrated farming with specific emphasis on pesticide use intensity', *European Journal of Agronomy*, 3, 461–70.

Di Iacovo, F. (2007), 'La responsabilità sociale dell'impresa agricola', *Agriregionieuropa*, 3(8), http://agriregionieuropa.univpm.it/dettart.php?id_articolo=204.

Di Iacovo, F. (ed.) (2008), *Agricoltura Sociale: quando le campagne coltivano valori. Un manuale per conoscere e progettare*, Milan: FrancoAngeli.

Dolan, C. and J. Humphrey (2002), 'Changing governance patterns in trade in fresh vegetables between Africa and the United Kingdom', *Environment and Planning*, 36(3), 491–509.

Drucker, P.F. (1954), *The Practice of Management*, New York: Harper & Row Publishers.

Drucker, P.F. (1967), 'The effective decision', *Harvard Business Review*, 45(1), 92–8.

Dyer, J.H. and N.W. Hatch (2006), 'Relation-specific capabilities and barriers to knowledge transfers: creating advantage through network relationships', *Strategic Management Journal*, 27, 701–19.

El Titi, A. and U. Ipach (1989), 'Soil fauna in sustainable agriculture: Results of an integrated farming system at Lautenbach', *Agriculture, Ecosystems and Environment*, 27(1–4), 561–72.

Elkington, J. (1992), 'Towards the sustainable corporation: win–win–win business strategies for sustainable development', *California Management Review*, 36(2), 90–100.

Elkington, J. (1997), *Cannibals with Forks: Triple Bottom Line of 21st Century Business*, New York: Wiley.

Farrell, T.C. and P.R. Tozer (1996), 'Strategic alliances and marketing cooperatives: a lamb industry case study', *Review of Marketing and Agricultural Economics*, 64(2), 142–51.

Freeman, R.E. (1984), *Strategic Management: A Stakeholder Approach*, Boston, MA: Pitman.

Gall, R.G. and B. Schroder (2006), 'Agricultural producer cooperatives as strategic alliances', *International Food and Agribusiness Management Review*, 9(4), 26–44.

Gilg, A.W. and M. Battershill (1998), 'Quality farm food in Europe: a possible alternative to the industrialised food market and to current agri-environmental policies: lessons from France', *Food Policy*, 23(1), 25–40.

Glaser, B.G. and A.L. Strauss (1967), *The Discovery of Grounded Theory: Strategies for Qualitative Research*, Chicago, IL: Aldine de Gruyter.

Hamel, G. and C.K. Prahalad (1994), *Competing for the Future*, Boston, MA: Harvard Business School Press.

Hinrichs, C.C., G. Gillespie and G. Feenstra (2004), 'Social learning and innovation at retail farmers' markets', *Rural Sociology*, 69(1), 31–58.

Holloway, L. and M. Kneafsey (2000), 'Reading the space of the farmers' market: a preliminary investigation from the UK', *Sociologia Ruralis*, 40(3), 285–99.

Holmlund, M. and M. Fulton (1999), *Networking for Success, Strategic Alliances in the New Agriculture*, Saskaton, Canada: Agriculture Institute of Management in Saskatchewan.

Hopwood, B., M. Mellor and G. O'Brien (2005), 'Sustainable development: mapping different approaches', *Sustainable Development*, 13(1), 38–52.

Ilbery, B. and M. Kneafsey (2000), 'Producer constructions of quality in regional speciality food production: a case study from south west England', *Journal of Rural Studies*, 16, 217–30.

Ilbery, B. and D. Maye (2005), 'Alternative (shorter) food supply chains and specialist livestock products in the Scottish–English borders', *Environment and Planning*, 37, 823–44.

King, R.P. and P.F. Phumpiu (1996), 'Reengineering the food supply chain: the ECR initiative in the grocery industry', *American Journal of Agricultural Economics*, 78(5), 1181–6.

Lal, R. and R. Rao (1997), 'Supermarket competition: the case of every day low pricing', *Marketing Science*, 16(1), 60–80.

Latouche, S. (2007), *La scommessa della decrescita*, Naples: Feltrinelli.
Lehtonen, M. (2006), 'The environmental–social interface of sustainable development: capabilities, social capital, institutions', *Ecological Economics*, 49, 199–214.
Lélé, S. (1991), 'Sustainable development: a critical review', *World Development*, 19(6), 607–21.
Lenucci, V. (2009), 'La qualità certificata cede. Domanda in calo, complice la crisi globale', *Mondo Agricolo*, 10, 12–13.
Lin, N. (2001), *Social Capital. A Theory of Social Structure and Action*, New York: Cambridge University Press.
Maloni, M.J. and M.E. Brown (2006), 'Corporate social responsibility in the supply chain: an application in the food industry', *Journal of Business Ethics*, 68, 35–52.
Marsden, T., J. Banks and G. Bristow (2000), 'Food supply chain approaches: exploring their role in rural development', *Sociologia Ruralis*, 40(4), 424–38.
McCullough, E.B., P.L. Pingali and K.G. Stamoulis (2008), 'Small farms and the transformation of food systems: an overview', in E.B. McCullough, P.L. Pingali and K.G. Stamoulis (eds), *The Transformation of Agri-Food Systems. Globalization, Supply Chains and Smallholder Farmers*, London: Earthscan, pp. 3–46.
Mussolino, D. (2008), *L'impresa familiare. Caratteri evolutivi e tendenze di ricerca*, Padova: CEDAM.
Nonaka, I. and H. Takeuchi (1997), *The Knowledge-Creating Company. Creare le dinamiche dell'innovazione*, Milan: Guerini e Associati.
Norberg-Hodge, H. (1999), 'Reclaiming our food: reclaiming our future', *The Ecologist*, 29(3), 209–14.
Passet, R. (1996), *L'Economique et le vivant*, 2nd edn, Paris: Payot.
Pawłowski, A. (2008), 'How many dimensions does sustainable development have?', *Sustainable Development*, 16(2), 81–90.
Payne, T. (2002), 'US farmers' markets 2000: a study of emerging trends', *Journal of Food Distribution Research*, March, 173–5.
Peteraf, M.A. and J.B. Barney (2003), 'Unraveling the resource-based tangle', *Managerial and Decision Economics*, 24(4), 309–23.
Rasul, G. and G.B. Thapa (2004), 'Sustainability of ecological and conventional agricultural systems in Bangladesh: an assessment based on environmental, economic and social perspectives', *Agricultural Systems*, 79, 327–51.
Reardon, T., C.P. Timmer, C.B. Barrett and J. Berdegué (2003), 'The rise of supermarkets in Africa, Asia, and Latin America', *American Journal of Agricultural Economics*, 85(5), 1140–46.
Reardon, T., C.P. Timmer and J. Berdegué (2008), 'The rapid rise of supermarkets in developing countries: induced organizational, institutional and technological change in agri-food systems', in E.B. McCullough, P.L. Pingali and K.G. Stamoulis (eds), *The Transformation of Agri-Food Systems. Globalization, Supply Chains and Smallholder Farmers*, London: Earthscan, pp. 47–65.
Renting, H., T. Marsden and J. Banks (2003), 'Understanding alternative food networks: exploring the role of short food supply chains in rural development', *Environment and Planning*, 35(3), 393–411.
Robertson, G.P., V.H. Dale, O.C. Doering, S.P. Hamburg, J.M. Melillo, M.M. Wander, W.J. Parton, P.R. Adler, J.N. Barney, R.M. Cruse, C.S. Duke, P.M. Fearnside, R.F. Follett, H.K. Gibbs, J. Goldemberg, D.J. Mladenoff, D. Ojima, M.W. Palmer, A. Sharpley, L. Wallace, K.C. Weathers, J.A. Wiens and W.W. Wilhelm (2008), 'Sustainable biofuels redux', *Science*, 322(5898), 49–50.
Ruben, R., M. Slingerland and H. Nijhoff (eds) (2006), *Agro-Food Chains and Network for Development*, Dordrecht: Springer.
Schaller, N. (1993), 'The concept of agricultural sustainability', *Agriculture, Ecosystems and Environment*, 46, 89–97.
Sciarelli, M. (2008), 'Resource-based theory e market-driven management', *Symphonya – Emerging Issues in Management*, 2, www.unimib.it/symphonya.

Senni, S. (2005), 'L'agricoltura sociale come fattore di sviluppo rurale', *Agriregionieuropa*, 1(2), http://agriregionieuropa.univpm.it/dettart.php?id_articolo=54.

Shapiro, B.P. (1988), 'What the hell is "market oriented"?' *Harvard Business Review*, 66(6), 119–25.

Sivadas, E. and F.R. Dwyer (2000), 'An examination of organizational factors influencing new product success in internal and alliance-based processes', *Journal of Marketing*, 64(1), 31–49.

Skinner, J.A., K.A. Lewis, K.S. Bardon, P. Tucker, J.A. Catt and B.J. Chambers (1997), 'An overview of the environmental impact of agriculture in the UK', *Journal of Environmental Management*, 50, 111–28.

Slater, S.F. and J.C. Narver (1999), 'Market-oriented is more than being customer-led', *Strategic Management Journal*, 20(12), 1165–8.

Smeltzer, L.R., G.L. Fann and V.N. Nikolaisen (1988), 'Environmental scanning practices in small business', *Journal of Small Business Management*, 26(3), 55–62.

Sporleder, T.L. (1992), 'Managerial economics of vertically coordinated agricultural firms', *American Journal of Agricultural Economics*, 74(5), 1226–31.

Tasch, W. (2009), *Slow Money. Per investire sul futuro della terra*, Bra: SlowFood.

Tillman, D., K.G. Cassaman, P.A. Matson, R. Naylor and S. Polasky (2002), 'Agricultural sustainability and intensive production practices', *Nature*, 418, 671–77.

Tippins, M.J., K.M. Rassuli and S.C. Hollander (2002), 'An assessment of direct farm-to-table food marketing in the USA', *International Journal of Retail and Distribution Management*, 30(7), 343–53.

Upton, S. (2002), 'Back to the basic', *OECD Observer*, 233, http://www.oecdobserver.org/news/fullstory.php/aid/778/Back_to_the_basics.html.

Van der Ploeg, J.D., H. Renting, G. Brunori, K. Knickel, J. Mannion, T. Marsden, K. De Roest, E. Sevilla-Guzmán and F. Ventura (2000), 'Rural development: from practices and policies towards theory', *Sociologia Ruralis*, 40(4), 391–408.

Venn, L., M. Kneafsey, L. Holloway, R. Cox, E. Dowler and H. Tuomainen (2006), 'Researching European "alternative" food networks: some methodological considerations', *Area*, 38(3), 248–58.

WCED (1987), *Our Common Future*, New York: Oxford University Press.

Yunlong, C. and B. Smit (1994), 'Sustainability in agriculture: a general review', *Agriculture, Ecosystems and Environment*, 49, 299–307.

16. Entrepreneurial functions by organic farmers[1]

Marcus Dejardin, Jean Nizet and Denise Van Dam

INTRODUCTION

Organic agriculture seeks to minimize the use of external inputs in the agricultural production process. It turns away from synthetic fertilizers and pesticides and aims at 'achieving optimal agro-ecosystems which are socially, ecologically and economically sustainable' (Codex Alimentarius, 2007: 2). The possible contribution of organic farming to worldwide sustainable development is receiving increasing interest (OECD, 2003). That being the case, organic farming is itself developing, and is considered to be an evolving industry. In order to explain its evolution and its growing importance, entrepreneurship and its contribution to the development and renewal of agricultural activities may be considered. Entrepreneurship represents a necessary factor for organic farmers to respond to competition. It means the creation or recognition of opportunities; innovation and differentiation. Entrepreneurship might furthermore be at the heart of the process providing answers to the growing concern for sustainability, although little is still known in this regard, and the immensity of our scientific ignorance calls for considerable efforts in terms of research. As Hall et al. (2010: 440) emphasize: '(w)hile the case for entrepreneurship having a central role in a transition to a more sustainable society has been proposed by many, there remain major gaps in our knowledge of whether and how this process will actually unfold'.

In light of the magnitude of the needs in terms of research, the contribution of this chapter appears rather modest. We focus on the three main contributions or functions of entrepreneurship identified in the scholarly economic literature: innovation, risk-taking and contribution to efficiency. We illustrate these functions by using some narrative elements extracted from experiences of organic farmers as they report them. In doing so, we seek very basically to show how these entrepreneurial functions may be transposed in the practice of organic farming, and to suggest the entrepreneurial contribution of organic farmers to the sustainable renewal of agriculture and, more broadly, of activities within the agro-food industry. The chapter relies on original material collected over 2006 and 2007, through first-hand fieldwork taking the form of semi-structured interviews of organic farmers active in three French regions (Alsace, Nord-Pas-de-Calais and Picardie). From the collected material, we have selected three interviews whose content appears more symptomatic of each of the three main functional definitions. We looked for the elements in concrete and direct evocation of the function. Our aim is to illustrate the entrepreneurial functions that are identified by economic analysis within the organic farming context and specificities.

Before going further, note that in reality the entrepreneurial functions may emerge simultaneously and be accomplished by the same individual or group of individuals. We consider them separately for the sake of simplicity. In addition, entrepreneurship is distinguished most often by singular acts that should be distinguished from regular activities, or routines, identified as managerial (rather than entrepreneurial) (Thurik and Wennekers, 1999). Only the entrepreneurial aspects of farmer activities are considered here.

First, we present the economic functions of entrepreneurship according to the classical authors, Joseph Schumpeter, Frank Knight and Israel Kirzner. The recognition of innovation as an entrepreneurial function is typically associated with Schumpeter, while risk-taking and the entrepreneurial contribution to (market) efficiency are respectively closely related to the work of Knight and Kirzner. Next, we briefly present the methodology adopted for collecting the original material and for developing this chapter. The following section reports on the concrete expression of entrepreneurial functions in organic farming through the narrated experiences of farmers.

THE ENTREPRENEURIAL ECONOMIC FUNCTIONS ACCORDING TO JOSEPH SCHUMPETER, FRANK KNIGHT AND ISRAEL KIRZNER

Joseph Schumpeter (1883–1950) is undoubtedly the economist whose name is most closely associated with the figure of the entrepreneur. The young Schumpeter especially identified the entrepreneur as a vector of innovation and the engine of economic development.

Innovation and development are intimately linked. Schumpeter describes their interrelationship as 'the carrying out of new combinations'. He distinguishes five cases: (1) the introduction of a new good or of a new quality of a good; (2) the introduction of a new production or commercial method; (3) the opening of a new market; (4) the conquest of new sources of raw materials or intermediate goods; (5) the carrying out of new industrial organizations (Schumpeter, 1963 [1934]: 66). Through innovation, the Schumpeterian entrepreneur seeks to create new profit opportunities. Innovation requires the entrepreneur to have the rare abilities that make them an exceptional agent, not only capable of leading change but also ready to withstand the opposition that change may produce in the social environment (van Praag, 1999).

If the function of the Schumpeterian entrepreneur is to bring innovation and development into the economic circuit, Frank Knight (1885–1972) gives entrepreneurs the role of risk-taking; more exactly, the role of bearing uncertainty. Indeed, Knight (1921) distinguishes between the concepts of risk and uncertainty. For Knight, risk enters into computations with known probabilities. On the contrary, although uncertainty takes into account the notion of risk, it also refers to non-foreseeable events; in other words, events where the probabilities are unknown. The uncertain nature of some events means that they enter the individual decision process jointly with the individual's subjective probabilities. This understood, an entrepreneur is the one who, taking expectations into account, would accept to bear uncertainty of production and trade. Expected profits would be payment for this specific activity.

Finally, for Israel Kirzner (1930–), the entrepreneur is the economic agent who assumes the equilibrating function in the market process. The imperfect information, or ignorance of economic agents about their respective buying and selling plans, explains market imbalance. Profit opportunities that may result from the market imbalance are seized by the entrepreneur. Through this entrepreneurial action, the imbalance will be reduced. One sees, through this process, the equilibrating action of Kirznerian entrepreneurs (van Praag, 1999). Moreover, in doing so, entrepreneurs contribute to the production of knowledge shared by economic agents. The entrepreneurial action is eventually followed by the mechanical action of imitators.

The stock of profit opportunities is also fuelled exogenously by changing economic conditions that may be determined by many non-entrepreneurial factors. For Kirzner, technical progress, when it results from conscious decisions supporting research and development and from managerial action, is considered to be exogenous from entrepreneurial action.

The production process, in contrast to the market process, is also not excluded from the conditions of realization of entrepreneurial profit. In this case, the entrepreneur discovers the profit they could make by considering not only trading activities but also better use of inputs in the transformation process leading to products and services.

At the origin of the discovery of profit opportunities is alertness, the hallmark of the Kirznerian entrepreneur. Alertness is not a case of prior knowledge. On the one hand, it is not possible to know what you ignore. On the other hand, if entrepreneurship is the capacity to exploit market knowledge, then there would be no reason to distinguish entrepreneurship from production factors, and pure entrepreneurial profit from production factor compensation. Alertness means more 'knowing where to look for market data' than 'knowledge of these data' (Kirzner, 1973: 67). If economic agents know of profit opportunities, they could grasp these opportunities, just as managers do for firms, by maximizing a profit function given the known technology, endowments and parameters. And, indeed, for this managerial activity (and for the lease of their knowledge), they receive compensation from the firms' owners. In line with Kirzner, the stake for managers is to run a programme; there is no discovery, no entrepreneurial decision and no pure entrepreneurial profit in this case.

METHODOLOGY

The original material that has been used for this chapter was collected at the occasion of a larger research project on organic farmers whose main results have been reported in Van Dam et al. (2009). The main research question was about organic farmers' motives regarding the adoption of organic farming from various disciplinary viewpoints: economics, sociology, anthropology and psychology. The variety of disciplines reflects the authors' academic and scientific backgrounds.

Alongside documents and secondary data, the research project exploits the content of semi-structured interviews that were conducted between February 2006 and June 2007 among French organic farmers. The latter are involved in cereals and/or dairy and/or vegetable production in Picardie; fruit tree cultivation in Nord-Pas-de-Calais; and viticulture in Alsace (Van Dam et al., 2009). In total, about 60 farmers were interviewed. Each interview was about 90 minutes long.

For developing this chapter, the interviews of three organic farmers were chosen. The criteria used for the selection of these three interviews were defined ad hoc. We read the interviews in search of rich narrative content that can be put into association with the main entrepreneurial functions that have been described in the classical economic literature on entrepreneurship. In so doing, we seek to exemplify entrepreneurial functions within the organic farming context as reported by organic farmers themselves. The fact that entrepreneurial functions are illustrated through events reported by actors that take part in them, as well as subjective representations and attitudes, is certainly to be emphasized. More specifically, it means that the following statements must be distinguished from statements that might be made by third parties; that they must be cautiously interpreted.

THE ENTREPRENEURIAL FUNCTIONS THROUGH ORGANIC FARMERS' NARRATED EXPERIENCE

The Entrepreneurial Function of Innovation: The Wetzel Experience

Schumpeter conceptualizes the entrepreneur as an innovation vector. The innovative behaviour of the entrepreneur is motivated by the creation of new profit opportunities. Regarding the organic farmers that we met, the motive for innovation can indeed be linked to the pursuit of production cost reduction, or looking for increased productivity in accordance with the required organic specifications. Here, we may cite the project of an organic farmer in the French Picardie region, who plans to introduce a new device for solar drying of the hay that he feeds his cows, with a resulting reduced cost attached to mechanical handling and packaging. But innovation can also be more selfless and be linked to the farmer's will to make a hardline application of organic farming principles. From this perspective, the Alsatian winemaker Ernest Wetzel (names have been changed) is quite exemplary.

Innovation appears repeatedly in the discourse of this winemaker and in many contexts. Thus, innovation results from the search for biological input best suited to the soil characteristics of his land, where he had to observe that the use of calcareous algae, although recommended by the Lemaire–Boucher method, was not effective. This exploration put him in contact with biodynamic farmers and with François Boucher, a biodynamic wine-grower in the French Maine-et-Loire region.

Wetzel is also a collective entrepreneur. He is among the initiators and founders of the Professional Organization of Organic Agriculture in Alsace (Organisation Professionnelle de l'Agriculture Biologique en Alsace, OPABA), whose goal is 'to organize, promote and develop organic agriculture in Alsace' (OPABA, http://www.opaba.org, March 2013). He also helped to found an event for the presentation of Alsatian Appellation d'Origine Contrôlée (AOC) organic wines. This event was set up without the support of the Interprofessional Committee of Alsatian Wines, even though he is a contributor to the organization. 'The Interprofessional Committee must always represent all growers. And since we [organic wine-growers] are a minority, it is limited in what it can do without alienating [the] majority. However, sometimes things must be done: We must stop the rhetoric and act.'

He offers a fully organic wine. Undoubtedly it is here that innovation is most striking. When we met Ernest Wetzel, the expression 'organic wine' did not officially exist. Only the expression 'wine made from grapes of organic agriculture' was officially recognized.[2] Wetzel, however, was already at that time making and selling wine labelled as 'organic wine':

> Wine with zero additives. A wine without added sulphur. And we prove that it is possible. Wine consumers may or may not like it: That is their palate and is both in the realm of freedom and in the realm of aesthetics. And we are one of a few that writes it on the bottle, to put 'organic wine', which is technically forbidden, but there are zero additives. And me, I reverse the burden of proof. This wine is sold, anyone can buy it, and anyone can test it. And me, I am fed up that people making effort have to prove what they do. [He says it loud and clear.] It is a militant act. I believe in the virtue of making a move forward in this way also, not just through accredited channels.

The absence of added sulphur has non-negligible effects on wine appearance and taste. This is a new product that requires a new approach: 'It is human to compare these wines with wines with added sulphur. It is natural. But we must also abstract ourselves from this. It is new learning.' If he gets official approval for these wines, he realizes however that he is able to receive the appellation of origin for his wines because he presents the wine shortly after production, thus before the flavour of the wine is affected by oxidation.

Risk and Uncertainty: The Marchand Experience

For Philippe Marchand, there is no entrepreneur who has not had their feet on the ground. If being in organic farming is a matter of conviction and response to specific aspirations, it is also necessary to have an accounting mind and to generate revenue. That said, Marchand accumulates risk factors, connecting him with the entrepreneurial function described by Knight. These risk factors relate to the characteristics of his business but also his own decisions. We may therefore consider the strategies that he uses to limit risk.

Marchand is active in organic fruit tree cultivation, an industry that involves technical knowledge. And it seems particularly difficult to get help and advice: 'In France, there are very few technicians to help us.' Yet, he decided to convert his entire orchard, not just part of it:

> Ten years ago exactly, when I decided to change the orientation of my production, I wanted to move radically towards organic farming and not partially. I really wanted to convert my entire orchard all at once in order to avoid suspicion from my clients and for myself as well. The risk that I took was converting everything in the same year.

Another risk factor is directly related to the specifications of organic farming. 'The peculiarity of organic farming is that if you are controlled positive for one single molecule, the penalty is a three year exclusion from organic farming. That is to say, for three years you are no longer able to label your products as organic.' The control provides protection for virtuous organic farmers and for consumers against unscrupulous organic farmers. But it still ignores the risk of suffering the negative externalities of his 'traditional' neighbours.

Risk is not just found in the technical nature of the activity, but is also related to the specifications of organic farming and the strategy of an immediate and complete conversion. Marchand is therefore active in looking for ways to reduce risk-taking.

Reducing risk-taking includes the quest for technical knowledge. With the Group of Organic Farmers of Nord-Pas-de-Calais (Groupement des Agriculteurs biologiques du Nord-Pas de Calais, GABNOR), he met the only person available in France, as far as he knew, able to pass on that knowledge. He also looked for practical experience:

> There are some growers in arboriculture in northern Paris. You see Paris and across northern France, which encompasses five counties (*départements*). There are few growers. So I turned to them, I went to see them and they also helped me to apply the biological theory to my orchard. Despite this, I had many challenges and, particularly during the first year, I had to hire staff to remove, branch by branch, aphids that had attacked my orchard.

Moreover, knowledge exchange often involved going abroad: 'In the Nord-Pas-de-Calais, we have only five or six farmers in the arboriculture industry. We meet two or three times a year to visit Belgium, England, Germany, in the South of France, or wherever, in order to visit other orchards, better understand our work and learn.'

Risk-taking finds also a response through the development of solidarity among organic farmers. 'You have to have it clearly in mind. This solidarity is very important. Already, there is less competition. You should know that when there is less competition, relationships are better. On top, this chain is spontaneous and natural between organic farmers.' In addition, we note the creation of an Economic Interest Group (Groupement d'Intérêt Economique, GIE) as well as a purchasing and marketing co-operative so that farmers can act together on pricing.

Finally, research is being enlisted to find remedies to certain risks associated with organic arboriculture:

> We work in collaboration with Gembloux in Belgium, with a research station in Kent, England, and with a research station in France. The projects relate to

varietal research. An ecosystem is required; that is to say, it is necessary that the auxiliary fauna helps you to avoid insecticide interventions, even natural ones. And regarding cryptogams, that is to say all the fungal diseases, we have to adopt varieties that are resistant.

Seizing Opportunities: The Briscot Experience

Joseph Briscot multiplies his activities. From the development of his farm and onwards, there is a reasoned diversification process: from apple production in his orchard through to the transformation of the product. However, 'it is not enough'. He plays safe and ensures himself a comfortable future. And despite all his activities, Briscot still works in the business where he was employed full time before becoming a farmer.

He reports himself to be very alert, seizing what he identifies as market opportunities. In what follows, we report on Briscot and his capacity, thus connecting him with the Kirznerian function of entrepreneurship. Opportunities for his farm include educational offerings aimed at school population. And this opportunity is big: 'We must be close to 4000 children. They come in groups of 50, now including many English.'

Briscot identifies the possibility of combining educational activities with other commercial activities. He wants to work more with the English and Belgians, for economic reasons. 'When the French visit, they really do not buy from the stores. The English have a budget and are here for 3–4 days. For us, in the store, when an English group visits, we make 400 euros. There is an economic reason.'

Considering the variety of vegetables from regional organic farming, he decided to start organic soup production. The potential is large: 'The interest for organic production is growing. This growing interest is what allows us to place our products in stores, even in supermarkets.' The soup is made from vegetables that were unsold, particularly cauliflower and the asparagus of a local producer who happens to be one of his friends:

> It is a great complementarity between production, processing, and marketing. And the little story explaining the origin of the organic soup is closely related to the production of organic asparagus. My friend is the only organic grower of asparagus in Nord-Pas-de-Calais; probably the only one. Each year, he throws away ten tons of organic asparagus because the stalks are broken or twisted. Organic products in stores must be impeccable. And he said 'we must find a solution' – and thus was born our first soup; a soup made with organic asparagus.

Choices between different activities must be made, meaning that some activities are not continued. Given his resources, he opts for the most profitable activities, the activities where competition is not too strong. He also develops his business through trial and error. For example, he tried to develop camping on his farm but was quickly overwhelmed by the task. Today, he is trying to develop farm tourism and shopping. He also seeks out other possibilities:

> I am the intermediary everywhere where there is a need; that is to say: when a job exists but there is nobody to do it, I act. For example, pumpkins. There are times early in the season when pumpkins cannot be found easily on the market. Me, what I do: I buy them directly from producers. I go with my van. I buy a ton of pumpkins that I collect myself in bulk from the field. I wash them, cut them into four parts, gut them, and then make containers of 150 kilograms each, ready to be used. If I buy them 0.80 euro per kilo, I can sell them to the agro-food industry for 2 euros per kilo.

CONCLUSION

Organic farming is receiving increasing interest as a way to attain sustainability in agriculture and, more broadly, in the agro-food industry. In addition, organic farming represents a growing but also evolving activity. To explain its development, entrepreneurship among organic farmers can be considered. In this chapter, we have detailed entrepreneurship contributions in terms of innovation, risk-taking and increasing efficiency. We then have considered what these contributions can mean more concretely in the practice of organic farming through the narrated experiences of three organic farmers.

While Wetzel offers for sale a totally organic wine, breaking away from legal rules of the time, Marchand accumulates risk factors and looks for the right strategies to avoid pitfalls. Briscot remains alert and, if necessary, calls into question his activities in order to enter the more lucrative business that awaits him. By being innovative, or fully assuming risk-taking, or seizing market opportunities, organic farmers report their entrepreneurial behaviours, breaking with routine management. This means that they might contribute to the vitality of their industry but also more widely, in their way, to the sustainable dynamism of the economy as a whole.

What is reported in the agricultural sector may be reported as well in other sectors. Entrepreneurial-type events can indeed be seen almost everywhere. Yet, they are in all probability, or by definition, more obvious in the new sectors. Whatever it may be, it is remarkable how entrepreneurship is apparent in what appear a priori highly mature sectors. The economic structures are perhaps changing and adapting more pervasively than expected. Provided these elements are moving in the right direction, they are rather encouraging for sustainability and future generations.

NOTES

1. The chapter is a lightly revised English version of a chapter published in French in Van Dam, Nizet, Dejardin and Streith (2009), *Les agriculteurs biologiques: ruptures et innovations*, Dijon: Educagri Editions. The authors are grateful to Martine Poillot (Educagri Editions) for authorization to proceed with this publication.
2. The interview was prior to the agreement on new European Union rules for organic wine. See the 'Commission Implementing Regulation (EU) No 203/2012 of 8 March 2012, amending Regulation (EC) No 889/2008 laying down detailed rules for the implementation of Council Regulation (EC) No 834/2007, as regards detailed rules on organic wine', published in the *Official Journal of the European Union* (dated 9 March 2012).

REFERENCES

Codex Alimentarius (2007), *Organically Produced Foods*, 3rd edn, Rome: Food and Agriculture Organization of the United Nations and World Health Organization.

Hall, J.K., G.A. Daneke and M.J. Lenox (2010), 'Sustainable development and entrepreneurship: past contributions and future directions', *Journal of Business Venturing*, 25(5), 439–48.

Kirzner, I.M. (1973), *Competition and Entrepreneurship*, Chicago, IL: University of Chicago Press.

Knight, F.H. (1921), *Risk, Uncertainty, and Profit*, Boston, MA: Houghton Mifflin.

OECD (2003), *Organic Agriculture. Sustainability, Markets and Policies*, Paris: OECD.

Schumpeter, J.A. (1963 [1934]), *The Theory of Economic Development. An Inquiry into Profits, Capital, Credit, Interest, and the Business Cycle*, Oxford: Oxford University Press, 1st edn 1934, translated by R. Opie from *Theorie der wirtschaftlichen Entwicklung. Eine Untersuchung über Unternehmergewinn, Kapital, Kredit, Zins und den Konjunkturzyklus* (1911).

Thurik, R. and S. Wennekers (1999), 'Linking entrepreneurship and economic growth', *Small Business Economics*, 13(1), 27–55.

Van Dam, D., J. Nizet, M. Dejardin and M. Streith (2009), *Les agriculteurs biologiques. Ruptures et innovations*, Dijon: Educagri Editions.

Van Praag, C.M. (1999), 'Some classic views on entrepreneurship', *De Economist*, 147(3), 311–35.

17. The entrepreneurial contribution of foreign-owned companies to the sustainable development of a small developing host economy

Tõnu Roolaht

INTRODUCTION

The sustainability of development is of ever-growing importance. From one viewpoint, sustainable development 'is a pattern of resource use that aims to meet human needs while preserving the environment so that these needs can be met not only in the present, but also for future generations to come' (Sorin and Irina, 2009: 230). In social sciences, the notion of sustainability is often used more generally to imply the viability and continuation of certain trends or development processes (which may incorporate environmental, economic and social aspects) in the future (e.g. see Chaudhury, 2010; Collins and Grimes, 2008).

Small economies are characterized by limited resources. The scarce domestic endowments of human capital and sometimes also knowledge resources are compensated for by using foreign resources, especially in the form of foreign direct investment (FDI) (see also Griffith, 2007). In addition to larger international companies, foreign direct investments are provided by foreign entrepreneurs and entrepreneurial small and medium-sized enterprises (SMEs). These entrepreneurs are likely to have business expertise and knowledge superior to that of domestic counterparts. However, not every investment received contributes to the sustainable development of the host economy. The entrepreneurial culture, which forms the basis for entrepreneurship, has been defined as 'the composite of personal values, managerial skills, experiences and behaviours that characterize the entrepreneur in terms of a spirit of initiative, risk-propensity, innovative capacity and management of a firm's relations within the economic environment' (Minguzzi and Passaro, 2000: 182). In this chapter, the focus is on entrepreneurial initiatives that relate to the application of more sustainable solutions. Sustainable entrepreneurship in a small-scale business is more elaborately analysed by, for example, Mathew (2009).

The size of a company is not the sole factor that determines its approach towards a host economy and sustainable development. Considerable importance can be attributed to the motivation for investing and to the corporate culture within the foreign-owned company (Collins and Grimes, 2008; O'Neill et al., 2009).

Foreign direct investments have a special role in developing, post-socialist economies. The capabilities and resources provided by foreign companies facilitate the economic reforms either directly on an intra-company level or more indirectly by various spillovers. Due to these specific properties of smallness and transformation, it is interesting to investigate the phenomenon of FDI contributions to the sustainable development of the host country in the setting of a small post-socialist transition economy.

The aim of this chapter is to identify how foreign-owned companies support the sustainable development of a small host economy through their entrepreneurial initiatives. The answer to this research question will be provided via exploratory interpretation of the economic performance, investment motives, management choices and behavioural examples of foreign-owned companies in Estonia. This somewhat descriptive and quali-tative approach does not seek strong causalities. The intention of this explor-atory study is to map the specific field of research and indicate possible research venues for a more detailed and advanced investigation of the cau-salities within the phenomenon. In this chapter, the exploration is not limited to various theoretical viewpoints, but includes three other viewpoints. This multilayered layout of several viewpoints is illustrated in Figure 17.1.

The novelty of this research relates to the unique combination of research streams. It builds upon elements of entrepreneurship literature,

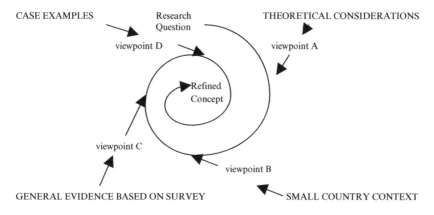

Figure 17.1   The exploratory logic of this chapter

sustainable development discourse and FDI impact analysis. This chapter should be seen as one of the first exploratory building blocks in the emerging discourse on sustainable entrepreneurship in foreign-owned companies. A small economy in transition has been chosen as the research context because in this setting the impact of foreign companies is likely to be more prominent. The role of foreign-owned companies as facilitators of sustainable development has so far found little research attention.

One might argue that experienced foreign companies only seek business opportunities and not entrepreneurial opportunities. Yet, the level of risk, uncertainty and the possibility of failure in a less developed host market setting are such that investors have to take a much more entrepreneurial approach in adjusting their business model. Thus, the unique market conditions create entrepreneurial opportunities. Even in sectors which seem highly regulated at the European Union (EU) level, the actual political discretion of providing subsidies and other support mechanisms on the national or local level is high and likely to provide entrepreneurial opportunities.

The chapter starts with two sections that clarify the research context. The first, theoretical, section offers a review of entrepreneurship, sustainability and sustainable entrepreneurship concepts, including aspects of foreignness. The next, contextual, section then discusses the general roles of sustainability and foreign-owned companies in Estonia. The rationale for choosing Estonia as an example relates to the fact that it has been very successful in building FDI-led growth. The following section describes the research data and methods of analysis. Subsequently, the empirical research results are provided and discussed in two stages: first, a more general discussion of sustainability orientation in foreign-owned companies; and then more detailed short cases highlight the complex interplay of environmental, economic and social aspects of sustainability in the activities of foreign-owned entrepreneurs. The chapter concludes with a discussion of how the exploratory results help to refine the view of foreign sustainable entrepreneurship as a contributor to the sustainable development of the host economy, followed by a final section on limitations and implications.

ENTREPRENEURSHIP, SUSTAINABLE DEVELOPMENT AND SUSTAINABLE ENTREPRENEURSHIP

Entrepreneurship is relevant for sustainable development because sustainability orientation at the corporate level requires innovative risk-taking and entrepreneurial shifts towards new, more sustainable technological approaches. An entrepreneurial culture is 'the composite of personal values, and managerial skills, experiences and behaviours that character-ize the entrepreneur in terms of a spirit of initiative, risk-propensity, inno-vative capacity and management of a firm's relations within the economic environment' (Minguzzi and Passaro, 2000: 182). It is highly dependent on the cultural, religious and intra-firm environments, among others. Covin and Slevin (1991) offer the list of important external variables that play a key role in determining the entrepreneurial environment. These variables include environmental technological sophistication, environmental dyna-mism, environmental hostility in the form of intensive competition, and early life-cycle stage in the industry. Thus, entrepreneurship is facilitated by a dynamic and highly competitive business environment, especially in sophisticated technological sectors that are still emerging and relatively young (Covin and Slevin, 1991). The challenge of sustainable development increases technological sophistication and dynamism, while being respon-sible for the emergence of highly competitive growth industries. These trends facilitate entrepreneurship. Therefore, an increase in sustainability orientation will create entrepreneurial opportunities.

Entrepreneurship can occur in various forms. An existing organization enters a new line of business, an individual or individuals champion new ideas for products and processes within a corporate framework (some-times labelled intrapreneurship), or the entire outlook and actions of an organization are led by an entrepreneurial philosophy (Covin, 1999). The sub-notion of intrapreneurship is especially interesting. It suggests that entrepreneurial resources can also be used within the framework of large organizations (Chang, 2001), and not only in smaller owner-driven companies.

Lee and Hsieh (2010) investigate the connection between entrepreneur-ship and sustainable competitive advantage. Their results suggest that entrepreneurial organizational culture should be supported by the devel-opment of marketing and innovation capabilities in a company because these capabilities have an additional influence on the sustainability of the competitive advantage. Networking provides yet another dynamic feature in entrepreneurial management that is used not only for exploit-ing entrepreneurial opportunities, but also for creating new opportunities (Moensted, 2010). Previous studies of foreign-owned companies have shown that they are more likely than domestic companies to possess such advantages (Roolaht and Varblane, 2008).

In terms of foreign impact on domestic entrepreneurship, there is evi-dence that in the short run import competition and foreign direct invest-ment discourage domestic entrepreneurs or stimulate their exit. However, the long-term positive effects of learning, demonstration, networking and linkages are likely to moderate or even reverse this initial crowding-out effect (De Backer and Sleuwaegen, 2003). The influence of foreign markets on entrepreneurial growth in an economy also depends on policy choices. Bhasin and Venkataramany (2010) argue that policies have to be market-oriented and demand-driven in order to promote entrepreneurial SMEs in production, distribution and service sectors in a global context. The demand-generating standards and the regulations imposed by governments are often associated with the need to introduce more environmentally friendly and sustainable solutions. Thus, governments facilitate entrepreneurial contributions to sustainability, whereas foreign-owned companies are likely to have more resources to capture these opportunities and profit from them.

In order to understand the concept of sustainable entrepreneurship, the essence of sustainable development has to be explained as well. With a back-reference to the United Nations: 'sustainable development is a pattern of resource use that aims to meet human needs while preserving the environment so that these needs can be met not only in the present, but also for future generations to come' (Sorin and Irina, 2009: 230). O'Brien (2002) indicates that the concept of sustainable economy is used to address problems related to energy conservation, reduction in greenhouse gas emissions, environmental protection, recycling and the conservation of natural resources. This narrow view of sustainability focuses predominantly on environmental concerns.

In terms of environmentalism and energy resources, the modern lifestyle brings paradoxical consequences. Horio and Watanabe (2008) argue that the transition has revealed the paradox of a service-oriented economy. In this setting, information was expected to substitute for constrained factors (like, for example, energy), but in fact energy consumption has relatively increased in comparison to the industrial era. Thus, the modern service-oriented economies are not in every respect more sustainable than earlier stages of development. Sirbu et al. (2009) stress, however, that building a knowledge-based economy facilitates accelerated and sustainable growth, while simultaneously strengthening social cohesion and concerns for environmental protection. Although service orientation and knowledge-based development are not entirely synonymous, there is still a strong connection between the two because information is an essential element of both concepts. Therefore, what seems to be more sustainable at first glance might actually be using more resources. This implies that sustainability is not just about the nature of end consumer solutions, but also about savings across the entire value chain and ultimately across society.

A longitudinal study of Dutch development shows that by 2005 the sustainability of the economy had been facilitated by offshoring manu-facturing to developing countries and by focusing retained manufacturing industries in niche markets and specialized machinery and installations (Lambert et al., 2010). Such industrial offshoring might have a detri-mental effect on ecosystems and social development in target economies. This argument has found support as a result of the economic analysis of unilateral sustainability in an open economy setting, where it is called the 'import of sustainability' (Klepper and Stahler, 1998). In terms of foreign-owned or international companies, this aspect indicates that their business activities could have a detrimental influence on social development in a host economy, especially when it is a less developed economy.

In social sciences, the notion of sustainability is often used more gener-ally to imply the viability and continuation of certain trends or develop-ment processes in the future (see Chaudhury, 2010; Collins and Grimes, 2008 as examples). In this broader context, the term 'sustainability' tends to remain defined inherently more vaguely, yet it might incorporate economic, social and environmental aspects. The related context often associated with sustainability is the socio-technical system or setting. The socio-technical system incorporates the production, diffusion and use of technologies in connection with societal functions (for example transpor-tation, communication, nutrition). Innovation should be understood in this setting as an outcome of the continuous alignment of technology and the user environment in a co-evolutionary manner where adaptation takes place on either side (Geels, 2004).

Gibbs (2009) argues that some socio-technical settings, be they coun-tries or regions, could be more supportive towards ecologically conscious sustainable entrepreneurship than others. Grundey (2008) shows similarly that applying sustainable development principles in an economy is a complex process that should involve micro, meso and macro levels of the economy. More developed countries have progressed further along this path towards sustainable thinking. Therefore, the foreign-owned compa-nies with ownership ties to these societies can transfer their experience in sustainable development to a host economy.

In a small country context, an interesting approach is taken by Norway in connection with European Economic Area (EEA) grants. According to this policy guide, the elements of sustainable development are often organized into three dimensions: environmental, economic and social. In terms of this division, for the purpose of sustainable development policy, environment is the basis, economy is the tool and social welfare is the target of sustainable development (European Economic Area, 2006). This basis–tool–target relationship offers additional possibilities to create more holistic policy schemes. Vitola and Senfelde (2010) suggest that the sustainability of economic development could be facilitated by improved national development planning. The new system should incorporate a unified process that connects different planning levels and documents as well as national and EU-funded investments.

The role of foreign-owned affiliates in facilitating sustainability is discussed by Collins and Grimes (2008). They show, using the example of Ireland, that the development led by inward FDI is not just about favourable tax policies and grant schemes offered by the host government. Several foreign-owned affiliates have benefited from the organizational changes and inward transfers in such a manner that their autonomy and importance in the multinational intra-corporate production network has grown. Such an increase in their long-term contribution does facilitate the sustainable development of the host economy. O'Neill et al. (2009) suggest that sustainable entrepreneurship is influenced by culture, and more particularly by differences in holistic value propositions. This aspect might determine the inherent acceptance of values related to the ecological and social sustainability dimensions of economic development, when it is relevant on the corporate level.

Sustainable entrepreneurs design companies with the intention of making a mutually supportive contribution to improved environmental quality and social well-being. These entrepreneurs can potentially function as catalysts to larger structural socio-economic transformations that support sustainability. This catalytic influence could be explained by using a co-evolutionary framework that links the interactive dynamics of change in technologies, institutions and business strategies (Parrish and Foxon, 2009). Entrepreneurship, as a dynamic force for change, has growing importance in contributing to sustainable development as a broad social goal. However, sustainability values prescribe a different approach to organizational design that diverges considerably from conventional principles of entrepreneurship. These focus on resource perpetuation, wider benefits, satisfactory outcomes of multiple objectives and worthy contributions to the enterprise (Parrish, 2010).

According to Crals and Vereek (2005), 'sustainable entrepreneurship is a spin-off concept from sustainable development that can be defined as the continuing commitment by business to behave ethically and contribute to economic development while improving the quality of life of the workforce, their families, local communities, society and the world at large, as well as future generations' (Crals and Vereek, 2005: 173). This broader view reintroduces the intertemporal aspect of future generations into the more specific notion of sustainable entrepreneurship. Cohen and Winn (2007) argue that while market imperfections (inefficient companies, externalities, flawed pricing mechanisms and information asymmetries) might contribute to environmental degradation, at the same time they provide opportunities for the creation of new technologies and innovative business models. A similar approach is offered by Dean and McMullen (2007). Brouwers (2006) shows that innovations for sustainability are often oriented predominantly towards process variables, such as reductions of resource use, energy savings and recycling, while the most sustainability-oriented companies make subsequent innovations in product design and develop new technologies. Larson (2000) uses the special term 'sustainable innovation' to distinguish changes undertaken in order to increase sustainability. The views on entrepreneurship and sustainability are summarized in Table 17.1.

In conclusion, the brief review of the literature allows us to propose that:

● Orientation towards sustainability creates new entrepreneurial opportunities.
● Depending on the corporate culture, larger non-family foreign-owned companies can also be entrepreneurial.
● Foreign-owned companies have more resources and capabilities than their domestic counterparts for capturing sustainability-related entrepreneurial opportunities, which are often facilitated by government policies.
● Sustainability is not only about the nature of solutions for consumers, but also about the savings across the entire value chain and ultimately across society.
● The business activities of foreign-owned companies could have a detrimental influence on social development in the target economy, especially when it is a less developed economy than the foreign owners' country of origin.
● Foreign-owned companies with ownership ties to sustainability-oriented advanced economies can transfer their experience in sustainable development to the host economy.
● Foreign-owned companies are likely to make sustainability-oriented innovations.

Therefore, foreign-owned companies support the sustainable development of the host economy potentially by capturing the entrepreneurial opportunities related to sustainability, while transferring their experience from more advanced home economies and international value chains. However, there can also be detrimental influences of foreignness on the sustainable development in the host economy; for example, on the social development dimension.

Table 17.1   The research contributions concerning entrepreneurship and sustainability

Authors and contributions	Research topics about entrepreneurship
Minguzzi and Passaro (2000)	Modern definition of entrepreneurial culture
Covin and Slevin (1991)	Key variables that determine entrepreneurial environment
Covin (1999)	The concept of intrapreneurship – intra-
Chang (2001)	company entrepreneurship
Lee and Hsieh (2010)	Dynamics of entrepreneurship and
Moensted (2010)	sustainable competitive advantage
De Backer and Sleuwaegen (2003)	International influences to
Bhasin and Venkataramany (2010)	entrepreneurship

Authors and contributions	Research topics about sustainability
Sorin and Irina (2009)	UN definition of sustainable development
O'Brien (2002)	and discussion
Horio and Watanabe (2008)	Sustainability paradox of service-oriented economy
Sirbu et al. (2009)	Sustainability and knowledge based development
Lambert et al. (2010)	Import of sustainability by exporting
Klepper and Stahler (1998)	sustainability burden to developing economies
Chaudhury (2010)	Sustainable development in social sciences
Collins and Grimes (2008)	
Geels (2004)	Socio-technical systems, setting, and
Gibbs (2009)	multi-level complexity
Grundey (2008)	
European Economic Area (2006)	The elements of sustainable development
Vitola and Senfelde (2010)	and development planning
Collins and Grimes (2008)	The role of foreign-owned affiliates and
O'Neill et al. (2009)	culture in facilitating sustainability
Parrish and Foxon (2009)	Sustainable entrepreneurs and sustainable
Parrish (2010)	entrepreneurship
Crals and Vereek (2005)	
Cohen and Winn (2007)	Market imperfections as sources for
Dean and McMullen (2007)	sustainable entrepreneurship opportunities
Brouwers (2006)	Innovations for sustainability or
Larson (2000)	sustainable innovations

THE RESEARCH CONTEXT OF A SMALL TRANSITION ECONOMY: EXAMPLE OF ESTONIA

Estonia is a suitable example of a small economy because its stable economic policy and development pattern have attracted various foreign direct investments, which provide additional resources and impetus for growth.

Estonia is a small open economy with a population of about 1.37 million people. In terms of natural resources, the country is highly forested (about 47 per cent of the land is forested) and uses oil shale mining as its primary energy source. Oil shale contributes extensively to the chemical industry as well. Other low-scale mining activities include the use of local limestone, sand and gravel as building materials. The oil shale industries are predominantly managed by state-owned and private domestic companies. All these companies have established sustainable development initiatives. In the timber and forestry industry, the sustainability and renewal of forest resources is controlled by relatively strict government policies aimed at preserving a balance between forest regrowth and economic usage. However, conifers are used in timber production more extensively than other types of trees and this creates a certain imbalance in forest management.

Domestic natural resources are relatively scarce in Estonia and several manufacturing industries rely on adding value by processing imported raw materials. Consequently, the environmental sustainability of Estonia is predominantly oriented towards pollution and recycling issues, while economic and social dimensions feature more prominently than in countries with abundant natural resources.

The role of foreign-owned companies in the development of this small transition economy relates predominantly to the provision of various additional resources, including knowledge resources. Despite its small size, Estonia has been successful in attracting foreign capital. The United Nations Conference on Trade and Development (UNCTAD) World Investment Report 2009 reveals that in 2007 there were about 2858 foreign subsidiaries in Estonia. The ratio of inward FDI stock to gross domestic product (GDP) has grown from a very low level in the early 1990s, to 68.8 per cent of GDP in 2008. In international comparisons, Estonia has a high intensity of inward FDI. In terms of the ratio of the total stock of inward FDI to GDP in 2008, Estonia had the second-highest ratio among new EU member states after Bulgaria, and across the EU only Luxembourg, Belgium, Malta and Cyprus had higher ratios. Inward FDI into Estonia grew considerably in the 1990s, but in terms of outward FDI, Estonia has become active in the new millennium (United Nations Conference on Trade and Development, 2009).

FDI into Estonia is characterized by the dominant role of services. This could be explained by domestic competition in several services: banking, leasing, real estate and retailing. Inward FDI has been mainly provided by Sweden (39.6 per cent), Finland (22.6 per cent) and Russia (3 per cent) (Bank of Estonia, 2011). The leading positions in terms of company-level inward FDI are held by the two largest banks in Estonia, Swedbank and SEB. FDI in Estonian manufacturing industries has developed differently. Estonia, as a small open economy, offered domestic manufacturers good exporting opportunities to neighbouring foreign markets. Due to the considerable cost advantages of domestic production, the role of outward FDI in the manufacturing sector was often to support the export process by establishing various distribution affiliations (for example, food, clothing, furniture, construction materials and wood products). By 1998, the majority of the Estonian outward investments were made by domestically owned firms. Since 1999, several of these companies have been acquired by foreign investors.

The key features of a sustainable development path in a small country are foreign openness in terms of exports and FDI, as well as knowledge sharing. Estonia has been very successful in attracting foreign investments, especially in the service sector. This has radically modernized the financial infrastructure and several other industries. The development status achieved should facilitate sustainable entrepreneurship initiatives in these industries.

RESEARCH METHODS AND DATA

The empirical analysis in this chapter continues to adopt an exploratory study as the primary research method. This means that instead of strict causalities, the focus is on approaching the phenomenon from several viewpoints in order to map the field of research and refine the concept by outlining possible research venues for more detailed and advanced investigation. The general logic of empirical analysis is illustrated in Figure 17.2.

The comparative analysis of foreign-owned and domestic companies is based on official business statistics. The purpose of this viewpoint is to clarify how these two groups of companies differ and what potential advantages foreign-owned companies possess. The survey evidence about the motivations and management choices of foreign-owned companies provides the opportunity to make generalizations about the sustainability orientation of these companies. Although based on survey data, the analysis focuses more on qualitative interpretation than on quantitative analysis. This choice was made partly because of the small size of the sample. The number of observations available is insufficient for the proper

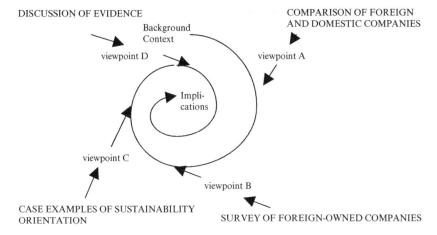

Figure 17.2   The exploratory structure of the data analysis

use of rigorous quantitative methods. The details of the dataset will be provided at the end of this section. The majority of the survey responses are evaluative responses using a five-point Likert scale (1 = not important at all; 5 = very important). Such responses are inherently more suitable for qualitative interpretation than for elaborate quantitative scrutiny.

The three case examples were selected on the basis of the theoretical reasoning that they should exemplify the interaction of environmental, economic and social aspects of sustainable entrepreneurship by foreign-owned companies. The methodological focus of the selected cases is to explain the sustainability-oriented initiatives taken by companies and their connection to sustainable development at the societal level. Therefore, the case evidence provided does not build on holistic in-depth case narratives, but focuses on sustainable entrepreneurship.

In general, such a triangulation of statistics, survey data and cases should help to obtain elaborate insights into the advantages of foreign-owned companies, as well as the motivations, beliefs and experiences of managers who have been responsible for the development processes in their companies. Yin (1992) argues that a case study is an empirical inquiry that investigates a contemporary phenomenon within its real-life context, when the boundaries between the phenomenon and the context are not evident, and in which multiple sources of evidence are used. In the case of the present chapter, the phenomenon under investigation is the support of foreign-owned companies for the sustainable development of a small economy. The earlier sections of this chapter indicated that foreign-owned companies are likely to have resource advantages which help them to capture entrepreneurial opportunities. In addition, they can benefit from experience acquired in the owner's home economy. These propositions make it relevant to investigate the advantages, motivations and management practices of foreign-owned companies, while the case examples offer a detailed understanding of particular situations in which foreign support becomes important. Further explanations of the case study approach and its uses can be found in Yin (1994).

The body of data used in this chapter was collected through a comprehensive study of foreign-owned companies in Estonia in the autumn of 2009 by a team of researchers from the University of Tartu Faculty of Economics and Business Administration. The author of the chapter was a member of this research team. Therefore, the gathered information represents the primary data. The dataset consists of 51 transcribed interviews with the managers of foreign-owned companies in Estonia. 'Foreign-owned' means 20 per cent or more of the voting right shares held by foreign owners. However, in most cases the respondents were either fully foreign-owned or greater than 50 per cent foreign-owned. The interviews each lasted about an hour or slightly longer. Usually one person per company was interviewed, but there were a couple of cases where several managers participated simultaneously. Based on these interviews and on background information about the companies, three companies were selected as case examples. The selection was based on the presence of the environmental, economic and social dimension in the activities of the chosen case company.

In addition, survey evidence from 96 companies was collected. The respondents were predominantly small (10–49 employees) and medium-sized companies (50–249 employees), providing 25.3 per cent and 46.3 per cent of the responses, respectively. Larger companies accounted for 22.1 per cent of the responses. Manufacturing companies made up 53.7 per cent of the respondents and 46.3 per cent represented various services. The primary foreign owners or parent companies of the participating companies originated predominantly from Finland (28.4 per cent), Sweden (14.7 per cent), Germany (8.4 per cent), Denmark (7.4 per cent), Norway (7.4 per cent), Austria (5.3 per cent), the USA (4.2 per cent), the UK (4.2 per cent) and the Netherlands (4.2 per cent). These distributions are similar in general terms to the investment pattern revealed in official statistics.

FOREIGN COMPANIES AS CONTRIBUTORS TO SUSTAINABILITY

The study of foreign-owned companies in Estonia included the comparative analysis of foreign-owned and domestic companies based on official statistics. These statistics revealed that foreign-owned companies are more productive in almost all sectors, with the exception of real estate and business services. In several sectors (for example telecommunications; trade; and energy, gas and water supply), they were more than twice as productive based on turnover per employee. The figures based on value-added reveal similar trends. If higher productivity is not the result of faster depletion of resources, it can be seen as favourable for sustainable development. Therefore, foreign-owned companies in Estonia produce and provide on average more sustainably. However, an intertemporal comparison shows that in several sectors domestic companies have become slightly more productive as well, because the differences in productivity have decreased over time. There could also be positive spillover effects from foreign to domestic companies. In the majority of sectors, the foreign-owned companies are more export-oriented, are better equipped with fixed assets, pay higher wages and are more profitable. All these elements suggest that foreign-owned companies are indeed in a better position for capturing the entrepreneurial opportunities created by sustainability orientation than domestic companies (Varblane et al., 2010).

The approach of foreign-owned companies and entrepreneurs to the facilitation of sustainable business operations, balancing economic goals with environmental and social considerations, depends on their motivation for entry into the host country. Resource-seeking and efficiency-seeking foreign direct investments could prescribe less sustainable business activities than market-seeking or strategic asset-seeking investments. The investment motives of foreign entrepreneurs entering Estonia are summarized in Table 17.2. In the table, 'current motivation' refers to the motivation to continue activities and investments in Estonia, while 'initial motivation' reflects retrospectively the motives of initial entry into the host economy.

The results in Table 17.2 allow us to conclude that the motivations for investing in Estonia increasingly support knowledge-based business activities, and continue to value stability. They are likely to render foreign investments that value a sustainable development path over an inherently more footloose resource or efficiency orientation. The main motivations potentially support sustainability across the value chain because they stress stability and technological advances that require qualified labour.

Besides the positive influences, there are somewhat negative aspects to foreignness as well. For example, the responses revealed that by far the most important determinant of withdrawal from certain export markets has been the strategy of the foreign owner. Therefore, the non-sustainability of some socially relevant economic activities might be caused simply by the discretionary decision of corporate managers or

Table 17.2   *The average scores of current and initial motivation for investing into Estonia (1 = not important at all; 5 = very important) and their standard deviations*

	Current motivation		Initial motivation	
	Average	Std dev.	Average	Std dev.
Qualified labour	3.83	1.05	3.55	1.18
Stability of Estonian economic environment	3.81	1.16	4.08	0.89
Favourable tax policy in Estonia	3.45	1.15	3.51	1.10
A good location in terms of logistics	3.24	1.37	3.69	1.15
Presence in Estonian market	3.16	1.56	3.29	1.65
Low labour costs	3.05	1.24	3.70	1.26
Modern infrastructure (e-services etc.)	3.04	1.26	2.76	1.32
Other cost motives (cheaper inputs, transportation costs)	2.86	1.25	3.60	1.35
Better access to the Baltic market	2.79	1.39	3.58	1.32
Rapid growth of the Estonian market	2.70	1.33	3.53	1.54
Access to raw materials, interm. products and components	2.61	1.51	2.46	1.35
Closeness to the parent company's customers	2.60	1.43	2.70	1.52
Following competitors	2.47	1.31	2.68	1.44
Acquisition of strategic assets (brand, distribution channel)	2.29	1.40	2.28	1.40
Access to the EU market	2.22	1.38	2.02	1.12
Access to new technology	2.12	1.21	2.10	1.24
Access to another foreign market	2.10	1.34	2.42	1.45

Note: The higher the standard deviation, the more variable the responses.

Source: Study of Foreign-Owned Companies in Estonia (2009).

foreign entrepreneurs. In most cases, such choices reflect a reaction to negative developments in the business environment; although in other situations they have little to do with the host economy. Consequently, withdrawals are caused either by corporate rearrangements or by radical shifts in the corporate vision. Therefore, due to the home country or international concerns, the interests of foreign-owned companies might not be aligned with sustainability-related policy intentions in the host economy.

The survey part of the study showed that the technological level in foreign-owned companies has improved considerably since the initial investment. The share of respondents who use completely modern technology has increased from around 15 per cent at the time of entry to 37.5 per cent in 2009. Only a few foreign companies use somewhat outdated technologies. Therefore, the technology has been renewed after the investment, and modern technologies are usually more productive, eco-friendly and socially comfortable than older ones. Because of these properties, inward transfers of technology as well as product and process development know-how should favourably influence the sustainability of the host economy's development.

To conclude, the evidence from the comparative analysis and survey shows that, in general, investment motivations and dynamics should favourably influence the sustainable development of a host country. The same holds for the technological advances and knowledge transfers that have commenced. However, the strategy of foreign owners or certain constraints on innovation and local cooperation might reveal adverse influences of foreignness on the sustainability of entrepreneurship and development in Estonia as the host economy.

CASES OF FOREIGN-OWNED COMPANIES CONTRIBUTING TO SUSTAINABLE DEVELOPMENT

Fortum

The Finnish energy production company Fortum Power & Heat Ltd has several subsidiaries in Estonia. One of them, Fortum Tartu, is the holding company for several units in the Fortum Tartu Group that produce heat energy, mediate, sell and purchase heat and electricity, as well as produce and supply local fuels. The main local fuels supplied are milled peat, sod peat, wood chip, sawdust and wood-waste. The specific contribution of this power company to the sustainability of the Estonian economy relates to large-scale investment in modern heat and electricity co-production plants, which can operate on local fuels instead of imported gas. This technological development towards more environmentally friendly approaches to power and heat supply has been a controversial story of entrepreneurial initiative in convincing the local municipality and investors of the viability of local fuels as an alternative to the gas-fuelled boiler houses used since the Soviet era.

> It can be said that this foreign owner made a difference. Previously, the heating companies in Tartu had numerous owners. With Fortum's investment, things moved along and important investment decisions were made between various owners, peat bogs were prepared for extraction in order to have peat for heating, and various studies made in preparation for installing a heat and energy co-production plant, which is now ready. Investments by Fortum helped to speed up these preparatory processes. (Manager of Fortum Tartu)

However, this case is also an example of potential conflict between the environmental and social dimensions of sustainability. Soon after opening the modern co-production plant, the company filed an application to increase the state-controlled price of heating. The need for the increase was said to be related to the shift in the price structure caused by the co-production of heat and electricity, as well as the size of the investment, which was larger than initially projected. This shows how the sustainable entrepreneurship concept may cause conflict between increased environmental concerns and the ability of lower-income members of the community to pay their heating bills in the winter season. Creativity and innovativeness as well as responsible and ethical behaviour through pursuing sustainable development are the core values of Fortum's culture. Therefore, the corporate culture at Fortum does entail elements of entrepreneurial and responsible business orientation.

4Energia – Energy of Four

4Energia is an innovative private company owned by three types of investors: Vardar Eurus, related to the Norwegian power company Vardar; financial investors (EBRD and Estonian private investors); and the company management. The company's business areas are the development of the renewable energy industry and power production. The number '4' indicates that the company focuses on four renewable energy sources: wind, water, biomass and solar. The company itself does not own the energy-generating installations. It manages subsidiary companies established separately for the specific projects through operating agreements. The company already has several onshore wind energy parks in Estonia and one in Lithuania. Several similar parks are still under development in all three Baltic countries, but mostly in Estonia and Lithuania. 4Energia is also planning a large-scale offshore wind energy park near Hiiumaa island in Estonia, and manages two biogas stations in Estonia that co-produce electricity and heat. The company is still in its expansion phase, both in terms of its presence in other Baltic countries and in terms of renewable energy production modes.

The main constraints that managers outlined during the interviews relate to the lack of well-developed long-term development plans for the entire energy sector, and the limited availability of qualified power engineers. According to one manager, in some respects the Lithuanian business environment seems more transparent than the energy sector in Estonia.

> The transparency of the competition policy is indeed important. If we look at what takes place in Estonia, Latvia and Lithuania: Latvia is the least transpar-

ent and nothing really happens there; then there is Estonia where something does occur, but more thanks to the need to keep up with other countries. Lithuania is the most transparent and has advanced the most. Of course, the biggest crisis in the energy sector will occur in Lithuania, because the Ignalina nuclear plant will close in the future. Maybe it is because of this that in recent years there has been very good cooperation with 4Energia in Lithuania. (Manager of 4Energia)

The more general discussion of renewable energy production relates to the problem of subsidies. The green energy price subsidy scheme enforced in Estonia has caused overshooting in terms of interest in investing in wind energy parks. There are still several projects under consideration, while public debate is raising concerns about the visual and noise pollution being potentially too extensive near protected areas in the countryside. Thus, somewhat paradoxically, foreign investment interest in sustainable entrepreneurship in the renewable energy sector might run counter to interests in keeping natural habitats undisturbed by wind energy parks. Despite the controversy, 4Energia has made innovative and sustainable development its core orientation by focusing specifically on advancing the use of renewable energy sources. This means development projects using cutting-edge emerging technologies. The management team at 4Energia combines knowledge in electro engineering and in business. Therefore, innovative approaches to the technology are a strong element of the company's corporate culture.

Ragn-Sells

Ragn-Sells is a subsidiary of a Swedish waste collection and recycling company that emerged out of AZ Sellberg and started to change its operations from transport services to waste collection around 1928 at the initiative of the entrepreneur Ragnar Sellberg, who led the concern until his death in 1995. The entry of Ragn-Sells into Estonia in 1992 was serendipitous. The owner-manager Ragnar, then around 80 years old, met people from the small Estonian town of Haapsalu at a trade exhibition. They invited him to visit their town. During the visit, a local waste collection company was discussed in terms of development prospects. Being an entrepreneur, Ragnar took up the offer to establish a joint venture in Haapsalu municipality. Subsequently, development continued with expansion to the larger cities in Estonia, and ultimately the service was extended to become a nationwide operation.

When Ragn-Sells came to Estonia, waste collection was at a relatively low-quality level. It was almost entirely manual labour. Even in Tallinn, waste was collected using Soviet-era haulage trucks. The first advantage for Estonia was that the foreign owner helped with newer technology in the form of modern waste collection equipment. Simple trampers, multiband type vehicles and collection containers were introduced in Estonia, and new modern Western-built trucks. New principles of waste collection were also introduced. For example, the idea of selective waste collection was transferred from Sweden. Not every village requires its own waste landfill; a few larger waste management centres would do the job instead. Läänemaa county was the first in Estonia to adopt a centralized county landfill, which gave it an environmental advantage. Waste management is now even more centralized. (Manager of Ragn-Sells Estonia)

One constraint on development in Estonia is related to difficulties in negotiating with municipalities about acceptable locations for waste management centres. Ragn-Sells faced opposition to selected locations from municipalities in both of the largest cities, Tallinn and Tartu. In keeping with the entrepreneurial spirit of the parent, the subsidiary in Estonia enjoys considerable autonomy in decision-making. This foreign-owned company in the waste collection sector has had considerable influence on sustainable entrepreneurship in Estonia by modernizing both the waste management and recycling technologies and procedures and the conceptual understanding of the role and importance of waste management in society. The knowledge transfer from Sweden has been invaluable in this respect. In the case of Ragn-Sells, entrepreneurial initiative has clearly been at the forefront of renewing the waste collection and recycling system in Estonia. Responsible behaviour is indicated by the fact that the company stresses the importance of recycling and reuse of various materials instead of incineration.

To summarize, the three cases show that foreign-owned companies do indeed contribute directly to sustainable development and entrepreneurship in the host economy. The opportunities taken in these cases are entrepreneurial, as opposed to simple business opportunities, because pre-existing technologies have been applied in a very different policy and regulatory setting, and in combination with local patterns of resource use. Novelty, innovativeness and risk-taking have all been essential elements of these foreign contributions, especially in the context of the host economy. These cases are about the reinvention of business models in light of entrepreneurial opportunities presented by the host country conditions. They might all seem to be environmental cases at first glance, but they actually involve important economic and social considerations as well, some of which might be controversial, at least in the short run. In the long-term perspective, however, such cases of sustainable entrepreneurship also facilitate the economic and social-communal transformations much needed for sustainable development.

REFINED VIEW OF SUPPORT FOR SUSTAINABLE DEVELOPMENT BY FOREIGN-OWNED COMPANIES

The concept of sustainable entrepreneurship integrates elements of entrepreneurship such as dynamic change (see Minguzzi and Passaro, 2000; Lee and Hsieh, 2010) with concepts of sustainability in development (O'Brien, 2002; Chaudhury, 2010; Collins and Grimes, 2008). This suggests a co-evolutionary organizational transformation of entrepreneurship and innovation towards more balanced values that target environmental, economic and social concerns simultaneously. The foreign input in terms of a sustainable entrepreneurial approach in a host economy can be both positive and negative.

Estonia, as the example of a small open transition economy, has scarce domestic natural resources and several manufacturing industries that process imported raw materials in order to add value. Environmental sustainability in Estonia is oriented towards pollution and recycling issues. The economic and social dimensions of sustainability in the Estonian context are more in focus than perhaps they are in countries with abundant natural resources.

The evidence from the survey is in line with the views of Grundey (2008) that sustainable development is a complex process that requires good coordination between micro, meso and macro levels. The foreign-owned companies in Estonia stress the importance of various macro-level policies in providing a framework for mutually beneficial long-term development. Several foreign-owned companies have taken the entrepreneurial initiative to invest in modern technologies that support sustainability. These sustainable innovations (as defined by Larson, 2000) have considerably improved the technological level in Estonia. Due to the smallness of Estonia, some entrepreneurial opportunities for foreign-owned companies are indeed presented by various market imperfections, which is in line with the views of Cohen and Winn (2007).

The three short cases illustrated how foreign-owned companies contribute directly to sustainable development and entrepreneurship in a small developing host economy. All three case companies have contributed to the improvement of socio-technical systems as described in the literature by Geels (2004). However, these processes are not only positive. Some social aspects of these environmentally more sustainable solutions are at least controversial, if not detrimental. For example, environmentally beneficial advances may increase certain social problems, at least initially, due to higher costs for consumers. This presents a potential trade-off between the foreign-owned economic interest (reflected through sustainable entrepreneurship) and the social-communal dimension of sustainability. However, it is likely that with an increase in living standards and the development of the host economy, some of these issues can be reconciled.

This chapter contributes to the literature by combining two contemporary streams of research, namely entrepreneurship and sustainability studies, within the international business context. It concludes that foreign-owned entrepreneurial companies have great potential to contribute to the sustainability of the development of small economies by taking a long-term strategic interest in the host market, and by transferring more contemporary technologies and capabilities. However, this potential might be undermined by corporate policies that discard host country interests or social realities in favour of global profit-seeking. Consequently, foreign entrepreneurs are more likely to contribute to sustainable development when host country policies favour their long-term commitment to that economy. This conclusion reflects the importance of national development planning, which would clearly pinpoint the role of cooperation with foreign-owned companies in providing sustainable solutions. The planning aspect has also been addressed in the literature by, for example, Vitola and Senfelde (2010).

This exploratory study revealed, on the basis of the literature, that sustainability orientation in an economy creates new entrepreneurial opportunities, and that larger foreign-owned companies can be entrepreneurial as well. Thus, even medium-sized foreign-owned companies in Estonia could be entrepreneurial in nature. The three case companies are indeed all entrepreneurial despite the differing nature of their ownership structure and the scale of their activities. The advantages of the foreign-owned companies over domestic companies also found support on the basis of official statistics. They have higher productivity, export orientation and better resources than domestic companies. The investment motivations of foreign investors are in accordance with sustainability orientations throughout their value chains. The survey evidence and cases revealed several positive aspects of foreign involvement, but also socially detrimental issues and cases of disinvestment and withdrawal from the Estonian market. Therefore, the strategic choices on the corporate level can cause a certain misalignment between the interests of foreign-owned companies and policy intentions in the host economy. However, foreign-owned companies are the initiators of several technological innovations that increase the sustainability of their processes. The theoretical, context-specific and empirical results of this exploratory approach allow us to offer a more detailed overview of how foreign-owned companies influence sustainable development in a small developing host economy. This overview summarizes the results of this chapter and is depicted in Figure 17.3.

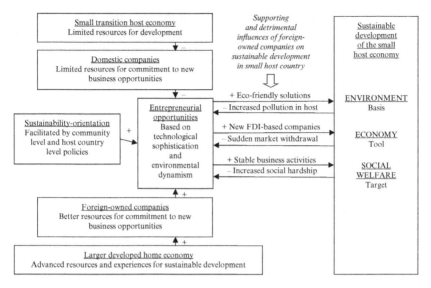

Figure 17.3   Refined overview of foreign-owned companies support to sustainable development

LIMITATIONS AND IMPLICATIONS

The results of this study should be interpreted with caution, because the evidence provided is limited by the configuration of available statistics, the survey questionnaire and the topics discussed during the interviews. The indications about sustainability are mostly indirect and contextual. Therefore, the interpretation of the results remains to some extent meta-analytical and subjective. The short case examples introduced are also context-specific, which does limit the generalizations that can be made about similar entrepreneurial initiatives in different economic settings. The results of this exploratory study are inherently bound by the interpretive and synthesizing capacities of the researcher.

The implications for theory suggest that the sustainable entrepreneurship concept should be viewed as more heterogeneous and multidimensional than several studies presume. The dynamics of and interplay between environmental, economic and social aspects of sustainability requires more detailed analysis in order to clarify their roles. From the theoretical perspective, it is equally important to analyse the influence of developmental level and living standards on the perception of the sustainability concept.

The policy implications relate to the need to re-evaluate established price controls and subsidizing schemes in light of the environmental, economic and social impact of sustainable development initiatives. More flexible promotion tools should include pre-agreed safeguards in order to avoid large-scale overshooting effects. From the perspective of foreign companies, these would maintain a relatively stable regulatory environment in the host country, while adjusting expectations about the stability of subsidies and controls. The study also indicated that government policies (which in the EU context should take community-level policies into account) and development plans often function as important catalysts of sustainability orientation in the context of a particular economy. This catalytic aspect of facilitating entrepreneurial initiatives towards sustainability could be advanced using awareness-building and other demand-side policy tools.

Foreign managers can benefit from this contribution by incorporating considerations of the local community more extensively into the planning and development of sustainable entrepreneurship initiatives. At present, they sometimes fail to deal proactively with social concerns to a sufficient extent. This indicates the need to orient corporate cultures and values more towards the living standards and social capabilities of host country customers, by adjusting expected pay-off periods to suit local living standards. This would serve as an important market-building tool by stressing the social aspect of sustainability within local communities.

Future research on foreign influences on sustainable entrepreneurship could investigate the role of regulations in creating or restricting entrepreneurial opportunities in the host economy. It is equally important to clarify the merits of risk-taking and innovativeness involved in foreign contributions to sustainability, and how this could be influenced by the regulatory environment. More research is required to explore the small versus the large country, or the developing versus the developed economy. It is important to stress the exploratory nature of this chapter, which is intended as a starting point for more elaborate analyses of these subjects.

ACKNOWLEDGEMENTS

This chapter has been prepared with financial support from the Estonian Research Council (Grants 8580, 8546 and IUT20-49).

REFERENCES

Backer De, K. and L. Sleuwaegen (2003), 'Does foreign direct investment crowd out domestic entrepreneurship?', *Review of Industrial Organization*, 22(1), 67–84.

Bank of Estonia (2011), 'Statistics', http://www.eestipank.info/pub/en/dokumendid/statistika/, accessed 2 February 2011.

Bhasin, B.B. and S. Venkataramany (2010), 'Globalization of entrepreneurship: policy considerations for SME development in Indonesia', *International Business and Economics Research Journal*, 9(4), 95–103.

Brouwers, H.E.J. (2006), 'Prime innovation and sustainable entrepreneurship in the Dutch rubber and plastic industry', paper for the High Technology Small Firms (HTSF) Conference, University of Twente.

Chang, J. (2001), 'Intrapreneurship and exopreneurship in manufacturing firms: an empirical study of performance implications', *Journal of Enterprising Culture*, 9(2), 153–71.

Chaudhury, R. (2010), 'A dual-model approach to measuring income convergence sustainability in European and Asian emerging economies', *Michigan Journal of Business*, 3(1), 45–78.

Cohen, B. and M.I. Winn (2007), 'Market imperfections, opportunity and sustainable entrepreneurship', *Journal of Business Venturing*, 22(1), 29–49.

Collins, P. and S. Grimes (2008), 'Ireland's foreign-owned technology sector: evolving towards sustainability?', *Growth and Change*, 39(3), 436–63.

Covin, J.G. (1999), 'Corporate entrepreneurship and the pursuit of competitive advantage', *Entrepreneurship: Theory and Practice*, 23(3), 47–63.

Covin, J.G. and D.P. Slevin (1991), 'A conceptual model of entrepreneurship as firm behaviour', *Entrepreneurship: Theory and Practice*, 16(1), 7–25.

Crals, E. and L. Vereeck (2005), 'The affordability of sustainable entrepreneurship certification for SMEs', *International Journal of Sustainable Development and World Ecology*, 12(2), 173–83.

Dean, T.J. and J.S. McMullen (2007), 'Toward a theory of sustainable entrepreneurship: reducing environmental degradation through entrepreneurial action', *Journal of Business Venturing*, 22(1), 50–76.

European Economic Area (2006), 'Sustainable development policy and guide for the EEA financial mechanism and the Norwegian financial mechanism', http://www.eeagrants.org/asset/341/1/341_1.pdf, accessed 21 September 2011.

Geels, F.W. (2004), 'From sectoral systems of innovation to socio-technical systems: insights about dynamics and change from sociology and institutional theory', *Research Policy*, 33(6–7), 897–920.

Gibbs, D. (2009), 'Sustainability entrepreneurs, ecopreneurs and the development of a sustainable economy', *Greener Management International*, 55, 63–78.

Griffith, W.H. (2007), 'Caricom countries and the irrelevance of economic smallness', *Third World Quarterly*, 28(5), 939–58.

Grundey, D. (2008), 'Applying sustainability principles in the economy', *Technological and Economic Development of Economy*, 14(2), 101–6.

Horio, H. and C. Watanabe (2008), 'The paradox of a service-oriented economy for sustainability: co-evolution between innovation and resources effectuation by a global complement', *Journal of Services Research*, 8(1), 155–75.

Klepper, G. and F. Stahler (1998), 'Sustainability in closed and open economies', *Review of International Economics*, 6(3), 488–506.

Lambert, A.J.D., W.H.P.M. Hooff Van, H.W. Lintsen, J.L. Schippers and F.C.A. Veraart (2010), 'Sustainability in the Dutch economy from 1850 to 2005', *Proceedings for the Northeast Region Decision Sciences Institute (NEDSI)*, pp. 672–7.

Larson, A.L. (2000), 'Sustainable innovation through an entrepreneurship lens', *Business Strategy and the Environment*, 9(5), 304–17.

Lee, J.-S. and C.-J. Hsieh (2010), 'A research in relating entrepreneurship, marketing capability, innovative capability and sustained competitive advantage', *Journal of Business and Economics Research*, 8(9), 109–19.

Mathew, V. (2009), 'Sustainable entrepreneurship in small-scale business: application, concepts and cases', *ICFAI Journal of Entrepreneurship Development*, 6(1), 41–61.

Minguzzi, A. and R. Passaro (2000), 'The network of relationships between the economic environment and the entrepreneurial culture in small firms', *Journal of Business Venturing*, 16, 181–207.

Moensted, M. (2010), 'Networking and entrepreneurship in small high-tech European firms: an empirical study', *International Journal of Management*, 27(1), 16–30.

O'Brien, C. (2002), 'Global manufacturing and the sustainable economy', *International Journal of Production Research*, 40(15), 3867–77.

O'Neill Jr, G.D., J.C. Hershauer and J.S. Golden (2009), 'The cultural context of sustainability entrepreneurship', *Greener Management International*, 55, 33–46.

Parrish, B.D. (2010), 'Sustainability-driven entrepreneurship: principles of organization design', *Journal of Business Venturing*, 25(5), 510–23.

Parrish, B.D. and T.J. Foxon (2009), 'Sustainability entrepreneurship and equitable transitions to a low-carbon economy', *Greener Management International*, 55, 47–62.

Roolaht, T. and U. Varblane (2008), 'Differences between inward–outward FDI and inward FDI in the context of Estonia', *International Business and the Catching-Up Economies: Challenges and Opportunities: Proceedings of 34th EIBA Annual Conference*, Technical University, Tallinn, pp. 1–36.

Sirbu, M., O. Doinea and M.G. Mangra (2009), 'Knowledge based economy – the basis for insuring a sustainable development', *Annals of the University of Petrosani, Economics*, 9(4), 227–32.

Sorin, A. and A.S. Irina (2009), 'Sustainable development in global economy', *Annals of the University of Oradea, Economic Science Series*, 18(2), 230–35.

Study of Foreign-Owned Companies in Estonia (2009), Survey response data files in MS Excel and interview transcripts in MS doc format, University of Tartu, Faculty of Economics and Business Administration, Tartu.

United Nations Conference on Trade and Development (2009), *The World Investment Report 2009: Transnational Corporations, Agricultural Production and Development*, New York, USA and Geneva, Switzerland: UNCTAD.

Varblane, U., I. Paltser, M. Tammets, K. Rõigas, D. Pavlov, A. Kljain and U. Varblane (2010), 'The comparative analysis of domestic and foreign-owned companies in Estonia' (in Estonian), in U. Varblane (ed.), *Foreign Direct Investments in Estonia* (in Estonian), Tartu: University of Tartu Press, pp. 48–86.

Vitola, A. and M. Senfelde (2010), 'The optimization of national development planning system as a precondition for competitiveness and sustainability of national economy', *Economics and Management*, 15, 325–31.

Yin, R.K. (1992), 'The case study method as a tool for doing evaluation', *Current Sociology*, 40(1), 121–37.

Yin, R.K. (1994), *Case Study Research: Design and Methods*, 2nd edn, Thousand Oaks, CA: Sage Publications.

Index

Printed and bound by CPI Group (UK) Ltd, Croydon, CR0 4YY

16/04/2025

14658375-0002